MODERN METHODS OF VALUATION

MODERN METHODS OF VALUATION

OF

LAND, HOUSES AND BUILDINGS

(*Eighth Edition*)

BY

WILLIAM BRITTON

B.Sc. (Estate Management) (Lond.), F.R.I.C.S., Associate Member of the Rating Surveyors' Association. Sometime Head of the Valuation Department, College of Estate Management and County Valuer and Estates Surveyor, Surrey County Council.

KEITH DAVIES

J.P., M.A. (Oxon.), LL.M. (Lond.) of Grays Inn, Barrister-at-Law. Professor of Law, University of Reading.

TONY JOHNSON

B.Sc. (Estate Management) (Lond.), F.R.I.C.S. Honorary Fellow of the College of Estate Management. Partner, Edwin Hill and Partners; sometime Senior Lecturer in Valuation, University of Reading and Principal Lecturer in Valuation, Polytechnic of the South Bank.

1989

THE ESTATES GAZETTE LIMITED
151 WARDOUR STREET, LONDON W1V 4BN

EIGHTH EDITION 1989

1943	FIRST EDITION	by	David M. Lawrance and Harold G. May
1949 and 1949	SECOND EDITION THIRD EDITION	by	David M. Lawrance, Harold G. May and W. H. Rees
1956	FOURTH EDITION	by	David M. Lawrance and W. H. Rees
1962 and 1971	FIFTH EDITION SIXTH EDITION	by	David M. Lawrance, W. H. Rees and W. Britton
1980	SEVENTH EDITION	by	William Britton, Keith Davies and Tony Johnson

ISBN 0 7282 0126 7

Printed in Great Britain at The Bath Press, Avon

Preface to the Eighth Edition

The Seventh Edition of this work was published in early 1980 just after the birth of Thatcherism. Much has, therefore, changed in the intervening years, certainly in the practice if not in the principles of valuation. Not all of the changes, however, represent progress and to provide but one instance of this, readers will note that in this edition we have reverted from metric to Imperial measurements. The valuation side of the surveying profession has shown considerable reluctance to adopt metric measurements and, except for the areas of rating, agriculture and minerals where metrication has certainly gained a foothold, most measurements and the figures which flow therefrom are at worst solely Imperial or at best Imperial with a metric translation. The next edition may well revert again to metric as the Government now shows signs of legislating to impose the metric system for 1992.

As with the previous edition, we have prepared this edition under the shadow of impending legislative and other changes, the most major being what have now become the Housing Act 1988 and the Local Government Finance Act 1988. The provisions of the Bills preceding these statutes are contained in the final Sections of Chapters 19 and 22 and further comment is contained in the Note to the Eighth Edition which follows this Preface.

As always we are indebted to many colleagues for advice and assistance in the preparation of this edition but in particular Raymond Stedman, F.R.I.C.S., F.A.A.V., for revising the Chapter on Agricultural Property, Owen Connellan, B.Sc., F.R.I.C.S., Dip.Rating, for revising the Rating Chapter, Roderick Innes, F.R.I.C.S., for revising the Chapter on Licensed Premises and Peter Fraser, F.R.I.C.S., for revising the Chapter on Minerals. We are grateful also to Diana Laming for transferring the text to a word processor and to Richard Johnson, B.A. (Oxon.), for preparing the Index and Tables.

Camberley, Surrey. 1989.

William Britton
Keith Davies
Tony Johnson

Note to the Eighth Edition

Two major pieces of legislation were making their way towards the Statute Book while this new edition was being prepared. Notes on the Bills were included in the Chapters concerned—Section 7 of Chapter 19 and Section 11 of Chapter 22—and this Note brings these matters and some further developments up to date.

RESIDENTIAL PROPERTIES

The Housing Bill 1988 received the Royal Assent and became the Housing Act 1988 on 15 November 1988, coming into effect in part on that date, in part 2 months later, and in part on various dates to be appointed subsequently. In addition to the matters in the Bill referred to in Section 7 of Chapter 19, the Act sets up "a body known as Housing for Wales" which will take over in Wales various functions in relation to housing associations which have hitherto been carried out by the Housing Corporation. The Act also makes further provision for consents by the Secretary of State to disposals of public authority housing stock, and for codes of practice under the Race Relations Act 1976 related to rented housing. It amends details of the Housing Act 1985 in regard to the "right to buy", repair notice procedure (e.g. in respect of flats) and letting conditions applicable to improvement grants; and various consequential amendments are made to the Housing Associations Act 1985 and to the Landlord and Tenant Act 1987.

RATING

The Local Government Finance Bill received the Royal Assent and became the Local Government Finance Act 1988 on 29 July 1988; its rating provisions are broadly in line with the summary of proposed changes indicated in Section 11 of Chapter 22. The following points, however, are worth emphasising:—

(i) "Net annual value" disappears for the purpose of future valuation lists and is replaced by "rateable value".

(ii) Rating appeals may be taken directly to the Lands Tribunal with the agreement of all parties, rather than being first heard by the Valuation and Community Charge Tribunal.

(iii) The Valuation List has been re-named the Local Rating List.

(iv) The decision of the House of Lords in the case of *Clement (VO)* v. *Addis Ltd.* [1988] RA 25, HL, is reversed to ensure that any valuation made between general revaluations should take account only of the physical condition and state of the locality at the time of the valuation but with the general market conditions being assumed to be those ruling at the time of the last general revaluation.

Planning Permissions

The 1977 G.D.O. (see Section 5 of Chapter 15) has been replaced by the Town and Country Planning General Development Order 1988. The procedure for making planning applications is now prescribed in the Town and Country Planning (Applications) Regulations 1988.

Value Added Tax

At the time of writing, proposals have been made by the Government for changes to the Value Added Tax (VAT) legislation which would result in VAT being charged on some commercial rents and certain disposals of land and buildings. The details of the legislation and its effect on the property market are too uncertain to enable detailed comment to be made at this stage.

VALUATION TABLES

A new (11th) edition of Parry's Valuation Tables is due to be published shortly after the publication of this book. It is understood that this work will contain a number of new tables including quarterly in advance Y.P., both single and dual rate, equivalent yields and equated yields. In addition the life tables are updated based upon the 1981 Census.

Table of Contents

PART 1

TABLES

CHAPTER 1

Principles of Value

1. THE VALUER'S RÔLE

THE SERVICES of a valuer may be sought by anyone with an interest in, or contemplating a transaction involving land and buildings. For example, a valuer may be required to advise a vendor on the price he should ask for his property, a prospective tenant on the annual rent he should pay, a mortgagee on the value of the security and on the mortgage loan he can advance, and a person dispossessed under compulsory powers on the compensation he can claim.

Knowledge of the purpose for which his valuation is required is usually vital to the valuer, for the value of a particular interest in landed property is not necessarily the same for all purposes. In many cases the valuer will also require to know details of the circumstances of the person for whom the valuation is being prepared because the value of a particular interest may be different to different individuals according to, for example, their liability to income tax.

In the majority of cases, however, the primary concern of the valuer is to estimate the market value; that is the capital sum or the annual rental which at a particular time, on specified terms and subject to legislation, should be asked or paid for a particular interest in property.

It might reasonably be asked next, what are the special characteristics of landed property which make the services of a person with special knowledge desirable, or in many cases essential, in dealing with it? There are three primary reasons:—

   (i) Imperfections in the property market.
  (ii) The heterogeneity of landed property and the interests which can exist therein.
 (iii) Legal factors.

The need for special knowledge of the law relating to

landed property will become apparent in the later Chapters;
the varied interests which can exist in landed property are
considered in Chapter 3.

2. THE PROPERTY MARKET

The nature of landed property, the method of conducting
transactions in it and the lack of information generally available of the transactions all contribute to the imperfection
of competition in the landed property market. Apart from
structural differences in any building, each piece of landed
property is unique by reason of location. The majority of
transactions in the property market are conducted privately
and even if the results of the transactions were available they
would not be particularly helpful in the absence of detailed
information on such matters as the extent and state of the
buildings and the tenure. The degree of imperfection does,
however, differ in different parts of the market. First-class
shop investments, for example, are fairly homogeneous and
this fact will decrease the imperfection of competition in the
market for them. The greater than average degree of homo-
geneity lies in the tenants of such properties rather than the
properties themselves, but the tenant is probably of greater
significance than the property.

It is, perhaps, misleading to talk of the property market
as though it were a single entity. In fact, there are a number
of markets, some local, some national and some international. For example, residential properties required for occupation are normally dealt with locally. A man looking for
a house to live in is rarely indifferent to its location because
it must be conveniently situated usually in relation to his
place of work and perhaps that of his wife, and to educational
facilities for his children. The market for first class investments on the other hand is national. This type of property
appeals to larger institutions such as insurance companies
who are largely indifferent to the situation of the property.
For example, they will tend to own commercial investments
such as shops, offices and factories in all the major urban
centres. The market for development properties can be local,
national or international. Small bare sites suitable for the

erection of a few houses are of interest to small local developers, large sites for residential or commercial development
to larger organisations operating in a much wider area. At
the extreme such organisations will be dealing with sites in
several countries to take advantage of the market conditions
in an international context.

3. A DEFINITION OF VALUE

Much paper can be, and indeed has been consumed in
discussing and defining value. It is not appropriate here to
contribute to this particular store of literature but merely
to provide a definition which will serve the present purpose.
Thus attention will be concentrated on value in a market
situation, value in exchange—or market value. Concepts of
social value, aesthetic value or other values are not appropriate to this work, but it should be remembered that value
can be considered from these points of view.

The market value or market price of a particular interest
in landed property may be defined as the amount of money
which can be obtained for the interest at a particular time
from persons able and willing to purchase it. Value is not
intrinsic but results from estimates, made subjectively by able
and willing purchasers, of the benefit or satisfaction they
will derive from ownership of the interest. The valuer must,
therefore, in order to value an interest, be able to assess
the probable estimate of benefit of potential purchasers. It
must be explained that what is valued is not the physical
land or buildings but the property interest which gives legal
rights of use or enjoyment of the land or buildings.

A potential purchaser is a person who proposes to tie up
a certain amount of capital in land or in land and buildings
and there are three main angles from which he may view
the transaction. First, if he wishes to occupy the property
he will be concerned with the benefits, commercial or social,
which he anticipates he will derive from that occupation.
Secondly, he may regard the property as an investment capable of yielding an annual return in the form of income.
Thirdly, his motive may be profit; that is buying at one price
now he hopes to sell at a higher price at some time in the

future, perhaps having injected further capital, and thus making a gain. These motives are not, however, mutually exclusive and a transaction may be entered into with more than one motive in mind. In any case the price which the purchaser will be prepared to pay at any given time will be influenced largely by the supply of that particular type of property and the extent of the demand for it. Supply and demand are discussed at length later in this Chapter but it might be noted here that demand must be effective; that is, that the desire to possess should be translatable into the action of purchasing.

4. VALUE AND VALUATION

Although the aim of the valuer is to provide an estimate of market value, it should not be assumed that the valuer's estimate of value and the market price or market value will always be the same. Different valuers could well place different values on a particular interest at a particular time because they are making estimates and there is normally room, within certain limits, for differences of opinion. In the majority of cases this is the most serious difference which should arise between competent valuers in times of stable market conditions because market prices result from estimates of value made by vendors and purchasers on the basis of prices previously paid for other similar interests; but in times when market conditions are not stable more serious differences may arise. In such unstable times the valuer's estimate of value will be based on prices previously paid but he must adjust his basis to allow for the changes since the previous transaction took place. The accuracy of his estimate will, therefore, depend on his knowledge of the changes and his skill in quantifying their effect.

Unstable times bring into focus the fact that in any market at any time there are many buyers and sellers, each of whom will have his own personal views, desires and judgments on what the commodity in question is worth. Thus a market constitutes an amalgam of individuals who will strike individual bargains, so that a "market price" can only represent an average view of all these factors. Where the commodities are all different, as in the case of property, then the problems of arriving at this average are multiplied. Where the valuer is making statutory valuations in hypothetical market conditions it is inevitable that differences of opinion as to value will become even more marked.

5. DEMAND, SUPPLY AND PRICE

It is axiomatic that quantity bought is equal to quantity sold regardless of price. This does not mean, however, that price is unimportant. Demand and supply are in fact equated at any particular time by some level of price. Other things being equal, at any given time, any increase in demand or decrease in supply will cause price to rise; conversely, any decrease in demand or increase in supply will cause price to fall. Therefore, whatever the given demand and supply, in a freely operating market, price will ration the supply and match it to the demand.

Price has, however, a wider role. If, over a long period, price remains persistently high in relation to the cost of producing more of the thing in question, it will call forth increased supplies which will gradually have the effect of pulling price down again to a long-run normal or equilibrium level. Price, therefore, acts also as an indicator and an incentive.

The extent of price changes caused by changes in demand or supply will depend upon the price elasticity of supply or demand. Thus, if supply is highly elastic, a change in demand can be matched quickly and smoothly by an expansion of supply and the price change, if any, will be small. Conversely, if supply is highly inelastic, a change in demand cannot be matched quickly and smoothly by an expansion in supply, thus the price change will be more marked. If demand is elastic, a change in supply will quickly generate an appropriate contraction or expansion in demand and the price change, if any, will be small; but if demand is inelastic this means that any change in supply is likely to generate a contraction or expansion in demand less quickly and the price change will be more marked.

This is a simple statement of economic laws which are

applicable to all types of commodity or service, but to consider their application to a particular type of commodity or
service it is necessary to look at the special characteristics
of the commodity or service in question. In the case of property a separate discipline of land economics has emerged
which reflects the unique status of property.

It is proposed, therefore, to look next at some of the principal factors which affect the demand for, and the supply of,
landed property.

6. Demand for, and Supply of, Landed Property

The term landed property covers such a wide range of
types of land and buildings and interests therein that generalisation is difficult but it is correct to say that, generally, the
demand for, and the supply of landed property are relatively
inelastic with respect to price changes.

The most important single factor restricting the supply of
land and buildings at the present time is planning. There
are, of course, natural limitations on the supply of land. First,
the overall supply of land is fixed and, secondly, the supply
of land suitable for particular purposes is limited, but these
natural limitations are overshadowed by planning limitations.

The powers of the planner are considered in more detail
in Part 2 but the following are the most important in this
particular context:—

(1) The power to allocate land for particular uses, for
    example, agricultural use or residential use. This allo-
    cation is shown in the development plan or local plan
    for the area. Thus, it would not normally be possible
    to erect a factory on a bare site in an area allocated
    for residential use.

(2) The power to restrict changes in the use of buildings.
    For example, before the use of a house can be changed
    to offices, planning permission must be obtained and
    this permission will not usually be forthcoming unless
    the change is in accordance with the provisions of the
    structure plan, the local plan or the planning policy
    for the area.

(3) The power to restrict the intensity of use of land. Thus the owner of a bare site in an area allocated for residential use is not free to choose between erecting on it, for example, a four storey or a fifteen-storey block of flats. Any permission is subject to the further restrictions of building regulations which may negate or limit that which the planners would allow.

To illustrate the operation of these powers in practice, assume that in a particular area in which all available office space is already taken up there is an increase in demand for office space. This increased demand might be met by an increased supply in three ways. Suitable buildings at present used for other purposes might be converted for use as offices; suitable bare sites might be developed by the erection of office blocks; and buildings which are not fully utilising their sites might be demolished so that larger office blocks could be erected. But planning may affect all three possibilities.

In the extreme case it might be that, although suitable buildings are available for conversion, planning permission for the change of use is not forthcoming; although bare sites are available, none is in an area allocated for office use and, although existing buildings do not fully utilise their site, they provide the maximum floor space the planner will permit. In such a case, in both short and long run, the effect of the increase in demand will be to increase the price of the existing office space to the point at which the high price so reduces demand as to equate it once again with the fixed supply.

In a less extreme case, where it would be possible to increase the supply by one or more of the three methods, some, perhaps considerable, time would elapse before any increased supply was available. In the case of conversion of existing buildings, it would be necessary to obtain planning permission, dispossess any tenants and carry out any necessary works of conversion. The time taken would depend on the administrative speed of the planning authority, the security of tenure of the tenants and the extent of the works. With the other methods planning permission would again have to be obtained and with the last method any tenants of the existing buildings would need to be dispossessed and the buildings demolished. The erection of the new buildings would take perhaps one or two years. Thus, in this less extreme case the effect of the increase in demand would be to increase the price of the existing space in the short run. In the long run, as the new space becomes available, the price would tend to stabilise or fall. If the increased supply was sufficient to satisfy the whole of the increased demand the price might return to its former level but if, as is more likely in practice, the increased supply was insufficient, or, if sufficient was of a higher quality, the new equilibrium price would be higher than the old.

A reduction in the supply of buildings is difficult to achieve; the existing stock of buildings can only be reduced by demolition or change of use and the loss involved in failing to complete buildings already started would almost certainly be higher than the loss resulting from a fall in price.

It has already been observed that the demand for land and buildings is also generally inelastic but the degree of inelasticity will depend to some extent on the purpose for which land and buildings are held.

Elasticity of demand for any commodity or service depends on whether the commodity or service is regarded as a necessity or not and on the existence of satisfactory substitutes.

Take, for example, the demand for landed property for residential occupation. This, viewed as a whole can generally be regarded as a necessity and no satisfactory substitutes exist. Thus, an increase in the price of living accommodation would probably not result in any marked contraction in demand because a particular standard of such accommodation is regarded as a necessity and a caravan or a tent would not, to the majority of people, offer a satisfactory substitute. This would not, however, be true in less prosperous times when an increase in price would probably, subject to legal restrictions on sub-division and over-crowding, lead to economies in the use of living space.

The importance of the difference between the desire of a prospective purchaser to possess a property and his ability to translate that desire into the actuality of purchasing was mentioned earlier, but further elaboration is desirable at this stage. The majority of purchases of landed property are not effected wholly by the use of the purchaser's own capital. To take houses as an example, the purchaser will normally pay only a small proportion of the purchase price out of his own capital and the remainder he borrows by way of mortgage from a financial institution such as a building society, an insurance company or a bank. In some cases this will be done because the purchaser prefers to invest the remainder of his capital elsewhere but, in most cases, the purchaser has insufficient capital to pay the whole of the purchase price although his income is sufficient to pay interest on the mortgage loan and to repay the capital gradually over a long period of years. Therefore, the ability of the majority of prospective purchasers of houses to make their demand effective depends on obtaining the necessary loan from a financial institution. Over the years these financial institutions have experienced two extremes in relation to money resources for lending which illustrate well the impact of effective demand on value. In the period 1970 to 1973 the lending institutions had plentiful sums available for lending, and borrowers were able to obtain mortgage sums for house purchase representing a large proportion of the purchase price and at low rates of interest. The effect of this lending situation was a rapid increase in house prices as borrowers competed fiercely for the houses available for purchase. At the end of 1973 the situation changed dramatically as lending institutions experienced a rapid fall in the sums they had available to lend. In the succeeding three years mortgages became difficult to obtain, certainly for any substantial proportion of purchase price, and then at high rates of interest, so that house prices actually steadied or even declined before returning to a slow rate of increase. This was particularly marked in the upper price ranges where in many cases they failed to reach the levels of 1973 even after three years of mortgage restriction. In 1976 the situation began to ease, and from 1980 the situation returned to that seen in the early 1970's. Indeed the decade starting in 1980 has seen conditions increasingly akin to those of the early 1970's with considerable funds available for borrowers wishing to buy houses. This has led to a sharp increase in house prices since 1980 in most parts of the country. The policy of financial institutions such as building societies and banks has, therefore, an important bearing on the demand for certain types of landed property.

Legislation often affects, either directly or indirectly, the demand for landed property. The various statutes affecting different types of landed property are considered in detail in Part 2 but as an example at this stage, the demand for smaller or poorer types of residential accommodation is directly affected by the Rent Acts which both restrict the income which the owner may derive from his property and also limit his powers to obtain possession.

The other principal factors affecting the demand for landed property are mainly long term so that their effects are felt only gradually over a long period of years.

Some of the effects of planning in relation to the supply of land and buildings have been noted but planning may also have important effects on the demand side. The creation of new towns, the extension of existing towns to accommodate overspill from the large conurbations and the redevelopment of central shopping areas are examples of planning schemes which may increase demand in and around the areas concerned although it may reduce demand in other areas. Thus, the new shopping centre may draw demand to adjacent properties but, in shifting the demand pattern, will diminish the demand for other nearby centres which decline in popularity.

Changes in the overall size, the location and the composition of the population will affect the demand for landed property. An overall increase in population, particularly if accompanied by an increase in prosperity, will increase the demand for most types of landed property. The increased population must be housed and its increased demands for necessities and luxuries will have to be met through the medium of such properties as shops, factories, offices, hospitals, schools and playing fields. The movement of population from one part of the country to another will have the dual effect of increasing demand in the reception area and reducing it in the area of origin. Changes in the composition of the population also have important effects. For example, a reduction in family size will increase the demand for separate dwelling units, or an increasing proportion of retired people will increase the demand for bungalows in the favoured retirement areas such as the South Coast or for flats specially developed for such people.

Improvements in transport facilities have encouraged people who work in towns to commute, sometimes over very long distances. As the number of commuters increases the transport facilities may become overburdened and the process may be reversed, particularly when coupled with above average increases in fares.

7. Landed Property as an Investment

Any purchase of an interest in landed property can be regarded as an investment. There is, first, the straightforward case of the purchase of an interest in a property which is to be let to someone in order to provide the benefit of an income. But purchase for occupation is also an investment, the benefit in this case being the annual value of the occupation. A businessman, for example, may make a conscious choice between investing his capital in purchasing a property for occupation for his business or alternatively renting a similar property, owned by someone else, so that he can invest his capital elsewhere. The point can be further illustrated by considering a case where a businessman has at some time in the past made the choice of investing part of his business capital by purchasing business premises for occupation. If he now wishes to realise the capital tied up in the property and invest it elsewhere in the business he might enter into a lease-back or a mortgage transaction. In the lease-back transaction he will sell his interest in the property but take the property back on lease paying the annual value by way of rent. In the mortgage transaction he obtains a loan on the security of his interest in the property paying annual interest on the loan.

CHAPTER 2
Methods of Valuation

1. VARIETY OF METHODS

A VALUER is called upon to give his opinion as to the value of many differing types of interest in many differing types of property for many differing purposes. Given such a multiplicity of situations the approach to the determination of value in one case may well be inappropriate to another and there have consequently evolved over the years several distinct approaches which constitute separate methods of valuation. The purpose of this book is to examine each of these and to explain their application to individual circumstances. At this stage it is useful to consider the methods in broad terms so as to provide the framework for the following Chapters.

2. COMPARISONS

Although, as will be seen, the methods of valuation differ significantly, underlying each of them is the need to make comparisons since this is the essential ingredient in arriving at a market view. In any market the vendors compete with other vendors in attracting the purchaser to them and the purchaser is thus faced with a choice. In reaching his decision the purchaser will compare what is available and at what price and he will purchase the good which in his opinion gives the best return for the price paid: he seeks value for money. This will be true in all but the most monopolistic or monopsonistic market.

The valuer, in arriving at his opinion of value, must try and judge what prices vendors generally would seek and do obtain and what choice purchasers would make. He must therefore assess what is now or has recently been available in the market place and make comparisons between them.

13

In this he acts no differently from any other person making a valuation: for example a person valuing a motor car would assess the number and types of cars available and the prices currently being obtained and so arrive at the price which in his opinion would attract a purchaser for the motor car in question. The key to the accuracy of the opinion is the knowledge of what prices have been obtained recently for similar goods with which comparison can be made. This evidence of comparable transactions in the property market is termed "comparables" and, as will be seen, the availability and the nature of comparables provide the basis of whatever method of valuation is adopted and, indeed, the choice of the method itself.

3. PRINCIPAL METHODS OF VALUATION

1. *Direct Capital Comparison*

The simplest and most direct approach in arriving at a value is to compare the object to be valued with the prices obtained for other similar objects. The method works best if the comparable objects are identical. For example, if ordinary shares in a company are each selling at 108p then the value of further shares is likely to be around 108p. Special factors may alter this view: if a large block of shares were offered which would give control of the company then a purchaser might be prepared to offer more than 108p per share. Thus even in the case of identical goods some judgment is required in arriving at a value. Property can never be absolutely identical so that the use of this method is limited to the simplest cases. The application of the method is shown in Chapter 4.

2. *Investment Approach*

A large part of the property market comprises properties where ownership and occupation are separated. The purpose of property is to provide an appropriate environment for different requirements—houses for living in, factories for making goods, shops for selling goods, and so on. For each property there is an occupier. However, in many instances properties are occupied under a contract whereby the occupier pays to the owner a sum of money, normally termed rent, in return for the right to occupy. Thus the owner surrenders occupation in return for money. This is attractive to those who wish to invest capital and obtain a return thereon and the property market is a major source of such investment opportunities. The ability to make such investments is closely allied to the various forms of interests in property which may exist, and which are set out in Chapter 3.

Thus the valuer is frequently called upon to make a valuation of an interest in property where the value is the amount of capital required to purchase the interest, and this value is clearly dependent on the amount of rent which an occupier would be prepared to pay for the right to occupy and the level of return which an investor would require on his capital. Hence there are several fundamental elements in the valuation each of which requires different types of comparables.

The basic principle is that an investor wishes to invest capital to obtain an annual return thereon in the form of a net income which represents an acceptable rate of return.

For example, A may wish to invest £100,000 in shop premises and he requires a return of 6% on his money. What net income will be required?

$$6\% \text{ of } 100,000 = 100,000 \times \frac{6}{100} = £6,000$$

as the net income.

However, in practice the position is generally reversed. The valuer will determine the net income which a property will produce. He knows that an investor will require a specific return on his capital. He can therefore calculate the capital sum which the investor will pay for the property.

For example, suppose that shop premises produce a net income of £8,000 p.a. The appropriate rate of return is 8%. What capital sum will an investor pay?

Let the capital sum be C, then

$$C \times 8\% = C \times \frac{8}{100} = £8,000 \text{ p.a.}$$

$$C = 8,000 \text{ p.a.} \times \frac{100}{8}$$

$$C = 8,000 \times 12 \cdot 5$$

$$\underline{C = £100,000}$$

As can be seen, the capital sum required is found by multiplying the net income by the reciprocal of the rate of return (the net income is "capitalised"). This reciprocal figure is termed a years' purchase or YP, a traditional expression in use for very many years, and might be said to represent the number of years to get back the capital invested, although this is a misleading concept as will become clear. It merely expresses the ratio of income to capital. The YP for any rate of interest can easily be found, e.g.

$$\text{YP at } 5\% = \frac{100}{5} = 20 \text{ YP}$$

$$\text{YP at } 7\% = \frac{100}{7} = 14 \cdot 28 \text{ YP}$$

$$\text{YP at } 10\% = \frac{100}{10} = 10 \text{ YP.}$$

It is clear that the lower the rate of interest the higher the YP. The determination of net income is explained fully in Chapters 5–7, and the determination of a YP and the capitalising of incomes in various situations in Chapters 8 and 9.

3. *Residual Approach*

So far the methods considered have been related to property which exists. Property is constantly being destroyed and created under the inevitable process of development or demolition and redevelopment which is required to meet the changing demands of society. Thus the valuer often needs to give a valuation of land or buildings which are to be developed or redeveloped. He may be able to arrive at such a value by direct comparison with the sale of other similar property which is to be developed in a similar manner, although this may be impracticable because of the unique nature of the property in question and the development proposed.

For example, it may be intended to develop some land with new warehouses in an area where no warehouses have been built in recent years. It will be possible to predict the rent which will be obtained from an occupier, and thus the capital sum which an investor would pay for the warehouses when built by adopting the investment approach. Further it is possible to predict the cost of building the warehouses and the profits which someone would require to carry out such an operation. Given the value of the finished product and the cost of producing it including required profits, it is clear that any difference represents the sum which can be paid for the land. For example, if the value of the finished warehouses is £800,000, the cost of producing them is £500,000 and the required profit is £70,000, then someone can afford to spend £800,000 − (£500,000 + 70,000) = £230,000 on the land. Thus the land value is £230,000. This sum represents the residue available and this approach is termed the residual approach.

This example represents a simple illustration of a method which has been developed in practice into an often complex calculation. The method and its application are explained in detail in Chapter 12.

4. *Profits Approach*

Many types of property depend for their value on various factors which combine to produce a potential level of business. In some instances the factors are so unique that comparison with other similar properties is impracticable and the value must therefore be determined by looking at the actual level of business achieved in the property.

A typical example of this is a petrol filling station. The design of such premises is relatively similar, and they tend to be located in prominent positions on busy traffic routes. Nonetheless a comparison of one with another is difficult

since each site is susceptible to unique factors which may
have a dramatic effect on the sales achieved. Two stations
may appear to enjoy almost identical qualities yet one will
sell 400,000 gallons a year and the other 700,000 gallons.
The level of sales clearly determines the level of profits, and
the profits determine the price someone will pay for the property and the opportunity to obtain the profits. It follows that
the value of the property can be determined from a knowledge of the profits. For example, if a property is producing
profits of £50,000 p.a. and a purchaser will invest capital
at 6 times the level of profits, the value of the property is
£300,000 (50,000 × 6). Alternatively, if an occupier is prepared to pay a rent of £20,000 p.a. out of the profits to be
able to earn the £50,000 and a purchaser will invest capital
at 15 times the rent, then again the value is £300,000
(20,000 × 15). Even here there is a need to obtain comparable
evidence, in this instance the ratio of profits or rent to capital.
This is a very simplified version of what is termed the profits
approach. The method is explained more fully in Chapters
22 and 32 when it will be seen that knowledge of the type
of business and the ability to interpret accounts and to analyse
the profits are needed to arrive at the value.

5. *Cost of Replacement Approach*

Within the wide range of properties which exist there are
some which are designed and used for a special purpose to
meet specific requirements and which are outside the general
range of commercial and residential properties. Typical
examples are churches, town halls, schools, police stations
and other similar properties which perform non-profitable
community functions.

In nearly all cases such properties are built by the authority
or organisation responsible for the provision of the special
service or use and commonly there is no alternative body
which requires the property. In such cases there are no sales
in the market and thus no comparables on which to base
a valuation. Indeed such properties are rarely sold and, when
they are, they generally need to be replaced by alternative
premises which have to be newly built since alternatives rare-

ly exist. As a result the price required by a body owning such properties is the cost of providing equivalent alternative accommodation. The price for the site will be based on the value of comparable sites whilst the cost of erection is derived from prevailing building costs.

Thus the valuation of such properties is derived from the value of alternative sites plus cost of building. This cost of replacement approach is sometimes referred to as the contractor's approach or contractor's test. Its application is restricted to special cases, as described in Chapters 21, 22 and 27.

This summary of the principal methods of valuation adopted by valuers indicates the need to take account of the special characteristics of each case. It may be possible to approach a valuation by adopting more than one method so as to check one against the other. It is clear that the accuracy of any method depends to a great extent on the comparable evidence which can be obtained by the valuer from his knowledge of the market. In the following Chapters the examples will make assumptions as to the nature of the evidence. It is stressed that any assumptions are solely for illustrative purposes and are not intended to indicate either levels for any specified factor or the relationship between factors currently obtaining in the market.

CHAPTER 3

Interests in Land

1. PROPERTY RIGHTS IN GENERAL

THE TWO principal interests or rights in land, or land and buildings, with which the valuer is concerned are known respectively as freehold and leasehold. Both must be distinguished from mere permission to enter upon land (even permission by virtue of a contract—e.g. for payment) which is known in law as a "licence", since permission can normally be withdrawn unilaterally on reasonable notice by the licensor (i.e. the landowner) to the licensee. A licence therefore has a negligible value in itself, at any rate at common law; but sometimes an "equitable" right is grafted on to it which does have some value or at least reduces the value of the licensor's legal title.

To the valuer the term freehold implies a property which the owner holds absolutely (i.e. unconditionally) and in perpetuity, and of which he is either in physical possession or in receipt of rents arising from leases or tenancies which have been created out of the freehold interest.

In law the term freehold has a wider general meaning and includes lesser interests such as entails and life interests. The legal term for the valuer's conception of freehold is the "fee simple absolute in possession". The Law of Property Act 1925 (Section 1) states that this and the leasehold (or "term of years absolute") are now the only forms of ownership capable of being a "legal estate" in land and thus existing at common law. Other interests are "equitable" merely. A "legal estate" is "good against the whole world", but an equitable interest is enforceable against some persons and not others. A "fee simple absolute in possession" exists in all land in England and Wales; whereas leaseholds and equitable interests are superimposed on (or "carved out" of) such

21

ownership, and subsequently terminated, depending on circumstances.

In the following sections it will be convenient to consider
first the position of the freeholder who is in physical possession of his property, and then note the nature and incidence of the various types of leasehold interest which may
be created out of the freehold. Later it will be explained
how successive interests in property—such as "entailed interests", "life interests" and "reversions and remainders",
which are "equitable interests" only—may sometimes arise
under wills or settlements.

Physical ownership of "land" extends indefinitely above
and below the surface of the land, within reason, and thus
in a normal case includes both air space and subsurface strata
of minerals.

2. FREEHOLDS

Under the Crown the legal freeholder is inherently the
absolute owner of the property, and is sometimes said to
be able to do what he likes with his land, subject only to
the general law of the land (notably planning control) and
to the lawful rights of others. He may thus in a normal case
develop it, transfer it, or create lesser interests in it, without
the consent of any other private person. His ownership of
the property is perpetual even though he is mortal. Buildings
may become worn out, the use and character of the property
may change; but the land remains the permanent property
of the freeholder and his successors, whether the latter obtain
it from him by gift, sale or disposition on death.

The legal freeholder, as absolute owner of his property,
usually holds it without payment in the nature of rent, though
in strict theory he is always nominally the tenant of the
Crown. But in some parts of the country freeholds will be
found to be subject to annual payments known as "rentcharges", "fee farm rents" or "chief rents". These usually
arise through a vendor of freehold property agreeing to
accept a rentcharge in perpetuity or for a limited term in
lieu of the whole, or sometimes part, of the full purchase

price. Although the rentcharge owner has the right, in the event of non-payment, to enter and take the rents and profits of land until arrears are satisfied, a freehold subject to a charge of this kind still ranks in law as a fee simple absolute in possession.[1] In many deeds creating such rentcharges there is a power of absolute re-entry where the rent has been in arrears for two years. The Rentcharges Act 1977, however, in general terms prohibits the creation of new rentcharges and makes provision for the gradual extinguishment of existing ones over the next sixty years.

A rentcharge or fee farm rent will be treated as an outgoing in arriving at the net income of the freehold for valuation purposes. As for the interest of the rentcharge owner (which is technically a form of legal estate in the land), although the rentcharge is commonly small in amount compared with the net rental of the buildings and land on which it is secured, and thus almost certain to be received in practice, it depreciates in real terms as does any fixed income in periods of inflation.

During a state of national emergency, statute may give the Crown drastic rights of user and possession over the property of its subjects. Even in normal times there are numerous Acts whereby an owner can be forced to sell his land to government departments, local authorities or other statutory bodies for various public purposes. Such compulsory purchases are to be paid for at market value; but this is determined statutorily under the Land Compensation Acts 1961 and 1973. To develop land an owner must obtain planning permission under the Town and Country Planning Act 1971. Public Health Acts, Housing Acts, Local Acts and Building Regulations also restrict the erection or reconstruction of buildings or compel the owner to keep them in a state of good repair and sanitation. The Leasehold Reform Act, 1967, gives certain long leaseholders of residential property the right to require their freeholder landlords to sell them the freehold reversion.

The owner's freedom to do as he likes with his property is also limited by the fact that he must not interfere with

---

[1] Law of Property (Amendment) Act 1926: Schedule.

the natural rights of others as, for instance, by depriving his neighbour's land of support or polluting or diminishing the flow of a stream. Often his enjoyment is lessened by the fact that some other owner has acquired an easement over his property or is entitled to the benefit of covenants restricting the use of it; these rights are discussed below.

Being a "legal estate", a freehold can normally be transferred (by a living owner) only on the execution of a deed, that is to say a document bearing a seal as well as a signature (Law of Property Act 1925, Section 52). In those parts of the country to which the Land Registration Acts 1925–86 apply on a compulsory basis, legal freeholds (and leaseholds for over 21 years) must, when transferred (or created), be entered in the Land Registry, and the title deed, or deed of "conveyance", will in such cases take the form of a "land certificate". Registration provides a state guarantee of the legal ownership or "title".

Occupation of land counts as legal "possession" if it rests on genuine "title", whether registered or unregistered. The common law remedy for an owner wrongly excluded from possession is a writ or order of possession obtainable from the court (and enforceable by the sheriff's officers); and damages for financial loss are also obtainable against a wrong-doer. But if an owner is excluded from possession and acquiesces in "adverse possession" by a trespasser who treats the land as his own, the Limitation Act 1980 provides that an action for possession against the latter must be brought within 12 years; if not, the owner's rights are extinguished and in their place the trespasser (or "squatter") acquires a lawful title himself.

It commonly happens that the freeholder, instead of occupying the property himself, grants or "lets" the exclusive possession of the premises to another for a certain period, usually in consideration of the payment of rent, under a "lease" or "tenancy".

A letting may be for quite a short period—e.g. yearly, quarterly, monthly or weekly—thus producing a "periodic" tenancy automatically renewing itself until terminated by notice to quit from either side; or it may be for any definite fixed period. A "building lease" of 99 or 999 years is often met with; but occupation leases for terms such as 15, 25 or 50 years are also commonly found in practice.

Like a freehold conveyance, a lease or tenancy taking effect as a legal estate must be granted by deed; but the Law of Property Act 1925, Section 54, provides that no formalities whatever are needed for the grant of a tenancy at a full market rent for not more than 3 years, taking effect immediately.

Grants of tenancies (but not the obligations contained in them) may be back-dated; or they may be made to begin at a future date ("reversionary leases") but not more than 21 years after the date of the grant.

When a freeholder grants a short-term lease or tenancy the lessee seldom has any valuable interest in the property not only owing to the shortness of his term but also to the fact that he is usually paying the full rental value which the premises are worth, as distinct from a lump-sum purchase price. The valuation of leasehold interests therefore tends to be significant only in those cases where property is leased for an appreciable term of years and where the rent reserved under the lease is less than the rental value and not subject to frequent adjustment under rent review clauses, so that the lessee is enjoying a "profit rent" from his possession of the property. Normally in such a case the rent is low because the lessee has also paid a lump-sum purchase price to the lessor. This low rent is often loosely called a "ground rent". It should be noted that a lease can be transferred—"assigned"—by gift or sale, or on death, just as a freehold can, unless the terms of the lease provide otherwise.

A freeholder who grants leases or tenancies retains the right at common law to regain physical possession of his property when these leases or tenancies come to an end. For this reason the landlord's interest in the land is known as his "reversion".

The common law right of a freeholder to regain physical possession of his property at the end of a lease granted by him (including, as a normal common law rule, any buildings or other "fixtures" added to the land by the tenant which are not removeable by him as "tenant's" fixtures) is now much restricted by legislation, the most important statutes being the Rent Act 1977, the Landlord and Tenant Act 1954, the Agricultural Holdings Act 1986 and the Leasehold Reform Act 1967. The provisions contained in these Acts (extending to control of rents as well as security of tenure) are considered in greater detail in later Chapters.

3. LEASEHOLDS

A leasehold interest, or "term of years", is normally subject to the payment of an annual rent and to the observance of covenants contained in the lease. The grantor of the lease is called the "lessor" and his interest while the lease lasts is the "reversion". The grantee is the "lessee" or "leaseholder". If the rent the lessee has covenanted to pay is less than the true rental value of the premises, the lessee will be in receipt of a net income from the property the capitalised value of which, for the balance of his term, will represent the market value of his leasehold interest. Even if the lessee is paying full rental value of the property this interest may have some value in that it confers a right on him to occupy the premises for the unexpired term of his lease and may enable him to claim a new lease or to continue in possession at the end of his term under the legislation mentioned above. If he is paying a rent above the full value, the lease will have a negative value owing to the liability which it creates.

The following are the principal types of lease met with in practice.

(i) *Building Leases.* These are leases of land ripe for building—i.e. development—under which the lessee undertakes to pay a yearly ground rent for the land, as such, to erect suitable buildings upon the land, and to keep those buildings in repair and pay all outgoings in connection with them throughout the term. The ground rent represents the rental value of the bare site at the time the lease is granted, and the difference between this and the net rent obtainable from the buildings when erected will constitute the lessee's profit rent or net income.

Building leases are usually granted for terms of 99 years, although 120, 125 and 150 year terms have become common in recent years, particularly for large scale commercial development. Longer terms of 999 years are found occasionally. Lesser terms than 99 years are met with, but it is obvious that no would-be leaseholder will incur the expense of erecting buildings unless he is granted a reasonably long term in which to enjoy the use of them, since they revert to the landlord with the land at the end of the lease. Leases of residential property exceeding 21 years (but not flats or maisonettes) may, under the Leasehold Reform Act 1967, be extended by 50 years at a modern ground rent; alternatively the lessee may buy the freehold reversion.

(ii) *Occupation Leases.* This term is applied to a lease of land and buildings for occupation in their present state by the lessee. In practice the length of the lease varies according to the type of property. Dwelling-houses and older types of commercial and industrial premises are often leased for fairly short terms, such as 3 or 5 years.

In the case of medium and long term leases of commercial or industrial premises, it has become standard practice to incorporate a "rent revision" clause which enables the rent to be revised, usually upwards, at fixed periods of time. The tendency in recent years, due largely to the effects of inflation, has been for review periods to become shorter, 5 years being a fairly standard period. Thus leases are normally granted for multiples of the review period, 10, 15, 20 or longer periods of years. Before this, multiples of 7 years were often met with.

Ground rents are now normally subject to review, the review periods often being the same as for the duration of occupation leases, although sometimes they are less frequent, 10 years being fairly common.

Where the rent reserved under an occupation lease represents the full rental value of land and buildings, or near it, it is called a market rent or rack rent. Where it is less than the full rental value, although obviously not a ground rent, it is called a head rent. It is on the difference between the head rent and the net rack rental value of the premises that the capital value (if any) of the leaseholder's interest depends in the case of an occupation lease.

The term head rent is also used to distinguish the rent paid by the head tenant to the freeholder from other rents paid in respect of the same property by a sub-tenant to that tenant as the sub-lessor.

(iii) *Subleases.* Subject to the terms of his headlease a leaseholder may sublease the property for any shorter term than he himself holds, either at the same rent or at any other figure he may be able to obtain. In this way the head lessee himself becomes entitled to a "reversion" on the falling in of the sublease. Often this reversion will be a purely nominal one of a day or a few days only. Thus, a head lessee having fourteen years of his lease still unexpired might sublease the property at an improved rent for a term of fourteen years less (say) ten days. The reservation of at least a day's reversion is necessary to preserve the nature of the sublease. An attempt to lease for the full term remaining would have the effect of an outright assignment, not a sublease.

A sublessee in occupation will often have the benefit of statutory security of tenure and control of rents already referred to.

Where a lessee has been granted a lease of building land at a ground rent he may sublease the land, as a whole or in smaller plots, either at the same rent as he himself pays, in which case the new rent is known as a leasehold ground rent, or, as is usually the case, at a higher rent than that reserved in his own lease, in which case the rent is known as an improved ground rent.

(iv) *Leases for Life.* It was possible until 1925 to grant leases for the duration of the life of the lessee or some other person. By the Law of Property Act 1925, these "leases for life" now take effect as leases for ninety years determinable on the death of the party in question by one month's notice from either side expiring on one of the usual quarter days. This is because a grant for life is an uncertain period and the aim of the Act of 1925 is to restrict leaseholds to ascertainable periods.

This provision has little effect on the duration of such a lease because if the premises are held at less than their true rental value the lessor will take the first opportunity of terminating the lease on the lessee's death, and if the lessee was paying a higher rent than the premises were worth his personal representatives will be equally anxious to determine.

From a valuation standpoint, therefore, the period of the lease may still be safely regarded as that of the lessee's life.

4. LEASEHOLD INTERESTS GENERALLY

A lessee is very much more restricted in his dealings with the property than is a freeholder. In many cases he will be under express covenant to keep the premises in good repair and redecorate internally and externally at stated intervals. Usually he cannot carry out alterations or structural improvements to the property without first consulting his lessor, and possibly covenanting to reinstate the premises in their original condition at the end of the term. Often he may not sublease or assign his interest or part with possession without first obtaining his landlord's consent, although that consent cannot be unreasonably withheld.

If the lessee subleases, even though the sublease contains precisely the same covenants as his own lease, there is still the risk of his incurring liability to his lessor if the sublessee fails to keep his part of the bargain. Similarly, if he assigns he may still be held liable on his express covenants—such as the covenant to repair—should his assignee prove to be a "man of straw".

For these and other reasons leaseholds are less attractive to the investor than freeholds and the income from a leasehold interest in a particular class of property will usually be capitalised at a higher rate per cent than would be used for a freehold interest in the same property.

5. RESTRICTIVE COVENANTS AND EASEMENTS

It has already been pointed out that land, whether leased or not, may be subject to restrictions as to user. Some previous conveyance of the freehold may have imposed easements or restrictive covenants, for example, to prevent land being used for business purposes or to prohibit the erection of houses costing less than a stipulated figure.

Such restrictions are often inserted in leases. For instance, the lessee of a house may covenant not to use it except as a private dwelling-house, or the lessee of a shop may covenant not to use it for any offensive trade, or to use it only for one particular type of trade.

A "covenant" is a contractual obligation in a deed. Normally at common law contracts are only enforceable against the individual party who has agreed to be bound (or assignees, in the case of normal leasehold covenants). But the rules of equity enable a covenant which "touches and concerns" land to "run" automatically with that land to burden all subsequent owners who have "notice" of it provided that it is negative ("restrictive") in nature, for the benefit of neighbouring landowners. Unless the covenant is an obligation in a lease it is registrable as a land charge (Land Charges Act 1972) and this acts as "notice to the whole world"—indeed, actual notice then becomes irrelevant. Failure thus to register such a covenant renders it void against a purchaser of a legal estate for money or money's worth. But the burden of a restrictive covenant cannot "run with the land" unless the benefit of it is annexed to nearby land capable of benefiting (often in the form of a scheme of development) or else is assigned with such land. Enforcement is principally by means of an injunction against infringement, though a court may also award damages.

Restrictions on the user of land are sometimes imposed solely for the benefit of neighbouring land which the vendor is retaining. In other cases they are intended to safeguard the general development of property in an area. For example, where a building estate is sold in freehold plots to various purchasers, each purchaser usually enters into the same covenants as regards the use of his land. Normally such covenants are mutually enforceable between the various purchasers and their successors in title, so that the owner of any one plot may compel the observance of the restrictions by the owner of any other plot. Yet although restrictive covenants which are reasonable in character may help to maintain values over a particular area, such as a building estate, in some cases—particularly when imposed a considerable number of years ago—they may restrict the normal development of a property and detract from its value.

The right to enforce restrictive convenants may be lost.

This may happen if the party entitled to enforce them has for many years acquiesced in open breaches of the covenant or has consented to a breach of covenant on one occasion in such a way as to suggest that other breaches will be disregarded, or if the character of the neighbourhood has so entirely changed that it would be inequitable to enforce the covenant.

There are also statutory means by which a modification or removal of restrictive covenants may be obtained. Thus the Housing Act 1985, Section 610, enables any interested persons or the local authority to apply to the County Court for permission to disregard leasehold or freehold covenants which would prevent houses being converted into maisonettes, if satisfied that changes in the neighbourhood render it reasonable to do so, and that, while the house is unlettable as a single house, it would readily let if converted into two or more tenements. More generally under the Law of Property Act 1925,[2] the Lands Tribunal may wholly or partially modify or discharge restrictive covenants on freeholds if satisfied that by reason of changes in the character of the property or the neighbourhood, or other material circumstances, the restrictions ought to be deemed obsolete or that their continuance would obstruct the reasonable use of the land for public or private purposes without securing practical benefits to other persons. Current planning policies of local planning authorities should be taken into account. These powers also extend to restrictive covenants on leaseholds where the original term was for over 40 years of which at least 25 years have elapsed.[3]

The Lands Tribunal may make such order as it deems proper for the payment of compensation to any person entitled to the benefit of the restrictions who is likely to suffer loss in consequence of the removal or modification of the restrictions.

The 1925 Act also gives power to the court to declare whether land is, or is not, affected by restrictions and whether

---

[2] Section 84 as amended by Lands Tribunal Act 1949, Section 1(4) and Law of Property Act 1969, Section 28.
[3] Landlord and Tenant Act 1954, Section 52.

restrictions are enforceable, and if so, by whom. This is a valuable provision which enables many difficulties to be removed where the existence of restrictions or the right to enforce them is uncertain.

Unlike restrictive covenants which only take effect as property rights in equity, easements are common law property rights and thus enforceable against the whole world regardless of notice or registration (though easements can also exist in equity, and these are registrable in the same way as restrictive covenants). An easement burdens particular land, termed a servient tenement, for the benefit of other land nearby, termed a dominant tenement, and its presence or absence obviously affects the value of each. Typical easements are private (not public) rights of way, and also rights of support, light and ventilation. Many other varieties of easement (for example, rights to instal and maintain pipes or cables) have been upheld from time to time. A right to support of land as distinct from buildings is, however, a natural right enjoyed by all owners, and not an easement.

Easements must, to be "legal estates", be granted expressly in a deed. But rules of law have been evolved whereby (for reasons of necessity or otherwise) the grant of easements is often implied into conveyances of land which in fact make no express mention of them. Also it is possible to have a presumed grant of an easement by "prescription", that is to say long user over the servient land provided it has been exercised "as of right" and not by permission of that land's owner. The Prescription Act 1832 provides that 20 years is the normal minimum period required. Easements can be terminated by express discharge or by allowing them to lapse. Similar to easements are "profits a prendre"; these involve taking such things as minerals, plants, game or fish from the servient land. A dominant tenement is not essential for a profit a prendre. Easements and profits are enforced by the same remedies as restrictive covenants.

It is also possible in some cases for a person to be allowed, on equitable grounds, a right to use property for his benefit even if at common law he is only present on it as a licensee, if the owner, who would otherwise be able by revoking the permission to exclude him, has misled him to his potential disadvantage into acting as if he had such a right. This is known as "equitable (or proprietary) estoppel".

6. Successive Interests in Property

Provisions are frequently made in settlements by deed or by will whereby, so far as the law permits, the future succession to the enjoyment of the property is controlled.

A once common example (now extremely rare in consequence of taxation) is the creation of an "entailed interest" in freehold or long leasehold property whereby the property is settled on a certain person for life and after his death on his eldest son and the "heirs of his body". In this way the property will descend from generation to generation unless the entail is barred or unless heirs fail, in which latter case the land will revert to the original grantor or his successors or else pass to any other person entitled under the settlement on termination of the entail.

Under this and other forms of settlement certain persons may be entitled, either alone or jointly with others, to successive life interests or entails in a property, the ownership finally passing to some other person in fee simple. The first owner enjoys his interest "in possession"; but each of the others has at the outset an interest which is only a future right and holds it "in remainder". Such a person is called a remainderman. Sometimes a party may be entitled to succeed to a property only subject to certain conditions—for example, that he reaches a prescribed age. In such a case the interest is spoken of as "contingent"; and if the contingency is too remote in the future the interest will infringe what in law is called the "perpetuity rule" and be void. The details of this are too complex to be given here; but it may be noted that a grantor is allowed to specify a period not exceeding eighty years in which prescribed contingencies (e.g. birth of grandchildren) may operate (Perpetuities and Accumulations Act 1964).

Life interests and future interests in property rank as equitable interests not legal estates. But from a valuation point of view the distinction is of little consequence. To a valuer the problem they present is that of finding the capital value of an income receivable for the duration of a life or lives, or the capital value of an income for a term of years or in perpetuity receivable after the lapse of a previous life interest. The valuation of such interests is considered in Chapter 11.

Under the Settled Land Act 1925, a person enjoying the interest of tenant for life has vested in him, and may sell, the whole freehold or leasehold interest (the legal estate) in the settled property, the capital money being paid to trustees and settled to the same uses (i.e. beneficial interests) as was the land itself. A valuer advising on a sale of this description is concerned not with the value of the party's life interest, but with the market value of the freehold or leasehold property which is the subject of the settlement; and in such a case the equitable (beneficial) interests in the settlement can be ignored for valuation purposes because the land will be sold free of them. They are said to be "overreached", that is to say preserved not against the land but against the capital of the settlement in its new form in money, investments, etc.

7. Co-ownership

Land may be concurrently owned by two or more persons, either by way of joint tenancy or tenancy in common.

In a joint tenancy the parties have equal rights to the benefits of the property, but when one joint tenant dies his share passes to the surviving joint tenants by "survivorship".

In a tenancy in common shares are "undivided" (i.e. there is no physical partition of the property) but not necessarily equal. Thus, one tenant in common might hold a quarter share in the property, another a half share and so on. Moreover, there is no survivorship, as in joint tenancies, for if one tenant in common dies his share passes under his will or intestacy. Thus the capital value and not merely the enjoyment of the property is shared between the co-owners.

Under the Law of Property Act 1925, the holding of "undivided shares" in the legal estate in land is abolished. This means that tenancies in common can only be equitable rights in the land. Where a tenancy in common exists, the legal estate of the property as a whole will be vested in trustees for sale as joint tenants, the owners of the shares (who may be the same persons as the trustees) being entitled in equity, though not at common law, to their respective proportions of the proceeds of sale and of net income from the land pending sale. Joint tenancies in equity are permissible, but may be "severed" into tenancies in common if their holders individually so desire.

From a valuation standpoint although a tenant in common or owner of a share in property no longer has any legal estate in the land he is entitled to all the benefits of ownership, such as participation in the rents and profits and a share of the capital sum realised by the property on sale. The best procedure is therefore to value the property as a whole and assign an appropriate fraction of the total to the value of the party's share.

It is generally recognised, however, that a share in property is less attractive to prospective investors than absolute owner-ship, and a percentage deduction varying according to the size of share and the degree of control it confers is usually made to allow for this.

As for joint tenancies, the survivorship rule prevents the rights of the joint tenants from having any market value. But the ultimate survivor will hold an absolute freehold (or possibly leasehold) which should be valued in the ordinary way. However, where joint tenants are trustees for other persons it is normally permissible to appoint new trustees, and this counteracts the working of the survivorship rule. Even if new trustees are not appointed the trust continues to exist and the court will if necessary take charge of it.

8. TRUSTS GENERALLY

Wherever an equitable interest is expressly or impliedly created in property separately from the legal estate there is a "trust" relationship. The legal owner is a "trustee", the equitable owner is a "beneficiary". Strict settlements, trusts for sale and co-ownership, for this reason all involve trusts;

and there can be trusts in other circumstances, such as when
X holds the legal title of property as nominee for Y. Unless
they can be and are "overreached" (see above) it is the equitable interests in a trust which are of value, not the legal
estate of the trustee or trustees.

9. TRANSFERS OF INTERESTS IN LAND

The rules of the law of property in land have evolved chiefly
in connection with transfers of ownership. A life interest
is a right which cannot be transferred at the life owner's
death because that is the time when it comes to an end,
but it can be transferred for so long as he remains alive (e.g.
for mortgage purposes). The legal freehold or "fee simple",
on the other hand, is perpetual in its duration, and so can
be transferred by a current owner during his lifetime ("inter
vivos") or at his death. The same is true in principle of leaseholds, except, of course, that the term of a leasehold may
end while its holder is still alive, in which case no property
right remains to him in respect of it (though, of course, he
may be able to secure a renewal).

The valuer needs to take proper account of these various
characteristics because what he is valuing is not "land" in
the purely physical sense, but property rights in land. Death
should perhaps be considered first. Transfer on death is governed by the deceased's (valid) will, if any. Failing that, it
goes by operation of law, under the Administration of Estates
Act 1925 (as amended), to the deceased's next-of-kin, in
accordance with various elaborate rules governing "intestacy". Frequently in practice this simply involves a sale by
his personal representatives; in which case what the next-of-
kin actually receive is a distribution of the money proceeds
of the sale. But, where necessary, the Inheritance (Provision
for Family and Dependants) Act 1975 empowers the courts
to order payments to be made out of a deceased person's
estate to any surviving spouses or other dependants who
would otherwise in effect be left destitute because no proper
provision has been made for them.

Transfer "inter vivos" occurs either by gift or by sale, that is to say either non-commercially or commercially. The latter can for this purpose be taken to cover transfers in return for a financial consideration in the form of a purchase price or a series of regular payments or both (long leases being often granted in return for both a lump sum purchase price and a "ground rent") or in the form of an exchange. Grants of new leases, assignments of existing leases and transfers of freeholds, are all varieties of transfer "inter vivos" whether as gifts or as commercial transactions.

A gift of land, on death or "inter vivos", requires the carrying out of the appropriate legal conveyancing formality, which is the execution of a deed of "conveyance" (or a written "assent" by personal representatives) of the legal freehold or leasehold as the case may be. The same is true of commercial transfers. An equitable property right, however, need only be in writing as a rule; indeed there are many circumstances where owners acquire equitable rights merely by implication of law. Thus if land is "conveyed" by legal deed of grant to a nominee, in equity the benefit goes by implication not to him but to the real purchaser. Legal leasehold tenancies, if at a market rent and taking immediate effect, do not, however, require to be granted by any formality at all, provided that they are created for a period not exceeding three years (thus oral short-term tenancies of this kind are still "legal estates" in land).

But commercial transfers, unlike gifts, involve another stage in addition to (and prior to) the "conveyance", namely the contract or bargain constituting the sale. Section 40 of the Law of Property Act, 1925, provides that a land contract cannot be enforced unless either it is evidenced in writing and signed by "the party to be charged" (or his agent) or the party seeking to enforce it (i) is claiming specific performance rather than damages (i.e. the defaulter is to be made to proceed to the conveyance and not to be allowed to buy himself out of liability) and (ii) can prove that he has "partly performed" the contract on his side. "Part performance" means some action "unequivocally referable" to the contract; and even the payment of money will do, if all the circumstances are such that it satisfies that test in a particular case. But the Court of Appeal has uttered a reminder that if in correspondence the phrase "subject to contract", or similar wording is used, there is no contract at all at that stage, merely negotiation (*Tiverton Estates Ltd. v. Wearwell* (1974) 1 All E.R. 209) from which either party can back out.

CHAPTER 4
Direct Value Comparison

1. GENERALLY

AS WAS described in Chapter 2, the simplest and most direct method of valuation is direct comparison. The method is based on comparing the property to be valued with similar properties and the prices achieved for them and allowing for differences between them, so determining the price likely to be achieved for the property in question.

The method is based on a comparison of like with like. Properties may be similar but each property is unique so that they can never be totally alike. As they move away from the ideal situation of absolute similarity so does the method become more unreliable. The reasons for dissimilarities are mainly:

(a) *Location.* The position of any property is clearly unique. The actual position is an important factor in the value of a property and for some, such as shops, the major factor. For example, on an estate built to the same design at the same time, some houses will be nearer to a busy traffic road than others: some will be on higher ground with good views whilst others will be surrounded by other houses: some will back south, others back north: some will have larger plots than others. Even in a parade of shops, some will be nearer a street crossing than others or be adjacent to a pedestrian exit from the car park or nearer to a popular large store.

(b) *Physical State.* The physical condition of a property depends on the amount of attention which has been given to maintenance and repair and decoration. Two otherwise physically identical properties can be in sharp contrast if one is well maintained and the other in poor order. Repair apart, occupiers of properties

39

typically make alterations, varying from a minor change to major improvements. This is perhaps most apparent with residential properties where occupiers may instal central heating, renovate kitchens and bathrooms, change windows, remove fireplaces, add extensions and so on, to the extent that houses which from external appearances are identical are seen to be totally different on closer inspection.

(c) *Tenure*. As was shown in Chapter 3 there are various interests in property. Apart from a freehold interest with no subsidiary leasehold interests, the likelihood of interests being similar is remote in view of the almost endless variations that may exist between them. Even on an estate with estate leases which allow for each tenant to hold on a similarly drafted lease, the terms are likely to vary as to expiry date or rent payable or permitted use. In the market at large the differences will multiply considerably and the method is strained to compare say a leasehold shop with 45 years to run at a rent of £100 p.a. with tenant responsible for all outgoings apart from external repairs and no limitations as to use, with the leasehold interest in a physically identical shop with 8 years to run at a rent of £4,000 p.a. with rent review in 3 years, tenant responsible for all outgoings and the use limited to the sale of childrens' clothes. If the first lease sells for £100,000 it is impossible to derive the capital value of the second lease directly from that figure—it is certainly less, but how much so? This contrast between the types and nature of interests is the principal barrier to the use of the direct comparison method for the valuation of interests other than freehold in possession.

(d) *Purpose*. The purpose of a valuation is an important element in deciding upon the method to be adopted. Where the valuation is for example for investment purposes, or for fire insurance purposes, the direct comparison method would be inappropriate since other methods will give a more realistic answer.

(e) *Time*. Transactions take place in the market regularly. The market is not static so that the price obtained for a property at one time will not necessarily be achieved if the same property is sold again. Thus the reliability of evidence of prices diminishes as time elapses since the transaction took place. In the volatile market which has developed in recent years, only a short time will pass before the evidence becomes unreliable.

Given the special characteristics of property and the drawbacks these create in adopting the direct comparison method, it is clear that it is of limited application. In practice only three types of property lend themselves readily to the use of the method and in each case only when the freehold interest free from any leasehold estate is being valued. The three types are considered below.

2. Residential Property

The great majority of all property transactions comprises the sale of houses and flats with vacant possession. As the direct comparison method is adopted for the valuation of such properties this is the method of valuation most commonly used. It is true that flats are generally held on leasehold interests but since these tend to be for a long period of years at a relatively small rent they often have the general characteristics of a freehold so allowing direct comparison.

Example 4–1

A owns the freehold interest in a house which is to be sold with vacant possession. The house was built in 1934. It is semi-detached with 3 bedrooms, bathroom and separate W.C. on the first floor and a through lounge and kitchen on the ground floor. There is a garage lying to the rear of the house with an access shared by the adjoining houses. Apart from taking down the wall between the former front and rear rooms to form a single lounge, and the installation of oil fired central heating, no improvements have been carried out. It is considered that both the bathroom and kitchen need to be modernised. The property is in a fair state of repair.

Several nearby similar properties have sold recently for prices in the range £38,000 to £44,000. The most recent include a house in the next pair to A's house, built at the same time and with identical accommodation but without central heating. However, the bathroom has had a new coloured suite installed with matching tiling, and new kitchen units were installed some 4 years ago. It is in good repair. The house sold for £41,500. Another house in the same street, also built at the same time and with the same basic accommodation but with modernised kitchen and bathroom, central heating and ground floor cloakroom, and also having an independent drive to the garage, in good repair, sold recently for £44,000.

Valuation. It appears that a house such as A's with the basic amenities and modernised and in good repair is worth around £41,500 without central heating.

Assume that with central heating the value would be £42,250. This appears to be realistic since a similar house but with ground floor cloakroom and independent drive to garage sold for £44,000 (an allowance of £1,750 for these further factors seems reasonable).

Allowing £2,000 for the cost and trouble of modernising the bathroom and kitchen, it appears that the value of A's house is £40,250 in good repair.

Allowing for the lower standard of repair, the value of A's house is £39,750.

It is clear from this example that it is necessary to make various allowances for the differences in quality between the houses. The level of allowance is subjective and depends on the experience and knowledge of the valuer. This example illustrates that the method is simple in its general approach but is dependent on considerable valuation judgment for its application.

The valuation of residential property is considered in detail in Chapter 19.

3. AGRICULTURAL PROPERTY

Agricultural land is divided between land let to tenants by the freeholder and land farmed by the freeholder. In the latter case, in any sale the freehold interest is offered with vacant possession. This allows the direct comparison method to be adopted. The valuer, considering the comparables available, must allow for differences such as the quality of the soil, type of farming possible, extent and condition of buildings, location, and quality of the farmhouse and other accommodation. Farms vary considerably in size and the valuer allows for this difference by adjusting the comparable evidence to a common unit of value, the price per hectare.

Example 4–2

Value the freehold interest in Whiteacre, a farm of 180 hectares. The farm is good arable land with a full range of modern buildings.

The evidence of recent sales includes the sale of Greenacre, a farm of 200 ha with better land than Whiteacre and all modern amenities at a price of £1,000,000; Blackacre, a farm of 170 ha with poor arable land and poor buildings which sold for £500,000: and Roseacre, a farm of 30 ha with good land but few buildings which sold for £170,000.

Analysis of Comparables
Greenacre 200 ha £1,000,000 good arable good buildings
£5,000 per ha
Blackacre 170 ha £500,000 poor arable poor buildings
£2,941 per ha
Roseacre 30 ha £170,000 good arable few buildings
£5,667 per ha

It appears that arable land has a value range of £5,667 per ha and £2,941 per ha. It is noted that the highest value is for a smaller area than usual which suggests that the overall farm size may have a special significance. It seems that the value of Whiteacre therefore lies around £4,750 per ha. Hence

Valuation 180 ha at £4,750 per ha = £855,000.

The valuation of agricultural property is considered fully in Chapter 17.

4. DEVELOPMENT LAND

In many instances property will be sold which is suitable for development or redevelopment and this is referred to as development land or building land. The types of development land range widely, reflecting the many forms of development which are possible and the variation in size and location of such land. There is one type, however, which tends to have many qualities common to each, development land for residential development. For this reason, residential building land may be valued using the direct comparison method.

The valuer, in analysing the comparables will need to allow for such factors as the type of development contemplated, e.g. from luxury houses to high density low cost accommodation; the site conditions, e.g. level or sloping, well drained or wet; and location in relation to general facilities, such as transport, schools, hospitals. The comparable sites will vary in size and the valuer therefore reduces the evidence to a common yardstick. This may be value per acre, value per plot or per unit, or value per habitable room. For example, the price of a site of 10 acres sold for £2,500,000 with permission to build either 90 4-room houses or 120 3-room flats may be expressed as:—

£250,000 per acre—£27,778 per plot—£20,833 per unit—£6,944 per habitable room.

The valuer will use whichever yardstick is appropriate to the type of sites he is valuing, the main essential being to apply the same yardstick to all cases.

Examples 4–3

Value the freehold interest in 5 acres of residential building land with the right to build 42 houses. Recent comparable land sales include

a) 7·5 acres with the right to build 60 houses, sold for £1,800,000.
b) 12·5 acres with the right to build 125 houses, sold for £3,125,000.
c) 1 acre with the right to build 6 houses, sold for £300,000.

Analysis of Comparables
a) 7·5 acres; 60 houses (8 houses per acre); £1,800,000:£240,000 per acre *or* £30,000 per house plot.
b) 12·5 acres; 125 houses (10 houses per acre); £3,125,000:£250,000 per acre *or* £25,000 per house plot.
c) 1 acre; 6 houses (6 houses per acre); £300,000:£300,000 per acre *or* £50,000 per house plot.

The analysis indicates that building land is worth £240,000 to £300,000 per acre or £25,000 to £50,000 per house. Where more houses are to be built on a given area (the "density") it is assumed that the houses will be smaller and less valuable, so that the value per house falls, and also the land on which it stands, although conversely the value per acre rises since the builder will have higher output and presumably higher profits overall. Site (c) has values outside the general range since it is a small development which would attract a different type of buyer, and it also has a low density so that large and high value houses are to be built. The higher value of (c) supports the general value evidence of (a) or (b).

Hence the site to be valued, which has a density of 8·4 houses per acre, appears to lie within the general band of values.

Valuation

5 acres at say £275,000 per acre = £1,375,000
or 42 houses at say £32,500 per house plot = £1,365,000
Value say £1,370,000

Although residential building land may be valued by direct

comparison, it is possible to cross-check the valuation by valuing the interest using the residual method of valuation which is the typical method for valuing development land, as was stated in Chapter 2. The valuation of development land is considered fully in Chapters 12 and 18.

CHAPTER 5
Rental Value

1. GENERALLY

IN CHAPTER 2 the basis of valuation using the investment method was described. It involves the determining of the present capital value of a future income flow.

In order to value a property by this method, two things must be known. First, the net income which the property will produce and, secondly, the rate of interest appropriate to the property from which the Years' Purchase can be found. The factors determining the yields from investments in landed property are discussed in Chapter 7. This Chapter and Chapter 6 are concerned with the factors affecting net income and the methods used in ascertaining it.

2. RENTAL VALUE AND NET INCOME

Some types of property are let on terms which require the landlord to bear the cost of certain outgoings such as repairs and rates. To arrive at the net income in such a case the outgoings must be deducted from the rent paid.

If the tenant undertakes to bear the cost of all outgoings whatsoever with the exception of income tax, which is a general charge on all incomes whatever their source, the rent is known as "net rent". "Net rental value" is the rent which may reasonably be expected to be obtained in the open market on the same terms as "net rent".

At this stage, therefore, where reference is made to "rent" it is to be understood that "net rent" is intended. The usual outgoings in connection with land and buildings are outlined in Chapter 6 and further considered in the Chapters dealing with particular types of property

47

Rent may be defined as "an annual or periodic payment for the use of land or of land and buildings". In fixing the rental value of a property a valuer is largely influenced in practice by the evidence he can find of rents actually paid, not only for the property being valued, but also for comparable properties in the same district. But it is essential that he should appreciate the economic factors which govern those rents. Knowledge of economic factors may not be necessary for the immediate purpose of his valuation, but it is vital in understanding fluctuations in rental value, and in advising on the reasonableness or otherwise of existing rents and market prices.

3. ECONOMIC FACTORS AFFECTING RENT

(a) Supply and Demand. In Chapter 1 it was observed that the general laws of supply and demand govern capital values and that value is not an intrinsic characteristic.

Variations in capital value may be due either to changes in rental value or to changes in the return that may be expected from a particular type of investment. Either or both of these factors may operate at any time.

The general trend is for rental value to change by rising over the years whilst returns follow the general market movements in interest rates which lead to returns rising and falling at different periods. It follows that at times rental values rise and returns fall, so combining to produce a sharp rise in capital values, whilst at other times the changes have opposing effects on capital values.

For example, shops in an improving position may increase in rental value over a period of years. At the same time, there may be changes in the investment market which cause that particular type of security to be less well regarded; a higher yield will be expected and consequently a lower Years' Purchase will have to be applied to the net rent to arrive at the capital value. The result may be that, whilst the rental value has increased, the capital value remains unchanged.

Example 5–1

Rental Value today £1,000	Rental value 5 years hence	£1,250
Years' Purchase (Y.P.) to show 8% yield	Years' Purchase (Y.P.) to show 10% yield	
12·5		10
Capital Value £12,500	*Capital Value*	£12,500

Both changes in rental value and changes in the yield required from property investments are the result of the operation of the laws of supply and demand. For rental value the influence of supply and demand is on the income which the property can produce: as for yield it is on the Years' Purchase which investors will give for the right to receive that income. In either case any variation has a direct bearing on the capital value of the property.

In this Chapter we are concerned with the influence of supply and demand on *rental value*.

When we say that value depends on supply and demand, it must be remembered that supply means the *effective* supply at a given price, not the total of a particular type of property in existence. In a particular shopping centre there may be perhaps thirty shops of a very similar type; of these the owners of twenty do not wish to let. The effective supply consists of the other ten shops whose owners are willing to let.

Similarly demand means the *effective* demand at a given price. Many people may desire a certain property or type of property, but all or many of them may be unwilling to satisfy that desire if the price is above the level which in money value expresses the strength of the desire. In the shopping centre example demand is derived from potential tenants who have weighed the advantages and disadvantages of the shops offered against other properties elsewhere.

The prevailing level of rents will be determined by the interaction of supply and demand, what is sometimes referred to as "the higgling of the market". If there is a large or increasing demand for a certain type of property, rents are likely to increase; if the demand is a falling one, rents will diminish.

As pointed out in Chapter 1, in two important respects landed property can be distinguished from other types of commodity in that the supply of land is to a large extent a fixed one and that in the case of buildings supply may respond slowly to changes in demand.

(b) Demand Factors. It is obvious that the prime factor in fixing rent is demand.

The demand for land and buildings is a basic one in human society, as it derives from two essential needs of the community:—

(i) the need for living accommodation:
(ii) the need for land, or land and buildings, for industrial and commercial enterprise-including the agricultural industry.

The demand for any particular property, or for a particular class of property, will be influenced by a number of factors, which it will be convenient to consider under appropriate headings.

General Level of Prosperity. This is perhaps the most important of the factors governing demand.

When times are good and business is thriving, values will tend to increase. There will be a demand for additional accommodation for new and expanding enterprises. There will be a corresponding increase in the money available for new and improved housing accommodation and for additional amenities in connection therewith.

The increase in rental values will not necessarily be exactly comparable to the increase in the general standard of living. It may not apply to all types of property and its extent may vary in different parts of the country owing to the influence of other factors.

Experience in this and other countries has shown, however, that rental values generally show a steady upward tendency in times of increasing prosperity.

Population changes. Times of increasing prosperity have in the past been associated with the factor of a growing population.

The supply of land being limited, it is obvious that an increase in demand due to increased prosperity or increase of population will tend to increase values. On the other hand, when these causes cease to operate or diminish in intensity, values will tend to fall.

Increase in population will, in the first place, influence the demand for housing, but indirectly will affect many other types of property the need for which is dependent upon the population in the locality—as, for instance, retail shops. Increases in population within a locality may occur in various ways. The birthrate may exceed the number of deaths so that there is a natural increase in the size of the existing population. Alternatively population may rise locally due to migration of people from other areas to the locality. A further change in population may arise for a temporary period, typically holiday centres, where the numbers rise significantly for certain periods of the year. The impact of tourists on demand can be very significant.

Changes in Character of Demand. Demand, in addition to being variable in quantity, may vary in quality. Associated with an increase in the standard of living, there is a change in the character of the demand for many types of property.

For example, in houses and offices, many amenities regarded today as basic requirements would have been regarded as refinements only to be expected in the highest class of property two decades ago. Similar factors operate in relation to industrial and commercial properties.

The increased standards imposed by legislation or technical improvements in the layout, design and equipment of buildings, tend to cause many buildings to become obsolete and so diminish their rental value.

Rent as a Proportion of Personal Income. In relation to residential property, the rent paid may be expressed as a proportion of the income of the family occupying the property. It is obvious that, in a free market, the general level of rents for a particular type of living accommodation will be related to the general level of income of the type of person occupying that accommodation. There will, of course, be substantial variations in individual cases owing to different views on the relative importance of living accommodation,

motor cars, television sets and other goods and services.
However, in this country, there is not, and has not been
for many years, a free market in living accommodation to
rent. Thus, although statistics are available showing the relationship between rent and income, they are of little assistance
to the valuer even as background information.

There is, however, a free market in residential properties
for sale and a useful parallel today in relation to capital,
not rental, values is that building societies in determining
an appropriate mortgage loan assume that an individual
should not pay more than a maximum proportion of his
income on mortgage repayment plus rates, typically one
quarter.

Rent as a Proportion of the Profit Margin. Both commercial
or industrial properties and land used for farming are occupied as a rule by tenants who expect to make a profit out
of their occupation, and that expectation of profit will determine the rent that such a tenant is prepared to pay.

Out of his gross earnings, he has first to meet his expenses;
from the gross profit that is left, he will require remuneration
for his own labour, and interest on the capital that he has
to provide; the balance that is left is the margin that the
tenant is prepared to pay in rent and rates. Obviously, no
hard and fast rule can be laid down as to the proportion
which rent will form of profit, but the expectation of profit
is the primary cause of the tenant's demand and the total
amount of rent and rates he will be prepared to pay will
be influenced by this estimate of the future trend of his
receipts and expenses and the profit he requires for himself.

Competitive Demand. Certain types of premises may be
adapted for use by more than one trade or for more than
one purpose, and there will be potential demand from a larger
number of possible tenants. For instance, a block of property
in a convenient position in a large town may be suitable
for use either as offices or for light industrial purposes. The
rent that can consequently be expected to be paid for either
use will reflect the relative demands, that having the greater
demand producing the greater rent.

In a free market it would be expected that the enterprise
yielding the largest margin out of profits for the payment

of rent would obtain the use of the premises. For where there are competing demands for various purposes properties will tend to be put to the most profitable use. In practice the operation of this rule will be affected by the fact that the use to which the property may be put will be restricted by town planning legislation.

(c) Supply Factors. It has already been stated that land differs from other commodities in being to a large extent fixed in amount. This limit on the amount of land available is the most important of those factors which govern supply.

Limitation of Supply. At any one time there will be in the country a certain quantity of land suitable for agricultural purposes and a certain quantity of accommodation suitable for industrial, commercial and residential purposes.

If these quantities were entirely static, the rents would be affected only by changes in demand. In fact, they are not static, but respond, although slowly, to changes in demand. There is, ultimately, only a certain quantity of land available for all purposes, but increase in demand will cause changes in the use to which land is put.

In agriculture, conditions of increasing prosperity will bring into cultivation additional land which previously it was not profitable to work. Conversely, in bad times land will go out of cultivation and revert to waste land. Similarly, increasing demand will render it profitable for additional accommodation to be built for commercial and residential uses and the supply of accommodation will be increased by new buildings until the demand is satisfied. These statements assume that the market is working freely. In practice there is considerable intervention by government, either to support and stimulate some uses or to dampen them down. For example, agriculture has generally enjoyed a strong measure of support for the past 40 years from all governments but this has now led within the EEC to substantial over-production. To reduce production to the level of demand within the EEC a number of restrictive measures, such as milk quotas, have been introduced but it is now clear that a substantial amount of land must be taken out of agricultural production and the current debate relates to other acceptable uses for that land. Office development has often been curbed too in parts of the country, despite a strong demand for new accommodation, in the largely mistaken belief that this will encourage similar development in other parts of the country.

The increase in rents that would occur if the supply remained unchanged will be modified by additions to the supply. But, as was pointed out in Chapter 1, adjustments in the supply of land and buildings are necessarily made slowly in comparison with other commodities.

Where there is a tendency for the demand to fall, the supply will not adjust itself very quickly; building operations may well continue beyond the peak of the demand period and some time may elapse before expansion in building work is checked by a fall in demand.

It would enlarge the scope of this book unduly to discuss the various causes of inelasticity in supply. But the principal ones are probably—(i) the fact that building development is a long-term enterprise, i.e., one where the period between the initiation of a scheme and completion of the product is comparatively lengthy; and (ii) the difficulty involved in endeavouring to forecast demand in any locality.

The above considerations introduce the subject of what economists call "marginal land". In the instance given of land being brought into cultivation for agricultural purposes, there will come a point where land is only just worth the trouble of cultivation. Its situation, fertility or other factors will render it just possible for the profit margin available as a result of cultivation to recoup the tenant for his enterprise and for the use of his capital. There will, however, be no margin for rent. This will be "no-rent" land or marginal land.

It is obvious that land better adapted for its purpose will be used first and yield a rent, but that also, with increasing demand, the margin will be pushed farther out and land previously not worth cultivation will come into use.

Similar considerations will apply to other types of property. For instance, there will be marginal land in connection with building development. A piece of land may be so situated that, if a factory is built on it, the rent likely to be obtained will just cover interest on the cost of construction, but leave no balance for the land. With growth of demand, the margin will spread outwards, the rent likely to be obtained for the factory will increase, and the land will yield a rent.

Land may have reached its optimum value for one purpose and be marginal land for another purpose. For example, land in the vicinity of a town may have a high rental value for market garden purposes and have reached its maximum utility for agricultural purposes. For building purposes it may be unripe for development—in other words, "sub-marginal"—or it may be capable of development, but incapable of yielding a building rent—in other words, "marginal". Such a case is rare today.

From the practical point of view, it is unlikely that land will be developed immediately it appears to have improved a little beyond its marginal point. Some margin of error in the forecast of demand will have to be allowed for, and no prudent developer would be likely to embark on development unless there is a reasonable prospect of profit.

Relation of Cost to Supply. Another factor which may influence supply is the question of cost.

If, at any time, values as determined by market conditions are less than cost, the provision of new buildings will be checked, or may even cease, and building will not recommence until the disparity is removed.

Thus, in the years immediately preceding the 1939–45 war, there was a considerable increase in the number of residential flats in and around London. In some areas the demand appeared to have been overtaken by supply and rents had fallen. At the same time costs had increased, and in such areas it was no longer very profitable to build flats. There was, accordingly, a contraction in the rate of building. Similar conditions can now be found in depressed industrial areas where the cost of providing new industrial units sometimes exceeds their value.

The disparity which may exist at any time between cost and value may be subsequently removed either by a reduction in cost or by an increase in demand. Governments may intervene by providing grants or other incentives so as to reduce the effective cost or to stimulate demand. It might be further modified by the non-replacement of obsolete buildings, which might in time bring about an excess of demand over supply and a consequent increase in value.

4. Determination of Rental Value

(a) Generally. It has already been pointed out that in estimating the capital value of a property from an investment
point of view the valuer must usually first determine its rental
value.

In doing so he will have regard to the trend of values in
the locality and to those general factors affecting rent discussed above. These will form, as it were, the general background of his valuation, although he may not be concerned
to investigate in detail all the points referred to when dealing
with an individual property.

The two factors most likely to influence his judgment are—

    (i) the rents paid for other properties and
    (ii) the rent, if any, at which the property itself is let.

In most cases when preparing an investment valuation it
will be assumed that the rental value at the time when the
valuation is made will continue unchanged in the future.
Experience proves that this is unlikely to be the case and
changes in value may result in the rent rising or falling over
a period. But, in the absence of special factors indicating
an abnormal future change in the rental value, the assumption is reasonable, as normal changes, either upwards or
downwards, are reflected in the rate per cent which an investment is expected to yield. The logic of the assumption is
considered in greater detail in Chapter 9.

In general, it may be said that if rental value is likely to
increase, a higher Years' Purchase will be applied; while if
there is a doubt of the present level being maintained, the
Years' Purchase will be reduced to cover the risk.

Future variations in rental value may sometimes arise from
the fact that the premises producing the income may be old,
so that it may be anticipated that their useful life is limited.
Together with the likelihood of a fall in rental value there
may be a possibility that in the future considerable expense
may be incurred either in rebuilding or in modernisation to
maintain the rental value. In such cases the rate per cent
which the investment will be expected to yield will be
increased and the Years' Purchase to be applied to the net

income correspondingly reduced. This particular aspect, commonly termed obsolescence, will be considered in greater detail in Chapter 9.

Where a future change in rental value is reasonably certain it should, of course, be taken into account by a variation in the net rent to which the Years' Purchase is to be applied. For example, a valuation may be required of a shop which is offered for sale freehold subject to a lease being granted to an intending lessee on terms which have been agreed. These terms provide for a specified increase in rent every five years. It has been ascertained that many similar shops in the immediate vicinity are let on leases for 10, 15 and 20 years with a provision for similar increases in the rents at the end of each 5 year period. Assuming that the position is an improving one and that the valuer is satisfied that such increasing rents are justified, he will be correct in assuming that the shop with which he is dealing can be let on similar terms, and he will take future increases in rent into account in preparing his valuation.

The method of dealing with such varying incomes from property will be considered in detail in Chapter 9.

(b) Basis of the Rent actually paid. Where premises are let at a rent and the letting is a recent one, the rent actually paid is usually the best possible evidence of rental value.

But the valuer should always check this rent with the prevailing rents for similar properties in the vicinity or, where comparison with neighbouring properties is for some reason difficult, with the rents paid for similar properties in comparable positions elsewhere.

There are many reasons why the rent paid for a property may be less than the rental value. For instance, a premium may have been paid for the lease, or the lease may have been granted in consideration of the surrender of the unexpired term of a previous lease. The lessee may have covenanted to carry out improvements to the premises or to forego compensation due to him from the landlord. In many cases the rental value may have increased since the existing rent was agreed. Differences between rent paid and rental value may also be accounted for by the relationship between lessor and lessee, e.g., father to son.

If, as a result of the valuer's investigations, he is satisfied that the actual rent paid is a fair one, he will adopt it as the basis of his valuation, will ascertain what outgoings, if any, are borne by the landlord and by making a deduction in respect thereof will arrive at net rental value.

If, in his opinion, the true rental value exceeds the rent paid under the existing lease his valuation will be made in two stages. The first stage will be the capitalisation of the present net income for the remainder of the term. The second stage will be the capitalisation of the full rental value after the end of the term.

If, on the other hand, he considers that the rent fixed by the present lease or tenancy is in excess of the true rental value, he will have to allow for the fact that the tenant, at the first opportunity, may refuse to continue the tenancy at the present rent, and also for the possible risk, in the case of business premises, that the tenant may fail and that the premises will remain vacant until a new tenant can be found.

As a general rule, any excess of actual rent over estimated fair rental value may be regarded as indicating a certain lack of security in the income from the property. But it must be borne in mind that rent is secured not only by the value of the premises but also by the tenant's covenant to pay, and a valuer may sometimes be justified in regarding the tenant's covenant as adequate security for a rent in excess of true rental value.

An example of such cases is where a shop is let on long lease to some substantial concern such as one of the large retail companies with several shops—a "multiple". Here, the value of the goodwill the tenants have created will make them reluctant to terminate the tenancy, even if they have the right to do so by a break in the lease. Where there is no such break, they will in any case be bound by their covenant to pay. Since rent is a first charge, ranking even before debenture interest, and since such a concern will have ample financial resources behind it, the security of the income is assured.

(c) Comparison of Rents. It has been suggested that the actual rent paid should be checked by comparison with the general level of values in the district. Not only is this desirable where the rent is considered to be prima facie a fair one,

but it is obviously essential where premises are vacant or let on old leases at rents considerably below true rental value.

In such circumstances the valuer has to rely upon the evidence provided by the actual letting of other similar properties. His skill and judgement come into play in estimating the rental value of the premises under consideration in the light of such evidence. He must have regard not only to the rents of other properties that are let, but also to the dates when the rents were fixed, to the age and condition of the buildings as compared with that with which he is concerned, and to the amount of similar accommodation in the vicinity to be let or sold.

In many cases, as for instance similar shops in a parade, it may be a fairly simple matter to compare an unlet property with several that are let and to assume, for example, that since the latter command a rent of £2,000 a year on lease it is reasonable to assume the same rental value for the shop under consideration which is similar to them in all respects.

But where the vacant premises are more extensive and there are differences of planning and accommodation to be taken into account in comparing them with other similar properties, it is necessary to reduce rents to the basis of some convenient "unit of comparison" which will vary according to the type of property under consideration.

For example, it may be desired to ascertain the rental value of a factory having a total floor space of 10,000 square feet. Analysis of the rents of other similar factories in the neighbourhood reveals that factories with areas of 5,000 sq. ft. or thereabouts, are let at rents equivalent to £2·50 per sq. ft. of floor space, whereas other factories with areas of 40,000 sq. ft. or thereabouts, are let at rents of £2 per sq. ft. of floor space. This indicates that size is a factor in determining the unit rental value. After giving consideration to the situation, the building, and other relevant factors, it may be reasonable to assume that the rental value of the factory in question should be calculated on a basis of £2·40 per sq. ft. of floor space.

The unit chosen for comparison depends on the practice adopted by valuers in that area or for the type of property. Notwithstanding the transition to metric units over past years valuers have shown a marked reluctance to abandon Imperial units. Thus the most commonly met units of measure are still values per square foot or per acre and most, if not quite all, comparative statistics are based on Imperial measures. Metric units are commonly adopted for agricultural purposes and in valuations for rating purposes. The student must be prepared to accept and work with either method. The practitioner will follow his normal practice.

The method of measuring also varies. Thus, some valuers exclude the areas occupied by lavatories, corridors, etc.; others work on external measurements of buildings, some including the space occupied by walls, others not. In an attempt to bring some uniformity, the professional societies have produced recommended approaches. Thus the Royal Institution of Chartered Surveyors has published a Code of Measuring Practice which both identifies various measuring practices, such as gross external area, gross internal area and net internal area, and also recommends the occasions when such practices would be appropriate, for example gross internal area for industrial valuation and net internal area for office valuation. Though persuasive, the valuer is not bound to follow the Code. Whether he does so or not, it is vital that analysis of comparable evidence and calculation of rental value are on the same basis.

When quoting rental figures the amount per annum should always be qualified by reference to such terms of the lease as the liability for rates, repairs and insurances, and by reference to the length of the term. The date of the valuation should also be stated.

(d) Rental Value and Lease Terms. The amount of rent which a tenant will be prepared to offer will be influenced by other terms of the lease. Rent is but one factor in the overall contract and if additional burdens are placed on the tenant in one respect he will require relief in another to keep the balance. For example, if a landlord wishes to make a tenant responsible for all outgoings in respect of a property, he cannot expect the rent offered by the tenant to be the same as where the landlord bears responsibility for some of them.

Similarly if a landlord offers a lease for a short term with regular and frequent upward revisions of the rent, he cannot expect the same initial rent as would be offered if a longer term were offered with less frequent reviews, particularly if his terms are untypical of the general market arrangements. Again, if a landlord seeks to limit severely the way in which premises may be used, the rent will be less than where a range of uses will be allowed.

It is clear therefore that rental value will reflect the other terms of the lease and cannot be considered in isolation.

In making comparisons, it must be remembered that the terms of the lettings of different classes of property vary considerably. It is convenient therefore, to compare similar premises on the basis of rents on the terms usually applicable to that type of property. Good shop property and industrial and warehouse premises are usually let on terms where the tenant is liable for all outgoings including rates, repairs and insurance. Thus, net rents are compared on this type of property, assuming a full repairing and insuring lease will be agreed. With blocks of offices let in suites, however, the tenant is usually liable for internal repairs to the suite and rates and the landlord for external repairs, repairs to common parts and insurance. The landlord provides services such as lifts, central heating and porters, but these are dealt with separately by means of a service charge on the tenants (and which may also include the landlord's liability to repair and insure). Thus, rents used for comparing different suites of offices would be inclusive of external repairs, repairs to common parts and insurance but exclusive of the service charge. Having arrived at the rental value of the office block on this basis, the net income would be arrived at by deducting the outgoings which are included in the rents and for which the landlord is liable. In cases where landlords include within the service charge their liability to repair and insure and also the supervisory management fees, the rental value will be the net income.

Example 5–2

A prospective tenant of a suite of offices on the third floor of a modern building with a total floor space of 2,500 sq. ft. requires advice on the rent which should be paid on a

five years' lease. The tenant will be responsible for rates
and internal repairs to the suite. The landlord will be responsible for external repairs, repairs to common parts and insurance. Adequate services are provided, for which a reasonable
additional charge will be made. The following particulars
are available of other recent lettings on the same terms in
similar buildings, all of suites of rooms:

Floor	Area in sq. ft.	Rent £	Rent £ per sq. ft.
Gd.	2,000	12,800	6·40
	3,000	18,000	6·00
1st	1,500	7,200	4·80
2nd	1,600	8,000	5·00
4th	4,000	20,000	5·00
5th	5,000	26,000	5·20
6th	2,000	10,000	5·00

Estimate of Rent Payable. As the particulars relate to lettings on the same terms as that proposed, it is unnecessary
for purposes of comparison to consider the outgoings borne
by the landlord or to arrive at net rental values.

The broad picture which emerges from the evidence is
that the highest rents are paid on the Ground floor but thereafter the rents are approximately the same. This is what
would be expected in modern buildings with adequate high
speed lifts. In older buildings with inadequate lifts or no lifts,
the higher the floor the lower the rent. The inconsistencies
in the rents may be due merely to market imperfections or
to differences in light or noise.

Subject to an inspection of the offices under consideration
so that due weight can be given to any differences in quality
and amenities, a reasonable rent would appear to be, say,
£5·00 per sq. ft. or £12,500 per annum.

The different methods used in practice for fixing rent by
comparison are referred to in more detail in later chapters
dealing with various classes of property.

(e) Rent in relation to Cost. A careful analysis of rent will show that, except in the case of undeveloped land, it is made up of two things—(i) an annual payment for the use of the land itself, and (ii) an annual payment for the use of capital expended on it in the form of buildings, improvements, etc.

This aspect of rent is seldom consciously present in the mind of either landlord or tenant. A prospective tenant, for instance, thinks of the house or shop he proposes to occupy in terms of land and buildings combined. The land will give him the advantages attaching to a certain situation; the buildings will provide him with accommodation in the form of rooms, floor space, etc. He thinks of the rent as the annual sum it is worth his while to pay for that amount and type of accommodation in that particular situation. But the valuer has from time to time to think in terms of (i) the rental value of the land, and (ii) the rental value of the buildings, etc., upon it.

That part of the rent which represents a payment for the use of buildings and other improvements should in normal cases consist of a reasonable return by way of interest on the owner's capital expenditure. What may be regarded as a reasonable return will depend upon the type of property in which the capital is sunk. But as between two properties of the same type there is likely to be little variation in the rate of interest expected.

Example 5–3

A owns two pieces of land, one in a good shopping street in the centre of a small provincial town and one in a somewhat inferior position. On both these sites he has erected shop premises costing £100,000.

The first shop is leased for 15 years at a net rent of £20,000. The second is leased on the same terms at £12,000. Analyse these rents.

Analysis

It is probable that the owner will expect approximately the same rate of interest from capital expended on either

site. Assuming 8 per cent to be a fair return in the circumstances, that part of the rent which represents a payment
for the use of the building will in both cases be £8,000.
Then:—

Shop No. 1.
  Net Rack Rent   £20,000
  Payment for use of buildings, 8% on
    £100,000   8,000
                                Payment for use of land £12,000

Shop No. 2.
  Net Rack Rent   £12,000
  Payment for use of buildings, 8% on
    £100,000   8,000
                                Payment for use of land £4,000

It is plain that the difference in rental between the two shops
lies in the value of the land. The higher rent of the first
shop is due to the advantage of situation of site No. 1, as
compared with site No. 2, and its effect on the profits which
prospective tenants are likely to make from their occupation
of the premises.

A possible method of estimating the rent of a property
is to reverse the process shown in the above analysis and
to add to the rental value of the site a fair percentage on
the cost of any buildings, etc., erected on it.

Where freehold land has been purchased, the usual practice is to take a percentage representing the return of ground
rental value to capital value on the purchase price. For
instance, assume that in the above example site No. 1 was
bought for £170,000 and the appropriate return is 7%, the
rack rent might be estimated as follows:—

  7% on £170,000 (value of land)   £11,900
  8% on £100,000 (cost of buildings)   8,000
                                Net Rack Rent   £19,900

The use of this method requires considerable care and experience. A price paid or a rent fixed for land some years ago may be misleading as a guide to its present rental value. The cost of building may have altered considerably since the premises were erected; also capital spent on buildings is not always laid out in the manner likely to give the best return. In any case, the method is an estimate of what the landlord may expect the property to be worth, whereas rents are finally determined by what prospective tenants are able and willing to pay.

For all these reasons it is very desirable that an estimate of rent based on a percentage of the cost of land and buildings should be checked where possible by comparison with rents actually paid for other similar buildings.

This method of estimating rental value is more often resorted to in valuing for rating or other special purposes and is rarely employed in an open market situation.

5. Effect of Capital Improvements on Rental Value

Since, in most cases, an owner is not likely to spend capital on his property unless he anticipates a fair return by way of increased rent, it is usually reasonable to assume that money spent on improvements or additions to a property will increase the rental value by an amount approximating to simple interest at a reasonable rate on the sum expended. The rate per cent at which the increase is calculated will naturally depend upon the type of property.

Since, however, the real test of rental value is not solely what the owner expects to obtain for his premises, but more importantly what tenants are prepared to pay for the accommodation offered, in practice any estimate of increased rental value should be carefully checked by comparison with the rents obtained for other premises to which similar additions or improvements have been made.

Capital expenditure is only likely to increase rental value where it is judicious and suited to the type of property in question. For example, a man may make additions or alterations to his house which are quite out of keeping with the general character of the neighbourhood and are designed solely to satisfy some personal whim or hobby. So long as he continues to occupy the premises he may consider he is getting an adequate return on his money in the shape of personal enjoyment, but there will be no increase in the rental value of the premises since the work is unlikely to appeal to the needs or tastes of prospective tenants.

Again, expenditure may be made with the sole object of benefiting the occupier's trade—as, for instance, where a manufacturer spends a considerable sum in adapting premises to the needs of his particular business. In this case the occupier may expect to see an adequate return on his capital in the form of increased profits, but it is unlikely that the expenditure will affect the rental value unless, of course, it is of a type which would appeal to any tenant of the class likely to occupy the premises—as, for instance, where an occupier of offices instals air-conditioning which significantly improves the working conditions.

On the other hand, the increase in rental value due to capital expenditure may considerably exceed the normal rate of simple interest on the sum expended. This will be so in those cases where the site has not hitherto been fully developed or where it is to some extent encumbered by obsolescent or unsuitable buildings. For example, a site in the business quarter of a flourishing town may be covered by old, ill-planned and inconvenient premises. If, by a wise expenditure of capital, the owner can improve these premises so as to make them worthy of their situation, he should secure an increase in rental value which will not only include a reasonable return on the capital sum expended, but also a certain amount of rental value which has been latent in the site and which will have been released by the development.

Example 5–4

Somewhat old-fashioned premises on a good shopping street are let at a rent of £24,000, which is a fair one for the premises as they stand. The occupier, who has a long lease of the premises, proposes to spend £45,000 on a new shop front, additional retail space, and other improvements.

These works will make the premises equal in every respect

to adjoining shops which readily let at £33,000 p.a.

Probable rental after improvements		£33,000
Present rental value	£24,000	
Normal return on capital expenditure of £45,000—8% on £45,000	3,600	27,600
Increase in rent due to release of latent site value		£5,400

In this case the total increase in rental value (£9,000) represents a return of 20% on the capital sum expended.

Since rental value is mainly determined by what tenants are prepared to pay for the accommodation offered, it follows that any capital expenditure on premises will have precisely the same effect on rental value whether the money is spent by the freeholder or by a lessee who has only a limited interest in the premises.

For instance, suppose that premises are worth £5,000 p.a. and the expenditure by the freeholder of £5,000 on improvements will increase the rental value to £5,500; a prospective tenant will certainly not pay more than £5,500 for identical premises next door where the same works have been carried out by a lessee whose term expires in thirty years' time.

Since, however, the lessee's interest in the premises will cease altogether when his lease runs out, the true annual cost of improvement to him will be greater than the increased rent he can hope to obtain for it, as will be shown in Chapter 7.

CHAPTER 6
Outgoings

1. GENERALLY

A MAJOR difference between property and most other forms of investment is that considerable sums of money need to be expended regularly to maintain it, to satisfy tax requirements and to protect it against the effects of damage. The duties of ensuring that sums are paid when due and work done when needed demand the attention of managers which itself has a cost. Such expenses are referred to as outgoings.

Where the property is occupied by the owner he will be liable for meeting all these costs. In the case of property which has been let, the terms of the lease will determine whether the landlord or the tenant is liable for any particular expense, subject to various statutes which impose duties on particular classes of persons notwithstanding their contractual arrangements.

It is common in practice for the landlord to seek to impose the duty of meeting all of the various expenditures on property on the tenant by means of a full repairing and insuring lease so that the rent payable to him is free from any deduction. This is particularly so in the case of non-residential property let to a single tenant. In the case of property in multi-occupation where services and other activities can only be met through a central or common approach, for example, the cost of maintaining a lift serving various tenants on different floors, landlords tend to attempt to recoup the expenditure by means of a charge additional to rent known as a service charge so as to separate rent from outgoings.

The reason for landlords' concern over this aspect is that rents tend to be fixed for a period, whereas some outgoings are subject to unpredictable and substantial changes, usually upwards in times of inflation. Where a rent is fixed for a period and the landlord has to meet certain outgoings from this income, if the cost of the outgoings rises it follows that the balance available to him will fall. A falling income is unsatisfactory in a time of stability, and in a time of inflation can be disastrous.

From a tenant's point of view, the burden of outgoings is a cost of taking a lease which is additional to the rent required and which, in aggregate, represents the cost to him of occupation. It is the aggregate cost which he will consider in deciding on whether or not to take a lease of property. Hence, if the burden and cost of outgoings are increased then he will have a smaller sum available out of his aggregate budget figure which he will be prepared to offer as rent.

For example, if two factories are offered of equal quality, but in one case the tenant must meet the cost of all outgoings, costing £6,000 per annum, whereas, in the other, the landlord will bear half, the tenant will have to spend £3,000 per annum less in the second case and would be prepared to pay around £3,000 per annum extra in rent in consequence. This aspect was referred to in Chapter 5 on rental value.

In the case of properties of similar facilities but different burdens, the tenant will pay a higher rent for the building with cheaper outgoings. For example, a prospective tenant may be offered two similar factory premises which, on other considerations, are of equal value; one of them he finds to be of indifferent construction and to have a considerable extent of external painting, with a consequent heavier liability to repair. In such a case he will be willing to offer a higher rent for the premises where the cost of repairs is likely to be less.

It is clear, therefore, that the level of outgoings has a significant effect on property dealings. It follows that it is important to determine the cost of meeting the various types of outgoings, and these are now considered.

2. Repairs

(a) Generally. The condition of repair of a property is an important factor to be taken into account when arriving at the capital value. Likewise the burden of keeping a prop-

erty in repair is an important factor in determining rental value.

Hence, regard must be had to the need for immediate repairs, if any, to the probable annual cost, and to the possibility of extensive works of repair, rebuilding or modernisation in the future.

The age, nature and construction of the buildings will affect the allowance to be made for repairs. Thus, a modern house, substantially built, with a minimum of external paintwork, will cost less to keep in repair than a house of some age, of indifferent construction and with extensive woodwork.

(b) Immediate Repairs. If such repairs are necessary, the usual practice is to calculate the capital value of the premises in good condition and then to deduct the estimated cost of putting them into that condition.

(c) Annual Repairs Allowance. It is obvious that the cost of repair of premises will vary from year to year.

For the purpose of arriving at the net income of a property where the cost of repairs has to be deducted, it is necessary to reduce the periodic and variable cost to an average annual equivalent. This may be done by reference to past records, if available; by an estimate based on experience, possibly, in some cases, expressed as a percentage of the rental value; by an estimate based on records of costs incurred on similar buildings, expressed in terms of units of floor space; or by examining in detail the cost of the various items of expenditure and their periods of recurrence.

Where reference is made to past records, it is essential to check the average cost thus shown by an independent estimate of what the same item of work would cost at the present day.

One of the dangers of using a percentage on rental value can be illustrated by the following example. Two shops are very similar physically, but one of them is so situated as to command a rent considerably in excess of the other; the cost of repair is likely to be similar, but different percentages would have to be taken to arrive at the correct answer. For example, one shop may be well situated and have a rental value of £10,000 per annum. Another similar shop may be in a secondary position with a rental value of £2,000 per annum. If the annual costs of repair for each are £400 per annum, in the first case this is 4 per cent of rental value whilst in the second it is 20 per cent. This discrepancy will remain even if the standard of repair of the better placed property is higher than the other: it is clear that the repair costs of the better shop would need to be £2,000 per annum if 20 per cent were to be the general percentage of rent spent on repairs. The percentage basis is therefore reliable only where the properties are similar physically and attract a similar rental value. While the percentage basis may be of some use, it is suggested that the only wise course is to judge each case on its merits and to make an estimate of the cost of the work required to put and keep the premises in good condition.

An estimate may be based on costs incurred on similar buildings. If the costs of keeping in repair several office buildings of similar quality and age are known, an analysis may show that they tend to cost a similar amount expressed in terms of a unit of floor space. For example, if the analysis showed that around 80p per sq.ft. was being spent it would be reasonable to adopt this sum in valuing a further office building in the area of similar qualities and age.

The fourth method of estimating the probable average annual cost of repairs is illustrated in the following example.

Example 6–1

A small and well-built house of recent construction, comprising 3 bedrooms, 2 reception rooms, kitchen and bathroom, is let on an annual tenancy, the landlord being responsible for all repairs, at a fair rental of £900 per annum. From inspection it is found that the house is brick built, in good structural condition, with a minimum of external paintwork. It is required to estimate the average annual cost of repairs.

    (a) Experience might suggest an allowance of 40 per cent of the rent.

(b) This estimate might be checked by considering the various items of expenditure and how often they are likely to be incurred as follows:—

(1)	External decorations every 4th year £600	£150 p.a.
(2)	Internal decorations every 7th year £700	£100 p.a.
(3)	Pointing, every 25th year, £1,000	£40 p.a.
(4)	Sundry repairs, say	£80 p.a.
		£370 p.a.

The method used in the example can be equally well applied to other types of property, regard being had in each case to the mode of construction, the age of the premises and all other relevant factors which will affect the annual cost.

(d) Conditions of Tenancy. Regard must be had to the conditions of tenancy in estimating the annual cost. Where premises are let on lease the tenant is usually liable for all repairs and no deduction has to be made (a full repairing lease). In other cases the liability may be limited to internal repairs (internal repairing lease), particularly where a building is in multi-occupation: in valuing the landlord's interest a deduction for external repairs will therefore be needed. This will be so even if the landlord has not covenanted to carry out external repairs and he is not therefore liable for such repairs (unless statutory provisions override the contractual position) since the rent paid includes an allowance for this element. In practice most landlords would regard it as prudent estate management to keep the property in repair. On the other hand it is common practice for landlords to impose a service charge on tenants which will include the cost of external repairs. In such cases no deduction from the rent will be made.

Reference should be made wherever possible to the actual lease or tenancy agreement to verify the exact liability to repair of the parties. In the case of short lettings, it must also be remembered that, on the conclusion of the tenancy, the premises will need redecoration before re-letting or sale even if in a fair state of repair at the date of valuation. The same may be true where a longer lease is coming to an end, depending on the extent of liability to repair imposed upon the tenant. A tenant under a general covenant to repair is liable to leave the premises in repair on termination of the lease and any works required at that time to bring the premises into proper condition are termed "dilapidations". Nonetheless, a valuer would need to decide if some allowance would be appropriate in valuing the landlord's interest, particularly if the tenant is a poor covenant and there is the risk of repairs not being done.

If the cost of repairs is expressed as a percentage of the rental value it must not be forgotten that this may have been estimated upon the basis that the landlord may also have undertaken to pay other outgoings besides repairs. The percentage to be adopted in such cases where applied to the inclusive rent will be somewhat less.

(e) Future Repairs. In considering the value of property it may be necessary to make allowance for the possibility of extensive works of repair, improvement, or even ultimate rebuilding in the future. Where the possibility of such works is long deferred it is not usual in practice to make a specific allowance therefor. However, where such works are possible in the near future (say up to 10 years or so) the present cost of the works deferred for the estimated period is deducted from the capital value. In the case of older properties the works will tend to reflect a considerable element of improvement to allow for the changes in standards that have occurred since the property was erected. In fact, the rate of improvement has tended to increase over recent years as changes in standards accelerate, and a generous allowance for repairs as an annual outgoing may be prudent to reflect the cost of these works which are often cosmetic rather than actual repair. Alternatively a provision for a capital investment in the property on the termination of the lease might be more appropriate. This would be so even where a tenant will contribute to dilapidations since these only cover putting into repair what was there, whereas the landlord might wish to carry out more extensive works of improvement or refurbishment.

3. SINKING FUNDS

It is sometimes suggested that provision should be made, in addition to the cost of repairs, for a sinking fund for the reinstatement of buildings over the period of their useful life. In some countries it is standard practice to do so.

In the case of properties where the buildings are estimated to be nearing the end of their useful life this provision may have to be made, but in most valuations the risk of diminution in the value of buildings in the future is reflected in the percentage yield to be derived from the property. This aspect is considered further in Chapters 9 and 20.

4. GENERAL RATES

Rates are normally the personal liability of a tenant, but in some cases, such as lettings on weekly tenancies, the landlord may undertake to pay rates.

Rates are levied on the rateable value at a poundage which varies considerably in different districts. This subject is considered further in Chapter 22 including the proposal to abolish rates on residential properties and replace them with a community charge and to fix a rate in the £ nationally on other types of property—a Uniform Business Rate (UBR).

To arrive at a fair amount to be deducted, regard must be had not only to the actual amount paid at the present time but also to possible changes in rate poundage and assessment in the future. This is particularly important if the rent cannot be increased on account of the increase in rates. However in most cases increases in rates will be borne by the tenant, either because he bears them directly or because the landlord is entitled to recover such increases from him.

As regards changes of assessment, the present rateable value of a property must not necessarily be taken to be correct. All assessments are capable of revision to take account of changes to the property or its use, or under a general revaluation. If an assessment appears too high, regard should be had to the possibility of its amendment at the earliest possible moment. If too low, the possibility of an upward revision should be anticipated.

It would obviously be incorrect, where no provision exists to adjust the rent paid in respect of alterations in rates, to base a valuation on the assumption that rates will continue at their present level, when there is every possibility of an increase in assessment.

With regard to possible variation in rate poundage, unless there is some clear indication of a higher than average change in the future it is usual to assume continuance at the present amount.

It should be borne in mind that any alterations in rates due to changes in assessment and in rate poundage are passed on to the tenant in the case of tenancies under the Rent Acts where the rent is inclusive.

In the case of other tenancies at inclusive rentals the provisions of the lease or tenancy agreement must be examined to see if a similar provision is made. Where such "excess rates" clauses are present no account need be taken of possible changes in the future for the term of the lease or agreement.

5. Other Charges Based on Rateable Value

(a) Water Services Charges. Except where metered, charges for water supplies are based on a poundage on rateable value fixed by Water Authorities.

(b) Sewerage and Environmental Charges. Again levied by Water Authorities and based on rateable value with some exceptions.

These charges, like general rates, are essentially occupiers charges and will normally be borne by tenants. Where they are borne by the landlord, they must be deducted as outgoings unless recovered through a service charge.

6. Income Tax

The income from landed property, equally with that from other sources, is subject to income tax, which is assessed in accordance with the rules of the Income and Corporation Taxes Act 1988.

It is customary to disregard income tax as an outgoing since it is a form of taxation to which all types of income are equally liable. This aspect of taxation is further considered in Chapter 9.

Allowance may have to be made for the tax, however, when valuing leaseholds and other assets of a wasting nature, such as sand and gravel pits. The reason for this is that the tax is levied on the full estimated net annual value of the property without regard to the necessity, in such cases, of a substantial proportion of the income having to be set aside as a sinking fund to replace capital. This aspect of taxation is further considered in Chapters 9 and 14.

7. INSURANCES

(a) Fire Insurance. This outgoing is sometimes borne by the landlord and will be deducted in finding the net income. A growing practice, when premises are let on lease, is that the lessee usually undertakes to pay the premium or to reimburse the premium paid by the landlord, unless the tenant's occupation is for some hazardous purpose such as a woodworking factory or chemicals store when the tenant may have to pay the whole or a portion of the premium.

The cost of fire insurance is often small in relation to the rental value, particularly for modern, high value premises. In the case of older premises of substantial construction, where the cost of remedying damage will be expensive, the premium may be significant, particularly as such property tends to command relatively lower rental values. The use of a percentage figure of rental value can therefore be misleading, and it is advisable to establish the current premium payable and to check the level of cover under the policy against current rebuilding costs. Valuations for fire insurance purposes are considered in Chapter 21.

(b) Other Insurances. In many cases of inclusive lettings e.g. where blocks of flats or offices are let in suites to numerous tenants, allowance must be made for special insurance,

including insurance of lifts, employers' liability, third party insurance and national insurance contributions. In the case of shops, the insurance for replacement of the plate glass shop windows is normally a duty placed on the tenant.

8. MANAGEMENT

Agency charges on lettings and management must be allowed for as a separate outgoing in certain cases. An allowance should be made even where the investor will manage the property himself, as his efforts must have an opportunity cost which should be reflected. In properties where there is a service charge, this charge often includes the cost of management but the valuer should check the service charge provisions in order to decide whether or not an allowance needs to be made.

In cases where the amount of management is minimal, as with ground rents and property let on full repairing lease, the allowance would be so small that it could be ignored.

In yet other cases, such as agricultural lettings and houses let on yearly tenancies or short agreements, the item is often included in a general percentage allowance for "repairs, insurance and management".

Where it is appropriate to make a separate deduction for "management" it can usually be estimated as from 5 per cent to 10 per cent of the gross rents.

It may be mentioned in this connection that the allowance to be made for this type of outgoing, and for voids and losses of rent referred to below, cannot be entirely dissociated from the Years' Purchase to be used. In making analysis of sales of properties let at inclusive rents the outgoings have to be deducted before a comparison can be made between net income and sale price to arrive at a Years' Purchase. If management is allowed for in analysis, the net income is reduced and a higher Years' Purchase is shown to have been paid than would have been the case if management was not allowed for.

Accordingly when, in making a valuation, a figure of Years' Purchase is used derived from analysis of previous sales, it is important that similar allowances are made for outgoings as were made in the cases analysed.

9. Voids

In some areas and for some properties, it is customary to make an allowance for those periods when a property will be unlet and non-revenue producing. For example, a poor quality block of offices in multiple occupation may expect to have some part of the accommodation empty at any time. These periods, termed voids, may be allowed for by deducting an appropriate proportion of the annual rental as an outgoing.

In addition, a landlord will be liable for rates and insurance during such periods, so there may be a need to allow for these outgoings in respect of void parts in a property where such costs are otherwise recoverable from the tenants.

10. Service Charges

Where buildings are in multiple occupation the responsibility for maintenance of common parts is inevitably excluded from the individual leases. As an example, the maintenance of the roof benefits not only the tenant immediately below it but all the tenants of the building. It would thus be inequitable for one tenant to be responsible for the repair of the roof.

The responsibility may be retained by the landlord although, in some cases, particularly blocks of flats which are sold on long lease, the responsibility may be passed to a management company under the control and ownership of the tenants.

Where a landlord does retain the responsibility he will commonly seek to recoup the costs incurred from all of the tenants by means of a service charge. The goal is to recoup the full costs so that the rent payable under the various leases is net of all outgoings. Such a situation typically arises with office blocks let in suites, but is also found in shopping centres, industrial estates and other cases of multiple tenancies.

Typical items covered by a service charge are repairs to the structure; repair and maintenance of common parts including halls, staircases and shared toilets; cleaning, lighting and heating of common parts; employment of staff such as a receptionist, caretaker, maintenance worker and security staff; insurance; management costs of operating the services. In addition to these types of expenditure which relate to the day-to-day functioning of the building, service charges are increasingly extended to provide for the replacement of plant and machinery such as lifts and heating equipment.

It is desirable for costs to be spread as evenly as possible over time so that an annual charge is normally levied, with surpluses representing funds which build up to meet those costs which arise on an irregular basis such as major repairs or replacements of plant.

Various methods of allocating the costs to individual tenants are adopted, including proportion of total floor area occupied by each tenant, and proportion of Gross Value or Rateable Value of each part to the aggregate value. Where some tenants do not benefit from services as much as others then special adjustments are needed. For example, where there is an office building but with lock-up shops on the ground floor, it would clearly be unfair to seek to recover costs relating to the entrance hall, staircases and lifts from the tenants of the shops who make no use of nor receive any benefit from these facilities.

It is clear that the existence of extensive service charges should allow the valuer to assume that the lease rents received are net of further outgoings, once he is satisfied that the charges are set at a realistic level, that the lease terms permit the landlord to levy such a charge and to include the items which are included and that statutory requirements which apply, for example, to blocks of flats are met. However, if there are any voids the landlord will become responsible for the charges relating to the empty space until a new tenant is found. If the valuer feels that voids are likely to occur fairly frequently and past evidence supports this view he may need to consider making some deduction on this account. For example, if the space is extensive it may be reasonable to assume that 4% or 5%, will be empty at any one time and so allow, as an outgoing for the landlord, 4% or 5% of the predicted service charges.[1]

11. VALUE ADDED TAX

At the time of writing, the Government has anounced its intention to allow landlords to charge value added tax (VAT) on rents. In such cases, VAT would be another outgoing to be deducted from the gross rent.

12. OUTGOINGS AND RENT

At the start of this Chapter it was emphasised that the level of outgoings will have a considerable influence on a tenant's offer of rent since he will be concerned with his overall budget. This can now be illustrated by the following chart.

Terms of lease	External Repairs	Internal Repairs	Insur-ance	Manage-ment	Rent	Budget Figure
Full Repairing & Insuring Lease (FRI)	300	200	60	40	2,000	2,600
Internal Repairing & Insuring Lease	—	200	60	40	2,300	2,600
Fully Inclusive Terms	—	—	—	—	2,600	2,600

It is assumed that a prospective tenant is offered a property on three different bases, and the costs of meeting the various liabilities are as indicated.

Although in practice the effects on rent will not be quite so clear cut, the chart does demonstrate how rents are affected by lease liabilities. It also shows that rents are at their

[1] For further reading on service charges, the reader is referred to "Service Charges—Law & Practice" by Philip Freedman and Eric Shapiro (Henry Stewart Publications).

lowest when a lease is on FRI terms. The valuer, when comparing rents on different terms of leases, will need to adjust by adding back or subtracting allowances for outgoings as appropriate.

CHAPTER 7

Yields

1. Generally

IN CHAPTER 2 it was shown that, in order to use the investment method of valuation, the valuer must determine the yield, which is the rate of interest appropriate to the particular interest in property being valued. He will normally do this by an analysis of previous market transactions. The valuer is not, however, merely an analyst. He must have a clear idea not only of what the market is doing but also why the market is doing it and, if he is to advise adequately on the quality of the investment, what the market is likely to do in the future. He should, therefore, have some knowledge of the levels of the interest rates on most types of investment and of the principal factors which influence them.

This Chapter is concerned with these points and in it will be considered the principles governing interest rates generally and yields on the main types of landed property.

Before considering these matters, however, it is necessary to dispose of two preliminary points which may be a source of confusion to the student.

2. Nominal and Actual Rates of Interest

The nominal rate of interest, or dividend, from an investment in stocks or shares is the annual return to the investor in respect of every £100 face value of the stock. Where stock is selling at its face value, that is at par, the nominal rate of interest and actual rate of interest, or yield, are the same. Thus, to take a Government Security as an example, the nominal rate of interest on $2\frac{1}{2}$ per cent Consolidated Stock ("Consols") is fixed at $2\frac{1}{2}$ per cent; that is £2·50 interest will be received each year for each £100 face value of the stock held. If the stock is selling at £100 for each £100 face value, an investor will receive £2·50 interest each year for every £100 invested which gives a yield of 2½ per cent. But assume now that £100 face value of 2½ per cent Consols is selling at £20, or below par. Each £20 of capital actually invested would be earning £2·50 interest annually

$$\therefore \text{Yield} = \frac{2\cdot5}{20} \times \frac{100}{1} = 12\cdot5 \text{ or } 12\tfrac{1}{2}\%$$

Thus the actual rate of interest is 12½% whilst the nominal rate of interest remains 2½%.

If a large industrial concern declares a dividend of, say, 25 per cent on its ordinary shares this means that the company will pay 25 per cent of the nominal value of each share as the dividend. Hence, if the shares are £1 shares the dividend per share will be 25 per cent of £1 = 25p per £1 share. But if the price of each £1 share on the market is £2 then:—

$$\text{Yield} = \frac{25p}{200p} \times \frac{100}{1} = 12\cdot5 \text{ or } 12\tfrac{1}{2}\%$$

If the price of these shares in the following year had risen to £2·50 and the same dividend of 25 per cent had been declared, then:—

$$\text{Yield} = \frac{25p}{250p} \times \frac{100}{1} = 10\%$$

From these examples two important points can be seen:—

(i) That a comparison of income receivable from various types of investment can only be made on the basis of yields and that nominal rates of interest derived from face values are of no significance for this purpose.

(ii) That a rise or fall in the price of a security involves a change in the yield of that security.

3. Timing of Payments and Yields

A yield is expressed as the interest accruing to capital in a year. Hence, if an investment is made of £1,000, and the investor receives £100 in interest payments in each year, the yield is said to be

$$\frac{100}{1000} \times \frac{100}{1} = 10\%$$

This assumes that the interest payment of £100 is made at the end of the year. However, if the payment of interest is made in instalments, then that produces a different result.

Suppose, for example, that the investor receives £50 after 6 months and a further £50 at the end of the year. He is receiving

$$\frac{50}{1000} \times \frac{100}{1} = 5\%$$

per half year. The payment received after 6 months can, in turn, be invested. If it is assumed that it is invested in a similar investment, then further interest of 5% for the remaining half year will be earned. The total interest payments at the end of the year are thus:—

£50 (after 6 months) + (5% of £50) + £50 (end of year payment)

In this case the total interest for the year is £102·50 representing

$$\frac{102 \cdot 50}{1000} \times \frac{100}{1} = 10 \cdot 25\%$$

As the payment patterns change, such as quarterly in arrears or quarterly in advance, so will interest for the year change. This phenomenon is recognised in everyday life by the adoption of APR (annual percentage rate) figures which are quoted in respect of loan rates for borrowers or interest payments for credit card borrowers. The APR reflects the timing of the interest charged on the loans (which will rarely be interest added at the end of the year).

When a reference is made to a yield, it is the yield as

determined by the total annual interest expressed as a return
to capital ignoring the timing of the payments. Thus in the
foregoing example the yield is 10% in the first case and
10.25% in the second. This approach is adopted by valuers
and property investors generally. It will be examined in more
detail in Chapters 9 and 14.

4. PRINCIPLES GOVERNING YIELDS FROM INVESTMENTS

The precise nature of interest and the relationship
between, and the level of, long-term, medium-term and
short-term rates of interest are subjects for the economist
and market analyst and are not dealt with in this book. The
valuer is interested primarily in long-term securities and the
relative yields from them. He is interested in why the investor
requires investment A to yield 6 per cent, investment B to
yield 3 per cent and investment C to yield 12 per cent.

A reasonably simple explanation of the many complex matters that the investor must take into account in determining
the yield he requires from an investment can be derived from
the creation, firstly, of an imaginary situation. For this purpose the following assumptions are made:—

  (i) That the real value of money is being maintained over
      a reasonable period of years—that is, that £1 will pur-
      chase the same quantity of goods in say, 10 years'
      time as it will now; and, either
 (ii) there is no taxation or that the rates of tax are so
      moderate as not to influence the investor significantly;
      or
(iii) the system of taxation is such that taxes bear as heavily
      on capital as on income.

In these circumstances the yield required by the investor
would depend on:—

  (a) the security and regularity of the income;
  (b) the security of the capital;
  (c) the liquidity of the capital;
  (d) the costs of transfer, i.e. the costs of putting in the

capital in the first instance and of taking it out subsequently.

Thus, the greater the security of capital and income, the greater the certainty of the income being received regularly, the greater the ease with which the investor can turn his investment into cash and the lower the costs of transfer, the lower will be the yield he requires.

Therefore, if investment D offered a guaranteed income payable at regular intervals, no possibility of loss of capital and the loan repayable in cash immediately on request at no cost to the investor, the investor would require the minimum yield necessary to induce him to allow the borrower to use his capital. If investment E offered the same terms as investment D except that six months' notice was required before the capital could be withdrawn, the investor would require a yield sufficiently higher than the minimum to offset this difference. If investment F offered the same terms as investment E except that there was some risk of fluctuation in, or occasional non-payment of, the income, the investor would require a still higher yield.

Now this imaginary situation must be adjusted to make it accord more closely with actual conditions in recent years.

With regard to the first assumption, that of money maintaining its real value, this does not happen during periods of inflation. Thus, where an investor investing during a period of inflation is guaranteed a secure income of, say, £100 a year, if the value of the pound is halved in 10 years, his "secure" income will in 10 years' time have a real value of only £50 a year. So also if "security" of capital means merely that if he invests £1,000 now he can withdraw £1,000 when he wishes, the real value of his capital would be halved over a period of 10 years. If, in these circumstances, 10 per cent, that is an income of £100 a year from an investment of £1,000, is a reasonable yield, the investor should be prepared to accept a lower rate of interest from an investment which will protect his capital and income from the erosion of inflation. Thus, he might be prepared to accept a yield of 5 per cent now on an investment of £1,000 if there is a reasonable chance that

(i) the income of £50 a year now will have doubled to £100 a year in 10 years' time thus maintaining its real value, and

(ii) that the capital of £1,000 will increase to £2,000 in 10 years' time thus maintaining its real value.

An investment which offers the investor the opportunity of maintaining the real value of capital and income in this way is described as a "hedge against inflation".

The second and third assumptions for the imaginary situation related to the level and incidence of taxation. Over recent years the occasions when a tax charge arises and the rates of tax charged have changed frequently. Tax tends to divide between tax on capital and tax on income.

In the case of capital, until 1962 there was no tax on capital apart from estate duty. This led to proceeds arising from the sale of a capital asset to be free of tax. In 1962 there was introduced a capital gains tax imposed on short-term gains, followed in 1965 by the establishment of capital gains tax on all gains. This tax remains today, though much changed, and the rate of tax was always 30% of the gain realised until 1987. In 1987 the capital gains tax charged on companies became the same as the corporation tax charged on income. In 1988 individuals were put in the same position as companies with the capital gains tax rate being the same as the income tax rate (see Chapter 23). On top of this, several other capital taxes have come and gone, all of which sought to impose a separate, and higher rate of tax on any capital gain arising from development value. These were betterment levy from 1967 to 1970, development gains tax from 1974 to 1976, and development land tax from 1976 to 1985.

Estate duty was a tax imposed on the assets of a person on his death, but careful tax planning made it possible to keep this down to modest levels or even to avoid it altogether: it was regarded as an avoidable tax. Estate duty was replaced by capital transfer tax introduced in 1975 which was a tax charged not only on assets at death but also on the value of gifts made during a person's lifetime. In 1986 capital transfer tax was replaced by inheritance tax which is more akin to estate duty. The rates of tax assessed on the value of the assets in the estate varied from 30% to 60%, but in 1988 a single rate of 40% was imposed.

As to tax on income, this has seen some significant changes in the rates of tax over the same period but the taxes imposed, corporation tax on companies and income tax on individuals, have existed throughout most of the period, the basic rules being set out in the Income and Corporation Taxes Act 1988, though with many changes in detail over the years. At the time of writing corporation tax has a basic rate of 35% whilst that for income tax is 25%. This contrasts with tax rates during the period when corporation tax had a basic rate of 52% for many years and income tax on investment income reached 98%.

It can be seen from this brief summary that tax is a significant factor in respect of investments, and that, in general, the tax on income has tended to be more penal than the tax on capital, particularly on capital gains. It also indicates that tax is prone to frequent change and fluctuation.

The four principles governing yields enumerated above, adapted to meet conditions of inflation and levels of income and capital taxation have, in fact, governed yields in the investment market in this country in recent years. This is apparent on examination of yields from different types of security during this period. British Government securities, which in times of stable prices and moderate taxation have been described as "ideal security", offered the minimum yield because they are practically riskless. Around 1955 the yield on Government securities rose above that on ordinary shares in sound companies for the first time and this position has prevailed since then.

There are many reasons for the fall in price, and consequent increase in yield, of Government securities, but one of the most important is that neither the capital invested in them nor the income issuing from them is secure in real terms. The lower yields on ordinary shares in, for example, many industrial concerns and retailing companies, can be accounted for by the security in real terms which they offer and, in many cases, the probability of substantial capital appreciation. By contrast the yields from shares in mining companies are often well in excess of those from Government securities, reflecting the insecurity of this type of company due to the uncertainty of production from uncertain reserves coupled with high costs of extraction.

5. YIELDS FROM LANDED PROPERTY INVESTMENTS

A prospective investor in landed property will be aware of the other forms of investment available and of the yields he can expect from them. He will, therefore, judge the yield he requires from a landed property investment by comparison with the yields from other types of investment such as insurance, building societies and stocks and shares. The principles governing yields discussed above are, therefore, applicable to landed property in the same way as to other forms of investments. However, landed property has certain special features which will be considered before looking at the yields from the main types of landed property.

First, there is the question of management. The investor has no management problems with, for example, Government securities as he will receive his income by cheque every six months. With most types of landed property, however, some management is involved. The actual cost of management of landed property is allowed for in computing the net income as discussed in Chapter 6. Apart from this factor a landowner will incur costs such as the agreeing of new rental levels and may incur legal and surveyors' fees in disputes with tenants over various matters affecting the property. He will, therefore, require the yield to compensate for this cost and risk. Where, in addition to being costly, management is also troublesome, the investor will require a higher yield to compensate for this.

The second special feature of landed property relates to liquidity of capital and costs of transfer. Ordinary shares, for example, can normally be bought or sold through a stock exchange very rapidly and the transfer costs are a small percentage of the capital involved. A transaction in landed property, however, is normally a fairly lengthy process and the costs of transfer, mainly legal and agents' fees and stamp duty, are somewhat higher. The effects of such costs on the yield, and in particular whether the yield is gross or net of such costs, is referred to in Chapter 9.

The last of the special features is legislation. Legislation does, of course, impinge on many types of investment but its effects, direct or indirect, on landed property are frequently of major significance. The Rent Acts and the Town and Country Planning Acts provide excellent examples. The former limit the amount of rent which can be charged for most categories of dwelling-house and the latter severely restrict the uses to which a property can be put.

As was seen in Chapter 3, there is more than one type of interest in landed property and different interests in the same property may have different yields. The yields considered below are from freehold interests in the type of property concerned. It is important to note that the yields given merely indicate the appropriate range for the particular type of property at the time of writing. The general level of yields from all types of investment, or from landed property investments only, may change and there are often substantial variations between yields from landed property investments of the same type. The age and condition of the buildings and the status of the tenant occupier are also factors which influence the yield. Other things being equal, the older the building and the poorer its condition, and the less substantial the tenant, the higher will be the yield. These comments cannot, therefore, be applied to actual valuations where the yield must be determined in accordance with market information.

Agricultural Land. Until the early 1980's it was said of agricultural land that it was a good investment, enjoying special tax advantages, support from the Government and the EEC and that a normal range of yields was 2–4 per cent. Since then the EEC has been imposing restrictions on agricultural production intended to reduce the supply of agricultural produce to the level of consumption within the EEC. This has had the effect of restricting or reducing farm incomes thus also restricting or reducing the rents which farmers are able to pay. In general it is the poorer quality land which is first affected by "demand" changes so that poor and medium quality agricultural land has become difficult to sell as an investment, although the best quality agricultural land is less affected. Investors are, however, requiring yields which reflect the risk of a reducing income, currently up to 10%.

Shops. A normal range of yields is $3\frac{1}{2}$ to 12 per cent, the lower figure being applicable to shops in first-class positions occupied by national retail organisations and the higher to shops in secondary positions occupied by small traders. Position and type of tenant are vital factors in judging a shop as an investment and these matters are dealt with in detail in Chapter 20. The substantial increase in the volume of retail trading in recent years has been a vital factor in determining yields from shop investments. The high level of demand for shops in the major shopping centres resulting from this has kept rents moving upwards at a sufficient rate to maintain income and capital in real terms and, indeed, in many cases to show a substantial appreciation.

Offices. A normal range of yields is from 5 to 10 per cent. The lowest yield would be expected from a modern block let to a single tenant who shoulders the management burden. The same block let in suites where the owner is responsible for a considerable amount of management, including the provision of such services as lifts and central heating, would yield a slightly higher rate, say $6\frac{1}{2}$ per cent. The highest yield would be expected from an older block, possibly let in suites and lacking modern amenities. As is apparent from the low yield, good office property is considered a good investment. In areas where the demand for offices is strong, rents have been increasing at a sufficient rate to provide a secure investment in real terms with a substantial appreciation.

Factories and Warehouses. Until recent years factories and warehouses have not been a popular investment and the range of yields, 7 to 12 per cent, to some extent reflects past unpopularity. However, significant changes have occurred over recent years which have blurred the distinction between factories and warehouses and other types of properties. In the case of factories, a strong demand has arisen for space to be occupied by companies in the computer and electronic fields where the requirements are for standards closer to those of offices than the traditional, more basic, factory. These are commonly termed "high-tech" buildings.

Similarly, alongside the traditional warehouse where the occupier houses his wares, there has grown up the development of retail warehouses, where the form of building is a single storey building but with extensive car parking and the occupier selling direct to the public. Thus the building form is similar to a warehouse but the activity is similar to that of a shop.

Yields will tend to be at the bottom of the range in the case of the high-tech and retail warehouse buildings, and also with modern single-storey factories and warehouses in areas of strong demand, since rents for these have been increasing at a rate to provide a secure investment in real terms. In the case of factories and warehouses in areas of poor demand, particularly in areas suffering from industrial decline generally accompanied by high unemployment levels, yields will be at the top of the range. For older buildings, which are frequently multi-storied, the yield may be well in excess of 12 per cent. Indeed, apart from buildings capable of conversion to small workshop units, they may even cease to be considered as investments and will change to other uses or remain vacant pending redevelopment.

Residential Properties. This expression covers a very wide range of properties and some sub-classification is required before even the broadest generalisation on yields can be made. Initially it should be stressed that whereas, in the past, residential properties formed a major part of the property investment market, in recent times they have shrunk to making a small contribution. The main impetus for this decline has been the growth in owner occupation coupled with restrictive legislation imposed on the powers of landlords. Even where property is let it is more likely to be seen by a purchaser as a speculation with the hope of obtaining possession followed by sale with vacant possession rather than as a long term income producing investment. Thus the yields referred to in this section are intended to apply to those instances where the property is likely to remain an investment (see Chapter 19).

With the tenement type of residential property the yield is high, from 12 to 18 per cent. Properties of this type will normally be old, rent restricted, subject to a great deal of legislation imposing onerous obligations on owners relating to repair, cleanliness and other matters, and many tenants may be unreliable in payment of rent. Capital and income are not, therefore, secure in any terms, income may not be regular and the property may be difficult to sell. In recent years such properties have tended to be acquired by public authorities or publicly financed organisations so that they are gradually ceasing to be investments found in the private sector.

Blocks of flats, on the other hand, particularly if they were modern, were, until recently, regarded as a good investment yielding about 8 to 10 per cent. Frequently they sold at much lower yields but these higher prices, known as "break-up" values, were based on the expectation that a substantial proportion of the flats could be sold to the sitting tenants usually on long leases at prices in excess of investment value. However, the Landlord and Tenant Act 1987 now gives the tenants a right of first refusal on the disposal of their landlord's interest and, in exceptional cases, a right to acquire their landlord's interest compulsorily. It remains to be seen how the market will respond.

The majority of houses are either local authority owned or owner-occupied but a considerable number of small houses are held for investment purposes and yield in the range 9 to 15 per cent. As was the case with flats, only more so, such properties when bought outside the public sector are purchased with a view to their ultimate sale so that investment criteria are not applicable and very low yields apparently emerge, but which are not to be interpreted as investment yields.

Ground Rents. A ground rent is a rent reserved under a building lease in respect of the bare land without buildings. In recent times the practice has been to grant the building lease once the buildings have been built, the developer holding an agreement to be granted the building lease during the period of development. Building leases are normally granted for a long term, 99 years at one time being fairly common, although modern leases are frequently for around 125 years, particularly in the case of commercial properties.

Secured ground rents where the lease has many years to

run yield in the range 6 to 15 per cent. Where the rent is a fixed amount throughout the term it is comparable in many ways with Government securities and the yield will be similar to, but slightly higher than, that on 2½ per cent Consols and at the top of the range. The investor obtains better security in real terms where the lease provides for upward revision of the rent at reasonable intervals and such an investment would provide a lower yield than where the rent is a fixed amount.

The amount of the rent is also a significant factor. A single rent of a few pounds may be unsaleable unless the occupier is in the market, since the cost of collection will absorb most of the rent received.

6. CHANGES IN INTEREST RATES

The landed property investment market normally responds to change less rapidly than other investment markets. The reason for this is probably the length of time taken to transfer ownership and the high costs of transfer. If, for example, circumstances are such that it is felt desirable to hold a greater proportion of assets in cash than hitherto, Stock Exchange securities can be realised immediately even if some loss is incurred. Landed property, however, cannot be realised with anything like the same speed. If, therefore, the change in preference is temporary the landed property market may remain unmoved while other markets are reacting violently.

The landed property investment market tends to respond to longer term changes. In recent years the movements in interest rates have been more marked and more rapid than in earlier times reflecting the closer integration of the property market into the general investment market brought about in the main by the growing involvement of pension funds and insurance companies ("the institutional investors").

CHAPTER 8

The Mathematics of Valuation Tables

1. GENERALLY

IT IS the valuer's business to make a carefully considered estimate of the worth of a property.

In making that estimate he must come to certain conclusions regarding the property—for instance, as to the net income it can produce, as to the likelihood of that income increasing or decreasing in the future, as to the possibility of future liabilities in connection with the property, and as to the rate per cent at which a prospective purchaser is likely to require interest on his capital.

The accuracy of his conclusions on these and other points will depend on the extent of his skill, judgment and practical experience. It is then the function of the valuation tables to enable the valuer, by a simple mathematical process, to express his conclusions as a figure of estimated value.

The object of the valuation tables is thus to save the valuer time and reduce the risk of error involved in elaborate mathematical calculations. Proficiency in their use can never be a substitute for practical experience of the property market or real appreciation of the factors which influence value: but it will assist the valuer very substantially in his work. The tables represent a mathematical tool for use by the valuer and he will gain by having a full understanding of their derivation and application.

The availability of calculators and computers in recent years has substantially changed the situation. These machines permit the carrying out of elaborate mathematical calculations speedily and without the risk of error inherent in manual calculations. However, the tables are still extensively used in practice and it remains essential for the student to understand the underlying mathematics. This and the immediately succeeding Chapters, therefore, remain of fundamental importance to the understanding of the valuation process.

The tables on which this Chapter is based are those in the current edition[1] of "Parry's Valuation and Conversion Tables". There are various sets of valuation tables available, some covering similar ground to Parry's, others of more limited application. Further comment on the use and limitations of tables are contained in Chapter 14.

The mathematical construction of the valuation tables and the formulae on which they are based are considered in this Chapter together with the nature of the various tables, what the figures in them represent and how they are commonly used in practice.

It should be emphasised at the start that all the tables which the valuer uses are based on the principle of compound interest.

It is for this reason that the following sections deal first with the "Amount of £1 Table"—the table of compound interest—instead of following the order in which the tables are arranged in *Parry's Valuation Tables*.

2. AMOUNT OF £1 TABLE
(Pp. 89–105 of *Parry's Valuation Tables*)

The figures in this table are simply figures of compound interest. They represent the amount to which one pound, invested at various rates of compound interest, will accumulate over any given number of years.

Such a calculation could, of course, be made manually as shown by the following example.

Example 8–1

To what amount will £1 invested at 5 per cent compound interest accumulate in three years?

---

[1] 10th Edition by A. W. Davidson (Estates Gazette).

Answer

	Principal	Interest	Total
Amount at end of 1 year (£1 plus interest at 5% on £1)	£1·0	£0·05	£1·05
Amount at end of 2 years (£1·05 plus interest at 5% on £1·05)	£1·05	£0·0525	£1·1025
Amount at end of 3 years (£1·1025 plus interest at 5% on £1·1025)	£1·1025	£0·0551	£1·1576

The above process is obviously a laborious one and it is a great saving of time to be able to take the appropriate figure direct from the valuation tables.

The importance of the Amount of £1 Table lies mainly in the fact that it has been used as the basis for the construction of the other valuation tables.

In practice the table is sometimes useful in calculating the loss of interest involved where capital sums are expended on a property which, for the time being, is unproductive of income.

Example 8–2

A building estate was purchased for £5,000,000. A sum of £1,000,000 was spent at once on roads and other costs of development. During a period of five years no return was received from the property. What was the total cost of this property to the purchaser at the end of the five years assuming interest at 15 per cent?

Answer

If the owner had not tied up £6,000,000 in the purchase and development of this land, he could presumably have invested that sum in some other investment producing interest at 15 per cent and have allowed capital and income to accumulate at compound interest. The cost of the property to him is therefore the sum to which £6,000,000 might have accumulated in 5 years at 15 per cent compound interest.

Capital sum invested	£6,000,000
Amt. of £1 in 5 years at 15%	2·0114
Cost to purchaser	£12,068,400

Alternatively an owner may have borrowed money to purchase a development property on the basis that interest will be charged but not payable until the development is completed (the interest is said to be "rolled up").

Example 8–3

A development property was purchased 3 years ago and a loan of £200,000 was obtained for this purpose at a fixed interest rate of 14 per cent rolled up until the development is completed. The development will be completed in 1 year's time. Calculate the sum due for repayment at that time.

Capital sum borrowed	£200,000
Amount of £1 in 4 years at 14%	1·689
Sum due for repayment (loan plus rolled-up interest)	£337,800

The formula for the Table is derived as follows:—

To find the amount to which £1 will accumulate at compound interest in a given time.

Let the interest per annum on £1 be i.
Then the amount at the end of 1 year will be $(1 + i)$;
The amount at the end of 2 years will be $(1 + i) + i(1 + i)$
$= 1 + 2i + i^2 = (1 + i)^2$;
The amount at the end of 3 years will be similarly $(1 + i)^3$;
By similar reasoning the amount in n years will be $(1 + i)^n$.
(The total interest paid on £1 in n years will be $(1 + i)^n - 1$).

3. PRESENT VALUE OF £1 TABLE
(Pp. 57–76 of *Parry's Valuation Tables*)

The figures in this table are the inverse of those in the Amount of £1 Table. Whereas the latter table shows the amount to which £1 will accumulate at compound interest over any given number of years, the Present Value of £1 Table shows the sum which invested now at compound interest will amount to £1 in so many years' time.

The figures in the table are the reciprocals of those in the Amount of £1 Table—i.e., it is possible to obtain any required figure of Present Value of £1 by dividing unity by the corresponding figure of Amount of £1.

Example 8–4

What sum invested now will, at 5 per cent compound interest, accumulate to £1 in six years' time?

Answer

Let V equal the sum in question
V × Amt. of £1 in 6 years at 5% = £1

$$\therefore V = \frac{1}{\text{Amt. of £1 in 6 yrs. at 5\%}}$$

$$= \frac{1}{1 \cdot 340}$$

$$= 0 \cdot 7462154$$

It is however, very much quicker to take the figure direct from the Present Value of £1 Table.

The Present Value of £1 Table is widely used in practice for calculating the value at the present time of sums receivable in the future and in making allowances for future expenditure in connection with property.

The value at the present day of the right to receive a capital sum in the future is governed by the fact that whatever capital is invested in purchasing that right will be unproductive until the right matures. So that if £x is spent in purchasing the right to receive £100 in three year's time, it follows that for those three years the purchaser's capital will be showing no return, whereas if the £x had been invested in some other security it might, during those three years, have been earning compound interest. The price which the purchaser can fairly afford to pay, therefore, is that sum which, with compound interest on it at a given rate per cent, will amount to £100 in three years' time.

Example 8–5

What is the present value of the right to receive £100 in three years' time assuming that the purchaser will require a 5 per cent return on his money?

Answer

Let V = sum which the purchaser can afford to pay. He will be losing compound interest on this sum during the three years he will have to wait before he receives the £100.

V must therefore be such a sum as, together with compound interest at 5 per cent, will in three years' time equal £100.

V × Amt. of £1 in 3 years at 5% = £100.

$$\therefore V = \frac{£100}{\text{Amt. of £1 in 3 yrs. at 5\%}}$$

$$= \frac{£100}{1 \cdot 1576}$$

$$= £86 \cdot 39$$

The above method has been used to show the principles involved. The same result would be obtained direct from the Present Value of £1 Table as follows:—

Sum receivable	£100
P.V. £1 in 3 years at 5%	0·863876
Present Value	£86·39

The process of making allowance for the fact that a sum is not receivable or will not be expended until some time in the future is known as "deferring" or "discounting" that sum. In the above example £86·39 might be described as the present value of £100 "deferred three years at five per cent".

Since, in the case of sums receivable in the future, the valuer is concerned with the temporary loss of interest on capital invested in their purchase, the rate per cent at which their value is deferred should generally correspond to that which an investor might expect from the particular type of security if in immediate possession. In other words, the rate should be a "remunerative" one.

Example 8–6

What is the present market value of the reversion to a freehold property let for a term of five years at a peppercorn rent but worth £350 per annum? Similar property in possession and let at its full market value has recently changed hands on a 5 per cent basis.

Answer

Since no rent is payable for the first five years (a "peppercorn rent" being a legal device for leases where no rent is to be paid), no value arises in respect of this period.

Value in five years' time	
Full rental value	£350 p.a.
Y.P. in perp. at 5%	20
	£7,000
P.V. £1 in 5 years at 5%	0.783
Present Value	£5,481

Where the sum for which allowance has to be made is a future expense in the nature of a liability which cannot be avoided, the valuer is not concerned with the question of loss of interest on capital invested, but rather with the rate per cent at which a fund can be accumulated to meet the expense. A future capital liability can be provided for either by the setting aside of an annual amount in the form of a sinking fund, or by the investment of a lump sum which at compound interest will certainly accumulate to the required amount in the given period. The first method will be discussed later in this Chapter. The second method can be effected through an insurance company by what is known as a single premium policy or some other investment with a guaranteed rate of interest for the whole period.

Unless the amount of the single premium is fairly considerable, the rate of compound interest on it allowed by insurance companies is low. It is therefore sounder, as a rule, to defer sums to meet liabilities in the future at a low "accumulative" rate rather than at the "remunerative" rate at which interest on capital is taken. The actual rate depends on the interest rates prevailing at the time and the financial market's view of future trends in interest rates. Historically such rates have tended to be around $2\frac{1}{2}\%$ to $3\frac{1}{2}\%$.

Example 8–7

A freehold factory was recently let to substantial tenants on a 40 years' lease at a rent of £40,000 per annum. The premises are in good repair, and the tenants are under full repairing covenants, but the owner has covenanted with the lessees that, after two years of the lease have expired, he will rebuild, in fire-resisting construction, a staircase which is now built of wood at a cost of £20,000; also that, after a further period of four years, he will rebuild the chimney shaft at a cost of £50,000 and that two years later (i.e. when the lease has 32 years unexpired) he will replace a wooden fence with a brick wall. This will cost £10,000. Current accumulative rates are $2\frac{1}{2}\%$.

Assuming that the works in question are necessary to maintain the present rent, and that no higher rent may be expected when the lease comes to an end, what is the value of the freehold interest?

Valuation

Net Rental Value (with improvements)			£40,000
Y.P. perp. at 8%			12.5
			500,000

Deduct cost of:

Fire-resisting staircase	20,000		
P.V. £1 in 2 years at 2½%	0·952	19,040	
Chimney shaft	50,000		
P.V. £1 in 6 years at 2½%	0·862	43,100	
New brick wall	10,000		
P.V. £1 in 8 years at 2½%	0·821	8,210	70,350

Value of Freehold Interest		£429,650
	say	£430,000

An exception to the above general rule occurs in cases where the future capital expense can be met out of moneys arising from the property itself, in which case there will be no need to provide for it by investment of a single premium at a low rate of interest and the sum can be deferred at the appropriate "remunerative" rate.

Where, as is frequently the case, future expenditure is of a kind which is optional—as distinct from a liability which cannot be avoided—it is probably preferable to allow for it at the higher (remunerative) rate, since in this type of case it is thought that the investor would not set aside a sum to accumulate at a low rate of interest—e.g., in a single premium policy.

The formula for this Table and its determination is as follows:—

To find the present value of £1 receivable at the end of a given time.

Since £1 will accumulate to $(1 + i)^n$ in n years, the present value of £1 due in n years equals

$$\frac{1}{(1 + i)^n}$$

If it is desired to take into account the payment of interest and its reinvestment at more frequent intervals i and n must be modified.

Let the number of payments in 1 year be m. Then the total number of payments is mn. As the annual rate of interest is i, the rate of interest for one period $\frac{i}{m}$, and the amount of £1 in n years equals

$$\left(1 + \frac{i}{m}\right)^{mn}.$$

The present value of £1 correspondingly will be

$$\frac{1}{\left(1 + \frac{i}{m}\right)^{mn}}.$$

4. AMOUNT OF £1 per ANNUM
(Pp. 107–122 of *Parry's Valuation Tables*)

The figures in this table represent the amount to which a series of deposits of £1 at the end of each year will accumulate in a given period at a given rate of compound interest.

A calculation in that precise form does not often come within the scope of a valuer's practice; but the table may be of use to him in calculating the total expense involved over a period of years where annual outgoings are incurred in connection with a property which is for the time being unproductive.

The following example serves to illustrate this use and also to emphasise the distinction between the nature and use of this table and the Amount of £1 Table.

Example 8–8

A new plantation of timber trees will reach maturity in 80 years' time. The original cost of planting was £2,000 per hectare. The annual expenses average £200 per hectare. What will be the total cost per hectare by the time the timber matures, ignoring any increase in the value of the land and assuming that interest is required on other outstanding capital at 5 per cent?

Answer

The £2000 per hectare spent on planting is in the nature of a lump sum which will remain unproductive over a period of 80 years. Its cost to the owner is represented by the sum to which it might have accumulated if it had been invested during that period at compound interest. This part of the calculation requires use of the Amount of £1 Table.

The expenditure of £200 per hectare on upkeep is an annual payment which will also bring no return during a period of 80 years. Its cost to the owner is represented by the sum to which a series of such payments might have accumulated if placed in some form of investment bearing compound interest. Here it will be necessary to the use the Amount of £1 per annum Table.

Original capital outlay per hectare	£2,000	
Amount of £1 in 80 years at 5%	49·56	£99,120
Annual cost per hectare	£200	
Amount of £1 per annum in 80 years at 5%	971·229	£194,246
Total cost per hectare for period of maturity		£293,366

The derivation of the formula for this Table is as follows:—

The amount to which £1 per annum invested at the end of each year will accumulate in a given time.

It is conventional to assume that interest is not paid until the end of the first year, hence the first payment £1 will accumulate for $n - 1$ years if the period of accumulation is n years.

The second payment will accumulate for $n - 2$ years and so on year by year.

The amount to which the first payment accumulates will, applying the Amount of £1 Table be $(1 + i)^{n-1}$; the second $(1 + i)^{n-2}$; and so on.

Let the amount of £1 per annum in n years be A.
Then $A = (1 + i)^{n-1} + (1 + i)^{n-2} + (1 + i)^{n-3} \ldots (1 + i)^2 + (1 + i) + 1$; or more conveniently

$$A = 1 + (1 + i) + (1 + i)^2 \ldots (1 + i)^{n-1}.$$

These terms form a geometrical progression for which the general expression is

$$S = \frac{a(r^n - 1)}{r - 1}.$$

Substituting therein $S = A$;

$$a = 1; r = 1 + i;$$

$$\text{Hence } A = \frac{(1 + i)^n - 1}{i}$$

5. ANNUAL SINKING FUND
(Pp. 77–88 of *Parry's Valuation Tables*)

This table is the inverse of the Amount of £1 per annum Table. Instead of showing the sum to which a series of deposits of £1 will accumulate over a given period, it shows the sum which must be deposited annually at compound interest in order to produce £1 in so many years' time. The figures in the one table are the reciprocals of those in the other, just as the figures in the P.V. of £1 Table are the reciprocals of those in the Amount of £1 Table. Thus, any required figure of Annual Sinking Fund can be found by dividing unity by the corresponding figure of Amount of £1 per annum, or vice versa.

The table is of direct use to the valuer when it is required to know what sum ought to be set aside annually out of income in order to meet some capital expense accruing due in the future, such as a possible claim for dilapidations on the termination of a lease or a sum likely to be required for the rebuilding or reconstruction of premises.

The provision of a sinking fund to meet future capital liabilities, although often neglected by owners in practice, avoids the embarrassment of having to meet the whole of a considerable expense out of a single year's income and enables the owner to see precisely how much of the annual return from the property he can afford to treat as spendable income. It is, however, met quite frequently in service charge agreements where a sinking fund provision is made to meet the costs of replacing lifts and plant when they reach the end of their useful lives.

Example 8–9

An investor recently purchased for £100,000 a freehold property which it is estimated will yield a net income of £20,000 for the next 15 years. At the end of that time it will be necessary to rebuild at a cost of £150,000 in order to maintain the income. How should the owner provide for this and what will be the result on the percentage yield of his investment?

Answer

The owner may provide for the cost of rebuilding by means of an annual sinking fund accumulating at, say, 3 per cent over the next 15 years, as follows:—

Cost of rebuilding	£150,000
Annual sinking fund to produce £1 in 15 years at 3%.	0·0538
Sinking fund required	£8,070 p.a.

The owner's true income for the next 15 years will therefore be (20,000–8,070) = 11,930, representing a return of 11·93 per cent on the purchase price instead of the 20 per cent which the investment might appear to be yielding.

The necessary provision may be made by means of a sinking fund policy taken out with an insurance company on terms and at rates of interest similar to those referred to in Section 3 of this Chapter for single premium policies, i.e. $2\frac{1}{2}\%$ to $3\frac{1}{2}\%$.

If the sum to be set aside annually is considerable, it is possible that an owner may find opportunity for the accumulation of it in his own business, or in some other investment, at a higher rate of interest than that usually allowed by an insurance company. It is probable that in most cases purchasers will be inclined to take this fact into account in considering the investment value of property, since otherwise the cost of allowing for replacement capital on ordinary sinking fund terms becomes prohibitive. However, the insurance policy approach guarantees a certain sum will be available at a future date which is rare in any form of investment other than those for a short term of up to around 5 years. In any event the purchaser will need to allow for any income tax or corporation tax which may be levied on the interest arising from other forms of investment. It is the interest *net of any tax payable* which he will need to adopt in comparing alternative forms of investment with an insurance policy approach.

It is proposed in the examples which follow to adopt 3 per cent net as a reasonable average figure where sinking fund is concerned.

The Annual Sinking Fund tables on pages 77–88 of the Valuation Tables are compiled on a net basis—that is assuming that the accumulations of interest on the sinking fund are free of income tax.

The allowance for income tax on interest on sinking fund accumulations which is made by using a net rate of interest should not be confused with the entirely separate adjustment for income tax on the sinking fund element of income which is made when using dual rate Years' Purchase. The latter point is dealt with in Chapter 9.

The derivation of the formula for this Table is as follows:—

To find the sum which, if invested at the end of each year, will accumulate at compound interest to £1.

Let the annual sinking fund be S and the period n years, then the first instalment will accumulate to $S(1 + i)^{n-1}$; the second to $S(1 + i)^{n-2}$; and so on.

Hence $1 = S(1 + i)^{n-1} + S(1 + i)^{n-2}\ldots\ldots$
  $S(1 + i)^2 + S(1 + i) + S$; more conveniently
  $1 = S + S(1 + i) + S(1 + i)^2\ldots\ldots S(1 + i)^{n-1}$

The sum of the series will be:—

$$1 = \frac{S[(1 + i)^n - 1]}{i} \text{ therefore } S = \frac{i}{[(1 + i)^n - 1]}$$

It will be observed that S is the reciprocal of Amount of £1 p.a.

It will be noted that investment of the sinking fund takes place at the end of each year. This is convenient when dealing with the income from real property, which is commonly assumed to be receivable yearly at the end of each year. For further discussion of this point see Chapters 9 and 14.

In comparing sinking fund tables with amounts payable under a sinking fund policy it must be remembered that under a policy the premium is payable at the beginning of each year.

By similar reasoning to the above in this case

$$S = \frac{i}{(1 + i)^{n+1} - 1}$$

6. PRESENT VALUE OF £1 PER ANNUM OR YEARS' PURCHASE TABLE
(Dual Rate pp. 1–25, Single Rate pp. 27–39 of *Parry's Valuation Tables*)

The figures in the table show, at varying rates of interest, what sum might reasonably be paid for a series of sums of £1 receivable at the end of each of a given number of successive years. By applying the appropriate figure from the table to the net income of the property the valuer arrives at his estimate of market value.

Where the income is perpetual the appropriate figure of Years' Purchase can be found by dividing 100 by the rate of interest appropriate to the property, or by dividing unity by the interest on £1 in one year at the appropriate rate per cent. Thus (as shown in Chapter 2), Years' Purchase in perpetuity can be expressed as

$$\frac{100}{\text{Rate per cent}} \text{ or } \frac{1}{i}$$

But where the income is receivable for a limited term only, as for example with a leasehold interest, the relationship between Years' Purchase and the rate of interest is more complex.

For example, if a certain property producing a perpetual net income of £500 per annum can fairly be regarded as a 5 per cent investment, a purchaser can afford to pay (£500 × 20 Y.P.) = £10,000 for it. Assume now that the income is receivable for 6 years only but that 5 per cent is still a reasonable return. In this case a purchaser could not afford to pay £10,000, for if he did so, although the income of £500 would represent 5 per cent on the purchase price throughout the term, at the end of the 6 years his interest in the property would cease and he would then lose both capital and income.

There are two ways to approach such a problem. The first of these is to consider the income flow for the next 6 years and take each year's income in isolation. Hence what is to be valued is in fact:—

End of year 1	£500
End of year 2	£500
and so on to	
End of year 6	£500

Now it has been shown that in valuing the right to receive a sum in the future the present "discounted" value is determined by applying the Present Value of £1 to the actual sum to be received. Hence, taking each in turn, it is clear that:—

End of year 1, sum receivable	£500	
× Present Value of £1 in 1 yr at 5%	0·9524	
		£476
End of year 2, sum receivable	£500	
× Present Value of £1 in 2 yrs at 5%	0·9070	
		£454
End of year 3, sum receivable	£500	
× Present Value of £1 in 3 yrs at 5%	0·8638	
		£432

End of year 4, sum receivable	£500	
× Present Value of £1 in 4 yrs at 5%	0·8227	
		£411
End of year 5, sum receivable	£500	
× Present Value of £1 in 5 yrs at 5%	0·7835	
		£392
End of year 6, sum receivable	£500	
× Present Value of £1 in 6 yrs at 5%	0·7462	
		£373
		£2,538

Hence it can be seen that the value of the right to receive £500 for each of the next 6 years is £2,538. This is a laborious approach, and if the period were extended would quickly become cumbersome. A tidier method would be as follows:—

	Sum receivable each year	£500
Present Value of £1 in 1 year at 5%	0·9524	
Present Value of £1 in 2 years at 5%	0·9070	
Present Value of £1 in 3 years at 5%	0·8638	
Present Value of £1 in 4 years at 5%	0·8227	
Present Value of £1 in 5 years at 5%	0·7835	
Present Value of £1 in 6 years at 5%	0·7462	
		5·0756
Present value of £500 p.a. for next 6 years		£2,538

In this way the annual rent is multiplied by the sum of the present values of £1 for each year. In fact, a formula can be derived to represent the sum of the present values of £1 p.a. for any number of years known as Years' Purchase Single Rate (see pp. 27–39 of *Parry's Valuation Tables*).

Hence in the above example:—	
Rent Receivable	£500
× Years Purchase (Single Rate)	
for 6 years at 5%	5·0757
Capital Value	£2,538

An alternative approach to the problem of valuing a terminable income is to recognise that a lower Years' Purchase will be required to capitalise the terminable income but at the same time the rate of interest must not be interfered with. If the rate of interest is merely increased to give the lower Years' Purchase necessary, it is no longer performing only its proper function as an indicator of the relative merits of different investments, it is also being required to function as an indicator of the period during which the income will be received. In order to leave the rate of interest to perform only its proper function, it is necessary to make the income comparable in terms of time. This can be achieved by allowing an amount out of the terminable income to be set aside annually as a sinking fund, sufficient to accumulate during the term to the capital originally invested. If this is done the purchaser, having paid £x for the interest in the first instance, will receive the income during the term and set aside out of that income a sinking fund, so that at the end of the term the sinking fund will have accumulated to the original capital of £x. In this way the terminable income has been perpetuated and is, therefore, directly comparable with the perpetual income.

Thus, the formula for finding the Present Value of £1 per annum for a terminable income is $\frac{1}{i+s}$, i being the interest on £1 in one year at the appropriate rate per cent and s being the sinking fund to replace £1 at the end of the term.

The next question is at what rate of interest should the annual sinking fund be assumed to accumulate? Again, the proper function of the rate of interest, that of indicating the relative merits of different investments, is the prime consideration. It was explained above that sinking fund arrangements can be made by means of a sinking fund policy with an insurance company. The interest on such a policy is low because the investment is riskless and as near trouble-free as possible. If it is assumed that the sinking fund is arranged in this way, all of the risks attached to the actual investment in the property will be reflected, as they should be, in the rate of interest the purchaser requires on the capital invested.

These two assumptions, (a) that a sinking fund is set aside and (b) that the rate of interest at which the sinking fund accumulates is the rate appropriate to a riskless and trouble-free investment, are in no way invalidated by the fact that many investors make sinking fund provisions in some way other than through a leasehold redemption policy or that many investors make no sinking fund provision at all.

Example 8–10

What is the value of a leasehold property producing a net income of £500 for the next 6 years assuming that a purchaser requires a return of 5 per cent on his money and that provision is made for a sinking fund for redemption of capital at 3 per cent?

Answer

Interest on £1 in 1 year at 5% $= 0.05$
S.F. to produce £1 in 6 years at 3% $= 0.1546$

$\therefore$ Y.P. 6 years at 5% & 3%

$$= \frac{1}{i+s}$$

$$= \frac{1}{0.05 + 0.1546}$$

$$= 4.888$$

Valuation

Net income	£500
P.V. of £1 p.a. or Y.P. 6 years at 5 and 3%	4.888
Value	£2,444

Notes

In practice the figure of 4.888 could have been obtained direct from the table of P.V. of £1 p.a. at 5 and 3% in *Parry's Valuation Tables*.

Proof

The fact that the estimated purchase price does allow both for interest on capital and also for sinking fund may be shown as follows:—

Interest on £2,444 at 5% (2,444 × 0·05)	£122
Sinking fund to produce £2,444 in 6 yrs at 3% (£2,444 × 0·1546)	378
Income from property	£500

The Years' Purchase used in the above example is called a dual rate Years' Purchase because two different rates of interest are used. The first rate (5% in the example) is called the "remunerative" rate, and the second (3%) is called the "accumulative" rate.

As is shown below, the sum of the Present Values of £1 p.a. has the same formula but the rate of interest for the sinking fund is the same as the remunerative rate—hence there is a single rate adopted throughout and so the result is a Years' Purchase Single Rate.

It will be noted that the terminable income of £500 p.a., when valued on a Y.P. Single rate produced £2,538 whereas on Y.P. Dual Rate the answer is £2,444. The choice of the appropriate Y.P. Table is determined by the nature of the income and surrounding factors, particularly the nature of the legal estate, as is illustrated in Chapter 9.

The derivation of the formulae for Years' Purchase Dual Rate and Years' Purchase Single Rate is as follows:—

a) Years' Purchase Single Rate

To find the value of £1 per annum receivable at the end of each year for a given time allowing compound interest.

The present value of the first instalment of income is $\frac{1}{1+i}$, that of the second $\frac{1}{(1+i)^2}$, the third $\frac{1}{(1+i)^3}$, and so on.

Let the present value be V and the term n years, then

$$V = \frac{1}{1+i} + \frac{1}{(1+i)^2} \cdots \frac{1}{(1+i)^{n-1}} + \frac{1}{(1+i)^n}.$$

Hence summing the series

$$V = \frac{1}{1+i} \left\{ \frac{\dfrac{1}{(1+i)^n} - 1}{\dfrac{1}{(1+i)} - 1} \right\}$$

changing the sign in the numerator and denominator

$$V = \frac{1 - \dfrac{1}{(1+i)^n}}{i}.$$

This expression has a three-fold aspect. V has been shown to represent the present value of a series of future payments allowing compound interest.

It also represents the sum upon which an income of £1 per annum will yield simple interest at i per annum and provide a sinking fund at i to accumulate to V at the end of n years.

Thus, the amount of simple interest on V is V.i, the sinking fund to replace V in n years is $V \dfrac{i}{(1+i)^{n-1}}$ (as shown above).

If these together are assumed to be equal to £1 then:

$$1 = V.i + V \frac{i}{(1+i)^n - 1}$$

$$1 = V.i \left(1 + \frac{1}{(1+i)^n - 1} \right) = V.i \frac{(1+i)^n}{(1+i)^n - 1}$$

$$V = \frac{(1+i)^n - 1}{i(1+i)^n}$$

Dividing numerator and denominator by $(1 + i)$

$$V = \frac{1 - \dfrac{1}{(1+i)^n}}{i}$$

which accords with the expression derived before.

b) Years' Purchase Dual Rate

To find the present value of £1 per annum for a given number of years, allowing simple interest at i per annum on capital and the accumulation of an annual sinking fund at s per annum.

As before, let the present value be V, then each annual instalment will consist of simple interest on V, that is V.i, and a sinking fund

instalment equal to $V. \dfrac{s}{(1+s)^n - 1}$.

$$1 = V.i. + V. \frac{s}{(1+s)^n - 1}$$

$$V = \frac{1}{i + \dfrac{s}{(1+s)^n - 1}}$$

This corresponds with the formula for $Y.P. = \dfrac{1}{i+S}$

when $S = \dfrac{s}{(1+s)^n - 1}$.

CHAPTER 9
Investment Method—Application and Use of Valuation Tables

IN CHAPTER 8 the principal Valuation Tables were examined and their functions explained. The valuer employs the Tables in many situations but their main use is in valuations using the investment method. This method is adopted for valuing both freehold and leasehold interests and these will be considered in turn.

1. VALUATION OF FREEHOLD INTERESTS

As has been previously explained the freehold owner of a property may choose to let the property and accept rent in lieu of occupation. Property is let on a lease and normally the freeholder will seek to obtain full rental value, by which is meant the highest rent obtainable from an acceptable tenant on the best appropriate terms. These terms may vary from a full repairing and insuring lease to a fully inclusive lease, as was set out in Chapter 5.

At the start of the lease, therefore, the tenant is paying full rental value. This level of rent remains payable until the end of the lease or until the rent is reviewed under the terms of the lease. This will be so regardless of any changes in the prevailing level of rental value. Suppose for example that a shop is let on 15 years' lease at an initial rent of £30,000 p.a. which is the rental value. The lease provides for the rent to be reviewed after 5 and 10 years. Assume that the rental value of the shop increases by £3,000 each year. It follows from this that rent and rental value coincide in year 1, but differ for the following 4 years, coinciding in year 6 as the rent review operates. Hence:—

Year	1	2	3	4	5	6	7
FRV	30,000	33,000	36,000	39,000	42,000	45,000	48,000
							and so on
Rent Payable	30,000	30,000	30,000	30,000	30,000	45,000	45,000

119

Now if the valuer is required to value the freehold interest in year 1 he will be valuing a freehold interest let at full rental value, whereas in, say year 3 the rent will be £30,000 p.a. whilst the rental value is £36,000 p.a. so that he has to value a freehold interest let at below full rental value. Each of these situations will be considered separately.

(A) Freehold Let at Full Rental Value

As was explained in Chapter 2, the principle of the investment method is

Net Income × Years' Purchase = Capital Value

Net Income is the rent receivable less any outgoings borne by the landlord, other than income tax. Income tax is ignored as this is a generally applicable impost and, insofar as it varies according to the personal status of the recipient, is a personal factor unrelated to the quality of the investment itself. The implications of valuing incomes net of income tax are considered in Chapter 14.

In the case of a freehold interest, as the interest is perpetual then income from the property will be perpetual. It is true that rent arising from buildings rather than land is unlikely to be perpetual since buildings eventually wear out. However, the life of the building rarely has a predictable end and, unless the building's life is relatively short, say up to 25 years, then the likelihood of rent from the building ending at some distant date is insignificant to the valuation. For example, suppose that a building has a predictable life of 30 years and produces a rent of £10,000 p.a. whilst a similar building will last for 100 years.

Then the rent from the 30 year building has a value of £10,000 p.a. × Y.P. 30 yrs at say 10% = 10,000 × Y.P. 9·427 = £94,270, whilst the second rent has a value of £10,000 p.a. at say 10% = 10,000 × Y.P. 100 yrs at 10% = 10,000 × Y.P. 9·999 = £99,990. The rent for 30 years has a value equal to 94·27% of the rent for 100 years.

The reason for this is that the value of £1 discounted for

a short period is higher than for a long period, and the effect of compound interest is to magnify this effect. Hence the Present Value of £1 in 1 year at 10% is £0·909, 2 years is £0·826, 3 years is £0·751 and so on for each succeeding year, the value falling for each subsequent year at an accelerating rate, so that for 30 years it is £0·057 and for 100 years £0·00007. This is illustrated on the graph on page 122. A similar pattern will apply at any rate of interest.

The rent in the earlier years is therefore more significant to the valuation than for later years. As was seen Y.P. for 30 years at 10% = 9·427, whereas Y.P. in perpetuity at 10% is $\frac{100}{10} = 10·0$. Thus in valuing any income to perpetuity at 10%, $\frac{9·427}{10·0} = 94·27\%$ of the total value lies in the next 30 years' income. An inspection of the Y.P. Single Rate Tables on Pages 27–40 of *Parry's Valuation Tables* will indicate the effect of this mathematical consequence at different rates of interest and as the graph on page 123 shows.

Quite apart from the mathematical reason a building is normally demolished because it is at the end of its economic life in that the rental value of the site for a new development exceeds that for the standing building. For example, the 30 year building will probably be pulled down after 30 years because the freeholder can obtain a rent of £10,000 p.a. or more from the site (or its equivalent capital value) and naturally prefers this to £10,000 p.a. from the old building. Hence in valuing the rent from a building the income may be regarded as perpetual although it is recognised that the rent will not always arise from the existing building.

It is true that in some special circumstances a building will have a predictably short life, for example, because of physical deficiencies or town planning restrictions, where a lower rent will subsequently arise. This situation is considered later.

The valuer is thus faced with a net income at full rental value which he can regard as perpetual. At present the rent is at the prevailing rental value, but he may feel that the rental value will change in future years. Indeed he would normally anticipate changes to occur as market forces change

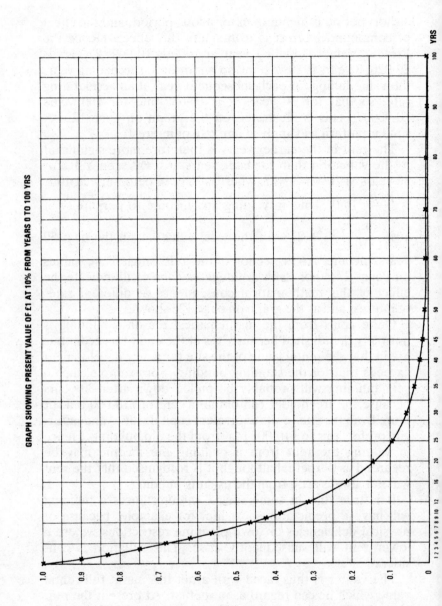

GRAPH SHOWING PRESENT VALUE OF £1 AT 10% FROM YEARS 0 TO 100 YRS

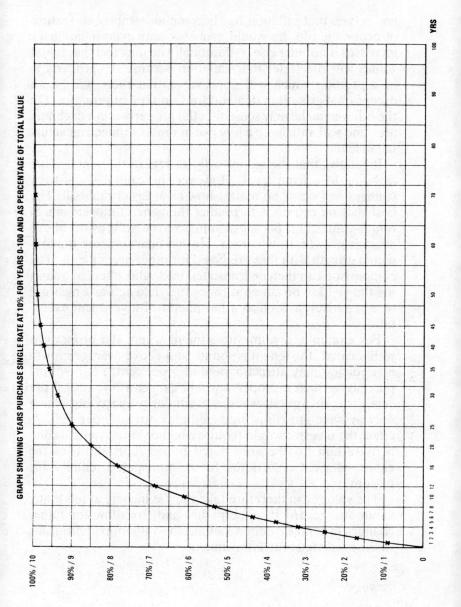

GRAPH SHOWING YEARS PURCHASE SINGLE RATE AT 10% FOR YEARS 0-100 AND AS PERCENTAGE OF TOTAL VALUE

and, given that inflation has become an established feature
of economic life, he would probably anticipate inflationary
increases if nothing else. Additionally he may feel that rental
values will rise faster than inflation because the property is
in a position which will improve or that there will be an
exceptional growth in demand for that type of property. On
the other hand he may sense that the property is in a declining
area and will anticipate a low rise in rents or indeed an actual
fall in levels.

It follows that the valuer will not regard the rental value
as being at a fixed level. However, he cannot know what
changes will occur no matter how clear his crystal ball. The
best that he can do is to predict the general movements in
rental values and perhaps estimate average growth, above
average growth, or whatever. He can then compare the predicted growth with that predicted for other investments. The
comparison can then be translated into value effect by adapting the yield to be adopted, since the yield acts as a measure
of comparison as well as a barometer of investment expectations.

For example, a prime investment where the property is
well located, the tenant is sound, and above average growth
is predicted may attract a yield of 5 per cent, i.e. investors
purchasing such a property would expect a return of 5 per
cent on their capital, whereas a similar property but where
only average growth is predicted may attract 7 per cent. In
effect the investor would require a higher initial yield to compensate him for the anticipated future shortfall. Thus the
choice of yield reflects the future anticipated rental value
pattern.

The valuer can therefore take the net income at full rental
value and regard it as perpetual and, to allow for future
changes in rental, adopt a yield in the valuation appropriate
to the predicted rental movement.

Example 9–1

Value the freehold interest in shop premises in a prime
location. The premises were recently let to a multiple company at £100,000 p.a. exclusive on full repairing and insuring

terms for 35 years with 5 yearly rent reviews. The rent is
at full rental value.

Valuation Rent Reserved (and		
F.R.V.)		£100,000 p.a.
Outgoings (NIL) ∴ Net Income		£100,000 p.a.
Y.P. in perp at 4%		25·00
		£2,500,000

Example 9–2

Value the freehold interest in shop premises in a secondary
location. The premises comprise a shop on the ground floor
with flat above which were let recently to a single tenant
at £10,000 p.a. exclusive on internal repairing and insuring
terms for 15 years with 5 yearly rent reviews. The rent is
at full rental value.

Valuation Rent Reserved (and		
F.R.V.)		£10,000 p.a.
less External Repairs say	£1,000	
Management at 5%	500	1,500
Net Income (and net F.R.V.)		£8,500 p.a.
Y.P. in perp at 9%		11·11
		£94,435
	Value say	£94,000

Note that the less attractive investment features of *Example 9–2* involve the adoption of a higher yield than in *Example
9–1*. A further significant factor in determining the yield is
that, in *Example 9–1*, the tenant is tied to the property for
a substantial period. If the new lease were for only a short
period, say 5 years, then there is no certainty that the property would be re-let to the same covenant or one of a similar
quality. Remember that the original tenant is responsible
for the rent throughout the period of the lease by privity
of contract even if he sells the lease and leaves the premises:
he acts in effect as a "guarantor" of the rent if he sells the

lease. Hence, if the lease were for a shorter term the yield might rise to say 5%.

It is worth noting that if a valuer chose to predict the future levels of rent at each review and thereafter and then chose to include them in the valuation, he would need to adopt a higher yield than that which was used, which does reflect growth potential, as he would otherwise double-count the growth. The problem then is the choice of a non-growth yield since yields excluding growth are not readily obtainable from comparables. The possibility of incorporating growth rental is discussed, together with comments on equated yields, in Chapter 14 where further aspects of this topic are considered.

It is also worth noting that the valuations determine the sum which an investor can invest to achieve a desired return. They do not, however, represent the whole cost of the investment since costs will arise in relation to the purchase such as professional fees and stamp duty. On all but small investments where no stamp duty is payable, these on-costs tend to average around 3 per cent for the purchasers and around $2\frac{1}{2}$ per cent for the vendor.

It follows, therefore, that the return on the actual sums spent on acquiring an investment will be slightly less than those adopted in the valuation which represents the return on the net purchase price. This in no way invalidates the valuation approach since the returns are based on the net purchase prices of comparable investments. As the on-costs tend to be a constant proportion there will be a fixed relationship between returns to net and gross sums invested.

For example, suppose that an investor pays £100,000 for an income of £10,000 p.a. The return to the net investment is

$$\frac{10,000}{100,000} \times 100 = 10\%$$

If on-costs are 3 per cent of £100,000 = £3,000, the return to the gross investment is:

$$\frac{10,000}{103,000} \times 100 = 9 \cdot 709\%$$

Thus an investor seeking a 10 per cent return recognises that he will achieve a 9·709 per cent return on gross sums invested. If any net income is valued at 10 per cent the return to gross investment will be 9·709 per cent in any event. When references are made to the return or yield on an investment this is normally a reference to a net investment. A valuer should of course be sure that this is so, particularly where large investment institutions are involved, since they do tend to talk in terms of returns to gross costs in many instances.

(B) Freehold Let at Below Full Rental Value

As has been illustrated a freeholder will frequently be receiving a rent below rental value because the rent was fixed some years ago and rental values have risen subsequently. An alternative reason might be that the lessee paid a premium to the freeholder when he took the lease which entitled him to pay a rent below rental value from the very start.

The valuer faced with such a situation may find that the approach adopted when rent equals rental value is inadequate. He could take the actual rent as net income and use the approach:—Net Income × Years' Purchase = Capital Value. However, he has a difficult problem in that, in addition to normal predictions as to underlying rental growth, he has a certain knowledge that the rent will change at a specific time when either the lease terminates or a rent review is to operate, and the rent will rise to a new level. This change is different from normal rental value variations resulting from general market movements. Consequently he will be unable to draw from market transactions the appropriate yield to apply unless he can find similar situations where the rent bears the same proportion to rental value, and the time for review or renewal is the same. Indeed in practice the only typical situation which tends to follow these requirements is the valuation of freehold ground rents where the rent is relatively nominal in relation to rental value and the time for rent change is distant.

Accordingly the valuer needs to adapt the general approach for this situation. For example, suppose that a valuation is required of a freehold interest where the rent receivable is £1,000 p.a. for the next 3 years. The current rental value is £4,000 p.a.

It is clear that for Years 1 to 3 the freeholder will receive £1,000 each year. At the end of Year 3 the rent will be revised to the then prevailing rental value. It is not known what the rental value will be at that time but it is known that the current rental value is £4,000 p.a. The valuation is made in two stages.

Stage 1.—Value current rent passing

The period for which the rent is fixed is known as the Term. The freeholder will receive £1,000 per year. It may be that it will be payable quarterly, half yearly, or annually, and in advance or in arrears. It is normally assumed for valuation purposes that the rent is payable annually in arrears. This is merely a convention of convenience although it is true that typically leases require rents to be paid in advance, and commonly quarterly in advance. This topic is further considered in Chapter 14.

Hence, following the normal convention, the valuer must value £1,000 receivable for each of the next 3 years. This he can do as follows:—

Year 1	£1,000	
P.V. £1 in 1 year	x	£1,000 x
Plus Year 2	£1,000	
P.V. £1 in 2 years	y	£1,000 y
Plus Year 3	£1,000	
P.V. £1 in 3 years	z	£1,000 z
		£1,000 (x + y + z)

However, as was shown in Chapter 8, a simpler method is to use the Years' Purchase Single Rate.

The valuer needs to adopt the appropriate yield to determine the Years' Purchase. He probably has no comparables of sales of similar incomes at one quarter of rental value receivable for 3 years only. What he does know is the yield adopted when valuing the rental value from similar properties: he can therefore derive the appropriate yield from this.

For example, suppose that if the property were let at its rental value of £4,000 p.a. the yield would be 6 per cent. What yield should be adopted in valuing the lower rent? One view is that the lower rent, being from the same property, has all the investment qualities of the rental value, but in addition it is even more certain of payment since the tenant is enjoying the accommodation at a cheap cost: thus a lower yield is appropriate. On the other hand, if the tenant did fail to pay the rent the freeholder could obtain possession and re-let at the higher rental value, so that this added security might be said to be of no real importance. Further, if the tenant is substantial, the chances of his defaulting at any level are remote if "a good covenant" has any meaning. Meanwhile, a low rent paid by a weak covenant is certainly more certain of being received than where the rent is at its maximum rental value. Yet again, if the low rent is fixed for a period beyond the normal review period then it has the disadvantage of providing a poorer hedge against inflation, a factor which will outweigh any additional certainty of payment: indeed if the rent is fixed for several years it takes on the characteristics of a medium fixed interest investment when the yield may be more realistically derived from yields for such investments than from the yield for the property producing the income.

From a purely practical point of view it will be found that, in cases where the term rent is small compared with the reversionary rent and the term is for a short period, the value of the term is only a small part of the whole value. The choice of yield in such cases can only have a limited practical significance since the overall value is hardly affected by whatever yield is chosen. Further it is practically impossible to analyse comparable transactions to demonstrate the yield being used for valuing the term for the same reasons.

The approach therefore is to weigh up the situation and make whatever adjustment appears to be appropriate—the valuer must make a subjective judgement. It is suggested that as a general rule the same yield should be adopted.

However, if the additional certainty of payment is specially attractive, for example where the tenants are not financially strong—as is generally the case in poorer properties—then a reduced yield is appropriate. On the other hand if the rent is fixed for a period significantly longer than the normal review period, it should be increased. In every case, however, the yield is derived from the prevailing yield applicable to the valuation of the rental value.

So, returning to the rent for the term, the valuation is:—

Rent Reserved	£1,000 p.a.
Y.P. 3 yrs at *say* 6%	2·673
	£2,673

Stage 2.—*Value Rent for Period After the Term*

The period following the Term is called the Reversion. The valuer must first determine the rent which will arise at the end of the Term. He has two choices, to adopt a predicted rental value or to adopt the prevailing rental value.

If he takes the former course he has two problems. First, he does not know what the rental value will actually be. Second, if he adopts a predicted future level he is contradicting the principle established in valuing a freehold interest let at rental value.

On the other hand if he adopts current rental value he can have reasonable confidence that this rent is currently obtainable. In addition the yield adopted in valuing rental value reflects the likely trends in rental value. If the property were now let at rental value this would anticipate a growth in rent receivable at regular periods in the future which will occur in the property being valued.

Hence the valuer should adopt the current rental value as the rent receivable on reversion, recognising that the yield he applies reflects the possible changes in rental value that will arise in the intervening period.

The valuer can therefore project himself forward to the end of the Term. At that time there will be a freehold interest

let at rental value. The valuation of such a situation has already been established.
Hence:—

Rental Value	£4,000 p.a.
Y.P. in perp at 6%	16·6667
	£66,667

However, that is the value in 3 years' time. What is required is the value now. This can be determined by applying the Present Value of £1 Table. The appropriate rate to use is that adopted for valuing the reversion since it is logical that an investor purchasing a future investment showing 6 per cent invests a sum today to grow at the same rate.
Hence:—

Value in 3 years' time	£66,667
× Present Value of £1 in 3 yrs at 6%	0·8396
	£55,974

The valuation of the Reversion is thus

Full Rental Value	£4,000
× Y.P. in perp at 6%	16·6667
	£66,667
× Present Value of £1 in 3 yrs at 6%	0·8396
	£55,974

As an alternative approach, it is known that the Years' Purchase Single Rate is the sum of the Present Values of £1. Hence Y.P. in perp = P.V. £1 in 1 yr + P.V. £1 in 2 yrs + P.V. £1 in 3 yrs + P.V. £1 in 4 yrs and so on. However, the valuation in this case requires the sum of the Present Values of £1 into perpetuity apart from the next 3 years. Hence one can apply Y.P. in perp (which includes P.V. for 1, 2 and 3 yrs) and deduct P.V. £1 in 1, 2 and 3 yrs (which equals Y.P. 3 years Single Rate). Thus:—

	Full Rental value		£4,000 p.a.
	Y.P. in perp. at 6%	16·6667	
less Y.P. 3 yrs at 6%		2·6730	13·9937
			£55,975

Note:

The deduction of Y.P.s does not apply to Years' Purchase Dual Rates as will be shown.

The valuer can short circuit either of these approaches where he is valuing a reversion to a term which goes on into perpetuity since *Parry's Valuation Tables* contain on Pages 42–55 Years' Purchase of a Reversion to a Perpetuity. Hence,

Full Rental Value		£4,000 p.a.
	Y.P. in perp. deferred 3 yrs at 6%	13·99365
		£55,975

(C) Term and Reversion

Thus it is seen that the valuation of a freehold interest let at less than full rental value requires the combined value of the term and reversion. The full valuation of the example becomes:

Term Rent Reserved		£1,000 p.a.	
	Y.P. 3 yrs at 6%	2·673	2,673
Reversion to F.R.V.		£4,000 p.a.	
	Y.P. in perp def'd 3 yrs at 6%	13,994	55,976
			£58,649

An alternative approach to the Term + Reversion is sometimes adopted where the initial rent is valued into perpetuity and the additional rent receivable at reversion is valued into perpetuity but deferred for the period of the term. Such an approach will give the same result as described above so long as a common yield is adopted throughout, but where the yield adopted in valuing the term should be different from the reversion, an artificiality is required for this layer method which makes it less reliable. The layer/hardcore method is considered in Chapter 14.

The following examples illustrate the valuation of freehold interests let at less than full rental value.

Example 9–3

Value the freehold interest in shop premises in a secondary location. The premises are let at £2,500 p.a. net on lease with 4 years to run. The current rental value is £6,000 p.a. net. The property is a 10% investment.

Term Rent Reserved	£2,500 p.a.	
Y.P. 4 yrs at say 9% (rent less than F.R.V. and more secure)	3·240	£8,100
Reversion to F.R.V.	£6,000 p.a.	
Y.P. in perp def'd 4 yrs at 10%	6·830	£40,980
		£49,080

Example 9–4

Value the freehold interest in well located factory premises let to a good covenant. The premises are let at £10,000 p.a. net on lease with 12 years to run without review. The current rental value is £16,000 p.a. net. The property is an 8 per cent investment (assuming a lease with 5 yearly rent reviews).

Term Rent Reserved	£10,000 p.a.	
Y.P. 12 yrs at 10% (rent less than F.R.V. but fixed for a long term)	6·814	£68,140

Reversion to F.R.V.	£16,000 p.a.	
Y.P. in perp def'd 12 yrs at 8%	4·964	£79,424
		£147,564

Example 9–5

Value the freehold interest in shop premises in a good location. The premises are let on ground lease with 60 years to run at £1,000 p.a. without provision for review. The current rental value is £50,000 p.a. net. The property is a 7 per cent investment.

Term Rent Reserved	£1,000 p.a.	
Y.P. 60 yrs at 14% (the rent is very secure but is fixed for a very long term)	7·14	£7,140
Reversion to F.R.V.	£50,000 p.a.	
Y.P. perp def'd 60 yrs at 7%	0·2465	£12,325
		£19,465

Note that the current rent provides a yield of $\frac{1000}{19465} \times 100 = 5\cdot137\%$ to capital invested. In practice it might be possible to show that similar ground rents sell on the basis of an initial yield of around 5 per cent—or put another way, they sell on a 20 Y.P. basis. This is one case where a direct valuation of the interest may be derived from the present rent, i.e. capital value is £1,000 p.a. × 20 Y.P. = £20,000. It is not as precise as the detailed approach but it may be considered sufficiently accurate in some circumstances.

2. VALUATION OF LEASEHOLD INTERESTS

Leasehold interests are commonly found in the property market. They arise in two principal ways.

One is where a freeholder of development land offers a

ground lease under which the leaseholder will carry out the development and enjoy the benefits of the property he develops for the period of the lease in return for the payment of a ground rent. Such leases are usually for a long term of years, typically 99 years or 125 years, to allow the lessee to recoup his capital investment in the buildings, and the ground rent is low relative to the rental value of the buildings.

The other principal source of leasehold interests is where either a freeholder or leaseholder offers a lease of premises which the tenant will occupy for his own use and enjoyment in return for the payment of a rent which will normally be the rental value of the premises.

As can be seen a lease may require the payment of a rent at less than full rental value or at full rental value. In addition, as was shown above, even where a lessee takes a lease at full rental value with provision for periodic reviews of rent, if rental values rise there will come a time when the rent paid falls below prevailing rental values.

The importance of the relationship between the rent payable under a lease and the full rental value is that a leasehold interest has no value unless full rental value is greater than the rent payable. The reason for this is that, as full rental value represents the maximum rent which a tenant is prepared to pay, he will not be prepared to offer any additional sum to purchase the lease. It must be remembered that when someone purchases a lease he becomes responsible for the observance of all the covenants set out therein including of course the duty to pay the rent. Hence, if someone purchases a lease for a capital sum and then is required to pay full rental value he is worse off than he would be if he had taken a lease direct of a comparable property.

Thus, as a first principle, a leasehold interest has a value where the full rental value exceeds the rent payable. The difference between these two figures is termed a "Profit Rent". For example, suppose that A holds a lease under which he must pay £800 p.a. when the full rental value is £1,500 p.a. The position is:—

F.R.V.	£1,500 p.a.
Less Rent paid	800

Profit Rent   £700 p.a.

Such a lease has a value because if someone purchases the lease he will be entitled to occupy the property under the lease terms and so pay £800 p.a. for something which is worth £1,500 p.a. or alternatively he may sub-let the property at a rent of £1,500 p.a. and so each year receive £1,500, pay £800 and retain the "Profit" of £700 as a profit rent. This benefit will continue until the lease ends or the rent is adjusted under a rent review clause to the higher value. The task of the valuer is to determine the price a purchaser would pay for the benefit — the value of the lease.

The valuation approach normally adopted is the investment method notwithstanding that the purchaser might intend to occupy. This is valid particularly in the case of commercial properties since, although the purchaser does not seek an actual return of rent on his capital investment, he will be receiving an annual rental benefit which will come to him as part of his profits on the capital he invests. That this is so can readily be demonstrated by assuming the facts of the example above, where the lessee will pay £800 p.a. as rent, also assuming in addition that another identical property is available at the full rental value of £1,500 p.a. In the first property he will pay £700 p.a. less than he would in the second property. Since all other conditions are identical his profits from trading in the first property will be £700 p.a. greater than for the second property. Similarly when in the first property the lease ends or the rent is reviewed, so that the rent is increased from £800 p.a. to £1,500 p.a. there will be an immediate reduction in the profits of £700.

Thus, when valuing a leasehold interest, the basic principle of the investment method will apply, namely:—

Net Income × Years' Purchase = Capital Value.

(A) Provision for Loss of Capital

Net Income for this purpose will be the Profit Rent, as has been shown above. However, when an investor purchases a leasehold interest he is faced with one factor which he will not meet in a freehold interest, namely that one day his interest must cease and he will have no further interest in the property: if he obtains a further lease in the property to follow the expired lease that will be a new investment.

The investor knows therefore that one day his interest will cease and he will have no capital asset remaining. His investment will therefore decline from whatever he paid to nothing. Such an investment is know as a wasting asset since the asset wastes away naturally and inevitably.

The investor faced with such a situation must therefore take steps to deal with the loss of his capital. This he can do by investing funds which grow to compensate for the capital he will lose. The sensible approach is to find these funds out of the income produced by the wasting asset so that it is self-compensating. Various methods are open to him but the conventional approach is to assume that he will invest part of his rent each year out of the net income in an annual sinking fund. Since he needs to guarantee the replacement of his capital he must seek a medium which is as certain as may be that the sums invested will reach a specific and certain figure and the only such medium is normally an insurance policy. Naturally the returns offered by insurance companies must be based on long term rates of interest which ignore abnormal movements in interest rates and which give a reasonable guarantee that they can meet their obligations. Consequently the returns offered will be low and an average yield of around 3 per cent has been found to be realistic.

If the investor places some of his net income in such a sinking fund he can be satisifed that his original investment capital will be available at the end of the lease for further investment. In that way he can continue indefinitely so that the return he receives after allowing for sinking fund costs will be perpetual. The effects of inflation on such an arrangement will be considered later.

An alternative approach to setting aside a sinking fund is to write off the investment over its life. This is an accountancy convention often followed where companies such as industrialists employ plant and machinery which by their nature have a limited life. A typical approach would be to adopt straight line depreciation where the capital cost is divided by the predicted years of useful life and this figure deducted as an annual cost of the item in the accounts. Such an approach does not lend itself readily to a valuation and fails to reflect the accelerating rate of depreciation suffered by a leasehold interest.

(B) Years' Purchase Dual Rate

The investor in a leasehold investment, if he provides a sinking fund, can regard the net income after sinking fund provision, as perpetual.

The valuer may now value any leasehold profit rent with this in mind. Assume, for example, that a valuation is required of a leasehold interest where the lease has 5 years to run at a fixed rent of £800 p.a. The current rental value is £1,500 p.a. The valuation approach is as follows:—

Stage 1 Determine Profit Rent

	F.R.V.	£1,500 p.a.
less	Rent paid	800
	Profit Rent (Net Income)	£700

Stage 2 Assess Annual Sinking Fund

As was shown in Chapter 8, the Annual Sinking Fund for the Redemption of £1 Capital Invested Tables shows the annual payments needed to reach £1. In this case the sum to be recouped will not be known until the valuation is completed, so assume value of interest is £V. Hence:—

Capital Sum required in 5 years	£V
× A.S.F. to replace £1 in 5 yrs at 3%	0·1884
Annual Sinking Fund Payment	£0·1884V

Stage 3 Assess Income Net of Sinking Fund

	Profit Rent	£700
less	A.S.F. to replace £V in 5 yrs	£0·1884V

Net Income   700–0·1884V

Stage 4 Value Net Income

Since the income net of A.S.F. is effectively perpetual notwithstanding that the lease will end, as has been demonstrated, the net income can be regarded as a perpetual net income as for freehold in possession. However, as the income is produced by a leasehold interest rather than a freehold, the investor has to collect rent and pay rent on to the landlord; he will have the trouble and expense of replacing his investment at the end of the lease; and he is subject to the restrictions on his actions which the covenants in the lease place upon him. Apart from these factors the investment is the same as the freehold investment in an identical property on which the yield will be known. Allowing for these adverse qualities the appropriate yield for the leasehold investment should be higher than the freehold yield. The amount of additional return required depends on the facts of the case but, as a general rule, the addition will be around $\frac{1}{2}$ per cent on a freehold yield of 4 per cent rising to 2 per cent on a freehold of 12 per cent. There is, however, no fixed adjustment to be made: the adjustment is a matter of judgment coupled with knowledge of adjustments found in analysis of comparables.

Hence, suppose in this case that the freehold yield is $7\frac{1}{2}$ per cent, the leasehold yield would then be say $8\frac{1}{2}$. Hence:—

Net Income	£700 − 0·1884V p.a.
× Y.P. in perp at $8\frac{1}{2}$– =	11·7647
Capital Value	£8235 − 2·216V

BUT the Capital Value was taken to be £V

$$\therefore £8235 - 2\cdot216V = V$$
$$\therefore V = £2,561$$

Thus, bringing the valuation together:—

F.R.V.   £1,500 p.a.

Less Rent Paid	800
	——
Profit Rent	700
Less A.S.F. to replace £V in 5 yrs	
at 3%	0·1884V
	————
	£700 − 0·1884V
× Y.P. in perp at 8½%	11·7647
	————
Capital Value	£8,235−2.216V

Capital Value (V) = 8235 − 2·216V = V

∴ Capital Value = £2,561

This is a straightforward approach but it was shown in Chapter 8 that there are Tables known as Years' Purchase Dual Rates. As was shown these Tables allow for the need to provide a sinking fund by incorporating within their formula an allowance for the appropriate sinking fund. They therefore perform the function of Stages 2 and 4 described above and their use will exclude the need for Stage 3. These Tables can therefore be applied directly to the Profit Rent. Hence,

F.R.V	£1,500 p.a.
Less Rent Paid	800
	——
Profit rent	700
× Years Purchase allowing for a yield of 8½ and annual sinking fund at 3% for 5 years	
(Y.P. 5 yrs at 8½% & 3%)	3·658
	——
	£2,561

Clearly this is a more convenient method and the one adopted in valuing a leasehold interest at full rental value. Nonetheless the valuer is aware that the method is the same as the valuation of a freehold interest at full rental value.

(C) Capital Replacement and Inflation

Mention was made earlier of the problem of inflation in the replacement of the capital invested. The problem is that an investor who invests capital in a leasehold interest and who replaces his original capital at the end may find that, with the erosion of the value of money over the period, the replaced capital is worth less, and perhaps significantly less, in real terms that at the start. As a general rule if he compares investments in freehold property, he will find that their value has risen to maintain more or less their real value. The implications of this situation which have led to some criticism of the approach described above are considered in Chapter 14.

(D) Annual Sinking Fund and Tax on Rents

The valuation set out above can be analysed to show that it achieves its goals as follows:—

Profit Rent	£700
Less A.S.F. to replace £2,561 in 5 yrs at 3% (2,561 × 0·1884) =	482
Income net of A.S.F.	218

$$\frac{218}{2{,}561} \times 100 = 8{\cdot}5\%$$

∴ the investor achieves his desired return.

OR Profit Rent		£700
Capital Invested	2,561	
Interest on Capital at 8½%	0·085	218
Sum available for investment in A.S.F.		482
× Amt. of £1 p.a. for 5 yrs at 3%		5·3091
		£2,559

∴ the investor replaces his capital.

This analysis ignores income tax. The reasons for ignoring income tax in determining the return on an investment were set out above. However, the annual sinking fund is a cost and the ignoring of the effects of income tax in respect of this leads to a misleading value as the following analysis where income tax is considered shows.

Assume that the investor pays income tax at a marginal rate of 40p in the £. Hence,

Profit Rent		£700
Capital Invested	2,561	
Interest at $8\frac{1}{2}\%$	0·085	218
Sum available for A.S.F.		£482

Thus the Profit Rent is divided as to £218 for return on capital and £482 for annual sinking fund investment. As to the £218, although income tax at 40 per cent is payable thereon (as part of the £700 p.a. on all of which 40 per cent tax is payable) this can be ignored for analysis purposes since the aim is to obtain $8\frac{1}{2}\%$ before tax. As to the sinking fund this is an actual investment exercise and the investor needs to put £482 each year into it. However, he must pay 40 per cent income tax on this since no tax relief is given on normal sinking fund investments. So he can only invest

A.S.F. before tax	£482
Less Income Tax at 40%	193
A.S.F. after tax	£289

It is obvious therefore that the investor will not be able to achieve his goal since he will not be able to pay £482 each year into the annual sinking fund and also meet his tax commitments. The true cost of the annual sinking fund therefore is not what he must invest but the annual income which, after payment of the tax, leaves £482 available to spend on the sinking fund.

This gross cost can be determined by multiplying the sum required by $\dfrac{100}{100-40}$ as is shown below.

Assume A earns £100 and pays tax of £40 (i.e. 40p in £).

Then A's income after tax is $(100-40)$p.

Thus for each £1 that A earns he will be left with $(100-40)$p out of each 100p.

Thus his net income (NI) will be $\dfrac{100-40}{100}$ of his gross income (GI).

$$\therefore \text{If} \quad GI \times \frac{100-40}{100} = NI$$

Then $$GI = NI \times \frac{100}{100-40}$$

The same will be true at any rate of tax. Thus, if tax is t, gross income can be reduced to net income by applying $\dfrac{100-t}{100}$.

Net income can be grossed up to gross income by applying $\dfrac{100}{100-t}$.

(E) Years' Purchase Dual Rate Adjusted for Income Tax

Applying the tax factor to the leasehold income, where an annual sinking of £482 was seen to be necessary to replace the capital, the amount of profit rent needed to be earned each year to leave £482 after tax is:

$$£482 \times \frac{100}{100-40} = £803.33 \text{ gross cost}$$

less Tax at 40p in £1 =

$$803.33 \times 0.4 = \quad 321.33$$

Net Income for A.S.F. = £482

If the investment is now analysed allowing for the true cost
of providing the sinking fund, the result is:—

Profit Rent	£700
less Gross A.S.F. to produce £482 p.a.	803·33
Hence Return to capital	− 103·33

Clearly the income has been over-valued if the price of
£2,561 is to be invested by a tax-payer paying 40p in the
£1 tax on income. Indeed it is obvious that the price of
£2,561 will only leave £482 p.a. available for A.S.F. after
the return of 8½% has been taken out if the investor is a
non tax-payer. Similarly the cost of providing a sinking fund
must vary with the individual tax-payer's marginal rate of
income tax, the higher the rate of tax the more gross income
needed before tax to produce the required net income for
A.S.F.

This presents a problem for the valuer called upon to prepare a "Market valuation" when it is clear that the potential
buyers in the market have differing rates of tax which have
a direct effect on their sinking fund costs. The solution is
for the valuer to adopt an "average rate" of tax, whilst recognising that investors whose personal rates differ sharply from
this have an advantage or disadvantage which renders the
valuation unreal for their own circumstances. If required he
can easily produce a valuation for a particular investor's
actual marginal tax rate.

Given that the valuer adopts an average rate of tax, what
is an average rate? In any year tax rates may vary from nil
for tax exempt persons to rates which have been as high
as 98 per cent with many different rates between, and these
rates tend to vary from year to year. Faced with such a variety
of rates the valuer needs to select a rate which is likely to
be most commonly met for the remaining years of the lease.
This rate is unknown, but a useful guide is the standard rate
of income tax for individuals and the corporation tax rate
for companies. The standard rate in recent years has come
down steadily from around 30 per cent plus 15 per cent invest-

ment surcharge to a basic rate in 1988 of 25 per cent coupled with a single higher rate of 40 per cent on incomes above £19,300. In similar fashion corporation tax has come down from 52 per cent for most companies to 35 per cent, with a rate of 25 per cent on small profits. This suggests that an average rate of around 35 to 40 per cent might be used. However, if rates of tax showed a tendency to rise or fall then the average rate should adjust to the trend.

Thus the valuer adopts a predicted average level of tax for coming years, and a rate of 35 per cent will be adopted for this purpose. In any event a small variation in the rate will only be significant if the term of years is short.

The valuer can now incorporate in the valuation approach a grossed up cost of an annual sinking fund by applying $\frac{100}{100-35} = 1.54$ to the required A.S.F. investment. This can readily be incorporated in the Years' Purchase Dual Rate formula. As was shown in Chapter 8, the formula is

$$\frac{1}{i + A.S.F.}$$

i represents the gross of tax rate of return and needs no adjustment. A.S.F. represents the annual sinking fund required to replace £1 of capital (after payment of tax).

It follows that $A.S.F. \times \frac{100}{100 - t}$ will represent A.S.F. required before payment of tax—the gross A.S.F.

Hence applying the facts of the example to the formula:—

$$i = 8\tfrac{1}{2}\% = 0.085$$

$$A.S.F. = A.S.F. \text{ to replace £1 in 5 yrs at 3\%} = 0.1884$$

$$\therefore A.S.F. \times \frac{100}{100 - 35} = 0.1884 \times 1.54 = 0.2901$$

$\therefore$ Y.P. 5 years at $8\frac{1}{2}\%$ and A.S.F. at 3% (adjusted for income tax)

$$= \frac{1}{0 \cdot 085 + 0 \cdot 2901} = 2 \cdot 6683$$

(Tables of Y.P. Dual Rate adjusted for varying rates of income tax can be found in Parry's Valuation Tables—Pages 30.1 to 52.32).

$\therefore$ *Valuation*

Profit Rent	£700 p.a.
× Y.P. 5 yrs at $8\frac{1}{2}$ & 3% adjusted for income tax at 35%	2·6683
Capital Value	£1,868

Analysis

Profit Rent		£700
less Interest on Capital at $8\frac{1}{2}\%$	£1,868	
	0·085	158
Gross A.S.F.		£542
less Income Tax at 35%		190
Net A.S.F.		352
× Amt. of £1 p.a. for 5 yrs at 3%		5.309
Capital Sum Replaced		£1,868

This shows that the adoption of a Y.P. Dual Rate adjusted for income tax allows the investor to achieve his required return and also permits him to replace his capital after meeting his tax liabilities.

With some exceptions, therefore, it is suggested that Y.P. Dual Rate adjusted for tax tables should be used for valuing leaseholds and other terminable incomes. The main exception is where the market comprises non-tax payers. It should be evident from the discussion so far that a person or organisation not liable to pay tax would be in a very advantageous position in relation not only to the actual yield from any investment but, with leaseholds, in relation to the rate of interest at which a sinking fund accumulates and to the amount which must be set aside—the gross annual sinking fund would equate to the net annual sinking fund. The shorter the lease, the greater the advantage. This advantage has been exploited by non-tax paying investors, in some cases to the point where they comprise the market (see Chapter 14).

(F) Leasehold Interest where Income less than Full Rental Value

So far the valuation of a leasehold interest has been restricted to those situations where the leaseholder receives full rental value, and the situation then compared with the valuation of a freehold interest in similar circumstances. However, as for freeholds, a leasehold owner may be receiving less than full rental value either because he sub-let in the past at the prevailing F.R.V. and rental values have risen, or he sub-let and took a premium.

Such a situation arose with freehold interests and, as was shown in such cases, the valuation values the existing rent whilst it is receivable—the "term", and then reverts to F.R.V. when this will be receivable—the "reversion". The same approach is adopted when valuing a leasehold varying income, with a Y.P. dual rate adjusted for tax being employed in place of Y.P. single rate or in perpetuity, as the following example shows.

Example 9–6

A took a lease of shop premises 23 years ago for 42 years at a fixed rent of £10,000 p.a. 17 years ago he sub-let the premises for 21 years at a fixed rent of £16,000 p.a. A valuation is now required of A's leasehold interest when similar shops are letting on 15 year leases with 5 yearly rent reviews at £40,000 p.a.

Term

A is receiving £16,000 p.a. for the under-lease. This will be payable for the next 4 years. Hence:—

	Rent Received	£16,000 p.a.
less	Rent Paid by A	10,000
	Profit Rent	£6,000 p.a.

A is receiving this profit rent for 4 years. Assume that the appropriate freehold rate for such a shop investment is $5\frac{1}{2}$ per cent. The appropriate leasehold rate would be 6 per cent. However, the rent is less than F.R.V., but assume this is not signifcant.

∴ Profit Rent		£6,000 p.a.	
× Y.P. 4 yrs at 6% and			
3% adj. for tax at 35%		2·338	£14,028

Reversion

After 4 years A will be able to re-let the shop at the prevailing rental value. For the reasons set out above when considering the valuation of a freehold interest let at less than F.R.V. the current rental value is adopted as the rent receivable at reversion. Hence:—

	Reversion to F.R.V.	£40,000 p.a.
less	Rent Payable by A	10,000
	Profit Rent	£30,000 p.a.

After 4 years, A will still have 15 years to run of his own lease. Hence, in 4 years' time the valuation will be,

Profit Rent	£30,000 p.a.	
× Y.P. 15 yrs at 6% and		
3% adj. for tax at 35%	7·007	£210,210

However, the value is required now, so that the value brought forward 4 years is:—

Value in 4 years	£210,210	
× P.V. £1 in 4 yrs at 6%	0·792	£166,486

Note that, as before, the discount rate is the same as that adopted for the valuation of the reversion.

Thus bringing the valuation together it becomes:—

Term Rent Received		£16,000 p.a.	
less Rent Payable		10,000	
Profit Rent		£6,000 p.a.	
× Y.P. 4 yrs at 6% and 3% adj. for tax at 35%		2·338	£14,028
Reversion to F.R.V.		£40,000 p.a.	
less Rent Payable		10,000	
Profit Rent		£30,000 p.a.	
× Y.P. 15 yrs at 6% and 3% adj. for tax at 33%	7·007		
× P.V. £1 in 4 yrs at 6%	0·792	5·550	£166,500
			180,528
Valuation of Interest say			£180,000

This method of deferring the reversion is the only one which may be adopted. There are no Tables in Parry's which combine Y.P. for a term of years × P.V. for the term (unlike Y.P. reversion to perpetuity Tables) and the Y.P. for the period from the time of valuation minus Y.P. for the term will give the wrong result (unlike Y.P. in perp minus Y.P. Single Rate for the Term). This latter aspect is considered in Chapter 14.

3. Marriage Value

The valuation of a freehold let at less than full rental value and of a leasehold interest have been considered. These interests will arise simultaneously in the one property since the lease held at less than rental value creates the freehold reversion and the lease profit rent. If the owner of one of the interests buys the other interest, the interests merge by operation of law so that the lease merges into the freehold to create a freehold in possession or, in valuation terms, a freehold at full rental value. It is interesting to consider the valuation implications of this situation.

Example 9—7

A owns the freehold interest in office premises. The offices were let 26 years ago for 40 years at £10,000 p.a. without review. The current rental value is £45,000 p.a. The freehold yield at F.R.V. is 6 per cent. A proposes to buy the leasehold interest following which he will re-let the offices at £45,000 p.a. on a new lease.

Value of A's Present Interest

Term Rent received	£10,000 p.a.	
× Y.P. 14 years at 9% (rent is fixed for long term)	7·786	£77,860
Reversion to F.R.V	£45,000 p.a.	
× Y.P. in perp def'd 14 yrs at 6%	7·372	£331,740
		£409,600

Value of Leasehold Interest

F.R.V.	£45,000 p.a.
less Rent Paid	10,000
Profit Rent	35,000

$\times$ Y.P. 14 yrs at 6½ and 3%
adj. for tax at 35%   6·45   £225,750

Value of freehold after Purchase of Lease

F.R.V.   £45,000 p.a.
Y.P. in perp at 6%   16·666   £750,000

Hence, if A buys the leasehold interest for £225,750, he will "lose" his existing interest valued at £409,600, but he will then have an interest worth £750,000. Thus there is additional value of £750,000 − (£225,750 + 409,600) = £114,650 which represents extra value arising from the merger (or "marrying") of the interests. This additional value is termed marriage value.

The reason that marriage value arises is that the profit rent element when owned by the lessee is valued at 6½ per cent dual rate whereas in the freeholder's hands it is valued on a single rate basis at 6 per cent in one case and 9 per cent in another. This marriage value phenomenon will arise in nearly all cases where interests are merged and can act as an incentive for owners of interests to sell to each other or to join together in a sale to a third party so as to exploit the marriage value.

The question which arises is who should take the benefit of the marriage value. Since the parties are interdependent they are of equal importance to the release of the marriage value, so as a general guide the marriage value is shared equally. Hence in *Example 9–7* above, A is able to offer the value of the lease £225,750 plus half the marriage value £57,325. In this way both A and the leaseholder make a "profit" of £57,325.

Marriage value may also arise where owners of adjoining properties marry their interests to form a larger single site. This will be particularly so where the united interests create a development site but the individual sites are incapable of or unsuitable for development. In these circumstances a person buying the interests (known as "assembling the site") can pay over and above normal value by sharing the marriage value among the parties.

Indeed in some cases site assembly will involve buying interests in adjoining sites and also buying up freehold and leasehold interests in particular sites, thus creating both forms of marriage value.

4. FREEHOLD INTEREST WHERE BUILDING HAS TERMINABLE LIFE

In considering the question of rental value in Chapter 5 it was stated that, as a general rule, the present rental value of a property is assumed, for the purpose of valuation, to continue unchanged in the future. Reference was also made in Section 1 of this Chapter to the fact that the majority of buildings are demolished when they reach the end of their economic life and at that stage the site value for redevelopment should exceed the value of the existing buildings and site. However, in circumstances where a building is approaching the end of its physical life, whether for structural or limited planning permission reasons, it may be that some loss of rental value will be incurred.

Example 9–8

Freehold shop premises built about 60 years ago are let on lease for an unexpired term of 30 years to a good tenant at £8,000 p.a. following a recent rent review.

It is considered that the buildings will have reached the end of their physical life at the same time as the current lease expires and that rebuilding will be required. The present cost of rebuilding is estimated to be £40,000 and the value of the site at £3,500 p.a., capital value £50,000.

The analysis of sales of properties similar in nature in the same district but more modern and whose structural life is estimated to be 75 years or more indicates that they sell at 12·5 Years' Purchase of the present rental value.

What is the present market value of the property?

Valuation

Method 1

Applying the evidence of other sales it would appear that the property in question could properly be valued at a higher rate of interest than 8 per cent because the buildings have only a 30 year life.

Rent on lease	£8,000 p.a.	
Y.P. in perp, say	10	£80,000

Method 2

Assuming a reversion to site value at the end of the lease.

That portion of present rent which will continue	£3,500 p.a.	
Y.P. for 30 years at 8%	11·3	£39,550
Remainder of rent	£4,500 p.a.	
Y.P. for 30 years at 8% and 3% adj. for tax at 35%	8·9	40,050
Reversion to site value	£3,500 p.a.	
Y.P. in perp at 7% deferred 30 years	1·88	6,580
		£86,180
	Value, say	£86,000

Method 3

Assuming continuance of rental value and making provision for rebuilding.

Rent on lease		£8,000 p.a.	
Y.P. in perp. at 8%		12·5	
		£100,000	
less cost of rebuilding	£40,000		
× P.V. £1 in 30 years at 8%	0·1	4,000	£96,000

Method 1 has the merit of simplicity but the increase in the rate of interest is very much a matter of opinion.

Methods 2 and 3 are open to objection on a number of grounds.

In Method 2 it may be argued that it is difficult to know what will be the value of the site upon reversion after the useful life of the building, 30 years hence. The only evidence of the value of the site is present-day selling prices, which suggest the figure of £50,000 (rental value £3,500 p.a.) used in the example, but this value may be considerably modified in the future. A similar objection applies to the figure of £40,000 for cost of rebuilding in Method 3, which, of necessity, has been based on present-day prices although these may be very different 30 years hence.

Another serious objection is the difficulty of predicting the life of a building with any degree of accuracy, particularly over a long period of years. Such an estimate of the life of the building as is made in the example, must necessarily be in the nature of a guess unless considerable data is accumulated over a long period showing the useful life in the past of similar buildings. Even such evidence, over perhaps 40 or 50 years in the past, is not conclusive of what the useful life of buildings will be in the future.

On balance it would appear that in many cases there is probably less inaccuracy involved in assuming the present income to be perpetual and using a higher rate to cover risks, than would be involved in the more elaborate method of allowing for possible variations in income.

On the other hand, the separation of land and building values and making provision for building replacement has the advantage of giving to an investor a more direct indication of the actual rate per cent he is likely to to derive from an investment than does Method 1, provided it is used in conjunction with analysis of sales made on similar lines.

In cases where it can confidently be assumed that existing buildings will be worn out in a few years' time, Method 2 may be the soundest.

In the case of properties where the building clearly has a very limited life but the site is incapable of being re-developed in isolation, whether for practical or for planning reasons, it may be impracticable to have regard to any future site value. In such a case the existing income might be valued for the estimated building life as a terminable income with no reversion.

5. PREMIUMS

A premium usually takes the form of a sum of money paid by a lessee to a lessor for the grant or renewal of a lease on favourable terms or for some other benefit. The term premium is frequently used by agents to describe the price required for a lease which is being sold, e.g. "Lease of shop premises for sale. Premium £8,000". This is a misuse of the word since what is sought is the price and since this is not a premium under the lease it is not a premium. The following comments refer to a premium payable as a term of a lease.

Where a premium is paid at the commencement of a lease, it is usually in consideration of the rent reserved being fixed at a figure less than the true rental value of the premises.

From the lessor's point of view this arrangement has the advantage of giving additional security to the rent reserved under the lease, since the lessee, having paid a capital sum on entry, has a definite financial interest in the property, which ensures that he will do his utmost throughout the term to pay the rent reserved and otherwise observe the covenants of the lease. Premiums are only likely to be paid where there is a strong demand for premises on the part of prospective tenants. On the other hand, in the case of leases of less than 50 years, the tax treatment of premiums is penal for lessors so that they may be discouraged from taking a premium (see Chapter 23).

The parties may agree first on the proposed reduction in rent and then fix an appropriate sum as premium, or they can decide the capital sum to be paid as premium and then agree on the reduction in rent which should be allowed in consideration of it.

The calculation of the rent or premium can be made from

both parties' points of view when it will be found that a different answer will emerge. The parties will then need to agree a compromise figure.

Where the premium is fixed first, in order to arrive at the reduction to be made in the rent it will be necesary to spread it over the term either by multiplying the agreed figure by the annuity which £1 will purchase, or by dividing by the Years' Purchase for the term of the lease.

Example 9–9

Estimate the premium that should be paid by a lessee who is to be granted a 30 years' lease of shop premises at a rent of £20,000 p.a. with 5 yearly revisions to $\frac{20000}{25000} = 80\%$ of rental value (a "geared" rent review). The full rental value of the premises is £25,000 p.a.

Note

The parties have agreed that the calculation shall be based on the dual rate table of Years' Purchase at 8 and 3 per cent adjusted for tax at 35 per cent for the leasehold interest and 7 per cent for the freehold interest.

Tenant's Point of View

Present rental value	£25,000 p.a.
Rent to be paid under lease	20,000
Future profit rent	£5,000 p.a.
Year's Purchase for 30 years at 8 and 3% adj. for tax at 35%	9·77
	48,850
Premium, say	£50,000

Landlord's Point of View

Present interest—		
F.R.V.	£25,000 p.a.	
Y.P. in perp, at 7%	14·28	£357,000
Proposed interest—		
Rent for term	£20,000 p.a.	
Y.P. 30 yrs at 7%	12·41	£248,200
Reversion to F.R.V.	£25,000 p.a.	
Y.P. perp at 7% def'd 30 yrs	1·88	47,000
		£295,200
add Premium		x
		£295,200 + x

$$\text{Present interest} = \text{Proposed interest}$$
$$\therefore 357,000 = 295,200 + x$$
$$\therefore x = 61,800$$
$$\text{Premium, say} = £60,000$$

Hence the Tenant's View suggests £50,000 and the Landlord's View £60,000. A compromise would be needed to arrive at the premium. Since the premium would be a compromise it would be impossible to analyse the premium to show the assumptions made by the parties.

Example 9–10

A shop worth £5,000 p.a. is about to be let on full repairing and insuring lease for 35 years. It is agreed between the parties that the lessee shall pay a premium of £10,000 on the grant on the lease. What should the rent be throughout the term assuming quinquennial geared rent reviews?

Tenant's Point of View

Present rental value	£5,000

Deduct: Annual equivalent of proposed premium of £10,000

$$\frac{10,000}{\text{Y.P. 35 yrs at 9 and 3\% adj. for tax at 35\%}}$$

	$= \dfrac{10,000}{8 \cdot 84} =$	1,131
	Rent to be reserved	£3,869

Landlord's Point of View

Present interest—		
F.R.V.	£5,000 p.a.	
Y.P. perp at 8%	12·5	£62,500
Proposed interest—		
Rent Reserved	x	
Y.P. 35 yrs at 8%	11·65	£11.65 x
Reversion to F.R.V.	£5,000 p.a.	
Y.P. in perp. def'd	0·845	£4,225
35 yrs at 8%		
add Premium		£10,000
		£11·65 x + 14,225

$$\text{Present interest} = \text{Proposed interest}$$
$$62{,}500 = 11 \cdot 65\,x + 14{,}225$$
$$x = 4{,}144$$
$$\text{Rent} = £4{,}144 \text{ p.a.}$$

In this case the Tenant's View suggests £3,869 p.a. and

the Landlord's View £4,144 p.a. No doubt a compromise rent around £4,000 p.a. would be agreed.

In some cases the parties may agree to a premium being paid in stages, perhaps a sum at the start of the lease, and a further sum after a few years have passed.

The calculation of the premiums or rent follow the same approach as before, the future premium being discounted at the remunerative rate from the landlord's point of view who will receive it, and the accumulative rate from the tenant's point of view for whom it is a future liability.

6. Surrenders and Renewals of Leases

Where the term of a lease is drawing to a close, lessees frequently approach their lessors with a view to an extension or renewal of the term so as to be able to sell the goodwill of the businesses which they have built up or so as to convert the lease into a more marketable form.

The usual arrangement is for the lessee to surrender the balance of his present term in exchange for the grant of a new lease, probably for the term on which he originally held, or for some other agreed period.

The Landlord and Tenant Act 1954, which gives tenants of business premises security of tenure, has not seriously affected this practice. It has undoubtedly strengthened the hand of the lessee in negotiation; but tenants prefer to hold their premises under a definite lease rather than to rely merely on their rights under the Act which in the end depend upon litigation, and an intending purchaser of a business held on a short lease will be reluctant to rely merely on rights under this Act. As for landlords, a surrender and renewal may give them the opportunity to obtain terms in a new lease not obtainable on a renewal under the 1954 Act, and this could make such a proposal attractive. They may, therefore, be prepared to give way on rental arguments for the new lease in order to achieve better overall lease terms.

If the true rental value of the premises exceeds the rent reserved under the present lease, it is obvious that the lessee will have to compensate the lessor for the proposed extension. The form which this compensation shall take is a matter of arrangement between the parties. It may be agreed that the fresh lease shall be granted at the same rent and on the same terms as at present, the lessee paying a premium to the lessor. More likely, the payment of a capital sum may be dispensed with in consideration of the lessee paying an increased rent throughout the proposed new term, or the parties may agree on the payment of a certain sum as premium and also on an increased rent throughout the term, with the possible additional obligation on the lessee of making some capital improvement to the premises when the new lease is granted.

The valuer usually acts for one side or the other but may be called upon to decide as between the parties the appropriate figure of increased rent or premium.

The calculation should be made from both the lessee's and the lessor's point of view, but the lessee must be credited with the improved value of the property for the unexpired term of the existing lease. For example, suppose the balance of the lessee's term is seven years and he is occupying the premises at a profit rent of £5,000 a year, it is clear that he has a valuable interest in the property which he will be giving up in exchange for the new lease. He is therefore entitled to have the value of the surrendered portion of his term set off against any benefits which he may derive from the proposed extension.

From both the lessor's and the lessee's point of view the principle involved is that of—(i) estimating the value of the party's interest in the property, assuming no alteration in the present term was made; and (ii) estimating the value of the party's interest, assuming that the proposed renewal or extension were granted. The difference between these two figures should indicate the extent to which the lessee will gain or the lessor lose by the proposed extension.

If a premium is to be paid, the above method will suggest the appropriate figure. If, instead of a premium, the parties agree on the payment of an increased rent, the required figure may be found by adding to the present rent the annual equivalent of the capital sum arrived at above, although the method used in the examples below is to be preferred.

The terms for the extension or renewal of a lease are sel-

dom a matter of precise mathematical calculation. An estimate of rent or premium made from the freeholder's standpoint usually differs from one made from the lessee's and
the figure finally agreed is a matter for negotiation. A valuer
acting for either lessor or lessee will carefully consider all
the circumstances of the particular case, not only as they
affect his own client but also as they affect the opposite party.
He will make valuations from both points of view as a guide
to the figure which the other side might be prepared to agree
in the course of bargaining.

In the three examples which follow, the calculation of premium or rent has been made from both the freeholder's and
lessee's points of view. A valuer acting for either party would
follow this practice in order to establish not only his own
client's position but also the likely requirements of the other
party. The effect of income tax at 35 per cent on the open
market value of the lessee's present and future interests has
been taken into account.

Example 9–11

A lessee holding a shop on a full repairing and insuring
lease for 40 years, of which six years are unexpired, desires
to surrender his lease and to obtain a fresh lease for 25 years
at the same rent with five yearly reviews. The rent reserved
under the present lease is £10,000. The true rental value
is £25,000 per annum. The rent at reviews will be 40% of
rental value.

What premium can reasonably be agreed between the parties?

(1) *Lessee's point of view:*
   Proposed Interest—
   Profit rent   £15,000 p.a.
   Y.P. 25 years at 8% and 3% adj.
      for tax at 35%   8·18
                                     £122,700

   Present Interest—
   Profit rent   £15,000 p.a.
   Y.P. 6 years at 8% and 3% adj.

	for tax at 35%	3·15	£47,250
	On this basis Gain to Lessee		£75,450

(2) *Freeholder's point of view:*
Present Interest—
Next 6 years

Rent reserved	£10,000 p.a.		
Y.P. 6 years at 7½%	4·694		
		£46,940	

Reversion to Full rental

value	£25,000		
Y.P. perp. def'd. 6 yrs at 7½%	8·639	£215,980	
			£262,920

Proposed Interest—
Next 25 years Proposed

rent	£10,000		
Y.P. 25 years at 7½%	11·15		
		£111,500	

Reversion to Full rental

value	£25,000		
Y.P. perp. def'd. 25 years at 7½%	2·19	£54,750	£166,250

On this basis Loss to Freeholder			£96,670

Depending on the negotiating strength of the parties, the premium will be fixed somewhere between £96,670 and £75,450.

Example 9–12

Assume that in the previous example it was agreed that the lessee should pay an increased rent throughout the new term in lieu of a premium; what should that rent be? It is assumed that the rent payable on review will bear the same proportion to rental value as at the start of the lease (a "geared review").

(1) *Lessee's point of view:*

Present Interest—		
as before		£47,250
Proposed Interest—		
F.R.V.	£25,000 p.a.	
less Rent Reserved	x	
Profit Rent	£25,000 − x	
Y.P. 25 yrs at 8½ and		
3% adj. for tax at 35%	8·18	
		£204,500 − 8·18 x

$$\text{Present interest} = \text{Proposed interest}$$
$$47,250 = 204,500 - 8\cdot18\,x$$
$$x = 19,223$$
$$\text{New Rent, say} \quad £20,000 \text{ p.a.}$$

(2) *Freeholder's point of view:*

Present Interest—		
as before		£262,920
Proposed Interest—		
Rent under Lease	x	
Y.P. 25 yrs at 7½%	11·15	11·15 x
Reversion to F.R.V. £25,000 p.a.		
Y.P. Perp. def'd.		
25 yrs at 7½%	2·19	54,750
		11·15 x + 54,750

$$\text{Present interest} = \text{Proposed interest}$$
$$262,920 = 11.15\,x + 54,750$$
$$x = 18,669$$
$$\text{New Rent, say} \quad £18,700 \text{ p.a.}$$

Depending on the negotiating strength of the parties, the rent will be fixed between £20,000 and £18,700.

The above approach from the freeholder's point of view rests upon the assumption that, so long as the capital value of his interest is not lowered, he will be satisfied with the arrangement.

Where, as part of a bargain for a renewal or extension of a lease, the lessee is to make an expenditure upon the property which will benefit the value of the lessor's reversion, the lessee must be given credit for the value due to his expenditure which will enure to the lessor at the end of the term, and the sum must be taken into account when considering the cost of the new lease to the lessee.

Example 9–13

A warehouse in a city centre is held on a lease having 5 years unexpired at £32,000 a year.

The present rental value is £40,000 per annum. The lessee is willing to spend £100,000 upon improvements and alterations affecting only the interior of the building, which will increase the rental value by £12,000 per annum, provided the lessor will accept a surrender of the present lease and grant a new lease for a term of 30 years. The lessee is willing to pay a reasonable rent under the new lease, or a premium. The lessor is agreeable to grant the new lease provided that the rent is fixed at £35,000 per annum, that a proper premium is paid and that the new lease contains a covenant that the lessee will carry out the improvements. What premium, if any, should you advise the lessee to offer if the new rent is £35,000 p.a.?

(1) *Lessee's point of view:*
    Proposed Interest—

Rental value	£40,000 p.a.
add value due to outlay	£12,000
	£52,000
less Rent payable	£35,000
Profit rent	£17,000 p.a.

Y.P. 30 years at 9% and 3%

adj. tax at 35%	8·17	
	£138,890	
Deduct expenditure on improvement	£100,000	
Value of proposed interest		£38,890

Present Interest		
Rental value	£40,000	
Rent paid	£32,000	
	£8,000	
Y.P. 5 years at 9% and 3% adj. tax at 35%	2·63	
		£21,040
Gain to lessee		£17,850

(2) *Freeholder's point of view:*
Present Interest—

First 5 years	£32,000	
Y.P. 5 years at 8%	3·99	
		127,680

Reversion

Note—Since the estimated increase in rent due to improvements represents 12 per cent on the sum expended, and since this is greater than the rate of interest which might reasonably be expected from such a property as this when let at its full rack rental, it would be worth the landlord's while, at the end of the present lease, to carry out the improvements at his own expense in order to obtain the increased income. The reversion

can therefore be valued on the basis
that the landlord would carry out the
improvement work on the expiry of
the lease, as follows:—

Reversion to rental value after improvements		52,000 p.a.	
Y.P. in perpetuity at 8%		12·5	
		£650,000	
Deduct cost of improvements		£100,000	
		£550,000	
P.V. £1 in 5 years at 8%		0·68	
			£374,000
Value of Present Interest			£501,680
Proposed Interest—			
First 30 years	£35,000		
Y.P. 30 years at 8%	11·26		
		£394,100	
Reversion to full rental value	£52,000		
Y.P. perp. deferred 30 years at 8%	1·24	£64,480	
			£458,580
Loss to freeholder			£43,100

Depending on the negotiating strength of the parties, the
payment would be agreed at around £30,000.

Suppose that it had been decided between the parties that
no premium should be paid and that the rent under the new
lease should be adjusted accordingly. What would be a reasonable rent in these circumstances?

(1) *Lessee's point of view:*
Rental value after improvements
have been carried out—   £52,000 p.a.
Deduct annual equivalent of—

Cost of improvements	£100,000	
Present Interest—as before	£21,040	
	—————	
	£121,040	
÷ Y.P. 30 years at 9% and 3% adj. tax at 35%	8·17	
	—————	£14,800
		—————
Reasonable rent from lessee's viewpoint		£37,200 p.a.
		—————

(2) *Freeholder's point of view:*

Value of present interest, as above		£501,680
Deduct value of proposed reversion to full rental value after improvements have been carried out	£52,000	
Y.P. perp. deferred 30 years at 8%	1·24	£64,480
	—————	
Value of proposed term		£437,200
		—————
÷ Y.P. 30 years at 8%		11·26
Reasonable rent from freeholder's viewpoint		£38,900 p.a.
		—————

Again a negotiated settlement could be reached at an initial rent of around £38,000 per annum.

CHAPTER 10

Discounted Cash Flow

1. GENERALLY

THE PRINCIPLE underlying the valuation of a future income flow within the investment method of valuation is that the future income should be discounted at an appropriate rate of interest to determine its present value. The valuation therefore represents the discounted future cash flow. This same principle has been adopted to evaluate investment proposals in business generally, with variations developed to meet different situations, under the general term of discounted cash flow (D.C.F.) techniques.

In recent years these D.C.F. techniques have been seen to be of assistance in decisions relating to property investment and appraisal. Their principal application is to the making of comparisons between choices of investment.

D.C.F. calculations involve the discounting of all future receipts and expenditures similar to the investment method of valuation, but they can readily be used to allow for inflation, taxation and frequent changes in the amount of income and receipts as may be required.

Two principal methods of D.C.F. calculations have emerged, the Net Present Value (or N.P.V.) method and the Internal Rate of Return (or I.R.R.) method.

2. NET PRESENT VALUE METHOD

In this method the present value of all future receipts from a proposed investment is compared with all future outgoings. If the present value of receipts exceeds the present value of outgoings then the investment is worthwhile. If the same calculations are applied to different investment possibilities, the investment which produces the greatest excess of present value of receipts over outgoings is the most profitable. This is clearly of great assistance in reaching a decision on the choices available although it does not follow that the most profitable will be pursued—for example, it may be that the "best scheme" requires a large amount of capital to be invested whilst other considerations make a scheme with a smaller capital outlay more attractive to the investor.

As has been said the future receipts and outgoings are discounted. The question then arises as to what is the appropriate discount rate. Commonly the rate adopted is the rate of interest payable on the money borrowed for investment in the scheme, representing the cost of capital. However, alternative choices may be the rate of return required by the investor—his target rate; or if the money is provided internally the rate of interest he could earn on the money in an alternative investment of a similar kind or in the alternative investment where the money will be invested if the scheme is not to proceed—the opportunity rate.

Example 10–1

A has been offered the freehold interest in a property comprising a large old factory for £70,000. The proposal is to modernise the factory in 3 stages spending £60,000 in the first year and £80,000 in the second year, and a further £100,000 in the fourth year.

A expects to let the first stage in year 2 at £9,000 p.a., the second stage in year 3 at £10,000 p.a. and the final stage in year 5 at £14,000 p.a. All leases will be 15 years with 5 yearly reviews. A will sell the whole interest in year 6 for £550,000 on which he will pay capital gains tax of £69,000.

A will borrow money for the scheme at 12 per cent.

Assess the Net Present Value of the scheme to advise A whether or not he should proceed. (See calculations on p. 171.)

Net Present Value = £330,346 − 282,128 = £48,218

This shows that the N.P.V. is positive and that the project is profitable at a cost of borrowing of 12 per cent.

It is clear from this Example that the investor can introduce other factors quite easily into the calculation. For example,

Example 10–1

Year	Details of Receipts/Payments	Cash Out	Cash In	Present Value of £1 at 12%	Discounted Cash Flow Cash Out	Cash In
0	Purchase Price	70,000		1·0	70,000	
1	Improvements—Stage 1	60,000		0.893	53,580	
2	Improvements—Stage 2	80,000		0.797	63,760	
	Rent—Stage 1		9,000	"		7,173
3	Rent—Stage 1		9,000	0.712		6,408
	Rent—Stage 2		10,000	"		7,120
4	Improvements—Stage 3	100,000		0.636	63,600	
	Rent—Stage 1		9,000	"		5,724
	Rent—Stage 2		10,000	"		6,360
5	Rent—Stage 1		9,000	0.567		5,103
	Rent—Stage 2		10,000	"		5,670
	Rent—Stage 3		14,000	"		7,938
6	Sale Proceeds		550,000	0.507		278,850
7	Capital Gains Tax	69,000		0.452	31,188	
					282,128	330,346

he may wish to allow for tax throughout including tax on
rents subject to tax allowances; anticipated inflation in costs
and rental values; any other costs which may arise. Further,
the calculation could be prepared on a quarterly or monthly
basis of expected costs and returns rather than annually as
shown and allowing for rent payable in advance or in arrear.
Indeed the major constraints are the tendency to mathematical complexity as one moves away from readily available
data such as Present Value Tables at annual intervals,
necessitating the use of formulae and possibly computers;
the level of accuracy possible in determining the timing and
level of payments in or out; and the problems of estimating
some items, particularly tax payments, where the underlying
rules of calculation are themselves complex. The level of
sophistication depends on the investor's requirements, and
certainly in very large scale investment proposals the effort
is likely to be justified.

As a general rule, where the method is used to compare
different investment possibilities, the one with the highest
positive N.P.V. is the one to adopt. However, this ignores
the different levels of capital which may be required to be
put into the investment. Where these are significantly different an alternative yardstick of comparison might be adopted
whereby the one with the highest benefit/cost ratio will be
adopted. The benefit/cost ratio is found by dividing the
N.P.V. of the receipts by the N.P.V. of the expenditures
(in *Example 10–1*, 330,346 divided by 282,128 = 1.17).

3. INTERNAL RATE OF RETURN METHOD

As an alternative to the N.P.V. method, an analysis can
be carried out which discounts all future receipts and payments of a project at a discount rate whereby the discounted
receipts equal the discounted payments. This discount rate
will then show the actual rate of return on the capital invested
in the scheme—the "internal rate of return". At this point
the N.P.V. will of course be nil.

The approach to this method is to adopt the same approach
as illustrated in *Example 10–1*, but, by trial and error, to
use different rates of interest until the correct rate is found.

Example 10–2

Take the facts as in *Example 10–1*. In this case, as the N.P.V. is positive it is clear that the investment is producing more than 12 per cent. The calculations of the return are shown on pp. 174 and 175.

It is clear from these that the project will produce a return of between 17 per cent and 18 per cent but nearer to 17 per cent. A close estimate of the rate can be determined by simple interpolation. At 17% N.P.V. = £1,972: at 18% N.P.V. = −£5,768: range £7,740. Assume a constant rate of change, then the exact rate is $17\% + \frac{1972}{7740}$ of 1% i.e. 0·255% = 17·255%. This is not of course absolutely exact since the difference in discount rates is based on geometric rather than linear expansion. However, it is probably sufficiently accurate for most cases.

This can be expressed as a formula which provides for linear interpolation. The formula is:—

$$R1 + \left\{ (R2 - R1) \times \frac{N.P.V\,R1}{N.P.V.\,R1 + N.P.V.\,R2} \right\}$$

Where R1 is the lower rate and R2 the higher rate

$$\text{Hence } 17 + \left\{ 1 \times \frac{1,972}{7,740} \right\} = 17·255\%$$

4. COMPARISON OF N.P.V. WITH I.R.R. APPROACHES

As has been shown the N.P.V. method compares the future costs and receipts on a discounted present capital value basis whereas the I.R.R. method shows the return earned on an investment. In the above examples the application of each method to the same investment shows that the investment is worthwhile on either basis. This will not always be so as sometimes it will be found that one method shows an investment proposal to be profitable whilst the other method suggests that it will show a loss, or that in deciding between investments A and B, N.P.V. method favours A whilst I.R.R. favours B. The reasons for this will lie in the choice of discount rate or in the pattern of costs and revenue.

The resolution of this contradiction can be found in the

Example 10–2

Try 17 per cent.

Year	Details of Receipts/ Payments	Cash Out	Cash In	Present Value of £1 at 17%	Discounted Cash Flow Cash Out	Discounted Cash Flow Cash In
0	Purchase Price	70,000		1·0	70,000	
1	Improvements— Stage 1	60,000		0·855	51,300	
2	Improvements— Stage 2	80,000		0·731	58,480	
	Rent—Stage 1		9,000	"		6,579
3	Rent—Stage 1		9,000	0·624		5,616
	Rent—Stage 2		10,000	"		6,240
4	Improvements— Stage 3	100,000		0·534	53,400	
	Rent—Stage 1		9,000	"		4,806
	Rent—Stage 2		10,000	"		5,340
5	Rent—Stage 1		9,000	0·456		4,104
	Rent—Stage 2		10,000	"		4,560
	Rent—Stage 3		14,000	"		6,384
6	Sale Proceeds		550,000	0·390		214,500
7	Capital Gains Tax	69,000		0·333	22,977	
					256,157	258,129

N.P.V. = 258,124 − 256,157 = £1,972

Example 10–2 contd.

Now try 18 per cent.

Year	Details of Receipts/Payments	Cash Out	Cash In	Present Value of £1 at 18%	Discounted Cash Flow Cash Out	Discounted Cash Flow Cash In
0	Purchase Price	70,000		1·0	70,000	
1	Improvements—Stage 1	60,000		0·847	50,820	
2	Improvements—Stage 2	80,000		0·718	57,440	
	Rent—Stage 1		9,000	"		6,462
3	Rent—Stage 1		9,000	0·609		5,481
	Rent—Stage 2		10,000	"		6,090
4	Improvements—Stage 3	100,000		0·516	51,600	
	Rent—Stage 1		9,000	"		4,644
	Rent—Stage 2		10,000	"		5,160
5	Rent—Stage 1		9,000	0·437		3,933
	Rent—Stage 2		10,000	"		4,370
	Rent—Stage 3		14,000	"		6,118
6	Sale Proceeds		550,000	0·370		203,500
7	Capital Gains Tax	69,000		0·314	21,666	
					251,526	245,758

N.P.V. = 245,758 − 251,526 = minus £5,768

standard tests on D.C.F. which provide various ways of over-coming the problem. As a general rule, however, the I.R.R. approach will be favoured by a valuer who is using D.C.F. for analysis since it will show the yield of the investment which will enable him to compare this with yields on other investments which he will know. On the other hand he will prefer the N.P.V. method if he wishes to compare the value of an investment proposition with others since the investment method of valuation and the N.P.V. method are closely allied in their approach.

5. APPLICATION OF D.C.F.

The principal use of D.C.F. lies in relation to investment decisions whereby a choice between alternatives can be made. In the case of development this may be a choice between development propositions on different sites or between different development schemes on the same site. For example, a landowner may be able to consider develop-ing a site with 100 houses over 3 years or 140 flats over 4 years or various other permutations. The analysis of each proposal by D.C.F. will show him which scheme is the more profitable.

Again an investor may be offered the choice of different investments showing different rental patterns. Although he can value each investment by the investment value approach, he will be able to make a further comparison between them by D.C.F. analysis to show the I.R.R. of each investment. In so doing he may if he wishes allow for projected rental increases. This approach has been developed by the determi-nation of the "equated yield" which is considered further in Chapter 14.[1]

---

[1] A great deal has been written about the theory, use and application of D.C.F. The reader is referred in particular to "The Valuation of Property Investments" by Nigel Enever (Estates Gazette) and to "Property Valuation Methods: Research Report", Ed. Andrew Trott (RICS).

CHAPTER 11
Valuation of Life Interests

1. GENERALLY

IN THIS Chapter it is proposed to give a brief outline of the principles of determining the values of life interests in property and of the methods used in applying them.

In the case of freehold or leasehold property, the property passes on the death of the freeholder or lessee to his heirs or to whom he may specify and the income is therefore considered to continue in perpetuity or for the length of the lease as the case may be. With lifehold property, on the other hand, the interest ceases on death and the lifeholder has no control over who obtains the property on his death.

A life interest may exist in either freehold or leasehold property. A life interest in leasehold property ceases on the death of the tenant for life or the expiration of the lease, whichever is the earlier.

On the death of a tenant for life, the property passes either to a reversioner or a remainderman. A remainderman is a person other than the original grantor and his heirs who succeeds to the property while the original grantor or his heirs would be reversioners. A "contingent remainder" is a remainder depending upon a certain event before it takes effect, such as, for example, a remainderman outliving a tenant for life.

A tenant for life of a freehold interest is a person who is, in effect, the owner of the freehold for his life, although he has power to sell the freehold absolute in the settled land subject to devotion of the proceeds of sale to specified purposes protecting the reversioner. He may wish to sell his own life interest, an interest entitling the purchaser to the property for the life of the tenant for life only and it is with the valuation of such interests and associated interests that this Chapter is concerned.

177

Leases for life can be made by a landlord granting a fixed term of years, terminable by himself or the lessee and his heirs on the death of a person named, usually the lessee. As one such party would gain by terminating the lease on the death, these interests are leases for life for all practical purposes.

The valuation problems which may arise when an interest in land is held for, or subject to, the life or lives of one or more persons, are various. Thus the valuer may have to determine:

(1) The value of a life interest in a freehold property.
(2) The value of the reversion to a freehold property after the death of a life tenant.
(3) The value of a life interest in a leasehold property.
(4) The value of the reversion to a leasehold interest after the death of a life tenant.
(5) The value of a life interest which will begin at the expiration of a certain period if the life is then in being (a contingent remainder).
(6) In any of the above cases the life interest may last only so long as two or more persons are alive, or it may last only so long as any one of two or more persons is still alive.

No new problems arise in the determination of the net income to be valued, nor in the choice of the appropriate remunerative rate per cent, except that, since the life of a particular individual is extremely uncertain, the purchase of any interest involving a life tenant must be speculative in nature and the demand for such interests is restricted. A rather higher rate would therefore be appropriate than that used for valuing incomes for terms certain. The new factor to be considered is the chance of life or death.

These chances are fairly well known, for although, to take an example, we have not the least idea how long a particular person now aged 50 will live, statistics show that, on the average, the mean expectation of life of men aged 50 is 22·68 years and of women of that age 27·57 years (see pages 232 and 233 of *Parry's Valuation Tables*—column e_x).

The Years' Purchase for life tables, however are not based

upon the "mean expectation" figures but upon the basic information from which the mean expectation figures were derived. This is the English Life Table No. 12 based on population enumerated in the 1961 census and mortality experience of the population during 1960, 1961 and 1962.

A "Life Table" (see pages 232 and 233 of *Parry's Valuation Tables*, column 1_X) shows how many, of some convenient number of infants born, may be expected to be alive at each year of life within the possible span of human existence. The number born in the English Life Table No. 12 is taken as 100,000. From this information, the table shows in column p_X the "probability factor", that is the probability that a person of a given age will survive at least one year. Other probabilities can easily be determined. Thus the table shows that of 90,085 males alive at 50, 68,490 will attain the age of 65. The probability of a man aged 50 living to enjoy his pension at 65 is therefore, $\dfrac{68,490}{90,085}$.

2. SINGLE AND DUAL RATE SYSTEMS

A lifehold interest is a depreciating asset and provision can be made for the replacement of the capital invested in purchasing such an interest by taking out an insurance policy insuring the life for the purchase price as soon as the interest is bought. Interest allowed on the insurance premiums payable is unlikely to be obtained at as high a rate as the remunerative rate required from the investment and there is therefore a case for the use of dual rate tables.

Dual Rate Life Tables are not included in the tenth edition of *Parry's Valuation Tables* (they are available in the eighth edition) but Section 5 of this Chapter shows how the Years' Purchase at a dual rate can be determined, if required.

Alternatively, the Years' Purchase for a Single Life tables on pages 189 to 195 of *Parry's Valuation Tables* (which are based on the Single Rate principle) can be used, with an upwards adjustment of the remunerative rate, if considered necessary.

3. Years' Purchase for a Single Life— Single Rate per cent

This problem can be worked from general principles as in the following example but it will be obvious that the amount of arithmetic involved will be very great unless the life tenant is of advanced age. The figures of Years' Purchase for ages 1–100 years, both male and female, are shown on pages 189 to 195 of *Parry's Valuation Tables*.

Example 11–1

What is the present value of an income of £1 per annum receivable for the life of a man now aged 102, interest being allowed at 5 per cent per annum?

The English Life Table No. 12 shows that of 100,000 males born, 25 will attain the age of 102. The table further shows that of these 25 persons, 15 will live to be 103. Thus the probability of a person who is just 102 living to receive an income payable if he lives to 103 is $\frac{15}{25}$ or 0·6 and this figure, the probability that a person of a given age will survive at least one year, is given in the English Life Table No. 12 (column p_X). *The "contingent present value" of the first year's income is therefore, the present value of £1 in 1 year at 5 per cent multiplied by the probability of living to receive it:—*

$$£0·952 \times 0·6 = £0·571$$

Similarly with the second year's income, the Life Table shows that only 9 persons will live two years more to be 104. The probability factor is, therefore, $\frac{9}{25}$ or 0·36, and the contingent present value of the second year's income:—

$$£0·907 \text{ (P.V. of £1 in 2 yrs at 5\%)} \times 0·36 = £0·327$$

Each year's contingent income is valued in this way. The tables show however, that no male will reach the age of 108. Thus the sixth and subsequent years' incomes will not be received by the tenant for life. The years' purchase (or present value of £1 per annum) is the sum total of these contingent present values as follows:—

Age	Probability Males alive	factor (a)	P.V. (b)	Contingent P.V. (a) × (b)
102	25			
103	15	0·60	0·952	0·571
104	9	0·36	0·907	0·327
105	5	0·20	0·864	0·173
106	3	0·12	0·823	0·099
107	2	0·08	0·784	0·063
108	0	Nil	0·746	Nil

Years' Purchase (male) aged 102 at 5%   1·233

4. Years' Purchase for a Single Life— Dual Rate per cent

The problem here is to find the present value of an income of £1 per annum, receivable for a life, when interest on the capital value is expected at a higher rate than the interest allowed in estimating the premiums paid to insure that life.

For this purpose we must ascertain the annual premium payable to insure the life. This could be obtained by enquiry from a prospective insurance company but a table of premiums required to insure £1 at the end of the year in which a person may die for ages from 1 to 100 years, based on the English Life Table No. 12 and at premium interest rates from 3 to 5 per cent is given on pages 226–229 of *Parry's Valuation Tables*.

The table also contains typical premium rates which may be offered by a Life Assurance Company for non-profit whole life assurance for ages 21–80 years.

Once the premium is known, the years' purchase can be obtained by an adaptation of the formula $Y.P. = \dfrac{1}{i + s.f.}$ which relates to leasehold interests.

The premium required to insure £1, can be substituted for "s.f." but in addition, allowance must be made for the fact that, unlike a sinking which is provided at the end of the year out of the year's income, the premium to insure the life must be paid as soon as the interest is purchased.

The formula is therefore adapted to allow for this and becomes:— $Y.P. = \dfrac{1 - P(1 + j)}{i + P(1 + j)}$

> where P = annual premium to secure £1
> i = remunerative rate required
> j = insurance premium interest rate.

Example 11–2

Calculate the Years' Purchase in respect of the life of a man aged 40. The investor requires an 8 per cent return on capital he invests. The life can be insured for an annual premium of 1·54 per cent which is based on an insurance premium interest rate of 5 per cent.

$$Y.P. = \frac{1 - 0.0154(1 + 0.05)}{0.08 + 0.0154(1 + 0.05)} = \frac{0.98383}{0.09617}$$
$$= 10.23$$

This compares with a Y.P. (Single Rate) male aged 40 at 8 per cent of 10·808.

In some cases insurance premiums are adjusted for tax relief before payment. Where the insurance premium has to be found out of taxable income, similarly to the case of leaseholds where the sinking fund to replace capital must be found out of taxable income, an appropriate adjustment may be made. With leaseholds the coloured Y.P. tables allow for this by increasing the sinking fund element to $\dfrac{100}{100 - t}$ s.f., where t is the tax rate expressed as a percentage. There are no coloured life tables but allowance can be made for this factor, if considered necessary, particularly where the life expectation is short and the premium to insure the life would be high, by an upward adjustment of the remunerative rate.

5. REVERSION AFTER DEATH TO A FREEHOLD INTEREST

The method used is that, from the present value of a perpetual income beginning at once, is subtracted the present value of the life interest.

Example 11–3

To find the Y.P. for a freehold reversion after the death of a man now aged 45, interest being reckoned at 8 per cent.

Y.P. perpetuity at 8%	12·500
Y.P. (male) aged 45 at 8%	10·206
Y.P. for reversion	2·294

This problem is one of the most important occurring in practice. The method used above may be compared with that employed in the valuation of perpetual incomes deferred for a term certain.

6. LIFE INTERESTS IN LEASEHOLDS

An interest of this nature can arise where a person inherits a life interest in a leasehold property or where a leaseholder grants a life interest in his lease. In either case, the maximum period the interest can last is the term of the lease, but the interest will cease beforehand if the tenant dies. The problem therefore, is to find the present value of £1 p.a. receivable for the life of the tenant or the length of the lease, whichever is the shorter.

This could be worked from the general principles used in the calculation of the Y.P. for life (Single Rate) detailed in Section 4 of this Chapter.

Example 11–4

To find the present value at 6 per cent interest of an income of £1 p.a. receivable for a maximum period of three years, provided a woman, now aged 55, lives so long, or otherwise for as long as she lives.

The English Life Table No. 12 shows 90,652 women living at age 55. Of this number, 90,034 will live to be 56

> 89,362 will attain the age of 57, and
>
> 88,631 will reach 58 in 3 years' time when the lease expires.

Thus the contingent present value of the first years income is

$$\frac{90,034}{90,652} \times \text{P.V. £1 in 1 yr at 6\% } (0.943) = 0.937$$

and of the second years' income

$$\frac{89,362}{90,652} \times \text{P.V. £1 in 2 yrs at 6\% } (0.890) = 0.877$$

and of the third years' income

$$\frac{88,631}{90,652} \times \text{P.V. £1 in 3 yrs at 6\% } (0.840) = 0.821$$

The Years' Purchase in respect of a life interest (female) aged 55 in a 3-year lease is the sum total of these contingent present values. $= \underline{2.635}$

It is obvious that if the term is a long one and the life not very advanced, the calculation becomes very lengthy and laborious or alternatively a very large book of tables would be required. In practice therefore, a method of comparing the Y.P. for the lease with the Y.P. for life may be used. If the Y.P. for the life is the lower, this may be taken as the lease will probably last longer than the life. This Y.P. may be too high mathematically as it will consist of contingent present values for the whole possible life span whereas it should be limited as above to the years of the lease. An adjustment might be made, if considered appropriate. If the lease Y.P. is lower, that Y.P. may be taken with an appropriate reduction to allow for the possibility of the tenant dying before the end of the lease. Thus, in the above example the exact Y.P. has been calculated at 2.635 whereas the Y.P.

for the lease period of 3 years at 6 per cent (Single Rate) is 2·673.

Example 11–5

What is the value of a life interest in a profit rent of £1,000 per annum held by a female aged 35 in a leasehold property having 55 years unexpired?

Valuation

As it is necessary to compare two Y.P.s but there are no dual rate life tables, the single rate table has been used in both cases to be consistent, the remunerative rate being adjusted upwards accordingly.

Profit Rent		£1,000
Compare Y.P. 55 yrs at 10%	= 9·947	
with Y.P. female aged 35 at 10%	= 9·540	

The Y.P. for the life interest is less and that figure, 9·54 Y.P., is therefore taken. It is slightly too high, as it consists of more than 55 contingent present values. However, the error is only very small in this case, therefore say 9·5.

	9·5
	£9,500

Example 11–6

As above, but the lease has only 10 years unexpired.

Profit Rent		£1,000
Compare Y.P. 10 yrs at 10%	= 6·145	
with Y.P. female aged 35 at 10%	= 9·540	

The lease Y.P. is less. That figure 6·145 Y.P., is taken and adjusted downwards to allow for the possible death of the tenant for life before the lease expires   *Years' Purchase say,*

	6
	£6,000

7. VALUE OF A LEASEHOLD REVERSION AFTER A LIFE INTEREST

Example 11–7

What is the value of the reversion to a net income of £25,000 per annum from a good class shop property after the death of a tenant for life (female) aged 83? The reversion is to a leasehold interest which has at present 63 years to run at a ground rent of £1,000 per annum.

Valuation

The method involves a comparison between the Y.P. for the lease and the Y.P. for the existing life.

Net Rent		£25,000
less Ground Rent		1,000
Profit Rent		£24,000
Compare Y.P. for the lease—Y.P. 63 yrs at 8% (single rate table used as we are comparing two Y.P.'s and there are no dual rate life tables— the remunerative rate has, there- fore, been increased to allow for this)	12·402	
with Y.P. for life aged 83 (female) at 8%.	3·456	
The tenant for life is likely to die before the lease expires and the differ- ence between the two Y.P.s is taken as the Y.P. for the leasehold reversion		
	8·946	
Value of leasehold reversion		£214,704

Example 11–8

What is the value of a reversion to a net income of £10,000 per annum from controlled tenancies of small houses after the death of a tenant for life (male) aged 40? The reversion

is to a leasehold interest which has at present 10 years to
run at a ground rent of £50 p.a.

Valuation

Net Rents from houses	£10,000
less Ground Rent	50
Profit Rent	9,950

Compare Y.P. for 10 yrs at 10%   6·145
   (single rate taken and remunerative
   rate increased for the reason given
   in the previous example)
with Y.P. for life aged 40(male) at 10%   9·053

Thus in this case, the chances are that the life tenant will
outlive the lease, in which case the reversioner will never
enjoy the profit rent. On the other hand, there is a possibility
that the tenant for life may die before the lease ends so that
the reversion must have some value, possibly only nominal.

The method may be criticised because the Y.P. for life
is the present value of the chances of receiving an annual
income for the whole possible life span of a male aged 40,
whereas it should represent the present value of his receiving
an income for 10 years only. The life Y.P. considered is,
therefore, too large, the degree of inaccuracy depending
upon the length of the lease and the age of the life tenant.
However, the alternative of calculating the probability of
receiving each year's income would involve considerable difficulty except where the lease is very short or the life tenant
very old.

8. VALUE OF A REMAINDERMAN'S LIFE INTEREST COMMENCING ON THE DEATH OF THE EXISTING LIFE TENANT, IF THE REMAINDERMAN IS STILL ALIVE

This is a "contingent remainder" as the remainderman's
interest is contingent upon his outliving the tenant for life.
The value of the remainder is obtained by deducting the
Y.P. for the existing life interest from the Y.P. for the remainderman's present age.

Example 11–9

Value the interest of a woman aged 24 who is a tenant for life of a freehold shop producing a net income of £2,000 per annum after the death of her father, aged 61.

Net Income		£2,000
Y.P. for life (female) aged 24 at 8%	12·054	
Y.P. for life (male) aged 61 at 8%	7·365	4·689
		£9,378

9. Years' Purchase for the Joint Continuation of Two Lives

Where an interest is dependent upon the continuation of both of two lives so that the interest terminates as soon as one of them ceases, the possibility of receipt of each year's income is reduced and the Present Value of each year's income will need to be multiplied by the probability of survival of each of the two persons. Otherwise the same method of computation is used as for the Y.P. for Single Life (Single Rate). The Y.P. for the joint continuation of two lives will thus be less than the Y.P. for either life. The tables are shown on pages 198 to 213 of *Parry's Valuation Tables*.

The same principle is used if the income is dependent on the joint continuation of three or more lives, the fractions of probability of each separate life being multiplied together to obtain the fraction of probability of their joint continuation.

Example 11–10

What is the value of a Net Income of £10,000 per annum secured upon a freehold shop property, held for the joint continuation of the lives of a man aged 60 and a woman aged 45?

Net Income	£10,000
Y.P. joint continuation of two lives aged 45 (female) and 60 (male) at 8%	7·306
	£70,306

10. Years' Purchase for the Longer of Two Lives

The problem here is to find the Years' Purchase of an income which is receivable as long as one or other of two persons is still alive. Thus, the probability of the receipt of the income is increased beyond that of either single life.

The rule to be used is to add together the Years' Purchase for each single life and to subtract from the total the Years' Purchase for their joint continuation.

The logic underlying this rule is as follows—the income lasts throughout both lives but if the Y.P.'s for each of the two lives are simply added together, the period during which both are alive has been double counted; the Y.P. for joint continuation must, therefore, be subtracted.

Example 11–11

To find the Y.P. at 7 per cent of an income receivable for the longer of two lives of two women, now aged 60 and 75.

The Y.P's for the single lives are obtainable from page 445 of *Parry's Valuation Tables* whilst that for their joint continuation is obtainable from page 465.

Y.P. life (female) aged 60 at 7%	9·477
Y.P. life (female) aged 75 at 7%	5·583
	15·060
Y.P. joint continuation of two lives aged 60 and 75 (females) at 7%	5·121
Y.P. longer of two lives aged 60 and 75 (females) at 7%	9·939

CHAPTER 12

Residual Method of Valuation

1. Concepts of the Residual Method

THE VARIOUS methods of valuation commonly employed were set out in Chapter 2. A more detailed consideration of the direct comparison and investment methods has been made in Chapters 4 to 11 which now allows further consideration of the residual method.

The residual method is adopted in the valuation of development property. This may be of bare land which is to be developed or of land with existing buildings which are either to be altered and improved, an exercise commonly termed refurbishment, or to be demolished and redeveloped with entirely new buildings.

The method works on the premise that the price which a purchaser can pay for such property is the surplus after he has met out of the proceeds from the sale of the finished development his costs of construction, his costs of purchase and sale, the cost of finance, and an allowance for profits required to carry out the project. This can be expressed as follows:—

	Proceeds of Sale
less	Costs of Development, and Profits
=	Surplus for land

These elements can be considered in turn in relation to an example.

Example 12–1

Value the freehold interest in 10 Main Road. The property comprises a house now vacant. Permission has been given to build a shop with offices above. The shop will have a frontage of 20 feet and a depth of 60 feet. Two floors of

191

offices will be built over the shop with separate access from Main Road and providing 940 sq. ft. net of floor space per floor. The house will be demolished.

The offices are expected to let at £10 per sq. ft. and the shop at £20,000 p.a. and the resultant investment should sell on the basis of a $6\frac{1}{2}\%$ return.

2. PROCEEDS OF SALE

These arise from the disposal of the developed property. In the case of houses they will be the price anticipated for each unit determined by the direct comparison method. In commercial developments they will be the anticipated price which will be obtained on a sale, usually after they have been let to create an investment: they will thus be determined by the investment method as previously described.

It should be remembered that the valuation approach is to determine the surplus available after meeting costs. The proceeds of sale are the whole of the anticipated money to be realised from the development. It is true that they will not be receivable until the work is completed which may be some considerable time in the future. Nonetheless it would be illogical to discount the proceeds to their present-day value. What the valuer is seeking to establish is the ultimate size of the development "cake" which he can then cut up into the various slices needed for costs and profits and so establish how much of the cake remains as the land slice.

Where a purchaser intends to occupy the property, or to let the property and then retain the investment, he will not actually sell and so receive the moneys. Nonetheless it is necessary to determine the realisable value of the development to carry out the residual valuation.

Applying this approach to *Example 12–1*; the Proceeds of Sale will be:—

Full Rental Value

Shop	£20,000 p.a.
Offices 1,880 sq. ft. at £10 per sq. ft.	18,800
	38,800 p.a.

Y.P. in perp. at 6½%   15·385

                            596,938

              say,   £600,000

3. COSTS OF SALE

The main costs incurred in a sale of the interest will be the agents' fees including advertising costs, and legal fees in the conveyance. In practice the general level of fees on a sale is in aggregate around 3% of sale price.

In the case of investment properties it may be considered desirable or even necessary in some cases to let the property before selling. If so the agents' and legal fees incurred in the letting should be brought into account. Agents fees will normally be 10% of the rents obtained or 15% if two or more agents are instructed. The aggregate fees will probably be around 20% of the rents obtained.

Where a purchaser intends to retain the property, it has been shown that the realisable value needs to be determined nonetheless. Since it is the net realisable sale proceeds which are required, the costs of sale which would be incurred are incorporated in the valuation.

Costs of Sale

Sale Costs—Agents' and Legal Fees, say 3%
of £600,000 =   £18,000
Letting Costs—Agents' and Legal Fees say
20% of £38,800 =   £7,760

                     Total Costs   £25,760

4. COSTS OF DEVELOPMENT

The major items normally met are the actual cost of building the development, and funding costs. Certain other miscellaneous items may be met on occasions.

(a) *Cost of Building.* In the preliminary stages the costs of development will need to be estimated. Estimates are normally based on the prevailing costs of building per square foot of the gross floor area. As the scheme details become more advanced it may be appropriate to prepare a priced specification or even a priced bill of quantities. In addition to the actual costs of building the professional services of the design team are payable. The membership of the team depends on the nature and scope of the development but commonly includes an architect and quantity surveyor and often an engineer. In the more complex schemes, structural, electrical, and heating and ventilation engineers will be needed. The fees payable depend on the circumstances but usually vary between 8% and 14% of the building costs, with 12% as the norm.

(b) *Miscellaneous Items*. All sites are different and have unique features which may require various special costs. Typically such items include costs of demolishing existing buildings, which will depend on the nature of construction and the salvage value: costs of obtaining possession, either by compensation to tenants on the site or even buying in minor interests: costs of agreeing compensation to neighbours such as buying rights over the land like easements or agreeing party wall rights and compensation: costs of providing above average quality boundary works: exceptional costs such as site clearance or filling of uneven land, and diversion of services: off-site costs such as highway improvements required as a condition for the grant of planning permission. As can be seen there are many possible problems which may need to be overcome, this list being far from exhaustive. Where possible an estimated cost should be adopted. As these items are sometimes difficult to predict so that they are not known at the time of valuation, it is possible to allow some general sum for such contingencies. On the other hand it can be said that these are part of the general risks of development which are reflected in the allowance for profits.

(c) *Costs of Finance*. Considerable sums of capital need to be spent on the carrying out of a development. Normally this money is raised from banks or other lending institutions, or it may be loaned as part of an overall deal with an investing institution such as an insurance company or pension fund, particularly in the case of medium to large scale commercial developments. The cost of borrowing the money which will be repaid on the completion and sale of the development is the interest charged at an agreed rate plus in many cases a commitment or fund-raising fee of around 1% of the money to be provided. The rate of interest depends on the prevailing rates being charged and will also vary with the status of the borrower and the risks attached to the development scheme. They commonly range between 1% to 4% above base rate or the minimum lending rate of one of the clearing banks. These rates have shown considerable fluctuation in recent years within a range of around 7% to 20%. The valuer will need to be aware of current rates at the time of the valuation.

In some instances the developer may have raised money on a long term basis which means that the rate of interest is now low compared with prevailing rates, or he may be able to provide money from his own resources. Nonetheless the prevailing borrowing rate should be adopted in the valuation as this is the opportunity cost of the capital. If the preferential rate is adopted, or none at all, this will produce a value to that person which is not necessarily the open market value.

Once the rate of interest is known the interest costs can be determined. The money to be borrowed relates to two items, building costs and land costs. As to land costs, these will be incurred at the start, so that the money is borrowed at the start and interest runs for the whole period of development. On the other hand money required for building works will only be needed in stages and, as a rule of thumb which experience shows is normally reasonably accurate, it may be assumed that the whole of the building money is borrowed for half the period of development. In the case of housing development the developer may obtain revenue from sales of houses as the development proceeds with consequent savings in the money to be borrowed. The implications of this are considered in Chapter 18.

Turning again to *Example 12–1*, the Costs of Development are:—

(a) *Building Costs*
    Shop 1,320 sq. ft. (gross)

at £30 per sq. ft.	=	39,600
Offices 2,150 sq. ft. (gross)		
at £60·00 per sq. ft.	=	129,000
		168,600

add Professional Services,		
say 12%	20,232	
		188,832

(b) *Demolition Costs*
    Assume   1,200

(c) *Costs of Finance*
    Assume development will
    take 1 year and interest is
    12%

Demolition Costs 1,200 for		
1 year at 12%	144	
Building Costs 188,832 for		
say ½ year at 12%	11,330	
		11,474
Total Costs of Development		£201,506

5. DEVELOPMENT PROFITS

As for any risk enterprise, a person undertaking a development will seek to make a profit on the operation. Target levels of profit will depend on the nature of the development and allied risks, the competition for development schemes in the market, the period of the development (the longer the period the higher the profit sought) and the general optimism in relation to that form of development. Consequently it is not possible to lay down firm limits of required profit levels. The profit is usually related to the costs involved but sometimes to the development value. The profit is the gross profit to the developer before meeting his general overheads and tax. Hence developers may seek say 20% gross profit on the capital invested, namely building costs and land costs, or say 17% of the development value.

If the profits are related to costs, at this stage in the valuation the land costs are unknown so profits on these will be calculated later as part of land costs.

Hence turning to *Example 12–1*

Developers Profits

Building Costs (including fees)	188,832	
Demolition Costs	1,200	
Costs of Finance	11,474	
Total Costs of Development	201,506	
Profits at 20%	0·20	
		£40,301

6. SURPLUS FOR LAND

At this stage the valuer has determined the net proceeds of sale, and the total cost of development and profits thereon. The difference between these figures represents the sum available to spend on land costs. In some cases building costs will exceed net proceeds of sale. If so this shows that there is negative value for that development and thus that the land is not suitable for development, unless some other form of development would be profitable.

Turning to *Example 12–1* the surplus available for Land Costs is:—

	Proceeds of Sale		600,000
less	Costs of Sale		25,760
	Net Proceeds of Sale		574,240
less	Costs of Development	201,506	
	Profits on Building Costs	40,301	241,807
	Surplus for Land Costs		£332,433

The land costs comprise four items. First there is the price to be paid for the land, the very purpose of the valuation. Secondly there are the professional fees and perhaps stamp duty in relation to the purchase. The fees will generally be for an agent and for legal services in the conveyance. These, together with stamp duty, are likely to be approximately 4 per cent of the price paid. The third item is the developer's profit on the sum invested in the land as explained before. Finally there is the interest on the money borrowed to be repaid on sale calculated for the period of development.

All of these items relate to the actual price of the land which in turn depends on the four items. The simple way of apportioning the surplus between them is to express the land price as a symbol, say x, and then solve the subsequent equation.

Turning to *Example 12–1*

(a) Land Price		1·00x
(b) Fees on Land Purchase at 4% of price	=	0·04x
(c) Finance Interest at 12% for period of development on (a) and (b) = 1·04x × 1 yr at 12%	=	0·1248x
(d) Developer's Profits at 20% of Gross Price = 0·20 × 1·1648x	=	0·2330x
Land Surplus Total		1·3978x

But the Land surplus is		£332,433
∴ 1·3978x	=	332,433
∴ x	=	237,826
Hence Value of Land is, say,		£238,000

Thus the Valuation is completed. The whole valuation is:—

Proceeds of Sale

F.R.V. Shop		£20,000 p.a.
Offices 1,880 sq.ft. at £10 per sq. ft.		18,800
		38,800
Y.P. in perp. at 6½%		15.385
	say	600,000

b/f £600,000

less Costs of Sale
    Sale Costs at 3% of
      £600,000   18,000
    Letting Costs at 20% of
      £38,800   7,760   25,760

    Net Proceeds of Sale   £574,240
less Development Costs
    Building Costs
      Shop 1,320 sq. ft. at £30
        per sq. ft.   39,600
      Offices 2,150 sq. ft. at
        £60 per sq. ft.   129,000

                          168,600
add Professional Fees at 12%   20,232   188,832

    Demolition Costs   1,200
    Costs of Finance
      £1,200 for 1 yr at 12%   144
      £188,832 for, say, $\frac{1}{2}$ yr
        at 12%   11,330   11,474

                          201,506
add Developers Profits at 20%
    of £201,506   40,301 £241,807

Land Surplus   £332,433

Land Price =   1·00x
    Add Fees on Purchase
      at 4%   0·04x
    Finance 1 yr at 12%
      of 1·04x   0·1248

                    1·1648x
    Developers Profits
      at 20% of 1·1648x   0·2330x

                1·3978x   =   332,433
             ∴   x   =   237,826
             Land Price   =   say £238,000

It is clear that this valuation contains many figures all of which are based on estimates of cost or value or derived from such estimates. As with any estimates, one person's estimate may differ from another so that in that way they are all variables. Given a calculation based on a large number of variables the actual range of answers which can be produced is wide. This uncertainty is the method's weakness but it is one which is acceptable so long as the estimates are prepared with as much information as is available to narrow possible errors.

The method is readily susceptible to computer programmes. Also it can be adapted to produce other information apart from the land value.

CHAPTER 13

Some Practical Points

1. GENERALLY

IT HAS ALREADY been emphasised that the primary problem of valuation is the ascertainment of present market value—that is, the price at which an interest in a property can be expected to sell as between a willing vendor and a willing purchaser, both of whom are fully informed regarding the interest in question, who are not forced to sell and are free to deal elsewhere if they choose.

But although most of the valuer's problems involve consideration of present market value, there are often other factors in the problem to which his attention must also be directed.

It is often necessary to have regard to future trends of value, to consider if prices at which interests in properties have been sold are reasonable or likely to be maintained, and to examine the possibilities of changes in rental value.

When valuations are made for certain purposes, e.g. for taxation or in connection with compulsory purchase for public undertakings, the valuation, although based on market value, may be regulated by statutory provisions as to the date at which the valuation is to be assumed to be made and as to the factors which may or may not be taken into account in making it.

Again where properties are purchased for investment, the valuer may be asked to advise on policy, to suggest what reserves should be created for future repairs, or in respect of leasehold redemption, and to advise generally on the many problems involved in good estate management.

The knowledge required to deal with all these matters can only be gained by experience but the student will find it of great advantage to keep abreast of current affairs, international, national and local, and in the light of them to make

201

a careful study of sale prices and rental values, particularly in areas with which he or she is acquainted and where there is an opportunity of seeing the properties which are the subject of recorded transactions.

The valuer needs to obtain as much information and evidence as possible so as to render the valuation as accurate as possible. Even so it should be emphasised that a valuation is only an expression of one valuer's opinion and it is not surprising that other valuers may hold different views. For this reason a valuation is at best an estimate of the price which will be achieved, but the best estimate must be the one based on the best evidence.

Some interesting observations on valuation in general including limits of accuracy are made in the decision on *Singer & Friedlander v John D. Wood & Co.* (1977) 243 EG 212 & 295.

2. The Analysis of Rents and Sales

In estimating the market value of an interest in property the valuer must consider all the evidence available.

The property may be let at a rent, in which event its reasonableness or otherwise must be considered in relation to the rents of other similar properties.

The rate per cent at which the net income is to be capitalised will be determined by reference to the rate shown by analysis of the sale price of other similar properties.

The keeping of accurate records of rents and sale prices, and of analyses of the latter to show investment yields is therefore of very great assistance to the work of the valuer.

An example is given in Chapter 5 of an analysis of rents made to determine the rental value of offices.

Similar methods, usually related to the superficial area of premises, can be used for the making and keeping of records in connection with a variety of properties.

Although in many offices manual records are still maintained, the availability of computers, from small micros to major mainframe systems, has added considerably both to the ease of maintaining records and to the ways in which information can be analysed, manipulated and retrieved.

In analysing sale prices the usual steps in making a valuation are reversed. The purchase price is divided by the estimated net income to find the figure of Years' Purchase, from which can be determined the rate per cent yield which the purchase price represents.

In the case of perpetual incomes the "yield", or rate per cent, at which the purchaser will receive interest on his money can be found by dividing 100 by the figure of Years' Purchase. In the case of incomes receivable for a limited term, it must be found by reference to the valuation tables.

Example 13–1

Freehold property producing a net income of £2,000 per annum has recently been sold for £20,000.

Analyse the result of this sale for future reference.

Analysis:—

$$\frac{\text{Purchase Price £20,000}}{\text{Net Income £2,000}} \text{ represents 10 Y.P.}$$

$$\left.\begin{array}{l} \text{Rate at which purchaser will} \\ \text{receive interest on money} \end{array}\right\} = \frac{100}{10 \text{ Y.P.}} = 10\%$$

Example 13–2

Shop premises held on lease for an unexpired term of 52 years at a rent of £15,000 have been sold for £135,000: the rental value is estimated to be £27,500.

Analysis

The profit rental is £12,500. The purchase price is £135,000 which divided by £12,500 represents 10·8 Years' Purchase. On reference to the dual rate tables for a term of 52 years this is seen to equate to 8 per cent and 3 per cent with tax at 35 per cent.

Example 13–3

Similar, but somewhat smaller, premises nearby are held on lease for an unexpired term of 45 years at £7,500; the lease was recently sold for £100,000. On the evidence of the previous example, at what do you estimate the rental value?

Answer

It would seem proper to apply the rate per cent derived from the previous analysis.

$$\frac{\text{Sale Price}}{\text{Y.P. for 45 yrs at } 8\% \text{ and } 3\% \text{ (tax at } 35\%)}$$

$$= \frac{100,000}{10 \cdot 353} = £9,659 \text{ profit rent}$$

$$add \quad \underline{7,500} \text{ lease rent}$$

Rental Value, say £17,000 p.a.

Although this means of ascertaining rental value must be resorted to where other evidence is not available, rental values should be estimated if possible by analysing the results of recent lettings of comparable properties and an estimate based on the analysis of a capital transaction should be avoided if at all possible. The object of analysing a capital transaction is usually to find the remunerative rate of interest.

In many instances comparisons of rental value will only be of value if restricted to a particular locality; this is obviously so in the case of shops, where wide variations in rent can occur within a distance of a few hundred yards.

On the other hand, with experience, the valuer may be able to identify a level of values which will be similar in locations of similar qualities within a region or even nationally. For example, in towns close to a common factor such as a motorway, the levels of office rents will tend to display regional rather than narrowly local characteristics.

In the case of industrial or warehouse properties the area for comparison purposes may be similarly extended; although evidence of value of a particular type of property in one town may have limited significance in relation to another town, say 30 miles away, even in respect of identical property. Whatever the general pattern, a comparison derived from nearby property will always be more significant.

In estimating the yield likely to be required from a particular type of investment, evidence over a much larger area can usefully be employed. Indeed there are two broadly defined markets found in practice—a national and a local market. Prime properties, such as first class shops or offices, or well designed modern warehouses or factories, tend to produce a similar yield nationally. On the other hand secondary properties are more prone to local factors influencing the yield so that they form a local market.

It is in the analysis of past sales and the application of the evidence derived therefrom to a particular case that the skill and experience of the valuer is called into play. He must consider carefully the extent to which the property to be valued is similar to those that have been sold. The correctness or otherwise of the rent must be determined; trends of value since the evidence was accumulated must be considered.

In some cases the prices at which properties have changed hands may be above or below "market value". The vendor may have been anxious to dispose of a property quickly and have taken a rather lower price than might have been expected; or a high price may have been given by a buyer in urgent need of a certain type of accommodation.

It follows that sales records cannot be used blindly. Sales transactions and lettings must be examined critically and allowances made for cases which depart from the general trend.

In some cases the general trend of sale prices or rents may be higher or lower than the valuer considers justified by the facts. In these circumstances, when advising on market value, he will no doubt point out that the present value is likely to change in the future by reason of factors that in his opinion have not received due consideration.

3. SPECIAL PURCHASERS

A valuation is prepared adopting certain assumptions as to the market conditions. In some instances the valuer will be aware that some people are in the market for whom the property in question will be of special interest. Typical examples are where marriage value exists—as described in Chapter 9.

The valuer must always consider if there are special purchasers since they are likely to pay the highest sum and one which is in excess of the value to the general market ("an overbid"). Even when the existence of the special purchaser is known it is often difficult to determine the price to which such a purchaser will go.

In Chapter 9 the price which might be agreed in marriage value situations was discussed. But in other cases the only way of discovering the over-bid is by marketing the property in a manner designed to draw out the final bid. The valuer must therefore be able to comment on the appropriate method of offering the property to the market. For example, it may be appropriate to sell at public auction, or by public tender, or by a closed tender (when the property is offered only to a selected group) or of course by a general offer for sale by private treaty.

The situation of special purchasers creating valuation difficulties is commonly found where leasehold interests are offered for sale in respect of shops in prime locations. In general, the major retailers will be established in such a location and they will be determined to remain whilst the centre continues to thrive. Hence the chance of obtaining a shop rarely arises since the leases will be renewed by the existing tenants. Thus when a trader does decide to move out and offers the balance of his leasehold interest he will find that there is considerable competition to purchase the lease. The valuer frequently discovers that if he applies the conventional methods of calculation, particularly the investment method of capitalising the profit rent with Y.P. Dual

Rate adjusted for Income Tax, the calculation figure will be far less than the price likely to be obtained. The most appropriate method might be a profits approach, perhaps valuing the profits for several years ahead beyond the term of the lease offered, since traders may be prepared to buy the right to be able to earn such profits. Whatever method is adopted it will often be found that the price paid defies analysis on any normal valuation method since it is the cost of getting into the centre. These exceptional prices offered by special purchasers are sometimes termed colloquially "key money" or "foot-in-value", the expressions' meanings being self-evident. This value phenomenon suggests that the prevailing rents which are accepted as rental values are falsely low, a situation which can arise in any artificial market, which a centre can become in the absence of actual market transactions.

The valuer may also experience the situation where a price is achieved considerably in excess of any valuation and in contradiction of all previous market evidence. The reasons may be many, such as the inexperience of the purchaser, a mistake being made, the property having a special sentimental value and so on. The valuer needs to recognise such fluke transactions and to disregard or distinguish them when considering them as market evidence.

4. RICS MANUAL OF VALUATION GUIDANCE NOTES

The Royal Institution of Chartered Surveyors intends to publish in late 1989 a Manual of Valuation Guidance Notes. These Notes are not directly concerned with valuation theory or method but with what are described as the mechanics of practice, including the assembly, interpretation and reporting of information relevant to the task of valuation. They will, therefore, become essential background reading both for the student and the practitioner of valuation.

5. THE COST OF BUILDING WORKS

It is often necessary, in connection with the valuation of land or buildings for various purposes, to estimate the cost of development works, of erecting new buildings, or of making alterations to buildings.

The following are examples of such cases:—

(i) In valuation of land likely to be developed in the future it is usually necessary to form some estimate of the cost of the necessary development works, including roads, sewers, public services, and the provision of amenities such as tree planting, open spaces and the like.

(ii) In connection with the development or redevelopment of urban sites for various purposes, estimates of the cost of building works are required.

(iii) Similar estimates are necessary where a valuer is called on to advise as to the sum for which existing premises should be insured against fire.

The principal methods used in preparing estimates of this character are outlined below.

Accuracy of estimate. The method to be adopted in arriving at approximate costs of buildings and development works will depend upon the accuracy desired and the information available.

In estimating the development value of large areas of land, it is necessary to make assumptions as to the value which the land, or various parts of it, will command in the future. These estimates will be based on the evidence available at the time when the valuation is made, but will necessarily depend on factors which may vary considerably in the future. Any greater degree of accuracy in estimating the cost of necessary development works will therefore be out of place.

In many cases estimates have to be made of the cost of works to be carried out in the future. In view of the fluctuations in cost that may occur before the works are carried out, undue refinement or accuracy in the methods used might again be out of place. However, in the case, for example, of major town centre developments where the planning stages are often prolonged, it may be necessary to project both income and costs into the future. Indices of past increases in rents and of building costs will provide some assistance but some additional technique which enables various assumptions on future increases to be tested will also be applied.

In many instances, both in connection with building estates and with the development of individual sites, the particulars available of the type of building to be erected, or which in fact can be erected, on a particular site may be very scanty. In the absence of detailed plans and specifications, any estimate of cost can only be arrived at by means of an approximation.

It is not possible to formulate any general rule in this connection. The circumstances of each case must dictate the degree of accuracy to be attempted, and the usefulness of the result achieved will depend largely upon the experience of the valuer in applying his knowledge, derived from other similar cases, to the one under review.

Bills of quantities. Where detailed drawings and a specification are available, it is possible for a bill of quantities to be prepared and for this bill to be priced by a quantity surveyor or contractor. This is the most accurate method of arriving at cost of works, but is often not practicable.

An approximate bill of quantities may be prepared whereby only the principal quantities in various trades are taken off, the prices to be applied being increased beyond what is customary, to include for various labours which normally would be measured and valued separately.

In the case of works of alteration, approximate quantities may be the only way of arriving at a reasonably accurate estimate where the works are extensive or present unusual difficulties.

Unit comparisons. The most common approximate method of comparing building costs is per square metre or square foot of gross floor area.

The gross floor area of a proposed building can be arrived at with an acceptable degree of accuracy from sketch plans or from a study of the site on which the building is to be erected, taking into account the likely requirements of the local planning authority, the restrictions imposed by building regulations and any rights of light or other easements.

The gross floor area having been determined the total cost

can be estimated by applying a price per square metre or square foot derived from experience of the cost of similar buildings or from a publication such as *Spon's Architects' and Builders' Price Book* which is revised annually. Costs are based on typical buildings and do not include external works. Adjustments will, therefore, be required if the building is not typical, if site conditions are abnormal and for external works.

Gross floor area is usually determined by taking the total floor area of all storeys of the building measured outside external walls and without deduction for internal walls. The price per unit will of course vary according to the method used.

It should be noted, however, that gross floor area will generally differ from net lettable area.

Other methods of comparison. In the case of building estates, the cost of road and sewer works is often estimated on a linear basis. This price should provide for the roads to be completed to the standard required by the local authority.

In the absence of a detailed development scheme, it is usually desirable to prepare a sketch plan of the proposed development in order to estimate the cost of the development works required. It may sometimes be possible, however, to make a comparison between one estate and another, whereby the total development cost per unit may be estimated by reference to the development costs of other land of a similar character in the neighbourhood.

The usefulness of these methods necessarily depends upon the extent of the information available and upon the experience of the valuer, who must make full allowance for any differences between the properties from which his experience is derived and the particular property to which such figures are to be applied.

Alterations and repairs. The use of an approximate bill of quantities in the case of alterations has already been referred to. A similar degree of accuracy may often be arrived at by preparing a brief specification of the works required to be done and placing a "spot" amount against each item.

Similar methods may be used in regard to repairs.

6. MANAGEMENT OF INVESTMENTS

The valuer may be required to advise on the policy to be adopted in the management of investment properties.

No attempt is made here to deal with general estate management issues or with the type of problem that can arise where, for example, a major estate forms part of the wider investment portfolio of a large financial institution. However, an attempt is made to comment on issues with a valuation connotation which are common to most types of estate, large or small.

Speaking very generally it may be said that good estate management should aim at securing the maintenance and maximisation of income and capital value.

To advise on a group of investment properties of varying types involves consideration of a number of factors, including:—

(a) The possibilities of increase or decrease in future capital value.

(b) An examination of present rents with a view to possible increase or reductions.

(c) Consideration of outgoings.

(d) The provision of reserves for future repairs or other capital expenditure, to enable the cost of repairs to be spread evenly over a period, and to provide sinking funds for wasting assets such as leasehold properties.

(a) *Maintenance of capital values*. From time to time it will be desirable to review the properties comprised in a landed estate to decide if some should be sold or otherwise dealt with and to consider whether or not they are likely to increase or decrease in value.

As an obvious and desirable objective is to maintain or enhance the capital value of the estate, properties likely to depreciate should be sold and other properties sought to replace them of a character which may increase in value or at least not depreciate. On the other hand such properties may produce a high rate of return and if a high level of income is desired they may nonetheless be suitable for retention in the portfolio.

Opportunities may arise where other interests in the properties can be bought, or adjoining properties, which will create marriage value. For example, an estate may own the freehold interest in properties let on leases granted some years ago when rents were considerably lower than to-day's and where no provision was made for rent review. It will be advantageous to purchase any such leases which come up for sale so that the lease can be extinguished and a new one granted on improved terms. This will not only increase income but probably increase the capital value of the freehold interest by more than the cost of the lease as marriage value applies. Re-structuring (or re-arrangement of the terms, including rent) of leases is a further possibility. Alternatively the freehold interest could be offered to the lessees on the basis of a shared marriage value with obvious benefit to both parties.

The possibilities of enhancement of capital value by re-development or refurbishment need to be kept in mind subject to the availability of finance for such works. In the case of large-scale developments they may be carried out by developers under ground lease so that external capital is imported into the estate.

There is also the possibility of investment in properties of a type where increases in value may be expected and which are not dependent upon the grant of planning permission.

For example, a block of shops offered for sale may be the subject of leases granted some time ago at rents which at the end of the lease may be expected to be substantially increased. An investment in property of this type offers possibilities of an inherent increase in capital value in the future.

Property in blocks may also offer the possibility of realisation of "break-up" value, the converse of marriage value. This happens when the sum of the parts exceeds the value of the whole and where individual occupiers are likely to be interested in purchasing the properties they occupy.

(b) *Examination of rents.* A periodic examination of rentals should be made to ensure that when a property comes into hand the rent is increased to the market value. In a few cases it may be found that, owing to a fall in values in the district, or for other reasons, a property is over-rented.

It will probably be wise to treat the excess over market value with caution; in making provision for the future it must be remembered that the only security for the enhanced rent is the tenant's covenant to pay, and in the event of his failure the rent will need to be reduced.

The general tendency is for rental value to increase. In order that landlords can secure the benefit of such increases, it is usual in the case of occupation leases to provide for upward only rent review clauses to operate at regular intervals, say every 3, 4 or 5 years. Hence terms are generally a multiple of the review periods, for example, 15 or 25 years' lease with 5 year reviews. In the case of building leases similar rent review clauses are incorporated but the rents commonly remain as a percentage of the full rental value so that they rise in parallel—they are "geared" to the full rental value.

(c) *Outgoings.* The present outgoings, particularly those liable to variation such as repairs and rates, need to be scrutinised. Where the landlord is responsible for outgoings it should be seen that rating assessments are correct, that void allowances are claimed where properties are empty and that adequate provision is made for repairs.

(d) *Reserves.* Certain outgoings, in particular repairs, will vary in amount from year to year. For instance, external painting may be required perhaps every five years. It is usually desirable that the available income from an estate should be reasonably constant, and in the years when such expenditure is not actually incurred an amount should be set aside for future use. So that if the cost of external painting every fifth year is estimated at say £5,000, a sum of £1,000 should be set aside each year to meet it rather than have an excessively large outgoing in one year which may swallow up the rental income.

Where property is held on lease with full repairing covenants, or where there is a covenant to reinstate after alteration, provision shoud be made for future expenditure either by setting aside a certain amount of income each year or on the lines indicated below.

Where income is derived from leasehold properties proper provision should be made for the replacement of capital at the end of the term. This may be done by means of a sinking fund policy or other amortisation plan or it may be possible to find a suitable investment—for example, ground rents with a reversion to rack rents which will come into hand at about the time when the leasehold interests run out. This portfolio mix can ensure that the estate overall maintains its rental and capital value.

The latter arrangement has certain advantages over the sinking fund method. The value of the reversion accumulates at a higher rate of interest in most cases; also a sinking fund, if established, has to be paid out of taxed income, and reduces the net available revenue. It may well be, however, that the capital resources of an estate do not permit of the purchase of suitable investments and provision for the future has to be made out of income.

A valuer may have to advise a particular investor in landed property on the type of investment best suited to him. In such a case, the valuer would have to take account of such a factor as the investor's liability to income tax.

CHAPTER 14

Developments in Valuation Methods

1. INTRODUCTORY

IN RECENT years critical attention has been given to valuation methods both from within the valuation profession and also from other quarters, particularly the financial sector. This has come about for various reasons. There has been a sharp growth in property values which has led to property transactions attracting considerable attention. There has been a growing involvement by institutional investors, mainly pension funds and insurance companies, who have invested a significant proportion of their funds in property. Public interest in and awareness of property has been fostered by press commentaries, most of the national newspapers carrying regular property articles. The importance of property to the economy is now clearly recognised: a fact which was highlighted by the collapse of the property market after 1973 when many companies were at risk though not being in business as property companies. Indeed many companies have substantial property interests as a natural consequence of their activities, and some companies such as retailers and banks have a property portfolio rivalling the major property companies and even institutions in value and quality.

Given the importance of property it is natural that the ways in which valuers work will be closely scrutinised. A valuation may be a vital factor in deciding whether shares or bonds will be purchased, companies remain solvent or expensive projects be carried out. Most importantly, a valuation may affect members of the public at large who could suffer seriously if the valuation is misleading.

Consequently the methods by which valuers arrive at a valuation, both as to assumptions and the detailed workings, have been increasingly examined. This is especially so in the case of the investment method of valuation. This is evidenced

215

by criticism of methods expressed in books, journals and other publications, and also by considerable academic research.

This body of critique has led to many suggestions as to alternative approaches to certain valuations or considerable adaptation of the general principles. However, until these methods receive wide acceptance such as to oust the methods set out in previous Chapters they cannot be set forth as the appropriate method to adopt. Indeed given the variety of views expressed it would be difficult to select any one against the others. This Chapter therefore will limit itself to a consideration of the aspects which give rise to criticism of investment valuations and some brief comments on the solutions offered so that the reader may be aware of the ideas being expressed.

2. Relationship of Y.P. Single Rate in Arrear and in Advance

The conventional approach to valuations has been to assume that rent will be paid and received annually in arrear and Valuation Tables have been based on this premise. However, current practice is for rents to be paid in advance, and commonly quarterly in advance. No change is made to the basic valuation approach if rents are taken to be paid on this basis.

If it is assumed that rent is payable either annually in arrear or annually in advance, the difference between Y.P. (rent in arrear) and Y.P. (rent in advance) is obviously $1 - $ (P.V. for nth year). The Y.P. (rent in advance) can be derived from $1 + $ Y.P. (rent in arrear) for $(n - 1)$ yrs e.g. Y.P. 3 yrs at 10% (rent in advance) = Y.P. 2 yrs at 10% + 1 = $1 \cdot 7355 + 1 = 2 \cdot 7355$. This compares with Y.P. 3 yrs at 10% (rent in arrear) of $2 \cdot 4869$, a difference of $0 \cdot 2486$ or 10%.

It follows that as the years are extended the difference between the Y.P.'s grows as the P.V. falls. For example Y.P. 50 yrs at 10% (rent in arrear) is $9 \cdot 9148$ whereas Y.P. 50 yrs at 10% (rent in advance) is $1 + $ Y.P. 49 yrs at 10% (rent in arrear) = $1 + 9 \cdot 9063 = 10 \cdot 9063$, an increase of $0 \cdot 9915$ on $9 \cdot 9148$, again a difference of 10%. In fact the difference will always be exactly 10% at a yield of 10% and it can be shown that the percentage increase at any rate will always be the rate adopted. Hence, for example, Y.P. 30 yrs at 6% (rent in advance) will be 6% greater than Y.P. 30 yrs (rent in arrear), Y.P. 40 years at 7% (rent in advance) will be 7% greater than Y.P. 40 years at 7% (rent in arrear) and so on.

However, rent paid annually in advance is probably as untypical as rent paid annually in arrear. In practice, where the rent is generally quarterly in advance, the method of approach is as follows.

Example 14–1

Value a rent of £1,000 p.a. receivable for 10 years, rents payable quarterly in advance. The rent is regarded as arising from a 12% investment.

(a) Conventional Approach (Y.P. S.R., rent annually in arrears)

Rent	£1,000 p.a.
Y.P. 10 yrs at 12%	5·65 p.a.
	£5,650 p.a.

(b) Valuation approach reflecting rent in advance

One method is to adapt the Tables by treating the income as being 4 payments per annum with an effective rate of $\frac{1}{4}$ of the annual rate, subject to adjustment as described above of $(1 - V)$ or adopting $1 + $ Y.P. $(n - 1$ year$)$.

Hence: Rent per quarter		£250
Y.P. $(4 \times 10) - 1$ quarters at 3% per		
quarter $(= $ Y.P. 39 yrs at 3%$)$	22·808	
add 1 =	1·000	
		23·808
Capital Value		£5,952

This alternative approach may be criticised in that it may not be a true comparison. A yield of 12% means that in

one year the investor earns 12% on his capital. The interest
may be added at the end of each year or may be added
half yearly or quarterly or at other periods. If the interest
is added at periods of less than a year it will normally be
on a compound basis. Thus, where the annual yield is 12%,
if interest is added quarterly and is compounded, the quarterly rate will not be 3% since this will produce an annual
yield of 12·55%.

Amt. of £1 for 4 periods at 3%	= 1·1255
less £1 invested	1·0000
Interest after 1 year	= 0·1255

The problem derives from what is meant by the yield. If
a yield of 12 per cent is meant to represent not only a nominal
annual yield but the effective annual return, or annual percentage rate (APR), then the quarterly equivalent is not 3
per cent but 2·874 per cent. If this appropriate quarterly
effective rate were adopted then there would be no difference
between quarterly in advance or annually in arrear.

The comparison of the treatment of rent in arrear and
in advance is explored fully in various works referred to at
the end of this Chapter under further reading.

3. TAXATION OF INCOMES

In Chapter 6 when identifying the outgoings commonly
found in property, reference was made to the taxation of
incomes, and in Chapter 9 it was established that, in the
investment method of valuation, income is valued gross of
tax payable on rents. The principal reason for this is that
the tax payable depends on the status of the recipient of
the income. Hence, the net income reflects this status as
indeed will the net yield to any investor. If net yields are
adopted as a measure of comparison they will no longer act
as a means of comparison between respective investments
since they will reflect, in addition to the qualities of the investment, a unique feature of an individual taxpayer/investor.

However, valuations may be made on a net of tax basis
and these will be of use in determining the value of an invest-

ment to an individual. It is interesting to consider such approaches, often referred to as a "true net" approach.

Consider first a freehold interest let at full rental value. The conventional gross of tax approach is as follows:–

Example 14–2

Value the freehold interest in commercial premises recently let at their full rental value of £10,000 p.a. The yield is 10%.

F.R.V. (and rent received)	£10,000 p.a.
Y.P. in perp. at 10%	10·0
Capital Value	£100,000

Now value the interest allowing for tax. Assume that the investor pays tax at 40% on rents.

F.R.V. (and rent received)	£10,000 p.a.
less Income Tax at 40%	
$0.4 \times 10,000 =$	4,000
True net income	£6,000

Before continuing the valuation, consider the appropriate yield. It is agreed that this is a "10% investment". But this is the gross of tax yield. The net of tax yield depends on the tax payable, and for an investor paying 40% tax, he will lose 40% of any return in tax leaving him with 60% of 10% = 6% as the net yield. This is the appropriate yield to adopt in a net of tax valuation.

Hence,

Income net of tax		£6,000
Y.P. in perp. at 6%		16·67
Capital Value	Say	£100,000

It is seen that each method produces the same value. This will be true of any valuation of a freehold at full rental value and at any rate of tax.

The same will be true of a leasehold interest let or enjoying full rental value as the following example shows:–

Example 14–3

Value the leasehold interest in commercial premises sub-let at full rental value of £12,000 p.a. The leasehold interest has 10 years to run at £2,000 p.a. This is a 10% investment. The investor pays tax at 40% on rents.

F.R.V. (and rent receivable)	£12,000 p.a.
less Rent Payable	2,000
Profit Rent	£10,000 p.a.
Y.P. 10 yrs at 10% and 3% (Tax at 40%)	4·075
Capital Value	£40,750

Now value the investment on a net of tax basis.

F.R.V. (and rent receivable)	£12,000 p.a.
less Rent Payable	2,000
Profit Rent	£10,000 p.a.
less Income Tax at 40% = 0·4 × 10,000 =	4,000
Net Profit Rent	6,000 p.a.

Before continuing the calculation, it is clear that the net yield should be adopted of 6 per cent. As to the sinking fund, as the net of tax profit rent is being valued, there is clearly no need to gross up the cost of the income tax element.

Hence:–

Net Profit Rent	£6,000 p.a.
Y.P. 10 yrs at 6% and 3%	6·792
	£40,750

Thus far it is clear that a valuation of a freehold or leasehold interest producing full rental value gives the same result whether valued gross or net of tax. From this it may be concluded that such investments present no advantage to one taxpayer as against another.

This should not be confused with the advantage to a non-taxpayer as against a taxpayer which a short leasehold interest offers for quite different reasons, as explained later.

The valuation of a freehold or leasehold interest where the present rent receivable is not at full rental value—a reversionary investment—does, however, produce different results as between gross and net approaches.

Example 14–4

Value the freehold interest in commercial premises with a rental value of £10,000 p.a. They are currently let for the next 5 years at £4,000 p.a. The appropriate yield is 10 per cent.

Term
Rent receivable	£4,000 p.a.	
Y.P. 5 yrs at 10%	3·791	£15,164
Reversion to F.R.V.	£10,000 p.a.	
Y.P. in perp. at 10% 10·0		
× P.V. of £1 in 5 yrs		
at 10% 0·6209	6·209	62,090
		£77,254

Assume the investor pays tax on rent at 40%
Term Rent receivable	£4,000	
less Income Tax at 40% of		
£4,000	1,600	
Net Rent receivable	£2,400 p.a.	
Y.P. 5 yrs at 10% gross, 6% net	4·212	£10,109
Reversion to F.R.V.	£10,000	
less Income Tax at 40% of		
£10,000	4,000	
Net F.R.V.	£6,000	
Y.P. in perp. at 6% 16·667		
× P.V. £1 in 5 yrs at		
6% 0·74726	12·45	74,700
		£84,809

It is apparent that the net of tax valuation gives a higher value. Indeed as the rate of tax is increased it will be found that the value rises on a net of tax basis. It should be noted that in 5 years' time, when the interest becomes a freehold interest let at full rental value and adopting current rental value and yields, it will be valued at £10,000 p.a. × 10 Y.P. or £6,000 p.a. × 16·67 Y.P. = £100,000. Clearly therefore the difference between gross and net of tax valuations arises because there is a term at a lower rent.

The reason for this can be seen in the mathematics in that, in valuing the term, although the rent is reduced by 40%, the Y.P. is not increased correspondingly. Similarly, in determining the present value of the reversion, the value at reversion is the same but the present values differ at different rates. Indeed the difference between the terms is more than offset by the difference in present values.

At the same time it should be stressed that the net of tax valuation shown above is incomplete if a full allowance for taxation is required in that no allowance has been made for capital gains tax. However, if an allowance for capital gains tax of 40% were adopted, in the net of tax approach the value still lies above the value on a gross of tax basis, as the following shows:–

Example 14–5

Term (as before)		£10,109
Reversion to Net		
F.R.V.	£6,000	
Y.P. in Perp. at		
6%	16·67	
		£100,000
less Capital Gains Tax		
(C.G.T.)		
Net value of		
interest = x		
∴ Gain = (100,000		
− x)		
∴ Tax = 0·4		
(100,000 − x) =		40,000 − 0·4x
∴ Reversion net of		
C.G.T.		60,000 + 0·4x

$\times$ P.V. £1 in 5 yrs
  at 6%   0·747   44,820 + 0·299x

Capital Value   £54,929 + 0·299x

But Capital Value = x
$\therefore$ x = 54,929 + 0·299x
$\therefore$ x = £78,360

Note. The CGT element has ignored indexation relief and other elements of the CGT computation for simplicity. A more detailed estimate of the liability could be made.

The full allowance for tax does therefore indicate that there will be a different value for investors with differing rates of tax. If a full allowance is to be adopted to analyse an investment to an individual it is probably more appropriate to use discounted cash flow techniques, discussed in Chapter 10. An allowance for tax in determining the open market value of an interest, on the other hand, is inappropriate since, as has been shown, the value would then depend on the choice of the rate of tax. Of course if it can be shown that a group at a certain rate of tax is dominating the market for a specific type of investment then it may become appropriate to adopt a net of tax approach applying that group's tax rate. Such a situation has arisen in the case of short leasehold investments, as described below.

It has been stated frequently that rates of tax vary. At one extreme an individual or company may pay tax at high rates whilst, at the other extreme, charities, and in particular pension funds, pay no income tax whatsoever—hence, their description as "gross funds".

In Chapter 9 the valuation of leasehold interests was described, including the need to allow for the gross cost of an annual sinking fund. Such a cost represents a high proportion of profit rent when the term is short. However, if a gross fund invests in such interests it is not faced with a tax liability so that the annual sinking fund costs do not need to be grossed up to allow for tax. The effect of this is that it can afford to pay significantly more for a short leasehold interest (say up to 15 years) than a taxpayer or, alternatively, if it can

buy such an interest on the basis allowing for tax then it
will obtain a higher than anticipated yield since the grossed
up element remains as a return to capital.

This has led to gross funds tending to be a major factor
in this part of the investment market. However, it cannot
be said that all short leasehold investments should be valued
ignoring the tax element; rather that it may be appropriate
to value grossing up the cost for tax and also ignoring this
factor, the price payable lying in between the two resultant
figures as the vendor and gross fund purchaser share the
benefits of the latter's tax-free status on the value. In practice
many gross funds adopt a single rate Y.P. approach or a
D.C.F. approach to the valuation of short leasehold investments, and it would be appropriate when valuing investments
likely to appeal to gross funds to consider these different
approaches.

4. Freehold Interests

Two aspects of the valuation of freehold interests cause
the greatest controversy, the yield to be adopted and the
effects of inflation.

(*a*) *Nature and Function of Yields.* The choice of, and the
function of, the yield appropriate to a particular investment
are both areas for comment. The fundamental issue turns
on the function of the yield itself.

As a matter of basic principle, the conventional approach
treats the yield as being a measure of comparison between
various investments available and the yield chosen reflects
all the different qualities between the investment in question
and others that are available. Thus it reflects the potential
for future growth, the strength of covenant, the likely performance in an inflationary economy, and any other factors
which are thought to be relevant. It is referred to as an "all-
risks" yield.

Another school of thought argues that the yield itself
should be analysed to reflect these different and distinct qualities. That view has been expressed in various articles, books
and theses where a "real value approach" is advocated.

It is not the role of this book to attempt to evaluate the different methods advocated but it is important for the student in particular to be aware of them.

(*b*) *Equated Yields*. The valuation of a freehold interest calls for the determination of the appropriate yield for the class of investment under consideration. Thus it may be said that the yield on first class shops is 4 per cent or modern factories 8 per cent and so on. What is meant by this is that where such a property is let at its full rental value on a normal market basis then that is the yield to be adopted in arriving at the Years' Purchase.

This is sufficient for valuation purposes but the converse of the method may be inadequate if an analysis is to be made of investments allowing for differing rent review patterns or projections of inflation in rents.

Indeed there may be difficulties in valuing. For example, if by analysis of similar properties let on 21 year leases with 7 yearly reviews the yield is known to be 5·3 per cent, what is the appropriate yield to adopt if one further similar property is found to have been let on a 21 year lease with 3 yearly reviews? In the absence of any comparables on this basis the valuer must use his judgment. The yield is probably lower, but by how much? 1 per cent, $\frac{1}{2}$ per cent, $\frac{1}{4}$ per cent? It is fair to say that in many cases the valuer's judgment, in conjunction with the investor's judgment, will determine the price offered in the market. But in some instances, and particularly where the investor is a fund or institution, a more reasoned approach would probably be demanded.

A solution to the valuation problem, and also to that of how to allow for projections of inflation, can be found in a technique that has been developed referred to as the equated yield.

The authors have found that the expression equated yield has been given different definitions so it should be made clear that in this instance the definition is taken to be the discount rate which needs to be applied to the projected income so that the summation of all the incomes discounted at this equated yield rate, equates with the capital outlay.

This definition follows the internal rate of return concept of D.C.F. as set out in Chapter 10. Thus an investment can readily be analysed allowing for actual and projected rent at whatever may be the review dates against the market price to show the I.R.R. or equated yield. Alternatively, given the actual and projected rents and review dates, and given the equated yield appropriate to the investment, the price which should be paid to maintain these factors can be determined.

Hence, in the valuation problem posed above, if the analysis of the investments where the rent reviews were 7 yearly is established, the appropriate price/value for 3 yearly reviews can be determined and thus the initial yield for valuation purposes.

Example 14–6

Similar properties have been letting for £1,000 p.a. on leases for 21 years with 7-yearly reviews. Rental growth is anticipated @ 12% p.a. The properties have been selling @ £18,750 (= 5·33% return). Value a similar property recently let @ £1,000 p.a. for 21 years with 3-yearly reviews.

Step 1: Find equated yield of properties sold @ £18,750.

Try 16%

Years	A £1 @ 12%	Expected Rent (1,000 × A £1)	PV £1 @ 16%	PV × YP 7 yrs @ 16%	PV of Rents
0–7	—	1,000	1·0	4·0386	4,039
8–14	2·2107	2,211	0·3538	1·4289	3,159
15–21	4·8871	4,887	0·1252	0·5056	2,471
22→perp	10·8038	10,804	0·0443	0·8306[1]	8,974

	18,643
Less Price Paid	18,750
NPV	−107

Note (1) 0·8306 = YP in perp @ 5·33% (18·75) × PV 21 yrs @ 16% (0·0443).

Try 15%

Years	A £1 @ 12%	Expected Rent	PV £1 @ 15%	PV × YP 7 yrs @ 15%	PV of Rents
0–7	—	1,000	—	4·1604	4,160
8–14	2·2107	2,211	0·3759	1·5639	3,458
15–21	4·8871	4,887	0·1413	0·5879	2,873
22 → perp	10·8038	10,804	0·0531	0·9956	10,756

	21,247
Less Price Paid	18,750
NPV	+2,497

$$\text{IRR} = 15\% + \frac{2,497}{2,497 + 107} = \text{say } 15\cdot95\%$$

Step 2: Apply IRR to the property to be valued.

Years	Expected Rent (1,000 × A £1) @ 12%	PV £1 @ 15·95%	PV × YP 3 yrs @ 15·95% (2·2477)	PV of Rents
0–3	1,000	1·0	2·2477	2,248
4–6	1,405	0·6415	1·4419	2,026
7–9	1,974	0·4115	0·9250	1,826
10–12	2,773	0·2640	0·5934	1,645
13–15	3,896	0·1693	0·3805	1,483
16–18	5,474	0·1086	0·2441	1,336
19–21	7,690	0·0697	0·1567	1,205
22 → perp	10,804	0·0447	0·0447x	482·9388x

	11,769 + 482·9388x
Less Price Paid	1,000x
NPV	0

$$\therefore 517\cdot0612x = 11,769$$
$$x = 22\cdot761 \text{ YP} (= \text{YP in perp @ } 4\cdot393\%)$$

Note: $x = $ YP in perp @ initial yield.

Hence initial yield on property to be valued is $4\cdot393\%$. The price that should be paid is £22,760.

It can be seen that the valuer making a subjective judgement as to the appropriate reduction to the prevailing yield would need to have reduced the yield by 1%, but this would be a matter of chance. On the other hand the calculations have produced a mathematical answer which is not necessarily acceptable as a true valuation. For this to be so it must be assumed that rents are unaffected by the review pattern. However, in practice, if identical properties are offered on leases with either three-year review patterns or seven-year review patterns it is most unlikely that the initial rent would be £1,000 p.a.

The more likely situation is that, if properties let on twenty-one-year leases with seven-year reviews command an initial rent of £1,000 p.a. and sell for £18,750, the valuer would be required to determine the approximate initial rent for a lease with three-yearly reviews so as to maintain the value @ £18,750.

The calculation is the same as for Step 2 above save that the initial rent is x, the value after twenty-one years is £18,750 × Amount of £1 for twenty-one years @ 12% (10·804) × PV £1 in 21 yrs @ 15·95% (0·0447) = 9055·103, and the Price Paid is £18,750. This produces a result of:–

$$11·769x + 9055·103 = £18,750$$
$$x = \text{say } £824$$

Thus the initial rent should be £824 p.a.

There are several Tables available which provide a simple means of adjusting rents to match changes in rent review patterns.

(*c*) *Effects of Inflation.* In recent times the impact of inflation has been experienced widely. It has led to widespread increases in the prices of many goods, and property has not been immune from its effects. The term inflation is often used imprecisely, so that any increase in price is treated as an effect of inflation. Thus, in property, as rents increase they are said to rise with inflation. If inflation is measured as the increase in the retail price index then the growth in rents of many types of property has been far in excess of inflation in the past decade.

Whatever may be the causes of increases in rents, such increases have led people to examine the investment method of valuation and to question whether adequate, or even any, allowance is made in the valuation.

Taking the simplest example of a property recently let at rental value, the valuation method is to multiply the rent passing by a Y.P. in perpetuity. As was explained in Chapter 9, the yield from which the Y.P. is derived reflects the likely future increases in rental value, be they real or nominal. In this way the valuation can be said to reflect fully the likely effects of inflation, used in its widest sense. Nonetheless it has been argued that a more explicit allowance should be made for growth. No generally accepted approach for making such an allowance has emerged, although the D.C.F. method or methods derived from D.C.F. techniques enable explicit allowance to be made quite readily.

(*d*) *Valuation of Varying Incomes.* It was shown in Chapter 8 that the valuer may be required to value a freehold interest where the rent receivable is currently less than full rental value. The method adopted was to capitalise the present rent until the full rental value could be obtained, the Term, and then to capitalise the rental value receivable thereafter, the Reversion. An alternative approach is sometimes adopted whereby the rent currently receivable is capitalised into perpetuity, and the incremental rental receivable at the expiry

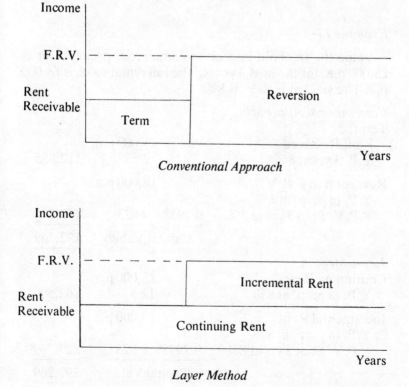

Conventional Approach

Layer Method

of the lease is capitalised separately. The present rent represents a hard core of rent which will continue into perpetuity whilst future rents are incremental layers. Hence, it is commonly referred to as the hardcore or layer method. This can be illustrated diagrammatically as above.

The valuation approach by the hardcore method involves applying a Years' Purchase in perpetuity to both the continuing rent and the incremental rent, the capital value of the incremental slice then being deferred by applying the appropriate Present Value. The problem which arises, and the major criticism of the method, is the choice of the appropriate yield for each slice. Where the Term and Reversion would be valued at the same yield, then that same yield can be applied throughout the hardcore method, and an identical result will emerge since each pound of future rent is being discounted at the same rate.

Example 14–7

Value the freehold interest in commercial premises let at £5,000 p.a. for the next 3 years. The full rental value is £8,000 p.a. The yield at F.R.V. is 8%

Conventional Approach
Term

Rent Received		£5,000 p.a.	
Y.P. 3 yrs at 8%		2·577	£12,885
Reversion to F.R.V.		£8,000 p.a.	
Y.P. in perp. at 8%	12·5		
× P.V. £1 in 3 yrs at 8%	0·7938	9·923	£79,384
		Capital Value	£92,269

Layer Method
Continuing Rent

		£5,000 p.a.	
Y.P. in perp. at 8%		12·5	£62,500
Incremental Rent		£3,000 p.a.	
Y.P. in perp. at 8%	12·5		
× P.V. £1 in 3 yrs at 8%	0·7938	9·923	£29,769
		Capital Value	£92,269

However, where it is felt that the rate for the term should be different from the reversion, perhaps lower because the covenant of the tenant makes the rent receivable more certain of receipt, or higher because the rent receivable is fixed for several years, then the layer method is likely to produce a different result. For example, where the term rent is valued at a lower rate, then the results will only coincide if the incremental rent is valued at an appropriate marginal rate.

The appropriate marginal rate may be derived by analysis. Take the rents in *Example 14–7*, but assume that the term rent is valued at 6%.

Hence, F.R.V.	£8,000 p.a.	
Y.P. in perp. at 8%	12·5	£100,000
less Rent received	£5,000 p.a.	
Y.P. in perp. at 6%	16·666	83,330
Capital Value of Incremental Rent		£16,670

$$\therefore \frac{3,000}{16,670} \times 100 = 18\%$$

Thus if the incremental rent is valued at 18 per cent and the continuing rent at 6 per cent the same results will emerge as the conventional approach adopting 6 per cent respectively for Term and Reversion. In practice the likelihood is that the valuer, whilst raising the yield in valuing the increment to reflect that it is the top slice, is unlikely to adopt what appears to be a very high rate of return. This leads to the criticism that, in the hardcore method, there is no yield adopted which can be checked by direct comparison with the yields of similar investments unless identical investments can be produced.

Similarly, where the term rent would be valued at a higher yield, the layer method tends to be difficult to apply. Assume again the facts in *Example 14–7* but assume that the rent of £5,000 p.a. is fixed for 15 years, following which the property can be let at £8,000 subject to regular reviews. Clearly the appropriate yield to apply to the £5,000 p.a. could be significantly higher than 8 per cent, based on medium term fixed interest investments. On the other hand it would be unrealistic to value £5,000 into perpetuity at such a high rate.

The argument in favour of the hardcore method is that it is simpler to apply, particularly where the rent varies at renewal stages.

The choice between the methods must be made by the individual valuer. This presents no problem in practice unless different results emerge, when it is left to the respective valuer to justify whatever approach he has chosen.

A further argument is advanced that the yield for the term and reversion should be the same in all circumstances since this is the yield for the investment as a whole. If this is accepted, then the case for the hardcore method becomes one of convenience only.

5. LEASEHOLD INTERESTS

A considerable amount of criticism has been expressed of the method of valuing leasehold interests. The criticism turns on two major areas, one being the concept of capital recoupment and the other of the inherent errors to be found in the valuation of varying profit rentals.

Capital Recoupment

As was explained in Chapter 9, the valuation of a leasehold interest recognises that a lease is a wasting asset and makes appropriate adjustments by the provision of a sinking fund for recoupment of capital. This leads to the adoption of a dual rate Years' Purchase.

The questions that are raised include how valid is it to allow for replacement of capital? If valid why not replace the capital in real terms allowing for the erosion of value due to inflation? Why allow for replacement of capital by an annual sinking fund at a leasehold redemption policy rate of around 3% interest when it can be demonstrated that few people actually take out such policies? If not valid, why use a dual rate Years' Purchase?

If these criticisms are valid then considerable doubt is thrown upon the method of valuation described in Chapter

9. Before considering the overall effects of the criticisms it is useful to consider the criticisms in turn.

(i) Replacement of Capital

The purpose within the valuation method of replacing the capital which must ultimately disappear in the case of a lease-hold investment is to isolate this factor, which is unique to leasehold interests as against freehold interests, and so to allow a ready comparison between freehold and leasehold interests. The alternative is to reflect this unique feature in the yield. This would lead to adjustments in the yield which would be partly subjective in the absence of direct compar-ables. The adjustments in the case of short leasehold terms would need to be considerable if it is accepted that investors who buy at prices allowing for a sinking fund accept such prices as being reasonable.

Example 14–8

Value the leasehold interest in commercial premises held for 5 years at £1,000 p.a. They are underlet for the term remaining at £11,000 p.a. The appropriate yield is 7%.

Conventional Approach

F.R.V. (and rent receivable)	£11,000 p.a.
less Rent payable	1,000
Profit Rent	£10,000 p.a.
Y.P. 5 yrs at 7% and 3% (Tax at 35%)	2·78
	£27,800

Value without A.S.F. at 3%	
Profit Rent (as before)	£10,000 p.a.
Y.P. 5 yrs at 23% single rate	2·80
	£28,000

If it is felt that 23 per cent is unrealistic and a lower rate is adopted, the value will rise which suggests that short lease-hold interests are under-valued by the conventional

approach. Such a view is supported in practice where gross
funds are in the market, as described above.

If a longer term lease is considered then the increase in
yield is lessened. For example, if the term were 50 years
at 7% and 3% adj. I.T. at 35% = 11·956 which is approximately equal to Y.P. 50 years at 8·2% single rate.

(ii) Replacement of Capital in Real Terms

It is true that the conventional method allows for an annual
sinking fund to replace the original capital invested. In times
of inflation there will be an erosion of capital value in real
terms. Clearly if £10,000 had been invested in a lease 20
years ago which now expires, then the £10,000 now available
under the sinking fund is not putting the investor in the same
position as he was when he made his original investment
in real terms.

The Y.P. dual rate can be adjusted quite simply if it is
decided to replace the capital in real terms. It would be
necessary initially to determine either the predicted rate of
inflation or the predicted rate of growth in an equivalent
freehold interest. The latter approach is more logical since
the aim is to put freehold and leasehold interests on an equal
footing. Once the rate of inflation or growth has been determined, then the annual sinking fund should be calculated
to replace not £1 invested but the amount of £1 at the chosen
rate over the period of the lease.

If this is done the leasehold interest is even more secure
so that the remunerative rate should be reduced, possibly
to the level of the yield on an equivalent freehold interest.
However, this is unlikely to counteract the increased cost
of the annual sinking fund, so producing a lower Years' Purchase and lower capital value.

Example 14–9

Assume a lease with 40 years to run and a freehold yield
of 9% and leasehold yield of 10%

Conventional Y.P.
   Y.P. 40 yrs at 10% and 3% (Tax at 35%) = 8·305

Inflation Proof Y.P.

Assume inflation at 7% p.a. leasehold rate now 9%

Formula =

$$\frac{1}{i + asf \text{ to replace A of £1 for 40 yrs at 7\%} \times \dfrac{100}{100 - 35}}$$

$$= \frac{1}{0{\cdot}09 + (0{\cdot}0148 \times 14{\cdot}974 \times 1{\cdot}538)}$$

$$= \frac{1}{0{\cdot}09 + 0{\cdot}3408}$$

$$= 2{\cdot}231 \text{ Y.P.}$$

This difference in Years' Purchase suggests that the conventional method greatly over-values leasehold interests. There is however a fallacy in the argument that the annual sinking fund under-provides without an allowance for inflation.

The fact is that a leasehold interest is a wasting asset by which is meant that it ultimately wastes away to nil. However, in the period between the start and finish of a lease the value may rise considerably before falling away. The reason for this is that, if rental values increase faster than the Years' Purchase for succeeding years' falls, then the capital value of the leasehold interest will rise in nominal terms. The effect of inflation is therefore reduced. If the investor sells his interest before the capital value starts to fall he will obtain more than he paid at the start.

Indeed an inspection of the Y.P. dual rate Tables will show that it is only in the last few years that there is a significant falling away of the value of the Y.P. figures such as to outweigh the inflation on rents. Thus it is only in the case of short leases that the ignoring of the effects of inflation in the sinking fund can be criticised, but the impact of any allowance is far less over such short periods.

Example 14–10

As for *Example 14–9*, but the lease has 4 years to run.

Conventional Y.P.
  Y.P. 4 yrs at 10% and 3% (Tax at 35%) = 2·138

Inflation Proof Y.P.

$$\frac{1}{0 \cdot 09 + (0 \cdot 2408 \times 1 \cdot 311 \times 1 \cdot 538)}$$
$$= 1 \cdot 738$$

(*iii*) *A.S.F. at 3 per cent*
It is suggested that few investors actually take out leasehold redemption policies. Instead it is said that they either invest their redemption funds in alternative investments showing a higher return than 3% or make no such provision at all. This may perhaps be so but such criticism misses the essential point of the annual sinking fund allowance, that it is a notional allowance to allow comparison between freehold and leasehold investments, as explained before. Given that the notional allowance makes such a comparison possible, it remains that only by means of insurance policies can an investor, if he so chooses, obtain a guarantee of a future specific capital payment, and the rates offered under such policies are naturally low. It is true that, in the case of short terms, there are investments which guarantee more than 3%, and it is in these cases where the dual rate Y.P. is less likely to be adopted as has been discussed.

(*iv*) *Why use Dual Rate Years' Purchase?*
The answer to this question is provided by the comments on the above points. Nonetheless it should be recognised that there is a body of opinion which argues for the abandonment of the dual rate approach and its replacement by a single rate Years' Purchase or D.C.F. or other alternatives.

Valuation of Variable Incomes
The usual method employed to calculate the capital value of a leasehold interest, where the income varies during the term of the lease, is inherently incorrect because of the use

of the dual rate tables. The method envisages more than one sinking fund being taken out to provide for the redemption of capital whereas in practice a purchaser would in all probability take out a single policy to cover the whole term. The concept of a variable sinking fund is not in itself incorrect and a valuation could be made on this basis if a method were employed which would enable the varying instalments to compound to the required amount over the full unexpired term.

The normal method of approach used in the valuation of varying incomes for a limited term does not allow for the correct compounding of the sinking fund accumulations. This type of valuation is made in two or more stages, so that each separate sinking fund instalment will be based on the number of years in the appropriate stage of the valuation and will not be based over the full length of the term. Consequently the sum provided by these sinking funds over the full length of the term will not equal the capital sum required for the redemption of capital.

The following examples illustrate the error which occurs when the normal method of valuation is used:–

Example 14–11

The valuation of a leasehold interest on an 8 and 2½ per cent basis. The lease has an unexpired term of 10 years and produces a profit rent of £1,000 p.a.

Profit Rent	£1,000 p.a.
Y.P. 10 years at 8% and 2½%	5·908
Capital Value	£5,908

Example 14–12

If the unexpired term of 10 years in *Example 14–11* is considered in two stages of say, 4 years and 6 years the valuation will take the following form:–

	Profit Rent	£1,000 p.a.	
Y.P. 4 years at 8% and 2½%		3·117	£3,117
	Profit Rent	£1,000 p.a.	
Y.P. 6 years at 8% and 2¼%	4·227		
P.V. in £1 in 4 years at 8%	0·735	3·107	£3,107
		Capital Value	£6,224

In these two examples, the profit rental of £1,000 p.a. has
been capitalised in each case for a total period of 10 years
at the same remunerative rate of 8 per cent; each example
should therefore produce the same result. The difference
of £316 is caused by the error which arises in *Example 14–12*.
The method of valuation used in this example is based on
the dual rate basis and is made in two stages; an incorrect
sinking fund instalment will therefore be implicit in the valuation and will introduce an error in calculation.

The degree of error which occurs in *Example 14–12* is
approximately +5¼%. If the 10-year term had been divided
into three stages (with the income varying in the third and
sixth year) the error would increase to over 8 per cent.

The Effect of Tax. If the incidence of income tax on the
sinking fund element is taken into account this must have
some effect on the degree of the error. In the following valuations the figures of Years' Purchase used in *Examples 14–11*
and *14–12* are adjusted to allow for the effect of income
tax assuming tax at 50 per cent for the purpose of the
Examples:–

Example 14–11(t)

	Profit Rent	£1,000 p.a.
Y.P. 10 years at 8% and 2½% (Tax at 50%)		3·87
	Capital Value	£3,870

Example 14–12(t)

In this example the 10-year term is again considered in two stages:–

	Profit Rent	£1,000 p.a.	
Y.P. 4 years at 8% and 2½%			
(Tax at 50%)		1·78	£1,780
	Profit Rent	£1,000 p.a.	
Y.P. 6 years at 8%			
and 2½%			
(Tax at 50%)	2·54		
P.V. £1 in 4 years			
at 8%	0·735	1·87	£1,870
	Capital Value		£3,650

These examples illustrate that when an allowance is made to reflect the incidence of tax, it will not always increase the error which exists, although this is often thought to be the case. They show that, in making the allowance for income tax, the adjustment has had a compensatory "pull" on the degree of the error which is reduced in the last example to approximately −5½ per cent from +5¼ per cent.

In many instances the effect of the tax adjustment will be more marked and will usually over-compensate for the "normal" error to such an extent that a much greater inaccuracy will be introduced. In some cases an error which is well in excess of 10 per cent may be involved.

The Double Sinking Fund Method. The following method, which is one developed by A. W. Davidson, enables this form of valuation to be made without involving any significant error. An attempt has been made to use the conventional methods of valuation and to avoid any involved mathematical approach.

Example 14–13

In this example the same leasehold interest is again considered and the term is divided into two stages as in *Example 14–12(t)*. It should be noticed that the dual rate principle is not used.

Let the Capital Value = P.

Profit Rent		£1,000 p.a.
less a.s.f. to replace P in 10 years		
at 2½%	0·0893P	
adj. for tax at		
50%	× 2·0	0·1786P

Spendable Income		£1,000 − 0·1786P.
Y.P. 4 years at 8%		3·312

£3,312 − 0·5915P

Spendable Income		£1,000 − 0·1786P
Y.P. 6 years		
at 8%	4·623	
× P.V. £1 in 4 yrs		
at 8%	0·735	

3·398

£3,398 − 0.6068P

£6,710 − 1·1983P

*Plus Repayment of the capital replaced
  by the Single Rate S.F.
P × P.V. of £1 in 10 years at 8%   0·4632P

£6,710 − 0·7351P

$$\therefore \qquad P = 6{,}710 - 0{\cdot}7351P$$
$$1{\cdot}7351P = £6{,}710$$
$$P = \underline{£3{,}867}$$

The spendable income has been valued on the single rate basis. This means that the "capital" has been replaced by allowing for a sinking fund at 8% in the capitalisation. Thus two "capital recoupments" have taken place one at 2½% and one at 8%.

*As the valuation has been reduced by allowing for the capital to be replaced twice, a figure equal to the deferred capital value has been added back to the valuation.

It will be seen that the capital value of £3,867 is higher than that produced in *Example 14–12(t)* of £3,650. Thus, removing the inherent error has increased the value by 5·9%.

to produce the same value as in *Example 14–11(t)* which is correct.

A simplified approach has been produced by P. W. Pannell which is probably sufficiently accurate for most cases. This again applies a single rate Y.P., the result being adjusted by applying the ratio of the Y.P. dual rate to the Y.P. single rate.

Example 14–14

The same facts are adopted as in *Example 14–13*.

1st 4 years	Profit Rent	£1,000 p.a.	
	Y.P. 4 yrs at 8%	3·312	£3,312

2nd 6 years	Profit Rent		£1,000 p.a.	
	Y.P. 6 yrs			
	at 8%	4·623		
	P.V. £1 in 4 yrs			
	at 8%	0·735	3·398	3,398

$$\text{6,710}$$

$$\times \frac{\text{Y.P. 10 yrs at 8 \& } 2\frac{1}{2}\% \text{ (IT 50\%)}}{\text{Y.P. 10 yrs at 8\%}} = \frac{3\cdot868}{6\cdot710} = \underline{0\cdot576}$$

$$\underline{\underline{£3,865}}$$

As can be seen the answer is almost exactly the same as that produced by the double sinking fund method (the difference being attributable to the rounding off of decimal places) and is much easier to produce.

This Chapter has considered some of the questions raised over valuation methods currently adopted. Its sole purpose has been to air some of the issues raised. The comments in the Chapter do not seek to accept or reject the views being expressed, nor is it suggested that all points of controversy have been introduced.

The hope is that the reader will appreciate that methods of valuation are under scrutiny and that this may result in changes in the approaches adopted to valuation. However, until such changes achieve general acceptance the authors believe that they have set out the principles and current practice of valuation in the preceding Chapters.

FURTHER READING

Research Report on Valuation Methods (RICS).
"The Valuation of Property Investments" by Nigel Enever (Estates Gazette).
"Property Valuation Tables" by Philip Bowcock (MacMillan Press).
"The Investment Method of Valuation: A Real Value Approach" by Neil Crosby in Journal of Valuation 1: 341–350 and 2: 48–59.
"Property and Building Appraisal in Uncertainty" by Ernest Wood (Liverpool Polytechnic).
"Property Investment Appraisal" by Andrew Baum and Neil Crosby (Routledge)

CHAPTER 15

Principles of the Law of Town and Country Planning

1. THE TOWN AND COUNTRY PLANNING ACT 1947

THE MODERN system of planning control, that is to say control of land use and development,[1] originated in the Town and Country Planning Act 1947. As is well known, there were several earlier planning statutes, but the system of control which they introduced was of limited scope and effect. The Act of 1947 is in a very real sense the starting point of planning as we know it in Britain.

There are two sides to modern planning law—physical (development control) and financial (compensation and taxation). They were meant to be logically complementary; but that principle has long been abandoned, and for purposes of analysis they must be considered separately. The original rigorous balance between the two sides disappeared in 1952 with the abolition of the "development charge" system introduced by the 1947 Act; and the "compensation-betterment problem", as it has sometimes been called, of deciding upon what financial principles, if any, public planning in the long term should be based has been shelved.

The following is a summary of those provisions of the 1947 Act which have a direct bearing on the subject of valuations. They are expressed in the past tense in order to give a complete picture of the Act as originally enacted, but only those which are printed in italics have been substantially affected by later legislation. The Third Schedule of the Act is now represented (with some important changes) by Schedule 8 of the Town and Country Planning Act 1971.

(i) Within three years from 1st July 1948 (the "appointed

---

[1] See "Planning Law and Procedure" (7th Edition 1986) by A. E. Telling (Butterworths Ltd.); "An Outline of Planning Law" (8th Edition 1981) by Sir Desmond Heap (Sweet & Maxwell Ltd.); Butterworths Planning Law Handbook (1987).

day") every local planning authority had to submit a "development plan" showing the way in which they proposed that land in their area should be used. Amongst other things, this "development plan" might define the sites of proposed roads, public and other buildings and works, airfields, parks, pleasure grounds, nature reserves and other open spaces; or allocate areas of land for use for agricultural, residential, industrial or other purposes. These development plans were to be subject to amendment at least once in every five years.

(ii) As from 1st July 1948, no owner might develop his property—e.g. carry out building, engineering or mining operations on it or "materially" change its existing use—unless permission for development was given under the Act, in most cases by the local planning authority. Subject to a right of appeal to the Minister, the local planning authority might refuse or grant it subject to conditions.

(iii) The fact that permission was refused, or restrictions on development imposed, did not, as a general rule, entitle the owner to compensation. But if the proposed development was a type specified in Part II of the Third Schedule to the Act which enumerated certain strictly limited forms of development—for example, an improvement or alteration to a building, involving an increase of not more than one-tenth of the existing cubic content at the "appointed day"—compensation was payable in the event of an adverse planning decision.

(iv) *Where permission was given for any development other than "existing use" development (i.e. development of the kind specified in the Third Schedule to the Act), the owner was required to pay a "development charge" based on the difference between (a) the value of the land with the benefit of the permission, and (b) its value with permission refused.*

(v) *Where land was acquired compulsorily for public purposes, the basis of compensation was its "existing use value"— i.e. its value assuming that any future development was restricted to those forms of development specified in the Third Schedule to the Act.*

(vi) *The effect of (ii) to (v) above was that owners were no longer entitled, as of right, to the development value of their land—i.e. that part of the market value in excess of the value the land would have if restricted to its existing use. For all practical purposes development values were under the control of—although not formally vested in—the Crown.*

(vii) Any owner who could prove that his land was depreciated in value in consequence of the above provisions of the Act might submit a claim—under Part VI of the Act—based on the difference between (a) the value of his property if restricted to "existing use" development only, and (b) the value it would have had if the Act had not been passed.

(viii) *A fixed sum of £300 million—known in practice as "the £300 million fund" or "the Global Fund"—was allocated to meet such claims so far as it would extend and this was to have been distributed in the form of Government stock by July, 1953, in accordance with a scheme to be prepared by the Treasury and approved by Parliament.*

(ix) *The consideration of claims for loss of development value, and the levying of development charges, was the duty of the Central Land Board established under the Act.*

To summarise the principles underlying the above provisions—the 1947 Act recognised an owner's right to some compensation in respect of development value existing at 1st July 1948, but not in respect of development value accruing after that date. In theory, at any rate, the recognised basis for all dealings in land after 1st July, 1948 was "existing use value".

"Existing use value" is a term which was first introduced into valuation practice by the provisions of the 1947 Act. It indicates the value which can be assigned to a property if it be assumed that no "development", within the meaning of the Town Planning Acts, will take place in the future except such forms of development as were formerly specified in the Third Schedule to the Town and Country Planning Act 1947, which has now been replaced by Schedule 8 to the Town and Country Act 1971 as modified by Schedule 18 to that Act.

Contrasting with "existing use value", therefore, is "development value", as described above. Before planning control existed, "development value" depended simply on market demand. If buyers would not offer more for a given property for purposes of development than for its existing use, then

its "development value" over and above "existing use value"
would be nil. But now "development value" depends on both
planning permission and demand. The then Master of the
Rolls, Lord Denning, said in *Viscount Camrose v. Basing-*
stoke Corporation (1966): "It is not planning permission itself
which increases value. It is planning permission coupled with
demand".

2. PLANNING AUTHORITIES AND DEVELOPMENT PLANS

The law regarding planning has been considerably
amended and re-enacted since 1947. The principal statute
to-day is the Town and Country Planning Act 1971. This
has been amended by later Acts; but the following account
will refer chiefly to the Act of 1971.

Planning authorities are both central and local. The central
authority is now the Department of the Environment. The
Secretary of State for the Environment does not usually
administer planning control directly; but appeals are made
to him from decisions of local authorities and he has the
power to "call in" applications from them for decision at
first instance. He issues orders and regulations, possesses
default powers and exercises a co-ordinating function by issuing circulars which give guidance and advice to local planning
authorities.

Detailed administration is entrusted to local planning authorities, which are county and district councils. The former
are "county planning authorities", concerned chiefly with
"strategic" matters; the latter are "district planning authorities", concerned normally with the routine planning control.

In order that they do not make their decisions at random,
they are required to make, and constantly revise, "development plans" for their area; and planning decisions should
always be made with the appropriate development plan in
mind even if for sound reasons they deviate from it. The
system of development plans under the Town and Country
Planning Act 1947 was gradually superseded by a new system,
introduced by Part I of the Town and Country Planning Act
1968, because of the delays caused by the requirement that

the Minister must approve all plans, in every detail, before they could become effective.

The 1968 system comprised two kinds of plans, structure and local plans (1971 Act, Part II, as amended). The structure plan was intended to formulate "policy and general proposals". The county planning authority made it in draft and submitted it to the Secretary of State, and publicised it. Objectors could then make representations which the Secretary of State dealt with by causing a "person or persons appointed by him for the purpose to hold an examination in public of such matters affecting his consideration of the plan as he considers ought to be so examined". Local plans dealt in detail with any part of the area covered by the structure plan, and were not normally to be submitted to the Secretary of State (in order to reduce delay), so that the local planning authorities must themselves deal with representations from objectors. Any parts of an authority's area which need to be generally replanned are to be specified in the structure plan as "action areas" and given their own local plans.

The latest change is a reversion in certain areas to the single development plans of 1947, under the Local Government Act 1985, section 4 and schedule 1, amended by the Housing and Planning Act 1986. In the areas of Greater London and the metropolitan counties, at dates to be prescribed, a new system of "unitary development plans" shall be introduced. When this becomes effective there will once again be, in those localities, all-purpose plans combining both strategic and detailed provisions.

The essence of any plan is a written statement. A local plan "shall consist of a map" as well; but detailed scale maps are to be avoided in structure plans. All these plans are to be based on a survey, which it is "the duty of the local planning authority to institute . . . insofar as they have not already done so".

Local planning authorities are required to keep various registers for public inspection. In addition to registers of local land charges, which include various orders, agreements and notices relevant to planning and compulsory purchase, there are separate registers of applications for planning permissions, for consent to display advertisements and for caravan site licences; and there are lists of buildings of special architectural or historic interest. Prospective purchasers and their solicitors should consult these registers and lists just as they normally apply for an official search of the local land charges registers.

3. JUDICIAL CONTROL OF PLANNING DECISIONS

No one holding public office has unrestricted freedom in decision-making, i.e. arbitrary power. Subject to alteration by Act of Parliament, the "discretion" of all public authorities has express or implied limits, enforced by the courts. Activities outside those limits are "ultra vires" and the courts can invalidate them. But there are stringent restrictions on recourse to the courts in planning as in other matters within the scope of the "ultra vires" principle.

Many, but not all, decisions of the Secretary of State (as distinct from those of local planning authorities) can only be challenged by application within six weeks to the High Court; and even so the court can only quash such decisions on the ground that they are "not within the powers of (the relevant Act), or that the interests of the applicant have been substantially prejudiced" by some procedural default. This represents a tightened definition of the "ultra vires" principle itself. Local planning authorities and other public bodies are, however, liable to have their "ultra vires" decisions challenged by a more general procedure in the High Court, "judicial review", in which the time limit is three months instead of six weeks (Rules of the Supreme Court, Order 53).

The House of Lords has stated that "the courts' supervisory duty is to see that (the authority) makes the authorised inquiry according to natural justice and arrives at a decision, whether right or wrong... they will not intervene merely because it has or may have come to the wrong answer, provided that this is an answer that lies within its jurisdiction".[2]

[2] *Anisminic Ltd. v. Foreign Compensation Commission* [1969] 1 All E.R. 208 at p. 237. "Wrong answer" presumably means "wrong on the apparent merits of the case".

The reference to "natural justice" is a reminder that the Secretary of State's decisions are usually reached after first granting a hearing to objectors. Many of the statutory provisions require him to "afford . . . an opportunity of appearing before, and being heard by, a person appointed by the Secretary of State for the purpose" (i.e. an inspector) to objectors, appellants, claimants or "persons aggrieved". Such proceedings must be conducted in accordance with "natural justice", which comprises two basic rules, namely that the person presiding must not be biased and that both sides are given a proper hearing on the points at issue. Though part of an administrative process, this private hearing or public inquiry is said to be "quasi-judicial"; so that the final decision can be quashed by the courts if "natural justice" is not observed.

Some inquiries are subject to safeguards additional to "natural justice". These include planning appeal inquiries, planning enforcement appeals inquiries, and compulsory purchase order inquiries. The various sets of Inquiries Procedure Rules governing these inquiries prescribe time limits and notice to be given to the parties and require written submissions to be made in advance by the authority stating the contentions on which they intend to rely. The Secretary of State has full discretion to make his eventual decision, so that he may reject any or all of the recommendations made by the inspector in his report; but he must hear any further representations if he disagrees on any finding of fact or considers any new issues or evidence of fact; and in the latter two cases he must reopen the inquiry if requested. In some cases the inspector who conducts the inquiry is himself empowered to take the decision instead of reporting back to the Secretary of State.

The "supervisory duty" of the High Court in regard to the "ultra vires" principle (natural justice included) is not an appeal jurisdiction; it does not relate to the merits of official decisions, as distinct from their general lawfulness, because those merits are questions of policy, not law.

4. LEGAL MEANING OF "DEVELOPMENT"

Section 22 (1) of the 1971 Act defines "development" as "the carrying out of building, engineering, mining or other operations in, on, over or under land, or the making of any material change in the use of any buildings or other land". Thus there will be development either if an "operation" is carried out, or if a "material change of use" is brought about. Often a project involves development because there will be one or more operations and a material change of use as well.

Section 22 (as amended) lists specific matters which either are or are not "development". The latter include "in the case of buildings or other land which are used for a purpose of any class specified in an order made by the Minister under this section, the use thereof for any other purpose of the same class". Thus we have the Town and Country Planning (Use Classes) Order 1987, which lists sixteen "use classes" in four groups A, B, C and D; and any change within a "use class" is not development at all, or in other words not "material".[3]

Whether any work amounts to an "operation" or whether any change of use is "material" is a "question of fact and degree" in each case. Examples include such difficult questions as whether demolition is an "operation", and whether the abandonment or the intensification of a use is a "material change". Building a model village as a permanent structure has been held to involve an "operation" but not placing a mobile hopper and conveyor in a coal-merchant's yard. Placing an egg-vending machine on the roadside of a farm has been held to involve a material change of use; but not altering part of a railway station yard from a coal depot to a transit depot for crated motor vehicles. The burden of proof rests heavily on that party who alleges that a finding in relation to development is ultra vires.

Ownership of land, or of things placed on land, is irrelevant to planning except in special circumstances: what matters is the nature of what is done on or to the land. Questions which may be relevant include (i) what is the actual area

<hr/>

[3] But a planning permission may lawfully be granted on condition that a use of premises must not be subsequently changed even within a "use class": *City of London Corporation v. Secretary of State for the Environment* (1972), 23 P. & C.R. 169.

involved; (ii) whether there are multiple uses on a given area of land and whether these are of equal importance, or are major and minor uses, or are confined to separate parts of the premises, or are intermittent, alternating or recurring; (iii) whether a project may amount to development for two or more quite separate reasons, for example the making of a reservoir in such a way as to involve an engineering operation (the work of construction) and a mining operation (the work of excavation and removal of mineral substances).[4]

5. PLANNING PERMISSIONS

Section 23 of the 1971 Act states that planning permission is "required" for carrying out development (subject to certain special exceptions). Section 24 empowers the Secretary of State to make "development orders", for the purpose (among others) of actually granting permission, on a general and automatic basis, for certain forms of development. The Town and Country Planning General Development Order 1977, known for short as the "G.D.O.", now (as amended) gives such permission for thirty classes of development which it carefully specifies. Apart from this there are other sections in the 1971 Act under which planning permission is "deemed" to be granted.

The G.D.O. prescribes the procedure for making applications to the local planning authority for planning permission. If a building is to be erected, an application may be made for "outline" permission, which means for approval in principle. If this is refused no time and expense need be wasted on detailed plans. If it is granted, separate application will need to be made for details to be approved—"reserved matters".

Any person may apply for planning permission; but an

---

[4] See *West Bowers Farm Products v. Essex County Council* (1985), 50 P. & C.R. 368.

applicant who owns neither a freehold nor leasehold in all
the land affected (normally a prospective purchaser) must
notify all freeholders, leaseholders with seven years or more
to run, and farm tenants, either directly or, if that is not
possible, by local press publicity. There are also certain
classes of controversial development which must be publicised. The persons notified by these methods may "make
representations" which the authority must take into
account.

A prospective developer who is not certain whether his
project amounts to "development" at all may request the
authority to "determine that question" (1971 Act, Section
53). It is also possible for a "person interested in land" to
make an agreement with the authority (enforceable against
him or persons deriving title under him) regulating development of that land on a more general basis than for a normal
planning permission (1971 Act, Section 52).

On receiving an application the local planning authority
must consult other authorities and government departments,
as appropriate, and "have regard to the provisions of the
development plan". Within two months they must notify
their decision to the applicant. They may grant permission
unconditionally, or "subject to such conditions as they think
fit", or refuse it (1971 Act, Section 29). Obviously if a developer acts on a planning permission he cannot continue any
previous use of the land which is inconsistent with it. The
possibility that a project could be regulated under some other
statutory procedure does not preclude a refusal of planning
permission, even if that other procedure might carry with
it a right to compensation.

Planning conditions are subject to a test of validity both
in principle and in detail. That is to say they must "fairly
and reasonably relate to the permitted development" and
they must be reasonable in their detailed terms. A condition
that cottages to be built must only be occupied by "persons
whose employment is or was employment in agriculture"
seems to have satisfied both tests. A condition that a project
of industrial development on a site next to a dangerously
congested main road must include the provision of a special
access road, and that this access road should be made avail-

able to members of the public visiting adjoining premises, seems to have satisfied the first test but not the second.[5]

Conditions which may be valid include those which cut down the use of other land of the applicant and also those which require a new use to cease after a stated time and thus take effect as temporary planning permissions. But permissions are normally permanent and "enure for the benefit of the land" (1971 Act, Section 33).

Other time conditions, which are so frequent as to be virtually standard-form conditions, specify the time within which development must take place, or at least begin. There is a statutory three-year deadline in "outline" permissions for seeking approval for all detail or "reserved matters", followed by a two-year deadline for starting development after final approval; alternatively there is an overall five-year deadline for starting development (if longer) as well as a five-year deadline for starting development under ordinary as distinct from "outline" permissions. The authority, however, can vary any of these periods. There is, moreover, an additional control by "completion notice". Where any of the above deadlines applies and development has duly begun in the time specified but has not been completed in that time, the local planning authority may serve a "completion notice", subject to confirmation by the Secretary of State (with or without amendments) specifying a time, not less than a year, by which development must be complete or else the permission "will cease to have effect" (1971 Act, Sections 41–44).

If he so wishes, the Secretary of State may direct that a planning application be "called in" (as it is usually termed), that is referred to him instead of being decided by the local planning authority. Such cases, however, are as rare as appeals are frequent. Appeal to the Secretary of State against a refusal of permission, or a grant made subject to conditions, or a failure to give any decision within the appropriate time-limit, must be made in writing within six months of the

[5] See: *Pyx Granite Co. Ltd v. Minister of Housing and Local Government* [1958] 1 All E.R. 625: *Fawcett Properties v. Buckingham County Council* [1960] 3 All E.R. 503; *Hall & Co Ltd. v. Shoreham Urban District Council* [1964] 1 All E.R. 1.

adverse decision or of the expiry of the time-limit. He may allow or dismiss the appeal or reverse or vary any part of the permission, and his decision is as free as if he were deciding at first instance. The procedure is now governed by Inquiries Procedure Rules (which have already been mentioned) and a hearing must be given if it is asked for (1971 Act, Sections 35–6).

The Secretary of State's decision on an application "called in" or on an appeal, or that made by an inspector on his behalf, is "final" and cannot be challenged in a court except in the circumstances described earlier in relation to the judicial control of planning decisions.

Planning permission can be revoked or modified (1971 Act, Sections 45–6). The authorities which do this must pay compensation for any abortive expenditure and for any depreciation in relation to development value which, having come into existence by virtue of the permission, disappears because of the revocation or modification. Revocation or modification orders must be confirmed by the Secretary of State except in uncontested cases. If permission is given automatically by the G.D.O. it may in effect be revoked or modified, if by an "article 4 direction" under the G.D.O. it is partly or wholly withdrawn and a specific application is then made which is refused or only granted subject to conditions; compensation is paid in these cases also.

Insofar as authorised development has actually taken place, even if only in part, revocation or modification orders and "article 4 directions" are ineffective. To put an end to any actual development or "established use" of land (except of course where it is the necessary consequence of acting on a planning permission that this should happen) requires a discontinuance order, which must also be confirmed by the Secretary of State (1971 Act, Section 51). Compensation must be paid for loss of development value and abortive expenditure and also the cost of removal or demolition; but as compliance involves physical action there is also an enforcement procedure in cases of recalcitrance, similar in essentials to ordinary enforcement of planning control. Discontinuance of mineral working, or its temporary suspension, is governed by a specially modified code of regulation and compensation (1971 Act Sections 51A–F, 170A–B, 178A–C, added by the Town and Country Planning (Minerals) Act 1981, Section 10).

Public authorities are subject to planning control with certain reservations. The most far-reaching concerns the Crown, to which planning control does not apply at all,[6] though as a matter of practice the relevant government departments do normally consult local planning authorities when proposing to develop land. But Crown lessees and other persons using Crown land are subject to planning control (1971 Act, Section 266). The Town and Country Planning Act 1984 empowers the Crown to obtain planning permissions or consents for the benefit of prospective purchasers, and also empowers local planning authorities to make tree preservation orders and issue enforcement notices in respect of Crown land so as to affect (where appropriate) persons other than the Crown.

Ordinary local authorities, however, have no such immunity, except that when any project which involves expenditure requires the approval of a government department such approval may also be expressed to confer "deemed" planning permission, with or without conditions, if needed (1971 Act, Section 40). This rule applies to "statutory undertakers" as well, that is the nationalised industries and public utility authorities; but with them there is also another factor, the difference between their "operational" and non-operational land (the latter being offices, houses, investment property and any other land which is not the site of their operating functions). "Operational" land has the benefit of special rules in planning law, for example in regard to compensation for restrictions on development (1971 Act, Part XI). As for local planning authorities, separate regulations are prescribed, whereby they are "deemed" to have planning permission from the Secretary of State (unless he requires a specific application) for any development they carry out in accordance with their own development plan; but they must normally apply to him specifically if they wish to go against the

[6] *Ministry of Agriculture, Fisheries and Food v. Jenkins* [1963] 2 All E.R. 147.

plan (1971 Act, Section 270; Town and Country Planning
General Regulations 1976).

6. ENFORCEMENT OF PLANNING CONTROL

It is not a criminal offence to develop land without planning
permission. If this happens the local planning authority
should first consider whether it would be "expedient" to
impose sanctions, "having regard to the development plan
and to any other material considerations". If they do, they
must serve an "enforcement notice" on the owner and occupier of the land (1971 Act, Section 87). It must specify the
"breach of planning control" complained of and the steps
required to remedy it, and also two time-limits, namely a
period of at least twenty-eight days before the notice takes
effect followed by the period allowed for compliance.
"Breach of planning control" occurs when development
takes place either without the necessary permission or in
disregard of conditions or limitations contained in a permission.

There is also what amounts to a limitation period, in that
the "breach of planning control" must have occurred after
1963; and if it comprises either a change of use to a single
dwelling-house or any kind of operation the time limit for
serving an enforcement notice is restricted to four years.

The period specified in the notice before it takes effect
is intended to allow for making an appeal, and the notice
is "of no effect" while any appeal is going forward. This,
of course, may encourage a recalcitrant developer to press
on with his activities in the meantime. The local planning
authority is therefore given additional power, during this
period, to serve a "stop notice" prohibiting "any activity...
alleged... to constitute the breach" (1971 Act, Section 90
as amended).

Appeal may be made against an enforcement notice by
the recipient "or any other person having an interest in the
land" within the time specified before it is to take effect
(1971 Act, Section 88 as amended). It must be made in writing
to the Secretary of State, and may be on one or more of
eight specified grounds: (a) permission ought to be granted

or a condition or limitation ought to be discharged; (b) the matters alleged do not amount to a "breach of planning control"; (c) the alleged breach has not taken place; (d) the alleged breach occurred more than four years ago, where that limit applies; (e) the alleged breach occurred before 1964; (f) the enforcement notice was not served on the proper parties; (g) the specified steps for compliance are excessive; (h) the specified time for compliance is too short.

The Secretary of State must arrange a hearing or inquiry before an inspector, if either side requires it; and he may uphold, vary or quash the enforcement notice and also grant planning permission if appropriate. He may "correct any informality, defect or error" in the notice if "satisfied" that it is "not material", and may disregard a failure to serve it on a proper party if neither that party nor the appellant has been "substantially prejudiced". The Court of Appeal has stated that "an enforcement notice is no longer to be defeated on technical grounds. The Minister . . . can correct errors so long as, having regard to the merits of the case, the correction can be made without injustice". That was said in a case in which it was held to be at most an immaterial misrecital for an enforcement notice to allege development "without permission" when in fact a brief temporary permission had existed under the G.D.O. "The notice was plain enough and nobody was deceived by it."[7]

Further appeal from the Secretary of State's decision on an enforcement notice lies to the High Court on a point of law (1971 Act, Section 246). Apart from these appeals as a general rule anyone may challenge the validity of an enforcement notice in appropriate legal proceedings, but normally no such challenge shall be made on any of the eight grounds in Section 88 otherwise than by appeal to the Secretary of State (1971 Act, Section 243). One obvious possibility of challenge is in defence to a prosecution, since although a breach of planning control is not a criminal offence the breach of an enforcement notice is (1971 Act, Section 89).

---

[7] *Miller Mead v. Minister of Housing and Local Government* [1963] 1 All E.R. 459, per Lord Denning. On the question of who may be served with an enforcement notice, see *Stevens v. London Borough of Bromley* [1972] All E.R. 712.

An owner who has transferred his interest to a subsequent
owner can if prosecuted bring the latter before the court.

In addition to prosecution after failure to comply with an
effective enforcement notice within the time specified in it,
the authority also have the power, after that time, to enter
on the land and carry out the steps prescribed by the notice,
other than discontinuance of any use, and recover from the
owner the net cost reasonably so incurred. He may in turn
recover from the true culprit, if different, his reasonable
expenditure on compliance (1971 Act, Section 91).

7. AMENITY AND SAFETY

The other major concerns of planning law are amenity
and safety. Amenity "appears to mean pleasant circumstances, features, advantages";[8] but it is not statutorily
defined, nor is safety. The provisions of planning law governing amenity covers trees, buildings of special interest, advertisements, caravan sites and unsightly land; those governing
safety cover advertisements and hazardous substances.

To grow or cut trees is not of itself development.[9] But
local planning authorities are specifically empowered, "in
the interests of amenity", to make "tree preservation orders"
for specified "trees, groups of trees or woodlands", restricting interference with the trees except with the consent of
the local planning authority. Dangerous trees, however, may
be cut if necessary. There are also provisions governing replanting. Unauthorised interference with any protected tree
calculated to harm it is a criminal offence (1971 Act, Sections
60–62, 102, as amended).

A T.P.O. must first be confirmed by the Secretary of State,
with or without modifications, unless it is not contested; also
in an emergency such confirmation may be dispensed with
for up to six months. Regulations are prescribed governing

---

[8] *Re Ellis and Ruislip-Northwood Urban District Council* [1920] K.B. at p. 370
per Scrutton, L.J.

[9] Conditions for replanting or preservation of trees should be imposed in planning
permissions where appropriate (1971 Act, Section 59). For control of timber felling
see the Forestry Act, 1967.

the procedure for making T.P.O.s, and their content.[10] Standard provisions in T.P.O.s lay down essentially the same procedure for applying for consents to interfere with protected trees as exists for applying for planning permission.

"Amenity" is not expressly mentioned in relation to buildings of special interest; but Section 277 of the Act of 1971 refers to "areas of special architectural or historic interest the character or appearance of which it is desirable to preserve or enhance", and requires local planning authorities to determine where such areas exist and designate them as "Conservation Areas". When one of these areas has been designated, "special attention shall be paid to the desirability of preserving or enhancing its character or appearance" by exercising appropriate powers under the Act of 1971, and also by publicising planning applications for development which in the authority's opinion would affect that character or appearance.[11]

The phrase "special architectural or historic interest" applies chiefly to buildings. The Secretary of State has the duty of compiling or approving lists of such buildings, after suitable consultations, and supplying local authorities with copies of the lists relating to their areas (1971 Act, Section 54). Such authorities must notify owners and occupiers of buildings included in (or removed from) these lists. The Secretary of State may, when considering any building for inclusion in a list, take into account the relationship of its exterior with any group of buildings to which it belongs and also "the desirability of preserving... a man-made object or structure fixed to the building or forming part of the land and comprised within the curtilage of the building".

If a building is not "listed" the local planning authority may give it temporary protection by a "building preservation notice" while they try to persuade the Secretary of State to list it (1971 Act, Section 58).

But certain kinds of buildings cannot in any case be "listed

[10]Town and Country Planning (Tree Preservation Order) Regulations 1969.
[11]The Town and Country Amenities Act 1974 amended and supplemented Section 277 of the 1971 Act. All demolition in a conservation area is prohibited without a listed building consent (see below); and proposals must be formulated publicly for enhancing conservation areas.

buildings", e.g. ecclesiastical buildings used for ecclesiastical purposes, and ancient monuments.

It is a criminal offence to cause any "listed building" to be demolished or altered "in any manner which would affect its character as a building of special architectural or historic interest", without first obtaining and complying with a "listed building consent" from the local planning authority or the Secretary of State, except when works have to be done as a matter of urgency. A consent may be granted subject to conditions, contravention of which is also a criminal offence. A planning permission which expressly specifies works involving interference with a listed building operates as a consent and may include conditions requiring works for preserving, restoring or reconstructing the building so far as is practicable (1971 Act, Sections 55–6; Housing and Planning Act 1986, Section 40 and Schedule 9).

The procedure for applying for listed building consents, and for appeals and revocations, is very similar to the procedure in ordinary cases of planning permission, as is the procedure for listed building enforcement notices and purchase notices (1971 Act, Schedule 11). Compensation is payable for restrictions on consent to works (other than demolition) not amounting to development (see Chapter 25). If an owner fails to keep a listed building in proper repair, a county council or other local authority or the Secretary of State may first serve a "repairs notice" and, if this is not complied with after two months, may then compulsorily purchase the property (1971 Act, Sections 114–17).

Control of the display of advertisements is provided for, in the interests of amenity and safety, but not censorship. The details are laid down in regulations. The use of any land for the display of advertisements requires in general an application to the local planning authority for consent, which in normal cases is for periods of five years. Appeal lies to the Secretary of State. There are several categories of display in which consent is "deemed" to be given, including the majority of advertisements of a routine nature and purpose; but "areas of special control" may be declared where restrictions are greater. But if the authority "consider it expedient to do so in the interests of amenity or public safety" they may serve a "discontinuance notice" to terminate the "deemed" consent of most kinds of advertisement enjoying such consent; but there is a right to appeal to the Secretary of State. Contravention of the regulations is a criminal offence. Consent under the regulations is "deemed" to convey planning permission also, should any development be involved (1971 Act, Sections 63–4; Town and Country Planning (Control of Advertisements) Regulations 1984).

The control of caravan sites may also be regarded as a question of amenity. Such control involves questions of public health, and there is authority for the view that control for purposes of public health must not be exercised for purposes of amenity. But there can be little doubt in practice that although control is concerned with health and safety on the caravan site itself it preserves amenity for the neighbourhood of the site.

Planning permission must be sought for caravan sites; but the detailed control of the use of each site is governed by a system of "site licences", obtainable from the local authority (Caravan Sites and Control of Development Act 1960). "There are two authorities which have power to control caravan sites. On the one had, there is the planning authority. . . . On the other hand, there is the site authority. . . . The planning authority ought to direct their attention to matters in outline, leaving the site authority to deal with all matters of detail. Thus the planning authority should ask themselves this broad question: Ought this field to be used as a caravan site at all? If "Yes", they should grant planning permission for it, without going into details as to number of caravans and the like, or imposing any conditions in that regard." Nevertheless—"Many considerations relate both to planning and to site. . . . In all matters there is a large overlap, where a condition can properly be based both on planning considerations and also on site considerations".[12]

It is the "occupier" of land who must apply for a site licence, which must be granted if the applicant has the benefit of a specific planning permission, and withheld if he has not;

[12] *Esdell Caravan Parks Ltd.* v. *Hemel Hempstead Rural District Council* [1965] 3 All E.R. 737, per Lord Denning, M.R.

and it must last as long as that permission lasts, perpetually in a normal case. The practical question, therefore, is what conditions a site licence shall contain. They are "such conditions as the authority may think it necessary or desirable to impose", with particular reference to six main kinds of purpose. Appeal may be made to a magistrates' court against the imposition of any conditions, or a decision or refusal to vary them at any time after imposition, on the ground that as imposed or varied they are "unduly burdensome".

There are several categories of use of land for caravans which are exempted from control, and also additional powers conferred on local authorities in special cases.

Next comes the question of unsightly land: neglected sites, rubbish dumps and the like. Local planning authorities are empowered, when "the amenity of any part of their area, or of any adjoining area, is adversely affected by the condition of land in their area", to serve a notice on the owner and occupier, specifying steps to be taken to remedy the condition of the land (1971 Act, Section 65 as amended). As with enforcement notices, two time limits must also be specified: a period (of twenty-eight days or more) before the notice takes effect, and the time of compliance. Failure to comply is a summary offence (1971 Act, Section 104 as amended).

Appeal lies, at any time before the notice takes effect, to a magistrates' court on any of the following grounds: (a) the condition of the land is not injurious to amenity; (b) the condition of the land reasonably results from a use or operation not contravening planning control; (c) the land is not of a kind to which such a notice applies; (d) the specified steps for compliance are excessive; (e) the specified time for compliance is too short. The magistrates may uphold, quash or vary the notice and "correct any informality, defect or error" if it is not material (1971 Act, Section 105). A further appeal lies to the Crown Court (1971 Act, Section 106).

Finally there is a newly devised system of control over the use of land for hazardous substances. This expression comes from regulations made under the Health and Safety at Work etc Act 1974, but has been imported into planning law by the Housing and Planning Act 1986, Part IV, which inserts a number of additional sections into the Act of 1971.[13] Control will relate to the placing of the "controlled quantity" of "hazardous substances" on land, and these expressions will be defined by the Secretary of State in appropriate regulations. The local planning authorities will act as "hazardous substance authorities"; and there will be a system of consents, conditions, appeals and enforcement very similar to planning control.

8. PLANNING COMPENSATION AND TAXATION OF BETTERMENT

After the abolition of development charges in 1952 there was, for thirteen years, no tax on the enjoyment of development value as such, which since 1947 has come to be regarded as synonymous with "betterment" (though the latter term previously meant the overall increase in the value of land caused by improvements of neighbouring land by public works). From 1965 to 1967 "betterment" was taxed as a "capital gain".

The Land Commission Act 1967 imposed a charge on betterment, this time called "betterment levy" and restricted initially to 40 per cent. A successor to the Central Land Board (referred to earlier in this Chapter), termed the Land Commission, was set up to collect it. The Land Commission was abolished in 1971; but "betterment" continued to be taxed, as a capital gain, and in 1974 this capital gain became treated for tax purposes as if it were income. The Development Land Tax Act 1976, introduced a tax on "realised development value", namely development land tax; but this was repealed by the Finance Act 1985, and "betterment" has fallen back once more into the scope of capital gains tax.

The converse of appropriating "betterment" to the community is awarding compensation to owners who are deprived of it by the community in consequence of planning restrictions. Detailed examination of planning compensation procedures is dealt with in later Chapters, but it will be

---

[13] Sections 1A, 1B, 58B to 58N, and 101B. The Town and Country Planning (Use Classes) Order 1987 excludes from its scope the use of land for keeping hazardous substances above "a notifiable quantity" thereon.

convenient here to explain the legal basis of this compensation in outline.

To begin with, the statutes require two main distinctions to be drawn. The first distinction is between (a) restrictions on development imposed at the outset by a refusal (or conditional grant) of planning permission and (b) restrictions imposed as an afterthought by revocation or modification of permission already granted. The second distinction is between (a) "new" development and (b) development set out in Schedule 8 to the Town and Country Planning Act 1971. "New development" is, by definition, such development as is not listed in that Schedule.

Part VIII of the 1971 Act provides that restrictions on development imposed by way of revocation, modification or discontinuance orders, since they are in effect regarded as interference with the enjoyment of development value previously conceded to an owner by the grant of planning permission, are fully compensatable by the local planning authority. Restrictions on development imposed at the outset—i.e. because the original application for permission is itself refused, or granted subject to conditions—are fully compensatable, by the local planning authority, but only if the restricted development is within Schedule 8. If, however, the restricted development is within Part I of the Eighth Schedule the compensation is only obtainable in the event of compulsory purchase (including purchase notices). Part I comprises (a) rebuilding of existing or demolished buildings, but only within certain limits, and (b) conversion of houses into flats. Part II development, where compensation is payable in the event of planning restrictions as well as compulsory purchase, comprises (a) alterations and extensions of buildings, within certain limits, (b) extensions of particular uses in land or buildings, again within certain limits, and (c) various other special cases. The compensation, when payable, will cover the loss of development value caused by the restriction of Schedule 8 development on the land in question.

Restrictions imposed at the outset on applications to carry out "new" development are only exceptionally compensatable; though when they are the compensation is payable by the Secretary of State. The underlying principle is peculiar. It will be remembered how the payment of compensation for expropriation of development values was suspended after 1952 when development charges were abolished. The Town and Country Planning Act 1954 enacted that rights to the benefit of "established claims" to that compensation, termed "claim holdings", were to be adapted to a new purpose. They would be transformed into a passport to future compensation for restrictions imposed at the outset on "new" development, in certain specific cases.

The "claim holding" was converted into a right in land and renamed the "unexpended balance of established development value" (or "U.X.B."). From 1955 onwards the sum (if any) certified by the Secretary of State as the U.X.B. for particular land represents the limit to which (and no further) compensation is payable by him for depreciation caused by restrictions at the outset on "new" development. Moreover, there are several categories of restriction which do not qualify for this compensation, so it is of limited application. This compensation code is now re-enacted in Part VII of the Town and Country Planning Act 1971.

The U.X.B., then, is used up by the payment of this kind of planning compensation, which, as far as it goes, is a way of realising the development value of land. Other ways, which also use up the U.X.B., include the receipt of compulsory purchase compensation and the actual carrying out of "new" development. Compensation over £20 is repayable to the Secretary of State if permission is later granted for certain substantial kinds of development, and such development is carried out; but this obligation to repay cannot be enforced unless a compensation notice has been recorded in the local land charges register for the area and disclosed to any subsequent owner of the land on the occasion of an official search of that register. The same applies where the original compensation was paid for a revocation or modification order; but, since in such a case the local planning authority would have paid it, the Secretary of State, who receives the repayment, must pass it on to that authority. For this reason he is empowered to contribute to revocation or modification compensation to the extent that U.X.B. compensation would have been payable had the restrictions been imposed in response to the original planning application; and if he has done this he is entitled to retain that amount of any repayment made to him in such circumstances.

CHAPTER 16

Principles of the Law of Compulsory Purchase and Compensation

1. LEGAL BASIS OF COMPULSORY PURCHASE

THERE ARE numerous Acts of Parliament under which Government departments, local or public authorities, or statutory undertakings, may carry out schemes for the general benefit of the community involving the acquisition of land or interference with owners' proprietary rights.

Where an owners' property is taken under statutory powers he is entitled to compensation as of right, unless the Act which authorises the acquisition expressly provides otherwise. Where no interest in land is taken but a property is depreciated in value by the exercise of statutory powers, the owner's right to compensation depends on the terms of the Act under which these powers are exercised.

For a detailed account of the law on the subject the reader should consult one of the standard text-books on the subject.[1] The present chapter is confined to a brief outline of the law such as will provide the necessary background to the principles involved in compulsory purchase valuations.

Compulsory purchase of land normally brings into play four main sets of statutory provisions, as follows. First, there is the authorising Act, normally a public general act authorising a public body or class of public bodies (e.g. county councils) to carry out some specified function, and going on to state (a) whether such a body may acquire land for the purpose, (b) whether they may buy it compulsorily, (c) whether they may obtain power to do this by compulsory purchase

---

[1] See "Compulsory Purchase and Compensation" 2nd Edition by B. Denyer-Green (Estates Gazette Ltd. 1985); "Law of Compulsory Purchase and Compensation" (4th Edition 1984) by Keith Davies (Butterworths Ltd.); "Guide to Compulsory Purchase and Compensation" (5th Edition 1984) by J. K. Boynton (Oyez Publications); Encyclopedia of Compulsory Purchase and Compensation (Sweet & Maxwell Ltd.).

order specifying the land required, and (d) if so what procedure is to be followed when making the C.P.O. There is now a standardised procedure laid down by the Acquisition of Land Act 1981, though alternative procedures are occasionally specified instead, for example, Part IX of the Housing Act 1985, which makes special provision for slum clearance. Second therefore, is the Act of 1981 (or such alternative code as the authorising Act may prescribe), which governs the making of the C.P.O.; and it may be said that the great majority of acquisitions are made under that Act. Third is the Compulsory Purchase Act 1965, which has to all intents and purposes replaced the Lands Clauses Consolidation Act of 1845 and governs the actual procedure for acquisition after the C.P.O. has sanctioned it, supplemented by provisions in the Compulsory Purchase (Vesting Declarations) Act 1981 and in the Land Compensation Act 1973. Fourth is the Land Compensation Act 1961, which contains the current rules for assessing compensation insofar as it relates directly to land values; these, too, are supplemented by provisions in the Land Compensation Act 1973.

Disputes over compulsory purchase fall broadly into two main classes, depending on whether or not they relate to the assessment of compensation. If they do (and also in one or two special cases to be mentioned below) they must be brought before the Lands Tribunal, a specialised body set up under the Lands Tribunal Act 1949 and staffed by valuers and lawyers. Otherwise they should normally be brought before the High Court. Appeal lies to the Court of Appeal not only from the High Court but also from the Lands Tribunal (though on a point of law only, by way of case stated, and within six weeks of the Tribunal's decision).

2. COMPULSORY PURCHASE PROCEDURE

Any acquiring authority who are empowered by an appropriate authorising Act to select and acquire compulsorily the particular land they need by C.P.O. procedure must normally make the C.P.O. in accordance with the procedure laid down in the Acquisition of Land Act 1981. This involves making the order in draft, and submitting it to a "confirming authority", which will be the appropriate Minister or Secretary of State unless of course he himself is acquiring the land. There must be prior press publicity and notification to the owners and occupiers of the land, and the hearing of objections by an inspector from the Ministry or Department concerned. Statutory inquiries procédure rules for hearings and inquiries are in force, closely parallel with those discussed above in relation to planning appeals. The order may be confirmed, with or without modifications, or rejected. If confirmed it takes effect when the acquiring authority publish a notice in similar manner to the notice of the draft order and serve it on the owners and occupiers concerned. The order cannot be challenged (except perhaps on the ground of nullity) apart from the standard procedure for appeal to the High Court within six weeks on the ground of ultra vires or a procedural defect substantially prejudicing the appellant.

The C.P.O. will lapse, in relation to any of the land comprised in it, unless it is acted on within three years. When the authority wish to act on the order they must serve a notice to treat on the persons with interests in the land to be acquired, requiring them to submit details of their interests and their claims for compensation. When the compensation is agreed in each case, it and the notice to treat together amount to an enforceable contract for the sale of the land. This is then subject to completion by the execution of a conveyance in the same way as a private land transaction.[2]

There is, however, an alternative procedure at the authority's option whereby the notice to treat and the conveyance are combined in a "general vesting declaration". The authority must notify the owners and occupiers concerned, in the same notice as that which states that the C.P.O. is in force (or a separate and later notice), that they intend to proceed in this manner by making a vesting declaration not less than two months ahead. This, when made, will by unilateral action vest the title to the land in the authority at a date not less than twenty-eight days after notification to the owners concerned; and it will by and large have the same consequences as if a notice to treat were served.[3]

[2] Compulsory Purchase Act 1965, Sections 4, 5, 23.
[3] Compulsory Purchase (Vesting Declarations) Act 1981.

Freeholds and leaseholds, both legal and equitable, are capable of compulsory acquisition. Leasehold tenancies with a year or less to run, including periodic tenancies, are not subject to acquisition and compensation but allowed to run out, after due service of notice to quit if necessary; although if the authority desire possession quickly they can take it subject to payment of compensation for the loss caused. An authority cannot normally, without clear statutory authorisation, take rights over land in the limited form of an easement or other right less than full possession (even a stratum of land beneath the surface). For example, in *Sovmots Ltd v. Secretary of State for the Environment* (1976) the House of Lords quashed a compulsory purchase order for acquisition of a lease and a sub-lease (not the freehold) of certain property, together with new easements of access and support which would be required because only the upper part of a building was to be taken, on the ground that appropriate statutory authority was lacking. But if the authority acquire a dominant tenement they acquire the easements appurtant to it, as in private conveyancing; and if they acquire a servient tenement they either allow the easements and other servitudes over it to subsist without interference or else pay compensation for "injurious affection" to the dominant land if they do so interfere.

If part only of an owner's land is to be acquired, this is "severance". The owner of "any house, building or factory" or of "a park or garden belonging to a house" can require the authority to take all or none; but the authority can counter this by saying that to take part only will not cause any "material detriment", and any such dispute has to be settled by the Lands Tribunal. Similar rules now apply to farms.[4]

Unjustifiable delay by the authority after service of a notice to treat may, in an extreme case, amount to abandonment of the acquisition.[5] As for making actual entry on the land, the authority are not normally entitled to do this until completion and the payment of compensation, unless they first

---

[4] Compulsory Purchase Act 1965, Section 8; Land Compensation Act 1973, Sections 53–8.
[5] *Grice v. Dudley Corporation* [1957] 2 All E.R. 504.

serve a "notice of entry"[6]; and entry before payment of compensation entitles an owner to receive interest on the compensation to be paid.

Many acquisitions by authorities are made by agreement, but are mostly under the shadow of compulsory powers and consequently involve the same rules of compensation. Obligations owed to third parties, as in restrictive covenants, do not normally involve the expropriated owner in liability, and the third party should seek compensation from the authority if there is any breach in such a case. On the other hand an owner must not increase the authority's liability to compensation by creating new tenancies and other rights in the land or carrying out works on it after service of the notice to treat, if any such action "was not reasonably necessary and was undertaken with a view to obtaining compensation or increased compensation".[7]

3. COMPULSORY PURCHASE COMPENSATION

The detailed rules of compensation are discussed later in Chapters 27–29. It will, however, be convenient to consider them briefly in outline here in order to demonstrate the legal basis on which they rest.

The acquiring authority must compensate the expropriated owner for the land taken, by way of purchase price, and for any depreciation of land retained by him, as well as for "all damage directly consequent on the taking".[8]

The basis of compensation for the taking or depreciation of land is "market value", namely "the amount which the land if sold in the open market by a willing seller might be expected to realise". "Special suitability or adaptability" of the land which depends solely on "a purpose to which it could be applied only in pursuance of statutory powers, or for which there is no market apart from the special needs of a particular purchaser or the requirements of any authority

---

[6] Compulsory Purchase Act 1965, Section 11.
[7] Acquisition of Land Act 1981, Section 4.
[8] *Harvey v. Crawley Development Corporation* [1957] 1 All E.R. 504, per Denning, L.J.

possessing compulsory purchase powers", must be disregarded. There must be no addition to nor deduction from market value purely on the ground that the purchase is compulsory, nor any addition specifically on account of the project to be carried out (on the claimant's land or any other land) by the acquiring authority. An increase in the value of adjoining land of the owner not taken by the authority, if it is attributable solely to the acquiring authority's project, must be "set off" against compensation.[9]

Special situations are, however, catered for. If the property acquired comprises one or more dwellings "unfit for habitation", then normally it is only the market value of the site (as distinct from the dwellings) which is to be taken into account.[10] And if the property has been developed and used for a purpose which has no effective market value, such as a church, then the Lands Tribunal may order that compensation "be assessed on the basis of the reasonable cost of equivalent reinstatement", if "satisfied that reinstatement in some other place is bona fide intended".[11]

These intricate legal rules are intended for the guidance of valuers rather than lawyers. Valuers engaged in the assessment of the compensation are required, subject to such guidance, to reach a figure which will put the expropriated owner in a position as near as reasonably possible to that in which he would find himself if there had been no compulsory acquisition and he had sold his land in an ordinary private sale.

Market value, however, has in any case two distinct main elements: "existing use value' and "prospective development value". Since development is not lawful without planning permission, the absence of permission will inhibit purchasers from paying any amount over and above "existing use" value, whether the land is built on or vacant in its present state of development. Before the days of planning control, "prospective development value" over and above "existing use value" depended on market demand. It must not be forgotten that this is still true. "It is not planning permission by itself

[9] Land Compensation Act 1961, Sections 5–9 and Schedule 1.
[10] Housing Act 1985, Section 585; Land Compensation Act 1961, Schedule 2.
[11] Land Compensation Act 1961, Section 5 (rule 5).

which increases value. It is planning permission coupled with demand."[12]

Assessing the existence of demand is essentially a question of valuers' expert evidence; though of course the Lands Tribunal is better qualified than a court to pronounce on such evidence.

Assessing the availability of planning permission, however, calls for special statutory rules. This is because there are many cases where planning permission is refused purely because some proposed private development, which might otherwise be acceptable and if so would be capable of giving rise to appreciable development value, is ruled out by the impending compulsory purchase notwithstanding that this purchase will often be for the purpose of a public works project giving rise to little or no development value.

"Assumptions as to planning permission" are therefore authorised by statute. The most useful of these turn on the allocation or "zoning" in the current development plan of areas of land which include the owner's property for uses which command a lucrative development value: residential, commercial or industrial. There may be a range of such uses. But permission can only be assumed it it is also reasonable to do so in relation to the particular circumstances of the land itself. If the development plan does not "zone" the land in this way the owner (or the authority) can apply to the local planning authority for a "certificate of appropriate alternative development" in relation to the particular circumstances of the land. Appeal lies to the Secretary of State; and from him in turn lies the usual limited right of appeal within six weeks to the High Court (Land Compensation Act 1961, Sections 17–22, as amended) on points of law.

In addition to purchase price compensation there is compensation for "injurious affection"—i.e. depreciation of land retained. This is "severance" if caused by a reduction in the value of the land retained greater than that caused by the reduction in size. Depreciation caused by what is done on the land taken by the acquiring authority is closely analogous

---

[12] *Viscount Camrose v. Basingstoke Corporation* [1966] 3 All E.R. 161 per Lord Denning M.R.

to damages in tort for private nuisance, though it may well include loss not compensatable in tort.[13] But if the harm done goes beyond what is authorised by the statutory powers of the acquiring authority, then it will in any case be unlawful and so compensatable (if at all) in tort and not as "injurious affection".

It is also possible to obtain compensation for "injurious affection" when no land has been acquired from the claimant. Here it is necessary to prove four things: (a) the loss is caused by activity authorised by statute, (b) it would be actionable at common law if it were not so authorised, (c) it is strictly a depreciation in land value, and (d) it arises from the carrying out of works on the compulsorily acquired land and not from its subsequent use. These four rules are customarily attributed to the decision of the House of Lords in *Metropolitan Board of Works v. McCarthy* (1874).[14] But depreciation caused by the use of public works, including highways and aerodromes, is in many cases now compensatable under Part I of the Land Compensation Act 1973, if attributable to "physical factors". The claim period runs from one to three years after the use begins.

Another head of compensation is "disturbance", which is not strictly land value but "must . . . refer to the fact of having to vacate the premises".[15] Thus it may include the loss of business profits and goodwill, removal expenses and the cost of acquiring new premises. It has been held that to claim for "disturbance" an owner must forego "prospective development value" in his purchase price compensation; that is to say his "true loss" is whichever is the higher: "existing use" value plus "prospective development" value or "existing use" value plus "disturbance".[16]

Disturbance compensation is (illogically) regarded in law as an integral part of land value. It is therefore not payable where the acquiring body, having expropriated the landlord,

[13] *Buccleuch (Duke of) v. Metropolitan Board of Works* (1872) L.R. 5 H.L. 418. On this see Chapter 28.

[14] L.R. 7 H.L. 243. The claimant's business premises in London became less valuable when an adjoining public dock (a public right of way) was destroyed by the construction of the Victoria Embankment at Blackfriars.

[15] *Lee v. Minister of Transport* [1965] 2 All E.R. 986 per Davies, L.J.

[16] *Horn v. Sunderland Corporation* [1941] 1 All E.R. 480.

do not expropriate a short-term tenant but displace him by notice to quit. In such cases the Land Compensation Act 1973 (Sections 37–8) provides for "disturbance payments" by the acquiring body to the tenant (unless he is an agricultural tenant, for whom separate compensation provisions exist). The 1973 Act also authorises the payment of "farm loss payments" to displaced owner-occupiers of farms (Sections 34–6) and "home loss payments" to displaced occupants of dwellings who have lived there for five years (Sections 29–33).

A claimant "must once for all make one claim for all damages which can be reasonably foreseen".[17] The date of the notice to treat fixes the interests which may be acquired, but does not govern compensation which, as the House of Lords held in the case of *Birmingham Corporation v. West Midland Baptist (Trust) Association (Incorporated)* (1969), must be assessed as at the time of making the assessment, or of taking possession of the land (if earlier), or of the beginning of "equivalent reinstatement".

4. COMPULSORY PURCHASE IN PLANNING

The Town and Country Planning Act 1971 (supplemented by the Land Compensation Act 1973) is itself the authorising Act for certain kinds of compulsory purchase of land; and Part VI of the 1971 Act authorises acquisition "in connection with development and for other planning purposes". This means "to secure the treatment as a whole, by development, redevelopment or improvement, or partly by one and partly by another method", either of the land itself or of adjoining land; or to relocate population or industry or to replace open space; or "to acquire the land immediately for a purpose which it is necessary to achieve, in the interests of the proper planning of an area in which the land is situated" (Section 112 of the 1971 Act, as amended). Local authorities in general have this power, subject to the standard compulsory purchase procedure. They can themselves develop land so acquired, but not without the Secretary of State's consent. More usually

[17] *Chamberlain v. West End of London etc. Rail Co.* (1863) 2 B. & S. 617, per Erle, C.J.

they dispose of the land to private developers, "in such manner and subject to such conditions as may appear to them to be expedient".

Another aspect of compulsory purchase in planning, under the 1971 Act (Part IX), is "inverse" compulsory purchase of which there are two species: "purchase notices" and "blight notices". The owners supply the compulsion in these cases, not the acquiring authorities. A purchase notice (Sections 180–191) is served in consequence of an adverse planning decision; but a blight notice (see below) is served in consequence of adverse planning proposals.

If planning permission is in a particular case refused, or granted subject to conditions, so that as a result "the land has become incapable of reasonably beneficial use in its existing state", then an owner may serve a purchase notice on the local borough or district council. If the council are unwilling to accept it they must normally refer it to the Secretary of State who must then exercise his own judgment as to whether the notice is justifiable and ought to be upheld. He must not uphold it merely on the ground that "the land in its existing state and with its existing permissions is substantially less useful to the server", since that is true of nearly all planning refusals. The land must in fact be virtually useless to justify a purchase notice.

A "blight notice" (1971 Act, Sections 192–208, amplified by the Land Compensation Act 1973, Sections 68–76) is served on a prospective acquiring authority. There are four principal requirements: (1) the situation affecting the owner's land must be within one of the "specified descriptions"; (2) the server must be an owner-occupier (or his mortgagee) with an interest "qualified for protection"; (3) he must have made genuine but unsuccessful attempts to sell for a reasonable price on the open market; and (4) the authority must in fact intend to acquire the land. Within two months the authority concerned may serve a counter-notice alleging that any of the above requirements has not been met. The claimant then has two more months in which to refer the dispute to the Lands Tribunal, before whom the burden of proof is on the authority if they deny an intention to acquire any or all of the land but on the claimant in all other cases.

The "specified descriptions" comprise the following situations. The land must be indicated as being required for the functions of a public body in a local plan or, failing that, in a structure plan or, failing that, indicated in a development plan as required for a highway; or as land in or beside the line of a trunk or special road, or sufficiently indicated in writing by the Secretary of State to the local planning authority as required for such a road or selected for a highway by a resolution of a local highway authority; or as land covered by a C.P.O. which has not yet been acted upon, or else subject to compulsory purchase by virtue of a special enactment. Inclusion of land in a slum clearance area, or in road-widening proposals, is also within the "specified descriptions".

To be "qualified for protection" it is necessary to be (a) a freeholder or a leaseholder with over three years to run, as well as (b) a resident owner-occupier of a dwelling or the owner-occupier of either an "agricultural unit" or of other premises with a rateable value not exceeding £2,250. The period of actual occupation must have been six months immediately before serving the blight notice or before leaving the premises unoccupied for not more than twelve months before serving the notice. A mortgagee of a person "qualified for protection" may also serve a blight notice provided that his power of sale has arisen, and he is given an extra six months in which to do so.

CHAPTER 17

Agricultural Property

THE AGRICULTURAL industry is facing a revolution unprecedented since the second world war. The former policy of guaranteed prices with full production regardless of market requirements has now been reversed under the Common Agricultural Policy of the EEC to one of limited production, regulated by price or quota controls, in an attempt to reduce the mountains and lakes of surplus produce in intervention stores. Failure to solve this problem could well bankrupt the EEC.

The valuation of agricultural property has always been a specialist activity but, at this time, even the expert approaches it with extreme caution.

1. FARMS

Valuation for rent

The valuation of farms whether for rent or for sale, is often a humiliating exercise. All the theoretical approaches may have been blended with thirty years' skill and experience to deduce that an annual value of Coldharbour Farm is one hundred pounds a hectare. It is put out to tender, and a genuine farmer—no speculator that is, but the current edition of ten generations never greater than "reasonably skilled in husbandry"—takes it on at one hundred and fifty pounds.

Farm rents are subject to the same laws of supply and demand as rents for other forms of property, but in many ways they seem to make their own rules. One well-established phenomenon is that although they fluctuate with farming prosperity, they have tended to lag behind to the landlord's disadvantage and it is an accepted fact that an investment in agricultural land will provide a modest yield in the form of rent.

However, once let, of the factors which shackle farm rents, most notable is security of tenure. This was first introduced for the life of the existing tenant by the Agricultural Holdings Act 1948; then extended by the Agriculture (Miscellaneous Provisions) Act 1976 to enable a limited class of close relatives satisfying specific requirements to claim a new tenancy on two occasions after the death of the existing tenant; reverting under the Agricultural Holdings Act 1984 to the 1948 Act position. The relevant provisions governing the relationship between landlords and tenants of agricultural holdings are now contained in the Agricultural Holdings Act 1986.

In effect, once a tenant has taken a farm and is farming it tolerably, the landlord cannot get rid of him except for a limited number of reasons. These reasons will be found in Section 26 and Schedule 3 of the 1986 Act. Briefly they are:—

(a) that the holding is let as a Statutory Smallholding by a Smallholding Authority the tenancy commencing after 12 September 1984 and the tenant has reached the age of 65;

(b) that the land is required for a use other than agriculture;

(c) that the tenant has not farmed in accordance with the statutory rules of good husbandry;

(d) that the tenant has not paid his rent, or has failed to remedy previously specified breaches of contract;

(e) that the tenant has caused damage to the reversion by some irremediable breach of contract;

(f) that the tenant has gone bankrupt;

(g) that the tenant has died;

(h) that the Minister has given advance consent to the notice to quit.

A tenancy for two years or more, however clearly specified the term, does not expire by effluxion of time but continues from year to year subject to a minimum of twelve months' notice to quit. If notice to quit emanates from the landlord the tenant can challenge it and, unless one or more of the limited exceptions apply, the notice will fail. Furthermore, Section 3 of the 1986 Act provides that most short-term tenancies are deemed for this purpose to be tenancies from year to year, and thus confers security of tenure upon the tenant.

Sections 35–38 of the 1986 Act extend this security of tenure in respect of tenancies granted before 12 September 1984 to certain defined relatives of a tenant on his death or retirement. Thus when a farm was let prior to this date, the landlord can be denied vacant possession for the life of the tenant and for up to 2 generations of the tenant's relatives. In respect of tenancies granted after 12 September 1984 there are no rights of succession.

The *quid pro quo* for eliminating the succession provisions was a new statutory definition for variation of rent through arbitration (originally in the 1984 Act) now contained in Section 12 of the 1986 Act. Agricultural rents may be referred to arbitration every three years by either the landlord or the tenant. The actual statutory provisions governing this review of rent will be discussed later but the new statutory definition was intended to reduce the rate of increase of agricultural rents. At the time of writing it is clear that previous levels of increase are not at present being achieved but it would be rash to attribute this change solely to the new statutory definition.

Current rents and trends

The 1984 Act was intended to encourage private landowners to offer more tenancies and there is limited evidence suggesting that this is happening. However, as with the new statutory definition of rent, it is questionable to what extent this is due to the legislation rather than the general upheaval which is taking place within the industry. The main stimulator in this matter is more likely to be the fiscal advantage or disadvantage to the landlord of letting land.

The Ministry of Agriculture, Fisheries and Food, in cooperation with the National Farmers' Union, the Country Landowners' Association and the Royal Institution of Chartered Surveyors, conducts an Annual Rent Enquiry covering 22,000 farms, being 33% of all tenanted land in England

and Wales. The latest report[1] indicates an average rent per
hectare for all farms in England of £97·34 which represents
a percentage rise of 1·9 over the mid-October 1986 figure.
This is the lowest increase for many years but, bearing in
mind the new definition of rent, is as expected.

The figures of average rent contained in this report are
of general interest and may also be of assistance to the reader
who has no conception whatever of the rent a farm will command. The valuer, however, is almost always concerned with
the rental value of a particular holding.

Factors affecting rent

Section 12 and Schedule 2 of the 1986 Act set down the
factors to be taken into account in the calculation of the
rent properly payable in respect of agricultural holdings as
follows:—

Amount of Rent

1.—(1) For the purposes of section 12 of this Act, the rent properly payable
in respect of a holding shall be the rent at which the holding might reasonably
be expected to be let by a prudent and willing landlord to a prudent and willing
tenant, taking into account (subject to sub-paragraph (3) and paragraphs 2 and
3 below) all relevant factors, (including in every case) the terms of the tenancy
(including those relating to rent), the character and situation of the holding (including the locality in which it is situated), the productive capacity of the holding and
its related earnings capacity, and the current level of rents for comparable lettings,
as determined in accordance with sub-paragraph (3) below.

(2) In sub-paragraph (1) above, in relation to the holding—
  (a) "productive capacity" means the productive capacity of the holding (taking
      into account fixed equipment and any other available facilities on the hold-
      ing) on the assumption that it is in the occupation of a competent tenant
      practising a system of farming suitable to the holding, and
  (b) "related earning capacity" means the extent to which, in the light of that
      productive capacity, a competent tenant practising such a system of farming
      could reasonably be expected to profit from farming the holding.

(3) In determining for the purposes of that sub-paragraph the current level of
rents for comparable lettings, the arbitrator shall take into account any available
evidence with respect to the rents (whether fixed by agreement between the parties
or by arbitration under this Act) which are, or (in view of rent currently being
tendered) are likely to become, payable in respect of tenancies of comparable
agricultural holdings on terms (other than terms fixing the rent payable) similar
to those of the tenancy under consideration, but shall disregard—

---

[1] MAFF Farm Rents in England and Wales—Results of 1987 Annual Rent
Enquiry. (Stats 42/88).

(a) any element of the rents in question which is due to an appreciable scarcity of comparable holdings available for letting on such terms compared with the number of persons seeking to become tenants of such holdings on such terms,

(b) any element of those rents which is due to the fact that the tenant of, or a person tendering for, any comparable holding is in occupation of other land in the vicinity of that holding that may conveniently be occupied together with that holding, and

(c) any effect on those rents which is due to any allowances or reductions made in consideration of the charging of premiums.

2.—(1) On a reference under section 12 of this Act, the arbitrator shall disregard any increase in the rental value of the holding which is due to—

(a) tenant's improvements or fixed equipment other than improvements executed or equipment provided under an obligation imposed on the tenant by the terms of his contract of tenancy, and

(b) landlord's improvements, in so far as the landlord has received or will receive grants out of money provided by Parliament or local government funds in respect of the execution of those improvements.

(2) In this paragraph—

(a) "tenant's improvements" means any improvements which have been executed on the holding, in so far as they were executed wholly or partly at the expense of the tenant (whether or not that expense has been or will be reimbursed by a grant out of money provided by Parliament or local government funds) without any equivalent allowance or benefit made or given by the landlord in consideration of their execution,

(b) "tenant's fixed equipment" means fixed equipment provided by the tenant, and

(c) "landlord's improvements" means improvements executed on the holding by the landlord.

(3) Where the tenant has held a previous tenancy of the holding, then—

(a) in the definition of "tenant's improvements" in sub-paragraph (2) (a) above, the reference to any such improvements as are there mentioned shall extend to improvements executed during that tenancy, and

(b) in the definition of "tenant's fixed equipment" in sub-paragraph (2) (b), the reference to such equipment as is there mentioned shall extend to equipment provided during that tenancy, excluding, however, any improvement or fixed equipment so executed or provided in respect of which the tenant received any compensation on the termination of that (or any other) tenancy.

(4) For the purposes of sub-paragraph (2) (a) above, the continuous adoption by the tenant of a system of farming more beneficial to the holding—

(a) than the system of farming required by the contract of tenancy, or

(b) in so far as no system is so required, than the system of farming normally practised on comparable agricultural holdings, shall be treated as an improvement executed at his expense.

3. On a reference under section 12 of the Act the arbitrator—

(a) shall disregard any effect on rent of the fact that the tenant who is a party to the arbitration is in occupation of the holding, and

(b) shall not fix the rent at a lower amount by reason of any dilapidation

or deterioration of, or damage to, buildings or land caused or permitted
by the tenant.

The main points to be considered in valuing a farm are:

The general situation. The position on the map, both large
and small scale, has an overall bearing on the value. The
point need not be laboured but, other things being equal,
a farm close to a town with suitable outlets for marketing
produce and perhaps "farm gate" sales is more esteemed
than one situated among untrodden ways.

The lie of the land. The height, aspect, contours and exposure of the farm are features which the practised valuer
instinctively takes into account. All have a bearing on the
cropping and livestock policy. For instance, steep slopes will
inhibit or prohibit arable cultivation and limit the enterprises
to sheep or cattle. High, exposed land will rule out dairying
and limit the livestock to the raising, not the fattening of
livestock; and so on.

Climate and rainfall also are bound up with the farm's
potentialities. Most crops of any value have their special
requirements. The better grasslands, for example, lie in the
wetter districts, while barley and wheat would sooner be
deprived of moisture than sunshine.

The size of the farm. The Ministry of Agriculture survey
of farm rents reveals that small farms normally have higher
rents per hectare than large ones. At the two extremes of
the farms sampled in 1985, those below 10 hectares averaged
£132 per hectare while those over 10 hectares averaged £90
per hectare.

The land itself, that is to say, the quality, the composition
and the texture of the soil. Fertilising and manuring will do
much to raise the productive capacity of any soil, but with
naturally infertile soils the law of diminishing returns—the
point at which the extra few units of nitrogen cost more than
the extra yield is worth—operates early. For this reason a
smallholding of good black fen is more valuable than a parish
of light sand. Whereas an unfamiliar soil needs a chemical
analysis to suggest its full potentialities, much can be learnt
by physical inspection. To this end a soil auger, or at second
best a spade, is an invaluable aid towards assessing quality,
depth and the height of the water table. At the same time

the valuer will note which fields have been tile or mole drained, and whether the drainage system is being maintained, particularly by attention to the outfalls.

Any quota allocated to the land. The valuer must have regard to any limitation on the cropping of the land that may be imposed by a quota restriction, of which milk quotas introduced in 1983 are an example. This book does not, however, deal with the complexities of quota which should be considered by a specialist adviser.

Water supply to fields. While much of the value of a farm may depend on measures taken to get water off, it may cost a good deal in labour and materials to get it on. Cattle are avid water bibbers and on a grass farm where the beasts do the round of the pastures a system of field troughs with a piped supply is essential. Few livestock farms lack this equipment today but any that do will command a very low rent, until the deficiency is remedied.

Roads and approaches. Apart from the desirability of concrete contact with the outside world, all-weather access is necessary within the farm itself from yard to field and from one field to another. Farm roads must be of adequate strength to stand up to tractors and machinery. This is an important matter bearing in mind the size of today's vehicles.

Fences and gates. Their maintenance is normally the tenant's job, legally so in the absence of written agreement to the contrary. Good fences, it is said, make good neighbours. With livestock farming they also make good bargaining points when negotiating rents.

Main water and electricity are virtually essential. If the installations are out of date or absent, and the landlord does not undertake to provide them, the tenant will reckon on providing them himself probably on borrowed money. The rent will suffer accordingly.

The cottages. Today's farm operatives are highly qualified employees, conversant with modern technology including new-fangled computers. Dwellings, therefore, should match the quality of the employee and, as a minimum, a bath, indoor sanitation and a shed for at least one car are required. Where the farm cottages fall appreciably short of this minimum, labour is hard to attract and the farm is correspondingly less valuable. In addition to the quality of the cottages, their quantity must be considered in relation to the farming system. There are no hard and fast rules, for an arable farm will need proportionately more workers than a hill sheep farm, but one service cottage per 50 hectares is some sort of guide. It is a fact that the number of cottages per holding has a direct bearing on rent: the greater the number the higher the rent per hectare.

The buildings are of paramount importance. At least they should be adequate to house the livestock, machinery and produce which the farm requires and yields. Those to do with dairying should conform to the provisions of the Milk and Dairies Regulations, while the growing demand for multi-purpose buildings adds a cachet to those adaptable for a variety of enterprises. Strictly specialist buildings, e.g., pig fattening or deep litter houses, should be regarded with some reserve, for it is not every farmer who aims to grow rich on the profits from bacon and eggs. They may be a liability, adding nothing to the rental value.

Other factors which influence rent include the responsibility for repairs and maintenance. If a tenant accepted a full repairing lease, he would naturally expect to pay a lower rent than if the landlord shared the burden. This factor, and the responsibility for outgoings, are discussed later on in connection with capital valuations.

Methods of Approach

There are now two principal methods of valuing for rent, based on:—

(1) The current levels of rents of comparable holdings. This is likely to include a field-by-field valuation suitably adjusted to take account of the differences in terms and conditions of tenancy, fixed equipment and other relevant factors to the subject holding.

(2) The productive capacity and the related earning capacity of the holding. For simplicity this is the profit achievable by a competent tenant practising a suitable system of farming.

To illustrate these methods, each will be applied to the same farm, namely:

A farm of 180 hectares in the south-east of England. The soil is brick earth of high fertility and the fields are large and easily worked. There is a fair range of buildings with yard and parlour suitable for a dairy herd of 100 cows with followers. A pleasant farmhouse is in a very good state of repair. The farm is in a good situation and there is an adequate labour supply locally.

A prospective tenant has had twenty years' experience of farming, much of it in dairying and cash cropping. He has sufficient capital to run a farm of the size. After careful inspection of the land and buildings he envisages the following farm plan:—

Cropping.—140 ha of tillage. This will give each year 85 ha of cereals, mainly wheat and oil seed rape. Previous experience on the farm indicates high yields with an average of 8·0 tonnes. 25 ha of sugar beet with an estimated yield of 36 tonnes. 26 ha one-year leys and 40 ha of permanent grassland complete the cropping. The leys and permanent grass will be used for grazing, silage and hay and this should provide sufficient forage for the dairy herd and followers. The cereals will all be sold off. There should be a surplus of straw and at least 100 tonnes should be available for sale.

Stocking.—100 Friesian dairy cows averaging 4,500 litres with 20 heifers in a self-contained dairy herd. The best twenty cows and heifers will be put to a dairy bull for replacements. The others will be crossed with a beef bull and the calves sold off at a week old.

Labour.—The farm will be run with a labour force of two regular workers consisting of a cowman and tractor driver with the tenant undertaking relief milking and standby duties. Most of the arable work, including the sugar beet harvesting, will be highly mechanised, but a considerable amount of contract labour will be required for thinning the sugar beet.

(1) The current levels of rent of comparable holdings

The Field-by-Field Valuation

This is the skill-and-experience method, astounding to client and pupil alike. Each field on the farm is inspected, and spot-figured at so much a hectare. If the farm is much of a muchness throughout, one figure per hectare may be applied to the whole. More likely the valuer will differentiate between the best arable, the medium and the poor.

A spot valuation requires a sound knowledge of rental values in the neighbourhood, since it is a comparative method. Because of the slow turnover in farm tenancies since the war, and the relative paucity of rental arbitrations, such knowledge is not always easily available. Where a farm has recently been let by agreement, or the rent adjusted by agreement or arbitration, the amount agreed upon or awarded does, however, have a habit of making itself known, either brazenly or through the grapevine.

In the course of his field-by-field assessment, the valuer will have in mind those factors outlined above: the physical features, the soil quality, the provision and state of cottages, fences, roads and other fixed equipment and the exclusions. The farmhouse and cottages are not normally valued separately; their adequacy is taken into account in assessing the thing as a whole. Thus if there were two farms otherwise indistinguishable, but one was better equipped than the other, there would be a case for rentally valuing A at a few pounds a hectare more than B.

A field-by-field valuation of our example farm might work out thus:

Arable land:
First class	120 ha at £110 =	£13,200
Second class	12 ha at £88 =	1,056

Permanent pasture:
First class	30 ha at £102 =	3,060
Second class	10 ha at £80 =	800

Coppices, roads,
buildings etc.	8 ha at £54 =	432
	180 ha	£18,548

The figure for "coppices, roads, etc." is to some extent arbitrary: the total can be satisfactorily rounded to £18,500. This represents an average of £103·00 per hectare.

The Comparison Method

In assessing the open market rent the evidence of comparables is invaluable but the following information is required by the valuer to analyse the results.

(1) The farm should be in the same district.
(2) The size and fixed equipment should be the same.

(3) The system of husbandry should be similar.
(4) The terms and conditions of the letting together with the tenancy agreement should be considered and compared.
(5) The valuer should consider all other relevant factors concerning the re-letting.

This method involves the direct comparison of facts and a conclusion. If no direct comparables are available then it is possible to make use of statistical evidence of rental levels and increases as follows:

(1) Guidance on an estate, county or national basis using a wide sample of farms of a similar type and system.
(2) Actual rents obtained when let on the open market normally by tender.
(3) Percentage increases of rents obtained over a certain period by open market lettings, by negotiations and by arbitrations.

Finally the present imbalance between supply and demand of farms to let previously mentioned must be considered and the extent to which this is reflected in the tenders received in the form of a premium or "key money" for which an adjustment must be made in accordance with Clause 1 (3) (a), (b) & (c) of Schedule 2 of the 1986 Act set out above.

(2) The productive capacity and the related earning capacity

With this method one tends to examine the matter from the tenant's point of view. It entails drawing up a budget of estimated annual returns and expenditure based on what a competent farmer would consider a suitable system for the farm in question, be it milk production, beef fattening, arable cropping, or a bit of everything. The balance between outgoings and incomings represents a combination of the farmer's personal income and what he would be prepared to pay for rent.

On our example farm the annual budget[2] might be estimated thus:

50 ha grass for dairy herd
16 ha grass for dairy followers
60 ha winter wheat
25 ha sugar beet
25 ha oil seed rape
 4 ha roads, buildings and coppices

GROSS MARGIN

100 Freisians diary cows at £500 per cow	£50,000
20 Friesian dairy followers at £270 per heifer	5,400
60 ha winter wheat at £510 per ha	30,600
25 ha sugar beet at £590 per ha	14,750
25 ha oil seed rape at £560 per ha	14,000
	£114,750

Less FIXED COSTS

Labour

Dairy cowman	£9,125	
Tractor driver	8,200	
Tenant	9,700	
		27,025

Machinery

Repairs, fuel oil, tax,			
etc., £105 per ha	18,900		
Depreciation	18,900		
Interest charges	10,000		
Miscellaneous	6,000		
		53,800	80,825
Net Farm income			£33,925

Having produced a net farm income of £33,925, the next

[2] The student seeking statistics from which he can make calculations similar to these is referred to: Farm Management Pocket Book by John Nix, 18th Edition, published by School of Rural Economics and Related Studies, Wye College, also the Ministry of Agriculture's "The Farm as a Business" and "Farm Incomes in England and Wales" published by HM Stationery Office.

question is what proportion of that might be earmarked for rent? Looking at it through the tenant's eyes, the more he pays in rent, the less he will have available for spending. A younger farmer eager to progress, would probably be content with a lower income for the sake of getting hold of such a desirable farm; indeed if he hasn't been long at the game he may have to borrow capital to stock and equip the farm. By contrast, an established farmer with family responsibilities and accustomed to high living may have firmer ideas about the income he requires.

In the witness box one might quite properly evade a categorical answer by submitting that, factually speaking, the collation of rents with profits on farms newly let within the past few years has shown considerable variation. If we take 55 per cent as an acceptable proportion, our example farm is worth £18,658 a year, or, say £18,500 or £103 per hectare.

Valuation for Sale or Purchase

As with other forms of real property, the capital value of a farm is ascertained by estimating the rental value, deducting various outgoings, and multiplying the result by so many years' purchase.

Unless the farm has been recently let at its full fair rent, it will be necessary to assess the rental value as already described.

Outgoings

This subject is dealt with in Chapter 6; the following summary includes a number of outgoings which are peculiar to agricultural property.

Drainage rates are levied by water authorities towards the cost of keeping rivers in order. There are two types:

(i) Owners' drainage rates, which are applied to new works or the improvement of existing works.
(ii) Occupiers' drainage rates, for the maintenance of existing works.

Both rates in the first instance are payable by the occupier, but if he is a tenant he can recover the owner's rate from his landlord. He may, however, covenant to be responsible for both.[3]

Drainage charges. Under the Land Drainage Act 1976 a water authority may meet the expenses of drainage works through "drainage charges". These are levied on the occupier, but a landlord may contract to pay them.

Repairs are likely to be the highest of all outgoings. What proportion of the gross rent should be deducted will depend on the general condition of the fixed equipment and, where a farm is let, the respective liabilities of landlord and tenant.

Repairing covenants and customs used to be diverse and incomplete, until a generally welcome uniformity was introduced in 1948 through The Agriculture (Maintenance, Repair and Insurance of Fixed Equipment) Regulations current edition 1973 (S.I. 1973 No. 1473) as amended 1988 (S.I. 1988 No. 281). Familiarly known as the Repairs Regs., or the Model Clauses, these regulations divide between the landlord and tenant of an agricultural holding the responsibility of maintaining, repairing and insuring the fixed equipment on it—and "fixed equipment" embraces not only buildings but fences, hedges, ditches, practically every immovable short of the land itself. Specific liabilities, from replacing the burnt-out farmhouse to cleansing the duckpond, occupy two closely printed pages.

The regulations apply to all farms which are let on an oral agreement; previously responsibility depended on local custom, an authority often so vague that the parties would drown in the Glebe Brook whilst arguing whose was the liability to renew the blocked culvert thanks to which the said brook was about to burst its banks.

Written agreement will still override the Model Clauses, although if it deals with the liabilities in a manner substantially different, either party may request an adjustment to conform with the regulations, and if need be refer the matter to arbitration.

In determining the landlord's liability for repairs, there-

---

[3] The Agriculture (Miscellaneous Provisions) Act 1968, Section 21 provides that drainage charges shall be charged per acre on chargeable land instead of on the annual value of hereditaments.

fore, the terms of any existing agreement must be reviewed in the light of the regulations and their trend towards universality.

The amount to be deducted for annual repairs will further depend on:

(a) the class, situation and character of the buildings and other fixed equipment;
(b) their construction, age, size and condition;
(c) the use to which they are put;
(d) their suitability to alternative systems of farming;
(e) any excess of buildings over the normal requirements of the holding.

As a rough check it is possible to express repairs as a percentage of the rental value say 15–25 per cent although with the wide variations of rents this is only a guide.

Valuers very often base their repairs allowance on so much a hectare rather than x per cent of the rent. This may vary from £6·00 to £20·00 a hectare.

Insurance and management are not always separately deducted. Where the Model Clauses apply to a farm, the landlord is under an obligation "to keep the farmhouse, cottages and farm buildings insured to their full value against loss or fire". The response to that may well be to take it automatically into account when estimating a figure for repairs. Frequently no allowance is made for management, especially when an individual farm, as distinct from an estate, is being valued. Where these two outgoings are separately assessed, 10 to 15 per cent is a reasonable range for insurance and management.

Other Tenancy Arrangements

Whilst by far the greatest number of tenancies follow the statutory division of responsibilities, the valuer will discover full repairing and insuring agreements and term leases with differing repair clauses. These were used primarily by the financial institutions when they were investing heavily in the agricultural market to meet their requirement of a clear uncomplicated return which could be forecast. They have not, however, proved generally popular.

Years' Purchase

A study of farm sales over the past twenty years shows a variation in Y.P. from 14 to 89 times the rent being paid for them. The average remained remarkably constant at 25 Y.P. Admittedly these figures were based on gross rents and on farms sold without vacant possession; nevertheless, they serve to illustrate the vanity of dogmatising At the time of writing, few tenanted farm sales are taking place and selecting a yield and a Y.P. is inspired quesswork.

Example capital valuation. For this we again exhibit the farm lately valued for rent at £18,500 per annum.

Rental value		£18,500
Less—Repairs and insurance at £14·50		
per ha, say	£2,610	
Management at 12%	2,220	4,830
Net income		13,670
Years' purchase at 6%		16·67
		£227,879
Capital value, say		£225,000

£1,250 per hectare is an acceptable figure for this kind of tenanted farm.

The valuation of farms with vacant possession is a very different matter, and is largely one of collecting and comparing recent market prices of similar farms. In areas where farming is the prime concern of potential purchasers, the factors to be considered are broadly similar to those set out above. In other areas, particularly those within commuting distance of a major business centre, the value of the house may be the prime consideration and the land merely an appendage thereto. Values of vacant possession farms in 1987 averaged £3,750 per acre[4] but this figure must be regarded as heavily distorted by the residential factor.

2. WOODLANDS

Woodlands comprise two forms of assets which are generally valued separately; the site and the trees growing on it. The valuation of woodlands is a specialised subject the details of which fall outside the scope of this book and the reader requiring further information is referred to Chapter 1 of "Valuation: Principles into Practice" (3rd Edition 1988) Ed. W. H. Rees.

There are a number of statutory constraints upon woodland, not least being the need to obtain a felling licence from the Forestry Commission before the timber may be felled and that licence may carry with it a requirement to re-plant which can be a costly operation. The woodland may also be Ancient woodland—woodland that has been consistently forest for 200 years—or the subject of designation under the Wildlife and Countryside Act 1981 as a site of special scientific interest. The leisure use of woodland is a new market; this can be either for war games or sporting but may prove a much needed alternative source of income for landowners.

3. COTTAGES

We have seen that in valuing a farm the house and cottages that go with it are not as a rule separately treated; the valuer takes into account their presence, condition or, indeed, absence as just one of those factors which influence overall rental-per-hectare.

So far as cottages for farm workers are concerned, prior to the passing of the Rent (Agriculture) Act 1976 they were normally "tied cottages", that is the tenant occupied the cottage on the basis that he was required to live there as a condition of his employment and, therefore, enjoyed no security. If the worker was paid on Agricultural Wages Board rates, he paid a nominal rent for the accommodation, which

---

[4] The Farmland Market. A six monthly review of farm prices published by the Estates Gazette and Farmers Weekly.

for several years has been £1·50 per week. The 1976 Act
gave such workers the protection of the Rent Acts with some
modifications. The modifications are first that the rent can
be agreed between landlord and tenant and this enabled rents
to continue at the nominal level. Secondly, the landlord can
regain possession, if the cottage is required for another
employee, when employment terminates, subject to suitable
alternative accommodation being available and the local
housing authority are required to use their best endeavours
to provide such accommodation if the applicant is unable
to provide himself with accommodation. The Housing Bill
1988 makes provision for a new type of agricultural occupancy—the "assured agricultural occupancy". The provisions of the Bill are outlined in Chapter 19.

Farm cottages are frequently subject to planning restrictions that they shall only be occupied by persons engaged
in agriculture or forestry. This can make cottages which are
surplus to farm requirements unmarketable unless a successful planning application is made for the removal of the restrictions.

4. Other Houses

Country houses in general are valued no differently from
their urban or suburban counterparts. The exception, fortu-
nately a rare one, is the mansion house: the Big House,
the pivot of the landed estate. It will probably have a large
garden attached and a few hectares of parkland, which can
be regarded either as an additional attraction or merely pad-
dock space for the white elephant. Although with the huge
growth in the leisure and recreation industry such properties
may now offer a source of income not previously considered
by their owners.

In making a cockshy at the rental value of a country mansion, the time-tested factors, *faute de mieux*, may be pro-
visionally applied. With the statelier homes the rent at which
they are worth to be let proportionally diminishes according
to magnitutude and the lack of modern comforts, or, where
these are installed, the expense of running them. The cost
of maintaining the gardens and the wages of the indoor ser-

vants are expenses reduced only by the impossibility of getting domestic help. The incidence of dry rot and death watch beetle, whose tastes are lucullan and whose preference for the more ducal houses is a proven phenomenon, is another factor to explain why the "hypothetical tenant" so often fails to hypothesise.

Conversion of the single residence into a number of residences, either in the form of separate wings or flats, has been carried out successfully in a number of cases. There is frequently a demand for the use of such houses for educational purposes, or as nursing homes or private hospitals and this type of use is often acceptable for planning purposes. There is also a demand in many areas for campus offices but this type of use is less likely to be accceptable in planning terms.

5. Sporting Rights

Sporting rights have increased in importance in recent years with greater demand for a shooting or fishing "experience". The valuer may even find purpose-made sporting lakes that provide a much better return than a few hectares of low-lying meadow.

Shooting rights may be let on a 3 or 7 year lease or managed direct by the landowner, but a whole gun in a shoot may be worth in the region of £2,000 per annum depending upon the expenditure of keepering and the variety of game which can include deer, pheasant, grouse, partridge also snipe, woodcock and wild duck.

Fishing rights relate to two distinct classes of fish, the "coarse" fish and the "game" fish. The demand for all fishing is strong today and clubs and syndicates will readily bid for any water. The more lucrative game fishing is let by the "beat" or stretch of river on one or both banks, the value of which depends on the type and quality of the fish available.

In valuing sporting rights it is necessary to examine the "bag" over the last five to ten years and apply a capital value according to results, e.g. salmon £2,000 per fish and grouse £500 per brace. Alternatively the more traditional capitalisation of rent at 10 Y.P. may be applied.

6. Summary—The Country Estate

For some generations past discussions on landed estates have been largely concerned with their break-up. There is life in them yet, each a self-contained entity with its large house and parkland, its dozen or more farms, its woodlands and sawmill, its houses and cottages, almshouses, watermill, minerals,[5] wayleaves and easements,[6] and its fear of death vis-a-vis Inheritance Tax.[7]

An agricultural estate which comes into the market is more often sold in parts than as one; its value therefore depends upon the nature of the individual properties of which it is composed rather than on its worth as a whole. Even when valuing the smaller estate for sale as a whole its components are more surely treated separately, particularly since some assets are better secured than others and so merit a higher years' purchase.

Apart from the concept of agricultural land as an indestructible investment in these times of continual inflation, purchasers are attracted by the physical value and by the concessions and advantages it enjoys in connection with income tax. There is, furthermore, the added attraction—particularly to the next in succession—of the reliefs from Inheritance Tax in respect of agricultural land and woodlands.

Despite existing legislation to the contrary investors are being influenced by the possibility of farmland in some situations being required later on, at enhanced values, for non-agricultural purposes. Finally, there is that "pride of ownership", an intangible attribute transcending even the pleasures of dining off the home-bred Hereford or running the Rolls on the farm accounts.

The Lands Tribunal decision in *Cuthbert v. Secretary of State for the Environment* (1979) 252 EG 921 provides an interesting commentary on the valuation of a large agricultural and sporting estate.

---

[5] See Chapter 33.
[6] See Chapter 31.
[7] See Chapter 23.

CHAPTER 18

Development Properties

1. GENERALLY

THE TERM "Development Properties" is used here to indicate the type of property the value of which can be increased by capital expenditure, by a change in the use to which the property is put, or possibly by a combination of capital expenditure and change of use. It has commonly been applied to areas of undeveloped land likely to be in future demand for building purposes; to individual sites in towns, at present unbuilt on; and to other urban sites occupied by buildings which have become obsolescent or which do not utilise the site to the best advantage. The value, which in these cases is latent in the property, can only be released by development and in all cases is subject to any necessary planning permission being granted.

2. VALUATION APPROACH

The method of valuation commonly applied to development properties is the residual method described in Chapter 12.

In making the valuation it is necessary to determine several factors. It is first necessary to decide the type of development or redevelopment for which the land is best suited, due regard being had to the planning permission likely to be granted. It is frequently necessary to work on an assumption as regards what consent will be forthcoming and the conditions attached to it, particularly in relation to density. Where this is done the valuer must state clearly what consent is assumed and what the conditions are. The valuer must then estimate the market value of the land when put to the proposed use: to consider the time which must elapse before the land can be

299

so used: to estimate the cost of carrying out the works
required to put the land to the proposed use together with
such other items involved as legal costs and agent's commission on sales and purchases and fees for planning applications: and to assess the cost of financing the project.

Where data of recent similar transactions exist, the valuer
may be able to use the comparison method of valuation.
He may do so even if he has to look outside the area in
which the land is situated, for example sales of office sites
in other towns with the same level of office rental values
or residential sites with closely similar house prices. The
above factors will then bear on his consideration somewhat
indirectly. Even when he can value by comparison he would
be wise to make an alternative valuation by the Residual
Method. Since this is essentially a forecast of sales and expenditure, it is possible to set out the figures in a different form.
Such a statement is known as a Viability or Feasibility Report
or Statement. Examples are given below but such a Report
or Statement contains the same figures as are employed in
a Residual Valuation.

When the residual method is employed it is obvious that
any errors made in the estimates of completed value, cost
of development, etc., will be reflected in the valuation arrived
at, so that considerable skill is required when applying this
method if consistent and accurate results are to be obtained.
Moreover, it frequently happens that the amount of the estimates of completed value and cost are very large compared
to the value of the property in its present state: a small error
in the estimates will entail a large error in the residue in
such cases.

Although at one time the residual method was frequently
used as the only method of valuation applied in any particular
case, direct comparison of the property being valued with
other similar properties may be a more reliable method, and
is certainly preferred by the Lands Tribunal[1] although the

---

[1] See, for example, *Fairbairn Lawson Ltd. v. Leeds County B.C.* (1972) 222
EG 566; *South Coast Furnishing Co. Ltd. v. Fareham B.C.* (1976) 242 EG 1057:
Essex Incorporated Congregational Union v. Colchester B.C. (1982) 23 R.V.R.
267.

residual method has been accepted by the Tribunal in some cases.[2]

The Tribunal's criticism of the residual method is essentially that of the inherent weakness referred to in the preceding paragraph.[3] If an optimistic view of values and costs is adopted a high land value will emerge, whilst a pessimistic view will produce a low value. If such opposing views are adopted by the parties to a dispute then the arbitrator will be faced with markedly different values. This is the common experience of the Tribunal. The residual method is thus mistrusted in such cases. However in commercial situations such as when a valuer is preparing a valuation for the purchase of a development site, a realistic view must be adopted and the residual method is accepted as a proper approach.

3. TYPES OF DEVELOPMENT

It can be said that there is at any given time a general demand for land for building purposes dependent upon factors applicable to the country as a whole, and that the extent to which this demand is localised in certain areas or in the neighbourhood of certain towns will depend upon local factors.

[2] See *Baylis's Trustees v. Droitwich Borough Council* [1966] R.V.R 158; *St. Clement's Danes Holborn Estate Charity v. Greater London Council* [1966] R.V.R. 333; Clinker & Ash Ltd. v. Southern Gas Board, [1967] R.V.R. 477; *Trocette Property Co. Ltd. v. Greater London Council and London Borough of Southwark* [1974] 27P & CR 256.

[3] See *Liverpool and Birkenhead House Property Investment Co. Ltd. v. Liverpool City Council* [1962] R.V.R. 162.

In *Wood Investments Ltd. v. Birkenhead Corporation* [1969] R.V.R. 137, Mr John Watson, a Member of the Lands Tribunal said, with regard to a witness's residual valuation, that it "provides a telling illustration of its [the residual method's] uncertainties. The key figures are (a) the value of the completed buildings estimated at £265,537 and (b) the cost of providing it estimated at £230,210. £35,327 which is (a) less (b) is the land but (a) and (b) are necessarily rough estimates and there must be some margin of error. If (a) turned out to be only 5 per cent too high and (b) 5 per cent too low the residual value of the land would be approximately £10,500 instead of approximately £30,000 and if the 5 per cent errors happen to be the other way round it would be over £60,000."

General factors affecting the demand for land include the state of prosperity of the country and population trends.

It is obvious that in prosperous times there will be a demand for sites for such buildings as offices, shops and the like. When the population is increasing there will be a larger demand for houses and for an improved standard of housing, both in quality and quantity, as family incomes increase.

It does not, of course, follow that because a certain type of development is provided for in the development plan for the area that the land can profitably be developed for such a use immediately or even within a reasonable period in the future. For instance, with a view to increasing employment in run-down areas such as inner cities, areas may be allocated for industrial use, but unless industrialists are willing to set up business in these areas the development of the land for this purpose will be unprofitable.

The prospect of profitable development of any particular piece of land within the conditions imposed, or likely to be imposed, by the planning authority will depend largely on local circumstances, and past evidence of trends of development in the neighbourhood will have to be taken into account. The valuer has also to consider general trends affecting development in the country as a whole.

In some cases of doubt or complexity it may be necessary to obtain an indication of the sort of planning consent likely to be forthcoming by informal discussion with the local planning authority before putting forward even a tentative valuation. In the course of such discussion any requirements for a "planning gain" will become apparent. For example, the planning authority may require the provision by the developer of children's play areas in residential developments or a community centre in a district shopping centre. The financial basis for such arrangements must be established and allowance made for any additional costs which may fall on the developer.

The nature of the development likely to be permitted having been ascertained or assumed, it is also necessary to assess its commercial possibilities. It does not follow that, because planning consent is likely to be obtained, there is necessarily a market for that particular form of development.

4. VIABILITY STATEMENTS

As explained above this is a statement of forecast of sales and costs of development. It can be presented in a number of different forms including that of a profit and loss account. The form used herein is one frequently employed.

Example 18–1

A developer has been negotiating for the purchase of a freehold site which could accommodate a small block of four self-contained flats each with garage. He can buy it for £80,000 subject to contract and to outline planning consent for the above development.

Sketch plans indicate that the flats will have floor areas of 700 sq.ft. each and investigation of sales of flats in the same area indicate that selling prices will be £63,500 including garage on a leasehold basis—99 years at a ground rent of £100 per annum per flat.

You are instructed to advise a finance house on the proposal generally and your report is to include a Viability Statement.

Viability Statement

Sales

4 flats at £63,500 each		£254,000
Ground Rents: 4 × £100 p.a. at		
7 Y.P.		2,800
		£256,800

Costs—

Land		£80,000
Cost of building:		
2,800 sq.ft. at		
£35 per sq.ft.	£98,000	
4 garages at £2,000 each	£8,000	
Site preparation, approach		
road and gardens	4,000	110,000
Stamp Duty on land		800
Architect's fee for plans (agreed)		3,000

Legal Costs on purchase of site	800	
Finance Costs:		
Land Costs £81,600 for		
12 months at 11 per cent	8,975	
Building Costs £113,000 for		
say 6 months at 11 per cent		
	6,215	15,190
Agents Commission on sale		
of flats (agreed)	4,000	
Legal Costs on sale of		
flats (agreed)	2,000	
		215,790 say 215,800
		Estimated profit £41,000

It is thought that many developers judge whether the profit level is sufficiently worthwhile to warrant undertaking the development by expressing the estimated profit as a percentage of the total costs of development. In the above case the return is 19 per cent since £41,000 represents 19 per cent of £215,800. This percentage can be used as a basis for comparison between one development and another of the same type. Alternatively the estimated profit can be expressed as a percentage of the total sales, £41,000 on £256,800 producing 16 per cent, or the amount of profit per flat, £10,250 per flat in the example.

5. Factors Affecting Value

In dealing with a particular area of land the local circumstances must be carefully considered, e.g., the prosperity of the town, the existing supply of houses, factories or other buildings, and the amenities of the particular property under consideration.

It is, of course, essential that proper access to the land is available. The proximity of public services is, also, of major importance, such as public sewers, gas, electricity, water and telephone supplies. The existence of restrictions and easements must be checked.

The factors vary according to the type of development

for which it is considered the land is most suitable due regard being had to town planning consent likely to be forthcoming or assumed.

In the case of land to be used for houses or flats, these will include the proximity of good travel facilities, and also the existence and proximity of shops, schools, churches, and the like or the possibility of the provision thereof in the future. Local employment conditions also affect demand. Regard must also be had to the presence of open spaces, parks and golf courses and the reservation of land under planning control for similar leisure purposes. The character of the neighbourhood must be considered to determine the most suitable type or types of development; also whether the character is changing.

The principal factor in the case of retail development is the location of the land. Where the land is in an established prime shopping location it is important to determine whether there are proposals such as road schemes or major retail developments nearby which might draw shoppers away from that location. Edge of town developments, normally large retail warehouse schemes or new shopping centres, depend on access to major roads in the area and the site being large enough to provide extensive customer car parking.

Offices depend on several factors, such as access by road and public transport generally and an adequate supply of suitable labour. Many occupiers need to be close to other companies in the same area of business, as witnessed by the grouping of professional firms, or those engaged in financial services.

The most important factors in the case of warehouse and industrial developments are access by road and an adequate supply of suitable labour. Proximity to ports and markets and to sources of power and materials, are now less important than they were due to the increase in road transport facilities.

Whether development is likely to be profitable or not is dependent upon the demand for the property when it has been completed. The physical state of the land, availability of services, etc., are also important factors to be taken into account. Until 1947 these were the only factors to be considered but since then the town planning provisions affecting

the land are the overriding factor which the valuer has to
consider.

6. RESIDENTIAL DEVELOPMENT SCHEMES

(*a*) *Generally*. In relation to small areas of land it may
be a comparatively simple problem to determine the best
use to which the land can be put, having regard to general
trends of development in the neighbourhood, the factors
affecting the particular piece of land under consideration and
the provisions of the relevant Development Plan.

Example 18–2

You are asked to advise on the value of land fronting a
residential road which has been made up and taken over
by the local authority. There are foul and surface water
sewers in the road and gas, water and electric services are
available. The property has a total frontage of 480 feet and
a depth of 120 feet. This is the remaining vacant land in
this road; the rest of the frontage has been developed for
houses currently selling at about £100,000 with frontages of
about 30 feet each. From the enquiries you have made you
find that similar plots in the area have sold at prices ranging
from £35,000 to £40,000 each. There is a demand for houses
of the character already erected; it is expected that all of
the plots could be built on and the houses disposed of within
a year.

You have ascertained from the local planning authority
that they would permit the development of this land for residential purposes. The land is in an area allocated for residential development.

Valuation

In this instance there cannot be very much doubt as to
the type of development that should take place.

After inspecting the land and the area and taking into

account the prices realised and the upward trend in values, it might be considered that a fair value per plot would be £40,000, giving a total valuation of £640,000 on the assumption that planning consent for this form of development would be granted subject only to usual conditions.

Note

In this instance the procedure has been a direct comparison with the sale prices of other similar properties in the vicinity. A speculative builder, before buying, even at a figure which he feels satisfied is a fair market value, would be wise to prepare a viability report on the following lines to forecast the probable rate of profit. A valuer advising on the sale price of the land would be wise to do the same since the forecast may bring to light some factor which might otherwise be overlooked or given too little weight.

Viability Statement

Selling prices 16 × £100,000			£1,600,000
Costs of development—			
Land		£640,000	
Building Costs—16 houses of 900 sq.ft. each at £40 per sq.ft. including garages, say		576,000	
Stamp Duty		6,400	
Plans		2,500	
Legal Costs—			
on purchase of land	6,400		
on sale of houses	8,000	14,400	
Sale Commission at £1,000 per house		16,000	
Finance at 12 per cent on say £600,000 for 8 months, say		48,000	1,303,300
Estimated Profit			£296,700

£296,700 represents 22·77 per cent of £1,303,300 or £18,540 per house.

Notes

1. The sale price of £100,000 is substantiated by reference to sales of similar houses in the same area. If there has been a rise in prices of such houses in the area the developer may deliberately increase his estimate to allow for a continuation of increase. If he adhered to prices current at the date of the purchase of the land he might find that he was constantly losing opportunities of purchase due to higher bids from others, if he worked on the same level of profit as them. The developer would probably do a number of such calculations within a price bracket. It is preferable to work on prices current at the date of purchase and a lower profit margin and to regard any increase in prices obtained in the event as "super-profits". To be too optimistic is likely to bring disaster.

2. There is an obvious interdependence between the figures of selling prices (£100,000 above) and building costs (£40 per sq.ft. above). The better the quality of the house offered the higher will be the price realised and the higher the cost of building. The object of the developer is to maximise the difference betwen the two figures by use of his experience, expertise and skill in design, and efficiency in sales organisation and building costs.

3. Most developers use stock plans or adapt plans they have used before and a full scale architect's fee would not be payable in most cases, Where fresh plans have to be prepared a much larger figure would have to be allowed: if the developer offers the designer too small a fee, the design and hence the saleability of the houses is likely to suffer. Many developers have their own in-house architects/designers so that the costs would be reflected in their profit targets with no specific allowance for architects' fees or plans.

4. There is a similar interdependence between the amount of the selling agents' commission and the prices obtained. If selling agents are paid too little they will not use maximum efforts to sell. On the other hand a developer is able to negotiate better terms for multiple instructions, particularly if the market is buoyant and the houses will sell quickly.

5. Since proceeds of sales will start to be received in say 6 months it will not be necessary for the developer to borrow

the whole of the estimated land and building costs (£1,230,000) for the whole period of the development (12 months). Under half the total figure for something over half the total period will give the cost of finance in this case.

If it is required to substantiate this figure, a "cash flow" forecast should be prepared. The Table on p. 310 assumes the sale of two houses per month starting in the sixth month and three houses per month in the last two months. Such a forecast would be useful to (and probably required by) any finance house providing the money for the development.

It may be necessary in the case of larger areas to prepare sketch plans of a suitable development, making provision, for instance, for certain portions of the estate to be developed for shops, others for flats, and others for houses, probably with varying densities. In such cases, the problem is more complicated but the principle is the same.

It is of course simple to set out the above figures in the form of a residual valuation.

Selling prices:		£1,600,000
Less Building costs—16 houses at 900 sq.ft.		
each at £40 per sq.ft.	£576,000	
Plans	2,500	
Stamp Duty	6,400	
Legal costs	14,400	
Commissions	16,000	
Finance	48,000	
	663,300	
Developer's profit—say $22\frac{1}{2}$ per cent, say	149,200	812,500
Land balance		787,500
Land price + $22\frac{1}{2}$% profit =	1.225x =	787,500
$\therefore$ Value of Land	x =	642,850
	say,	£640,000

(*b*) *User of land*. When preparing a scheme in outline, the extent of the various uses to which the land is to be put must be determined, and a lay-out prepared to indicate the plots that will be provided and the roads and sewers that will have to be constructed; regard must be had to the

Month

Items	1	2	3	4	5	6	7	8	9	10	11	12
	£	£	£	£	£	£	£	£	£	£	£	£
Land	640,000											
Stamp duty	6,400											
Building costs		52,360	52,360	52,360	52,360	52,360	52,360	52,360	52,360	52,360	52,360	52,500
Plans			2,500									
Legal fees	6,400											
Interest at 1 per cent per month		6,528	7,117	7,737	8,338	8,945	7,588	6,217	4,833	3,435	2,023	137
	652,800	711,688	773,665	833,762	894,460	955,765	818,713	680,290	540,483	399,278	256,661	13,798
Net proceeds of sales, i.e., 2 or 3 houses at £100,000 each less £1,500 per house (legal costs and sale commissions)		—	—	—	—	197,000	197,000	197,000	197,000	197,000	295,500	295,500
Net balance of drawings	652,800	711,688	773,665	833,762	894,460	758,765	621,713	483,290	343,483	202,278	CR 38,839	CR 281,702

Total interest = £62,898

Note how the amount drawn builds up from the initial payment for the land to the point in time when the first sales are made from when it decreases until it is all repaid. The profit in cash all accrues to the developer in the last two months.

In the above table it is assumed that the interest is added to the loan, i.e., it is "rolled up", as distinct from being paid regularly by the borrower from his own resources.

provision of suitable size plots and to any restrictions in force relating to the density of buildings and to the proportion of site that may be covered.

In the case of large estates, it may be necessary to make reservations for special plots for open spaces, for a school or a church or community centre, and similar local amenities.

In relation to those parts allocated for commercial purposes, it may be considered that a site should be set aside for a petrol-filling station, public-house or neighbourhood shopping centre.

Even though a scheme is prepared primarily for the purpose of arriving at the value of the land it is usual to discuss the scheme informally with the local planning authority. Such discussions will identify whether different densities should be allowed for in different parts of the land and what provision is to be made for roads, open spaces, etc. Indeed as the scheme is worked up further valuations will be required to monitor the value implications.

(*c*) *Infrastructure*. In a scheme of even a modest size close attention must be given to the provision of infrastructure such as roads and services since these will represent a significant cost. This applies not only within the area of the scheme but also to off-site works.

The internal road layout should be such as to provide good and easy access to all parts of the estate. If there are any changes of level, regard must be had to the provision of easy gradients. So far as is practicable, plots of regular shape and of suitable size must be produced by the road lay-out, at the same time avoiding undue monotony and lack of amenity. Roads producing no building frontage should be kept to a minimum.

The lay-out of soil and surface water sewers must be determined in relation to the available outfall. Both roads and sewers will need to be constructed to the requirements of the local authorities prior to them being taken over (or "adopted") by the highway authority or statutory undertaker.

In addition to agreeing the internal road and sewer provisions with the appropriate authorities it may well be necessary to agree off-site works. For example, the local road serving the site may need to be widened or a roundabout or traffic lights provided. Similarly, the existing sewerage system may be inadequate and need to be upgraded with larger pipes or by enlarging the sewage works. Such works will be carried out by the authorities with the developer bearing all or part of the costs.

It may be found that the land is so situated that it would not be possible to connect to a public sewer by gravity and allowance would have to be made for the cost of constructing a pumping station. Surface water disposal might require the provision of a balancing pond, although they can often provide an attractive amenity feature within the overall design.

Enquiries must also be made as to the terms upon which supplies of gas and electricity and the installation of telephone cables can be obtained, as the nearest mains or cables may be at some considerable distance and supplies inadequate.

7. PERIOD OF DEVELOPMENT

There are two main factors which will determine the speed of development. The first is the physical factor of how quickly the actual construction work can be carried out and the second is the rate at which the completed buildings can be sold.

In the case of a small housing estate it may be reasonable to assume that each house will be sold immediately it is completed so that no deferment of development costs and sale proceeds is necessary.

However, in the case of an estate of several hundred houses it will be necessary to estimate the rate at which the market will take up the houses, which will depend on a number of factors including the strength of demand in the area and any competing developments being carried out, and to assume that the development will be appropriately phased over a period of years. In this case deferment of some costs and of sale proceeds will be necessary. Quite often the original purchaser of a large scheme will sell off parcels of serviced land to other developers. One reason is to recoup some of the initial heavy costs of providing the basic infrastructure. However the introduction of a different developer with his own design standards can add variety to the house types and layouts on offer and so give an impetus to interest in the whole scheme with benefits to the vendor developer through increased take up of houses. Developers might even join together from the very start and form a joint venture consortium to carry out the scheme.

8. INCIDENTAL COSTS

In most cases certain additional expenses will be incurred beyond the bare constructional costs of roads and sewers.

If open spaces or other amenities such as belts of trees are provided by the developer the cost must be taken into account.

Professional services are required for the preparation of detailed lay-out schemes and the drawings and specifications for constructional works: fees for this may be taken from 4 per cent to $12\frac{1}{2}$ per cent on the cost of the works, depending on the amount of professional input required. Even where a developer has an in-house design department some independent professional advice may still be required, particularly from highway and civil engineers. In the case of large and contentious schemes where the planning permission must be pursued through the appeals procedure with a public hearing, the fees of planning lawyers, town planners and other professional advisers can amount to very large sums.

Legal charges may be incurred both in respect of the purchase of the land (and stamp duty) and of the sales. The amount to be allowed will depend on whether the land is registered or unregistered. Further legal charges may be incurred where planning, highway and other legal agreements are required.

A detailed estimate of the cost of advertisements and commission on sales payable to agents must also be made. This should include the costs, where appropriate, of furnishing and staffing a show house.

9. Site Assembly

The acquisition of land for large schemes almost invariably involves the purchase of several landholdings. The problem for the developer is that he is usually buying land without planning permission. He will be unwilling, and probably unable, to commit large sums of money without the certainty of being able to carry out development and so justify the expenditure.

The normal solution to this problem is for the parties to enter into option agreements. These may be call options, whereby the developer can require the owner to sell to him on grant of planning permission, or put and call options, whereby either party can require the other to carry out the sale/purchase of the land.

The option agreement must cover many matters, including the means of determining the price payable. Sometimes this will be at a stated figure, although when land values are rising this is unfavourable to the landowner. Alternatively the price will be market value, to be determined at the time of the exercise of the option. Commonly the price will be a percentage of market value, say 70% to 90%, to reflect the costs of assembly and of obtaining planning permission which will be borne by the developer.

It is essential that the provisions for determining the price should be set out to enable the valuers for the parties to have a clear understanding of the approach to the valuation. For example, where the price is to be assessed at an agreed price per acre, it must be clear whether this is the gross area or some lesser area such as the net developable area which needs to be defined: where it is price per plot, how the valuer should deal with plots which straddle the boundaries of land ownership needs to be stated: if a landholding controls the access to other land, the valuer needs to know whether the special value of this strategic land must be reflected—"ransom value": in options where a developer may exercise the option without planning permission having been granted, the planning assumptions for the valuation should be present: if, as is usual, the developer has to bear the cost of extensive and expensive infrastructure, the valuer needs to know how this factor should be reflected in the valuation.

It is clear that considerable care is required in the preparation of an option if extra complications in what is in any event a difficult and contentious area of valuation are to be avoided.

10. HOPE VALUE

The development value of land can be identified by the existence of a planning permission. It is obvious however that planning permissions do not appear out of the blue so that, on one day, a planning permission for residential development is given when the land acquires a residential development value. What happens in practice is that a view is taken as to the likelihood of planning permission being given, either now or at some time in the future. If the likelihood is nil, such as prime agricultural land in the Green Belt in an Area of Outstanding Natural Beauty and with rare wild flowers found nowhere else, it is unlikely in the extreme that anyone would pay more than agricultural value.

In other cases, whilst it is agricultural land with no immediate prospect of development, it may be felt that in a few years, when say a proposed new road has been built nearby, some form of development might be allowed. In such cases purchasers might be found who will pay above agricultural value in the hope that, after a few years, they will realise development value and make a large profit. This price above value reflecting the existing use but below full development value, is termed hope value.

A valuation to determine hope value is often impossible other than by adopting an instinctive approach, particularly in the stages when the hope of permission is remote. It can only be a guesstimate of the money a speculator would be prepared to pay. As the hope crystallises into reasonable certainty of a permission at some stage a valuation can be attempted based on the potential development value deferred for the anticipated period until permission will be forthcoming, but with some end deduction to reflect the lack of certainty. Indeed, since most developers will buy only when permission is certain, preferring an option to buy or a contract conditional on the grant of permission before certainty has been reached, any sale in the period of uncertainty will probably require a significant discount on what might otherwise appear to be the full hope value.

11. Urban Sites

(a) New Development

The previous sections of this Chapter have been concerned mainly with land, not built upon, in the vicinity of existing development, commonly referred to as greenfield sites.

In the centre of towns, in built-up areas, it is often necessary to consider the value of a site which has become vacant through buildings having been pulled down, sometimes termed a brownfield site, or which is occupied by buildings which are obsolescent or do not utilise the site to the full.

The general method of approach suggested in Section 2 can be used, i.e. to value by comparison with sales of other sites by reference to an appropriate unit, e.g. per square foot or foot frontage and to check the result by drawing up a viability statement or by a valuation by the residual method. For example, with office sites, there is a correlation between rental value, building cost and site value. In areas with closely similar rental values and site conditions, an office site might be valued at £x per gross square foot of offices to be built. Thus in an area where offices are letting at £16 per square foot analysis of site purchase prices might show that prices represent £100 per square foot of the gross floor area of the offices to be built.

As in the case of building estates, the type of property to be erected and the use to which it can be put when completed is entirely dependent upon the planning permission which will be granted. An indication will probably be obtained by an inspection of the development plan and discussion with the local planning authority.

Sites are often restricted as to user, height of buildings, the percentage of the site area that may be covered at ground floor and above, and by conditions imposed when planning permission is granted.

There may be further restrictions on user owing to the existence of easements of light and air or rights of way.

A site may be bare, but may contain old foundations and the cost of clearing may be considerable, whilst on the other hand advantage may be taken of existing runs of drains.

In many areas the cost of development may be seriously increased by the presence of underground water or the difficulty of access with building materials in a crowded and busy thoroughfare.

Factors of this kind must be carefully considered both in relation to any suggested scheme of development and also when comparing two sites which apparently are very similar but which are subject to different restrictions or conditions.

The existence of restrictive covenants may reduce the value of a site although the possibility of an application for their modification or removal under Section 84 of the Law of Property Act 1925,[4] must not be lost sight of. It is frequently possible to insure against restrictions being enforced where these are contained in old documents and where there is considerable doubt as to whether they are any longer extant. Where applications are made to the Lands Tribunal it must be remembered that the Tribunal can award compensation to the person having the benefit of the covenant. In the case of restrictions preventing the conversion of houses it may be possible to take similar action to that under Section 84 of the Law of Property Act 1925, under the Housing Act 1985.[5]

Where possession of business premises is obtained against tenants in occupation at the termination of their leases for purposes of redevelopment under Section 30 of the Landlord and Tenant Act 1954,[6] the amount of compensation to be paid must be deducted as part of the costs of development.

As in the case of a building estate, the value of urban sites is best found by direct comparison using an appropriate unit. However urban sites are not generally susceptible to direct comparison since they commonly provide a mix of

---

[4] As amended by the Landlord and Tenant Act 1954, Sec. 52 and by the Law of Property Act 1969.

[5] Sec. 610.

[6] See Chapter 20.

uses. The residual method is therefore usually adopted. The nature of the method lends itself readily to computer programmes. These not only make it easier to prepare the valuation but allow for sensitivity testing which enables the valuer to identify those matters on which he needs to concentrate.

(b) Refurbishment

In urban areas, development can take the form of work to existing buildings rather than the erection of new buildings. In conservation areas or with listed buildings, this may be the only possible form of development. Even in other cases it may be found that it is more profitable to modernise a property rather than to demolish it and replace it. This approach is known as refurbishment.

When considering refurbishment it is necessary to consider whether any planning permission will be required. This may be so because alterations will be made to the external appearance such as inserting new windows or making additions such as plant rooms on the roof. Equally where a change of use is contemplated then the need for planning permission must be considered.

The other important factor to be considered is the estimated cost of the works. A typical refurbishment scheme of an office building would include installation of suspended ceilings and raised floors where possible, upgrading of all services including heating, toilets and lifts, redesign of the entrance hall and common parts, and even the recladding of external parts. Similar considerations apply to blocks of flats, shopping centres and other buildings. Unlike new development, where building costs may be available by comparison with other new buildings, each refurbishment is unique and needs the services of a building cost surveyor to estimate the costs involved.

A growing practice is for planning authorities to allow new buildings subject to the retention of existing façades. This film set architecture produces a hybrid new development/refurbishment scheme which draws upon the elements of both.

Since refurbishment is a form of development the residual method of valuation is appropriate in valuing such property. Indeed the valuer will often need to prepare a residual valuation assuming refurbishment and also one assuming redevelopment. A comparison of the valuations will provide a strong indication of which approach is to be favoured.

Example 18–3

A freehold office building erected 30 years ago is on 5 floors with 4,000 sq.ft. net on each floor. There is surface car parking for 40 cars. The site area is 12,000 sq.ft.

The property is occupied by tenants whose lease has 2 years to run at a current rent of £40,000 p.a. The rateable value is £15,000.

The property is lacking in modern amenities. It would cost £700,000 to bring the property up to current standards when the rental value would be £12 per sq.ft. The planning authority has indicated that a new office building would be permitted at a plot ratio of 2·5 : 1 producing 30,000 sq.ft. gross, 23,000 sq.ft. net with 15 car spaces at basement level. The rental value would be £15 per sq.ft.

What is the value of the freehold interest?

Valuations

The first step is to establish the value assuming refurbishment and the second the value assuming redevelopment.

A. Refurbishment
  GDV—
    Offices 20,000 sq.ft. at
      £12 per sq.ft.   £240,000 p.a.
    Car Spaces 40 spaces at
      £200 per space p.a.   8,000

                                              £248,000 p.a.
      Y.P. perp. at 6¾%   14·81 say £3,673,000

  Less Building Costs
    Estimated Costs   £700,000
    Add Fees at
      say 10%   70,000 770,000

Finance
Assume 8 months scheme
    £770,000 for 4 months at
    12% say   30,800
Letting Costs say 15%
    of £248,000   37,200
Developer's Profit at
    20% of £800,800   160,160   998,160

Land Balance   £2,674,840

Land	$= 1 \cdot 00x$	
SD + Fees	$= 0 \cdot 03x$	
Finance $= 0 \cdot 08 \times 1 \cdot 03x$	$= 0 \cdot 08x$	
Profit $= 20\%$ of $1 \cdot 11x$	$= 0 \cdot 22x$	$1 \cdot 33x = 2{,}674{,}840$
		$\therefore x = 2{,}011{,}158$

Value   say £2,000,000

B. New Development

GDV—
    Offices 23,000 sq.ft.
        at £15 per sq.ft.   £345,000 p.a.
    Car Spaces 15 spaces at
        £300 per space p.a.   4,500

                                      say 350,000 p.a.
    Y.P. perp. at $6\frac{1}{4}\%$ 16·0   £5,600,000

Less Building Costs
    30,000 sq.ft. at £50
        per sq.ft.   £1,500,000
    Basement say 4,000
        sq.ft. at £40 per
        sq.ft.   160,000
                          1,660,000
    Add Fees at 12%   199,200 £1,859,200

Finance
Assume 18 months scheme
    £1,859,200 for 9 months at
    12%   167,328

Letting Costs say 15% of £350,000		52,500	
Developer's Profit at 20% of £2,079,028		415,806	say 2,495,000
Land Balance			£3,105,000

$$\begin{aligned}
\text{Land} &= 1\cdot00x \\
\text{SD + Fees} &= 0\cdot03x \\
\text{Finance} = 0\cdot18 \times 1\cdot01x &= 0\cdot19x \\
\text{Profit} = 20\% \text{ of } 1\cdot19x &= 0\cdot24x \quad 1\cdot46x = 3{,}105{,}000 \\
&\therefore \quad x = 2{,}126{,}712
\end{aligned}$$

Value say £2,100,000

Hence it appears that redevelopment and refurbishment are of about the same value. The decision on what course to follow would depend on resources available and the state of the market at the end of the lease.

Valuation

Term—Rent reserved	40,000 p.a.	£72,000
Y.P. 2 yrs at 7½%	1·80	
Reversion—to		
Development Value say	2,000,000	
Less Compensation to Tenants say		
3 × R.V. £15,000	45,000	
	1,955,000	
P.V. £1 in 2 yrs at 6¾%	0·88	£1,720,400
Value		say £1,800,000

Note—In practice valuations should also be made on the basis that the building would remain in its existing state, or be modernised to lesser standards at reduced costs of improvement.

If the work could be carried out with the tenants remaining this might also be a significant factor.

12. GROUND RENTS

A common feature in the development process is the release of land to developers by landowners who wish to retain an interest in, and some control over the future use of, the land to be developed. This is achieved by the grant of a ground lease to the developer.

Ground leases have been a common feature of the development process for several centuries. The best known examples from the past are the large estates controlled by families or charities whereby the overall estate remained in the ownership of the estate owner who controlled the development of the estate in accordance with a general estate plan. The Grosvenor and Cadogan estates in central London, Alleyn's estate in Dulwich, and the Calthorpe estate in Birmingham are typical examples. Control was, and still is, exercised by the granting of ground leases which imposed restraints on the manner in which any parcel of land was developed for the benefit of the estate at large.

In recent times the ground lease has been adopted by local authorities and new town corporations whereby areas of land can be developed by the private sector whilst control of such development can readily be exercised through the landlord's powers under the ground lease, notwithstanding the powers they may have in addition as planning authorities.

Ground leases however are not confined to large scale, estate development. Many individual sites may be offered on a ground lease basis since such an approach may be attractive to others who are taking a long term view. This is particularly so with the advent of rent review clauses. A further significant area where ground leases have become common is that of developments of flats and maisonnettes. The legal system in the United Kingdom, apart from Scotland, is so structured that a freehold interest in a flat which is part only of a property raises considerable problems. These are readily solved by the grant of a ground lease of the flat.

In earlier times ground leases were usually granted for 99 years at a fixed rent, although other terms were sometimes adopted. For example there are in existence many leases granted for 999 years at a peppercorn ground rent which are effectively freehold interests.

In recent times two important changes have taken place. First, there has been a movement towards leases of 125 years' duration. The pressure for this appears to be two-fold. One is that the pace of change is such that it is felt that the life of buildings is shortened. Hence if a building will last around 60 years then a 99 years lease does not allow sufficient time to justify the redevelopment of the building after 60 years. The other is that the major funding institutions, the pension funds and insurance companies, have argued forcefully that a 125 year lease is the minimum period to justify their investing in such interests. Hence building leases for 125 years are becoming more common. However the power of local authorities to grant leases of more than 99 years was for some time tightly controlled by central government so that they normally granted leases for the traditional term of 99 years.

The other change which has occurred is far more significant. This is the adoption of rent review clauses. At first rent reviews were introduced into 99 year leases after 33 years and 66 years, but over time these intervals have shortened and it is not now uncommon for a rent review to operate each 5 years, as in occupation leases.

The valuer therefore is likely to be faced with a variety of ground leases. The general principles to be adopted in valuing a freehold interest subject to a ground lease are set out in Part 1. In this Chapter the current forms of ground lease are considered since these are the ones to be found in properties suitable for development. They are considered in two broad categories, residential and commercial.

Residential Ground Leases

As has been explained, developers of flats have overcome the problems of divided freehold interests by the grant of long leases. Typically such flats will be offered for sale at a stated price plus a ground rent. The ground rents are commonly quite small with few reviews. Technically what is offered is a lease at a lower rent and a premium but such terminology is rarely, if ever, used when they are marketed.

The determination of the ground rent bears no relationship to the rental value of the land but tends to be derived from prevailing levels of such rents charged in the area. For this reason they are not truly ground rents though so described.

In valuing such ground rents the principal characteristics to note are that the sums tend to be small with a consequently disproportionately high management cost and that the income, though secure, is fixed for a long period. Returns tend to equate with those on medium dated government stock.

Example 18–4

Value the freehold ground rents derived from a block of 24 flats erected 2 years ago. Each flat owner pays a ground rent of £30 p.a. rising to £60 p.a. in 32 years' time and £90 p.a. in 65 years' time.

Income 24 flats at £30 p.a.	£720 p.a.
Y.P. in perp. at 15 per cent	6
	£4,320

Where the unexpired period of the ground lease is shortening to the point where purchasers of the ground lease have difficulties in raising mortgages, the ground lessee may be prepared to offer a sum significantly in excess of the normal investment value to the freeholder in order to overcome the problem. Alternatively the ground lessee may be prepared to pay a premium for a new lease or an extended lease.

Commercial Ground Leases

Where commercial sites are offered on ground lease, the ground rent will tend to represent the annual rental value of the site. The rental value clearly depends on the surrounding conditions under the lease.

A typical approach to the matter is that the freeholder offers the site on ground lease. Initially the developer/lessee will be granted a building agreement which requires him to carry out the proposed development. The agreement provides that, on satisfactory completion of the development, a building lease will be granted in the form of the draft lease attached to the agreement. The lease will provide that the lessee is responsible for the property under the normal repairing and insuring obligations. As to the ground rent, the initial rent will be agreed as the prevailing ground rental value. Current practice is to provide for the ground rent to be reviewed at frequent intervals, commonly five years, and for the basis of review to be a geared rent. This means that, at the grant of the lease, the parties will agree what is the estimated rental value of the property to be built. This establishes a relationship between initial ground rent and full rental value, normally expressed as a percentage. Thereafter, at each review, the ground rent will rise to that same percentage of the then prevailing rental value.

For example, on the grant of a ground lease of an office site, the ground rent may be fixed at £20,000 p.a., and it is agreed that the rental value of the offices, if they were already built, would be £80,000 p.a. It is clear that the initial ground rent is 25 per cent of the rental value of the offices. At the first review, it may be agreed that the rental value of the offices is £140,000 p.a. If so, the ground rent will become 25 per cent of £140,000 = £35,000 p.a.

In this way the ground rent will follow the rental pattern of the finished building rather than movements in land values. This tends to be preferred since it brings greater certainty in the rental value pattern, links movements in income to larger and more acceptable types of investment, and obviates arguments over land values at each review which tend to be less easily determined and thus less certain of agreement.

There are therefore two principal matters which demand the valuer's skills. One is determination of the initial ground rent, the other is the valuation of the freehold ground rent once in being.

Ground Rental Value

Since the ground rental value is the annual equivalent of the site capital value, ground rents may be derived from the capital value of the site which can be determined in the manner described in this Chapter.

From the freeholder's point of view, the ground rent should be at a level which, when capitalised, will produce the capital value of the site which it has before the grant of the lease.

This level is therefore the level derived from applying the prevailing yield for such ground rents.

Hence if a site has a capital value of £300,000, and ground rents are valued at 7 per cent at full rental value, then the freeholder will require a ground rent of 7 per cent of £300,000 = £21,000 p.a. Such a result might not emerge in practice since a developer offered a ground lease might prefer such an arrangement, as he has to raise less building finance, and might therefore go above this level. On the other hand he might find it more difficult to raise development funds if he can offer only a lease as security and so might reduce his offer to encourage an outright sale of the freehold. These factors depend on the state of the market and the nature of development, but the general rental value can be derived from such a strightforward approach, which at least provides a starting point.

The developer/lessee's approach to ground rents is different from a landlord's. To him a ground rent is an outgoing, and he may choose to determine the ground rent he can afford by a residual approach. The same principles will apply as to the residual method adopted to determine capital value, as described earlier, save that the annual cost of the development coupled with an annual profit will be deducted from the prospective annual income, any difference representing the "surplus" he can offer on a ground rent.

Example 18–5

X has been offered a ground lease of a site for which planning permission exists to erect a warehouse of 50,000 sq.ft. The lease is to be for 99 years from completion of the building. What rent can X afford to pay for the ground lease?

Rental Value of completed building
50,000 sq.ft. gross, say
45,000 sq.ft. net at £6 per sq.ft.   = £270,000 p.a.

Development Costs
Building costs 50,000 sq.ft.
at £30 per sq.ft.   £1,500,000

Professional fees at 10%	150,000
Finance say 6 months	
at 12%	99,000
Acquisition Costs	
Legal and agents fees and	
stamp duty say	40,000
Letting Costs	
Legal and agents fees say	30,000
	say £1,820,000

Annual Equivalent of Costs			
Interest at 8%	0·08		
A.S.F. 50 yrs at 2½%	0·02		
Profits at 2%	0·02	0·12	218,400
Surplus for Ground Rent			£51,600 p.a.

Capital Value of Ground Rents

Once a building lease is in operation the valuation of the ground rents produced follows the general principles in determining the capital value of any investment, as described in Part 1.

However a ground rent is generally less than the full rental of the property so that, in the case of a ground rent with geared reviews, apart from having the same qualities as the investment from which it derives, the rent is that much more certain of receipt, and has no risk of income interruption because of voids. For these reasons a ground rent will generally be valued at or slightly below the prevailing yields for the type of property from which it derives.

On the other hand it must be stressed that the general content of the ground lease will determine the yield. If rent reviews are widely spaced, so that the rent is fixed for longer than acceptable periods, then the yield will rise to reflect this. Similarly at one time developers commonly entered into leasing arrangements whereby the landlord received a certain minimum proportion of the rent of the buildings, leaving the developer with a share of the marginal rent (a "top slice" arrangement). Clearly the valuation of the landlord's interest would reflect his added security, whereas the valuation of the ground lessee's interest would need to reflect his exposure to the changing fortunes of the market place.

The foregoing comments have concentrated on the traditional situation where the freeholder grants a ground lease to the developer. Recent times have seen the use of ground leases where several parties come together to carry out large scale schemes, typically town centre redevelopments. The parties will include a developer, who will carry out the development and manage it thereafter, a funding institution which will put up the development funds, and the local authority who will provide planning and other support including the use of compulsory purchase powers to ensure site assembly. In these cases the agreement might be that the freehold interest will vest in the local authority who will grant a head lease to the funding institution who in turn will grant an under ground lease to the developer. The terms of the ground leases will reflect the agreement between the parties and their financial involvement. In these cases the ground lease terms will be arrived at in a different manner from that previously described. For example, the under ground lease might well provide for a rent which is a percentage of money given to the developer and, as such, the agreement is more of a funding document than a traditional ground lease. Even so the agreements must be related to the development and "side by side" agreements are common whereby all the parties share in the growth in rental value whilst sharing the downside risks of a fall.

Ground rents and ground leases have seen a fairly rapid development in their nature and make-up over recent years. At one time the valuer was concerned with whether they were "well secured" or not and, if so, they attracted minimum yields. Today the ground lease has evolved into the expression of a commercial arrangement and the valuation of ground lease investments has changed accordingly. They are now seen as an investment to be judged critically along with the other investment opportunities available.[7]

---

[7] For a more detailed consideration of the development process and associated valuation aspects see "Valuation and Development Appraisal" Ed. C. Darlow (Estates Gazette).

CHAPTER 19
Residential Properties

1. GENERALLY

THE RANGE of properties to be considered in this Chapter is a wide one, including tenements, cottages and small houses let at weekly or monthly rents, moderate-sized houses, large houses and flats. The main statutory areas of law which will be looked at are those concerned with (i) the protection of residential tenants; and (ii) the availability of financial assistance for the acquisition, provision and improvement of dwellings.

At the outset it is necessary to distinguish between properties let at rents under existing tenancies and bought for investment and properties offered on the market with vacant possession.

The former may be valued by the investment method of multiplying the net income by an appropriate figure of Years' Purchase; but in the case of the latter, the method of valuation is that of direct comparison of capital values based on records of recent sales in the same or comparable districts. There is a substantial disparity between these two values, investment value and vacant possession value, of the same property and valuation difficulties arise whenever there is a possibility of converting an investment value into a vacant possession value. This will be discussed later.

Whatever the method of approach to a particular problem, however, the two principal factors which influence the value of residential properties are (i) accommodation, and (ii) situation. The prospective tenant or purchaser will consider the nature and extent of the accommodation offered, and will at the same time have regard to the situation of the property as it affects the general amenities of life, time of travel to work, proximity to schools and like matters.

For example, a prospective occupier viewing an ordinary

three-bedroomed, semi-detached, suburban house, will probably already have in his mind some idea of the number of rooms he requires and their approximate size. He will consider the arrangement of the rooms for convenience in use, the adequacy of the domestic offices—kitchen, bathroom, etc.—the presence of central heating and the type of fuel used, the aspect of the rooms, the presence of a garage or parking space, the size of the garden, the state of repair, and all the other details which make the property attractive to him or otherwise.

It is true that in some cases all such proper considerations may be swamped by the urgent desire to secure a house of any kind; but, even allowing for this factor, it is not difficult to imagine two houses of the above type identical in construction, size, accommodation and state of repair, and yet so different in their situation that one may readily fetch £70,000 in the open market, while the other may only be worth £55,000.

The effect of position on value is influenced not only by such concrete considerations as have already been referred to, but also by such uncertain factors as changing fashions and the value of a good address. In valuing residential property it is often important to have regard not only to the present character of the neighbourhood but also to the possibility of changes in the future, dependent on an increase or decline in its popularity.

To summarise the effect of position and accommodation, it can be said that the general level of values in a neighbourhood is determined by situation factors, while differences in value between individual properties are determined by the nature and extent of the accommodation they offer.

2. STATUTORY CONTROL OF RESIDENTIAL TENANCIES

Although it is beyond the scope of this book to examine in detail the legislation directly affecting the valuation of residential property, a brief summary of this legislation is necessary as a background.

(i) The Rent Acts

Subject to proposed changes (see Section 7 of this Chapter on the Housing Bill 1988), the main body of legislation concerned with rent control of dwelling-houses is contained in the Rent Act 1977.

The Legislation—Historical Development. The first Act restricting rents and mortgage interest (passed in 1915) limited the rent which could be charged for a house coming within its provisions and restricted the landlords' right to recover possession of such houses. Jurisdiction over these matters was given to the county courts.

The provisions of the original Act were amended after the 1914–18 War by a number of Acts passed between 1920 and 1939 and the scope of the properties falling within the Rent Acts was reduced. The scope was determined mainly by reference to rateable value and by 1939 all but comparatively small dwellings had been freed. In 1939, a new Act was passed at the outbreak of war and brought into control all but comparatively large houses. From 1939 onwards there were therefore two categories of controlled houses, those under legislation prior to 1939 and those brought into control in 1939 known respectively as "old" and "new" controlled houses. In each case the rent recoverable was determined by reference to the rent at which the house concerned was first let and additions could only be made for increases in rates and for improvements. In addition, in the case of old controlled houses overall percentage additions were possible as well as certain increases in the case of properties sub-let. Furnished lettings were outside the scope of control, but limitation of rents and security of tenure were applied to them by a separate code under the Furnished Houses (Rent Control) Act 1946. This involved adjudication by a rent tribunal, not the county court.

Until 1949, there was no control of the rent which could be charged for a newly-erected house, except under the Building Materials and Housing Act 1945. The Landlord and Tenant (Rent Control) Act 1949, enabled either the landlord or the tenant to apply to the tribunal appointed under the Furnished Houses (Rent Control) Act 1946, to determine the reasonable rent in the case of dwelling-houses let for the first time since 1 September 1939. The Housing Repairs and Rents Act 1954, provided that new properties completed after 29 August, 1954, were free from control.

The Rent Act 1957, de-controlled dwelling-houses with rateable values on 7 November, 1956, of over £40 in London or £30 elsewhere. It also provided that the Rent Acts should not apply to "long tenancies" (granted for terms exceeding 21 years), nor to tenancies created after the commencement of the Act—"creeping de-control". For properties below the limits of rateable values specified which remained controlled, the maximum recoverable rent was determined on the basis of applying a multiplier to the 1956 gross value of the property.

The Rent Act 1965, left unaffected tenancies controlled under the Rent Act 1957, but re-imposed control on the majority of houses de-controlled under the 1957 Act. The tenancies which continued to be subject to control under the 1957 and 1965 Acts were "controlled tenancies"; but those brought under control in consequence of the 1965 Act are "regulated tenancies", and all "controlled tenancies" were converted into "regulated tenancies" by the Housing Act 1980. Tenancies at "low rents" (less than two-thirds of the rateable value of the premises on 23 March 1965, or when first rated thereafter) are outside the scope of the Rent Acts; though if they are "long tenancies" granted for terms exceeding 21 years the Landlord and Tenant Act 1954, Part I, protects them in a manner to be described below, provided that they would otherwise come within the scope of the Rent Acts. "Long tenancies" at full rents were put back within the scope of Rent Act protection by the Leasehold Reform Act 1967. The 1965 Act applied to dwelling-houses with rateable values on 23 March 1965, not exceeding £400 in Greater London or £200 elsewhere. The Counter-Inflation Act 1973, Section 14, raised these limits to £600 and £300 respectively as from 23 March 1973 and again to £1,500 and £750 respectively as from 1 April 1973 (when new rateable values came into effect). The 1965 Act introduced the system of "regulated rents", which are now governed by the Rent Act 1977.

The Rent Act 1968 consolidated the previous legislation,

including the unrepealed provisions of the 1957 and 1965 Acts. The special protection afforded by the Act of 1946 to furnished tenancies was first separately preserved under Part VI of the 1968 Act.

The Rent Act 1974 extended the scope of regulated tenancies to cover furnished tenancies and retained the special form of protection which these hitherto enjoyed (under Part VI of the 1968 Act) for a more limited class of tenancy, namely tenancies granted after 13 August 1974, by a "resident landlord", whether furnished or unfurnished and whether or not the rent covered payment for services (only cases of rent including board now being excluded). "Resident landlord" tenancies are those in which the landlord for the time being has continued to occupy a dwelling within the same building as a residence for himself.

The Rent Act 1977 now contains the law enacted in the previous statutes, in a consolidated form, and will be referred to in the remainder of this account of the law, together with later amendments. It should be noted that certain kinds of tenancy are excluded from Rent Act protection even if they are not at "low rents" and do not exceed the rateable value limits. Examples are holiday lettings, lettings by certain educational institutions to their students, lettings where the rent includes payment for board or attendance, lettings by the Crown or other public bodies, and lettings of parsonage houses, public houses or farms.

It should be noted also that the 1977 Act prohibits the evasion of new control by charging the tenant a "premium" (i.e., a lump sum over and above the rent). This is a criminal offence and the tenant can claim repayment.

The Housing Act 1980

Part I, Chapter I (re-enacted in the Housing Act 1985, Part V, and amended by the Housing and Building Control Act 1984, Part I, and the Housing and Planning Act 1986, Part I) confers on tenants of property in the public sector— i.e. council house tenants, and others in similar accommodation, referred to as "secure tenants"—the right to buy their dwellings (with registered title and at a concessionary price) and also the right to be granted a mortgage for that purpose. With some exceptions, tenants of houses are empowered to buy the freehold; while tenants of flats and maisonettes are empowered to buy a long lease (which will normally be for a term of 125 years at a ground rent of not more than £10 a year). The landlord's reversion may be a leasehold (21 years or more) in which case the tenant is entitled to a lease expiring five days earlier than the expiry of the landlord's lease. A qualifying minimum of two years' occupation is necessary, of one or more dwellings in succession.

The purchase price is the open market value with vacant possession at a discount of 32 per cent rising by 1 per cent for each year of occupation beyond 2 years, up to a maximum of 60 per cent for 30 years (but not more than £35,000); but for flats it is 44 per cent rising by 2 per cent yearly to a 70 per cent maximum. The discount is repayable on early re-sale, i.e. within 3 years of purchase, at a rate of one-third of discount for each of the years up to 3. Up to the entire discounted purchase price plus costs may be left on mortgage with the landlord authority or (in the case of housing associa-tion dwellings) the Housing Corporation. The right to buy and to mortgage may be enjoyed successively by surviving spouses, or children, of deceased secure tenants.

If the tenant claims a mortgage from the local authority or Housing Corporation after serving notice of exercising his "right to buy", and he does not or cannot seek an advance covering the entire (discounted) purchase price plus costs, he can now, in addition to claiming a deferment of completion for three years from his original notice to buy, also claim a "shared ownership lease" (Housing Act 1980, amended by Part I of the Housing and Planning Act 1986). The claim for deferment must still be made (plus £150 deposit) within 3 months of receiving the authority's answer to the claim for a mortgage; and that answer must inform the tenant of his right to a "shared ownership lease" as well as deferment. The "shared ownership lease" is to be for the period of 125 years (or longer) specified in Sched. 2, para. 11, of the Hous-ing Act 1980. The tenant can buy an initial share in value, and later increase this up to full value; the shares are in eighths of the full value from one half upwards (though the

Secretary of State can vary these fractions). The basic rules
as to rent, valuations, mortgages and discounts apply, but
with amounts properly scaled down in proportion. When the
tenant has paid the *full* value he is then entitled to an outright
transfer of the landlord authority's interest, if freehold, or
a sub-lease expiring five days before the expiry of that interest, if leasehold, taken in his own name or that of a nominee.
The "shared ownership lease" must provide accordingly in
each case.

Part I Chapter II (re-enacted in Part IV of the Housing
Act 1985 and amended by the Housing and Building Control
Act 1984, Part I) provides, for the first time, a system of
security of tenure for "secure tenants" who do not avail themselves of the above-mentioned right to buy their dwellings,
whether their tenancies were granted before or after the commencement of these provisions. Section 28 defines "secure
tenants" as tenants of dwellings owned by local authorities,
new town authorities, the Development Board for Rural
Wales, housing associations and housing trusts. Long tenancies (over 21 years) are excluded, as are various tenancies
for special purposes such as temporary accommodation,
student lettings, occupation for purposes of the tenant's
employment and other such matters. Residential properties
let to corporate bodies are excluded from protection.
Licences, however, are included in protection on the same
basis as tenancies. Fixed-term tenancies continue after the
end of their term as periodic tenancies. There is one statutory
succession on the death of a secure tenant on a periodic
tenancy (not *two* as in the private sector) to the surviving
spouse, if any, or else to another member of the family who
has resided in the dwelling for the past year. The landlord
authority can only recover possession by application to the
county court on grounds similar to those available in the
private sector under the Rent Act 1977. As to the terms
of a "secure tenancy", the tenant is given an absolute right
to take in lodgers, but cannot sublet, or part with possession
of *part* of the premises without permission (which must not
however be unreasonably withheld); while subletting, assign-
ing or parting with possession of the whole (or the remainder)
of the premises normally terminates the security of tenure.

Special rules deal with variation of terms of secure tenancies, information to tenants, consultation, management and improvements.

Part II deals with protected residential tenancies in the private sector. It introduced "protected shorthold tenancies" (as from 28 November 1980). These may be granted for a term certain of from 1 to 5 years. Private landlords may apply to the county court to recover possession at the end of the term granted: but apart from that the tenant is protected under the Rent Act 1977, particularly as regards his rent (certificates of fair rent and registration of rents). Also introduced were "assured tenancies" to be granted by "approved bodies" (i.e. approved by the Secretary of State), of dwellings constructed after 8 August 1980. Such tenancies are protected in the same way as business tenancies under Part II of the Landlord and Tenant Act 1954. As for protected tenancies under the 1977 Act, all controlled tenancies[1] became regulated tenancies; various amendments were introduced into the system of rent registration; and improved rights of recovery of possession were given to intending owner-occupiers, retirement home owners and servicemen. "Restricted contracts" of letting by resident landlords were also dealt with (separate rent tribunals were abolished, but rent assessment committees now deal with such lettings as "rent tribunals"; while security of tenure was transferred to county courts, and reduced from six to three months). The right of charging of premiums for tenancies at low rents was extended.

Part III empowers "secure" and "protected" tenants to improve the tenanted property with the landlords' consent, which must not be unreasonably withheld.

Rents under Regulated Tenancies (1977 Act, Part III)

Under the regulated tenancy system, the landlord or tenant or both can apply to the rent officer for the registration of a fair rent (subject to a right of appeal to the local rent assessment committee). Once such a rent has been determined

---

[1] Except for mixed residential and business premises, which are protected in the same way as assured tenancies (above).

and registered it is the maximum rent which can be charged for the property.

A fair rent is an open market rent subject to certain special rules laid down in section 70 of the 1977 Act, which states that in determining a fair rent regard must be had to all circumstances (other than personal circumstances) and in particular to the age, character and locality of the dwelling-house and to the state of repair. It must be assumed that the number of persons seeking to become tenants of similar dwelling-houses in the locality on the terms (other than those relating to rent) of the tenancy is not substantially greater than the number of such dwelling-houses in the locality available for letting on such terms. To be disregarded are disrepair or other defects attributable to the tenant and any improvements carried out, otherwise than in pursuance of the terms of the tenancy, by the tenant or his predecessors. Section 55 of the 1977 Act, which enacted a system of phased increase of rent for regulated tenancies, has now been nullified by the Rent (Relief from Phasing) Order 1987, made under the Housing Act 1980.

Security of Tenure (1977 Act, Part VII)

Limitation of rents would be of little use to protected tenants if they did not also have security of tenure, because otherwise their landlords could at common law terminate their tenancies by notice to quit (in the case of periodic tenancies) or refuse to renew them (in the case of fixed-term tenancies). The 1977 Act therefore provides also that when the contractual ("protected") tenancy comes to an end in this way it is prolonged indefinitely in the form of a "statutory tenancy", which is transmissible on the tenant's death (though not otherwise except by agreement) to a surviving spouse or other relative (if resident), and similarly a second time on that person's death. This security of tenure, however, can be terminated if the county court grants possession to the landlord; though the court can only do this in certain specified cases, some of which arise because of the requirements of the landlord and others because of some default by the tenant. These various grounds will be found in

Schedule 15 of the 1977 Act. The landlord may succeed if he can satisfy the court: (a) that it would be reasonable for him to be awarded possession; and (b) that there is suitable alternative accommodation or that one of certain "discretionary" grounds listed in Part I of Schedule 15 applies; and (c) that there exists no special reason for withholding the award of possession; but the court must award possession on proof of one of the "mandatory" grounds set out in Part II of Schedule 15 (as amended by the Rent (Amendment) Act 1985). County courts also have jurisdiction over "rental purchase agreements", which were previously outside the scope of statutory protection (Housing Act 1980, Part IV).

(ii) THE LANDLORD AND TENANT ACT 1954 (PART I) AND THE LEASEHOLD REFORM ACT 1967

The protection of tenants occupying dwelling-houses on ground leases has caused concern for a number of years and these two pieces of legislation represent the two major steps taken to ensure that such tenants are not automatically dispossessed when their contractual right to remain in occupation has expired.

The Landlord and Tenant Act 1954, (Part I), which came into effect on 1 October 1954, applies to houses let on "long tenancies" (i.e., for more than 21 years) which, on account of the rent being a "low rent" (i.e. less than two-thirds of the rateable value on 23 March 1965, or when first rated thereafter) are outside the protection of the Rent Acts. The limits of rateable value within which Part I of the 1954 Act applies are those applicable under the Rent Act 1977, referred to above. A tenant is not protected if the landlord is the Crown or a local authority, the Development Corporation of a new town or certain housing associations and trusts.

The effect of the 1954 Act is to continue the tenancy automatically after the date when it would normally expire, on the same terms as before, until either the landlord or the tenant terminates it by one of the notices prescribed by the Act; though the landlord and the tenant can agree on the terms of a new tenancy to take the place of the long tenancy.

A long tenancy can be terminated by the landlord by giving

one of two types of notice, each of which must be in prescribed form. If the landlord is content for the tenant to stay in the house he must serve a landlord's notice proposing a statutory tenancy. If he wishes the tenant to leave he must serve a landlord's notice to resume possession.

Should a tenant wish to terminate a long tenancy he must give not less than one month's notice in writing.

A landlord's notice proposing a statutory tenancy would set out the proposed terms as to rent and repairs, including "initial repairs". The landlord and tenant can negotiate on these terms and come to an agreement in writing. If they cannot do so the landlord can apply to the County Court to decide those items which are in dispute.

The 1977 Act procedure already referred to for the determination and registration of fair rents applies to tenancies arising from these provisions.

Where a tenant remains in possession after the end of the long tenancy he is relieved of any outstanding liability in respect of repairs arising under that tenancy. The terms proposed by the landlord may provide for the carrying out of repairs when the new terms come into force. These repairs are known as "initial repairs" and the tenant may have to bear some or all of the cost of them. Where a tenant leaves at the end of the long tenancy his liability under the tenancy is not affected by the 1954 Act. "Initial repairs" may be carried out either by the landlord or by the tenant or partly by one and partly by the other; neither need do any unless he wishes. If the landlord carries out the repairs he is entitled to recover from the tenant the reasonable cost of the repairs insofar as they are necessary because the tenant did not meet his obligations under the long tenancy. Payment can be made by the tenant either by a lump sum or by instalments, as agreed between the parties or as determined by the county court.

Where a landlord serves notice to resume possession the tenant if he wishes to remain in the house should so inform the landlord. If he does not agree to giving up the house, the landlord can apply to the county court for a possession order. The grounds upon which a landlord can apply for possession include the following: (i) that suitable alternative accommodation will be available for the tenant; (ii) that the tenant has failed to comply with the terms of his tenancy as to payment of rent or rates or as to insuring or keeping insured the premises; (iii) that the tenant, or a person residing with him, or any sub-tenant of his has caused nuisance or annoyance to adjoining occupiers; (iv) that the premises, or any part of them, which the tenant is occupying are reasonably required by the landlord for occupation as a residence for himself or any son or daughter of his over 18 years of age or his father or mother. In the last case the Court must not make an order for possession where the landlord purchased the property after 21 November 1950, or where it is satisfied that having regard to all the circumstances of the case, including the availability of other accommodation, greater hardship would be caused by making the order than by refusing to make it. Where the landlord's interest is held by any of certain specified public or charitable bodies (Leasehold Reform Act, 1967, section 38), there is an additional ground for obtaining possession, namely that the landlord proposes to demolish or reconstruct the premises for purposes of redevelopment, and will require possession for this purpose at the end of the long tenancy, and has made reasonable preparation for the redevelopment.

The Leasehold Reform Act 1967 came into force on 27 October 1967, and represents a very radical departure from previous property law. The White Paper[2] which preceded the legislation stated the Government's view that "the basic principle of a reform which will do justice between the parties should be that the freeholder owns the land and the occupying leaseholder is morally entitled to the ownership of the building which has been put on and maintained on the land". This principle has, however, only been extended to the limited range of properties to which the 1967 Act applies; and this (unlike the Landlord and Tenant Act 1954, Part I) excludes flats and maisonettes, and any similar units produced by subdivisions of buildings where the dividing line is horizontal instead of vertical.

The 1967 Act enables qualified leasehold owner-occupiers

---

[2] Cmnd. 2916 of 1966 "Leasehold Reform in England and Wales".

either to purchase the freehold reversion from the ground landlord or to obtain an extension of the term of the lease.

The following requirements must be met before a leaseholder is qualified and entitled to the benefits conferred by the Act:

(a) The term of the existing lease must be more than 21 years and the rent reserved must be less than two-thirds of the rateable value.

(b) The leaseholder must have occupied the house for three of the last ten years as his main residence. Use of part of the premises for another purpose, for example as a shop, does not necessarily disqualify.

(c) The rateable value of the house on 23 March, 1965, or when first rated therafter, must not exceed £400 in Greater London and £200 elsewhere. The Housing Act 1974, Section 118(1), increased these limits, with effect from 1 April, 1973, to £1,500 and £750 respectively for tenancies created on or before 18 February, 1966, and to £1,000 and £500 respectively for tenancies created after that date.

"Shared ownership leases" granted by various public authorities and housing associations are excluded from the operation of the 1967 Act (Schedule 4A, added by the Housing and Planning Act 1986).

Enfranchisement

Where a leaseholder is qualified under the 1967 Act and gives his landlord written notice of his desire to purchase the freehold interest, then, except as provided by the Act, the landlord is bound to make to the leaseholder and the leaseholder to accept (at a price and on the conditions provided) a grant of the house and premises for an estate in fee simple absolute, subject to the tenancy and to the leaseholder's incumbrances but otherwise free from incumbrances.

The price payable, as defined in Section 9(1A) of the 1967 Act as amended by Section 23 of the Housing and Planning Act 1986, is the amount which the landlord's reversion to the house and premises might be expected to realise on the assumption that it is to be sold in the open market by a willing seller (the tenant and members of his family who reside in the house having no right, for the purpose of this assumption, to buy the freehold or an extended lease). It must be assumed also that the freehold interest is subject only to the existing lease, ending on the original date of termination even if extended under the 1967 Act.

Within one month of the ascertainment of the price payable the tenant may give written notice to the landlord that he is unable or unwilling to acquire at that price, in which case the notice of his desire to have the freehold ceases to have effect. In such circumstances the tenant must pay just compensation to the landlord.

Valuations to Determine Enfranchisement Price—"Original Method"

The valuation approach to determine the price payable under Section 9 of the Act (as amended) has proved in practice to be a highly contentious area and there have been many cases referred to the Lands Tribunal.

One of the earliest cases turned on whether the valuation approach should reflect the tenant's position as a special purchaser and so allow for marriage value.[3] This led to the amendment which provided that the tenant's bid should be disregarded (but see, in relation to higher value properties, the amendments introduced by the Housing Act 1974 and the "new method" of valuation referred to later).

Subsequent cases have turned chiefly on two aspects, the method of determining the modern ground rent and the choice of the capitalisation rates, within the valuation of the freehold interest.

A typical situation is where the freehold interest is subject to a ground lease granted several years ago at an annual ground rent which is now considered to be a nominal sum. At the end of the lease it must be assumed that the tenant will extend the lease for a further period of 50 years at the

---

[3] *Custins v. Hearts of Oak Benefit Society* (1968) 209 EG 239.

current ground rental value (a "modern ground rent") subject to review after 25 years. Thereafter the house and land will revert to the freeholder. This involves a three stage valuation:

(a) *Term of Existing Lease.* This will be the valuation of a ground rent for the outstanding period of the lease. From an investment viewpoint this is an unattractive proposition since the income is fixed and it is small so that management costs are disproportionately high. This has led to disputes as to the appropriate capitalisation rates to be adopted.

As a general rule, the Lands Tribunal decisions tended to adopt rates between 6 and 8 per cent,[4] but since 1980 most leasehold valuation tribunal decisions have adopted 7 per cent. Higher rates have been employed where the outstanding term is relatively long or where there is market evidence.[5]

(b) *Reversion to Modern Ground Rent.* At the end of the existing lease the rent will rise to a "modern ground rent" which will be receivable for 50 years, subject to one review after 25 years.

The "modern ground rent" is in essence the current ground rental value. However, it has been accepted that the rental value is not that of a site cleared and ready for development but of a site with house "parked" on it. Thus one approach has emerged which is commonly adopted whereby the value of the freehold interest in the house and land is apportioned between land and buildings and the modern ground rent is then derived from the value of the land as apportioned. This is known as the "standing house approach".[6]

Alternative methods may be adopted involving a valuation direct to site value or to site rental value and are generally to be preferred where evidence exists.[7]

The standing house approach starts therefore with the

[4] See for example *Carthew v. Estates Governors of Alleyn's College of God's Gift* (1974) 231 EG 809; *Nash v. Castell-y-Mynach Estate* (1974) 234 EG 293.

[5] See for example *Lead v. J and L Estates Limited* (1974) 236 EG 819.

[6] See for example *Hall v. Davies* (1970) 215 EG 175: *Kemp v. Josephine Trust* (1971) 217 EG 351: *Nash v. Castell-y-Mynach Estate* op. cit.

[7] *Farr v. Millerson* (1971) 218 EG 1177: *Miller v. St. John Baptists College, Oxford* (1976) 243 EG 535: *Embling v. Wells and Campden Charity's Trustees* (1977) 247 EG 909.

valuation of the freehold interest in the house and land. The valuation assumes vacant possession, ignoring for example the fact that part is let to tenants at a controlled or fair rent, or any disrepair.[8] The reason for this is that what is sought is the full unencumbered value of the property. For the same reason it will reflect any potential for conversion into separate flats to be sold with vacant possession.[9]

Once this full value has been determined it is necessary to apportion the value between land and buildings. The amount apportioned to the land will depend on the facts of the case, but in general the proportion attributable to the land value of houses in high value areas will be greater than that in low value areas in the same way that values per plot for high value houses are greater than values per plot for cheaper housing. There can be no hard and fast rules but tribunal decisions have tended to adopt around 40 per cent for houses in London and around 30 per cent for houses elsewhere as a reflection of this general proposition.[10]

Having determined the land value the final stage is to determine the modern ground rent. This is found by decapitalising the value applying the appropriate yield. This again has been an area of dispute, coupled with the choice of yield with which the modern ground rent will be capitalised. Clearly if both yields are the same then the whole exercise can be short-circuited by simply deferring the land values at the chosen yield. However, a line of argument was developed which required the decapitalisation rate to be lower than the recapitalisation rate, an approach known as the adverse differential.

The Lands Tribunal adopted this approach in many decisions but the correctness of the approach was challenged in the Court of Appeal in one case[11] when the Court held that there was no justification for adopting different rates.

Since then the tribunal decisions generally have not

---

[8] *Official Custodian for Charities v. Goldridge* (1973) 26 P & CR 191, 10.
[9] *Official Custodian*, etc. op. cit.
[10] See for Example *Graingers v. Gunter Estate Trustees* (1977) 246 EG 1286.
[11] *Official Custodian*, etc. op. cit.

adopted the adverse differential, although they may do so if they feel the particular circumstances justify it.[12]

When the adverse differential approach is adopted the land value is commonly decapitalised at around 6 per cent and the resultant modern ground rent then recapitalised at around 8 per cent. In other cases a common rate will be adopted normally between 6 per cent and 8 per cent. These yields do not form absolute precedents, the yield depending on the facts of the case and the valuation implications thereof.

(c) *Reversion to House.* Following the expiry of the 50 years deemed extension the whole property reverts to the freeholder. However, if the existing lease does not expire for a considerable period, by the time account is taken of the 50 year extension, the reversion to the standing house will have an insignificant value and can be ignored so that the modern ground rent is valued to perpetuity. However, if the unexpired term of the existing lease is short, the reversion in just over 50 years may be sufficiently significant to be included, as in the case of *Haresign v. St. John the Baptist's College, Oxford.*[13] Such a reversion is termed a "Haresign reversion".

Market Transactions

One of the principal causes for the valuation arguments which have emerged is that the statutory approach is not usually found in the open market, thereby leaving the valuer to draw upon valuation principles to carry out the valuation. The only comparables which will generally be found are of sales to tenants who are also enfranchising and where it may be assumed that the statutory approach has been adopted. However, in practice a tenant may be prepared to pay over the odds to effect a purchase rather than go to the Lands Tribunal with the contingent risk of additional costs and uncertainty of outcome. The Lands Tribunal has recognised this factor when considering comparables by discounting the

---

[12] *Gallagher Estates Limited v. Walker* (1974) 230 EG 359: *Leeds v. J & L Estates Ltd.* (1974) 236 EG 819: it is suggested that the Lands Tribunal will normally be reluctant to accept the adverse differential.

[13] (1980) 255 EG 711.

prices paid since the case of *Delaforce v. Evans*;[14] the pressure on tenants and the consequent over-bidding being termed the "Delaforce" effect.[15]

Example 19–1

The leaseholder of a late 19th century, brick-built four-bedroom semi-detached house with garage, in a fairly good residential area, wishes to purchase the freehold interest. The lease is for 99 years from 1 January, 1908, at an annual ground rent of £5.

On 1 January, 1989, the leaseholder, who is qualified under the Act, serves the necessary statutory notice under the Leasehold Reform Act 1967, claiming the right to have the freehold.

The house occupies a site with an area of 300 square yards. Comparable residential building land in the area has recently changed hands at £120,000 per acre. Similar houses in the area have been sold on the open market with vacant possession at figures ranging from £28,000 to £32,000.

Valuation

In order to value the reversion after the existing lease it is necessary to estimate a modern ground rent:

(a) Standing House approach

Standing House Value, say	£30,000	
Land Apportionment, say 30%	0·3	
Site Value	£9,000	
Modern Ground Rent at 8%	0·08	£720 p.a.

(b) Capital value of site with all services £9,000
Modern ground rent at 8%   0·08   £720 p.a.

Modern Ground Rent   £720 p.a.

---

[14] *Delaforce v. Evans* (1970) 215 EG 315.
[15] For an example of the application of the "Delaforce" effect see *Guiver v. Francine Properties Limited* (1974) 234 EG 741.

Term

Present ground rent	£5p.a.	
Y.P. 18 years at 8%	9·37	£47

Reversion

After 31st December, 2007, to modern ground rent based on 1989 site value	£720p.a.	
Y.P. perpetuity at 8% deferred 18 years	3·12	£2,246
Price payable for enfranchisement, say		£2,300

Amendments under Housing Act 1974

As was stated above, the Housing Act 1974 extended the rights of enfranchisement to houses with a rateable value up to £1,500 in Greater London (£750 elsewhere) or, for tenancies created after 18 February, 1966, £1,000 (£500). The rateable value may be adjusted so as to ignore tenants' improvements and a certificate may be obtained from the Valuation Officer for this purpose.[16] Thus a house in London with a rateable value of say £1,570 may come within the 1974 Act if, for example, the tenant put in central heating and added a garage all of which has added more than £70 to the rateable value.

Valuations to Determine Enfranchisement Price—"New Method"

In respect of houses within the extended rateable value limits set by the 1974 Act, the valuation approach for enfranchisement differs in two important respects from "the original

[16] Section 118 and Schedule 8 Housing Act 1974 as amended by section 141 and Schedule 21 Housing Act 1980, now section 1(4A) 1967 Act.

method" already considered. The first is that the price may reflect the tenant's bid, so allowing for marriage value.[17] The second is that the valuation should reflect the tenant's right to remain in possession under Part I of the Landlord and Tenant Act 1954 and not his right to extend the lease by 50 years at a modern ground rent. This basis of valuation is described as "the new method" and the provisions are in Section 9(1A) of the 1967 Act.

Extension of the Existing Lease

Where a leaseholder is qualified under the Act and gives the landlord written notice of his desire to extend his lease then, except as provided by the Act, the landlord must grant and the leaseholder must accept a new tenancy for a term expiring fifty years after the term date of the existing tenancy.

With the exception of the rent the terms of the new tenancy will be the same as the terms of the existing tenancy. Rules for the ascertainment of the new rent are laid down in Section 15 of the 1967 Act but the main point to be noted is that the rent must be a ground rent in the sense that it represents the letting value of the site excluding anything for the value of the buildings on the site. This modern ground rent which is payable as from the original term date can be revised if the landlord so requires after the expiration of twenty-five years.

Landlord's Over-Riding Rights

In certain circumstances the leaseholder's right to purchase the freehold or to extend the lease may be defeated. If the landlord can satisfy the Court that he requires possession of the house for redevelopment or for his own occupation or occupation by an adult member of his family, the Court may grant an order for possession. The tenant is entitled to receive compensation for the loss of the buildings. The

---

[17] *Norfolk v. Trinity College, Cambridge* (1975) 238 EG 421.

compensation will be the value of the 50 years lease at a modern ground rent.

Retention of Management Powers

In circumstances specified in section 19 of the 1967 Act, landlords could retain certain powers of management on enfranchisement in order to maintain adequate standards of appearance and regular redevelopment in an area.

For a more detailed consideration of the Leasehold Reform Act 1967, the reader is referred to Chapter 3 of "Valuation: Principles into Practice" (3rd Edition 1988) Ed. W. H. Rees and "The Handbook of Leasehold Reform" by Charles Hubbard and Delyth Williams (Sweet & Maxwell).

(iii) THE HOUSING ACT 1985

The provisions of the Housing Act 1985 give local authorities wide powers to prevent overcrowding within houses, to ensure that they are kept in reasonable repair and condition, and to have them improved or removed as the case may be.

Individual houses unfit for habitation can be dealt with by closing and demolition orders, or by repair notices ordering the owner to carry out the necessary repairs. Obstructive buildings detrimental to good housing around them may be compulsorily demolished. Areas of substandard housing may be cleared for redevelopment, the compensation payable to owners of unfit houses being in principle limited to "cleared site" value. Other areas may be subject to renovation by encouragement of improvement works by house owners themselves (grant-aided, as described later in this Chapter); these are "housing action areas" and "general improvement areas", but the availability of grants is not confined to them, as will be seen.

The compensation provisions of the 1985 Act are dealt with at length in Chapter 30.

(iv) LOCAL AUTHORITY PARTICIPATION IN PRIVATE HOUSING FINANCE

Home Loans

There were formerly two main statutory codes under which local authorities participated in the lending of money for private housing: the Small Dwellings Acquisition Acts 1899–1923, and the Housing (Financial Provisions) Act 1958, as subsequently amended. The Housing Act 1985, Part XIV, has abolished the former and re-enacted the latter. A third code, the "option mortgage" scheme under Part II of the Housing Subsidies Act 1967, was abolished by the Finance Act 1982, section 27.

The Housing Act 1985, Part XIV, empowers local authorities to make advances on mortgage for acquiring existing houses, erecting new houses, converting buildings into houses, and altering, enlarging, repairing or improving houses. The authority must be satisfied that the house is, or will be made, in all respects fit for human habitation; and no advance may be made unless the interest to be mortgaged is the freehold or a leasehold with an unexpired term at least 10 years longer than the period for repayment of the loan. Easier terms may in some circumstances be available for purchasers of older properties which are in need of repair or renovation ("homesteading"). Authorities may also agree to indemnify building societies and other bodies making "home loans", so that if a mortgagor defaults the loss will fall on the authority instead of the mortgagee.

There is also a power for the Secretary of State to advance money to local housing authorities, building societies and such other "recognised lending institutions" as may be specified, to assist "first-time buyers" who have been "saving with a recognised savings institution" (local authority, bank, friendly society, National Savings, etc.) for at least two years.

Grants to Improve Dwellings

In addition to loans there are grants, payable by local housing authorities to house owners, "towards works of improvement, repair and conversion" of dwellings, in accordance with Part XV of the Housing Act 1985, which re-enacts the substance of earlier legislation and is itself extended by section 15 and Schedule 3 of the Housing and Planning Act 1986.

These are "improvement", "intermediate", "special", "repairs" and "common parts" grants, payable towards the cost of works for conversion to, or improvement or repair of, dwellings generally, and also for improvement of dwellings in multiple occupation and the improvement or repair of the "common parts" of a building including one or more flats.

An application must be made to and approved by the local authority, must normally be made and approved in advance, and must not duplicate previous grant-aided works applied for within the past two years; and the building for which it is made must normally have been erected before 3 October 1961. If works specified in an application though appropriate in principle seem excessive in amount the local authority can scale it down accordingly.

Applicants must normally have an "interest" in the property. This means they must be freeholders, or leaseholders with five years to run, or statutory or secure tenants, or protected tenants or occupants, or leaseholders on long tenancies (over 21 years) at low rents with less than five years to run which come within section 1 of the Landlord and Tenant Act 1954.

Applications (except for "common parts grants"), must normally be accompanied by either of two kinds of "certificates as to future occupation". A "certificate of owner—occupation" certifies that the dwelling will be occupied exclusively as the sole or main residence of the applicant (or of a beneficiary if the application comes from a trustee or personal representative) or a member of his family or a member of his or their household, throughout the period from one to five years after the "certified date" when the dwelling becomes fit for occupation after completion of the grant-aided works. A "certificate of availability for letting" certifies that for five years after the "certified date" the dwelling will be available for letting to anyone outside the applicant's family, if any, or for occupation as an agricultural tied dwelling, or as a residence other than for holiday use.

"Improvement grants" are payable at the local authority's discretion. They are for conversion or improvement works which go beyond works qualifying for "intermediate grants" (to be described below) and which are expected to bring the premises up to the "required standard"—i.e. so as to have all the "standard amenities", to be in repair, and to comply with a list of ten requirements currently specified by the Secretary of State (in DOE Circular 21/80, Appendix A, para. 5). Except for dwellings located in housing action areas or occupied by disabled persons, there are rateable value limits: £400 in Greater London and £225 elsewhere for improvements, and £600 in Greater London and £350 elsewhere for conversions (SI 1977 no. 1213).

The authority must, if approving a grant application, determine the proper cost of the "relevant works"; and not more than 50% of that cost can be for repairs or replacements (70% for a building in need of substantial structural repair— SI 1982 no. 1205). To the "estimated expense" of these approved works an "eligible expense" ceiling is applied. Under SI 1983 no. 613 this depends on whether the dwelling is within Category A or Category B. Category A covers dwellings which are: (i) located in housing action areas, or (ii) subject to repair notices or undertakings, or (iii) lacking in one or more "standard amenities", or (iv) in need of substantial structural repair, or (v) occupied by a disabled person. All other dwellings are in Category B. The ceiling of expense currently prescribed for conversion of buildings of less than three storeys, or for improvements generally, is £13,800 in Greater London and £10,200 elsewhere for Category A and £9,000 in Greater London and £6,600 elsewhere for Category B; but higher figures are prescribed for listed buildings and for buildings of three or more storeys. The actual grant payable must not exceed the "appropriate percentage" of the "eligible expense" (at or below the ceiling as the case may be). This is 50% as a general rule but 75% for all Category A cases and 65% for Category B cases in general improvement areas. The 75% grants can be further raised to any figure up to 90% in cases of hardship, and 50% grants up to 65%. Grants amounting to less than the "appropriate percentage" can be awarded, but only if a written statement of reasons is given.

Thus for example a property with a rateable value of £450, provided that it is situated in Greater London, can qualify for an improvement grant, but only in respect of conversion works. If in addition the building is in need of substantial structural repair, it comes within Category A. This in turn means that up to 70% of the proper cost of "relevant works" can relate to repairs or replacements. The "eligible expense" ceiling which applies to this cost figure is currently, on the figures given above, £13,800, up to £9,660 of which can relate to repairs or replacements. It follows from these details that 75% is the "appropriate percentage" payable as grant (less, if written reasons are given). If the proposed works of conversion are reasonably acceptable, the council should accept them and approve the grant—i.e. it would be capricious not to do so. If the proper cost of the works is at or above the "eligible expense" ceiling of £13,800 (above) the grant at 75% will be £10,350. If the council decide to give less, that decision must be justified in writing. If they decide to give more, they must genuinely believe that it is a case of hardship, justifying an amount up to 90% of the "eligible expense"— i.e. £12,420.

Moving on to "intermediate grants", it is to be noted that payment is mandatory upon the local authority, provided that they are reasonably satisfied that the prescribed requirements are met. These grants are intended to contribute to the proper cost of installing in a dwelling any or all of the "standard amenities" which have been lacking or defective for at least a year, or are unsuitable for a disabled occupant. If the installation work necessitates in addition works of repair or replacement, the cost of these should be taken into account also. As with an "improvement grant" the application, accompanied by the estimate of the cost of the works, must be approved in advance; and for the "estimated expense" there is an "eligible expense" ceiling. This figure is an aggregate of separate "ceilings" for each "standard amenity" which it is necessary to instal and also for any necessary work of repair and replacement. The seven "standard

amenities" with their "eligible expense" ceiling are currently
as follows:

	Greater London	elsewhere
(1) Fixed bath or shower	£450	£340
(2) Hot & Cold water supply to (1)	£570	£430
(3) Wash-hand basin	£175	£130
(4) Hot & cold water supply to (3)	£300	£230
(5) Sink	£450	£340
(6) Hot & cold water supply to (5)	£380	£290
(7) WC	£680	£515
Totals	£3,005	£2,275

For works of repair or replacement the "eligible expense"
ceiling is currently £4,200 in Greater London and £3,000 elsewhere if the dwelling will have been put into reasonable
repair after the works have been completed, or if the case
is one of financial hardship; but in other cases it is a prescribed
sum, in addition to the amount listed above, per "standard
amenity" installed, namely £420 in Greater London and £300
elsewhere but not higher than a ceiling total of £1,680 and
£1,200 respectively—i.e. for four of the "standard amenities". (These figures are as prescribed in SI 1983 no. 613).
The amount of grant is the "appropriate percentage" of the
total "eligible expense", calculated at or below the ceiling,
or ceilings, applicable to the various parts of the "estimated
expense" of the works which are approved. This is currently
set at 75% if the premises are within Category A as described
earlier, 65% if they are in Category B but in a general improvement area, and 50% otherwise. In cases of hardship
the percentage can be raised to any higher level up to, but
not beyond, 90% (from 75%) and 65% (from 50%). (These
figures are as prescribed in SI 1980 no. 1735).

Moving on again to "special grants", it should be noted
that these are payable in respect of works for improvement
of any "house in multiple occupation" by installing missing
or defective "standard amenities" or fire escapes. They are
mandatory if the works are necessary to comply with an
official notice requiring them to be carried out, but discretion-

ary in other cases. "House in multiple occupation" means a house occupied by a number of people who do not "form a single household", excluding any part occupied *as a separate dwelling* by any people who actually do "form a single household". A "certificate as to future occupation" is not required; but for discretionary "special grants" it is necessary for the applicant to have a property "interest" in the premises and for the works to be such as can be expected to put the premises into reasonable repair, whereas for mandatory "special grants" these requirements are dispensed with and the works can have been put in hand already. The "estimated expense" of the works acceptable for grant must be calculated under the three heads of "standard amenities", fire-escapes, and works of a repair or replacement, and so must the "eligible expense" ceilings(s). For "standard amenities" the ceiling is the same as for "intermediate grants" (above); for fire-escapes it is currently £10,800 in Greater London and £8,100 elsewhere; for repair or replacement it is currently £4,200 in Greater London and £3,000 elsewhere (SI 1983 no. 613). The "appropriate percentage" of the "eligible expense" at or below its ceiling(s) payable as grant is 75% if the grant is mandatory, or if it is required to make up a sufficient number of "standard amenities" or fire-escapes for the number of occupants, or if the premises are within Category A as described earlier; otherwise it is 65% in a general improvement area and 50% elsewhere. In cases of hardship there is discretion to raise 75% grants to a level up to but not above 90%, and 50% grants up to but not above 65%. The "appropriate percentage" must be given in full in a mandatory "special grant"; but less can be given in a discretionary "special grant" if written reasons are supplied.

Moving on once more to "repairs grants" which are payable only in respect of 'old dwellings" (currently defined as pre-1919 houses) and later houses built before 3 October 1961 which contain lead water-pipes which should be replaced (SI 1982 no. 1205), it should be noted that these are confined to repair or replacement works unrelated to conversion or improvement. Like "special grants" they are mandatory if the works are necessary to comply with an official notice requiring them to be done (in this case a repair notice) but discretionary in other cases; and in the case of mandatory "repairs grants" the applicant need not have a property "interest" in the premises nor furnish a "certificate as to future occupation" and the works can already have been put in hand. The authority must be satisfied that works proposed for a discretionary "repairs grant" will put the premises into reasonable repair and be of substantial and structural character in various respects—i.e. as to matters such as roofs, external walls, foundations, floors, or staircases and other internal features (Department of the Environment Circular 20/81). If the "certificate as to future occupation" required for a discretionary "repairs grant" is a "certificate of owner-occupation" there is a rateable value limit for applications which is currently set at £400 in Greater London and £225 elsewhere (SI 1982 no. 1205) unless the premises are in a housing action area. There is an "eligible expense" ceiling in relation to the "estimated expense" of the approved works, which is currently set (SI 1983 no. 613) at £6,600 in Greater London and £4,800 elsewhere, but at higher amounts for "listed buildings" (respectively £7,480 and £5,680 for "Grade I" buildings, £7,130 and £5,330 for "Grade II starred" buildings, and £6,860 and £5,060 for "Grade II unstarred" buildings). The "appropriate percentage" of the "eligible expense" at or below the ceiling, payable as grant, is 75% for dwellings in Category A (above), and for other dwellings 65% in general improvement areas and 50% elsewhere, with the power already mentioned to raise the 75% level to any level up to 90%, and the 50% to any level up to 65%, in cases of hardship. The "appropriate percentage" must be paid in a mandatory "repairs grant", but in a discretionary "repairs grant" the authority may pay less provided that they give reasons in writing.

Various provisions apply generally to these different grants. Thus an authority can increase a grant to cover necessary additions to estimates or works; and they can require an owner to furnish a certificate giving further information about the occupation of a dwelling to which any grant relates. The "certificates as to future occupation", referred to above at the outset of this discussion of grants, have the effect of imposing conditions upon the making of the grant that the undertakings in the certificates will be complied with. Additional conditions may be imposed if the dwelling is to be available for letting; these are to the effect that it will be protected under the Rent Act 1977 (by regulated tenancy or restricted contract); indeed the authority must impose such conditions in a housing action area or general improvement area. Grant conditions are in force for seven years in housing action areas and five years elsewhere and are binding on each owner of the dwelling for the time being; and breach of any condition empowers the authority to demand repayment from him, with compound interest, of any or all of the grant. Voluntary repayment in full (interest included) by owner or mortgagee will free the dwelling from the condition, and if a mortgagee repays the grant the amount will be added to the mortgage loan. An authority must be satisfied as to the proper execution of the works before paying any grant. They may pay by instalments in proportion to the stage in the works reached at any given time. If they are satisfied with the works then payment of grant becomes a duty; but a specified time-limit of a year or longer for completion of works may be imposed at the time the application is approved, plus extensions where necessary. Failure to complete on time makes the recipient liable to repay any instalments which he may have received. Note that the conditions are to some extent relaxed in respect of dwellings belonging to charities.

Authorities have power to execute on an owner's behalf works which would attract grant, at his expense but offsetting the grant, if he is a freeholder or a leaseholder with five years or more to run. If an applicant dies his personal representatives take his place under these arrangements; if he gives up his ownership or tenancy otherwise than on death any right to grant ceases and sums already paid must be refunded. As far as the central government is concerned, the Secretary of State is empowered to subsidise local authorities' expenditure in respect of grants to the tune of 75% of the loan charges incurred, or 90% in a housing action area or general improvement area, spread over 20 years. The Secretary of State may also authorise and assist authorities to pay grants towards the cost of thermal insulation works to dwellings in their area. Authorities are empowered in addition to pay all or any part of the cost of providing separate piped water to a dwelling which has hitherto had to share a mains water supply.

"Common parts grants" are new discretionary payments by local housing authorities for works of a repair or improvement to "common parts" of blocks of flats needed to put them into reasonable repair. Amounts payable will be in accordance with rules to be prescribed by the Secretary of State. Applicants must be under a duty to carry out the works or have a right to do so (as freeholder, leaseholder with 5 years to run, or a statutorily protected tenant of a prescribed kind). Rateable value limits will apply (except in housing action areas) as specified by the Secretary of State. These grants are authorised under sections 464A and 498A of the Housing Act 1985.

It should also be noted that local authorities can, if a tenanted dwelling is situated in a housing action area or a general improvement area, order the landlord (unless the property is let on a "long tenancy", i.e. over 21 years) to carry out works for the provision of deficient "standard amenities" up to the "full" or "reduced" standard. Under Part VII of the Housing Act 1985, a "provisional notice" specifying the works to be done is first served; and if the landlord fails to do the work by agreement the authority can serve an "improvement notice" ordering him to do so. Appeal lies to the county court. Moreover the landlord can serve a purchase notice requiring the local authority to buy the dwelling from him. In default of compliance with an improvement notice the authority may do the works at the landlord's expense.

3. SMALLER RESIDENTIAL PROPERTIES AND TENEMENTS

(a) *General Method of Valuation.* The rents of small houses, cottages and tenements are usually payable weekly or monthly.

In free market conditions slight differences in style and accommodation—for instance, a few feet of front garden with a dwarf brick wall and railings, or the fact that the front living room opens out of a small hall-passage, instead of direct on to the street—may cause a considerable difference in rental between houses within a short distance of each other.

The gross yearly income is estimated by taking 48 to 52 weeks' rent, according to whether or not it is thought necessary in the circumstances to make allowance for loss by irrecoverables. The effect of control is greatly to reduce the risk of loss of rent by bad debts.

If, owing to overcrowding, a house is let at what may be regarded as an excessive rent the excess should be disregarded, since it will certainly be lost should the local authority exercise its powers under the Housing Act 1985.[18]

Repairs, insurance and management will be the main outgoings and, in some cases the landlord may also pay rates and water and drainage charges.

Yields vary widely according to the circumstances of the particular case and the state of the local market. In the case of freeholds they may range from 5 per cent or less where the security is good to figures of 15 per cent or more where property is old, in poor repair and occupied by an unsatisfactory type of tenant. Where the rate of interest is low this is probably because of the large increase in capital value which occurs if vacant possession is obtained. In this connection it may be noted that the market for what may be described as "tenements", i.e., large buildings let out to a number of tenants—is usually poor and uncertain compared with that for small, fairly modern houses let to single families. This is particularly so at the present time owing to the high cost of repairs in the case of the "tenement" type and to the large increase in capital value if vacant possession is obtained of a house let to a single family.

Indeed there has been a sharp decline in the number of investors who are interested in holding residential properties as long term investments. The growing tendency has been either for owners to sell to "sitting tenants", or not to re-let properties when they become vacant but to sell them off with vacant possession. A sale to a sitting tenant would realise

---

[18] Part X; see also the provisions in Part XVII relating to compensation for compulsory purchase.

360 Modern Methods of Valuation

a figure between investment value and vacant possession value whereas a sale with vacant possession would realise the full vacant possession value. In most cases where a tenanted property is being valued, it is suggested that a normal investment valuation should be performed, i.e. the net income should be multiplied by the appropriate Y.P., and that the resultant value should be checked as a percentage of vacant possession value. This will be found to fall within a range of 40 to 60 per cent depending on how the market assesses the possibility of vacant possession being obtained. The smaller houses will tend to be at the lower end of this percentage range. Where there is certainty of obtaining possession, as in the case of a shorthold tenancy, the vacant possession value should be deferred for the period of waiting.

(b) *Outgoings*. The principal outgoings are repairs, insurance and management. In some cases the landlord may also pay rates and water and drainage charges. Under the Rent Act 1977, any increase in rates due either to changes in assessment or poundage can be passed on to the tenant. The community charge will replace general rates in 1990 but that charge is entirely unrelated to the occupation of property and the responsibility for payment will be on the individual assessed. Water and drainage charges will continue.

Apart from any contractual liability to repair, in the case of leases granted after 24 November 1961, for terms less than seven years of dwelling-houses which the statutory protection of business or agricultural tenancies does not cover, the Landlord and Tenant Act 1985, sections 11–16, implies a covenant by the lessor to keep in repair the structure, exterior and installations for water, gas and electricity supplies, for space and water heating and for sanitation (contracting out is prohibited except with the approval of the county court).

It is generally preferable to make the allowance for repairs by deducting a lump sum per property which should be checked by reference to past records and to the age, extent and construction of the premises.[19] For example, the allowance in the case of a house stuccoed externally and requiring

---

[19] See Chapter 6.

periodic painting will naturally be higher than in the case of a similar house with brick facings in good condition. It has been customary in the past to estimate the amount to be allowed for repairs as a percentage of the rent but this method is unreliable.

Where in the past the work of repair has been left undone it may be necessary to include in the valuation a capital deduction for immediate expenditure to allow for the cost of putting the property into a reasonable (but not necessarily a first-class) state of repair.

The annual cost of insurance can usually be determined with sufficient accuracy, either by using the actual premium paid or by assessing it on the basis described in Chapter 21. Fire insurance premiums are becoming significant sums so that, where the landlord is responsible, care must be taken to ensure that the appropriate deduction is made.

Management may cost from 10 per cent upwards plus VAT according to the circumstances and the services rendered.

Reference so far has been made to the estimation of net income by calculating each outgoing separately. It is useful as a check to determine the percentage which they represent of the gross rents.

(c) *State of Repair.* Careful consideration must be given to the condition of repair as affecting the annual cost of repairs, the life of the building and the possibility of heavy expenditure in the future. Particular attention should be paid to the structural condition, the presence or absence of dampness in walls or ceilings, the proper provision of sanitary accommodation and of cooking and washing facilities.

Regard should be had to the possibility of the service of a dangerous structure notice in respect of such defects as a bulged wall.

Where premises are in such a condition as to be a nuisance or injurious to health, the local authority may require necessary works to be done.[20] They may also serve a notice to repair a house, which is in substantial disrepair or unfit for human habitation.[21] The standard for deciding whether a

---

[20] Building Act 1984, section 76; Public Health Act 1936, sections 92–100.
[21] Housing Act 1985, Part VI.

house is "unfit for human habitation" is that laid down by Section 604 of the Housing Act 1985.

Where a house cannot be made fit for human habitation at a reasonable cost, the local authority may serve a demolition order. In respect of any part of a building unfit for habitation including any underground room or any unfit house from which adjoining property obtains support, or which can be used for a non-residential purpose, or is of special historic or architectural interest, they may serve a closing order[22] instead of a demolition order.

In lieu of making a demolition order a local authority may purchase a house which is unfit if they consider that it can be rendered capable of providing accommodation of a standard which is adequate for the time being.[23]

Special provision is made in the Housing Act 1985 as regards houses in multiple occupation (Part XI), and as regards houses which are overcrowded (Part X).

Where, on inspection, a property is considered not to comply with statutory provisions currently in force, allowance should be made in the valuation for the cost of compliance.

The allowance for annual repairs included in the outgoings is usually based on the assumption that the property is in a reasonable state of repair, at least sufficient to justify the rent at which it is let. If it is not, a deduction should be made from the valuation for the cost of putting it into reasonable repair, less any grant payable.

(d) *Clearance Areas.* There are many houses, let either as a whole or in parts, which are of considerable age, indifferent construction, or so situated as likely to be included in a Clearance Area in consequence of which the local authority may acquire houses and buildings for the purpose of demolishing them and re-planning the area.[24]

Particular regard must be had to the possible application

---

[22] Ibid., Part IX.

[23] Ibid., Part VI, section 192.

[24] Housing Act 1985, Part IX. They are empowered to preserve unfit houses from demolition which can provide accommodation that is of a standard "adequate for the time being" (sections 300–302); but this does not confer on them an immunity from proceedings before the magistrates if any such house is either "dangerous to health" or "a nuisance" under the Public Health Act 1936 (*Salford City Council v. McNally* [1976] AC 379.

of this procedure, and to the statutory provisions applying to individual houses in a clearance area, when valuing old or defective property.

It must be remembered that a house, although not unfit in itself, may be included in consequence of its being in or adjoining a congested or overcrowded area.

For a detailed consideration of the provisions of the Housing Acts governing these matters see Chapter 30.

(e) *Duration of Income.* In addition to the factors already considered, regard must also be had to the length of time during which it is expected that the net income will continue.

In the case of houses of some age, it is sometimes suggested that an estimate should be made of the length of life of the property, and the net income valued for that period with a reversion to site value. But, as explained in Chapter 9 it is more usual for the factor of uncertainty of continuance of income to be reflected in the rate per cent adopted.

In such cases a net yield of up to 20 per cent may well be expected, whereas, in the case of more modern properties, the yield may be as low as 5 per cent.

Where, however, there are strong reasons for assuming that the life of the property will be limited, allowance should be made for that factor in the valuation.

If demolition of existing buildings is likely in the future under the provisions of the Housing Act 1985 (Part IX), the income may properly be valued as receivable for a limited term with reversion to site value. Similarly, if unfit property is likely to be acquired compulsorily as part of a "clearance area" the compensation may be restricted to cleared site value, so that again it may be proper to treat the present income as of limited duration only.

In each of the above cases cleared site value will be governed by the provisions of the Land Compensation Act 1961 and Part XVII of the Housing Act 1985.

Example 19–2

A terrace house in a suburban area built about 70 years ago comprises ground, first and second floors, with two large and one small room on each floor. There is a W.C. on each floor and each of the small rooms has been adapted for use as a kitchen and a sink and ventilated food storage provided. The house is situated in a neighbourhood where the development is open in character. The general structural condition is good, with the exception of the flank wall of the back addition, which is badly bulged, and the front wall where there are extensive signs of rising damp.

There are three tenants: the ground floor producing £10·00 per week, the first floor £12·00, and the second floor £10·00. These rents are the maximum rents permitted under the Rent Act 1977.

The total rateable value is £200. Rates and drainage and water charges total £2·00 in the £.

What is the present market value?

Valuation

	per week	per annum
Gross Income—		
Ground Floor	£10·00	
First Floor	£12.00	
Second Floor	£10·00	
	£32·00	£1,664
Less Outgoings—		
Rates, drainage and water	£400	
Repairs and Insurance	£600	
Management at 10% + VAT	£192	£1,192
Net Income		£472
Y.P. perpetuity, say		10
		£4,720
Estimated cost of repair of flank wall and damp in front wall, net of grant, say		£3,000
Value, say		£1,700

4. LARGER RESIDENTIAL PROPERTIES

(a) *Generally*. For many years after the 1914–18 war the shortage of housing accommodation led to very much higher prices being paid for properties with vacant possession than for those let to tenants and purchased as an investment.

At the outbreak of the second world war in 1939 the shortage had been largely overcome. The disparity in value between the houses with or without vacant possession had disappeared except in the case of properties which had not been freed from rent control; in some areas, new houses were more easily let than sold and houses let at good rents to reliable tenants sometimes commanded a higher value than the same house with vacant possession.

However since 1945 there have been considerable differences between the values of houses let to protected tenants (a) for investment, and (b) for occupation. Over the same period there has been a general upward movement in the value of all types of houses with vacant possession.

When valuing with vacant possession, as already pointed out in Section 1 of this chapter, the capital value must be fixed by direct comparison with prices actually realised on sale.

In the case of larger houses which are let, the method recommended earlier in this Chapter in relation to smaller houses, of performing a normal investment valuation and comparing the resultant figure with the vacant possession value, is again appropriate.

(b) *Factors Affecting Value*. The factors in question may be briefly summarised as follows:

(i) Size and number of rooms. A prospective occupier is primarily in search of a certain amount of accommodation. He is likely, in the first instance, to restrict his enquiries to properties having the number of rooms of the size he requires.

(ii) Position. The price he is prepared to pay for this accommodation will be influenced by all the factors associated with position.

Proximity to shops, travelling facilities, open spaces, golf courses and schools: the character of surrounding property,

building development in the neighbourhood, the presence
and cost of public services, the rate in the £ for the district
and the level of assessments, are all matters to be taken
into account.

(iii) Planning, etc. In viewing property itself the prospective occupier will also consider such points as the arrangement, aspect and lighting of the rooms, the adequacy of the
domestic and sanitary offices, the methods of heating, the
presence or absence of a garage, the size and condition of
the garden.

The value of the accommodation provided by a house will
be increased or diminished according to the way in which,
in the details enumerated, it compares with other properties
of a similar size.

(iv) Age and condition of repair. Changes in taste and
fashion and the greater amenities provided in modern houses
tend to reduce the value of older houses.

The condition of repair must be considered both as regards
the cost of putting the premises into a satisfactory state of
repair now and the cost of maintenance in the future.

A number of the points already mentioned in connection
with smaller property must be considered.

The principal points include the condition of the main
structure and roof; the penetration of damp, either by reason
of a defective damp-proof course or insufficient insulation
against wet of the external walls; the presence of conditions
favourable to dry rot; the presence or absence of such rot
or of wet rot or attack by woodworm or beetle; the arrangement and condition of the drainage system; the condition
of external paintwork; internal decorations.

Houses with a large expanse of external paintwork or complicated roofs with turrets and domes will cost more in annual
upkeep than houses of plainer design. The annual cost of
repairs will also be influenced by the age of the premises.

When houses are let, the incidence of the liability for repair
as between landlord and tenant is an important factor in
their valuation. In the case of the larger houses let on long
lease the tenant usually undertakes to do all repairs; but
in the case of short term lettings of small or moderate sized

houses, the bulk of the burden has usually fallen on the landlord. The implied repairing obligations placed on the landlord by the Landlord and Tenant Act 1985, sections 11–16, (already referred to under small houses), must also be borne in mind.

(c) *Methods of Valuation.* At the present day estimates of open market rental value for house property are seldom made. If a house is vacant, it will almost certainly be put on the market with vacant possession, and its capital value arrived at by direct comparison with recent sales, without reference to rental value. Comparisons are made between houses (or flats) to find fair rents on the basis of so much per unit of net floor space.

Example 19–3

A small semi-detached, brick-built modern house in good repair, on a plot with a 30 ft. frontage, contains two reception rooms and W.C. on ground floor, two large and one small bedroom, bathroom and W.C. on the first floor.

What is its market value?

Valuation

Direct comparison of capital value. Similar houses in the neighbourhood sell for prices ranging from £55,000 to £60,000; by direct comparison of position, size of rooms, condition of repair and the amenities provided, the value is estimated to be £57,500.

In the case of tenant-occupied houses where the tenant is protected by the Rent Acts or where he holds the house under a lease or agreement with a reasonable term to run at a low rent, the tenant himself may be anxious to purchase the property. In these circumstances the price he will pay is likely to be the result of bargaining between the parties. The tenant is obviously not going to pay full vacant possession value; the landlord is not likely to be content with investment value only; the result will usually be a purchase price between these two extremes.

(d) *Sales Records.* The systematic recording of the results of sales is essential to the valuer; the form such records can take varies widely.

5. BLOCKS OF FLATS

(a) *Generally.* The valuation of a block of flats does not differ in principle from the valuation of properties already considered.

The problem is only complicated by the greater difficulty in forming a correct estimate of gross income and of outgoings.

(b) *Gross Income.* In a few cases flats are let at inclusive rents, the tenants not being liable for any outgoings, although extra charges for special services are usually encountered.

In estimating gross income, it should be borne in mind that fair rents can be reviewed every two years or, if tenants are not protected, existing agreements may permit rents to be reviewed.

Among the many factors affecting the present rental value are the presence of lifts, central heating, constant hot water, refrigerators, the adequacy of natural lighting, the degree of sound insulation between flats, convenience of proximity to main traffic routes offset by possible nuisance from noise.

(c) *Outgoings.* In estimating the allowance to be made for outgoings on an existing block of flats it is necessary to study the tenancy agreements carefully in order to determine the extent of the landlord's liabilities. In recent years there has been a marked tendency to make tenants responsible for all possible repairs but the provisions of the Landlord and Tenant Act 1985,[25] must be kept in mind.

Rates. The present cost of rates and water and drainage charges can easily be ascertained and the replacement of general rates by the community charge in 1990 should be borne in mind. Generally flats are let at rents exclusive of general rates.

Repairs. It is difficult to give any general guide to the allowance to be made for repairs, since the cost will depend upon many factors.

[25] Sections 11–16 (referred to earlier in this Chapter).

An exterior of stucco work, needing to be painted approximately every five years, will cost much more than one of plain brickwork, which is only likely to involve expenditure on repointing every 25 or 30 years. Regard must also be had to the entrance hall, main staircase and corridors, those having marble or other permanent wall coverings will have a low maintenance cost; other types of decoration requiring considerable expenditure to keep in a satisfactory condition will have a much higher maintenance cost.

Services. Until the Rent Act 1957, rents were frequently inclusive of services. Now these are generally covered by a separate service charge payable in addition to the rent in the case of decontrolled tenancies. Such service charges are usually variable according to cost. It is necessary for the valuer to check that the charge is sufficient to cover costs and depreciation. Where services are included in rents paid, the cost must be deducted from the gross rents together with other outgoings to find the net income.

Section 136 and Schedule 19 of the Housing Act 1980 now provide that tenants of private flats who pay service charges (covering services, repairs, maintenance, insurance, or landlord's management costs) are entitled to receive a written summary certified by a qualified accountant justifying the amount charged. Service charges must be such as a court considers reasonable both as to standard of services and amounts charged. Before ordering any "qualifying works", the landlord or his agent must obtain two estimates, one of which must be from a genuinely independent source, and notify the tenants (including any association representing the tenants).

Similar protection is extended to "secure tenants" (i.e. tenants in the public sector) by the Housing and Building Control Act 1984, section 18 and Schedule 4, amplified by the Housing and Planning Act 1986, sections 4–5. The latter Act (section 4) inserts an elaborate code into the Housing Act 1985, Part V, concerning information which tenants are entitled to receive from landlords when exercising the "right to buy". This code, contained in sections 125A, B and C inserted into the 1985 Act, deals with "improvement contributions" as well as service charges.

(d) *Net Income and Yield.* A reasonable deduction from gross income having been made in respect of the estimated outgoings, a figure will be arrived at representing prospective net income.

However carefully this figure may have been estimated, it is likely to vary from time to time, particularly in relation to expenditure on repairs. The valuer will have regard to this fact in selecting the rate per cent of Years' Purchase on which his valuation will be based.

The rate per cent yield on the purchase prices of blocks of flats varies considerably. At the time of writing first-class flats are showing about 8 per cent. A considerably higher return is likely to be expected from "converted" houses, probably 10 to 12 (or even more) per cent.

Example 19–4

You are instructed to value a large freehold property comprising eight blocks of flats, some of three storeys and some of two, erected about six years ago. The Vendor's agents inform you that the flats are all let, at recently reviewed fair rents from £2,000—£2,400. The standard form of tenancy agreement provides that the tenants are liable for internal decorative repairs.

The following particulars are also supplied. Total rent roll, £171,200 including 18 garages, £3,600. Outgoings last year: repairs, £10,000; lighting, £1,000; upkeep, £1,500; insurances, £4,000.

As a result of your inspection the following additional facts are established:

The tenants pay the rates on both flats and garages, the rents for the latter averaging £4 per week. The agreements are for three years.

The gardens are extensive. The general condition of repair is satisfactory.

The flats are brick-built with tiled roofs, concrete floor, and a modern hot water system: there is no lift.

There is a long waiting list for flats.

The landlord provides no services other than lighting of common parts and upkeep of the gardens.

The outgoings seem to be reasonable except for the amount for repairs and maintenance which is obviously too low.

Total Rent Roll			£171,200
Less Garages			£3,600
			£167,600
Less Outgoings—			
Lighting		£1,000	
Garden		£1,500	
Insurances		£4,000	
Repairs—say		£20,000	
Management, say		£8,000	£34,500
Net Income			£133,100
Y.P. at 8%			12·5
			£1,663,750
18 garages, gross		£3,600	
Less Outgoings			
Repairs	£400		
Management, say	£360	£760	
Net Income		£2,840	
Y.P., say		8	£22,720
			£1,686,470
Value, say			£1,650,000

(e) *Flats Held as Investments.* The provisions of the Housing Act 1980 in relation to statutory controls on management of blocks of flats have already been mentioned. The next part of this Chapter outlines the provisions of the Landlord and Tenant Act 1987 which tighten these management restrictions and also provide for tenants to be given first refusal when a landlord wishes to dispose of his interest. Although the Government's intention to protect tenants from bad landlords (and bad managers) is both understandable and laudable, it is difficult to see that there will be any incentive in the future for holding flats as investments. At the same time, it will be difficult for existing investors to withdraw except by selling to the tenants at what is submitted must be a basic investment value. Even this basic investment value presents difficulties if there are in fact no potential purchasers in the investment market. This is not to say there is no future for private blocks of flats but it seems likely that each flat will be individually owned, most probably on a long lease, with the freehold held and management arranged on a communal basis.

Landlord and Tenant Act 1987

This statute deals with privately owned blocks of flats, and implements a number of recommendations contained in a report on the management of such flats, produced by a committee chaired by Mr. E. G. Nugee, Q.C. Its provisions come into force on dates prescribed by order, some of which are stated below.

Part I of the Act (secs. 1–20), which was brought into effect on 1 February 1988, applies to flats occupied by "qualifying tenants"—i.e. those whose tenancies are not shorthold tenancies (under the Housing Act 1980, sec. 52), or business tenancies (protected under the Landlord and Tenant Act 1954, Part II), or tenancies which go with the tenant's employment, or tenancies comprising more than one flat; but a "qualifying tenant" can hold two or more tenancies of up to 50% of the flats in the block. In regard to such tenants, the immediate landlord must serve on them a notice giving them first refusal before making a "relevant disposal". This means any disposal by way of a legal estate or equitable interest (which may extend to "common parts" of the block), other than certain prescribed exceptions such as disposals to the Crown, to a compulsorily purchasing authority or to an associated company, and non-commercial disposals within the landlord's family or for the purposes of trusts, charities, bankruptcy, etc. "Qualifying tenants" must occupy more than half the flats in the block. Flats of which more than 50% of the internal floor area is used for non-residential purposes are excluded. If the landlord also holds under a tenancy which will be or can be terminated within 7 years the superior landlord also counts as "the landlord", and so on up the scale. Flats owned by public sector landlords are not within the scope of these provisions, nor are those owned by resident landlords.

The "notice conferring rights of first refusal" which must be served on the "qualifying tenants" must set out the terms of the proposed disposal and serves as an offer which may be accepted by a majority vote of the tenants—i.e. more than 50% of the votes on the basis of one flat one vote. A period of at least two months must be allowed for acceptance, and a further period of at least two months must be added if the tenants (by a majority) nominate a person or persons for the purposes of acquiring the interest to be disposed of. If the offer is not accepted within the specified time, the landlord may within 12 months thereafter dispose of the "protected interest" to be disposed of (i.e. the interest which is subject to the tenant's right of first refusal) to anyone he chooses, so long as he does not undercut the terms of his offer to the tenants. If the tenants do not propose to accept the offer they can, within the time limit specified, make a counter-offer. The landlord may accept or reject this; but his rejection may also contain a counter-offer of his own, provided that it sets out the terms of such counter-offer and specifies a further period of time for acceptance. If the tenants do not accept within that time the landlord may within 12 months dispose of the protected interest in the manner stated above. Short of the conclusion of a binding contract, either the landlord or the person(s) nominated by the tenants may withdraw, and the nominated person(s) must do so if the number of tenants wishing to proceed falls below a majority.

If the landlord wrongfully disposes of the protected interest in disregard of the tenants' right to have "first refusal", the new landlord—i.e. the transferee—can be required to give them details of the offending transaction within one month.

The tenants by a majority (as above) may then within three months serve a "purchase notice" on the new landlord requiring him to sell the interest he has acquired to a person or persons nominated by them on the same terms as those on which it was acquired by him. If any dispute arises over the terms of such a purchase notice it is to be referred to the local rent assessment committee (as constituted under the Rent Act 1977). The "new landlord" may be the previous landlord's own landlord if the wrongful disposal took the form of a surrender. If a prospective purchaser from the landlord is unsure whether rights of first refusal exist or not, he may serve notices on the tenants concerned so that the question can be resolved in advance. It should be noted that the Secretary of State for the Environment is empowered to modify the operative provisions concerning the "notice conferring rights of first refusal" and consequential procedures, by making regulations to that effect.

Part II (secs. 21–24) concerns the appointment by order of the court of managers for flats in buildings or parts of buildings containing at least two flats not held on business tenancies protected under the Landlord and Tenant Act 1954, Part II. The High Court or county court must be satisfied that the landlord is in breach of some obligation owed by him to the tenant which relates to the management of the premises, and that these circumstances are likely to continue, and that in all the circumstances it is just and convenient to make the order. These provisions do not apply to flats which are owned by public sector landlords or resident landlords or "included within the functional land of any charity".

Proceedings are to start with a preliminary notice served by the tenant on the landlord stating that an application to the court is intended on grounds referred to above, as appropriate. Only if the landlord does not take steps to rectify the situation within a reasonable period of time which the tenant must specify (if applicable) can the tenant apply to the court, which can then make an order appointing a manager on such terms as it thinks fit, in a similar manner to the appointment of a receiver. The order may be provisional or final, may be suspended, and may extend to more or less than the premises in respect of which it has been sought.

Part III (secs. 25–34) confers on tenants a power of compulsory purchase of the interest held by their landlords. As with Parts I and II, premises owned by public sector landlords, and also resident landlords, are excluded. Included are buildings or parts of buildings containing two or more flats occupied by "qualifying tenants"—i.e. tenants holding under "long leases" (21 years or more or leases granted under the "right to buy" in the Housing Act 1985, Part V) but not business tenancies protected under the Landlord and Tenant Act 1954, Part II. At least 90% of the flats in such a block must be held by "qualifying tenants" (all but one, if there are five to nine flats; all, if there are four flats or less). If more than 50% of the internal floor area of a block is in non-residential use (excluding common parts) then it too is excluded. A tenant under a lease covering more than a single flat is not a "qualifying tenant", though qualifying tenants are not restricted to one lease of one flat.

The power given to "qualifying tenants" is to nominate a person to acquire the landlord's interest under an "acquisition order" to be made by the court. At least 50% of the "qualifying tenants" (one tenant one vote) must first serve a "preliminary notice" on the landlord stating that they will apply to the court for such an order: but will not do so if the landlord remedies specified defaults which are capable of remedy within a reasonable time where this is the case. The pre-requisite for the procedure is that the landlord is in breach of his obligations to the tenants under their leases in respect of repair, maintenance, insurance or management, in circumstances which are likely to continue, and the appointment of a manager under Part II "would not be an adequate remedy". If the landlord fails as stated above to remedy specified defaults (if that is the case), or if his defaults are not remediable, the "requisite majority of such tenants" must then apply to the court for the "acquisition order", the application being registrable as a "pending land action" (i.e. a land charge), and inhibitions are obtainable if it is registered land. The court must not make the "acquisition order" unless satisfied that the above requirements are broadly met and that it would be appropriate to do so in all the circumstances. If a manager has already been appointed under Part II it is necessary to wait until that appointment has lasted three years. The landlord's interest will, under the "acquisition order", be vested in the nominated person referred to above, on terms settled (in default of agreement) by the local rent assessment committee; but if the landlord is a leaseholder who needs the consent of a third party to the transfer of his own lease and this consent is genuinely not forthcoming, the order will not take effect. The market price to be paid must assume that the landlord's interest is subject to all the existing leases and that the tenants are none of them buying it or seeking to buy it. Subject to any agreement or court decision otherwise, mortgages, liens and charges—other than rent charges—are to be paid off in accordance with a procedure laid down in Schedule 1. If the landlord is not traceable, the acquisition terms are settled by the court, and the price is paid into court after being assessed by a surveyor chosen by the President of the Lands Tribunal. Conversely, if acquisition proceedings are abortive the order can be discharged and the landlord, in a proper case, can recover reasonable costs.

Part IV (secs. 35–40) deals with variation of leases of flats. In theory its scope is wider than the foregoing provisions in that only tenancies protected as business tenancies under the Landlord and Tenant Act 1954, Part II (this does not here include assured tenancies) are excluded; but since the provisions apply only to long leases—i.e. for 21 years or more—public sector leases will only rarely be affected in practice. As with the foregoing provisions, leases covering more than individual flats are excluded, but there is nothing to exclude tenants who hold more than one lease in any building. Anyone who is a party to a long lease within these provisions may apply to the court for an order varying, or directing parties to vary, that lease if it is defective because it does not (for whatever reason) make satisfactory provision in regard to the premises for any of the following matters: (a) repair or maintenance of the premises or of ancillary features such as garages, access, etc.; (b) insurance; (c) repair or maintenance of installations which are reasonably necessary for proper enjoyment of the premises; (d) provision or maintenance of services which are reasonably necessary for proper enjoyment of the premises; (e) re-imbursement of any party to the lease for expenditure reasonably incurred or to be incurred by him for the benefit of any other party.

Parties to any lease, other than the applicant, may thereupon apply to the court for other orders making corresponding variations of other leases, particularly in cases where any variation would not be satisfactory in isolation. If the court is satisfied it may by order make the variations applied for, or any other variations which it thinks should be made; but no variation is to be made if any person would be substantially prejudiced thereby in a way that cannot fairly be met by financial compensation, or if on any other grounds the variation would not be reasonable. Third parties (including predecessors in title) are bound by any variations which are made. No variation in regard to insurance must interfere with provisions in a lease for nominated or specified insurers; on the other hand the right to apply to vary in respect of insurance is extended to dwellings *other* than flats.

Part V (secs. 41–45) relates to management of leasehold property more generally in the residential private sector. Section 45, which took effect on 1st February, 1988, amends the Housing Associations Act 1985, sec. 4 (but not in Scotland) by extending the "permissible objects" of housing associations registered with the Housing Corporation so as to include management of any house or any block of flats (i.e. a building with two or more flats "held on leases or other lettings" which is "occupied or intended to be occupied wholly or mainly for residential purposes").

Sections 41–44 amend the Landlord and Tenant Act 1985 in respect of "service charges" payable by residential tenants. Detailed procedural amendments are made to the 1985 Act to put tenants who are represented in dealings with their landlord by a recognised tenants' association on the same footing as those who are not (long leases are no longer to be treated differently from other leases). Also worthy of note is a provision that the retrospective effect of service charges is to be limited to 18 months (sec. 41 and Sched. 2). The basic point about service charges is that they relate to *variable* costs towards which two or more tenants are required by their tenancies to contribute periodically because of the benefits which accrue to them (thus "fair rents" registered under the Rent Act 1977 are to be excluded except where there are elements producing variable rents). The 1987 Act (sec. 42) now provides that without prejudice to any pre-existing trust, the recipient of service charges—the landlord or management company, or other person—is to hold the money (with interest) on trust to defray all the relevant costs, and then to hold the balance for the tenants in shares in proportion to their liabilities (presumably to set against subsequent costs, because persons ceasing to be tenants will not recover their shares). Further safeguards are provided for tenants (sec. 43 and Sched. 3) in respect of their insurance cover as paid for by service charges. Tenants' associations are given rights of consultation in relation to the appointment of managing agents for premises where service charges are payable (sec. 44 inserting a new sec. 30B into the 1985 Act).

Part VI (sec. 46–51), which took effect on 1st February, 1988, requires the giving of information to tenants of dwellings other than premises covered under the protection of business tenancies in the Landlord and Tenant Act 1954, Part II. Written demands for rent or other payments must contain the landlord's name and address (and also if necessary "address for service" in England and Wales) failing which no service charge can be recovered (secs. 47–49, which also modify sec. 196 of the Law of Property Act 1925). If the landlord's reversion is assigned, the assignor continues to be liable to any tenant until *either* the assignor or the assignee gives notice, to that tenant, of the assignee's name and address; and the old and new landlords are jointly and severally liable for breaches occurring between the date of assignment and the date when notice is given (sec. 50). In regard to registered land, the tenant of any dwelling is given the right (on payment of a fee) to search the proprietorship register in the Land Registry for details of his landlord's name and address (sec. 51, adding a new sec. 112C to the Land Registration Act 1925).

Part VII (secs. 52–62) contains various general provisions. It should be noted that, except in regards to secs. 41, 43–45, and 49–51, "the court" means the county court, for the purposes of this Act; and in the absence of some specific justification anyone bringing High Court proceedings will be penalised in costs (sec. 52). The Act does not bind the Crown, but applies to Crown Land in the sense that a Crown interest may subsist in the premises provided that it is both separate from and superior to the private landlord's (leasehold) reversion as well as the interests of the various tenants of that landlord (sec. 56).

6. HOUSING ASSOCIATIONS

In addition to the grants and loans for assistance to private housing mentioned earlier in this Chapter which are furnished by local authorities, public financial help is also made available by central government for the provision of dwellings by "housing associations". These are non profit-making bodies composed of private persons, corporations and charitable organisations; and the financial assistance is chiefly available in the form of grants from the Secretary of State for the Environment and loans from the Housing Corporation. The system of grants is similar in many respects to the housing subsidies paid by the Secretary of State to local authorities and new town corporations under the Housing Act 1985, (Part XIII), and earlier legislation (these subsidies are not within the scope of this book); but it is legitimate in this matter to regard housing associations as private rather than public bodies operating in the housing field. The law as to housing associations is now consolidated in the Housing Associations Act 1985.

The Housing Corporation is a national body which has the function of registering housing associations and making (or guaranteeing) loans to them or to persons buying or leasing dwellings from them or from itself (it can provide dwellings and hostels directly). Such loans may be made to the housing associations that it registers, and also to those that it does not register provided that they are "self-build societies", that is to say associations which provide dwellings for purchase or occupation by their members using chiefly labour of such members in the work of construction or improvement.

This system of registration applies only to housing associations which are already registered either as charities or as industrial and provident societies. Further financial provision for the assistance of registered housing associations takes the form of grants payable by the Secretary of State for the Environment. These are: "housing association grants" towards the cost of approved general expenditure on the provision of dwellings; "revenue deficit grants" to make up for deficits in associations' annual revenue accounts; and "hostel deficit grants" in respect of revenue deficits in the management of hostels. This system of grants replaces the subsidies payable to housing associations under previous legislation.

Apart from loans and grants there is the question of control of rents and security of tenure. Section 5 of the Rent Act 1968 excluded from the protection afforded to tenants by that Act tenancies held from housing associations where the dwellings had been provided with the assistance of grants of public money (under legislation ante-dating the Housing Act 1974) or where the associations were registered as charities or industrial and provident societies. Accordingly there was a basic distinction between housing associations in the public sector, which were exempt from the Rent Act, and those in the private sector, to which that Act applied. Thus "private sector" lettings by housing associations enjoyed rent control under the "fair rent" system and security of tenure: in other words, they were included within the category of "regulated tenancies".

Housing association tenants are within the private sector for statutory protection purposes if their association is not registered with the Housing Corporation, and such tenants enjoy protection under the Rent Act 1977; but registered housing associations are within the public sector, and in consequence their tenants are "secure tenants" under the Housing Act 1980 like other public sector tenants, unless the association is in addition a "registered society" under the Industrial and Provident Societies Act 1965.

7. THE HOUSING BILL 1988

The Bill aims at "transforming the rented housing market" in furtherance of various proposals outlined in the White

Paper "Housing: The Government's Proposals" (CM. 214 of 1987).

Part I: Rented Accommodation

Chapter I (clauses 1–17) re-casts "assured tenancies", originally created under the Housing Act 1980. Tenants will have security of tenure; but a landlord may recover possession on various grounds: mandatory grounds on which a court must order possession, and discretionary grounds on which it may do so. Rent payable under an assured periodic tenancy may be increased and in some cases other terms of a tenancy can be varied. A rent assessment committee will be empowered to fix a new rent in certain cases.

Chapter II (clauses 18–21) introduces "assured shorthold tenancies", under which landlords can recover possession at the end of the tenancy by a specified procedure. Tenants will have the right to refer rent payable under a shorthold tenancy to a rent assessment committee on the ground that it is "significantly" higher than comparable rents in the locality; but the Secretary of State may withdraw this right in specified areas or circumstances.

Chapter III (clauses 22–24) introduces "assured agricultural occupancies" when future tenancies are granted to former or current agricultural workers. These will include security of tenure and a right to be rehoused if the landlord wishes to recover possession.

Chapter IV (clauses 25–31) amends the Protection from Eviction Act 1977 by extending it in certain cases to licensees and by creating a new offence of harassment. It gives a right of compensation to residential occupiers unlawfully evicted from or harassed into leaving their homes.

Chapter V (clauses 32–37) aims at "phasing out" statutory protection of residential tenants under the Rent Act 1977. With some exceptions, no future tenancies will be "protected tenancies" or protected housing association tenancies under that Act or secure tenancies under the Housing Act 1980 or other similar tenancies. No future "restricted contracts" or "assured tenancies" under the Housing Act 1980 will be granted. Interim arrangements will take effect, with particular reference to restricting the statutory succession to tenancies under the 1977 Act.

Chapter VI (clauses 38–44) deals with procedural matters, and gives jurisdiction over "assured tenancies" to the county court.

Part II: Housing Associations (clauses 45–55)

This extends the powers of registered housing associations and the power of the Housing Corporation to pay (and recover) grants, tightens the Secretary of State's control over registered associations' finances, redefines "housing activities" under the Housing Associations Act 1985, and provides for delegation of certain functions of the Secretary of State to the Housing Corporation.

Part III: Housing Action Trusts (clauses 56–85)

This provides for areas to be designated for these Trusts, and their functions and duration. The main purpose is to repair, maintain and manage houses, with diversity of tenure, and to improve living conditions. Trusts are to own, manage and dispose of properties, provide main services, and consult local authorities and local residents; and they may be given housing, planning and public health functions, and have local authority dwellings transferred to them.

Part IV: Change of Landlords of Secure Tenants (clauses 86–103)

This provides for the transfer of tenants of "public sector landlords" to other landlords to be approved by the Housing Corporation. Prospective transferee landlords will be entitled to apply, under a prescribed procedure; tenants may be entitled to choose to retain their existing landlords, and if over 50% of the tenants consulted by any applicant oppose a transfer it will not go ahead. The Secretary of State's consent will be needed for completion of the transfer and for subsequent disposals, except that the "right to buy" is to be preserved. Disputes will be within the county court's jurisdiction.

Part V: Miscellaneous (clauses 104–109)

In most cases it will become possible to charge premiums for long leases. Landlords' repairing obligations under short leases are to be extended. Rent officers may be given functions relating to housing benefit and rent allowance subsidy. Housing benefit expenditure is expected to rise to meet increases in rents which will be charged as private landlords undertake an increasing number of grants of tenancies.

CHAPTER 20
Commercial Properties

1. GENERALLY

THERE ARE several categories of property which come under the general heading of commercial properties, and the categories can in turn be sub-divided into types within each category. As a start the main categories can be identified as:—

(a) Retail
(b) Industrial
(c) Warehouses
(d) Offices

Not only can each category be sub-divided but there is also considerable overlap between categories. Take, as an example, Retail and Warehouses. Retail properties come in various forms. The obvious example is a shop in a street, but even there they vary from kiosks to standard shop units to departmental stores. Over recent years there has been extensive development of shopping centres where the shopper enters off the shopping street into a development of various retail units under one roof frequently with its own multistorey car park. A further development has been the creation of edge-of-town centres where the shopping centre is surrounded by extensive car parking. A yet further trend has been the development of out-of-town stores of large size, generally food based, again with extensive car parking, described as superstores or perhaps hypermarkets. In the nonfood sector there has been the creation of one-off or groups of retail warehouses selling furniture, DIY or carpets, each of a size larger than the traditional shop units, with extensive car parking as a key element. These are often referred to as retail warehouses, to distinguish them from the traditional

385

warehouse where goods (wares) are housed in bulk prior to distribution to other smaller traders or retail outlets.

Thus "retail" covers several types of properties where goods are sold to the public, some retail properties being similar to warehouses save that the public at large can visit them and purchase goods; whilst a non-retail warehouse is a property where goods are centrally assembled prior to distribution to trade purchasers.

Another example is the comparison between offices and industrial. Offices themselves range from small shop-type units in shopping streets used by building societies or estate agents, to floors above shops occupied by solicitors, accountants or employment agencies, to free-standing buildings given over to office activities which themselves can range up to the very large and high office blocks found in major City Centres. A recent development has been that of buildings where office activity runs alongside research and manufacturing activity but where the whole building is of a more or less uniform standard of fitting and finish, commonly termed "high-tech" buildings. This manufacturing activity, generally in electronics or similar modern activities, can properly be described as industrial, but differs substantially from other, more traditional industrial activities, in small to large factories, and even more from the large "heavy" industrial plants given over to engineering and other large scale manufacturing activities.

The traditional dividing line between these various activities of retail, industrial, warehouse and office is, in the interests of business efficiency, becoming less rigid—a fact acknowledged by the introduction of new Use Classes for planning purposes by the Town and Country Planning (Use Classes) Order 1987 (S.I. 1987 No. 764). Nevertheless, most properties tend to relate principally to one of these activities.

The feature common to all the above four classes of property is that, generally speaking, they are occupied for the purpose of carrying on an industry, trade or profession in the expectation of profit: and it is the profit which can reasonably be expected to be made in the premises which in the long run will determine the rent a tenant can afford to pay for them.

The principal factors affecting each class are considered in detail later and they fall under three broad categories, viz: the quality and quantity of the accommodation and the location of the premises.

There are some types of property which, although capable of inclusion in one or other of the above classes, are seldom let to a tenant for trading purposes and in respect of which there may be little or no evidence of rental transactions to guide the valuer in arriving at a proper valuation. Typical examples are premises given over to a special purpose, such as chemical, gas or electricity plants or works, and premises occupied for charitable purposes.

In many cases such properties are only likely to come onto the market if the use for which they were built has ceased. In these circumstances it will be necessary to consider the alternative use to which they can be put—if planning permission is likely to be forthcoming to enable such a change of use to be made—the cost of converting them to or redeveloping them for such use and the value they will have when converted or redeveloped. Where any have to be valued for the particular purpose for which they are used resort may be had to the Cost of Replacement Approach described in Section 3.5 of Chapter 2.

Another feature common to the four classes of property is that certain pieces of legislation apply to them—the Landlord and Tenant Act 1927 (Part I) as to compensation for improvements; the Landlord and Tenant Act 1954 (Part II), as amended by the Law of Property Act 1969, as to security of tenure; and various statutes concerned with working conditions such as the Health and Safety at Work etc. Act 1974. Before considering each type of property in detail, it has been thought desirable to outline these provisions.

2. Landlord and Tenant Acts 1927 (Part I) and 1954 (Part II)

(a) *Landlord and Tenant Act 1927 (Part I).* This Act gives tenants of premises let for trade, business or professional purposes the right to compensation for improvements made during the tenancy. (It also gave a right to compensation for "goodwill" in the case of premises let for trade or business purposes but this was made redundant by the security of tenure given by Part II of the Landlord and Tenant Act 1954 and was repealed). The provisions as to compensation for improvements remain, subject to certain amendments made by Part III of the 1954 Act, but are comparatively unimportant in practice and in their effect on values.

The tribunal for the settlement of questions of compensation for improvements under the Act is the County Court, but claims are referred by the Court to a referee, who is selected from a special panel.

The notes which follow do not attempt to give details of procedure under the Act, but merely to indicate the possible effect on value of the tenant's right to claim.

A tenant's claim for compensation for improvements[1] is limited to (*a*) the net addition to the value of the holding as a whole which is the direct result of the improvement, or (*b*) the reasonable cost of carrying out the improvement, at the termination of the tenancy, whichever is the smaller. In determining the compensation, regard must be had to the purpose to which the premises will be put at the end of the tenancy and to the effect that any proposed alterations or demolition or change of user may have on the value of the improvement to the holding.

It may be said, therefore, that in principle the basis for determining the compensation payable to the tenant is the benefit which the landlord will derive from the improvement.

In order that an improvement may carry a right to compensation under the Act, the tenant must first have served notice on the landlord of his intention to make the improvement, together with full particulars of the work and a plan. If the landlord does not object, or, in the event of objection, if the tribunal certifies that the improvement is a "proper" one, the tenant may carry out the works. Alternatively, the landlord may offer to carry out the improvement himself in consideration of a reasonable increase in rent.

In practice it is found that despite the tenant's right to

---

[1] Landlord and Tenant Act 1927, Sections 1–3.

compensation for improvements very few notices under the Act are served on landlords.

In valuing any given property it is desirable to ascertain whether or not improvements have been made by the tenant within the terms of the Act which may give rise to a claim for compensation at the end of the tenancy. The way in which a potential claim for compensation should be taken into account when preparing a valuation must depend on the circumstances. An example is given later in this Chapter.

(*b*) *Landlord and Tenant Act, 1954 (Part II)*. Subject to certain exceptions and qualifications, this Part of the Act (as amended by subsequent legislation, in particular the Law of Property Act 1969, Part I), ensures security of tenure where any part of a property is occupied by a tenant for the purposes of a business carried on by him—provided it is not carried on in breach of a general prohibition in the lease.

The term "business" in the 1954 Act means any trade, profession or employment and also any activity carried on by a body of persons corporate or unincorporate. The Act therefore covers not only ordinary shops, factories and commercial and professional offices, but also premises occupied by voluntary societies, doctors' and dentists' surgeries, clubs, institutions, etc.[2] The scope of premises to which the 1954 Act applies is wider than that of the 1927 Act which applies to premises let for trade, business or professional purposes.

The Act extends not only to lettings for fixed terms, e.g., twenty-one or ninety-nine year leases, but also to periodic

---

[2] A tennis club registered under the Industrial and Provident Societies Act 1893 was held by the High Court (Queen's Bench) to be a business letting within the 1954 Act in *Addiscombe Garden Estates Ltd. and Another v. Crabbe and Others* [1958] 1 Q.B.513; but sub-letting part of premises as unfurnished flats with a view to making a profit out of the rentals was held by the Court of Appeal not to be a business letting within the Act in *Bagettes Ltd., v. G.P. Estates Co. Ltd.* [1956] Ch. 290. In the former case the *use* of the premises was "an activity carried on by a body of persons", but in the latter case it was ordinary residential use. Yet occupation of premises by a medical school for the purpose of student residences was held by the Court of Appeal to be a protected business use in *Groveside Properties v. Westminster Medical School* (1984) 47 P & C.R. 507. A government department can have a protected business tenancy even if the premises are occupied on its behalf by another body, rent free: see *Linden v. D.H.S.S.* [1986] 1 W.L.R. 164.

tenancies, e.g. quarterly, monthly or weekly tenancies. But the following types of tenancy are excluded:—

  (i) tenancies of agricultural holdings;
 (ii) mining leases;
(iii) tenancies within the Rent Act 1977, or which would be but for the tenancy being a tenancy at a low rent.
 (iv) tenancies of on-licensed premises, with some exceptions;
  (v) "service" tenancies, i.e, tenancies granted by an employer only so long as his employee holds a certain office, appointment or employment;
 (vi) tenancies for a fixed term of six months or less, with no right to extend or renew, unless the tenant and his predecessor (if any) have been in occupation for more than twelve months.

The general principle upon which this Part of the Act is based is that a tenancy to which it applies continues until it is terminated in one of the ways prescribed by the Act. Thus, if it is a periodic tenancy, the landlord cannot terminate it by the usual notice to quit. If it is for a fixed term, it will continue automatically after that term has expired, on the same terms as before, unless and until steps are taken under the Act to put an end to it.

One way in which a tenancy can be determined is by the parties agreeing on the terms of a new tenancy to take effect from a specified date. A tenancy may also be terminated by normal notice to quit given by the tenant, or by surrender or forfeiture. In the case of a tenancy for a fixed term, the tenant may terminate it by three months' notice, either on the date of its normal expiration or on any subsequent quarter day.

Apart from the above cases, the methods available to landlord or tenant to terminate a tenancy to which Part II of the Act applies are as follows.

The landlord may give notice, in the form prescribed by the Act, to terminate the tenancy at a specified date not earlier than that at which it would expire by effluxion of time or could have been terminated by notice to quit. Not less than six months' nor more than twelve months' notice must be given. It is to be noted that a landlord must give six months' notice to terminate a quarterly, monthly or weekly tenancy. The notice must require the tenant to specify whether he is willing to give up possession and must state whether, and if so on what grounds, the landlord would oppose an application for a new tenancy.

After notice has been served the parties may negotiate on the terms of a new tenancy or may continue negotiations begun before the notice was served. If they cannot agree on the terms, or if the tenant wishes to remain in the premises but the landlord is unwilling to grant him a new tenancy, the tenant can apply to the County Court for a new tenancy and the Court is bound to grant it unless the landlord can establish a case for possession on certain grounds specified in the Act.

A tenant holding for a fixed term of more than one year can initiate proceedings by serving a notice on his landlord in prescribed form requesting a new tenancy to take effect not earlier than the date on which the current tenancy would come to an end by effluxion of time or could be terminated by notice to quit. This notice must state the terms which the tenant has in mind. If the landlord opposes the proposed new tenancy, the tenant can apply to the Court for the grant of a new tenancy, the terms of which can be agreed between the parties or, in default of agreement, will be determined by the Court.

The Court must have regard to the following points in fixing the terms of a new tenancy[3]:—

(i) The tenancy itself may be either a periodic tenancy or for a fixed term of years not exceeding fourteen;
(ii) The rent is to be fixed in relation to current market value and the following are to be disregarded in determining it:
   (a) the fact that the tenant is a sitting tenant;
   (b) any goodwill attached to the premises by reason of the carrying on of the tenant's business on the premises;

[3] Landlord and Tenant Act 1954, Sections 34 and 35, as amended by Law of Property Act 1969, Sections 1 and 2.

(c) any improvement carried out by a person who was the tenant at the time of improvement but only if the improvement was made otherwise than in pursuance of an obligation to the immediate landlord and, if the improvement was not carried out during the current tenancy, that it was completed not more than 21 years before the application for the new tenancy.

(d) in the case of licensed premises, any additional value attributable to the licence.

(iii) The terms may include provision for varying the rent.

(iv) Other terms of tenancy must be determined having regard to the terms of the current tenancy and to all relevant circumstances.

In practice some terms may be agreed between the parties so that the Court is required only to settle those not agreed. For example, they may agree that the new lease shall be for 25 years rather than the maximum period of 14 years which the Court can allow. Commonly all terms are agreed other than the rent payable. The Courts, in "having regard to the terms of the current tenancy" tend to retain the same covenants as in the existing lease unless sound reasons can be advanced for a change (*O'May and Others v. City of London Real Property Co. Ltd.* (1982) 261 EG 1185).

Subject to certain safeguards, the Court will revoke an order for the new tenancy if the tenant applies within fourteen days of the making of the order, so that a tenant is not bound to accept the terms awarded by the Court.

During the period while an existing tenancy is continuing only by virtue of the Act and provided the landlord has given notice to determine the tenancy or the tenant has requested a new tenancy, the landlord may apply to the Court for the determination of a "reasonable" rent (an Interim Rent).[4] The interim rent is determined in accordance with the same rules which apply to a rent for a new tenancy but is on a year to year basis having regard to the rent payable under the expiring lease. The interpretation of these rules has led to a general approach whereby the rental value established

---

[4] Law of Property Act 1969, Section 3.

for the new fixed term lease is reduced by 10% to convert it to a year-to-year basis, and then by a further 10% so as to have regard to the existing rent (supported, for example, by *Janes (Gowns) Ltd. v. Harlow Development Corporation* (1979) 253 EG 799 and *Ratners (Jewellers) Ltd. v. Lemnoll Ltd.* (1980) 255 EG 987). However, this is not a fixed rule and the Courts may vary the approach depending on the facts of the case. For example, in *Charles Follett Ltd. v. Cabtell Investments Ltd.* (1987) 19 CSW 74, the new lease rent was fixed at £106,000. This was reduced to £80,000 as being the rent on a year-to-year basis. The further reduction so as to have regard to the existing rent was fixed at 50%, producing an Interim Rent of £40,000. This was because the rent is not a reasonable rent but "the rent which it would be reasonable for the tenant to pay" and this, coupled with the need to "have regard to the rent payable under the (old) tenancy" (in this case £13,500 p.a.) justified such a large percentage deduction.

A landlord can successfully oppose an application for a new tenancy on the following grounds:—(a) That the tenant has not complied with the terms of his tenancy. (b) That the tenant has persistently delayed paying rent. (c) That the landlord can secure or provide suitable alternative accommodation for the tenant, having regard to the nature and class of business and to the situation and extent of, and facilities afforded by, his present premises. (d) That the landlord will suffer substantial loss if new tenancies are granted of parts of the premises where the landlord is in a position to let or sell as a whole. This applies only where such tenancies were granted by an intermediate landlord or landlords. (e) That the landlord intends to demolish or reconstruct the premises.[5] (f) That the landlord requires the premises for his own occupation—but a landlord is debarred from using this ground if he acquired the premises less than five years

[5] There are many decided cases relating to this ground. Note that the Law of Property Act 1969, Section 7, inserts an additional section (31A) into the 1954 Act which entitles a tenant to a new tenancy despite reconstruction works by the landlord if terms reasonably facilitating the performance of those works can be included, or if "an economically separable part of the holding" can be substituted for the entirety of the holding.

before the end of the tenancy. This five-year limitation gives rise to difficulty when purchasers wish to reconstruct premises for their own occupation.[6]

A tenant who is refused a new tenancy is entitled to compensation from his landlord if either the landlord or the Court refused on grounds (d), (e) or (f) above, and there is not an agreement which effectively excludes compensation. Such compensation is in addition to any the tenant may be entitled to under the Landlord and Tenant Act 1927, in respect of improvements.

If the business has been carried on in the premises for less than fourteen years, the compensation is equal to three times the rateable value of the premises. If it has been carried on for fourteen years or more, the compensation is six times the rateable value (S.I. 1984, No. 1932—L.T.A. 1954 (Appropriate Multiplier) Order). Where net annual value differs from rateable value, net annual value is to be taken as the basis for compensation. The compensation multipliers are fixed by Orders and change on the introduction of new Valuation Lists or even during the life of such lists.

In general it is not possible to contract out of Part II of the Act but Section 5 of the Law of Property Act 1969 introduced an important exception whereby the Court may, on the joint application of landlord and tenant prior to the grant of the lease, authorise an agreement to exclude the provisions of the 1954 Act regarding compensation (and indeed other provisions). Section 38 of the 1954 Act allows the parties to exclude the compensation provisions where the tenant or his predecessors in business have occupied the premises for less than five years.

The effect of all these provisions on the value of business premises falling within Part II of this Act has, generally speaking, been slightly to lower rents obtainable from sitting tenants when leases are renewed. There is no doubt at all that it strengthens the hand of a tenant very considerably indeed in negotiations for a new lease or in negotiations for the surrender of an existing lease in return for a new lease.

---

[6] See *Atkinson v. Bettison*, [1955] 1 W.L.R. 1127; and *Fisher v. Taylor's Furnishing Stores Ltd.*, [1956] 2 Q.B. 78 (both Court of Appeal decisions).

Nevertheless, lessees still prefer to have a lease for a definite term of years rather than to rely solely on their rights to a new lease under the Act. Tenants who have only a few years of their lease unexpired and who wish to sell the goodwill of their businesses or to invest in the property or the business nearly always have to surrender their existing short leases to secure a sufficiently long term to realise the full potential of their business. In practice purchasers require the security of a term of years rather than the rights under this Act.

With few exceptions, it would seem that reversions after an existing lease should be valued on a capitalised rental value based on the terms—referred to above—to which a Court must have regard when settling disputes between the parties for new tenancies. If a landlord's interest is valued on the assumption that a new tenancy will not be granted, allowance should be made for compensation which may have to be paid to the tenant.

There is little doubt that the security of tenure afforded by Part II of the Act increases the value of a tenant's interest. If his interest is valued upon the basis that he will have to give up possession at the end of the lease for one of the reasons set out above which attract the payment of compensation, an appropriate addition should be made. Conversely the effect is to decrease the value of a landlord's interest. Only in a comparatively few cases can reversions be valued on the basis of vacant possession.

In general, the 1954 Act has had a much greater effect in practice than the 1927 Act.

The following example illustrates the possible effect of both the 1927 and the 1954 Acts in various circumstances:—

Example 20–1

Shop premises are let on a lease granted 15 years ago and with 3 years unexpired at a rent of £4,000 per annum. Improvements were carried out seven years ago at a cost of £30,000 by the tenant, who served notice of his intention on the landlord under the Landlord and Tenant act 1927, and received the landlord's consent thereto.

It is considered that without these improvements the rental value is £5,000 per annum, but that in consequence of the work done the annual rental has been increased to £7,500 per annum. The present Rateable Value is £1,000. Prepare a valuation of the freehold interest.

Valuation

As the tenant has a right to a new lease which excludes the value of the improvements made by him, the rental value of £7,500 per annum should be ignored for the probable period of the new lease, a maximum of 14 years if fixed by the Court. The landlord might not wish to grant a lease for longer than this so as to obtain the rental value of the improvements at the earliest opportunity (21 years from improvement being made). He would weigh this consideration against possible disadvantages of a lease for a "non-standard" term.

Term—rent payable under lease		£4,000	
Y.P. for 3 years at 6%		2·67	
			£10,680
Reversion—to new lease (say 14 years) at rental value ignoring improvements		£5,000	
Y.P. 14 years at 6%	9·295		
P.V. £1 in 3 years at 6%	0·84	7·81	
			39,050
—to rental value reflecting improvements		£7,500	
Y.P. perp at 6% deferred 17 years		6·19	46,425
			96,155
Value, say			£96,000

If it is known that the landlord wishes to occupy the premises himself when the present lease terminates, the value would be:—

Term—rent reserved under lease	£4,000	
Y.P. for 3 yrs at 6%	2·67	
		£10,680
Reversion—to	£7,500	
Y.P. in perpetuity at 6% deferred 3 years	13·99	104,925
		£115,605

Deduct—

Compensation under the Landlord and Tenant Act, 1954—6 × R.V. £1,000	£6,000	
Compensation under the Landlord and Tenant Act 1927		
(a) Increase in rental value of landlord's reversion	£2,500	
Y.P. in perpetuity at 6%	16·67	
say	£42,000	
(b) Cost of carrying out improvements at end of lease, say	£45,000	
Less depreciation, say 30%	13,500	
	£31,500	
Take lesser of (a) or (b)	£31,500	
	£37,500	
P.V. £1 in 3 years at 6%	0·84	31,500
		84,105
Value, say		£84,000

It is assumed for the purposes of the above that the landlord is not debarred by the five-year restriction. It is also assumed that the tenant has been in occupation for over fourteen years and thus the amount of compensation under the Landlord and Tenant Act 1954, is six times the R.V. The cost of meeting the compensation has been deferred at the remunerative rate as it is the landlord's choice to take possession and the compensation is the payment required to obtain the advantages sought.

If the landlord intended to demolish the premises, the valuation would be:—

Term—rent reserved under lease	£4,000	
Y.P. for 3 years at 6%	2·67	
		£10,680
Reversion to site value, say	£200,000	
Deduct—		
Compensation under the Landlord and Tenant Act 1954	6,000	
Net value of reversion	194,000	
P.V. £1 in 3 years at 6%	0·84	162,960
		173,640
Value, say		£170,000

In this case no compensation would be payable under the 1927 Act as the demolition would entirely negative the effect which the improvements would have on the value of the holding.

3. HEALTH AND SAFETY AT WORK, ETC. ACT 1974

This Act "to make further provision for saving the health, safety and welfare of persons at work, for protecting others against risks to health and safety in connection with the activities of persons at work" provided[7] for the progressive replacement by a system of Health and Safety Regulations and Approved Codes of Practice of such legislation as the Factories Act 1961, and the Offices, Shops and Railway Premises Act 1963 which remain in force.

Health and Safety Regulations may be made for any of

---

[7] Section 1.

the general purposes of Part I of the Act[8] and Schedule
3 sets some of these matters out in detail including such things
as structural condition and stability of the premises, means
of access and egress, cleanliness, temperature and ventilation, fire precautions and welfare facilities.

These requirements must be borne in mind when leases
are being granted and freehold and leasehold interests are
being valued. In appropriate circumstances deductions may
have to be made to allow for the cost of complying with
the regulations.

4. RENT REVIEWS

A major development in commercial leases over recent
years has been the provision for the review of the rent during
the currency of the lease. In the early 1960's landlords began
to give close attention to the fact that, when a lease is granted
for several years, if the rent is fixed it becomes less valuable
in real terms as inflation takes its toll, and further that the
steady increase in rental value accrues wholly to the lessee
who is not in essence a property investor.

Two solutions are obvious. One is to shorten the length
of the lease so that the landlord can adjust the rent frequently
on the grant of a new lease. This is unattractive both to
investors and occupiers because, for the investor it increases
the possibility of voids since lessees have regular opportunities to vacate, whilst the occupier has no long-term certainty
of occupation. Not only that, the frequent grant of new leases
is costly. The other solution is to retain the long term of
years but provide for rent increases during that term. Initially, such increases were often effected by fixing the rent
for the first few years at the agreed rental value, and then
fixing a higher rent for the subsequent periods. For example
a shop might be let for 21 years at £1,200 p.a. for the first
7 years, rising to £1,500 p.a. for the following 7 years and
£1,800 p.a. for the final 7 years.

This approach went some way to overcoming the problem
but it soon became apparent that it was far from ideal. At

---

[8] Section 15.

the time when the first increase came into operation it was
seen to be quite fortuitous if the new rent represented rental
value at that time. Quite often it would be less, so that the
landlord was still losing ground. Where it was more the tenant
would be unhappy at the injustice as he saw it.

This led to the introduction within leases of a machinery
for the rent, at intervals, to be re-determined at the then
prevailing rental value. The machinery was contained in rent
review clauses. In the absence of precedents, rent review
clauses took many different forms reflecting the differing
views of lawyers, some of whom initially raised doubts as
to whether such clauses were valid.

In time however the practice of providing for rent reviews
grew and became accepted. In occupation leases the reviews
tended to be at 7 year intervals but this came down to 5
years, and in the early 1970's pressure grew for 3 yearly
reviews. The market seems to have settled in the main for
5 year reviews with the consequential effect that leases tend
to be granted for multiples of 5 years. Ground leases have
seen a similar development, initially the review period being
33 years or perhaps 25 years, but now 5 year reviews tend
to be commonly found.

The introduction and acceptance of rent reviews took
several years but by the early 1970's they were the rule rather
than the exception. The period 1970 to 1973 saw a sharp
rise in property values, both capital and rental. The government became alarmed at the sharply rising costs to occupiers
of rental payments, and this led to the introduction of a rent
freeze on business properties in 1972, which lasted until 1974.
In that period rent review clauses became ineffective, so that
new rentals were agreed but could not be claimed by the
landlords. This meant that, following the lifting of the freeze,
rents rose in 1974 and into 1975 when capital values were
declining rapidly. It is not possible to prove, but experience
does suggest that in that period tenants began to be far more
sensitive to the fact of increasing rents and since then rent
reviews have attracted considerable attention. This has been
magnified by the fact that the first effects of the practice
of 5 year reviews begun in the early 1970's coincided with
the falling in of many leases granted in the 1950's at fixed

rents, as well as joining with the period of business depression. Tenants, and particularly companies such as multiple retailers who are tenants of many properties, faced with sharp increases in their rent bills in such circumstances, naturally seek to restrict increases to the minimum.

Inevitably, with closer attention being paid to the actual wording of the rent review clause in conjunction with the other terms of the lease, valuers have begun to develop valuation theories and ideas. Disputes between the parties have become more common, leading to a marked increase in the use of arbitration and also to a considerable number of cases heard by the Courts. There have thus emerged certain principles applicable to rent reviews.

A typical rent review clause will cover the following areas:—

(a) The machinery for putting into effect the review.
(b) The factors to be taken into account and assumptions to be made in arriving at rental value.
(c) The machinery for determining disputes in the absence of agreement.

Most of these aspects can be considered in turn.

(*a*) *Machinery for review.* In general the review is triggered by the service of a notice by the landlord on the tenant, following which the parties' valuers have a period of time in which to reach agreement. Failing agreement the matter is referred to arbitration. Although a time scale is laid down for all these matters it seems that the time scale is not so restrictive as to compel absolute compliance therewith,[9] unless it is clearly stated or indicated that time is to be of the essence,[10] or some other terms of the lease (such as a tenant's option to break the lease following review) make it essential for time to be of the essence.[11]

(*b*) *Rent payable.* The rent review clause sets down the factors which are to be taken into account in arriving at the

[9] *United Scientific Holdings Ltd. v. Burnley Borough Council* (1977) 243 EG 43.

[10] *Drebbond Ltd. v. Horsham District Council* (1978) 246 EG 1013.

[11] See for example, *Al Saloom v. Shirley James Travel Services Ltd.* (1981) 259 EG 420. For a full discussion of time of the essence see 284 EG 28.

rent. These take many forms and each clause must be read carefully to see which apply to any particular case. In general they have tended to vary between two extremes. At one the various factors affecting rent are set out in great detail including a definition of the rent payable—"rack rent", "open market rent", "open market rent as between willing lessor and willing lessee", etc.: assumptions as to use: whether to disregard tenant's improvements: whether to disregard tenant's goodwill: whether to assume the lease has its full term to run or merely the actual unexpired term: assumptions as to general lease covenants. At the other extreme the clause is limited to saying that "market rent" or some similar phrase shall be adopted.

The assumptions may have a considerable effect on rent. For example:—

(*i*) *Rent description.* Generally where the phrase used is one commonly adopted and widely understood no problems arise. However, where less familar terms are used then they may have a considerable impact on the rent finally determined. For example, "a reasonable rent for the premises" led to the Court fixing a rent reflecting the improvements carried out by the tenant, even though they would be ignored on renewal of the lease.[12]

(*ii*) *User.* Normally the use assumption follows the user covenant of the lease under the general lease covenant assumptions but sometimes an assumption is imposed which is different. In either case, where a lease severely limits the use to which a property may be put, this will tend to reduce the rent below the level acceptable where the tenant has flexibility of approach. Thus the rental value of a shop whose use is strictly limited to the retail business of cutlers is clearly worth less than one where the tenant may adopt other activities with the landlord's consent which is not to be unreasonably withheld.[13] This contrasts the difference between restricted user clauses and open user clauses. The class of person who may use a building may be restricted. Thus offices held under a lease which limits occupation to civil engineers

[12] *Ponsford v. HMS Aerosols Ltd.* (1978) 247 EG 1171.
[13] *Charles Clements (London) Ltd. v. Rank City Wall Ltd.* (1978) 246 EG 739

are likely to be worth less than the same offices if they can be occupied by anyone in the market, since the competition therefor is so restricted. Such was the situation in the *Plinth Property* case[14] when it was agreed that the "open" use rental value was £130,455 p.a. whereas in the market limited to civil engineers it became £89,200 p.a. The possibility that landlords might well relax the provisions was ignored.

Where the use is even more restricted to that of a named tenant only then it is assumed that there is a "blank lease" with the name to be inserted, and the generally prevailing rental values for that type of property will be adopted.[15] If there is an assumed use for rent review purposes which displaces the actual use covenant in the lease it is assumed that planning permission exists for that use[16] although the need to carry out works to achieve the assumed use would need to be reflected in the rent.[17]

(*iii*) *Improvements.* It is widely accepted that tenants should receive the benefit of any improvements carried out by them not as a condition of the lease, a view reflected in successive Landlord and Tenant Acts, including the 1954 Act which requires their effect on rents to be disregarded. The wording of the 1954 Act is commonly adopted in rent review clauses.

A problem arises as to how the valuer should disregard the effect of improvements. Approaches commonly adopted include assessing the rental value as if the improvements had never been carried out, or to assume that the improvements are to be carried out at the time of review at current building costs, amortising the cost over the remaining years of the lease, and deducting the amortised cost from the rental value which reflects the improvements. A further approach is to adopt a "gearing" approach whereby if, at the time of the improvements being carried out the rental value was increased by 50%, then the rent at review, ignoring the effect

[14] *Plinth Property Investment Ltd. v. Mott Hay & Anderson* (1979) 249 EG 1167.

[15] *The Law Land Company v. Consumers' Association Ltd.* (1980) 255 EG 617.

[16] *Bovis Group Pension Fund Ltd. v. GC Floorings and Furnishings Ltd.* (1984) 269 EG 1252.

[17] *Trust House Forte Albany Hotels Ltd. v. Daejan Investments Ltd.* (1980) 256 EG 915.

of the improvements, is taken to be two-thirds of the rental value reflecting the improvements. The Courts have rejected these approaches,[18,19] but notwithstanding such criticisms, the methods are still commonly applied as providing a practical valuation solution even though not perhaps a true legal interpretation.

(*iv*) *Goodwill.* Although valuers are commonly required to ignore goodwill attributable to the carrying on of the tenant's business, this is not normally a matter which raises specific valuation issues. It would generally apply only to special properties, such as hotels and restaurants, where the history of trading by the the the tenant generates rental valuation evidence by analysis of the trading record of the tenant.

(*v*) *Length of Lease.* A rent review clause commonly provides that, on review, the actual unexpired term is to be adopted in determining the rent. Thus, on a 20 year lease with 5 yearly reviews, at the first review it is to be assumed that a new lease of 15 years is being offered (with 5 yearly reviews), at the second one of 10 years, and at the third a lease of 5 years. This is unlikely to have any significant effect apart from the final review when such a short term might be argued to be very unattractive to tenants. Where the tenant has carried out major improvements which are to be ignored, then the effect might be significant at later reviews as the time left to recoup the expenditure by adjustment of rent could require a considerable reduction. However, the possibility of the tenant obtaining a new lease under the 1954 Act should be reflected in the approach and this will tend to negative the tenant's argument for a lower rent.[20]

On the other hand some leases do provide that it shall be assumed that on each review a lease for the original term is being offered. This overcomes such problems but tenants may resist such an assumption as being unrealistic.

(*vi*) *General Lease Covenants.* The rent review clauses will generally provide that the other terms of the lease are to be assumed to be included in the hypothetical new lease.

[18] *GREA Real Property Investments Ltd. v. Williams* (1979) 250 EG 651.
[19] *Estates Projects Ltd. v. London Borough of Greenwich* (1979) 251 EG 851.
[20] *Secretary of State for the Environment v. Pivot Properties Ltd.* (1980) 256 EG 1176.

Commercial Properties

405

Thus covenants as to repair, insurance and alienation are
to be the same as in the lease subject to review. The more
restrictive or onerous they are to one party, so the rent will
be adjusted upwards or downwards to reflect this quality,
as is the case on the grant of a lease.

One problem area concerns a phrase commonly adopted,
whereby the hypothetical lease is assumed to contain the
same covenants as in the existing lease "other than as to
rent" or some such exclusion. It seems probable that the
purpose of this exclusion is to indicate that the rent itself
will be different. However, the Courts have considered the
meaning of this exclusion clause in the various forms it takes,
and in particular whether it meant that the actual clause
requiring the rent to be reviewed should be assumed to exist
or not.

Initially the Courts adopted a strict literal interpretation
and decided that ignoring the provisions as to rent meant
that the rent review clause itself should be ignored.[21] Later
cases adopted a more commercial view so that, unless the
words in the clause clearly required the provisions as to rent
review to be disregarded, then a rent review clause should
be assumed.[22] In a yet later decision on appeal to the Court
of Appeal, the more literal approach was favoured.[23] Thus
it seems that a seemingly innocent phrase which requires
the valuer to take account of the clauses in the actual lease
"other than as to rent" might require the rent to be determined assuming no rent reviews for the remainder of the
term. The effects of these are considered below.

These examples illustrate that the valuer needs to weigh
up the effects of the assumptions in determining the rent,
as the rental valuation is of the hypothetical world which
the assumptions create rather than the real world if the property were being put on the market with full flexibility of
action. Even where the clause requires the rent to be the
market rent as between willing lessor and willing lessee, if

---

[21] *National Westminster Bank plc v. Arthur Young McClelland Moores & Co.*
(1984) 273 EG 402.
[22] *British Gas Corporation v. Universities Superannuation Scheme Ltd.* (1986)
277 EG 980.
[23] *Equity & Law Life Assurance Society plc v. Bodfield Ltd.* (1987) 281 EG 1448.

the parties are not willing then a hypothetical willing lessor and lessee must be assumed to exist.[24]

Another problem which may arise in the welter of different lease covenant assumptions is the actual period between reviews. Clearly if the lease in question has 5 year rent reviews and the rental evidence is of similar leases with 5 year rent reviews then a direct comparison can be made. But what if the review period is shorter, say 3 years, or the period is actually longer, say 7 or 21 years, or assumed to be longer by the interpretation of the phrase "other than as to rent" referred to above, when no rent review is to be assumed? As a general rule it can be said that the longer the period between the reviews, the higher should be the rent, and vice versa. The mathematical analysis by using discounted cash flow techniques is considered in Chapter 10.

Landlords tend to resort to a mathematical solution which puts them in the same position on a discounted rent basis whatever the review period. Where the period is relatively long this can produce a rent fixed well above the rents paid with the common 5 year review pattern. In the Arthur Young case referred to above[21] the Court recognised that the uplift was 20·5%. In practice there is strong tenant resistance to significant increases as rents reach levels which tenants argue they cannot afford, particularly in the early years after the review. They may accept an uplift up to 10% but argue that tenants would not afford more than this. A "rule of thumb" approach has emerged whereby 1% for each additional year beyond 5 years is added to the rent on a 5 year basis. These arguments can only be tested by marketing properties on different rent review bases but this is rarely attempted.

(*c*) *Machinery for Settling Disputes.* Where the parties cannot agree then the clause provides for the matter to be referred to an arbitrator, commonly a valuer agreed between the parties or one appointed by the President of the Royal

---

[24] *F.R. Evans (Leeds) Ltd. v. English Electric Co. Ltd.* (1977) 245 EG 657. In this case the Court held that, as each party was willing, the actual market conditions which showed an absence of any demand was to be ignored so as to reflect the existence of the tenant willing to take the premises. A more realistic view of market conditions can be taken following *Dennis & Robinson Ltd. v. Kiossos Establishment* (1987) 282 EG 857.

Institution of Chartered Surveyors. He may be required to
act as an arbitrator or as an expert.

The considerable attention given to aspects of rent reviews
has led to some standardisation of the contents of rent review
clauses. Nonetheless they still vary considerably and the
valuer needs to pay close attention to their actual wording
in each case as the rent review clause represents the instructions to the valuer as to how he shall prepare his valuation.
As a general rule, the more onerous or restrictive the covenants are on the freedom of action of the tenant, the lower
the rent, and vice versa. The consequences on the rent payable can be considerable.

5. RETAIL PREMISES

(*a*) *Location*. These may vary from small shops, with upper
floors, in secondary positions likely to let at rents of a
thousand pounds or so per annum to out of town superstores
with floor areas of thousands of square feet and town centre
enclosed air-conditioned centres with shops on a number of
levels and the rent of a small standard unit measured in terms
of many thousands of pounds per annum.

As already indicated, the chief factor affecting values is
that of position and its effect on trade. The prospective purchaser or tenant is likely, in nearly every case, to attempt
some estimate of the trade in those premises in that position.
The degree of accuracy that he will attempt to achieve will
depend largely on circumstances. It is well known that many
of the bigger concerns, with a large number of branches,
have arrived from experience at certain methods of assessing,
with a fair degree of accurcy, the turnover they are likely
to be able to achieve in a given shopping position. From
such an estimated turnover it is necessary to deduct the cost
of goods to be sold; from the gross profit remaining will
fall to be deducted wages, overhead charges and a margin
for profit and interest on capital. There remains a balance
or residue which the tenant can afford to pay in rent, rates
and repairs.

The use of shop premises for one particular retail trade
can, with some exceptions, be changed to its use for another

retail trade without the necessity of obtaining planning permission. If, therefore, premises are capable of occupation
for a number of different purposes, and are likely to appeal
to a number of different tenants, there will be competititon
between the latter, and the prospective occupier whose estimate of the margin available for rent, etc., is largest, is likely
to secure the premises by tenancy or purchase.

It is not suggested that in the majority of cases a valuation
of shop premises should be based on an analysis of the probable profits of any particular trade in order to arrive at the
rent a tenant can afford to pay for them, largely because
the probable profits are based on amounts which in practice
are very difficult to assess with any reliable degree of accuracy. But the general factors likely to influence prospective
occupiers in their estimate of turnover and margin available
for rent will certainly have to be taken into account by the
valuer.

It is a commmonplace that shops in a prime position such
as the main thoroughfare of an important town with large
numbers of passers-by will command a much higher rent than
those in secondary positions. Again, the potential purchasing
power of the passers-by must be considered: for instance,
the amount of money they have available to spend in the
shops is likely to be greater in Bond Street, London, than
in the main shopping street of a small provincial town.

In some instances large variations in value may be found
within a comparatively short distance. A location at the corner of a main thoroughfare in a side street may be of considerable value, whereas a short distance down the side street
the shops will be of comparatively small value. Location is
therefore a factor to which most careful consideration must
be given. It has been said that the three main qualities which
determine value are location, location and location, and this
is particularly so in the case of shops.

Some of the most important points in regard to location
are: in what class of district is the shop situated? What is
the type of street and what sort of persons use it? What
is the position of the shop in the street? It is a focal point
such as the corner of an important road junction? Are there
any multiple shop branches nearby or any "magnet" such

as a big store? Is the property close to premises which break the continuity of shopping, such as a town hall, bank or cinema? How does it compare with the best position in the town? How close is it to car parks or public transport?

(*b*) *Type of Premises.* The next most important factor is the type of premises and their suitability for the display and sale of goods. The available frontage for the display of goods needs first consideration, together with the condition and character of the shop front. The suitability of the interior must then be considered; the adequacy of its lighting; the presence or absence of access at the rear for receipt or delivery of goods (this is becoming increasingly important as parking, waiting and loading restrictions become imposed over more and more roads in the centres of towns); the character of the upper floors, whether separately occupied or only usable with the shop; the general condition of repair and the ancillary staff facilities.

In the case of newly erected premises, shops are often offered to let on the basis that the tenant fits out the shop and installs his own shop front at his own expense; what is offered is a "shell" often with the walls and ceiling to be plastered and the floor in rough concrete. In more established districts premises will be offered to let complete with shop front. If the latter is modern and likely to be suitable for a number of different trades, the value of the premises may be enhanced thereby. If, however, the shop front is old-fashioned, or only suitable for a limited number of types of business, it will be necessary to have regard to the fact that any prospective occupier will need to renew the shop front. Most multiple retailers have their own style of shop front so that they will be indifferent to the existence and quality of any existing shop front. This will apply also to the internal fittings since extensive shop fitting work is carried out before trading begins.

Sometimes a factor of importance is the right of a tenant to display goods on a forecourt. There are many shops where the enforcement of a building line or the like has created a forecourt of considerable extent and of value to a number of trades, such as DIY, greengrocers and others, for the display of goods.

In considering particular premises it may be necessary to have regard to the possibility of structural alterations in the future for the purpose of improving the premises. In the case of large premises the division of the premises to provide a few "standard" units or, for very large premises, the creation of a shopping precinct should be considered.

In valuing premises of some age, regard may have to be had not only to their probable useful life but also to the possibility of their being redeveloped in whole or in part or of additions being made, for example to extend the selling space to a greater depth, subject to the necessary planning consent.

As regards accommodation on upper floors, it is necessary to consider the best purpose to which it can be put. In the more important positions it is frequently found that such floor space can be used for the display and sale of goods. In less prominent positions it may be more profitable for the upper part to be let off separately for use as offices or dwelling purposes, but in such cases it must be borne in mind that planning permission for a change in use may not be forthcoming.

The extent to which large basement areas are of value will again depend largely upon position. In valuable situations where rents are high any prospective tenant is likely to wish to use the whole of the ground floor area for the display of goods and an extensive and dry place for storage will enhance the rental value of the premises considerably. In less important positions the use of the rear portion of the ground floor for storage purposes may be more practicable, and the enhancement of value due to the presence of a basement may be quite small.

The comments so far have concentrated on the traditional shop premises found in shopping streets. Nonetheless the same considerations apply to out-of-town superstores or retail warehouse parks or to shopping centres, but will have a different emphasis.

For example the quality of location for out-of-town premises will be tested more against accessibility for customers who will be mainly motorists, although the availability of public transport may be important. Thus the location should be well placed for the road network, with sites near to motorway junctions being preferred. Extensive parking will also be required to accommodate the motorist customer on arrival, ideally at ground level only. In the case of in-town shopping centres a good road access is less easy to achieve but extensive parking is also required, commonly on several levels within the shopping centre.

Similarly the type of premises is important. Retail warehouses require large open lofty spaces although a high standard of internal finish is not generally sought. On the other hand food superstores require a high standard of design both internally and externally. Indeed the cost of fitting out such stores can match or exceed the cost of the building itself. Similar requirements as to design and finish apply to shopping centres, not only to the shop units themselves but increasingly to the common parts. The early shopping centres are more and more being extensively refurbished with the roofing over of public malls, the upgrading of floor surfaces, and improvements to lighting and general design being areas of special attention. The effect on rental values of such works can be significant with tenants accepting considerable rental increase in recognition of the improvement to trading potential which the works generate.

(*c*) *Type of Tenant.* This is of considerable importance to the value of property from an investment point of view.

The tenancy of a large multiple concern is considered to give exceptional security to the income, since the mere covenant to pay rent by such an undertaking can be relied on for the duration of the lease even if the profits from the particular branch are less than was expected or even if the lease is assigned to another trader.

This contrasts with premises let to individuals or small companies with limited resources where the chance of business failure is far higher.

Since multiple concerns tend to occupy prime property and the tenants of poor covenant the poorer property, this contributes to the sharp difference in yield between prime property at low yields and secondary or tertiary property at high yields.

(*d*) *Terms of the Lease.* Shop property may be let on various repairing terms; on the one hand the tenant may be responsible for all repairs and insurance and at the other extreme the landlord may be responsible for all repairs. In between these extremes a variety of different responsibilities is found. The tendency in the last twenty years or so is for the responsibility to be put on to the tenant. Where the landlord has any responsibility for outgoings an appropriate allowance must be made in valuations.

The length of the lease is important. An investor will prefer a long lease with provision for regular rent reviews.

The terms of letting of the upper portion (if separate from the shop) must also be noted and the presence of any tenancies under the Rent Acts.

(*e*) *Rental Value.* When making comparisons of rental value between shops in very similar positions, regard must be had to size. Lock-up and small or medium size shops may provide sufficient floor space to enable a large variety of businesses to be carried on profitably and may be in great demand whereas, in the case of larger shops for which there is less demand it may be found that the rent is not increased in proportion to the additional floor space available.

For example, in a given position a lock-up shop with a frontage of 20 feet and a floor space of 1,000 square feet may command a rent of £10,000 per annum, equivalent to £10 per square foot; whereas, nearby, in a very similar position, a larger shop with a frontage of 30 feet and a depth of 60 feet may only command a rent of £12,600 per annum, equivalent to a rent of £7 per square foot.

In recent years the demand has grown for large units as patterns of retailing change so that it could be that, in prime positions, the rent for larger units will be proportionately larger than that for small units. The valuer will need to assess the relative demand for different sized units within the shopping area before preparing a valuation.

Although various "units of comparison" can be adopted by a valuer in comparing rents paid for other units with the unit to be valued, such as frontage or standard unit comparisons, the method most commonly adopted is that of "zoning" as described in detail in Chapter 22.

In valuing extensive premises comprising basement,

ground, and a number of upper floors, there is some difficulty
in deciding upon the comparable rental values of the different
floors. Generally speaking, the zoning method allows for this
by adopting a proportion of the Zone A rent. Thus a first
floor retail area may be valued at one-sixth of the ground
floor Zone A rental value, whereas first floor storage might
be one-tenth. The actual rent per square foot would need
to be considered to assess whether it is unrealistic for such
a use. For example if the ground floor Zone A rent is £150
per square foot then one-tenth, or £15 per square foot, might
be regarded as excessive for storage space on the first floor
if warehouse or storage buildings in the area have a rental
value of only £4 per square foot.

The method of approach to problems of this type is illustrated by the following example:—

Example 20–2

You are asked to advise on the rental value of shop premises comprising basement, ground, 1st and 2nd floors, in a
large town. The premises are old but in a fair state of repair;
the basement is dry, but has no natural light; the upper part
is only capable of occupation with the shop. The net floor
space is as follows:—Basement, 1,100 square feet; Ground
Floor, 900 square feet; 1st Floor, 800 square feet; 2nd Floor,
300 square feet. The shop has a frontage of 20 feet and a depth
of 45 feet. The 1st floor is retail and the 2nd floor staff rooms.

The following particulars are available of recent lettings
of shops in comparable positions, but all of them are more
modern premises:—

(1) Premises similar in size let at £37,000 p.a.: areas—
    Basement, 1,000 square feet; Ground Floor, 960
    square feet; 1st Floor, 700 square feet retail space;
    2nd Floor, 600 square feet storage. The ground floor
    has a frontage of 16 feet and a depth of 60 feet.
(2) A lock-up shop, 12 feet frontage and 15 feet depth,
    let at £9,000 p.a.
(3) A shop and basement, frontage 45 feet and depth 80
    feet, with a basement of 1,000 square feet let at £83,500
    p.a. The upper part is used as offices and is separately

let in floors as follows: 1st Floor, 1,400 square feet at £7,000 p.a.; 2nd Floor, 1,300 square feet at £5,200 p.a.
(4) The basement under lock-up shop No. 2 and three more shops, is dry and well lit with direct street access; floor space is 1,200 square feet and it is let for storage purposes at £3,600 p.a.

Note.—In practice these lettings might be on different terms and adjustments would be required to the rents to reduce them to net figures.

Analysis—

Analysis of the first letting is best deferred until other lettings of various parts of premises have been dealt with:—

Letting	Floor	Area in sq. ft.	Rent £'s	Rent £'s per sq. ft.
2	Ground	180	9,000	50
4	Basement	1,200	3,600	3
3	1st	1,400	7,000	5
3	2nd	1,300	5,200	4

The evidence from these lettings can be used to analyse the letting of shop No. 3 as follows:—

Rent for shop and basement	£83,500
Less Basement	
1,000 square feet at say £2·50 per sq. ft.	2,500
Rent for shop	£81,000

Zone A—45 ft. × 20 ft. =   900 sq. ft.—in terms
                                     of Zone A   =   900 sq. ft.
Zone B—45 ft. × 20 ft. =   900 sq. ft.—in terms
                                     of Zone A/2 =   450 sq. ft.
Remdr.—45 ft. × 40 ft. = 1,800 sq. ft.—in terms
                                     of Zone A/4 =   450 sq. ft.

Total area in terms of Zone A   1,800 sq. ft.

1,800 sq. ft. at £81,000 gives Zone A value of £45 per sq. ft.

This evidence can then be used to check the letting of shop
No. 1, as follows:—

Basement:	1,000 sq. ft.	at £2·50	2,500
Ground Floor:	560 sq. ft.	at £50·00	28,000
1st Floor:	700 sq. ft.	at £8·33	5,830
2nd Floor:	600 sq. ft.	at £2·50	1,500

£37,830

Actual Rent £37,000

Note: The Ground Floor is Zone A (16 × 20) + Zone B
(16 × 20)/2 + Remainder (16 × 20)/4 = 560 sq. ft. in terms
of Zone A. The 1st Floor being retail is valued at A/6. The
Zone A rent is higher than Shop No. 3 which is larger than
usual.

Valuation

Bearing in mind age, position and all other relevant factors,
the valuation might be as follows:—

Basement:	1,100 sq. ft.	at £1·75	1,925
Ground Floor:	625 sq. ft.	at £48·00	30,000
1st Floor:	800 sq. ft.	at £8·00	6,400
2nd Floor:	300 sq. ft.	at £2·00	600

£38,925

Rental Value say £39,000

The preceding comments on the rental valuation approach
apply to shops in town centres and shopping parades.

However, the zoning method has limitations and is not generally applied to the larger types of shop found particularly in town centres such as supermarkets, chain stores and departmental stores. In these cases ground floor retail areas will be valued at an overall rate per square foot and upper floor retail areas again at an overall rate per square foot which might be related to the ground floor rate on the basis of turnover.[25]

In the case of retail warehouses or out-of-town food stores the rental value will generally be determined by comparison with similar units in the area or even in comparable locations in relation to other urban centres. The rental value analysis will produce rental values per square foot applied to the total retail floor space, perhaps with a differential rental value for storage space. Unlike town centre shopping centres, the factors in determining rental value will depend more on accessibility and customer parking and visibility.

A further form of rental approach may be found where the rent payable is related to the level of business done by the occupier. Commonly this is a "turnover rent" since the gross takings will be the determining factor. Generally the rent payable has two elements, a base rent payable whatever the turnover, and a further rent payable being a proportion of the turnover in excess of a specified amount.[26]

(*f*) *Capital Value*. Similar methods of analysis and comparison can be used in determining the appropriate rate per cent to use in capitalising rental value.

Shops let to good tenants can generally be regarded as a sound security since rent ranks before many other liabilities, including debenture interest and preference dividends in the case of limited liability companies.

Present day rates per cent may vary widely from around 4 per cent to 11 per cent, the lower rates reflecting the above

[25] See Chapter 7, "Valuation: Principles into Practice", Ed. W. H. Rees, 3rd Edition 1988 (Estates Gazette).

[26] For a detailed examination of turnover rents see Paper Five, "Turnover Rents for Retail Property" by Dr. R. N. Goodchild in the Property Valuation Method Research Report published by the RICS and South Bank Polytechnic in July 1986.

average and above inflation rate of growth anticipated for shops in prime positions which has been seen over recent years.

Where the upper part of freehold shop premises is let separately, e.g., for residential purposes, it is probably desirable to value it separately at a different rate from that used for the income from the shop. In the case of leaseholds, however, this would involve an apportionment of the ground rent, and a more practical method may be to deduct the ground rent capitalised at a fair average rate per cent for the whole premises.

In any particular case, evidence of the actual transactions is usually the best basis for capitalising rental values.

6. INDUSTRIAL PREMISES

(a) *Generally.* Reference was made in Chapter 5, Section 4, to the method of ascertaining the rental values of this type of property on a floor space basis in terms of square feet.

The range of properties to be considered is extensive and varies from shop or residential property, converted for use as storage or for factory purposes, to well-constructed, well-lighted, up-to-date premises with many amenities.

Situation is one of the chief factors affecting value, including such points as access to motorways or link roads and railways, also proximity to markets and, in particular, to the supply of suitable labour.

In making comparison between premises otherwise similar, the influence of these matters must be carefully considered.

(b) *Construction.* Good natural lighting is essential in many trades; and premises in which the use of artificial light during day-light hours can be kept to a minimum might well command a higher rent than those where a good deal of work has to be done under artificial light.

Adequate working heights are essential and in new single storey factories 18 to 20 feet to eaves is regarded as a minimum.

The rates of insurance for many trades are comparatively high. The risk of fire will be minimised by fireproof
construction and by the presence of sprinklers. For the purpose of insurance, premises are graded by Insurance Companies in accordance with the rules of the Fire Offices
Committee.

The means of escape from fire will need to be considered,
also the provision of adequate sanitary accommodation and
adequate ventilation. It must be ascertained that the premises
under consideration comply with the requirements of the
Health and Safety Regulations. The mode of construction
may also be important in relation to the annual cost of repair.
The rental value on lease will be diminished, for example,
where the roof is old and by reason of age or construction
is likely to leak.

Consideration must also be given to the services available,
the type of central heating plant, electricity supply and equipment and the availability of a gas supply.

The lay-out of the premises should be such as to give clear
working space, to facilitate dealing with the delivery and
despatch of goods, and the handling of goods within the
premises without undue labour.

For many trades the floor space on the ground floor is
of considerably greater value than that on upper floors,
although this may be offset in the case of valuable sites, particularly in central districts, by adequate provision for handling goods by lifts or conveyors between floors. Particularly
in the case of ground floors it is a disadvantage if the whole
of each floor of each building is not at the same level, i.e.,
if there are steps or breaks in the floor.

The artificial lighting system should be considered, to see
that there is an adequate standard of illumination to enable
work to be done satisfactorily.

In large factories the provision of adequate canteen, welfare and car parking facilities is an essential point.

(*c*) *Rental and Capital Values*. In some cases it may be
found that land is sold and factories erected to the requirements of an occupier who purchases the freehold, and there
may be little evidence of rental values. In such cases regard
must be had to the selling price rather than the rental value

of the accommodation when making a valuation. Wherever possible, values arrived at on this basis should be checked by consideration of rental value.

In the centres of towns a large building is often let off in floors, the tenants paying exclusive rentals, the landlord being responsible for the maintenance of common staircases, lift, and sometimes the provision of heating or the supply of power. The method of valuation in such cases will be on the lines indicated in this Chapter in respect of office premises, an estimate of the net income being made by deducting the outgoings from the gross rentals and, where necessary, the actual rentals being checked against comparable values for other similar properties. The cost of services may, however, be recovered by a service charge. Service charges are also found on industrial estates where, although individual factories will be let on full repairing and insuring terms, the landlord provides other services the cost of which is recovered through a service charge.

Currently the range of yields for modern single storey factories is from 7% in the South East up to 13% in the North East. The range of rents for similar properties shows a similar wide disparity—from up to £8 per square foot in the favoured areas of the South East down to £2 per square foot in the less-favoured areas. The major conurbations, particularly London, provides exceptions to these rental generalisations.

In making comparisons between one property and another careful note must be made of the factors already mentioned. It may be found that one factory in a similar position and of a similar area and construction has a modern central heating system, sprinklers, road and rail access, whereas the other lacks these amenities. Such differences are usually taken into account by modifying the price per unit of floor area. But it must not be overlooked that the provision of additional facilities of this kind may be possible at a comparatively small cost and it may be more realistic to value the property as if the improvement had been carried out and to deduct the cost.

It may sometimes be found that extensive factory premises

comprise new and old buildings, some of which may be of little value in the open market. They may, for instance, have been erected for the purposes of a particular trade and although the covered floor space area may be extensive, they may have a comparatively low market value.

The following example is typical of fairly modern factory premises.

Example 20–3

You are instructed to prepare a valuation for purposes of sale of a large factory on the outskirts of an important town.

The premises are in the occupation of the owners, by whom they were acquired in 1968; the premises are of one storey only for the greater part, with offices, canteen and kitchens in a 2-storey block fronting the main road. The factory is brick built with steel span roof trusses covered externally with corrugated asbestos and lined internally, eaves height 20 ft. There is good top light. The floor is of concrete finished with granolithic paving. There is an efficient central heating system. Gas, electricity and main water supplies are connected. The site has a frontage of 300 ft. to a main road and has a private drive-in with two loading docks. There is adequate lavatory and cloakroom accommodation. The site area is 3·0 acres.

Temporary buildings for storage purposes with breeze-slab walls and steel-truss roofs carried on steel stanchions have been erected since the property was purchased.

The available areas in terms of sq. ft. are as follows:—Main factory, 30,000; boiler house, 700; loading docks, 1,200; outside temporary stores, 2,000; Gd. floor offices, 2,000; 1st floor offices, 1,200.

There are a number of similar factories in the vicinity, of areas from 10,000 to 25,000 sq. ft., let within the last five years at rents of from £2·50 to £3·50 per sq. ft. The rents show a tendency to increase.

Valuation—

It is usual for valuations of industrial premises to be based on the gross internal area (inside external walls) except for multi-storey premises where the net internal area (broadly usable space) is adopted.

As a result of an inspection, it will be possible to decide a fair basis of valuation in comparison with those factories where there is evidence of rental value.

A reasonable basis for a valuation might be as follows:—

		sq. ft.	£
Ground Floor:	Main factory floor	30,000 at £3·25	97,500
	Loading docks	1,200 at £3·25	3,900
	Outside stores	2,000 at £1·25	2,500
	Offices	2,000 at £5·00	10,000
First Floor:	Offices	1,200 at £3·50	4,200
	Full rental value—net		118,100
	Y.P. perpetuity, say		10
			£1,181,000
		Value, say	£1,200,000

Notes—
(1) The increased value placed on floor space used as offices reflects the higher standard of finish and amenity compared with the main factory. The office content, just under 10% of the total floor space, accords with the norm.
(2) It will be observed that the total area covered by buildings, allowing for outside walls, etc., is probably about 40,000 sq. ft. so that on a site of 3·0 acres and working on a site coverage of 40%, there is room for extension. Depending on the particular circumstances, this might justify some specific addition to the value but has been accommodated in this case in the rounding up.

7. "High-Tech" Industrials

Reference was made earlier in this Chapter to the new types of building which are now being provided to house new types of high technology based industry. Although many of the locational requirements which apply to light industry apply also to this type of industry, there are some differences to be noted. The first is general environment, where higher standards are required. The second is proximity to residential areas and other facilities appropriate to the level of staff employed, which again must be of a higher standard. The third, and this affects the building form more than immediate location, is a much higher standard of internal working environment. "High-tech" buildings tend to be two or perhaps three storey and the internal finish is of office rather than industrial standard. The essential feature, however, is flexibility so that any part of the building can be used for any of the various activities which form part of the total process. Finally, a higher standard of car parking is required.

Rents for these types of premises range at the time of writing from £8 to £12 per sq. ft. overall and yields tend to be slightly lower than for the best industrial, from about 7%.

A matter which has led to some difficulty has been the terms of leases. Landlords seek the traditional pattern of 20 or 25 years with 5 year reviews but the type of occupier concerned often desires a shorter term commitment.

8. Business and Science Parks

Reference has already been made to the industrial estate which has been a feature of the industrial scene since the early part of this century.

The business park is a fairly recent development which exploits the greater flexibility between business uses permitted by the 1987 Use Classes Order. Access to a motorway tends to be the chief locational requirement but insofar as "high-tech" and office uses will be accommodated, their specific locational requirements must also be met.

The science park caters for research and development

activities primarily and the essential locational requirement
is proximity to a university or other academic institution with
which the occupiers co-operate.

9. WAREHOUSES

A warehouse is, by definition, a place where people house
their wares. At one time warehouses were found in the main
at docks. Goods were brought to the docks where they
awaited being loaded on to ships, or they lay there having
been unloaded from ships and prior to being distributed
around the country. Indeed in many of the older docks there
may still be found former spice warehouses, sugar warehouses, and others designed for specific commodities.

After a decline, warehouses have now taken on a greater
significance in the development of the economy, so that today
they represent an important element in the economic structure. For example, the growth of major retailing groups has
led to demands by them for large warehouses to which the
various goods they offer for sale can be delivered by the
manufacturers and there assembled with other items for delivery to their stores.

Similarly shippers, having moved towards containerisa-
tion, require warehouses where they can have goods delivered and where they can join with others to fill the containers
for various destinations. Indeed the many developments in
the manufacturing, retailing and distribution industries have
led, in recent years, to considerable demand for warehousing
facilities which were not contemplated previously and which
led to the development of warehouses and whole warehouse
estates, to meet these demands. In consequence the warehouse has become a major attraction to investors in contrast
to former times when it was generally of secondary importance and interest.

These comments on warehouses refer to what are commonly known as wholesale warehouses to distinguish them
from retail warehouses which were considered earlier in this
Chapter.

The investor in warehouses is looking for various qualities

when judging any particular warehouse; qualities which will also attract the occupier. The principal qualities are:—

(*i*) *Location*. Ideally a warehouse should be well located within the general transport network. In general this means it should be close to the motorway network.

(*ii*) *Site Layout*. A warehouse is a building to which products are brought and subsequently removed. This involves lorries bringing in goods and then removing them. Thus there will be a flow of vehicles and the best planned warehouses have facilities to accommodate lorries waiting to unload, good unloading facilities, and easy means of access. Contrast this with old warehouses where lorries have to park in the streets when waiting to deliver; a narrow access requires several manoeuvres before the lorry can back into the narrow access to the yard space, and all set in areas of narrow streets.

(*iii*) *Design*. A modern warehouse will have easy access to vehicles, and loading bays, or docks, so that lorries can readily be brought up to the premises to load or unload. It will be single-storey to avoid raising goods by lift or crane or gantry. It will have clear floorspace to allow fork lift trucks to transfer goods around the property unhindered by columns or walls. The headroom will allow bulky goods to be moved around without hindrance and will allow smaller items to be stocked to the height limit of the fork lift trucks or other mechanical devices.

If these qualities are brought together it is seen that a modern warehouse is normally a single-storey building, of clear space, with minimum height to eaves of around 18–20 ft. with loading/unloading facilities to accommodate the largest lorry, high floor loading capacity, and located close to a motorway and urban centres. Such a building is totally different from the "traditional" warehouse, usually multi-storey, close to docks or a railhead, in an area with poor street access and no off-street loading/unloading facilities. It is important to keep this sharply contrasting picture in mind when warehouses are mentioned.

The valuation of a warehouse reflects these various qualities. In determining the rental value, the actual quality judged against the desirable qualities must be considered. The common approach is to apply a rental value based on the floor area. Thus, in a locality, warehouses which exhibit the most desirable qualities might command a rent of £5 per square foot whereas old multi-storey warehouses command rent of £2 per square foot on the ground floor with reducing rental values on the upper floors.

This appears to be the general approach, so that cubic content tends not to be considered in assessing rental value even though it would appear that the capacity for storage should be a critical factor. It is true that warehouses with low headroom tend to attract lower rental values than warehouses with high overall clearance but nonetheless the cubic capacity is rarely determined and noted. An exception to this is specialist warehouses. For example cold stores, which are essentially warehouses of a special type, are generally described in relation to their cubic content. Apart from such special cases a warehouse is typically described and considered in relation to its floor area.

As to the yields required by investors in warehouses, these tend to be at or around the yields required for industrial premises of a similar age and quality. There are however two qualities which might lead to the acceptance of a lower yield as against a comparable industrial unit. First, the amount of wear and damage which a warehouse suffers by use will tend to be less than an industrial unit. Secondly a warehouse is an adaptable building. It is usually a simple building, sometimes referred to familiarly as "a large shed", which enables it to be switched to other uses speedily and for a low cost. Hence if the demand for warehousing falls away a modern warehouse can readily be adapted to industrial use, or to retail use. Indeed there has been a strong demand for the adaptation and use of warehouses as retail stores for discount stores, superstores or "retail warehouses", which were considered earlier in this Chapter.

Thus the warehouse is again an important building in the economy both to users who require well planned storage space for their operations, to investors who feel that they offer a sound investment because of this demand by users, and to developers who are happy to meet the demand since the actual development of warehouses generally presents fewer problems than most other forms of development.

10. OFFICE PROPERTIES

(*a*) *Generally.* The range of properties to be considered is extensive. At the one extreme there are converted dwelling-houses, perhaps in a small provincial town where the demand for office accommodation is limited; at the other, there are modern buildings in large towns constructed specifically for offices, containing considerable floor space and providing within one building many amenities, which may include restaurants, club rooms, shops, post office, etc., and equipped with central heating, air conditioning and lifts. In the latter case the services provided by the landlord may be considerable, and may include not only lighting and cleaning of the common parts of the building but also the cleaning of offices occupied by tenants. The cost of such services is usually covered by a service charge payable in addition to the rent. Recent years have also seen the development of out-of-town offices in spacious, well landscaped sites, sometimes referred to as campus offices.

The method of valuation usually employed will be to arrive at a fair estimate of the gross income, deduct therefrom the outgoings borne by the landlord, and apply to the net income so arrived at an appropriate figure of Years' Purchase.

At the time of writing, rents of best quality offices range from £70 per square foot in prime City of London positions, through £50 in the West End of London, £14 to £25 in the best London suburban locations to £7 to £10 in major provincial cities.

(*b*) *The Income.* The annual value is usually considered in relation to area, and in advertisements of floor space to let in office buildings the rent is often quoted at so much per unit of floor area. Before buildings are erected this practice is difficult to avoid but it gives rise to disputes as to the actual area involved, notwithstanding that a code of measuring practice has been produced by the RICS. Once buildings are erected rentals should be quoted in terms of pounds per annum; this will avoid disputes as to the actual floor area.

Actual lettings will require careful consideration and analysis and may often appear to be inconsistent. This may be accounted for by the fact that tenancies were entered into at various dates and that the landlord will have sought to make the best bargain he could with each tenant. A further factor is connected with the question of varying areas of floor space. It may be, for example, that the whole of the fifth floor of a building is let to one tenant, whereas the sixth floor is let to seven or eight different tenants, so that the total net income derived from the higher floor may be greater than that from the one below.

The valuer's estimate of a fair and proper rental will depend upon the circumstances of each case and upon his judgment of the way in which the building can best be let. He will be guided primarily by the level of rental value obtaining in the district, found by analysing recent lettings of similar accommodation in comparable buildings in the area.

When dealing with office premises which are empty, or when estimating the rents at which a proposed new building will let, it is usual to make comparison with other properties on the basis of the terms on which such accommodation is usually let. In general, offices are let on full repairing and insuring leases. In the case of buildings in multiple occupation, the tenant will be limited to internal repairs but a service charge will be levied in addition to cover external repairs and maintenance of common parts and services.

It is important that the same basis of area is used in analysis as is employed in the subsequent valuation. This may be gross internal area, or net usable area excluding lobbies, toilets and the like. The RICS code of practice recommends net internal areas. Agreement of the basis of measurement and the area which results is one of the most contentious factors in negotiations between valuers.

(c) *Terms of Tenancy.* These, as has been stated, will vary considerably. Lettings are today almost always exclusive of rates. The cost of external repairs, maintenance of staircases, lifts and other parts in common use, in the case of buildings let in suites, will be covered by a separate service charge. The tenants may be liable for all repairs to the interior of the offices. Where whole buildings are let to single tenants, the lease is normally a full repairing and insuring one.

Where accommodation is let in suites it is quite likely that individual variations will be found in the tenancies within the same building, and careful examination of the terms of tenancy for each letting is necessary.

(*d*) *Outgoings.* The use of a percentage deduction from gross rentals to arrive at a net income, or even to give any accurate indication of costs in regard to the principal outgoings likely to be found, is in most cases very unrelible. Where available it will usually be found desirable to examine the actual cost of the outgoings for the property under consideration, and to consider them critically in the light of experience and by comparison with other similar properties.

Repairs.—The average cost of repairs will depend upon the type of construction, the planning and age of the building, and the extent of the tenants' liabilities under their covenants. Where tenants are only liable for internal decorative repairs (fair wear and tear excepted) the landlord must expect to bear practically the whole of the cost and a comparatively large allowance must be made.

Probably the soundest method is to make an estimate of the periodic cost of external and internal repairs by reference to the actual building and reduce this to a yearly allowance, checking the result by comparison with a similar building.

Rates.—In the case of existing buildings in assessment the present rates can be easily ascertained. In the comparatively few cases found today where the landlord pays the rates a most important point is whether the terms of the tenancy permit of any increase being passed on to the tenant.

Services.—There is no hard and fast rule as to the items covered by this term. The general tendency is to increase the scope and to recover from tenants not only the actual cost but also an amount for supervision of services and repairs to buildings let in suites. As stated above the items are usually covered by a separate service charge payable as additional rent. Where this is the case the valuer concerned should satisfy himself as to the conditions of the charges, in particular he should ascertain if increases in costs can be passed on to tenants. He should also ascertain if the amount of the charge is sufficient to cover the cost of the services, allowing for depreciation to installations.

The following items usually fall under the heading of services. The remarks given against each item give the considerations to be kept in mind when examining the cost of individual services to ascertain if the service charge covers the cost of provision adequately.

Heating and Domestic Hot Water. The annual cost of central heating will depend largely on the type and age of the system and the type and amount of fuel used.

Air Conditioning Plants. Many offices now have complete air conditioning plants. As a generalisation such plants are expensive both to operate and maintain.

Lighting. Tenants are usually responsible for the cost of lighting the offices, but the service charge will cover lighting of staircases and other parts of the building in common use. The cost will depend upon the extent of the lighting provided, including the replacement bulbs.

Lifts. The annual cost of the maintenance of lifts will vary considerably. Much will depend upon the age and type of lift, and the amount of traffic carried.

Cleaning. When provided, this will depend on the number of staff employed.

Where tenants are responsible for providing their own services, e.g. heating, no account need be taken of the cost except in so far as it will affect the rental value of accommodation.

Staff. The cost of staff again must be ascertained in respect of each particular case, and consideration should be given as to whether or not the actual number of staff employed is adequate for the building.

Insurance. There will be a number of insurances included in the service charge. Fire insurance is the main item but in addition there are insurances for public liability, lifts (if any), boilers and heating, and National Insurance.

Management. An allowance for management is usually considered to be necessary, and this is likely to vary between 3 per cent and 5 per cent on the gross rents.

An allowance may have to be made for voids in areas or in respect of types of building where supply exceeds demand.

(*e*) *Net Income and Capital Value.* The estimates of net

income made on the lines indicated above will not necessarily accord with the actual net income of any recent year. It should, however, represent what can be taken to be a fair expectation over a considerable period.

The basis upon which it is to be capitalised will depend on the type of property, its situation and neighbourhood, the competition of other properties in the vicinity, and the valuer's estimate of the general trend of values for the type of investment under consideration. The rate of return for the high class of modern building let to first-class tenants, will at the time of writing range from $4\frac{1}{2}\%$ in Central London, through $5\frac{1}{2}$ to $6\frac{1}{2}\%$ in the South East to 9% in the North East. Similar buildings in multi-occupation will produce slightly higher yields. Older, poorer buildings and conversions will produce upwards of 10%.

Care should be taken, in analysing sale prices to arrive at yields, to ensure that the methods used are similar to those it is intended to apply to the valuation. For example, reliable evidence of years' purchase and yield can only be deduced from the result of a sale where an accurate estimate of net income is first made to compare with the sale price.

In some cases an investment that has to be valued may comprise different types of property, which in themselves might be valued at differing rates per cent. For example, a property might comprise shops on the ground floor, basement restaurant, and offices in the upper parts. The rates per cent applicable separately might be $7\frac{1}{2}$ per cent for the shops, 9 per cent for the restaurant and 8 per cent for the offices. Where the property is held on lease at a ground rent considerable difficulty may arise in determining how this should be apportioned so as to arrive at a fair net income in respect of each of the different types of letting. It is probably best in practice for the valuer, having capitalised the occupation rents individually at appropriate yields, to deduct the ground rent capitalised at an average of those yields.

Example 20–4

You are required to make a valuation for sale in the open market as an investment of a block of offices on ground and five floors over. You are furnished on receiving your instructions with the following details:—

The block is leasehold having 56 years to run at a fixed ground rent of £600 p.a.

The landlord supplies services consisting of automatic lifts, central heating to the offices (but not hot water to lavatory basins for which the tenants are responsible), and lighting and cleaning those parts of the building not let to tenants. The costs of these services, of repairs for which the tenants are not directly liable and of all insurances are recoverable from the tenants by a service charge which you investigate and find is reasonable. The provisions in the leases as regards the service charge have the normal escalator clause which covers rises in costs. The tenants arrange for their own office cleaning and pay for their own lighting.

All leases make tenants responsible for internal repairs and incorporate 5 year upward only rent review clauses.

Ground Floor
Let to an insurance company for offices at £35,000 per annum exclusive for twenty years from this year.

First Floor
Let at £20,000 p.a. exclusive, for ten years now having two years to run.

Second Floor
Let at £19,000 p.a. exclusive, for ten years now having two years to run.

Third Floor
Let at £21,500 p.a. exclusive, for fifteen years now having five years to run.

Fourth Floor
Let at £17,000 p.a. exclusive, for ten years now having seven years to run.

Top Floor
Let at £4,000 p.a. exclusive, for five years, now having two years to run.

On internal inspection the premises are found to be in good condition and to provide an acceptable modern standard of accommodation having been originally constructed in the 1930's of brick and stone with slated roof and completely refurbished internally about 10 years ago. You have been given a plan of the building from which you ascertain the following to be the net floor areas:—

Floor	Area in square feet
Ground	3,500
First	3,100
Second	3,000
Third	2,850
Fourth	2,850
Top	1,000

Valuation—

The first stage in the valuation is to draw up a schedule collating the information to hand. This is best done in columnar form and, in this instance, would be as follows:—

See Schedule I (page 433).

Columns 1, 2, 3, 5, and 6 present no difficulty. Column 4 is completed from Columns 2 and 3. Column 7 is completed by a careful scrutiny of the whole schedule: those floors marked * are the most recently let and form the basis for the other figures. The valuer would rely, not only on the rents obtained for this building, but also on his local knowledge of similar recent lettings of comparable accommodation. Column 8 is obtained from 3 and 7.

The actual and estimated gross income is now apparent as:—

For the next two years	£116,500 p.a.
Then onwards	£128,625 p.a.

Outgoings

All outgoings are included in the service charge except management and the ground rent.

SCHEDULE I

1	2	3	4	5	6	7	8	
				Tenancy Details		Estimated Rental Value	Estimated Rental Value	
Floor	Present Rent £'s	Area sq. ft.	Present Rent £/sq. ft.	(a) Term years	(b) Time to Review (or expiry) years	£/sq. ft.	£'s	Remarks
Ground*	35,000	3,500	10·00	20	5	10·00	35,000	Recent letting
First	20,000	3,100	6·45	10	(2)	7·50	23,250	
Second	19,000	3,000	6·33	10	(2)	7·50	22,500	
Third*	21,500	2,850	7·54	15	5	7·54	21,500	Recent review
Fourth	17,000	2,850	5·96	10	2	7·50	21,375	
Top	4,000	1,000	4·00	5	(2)	5·00	5,000	
TOTAL	£116,500	16,300 sq. ft.					£128,625	

Gross Rents for next 2 years		£116,500	
Less Management, say	£5,000		
Ground Rent	600	5,600	
Net Income		110,900	
Y.P. 2 years at 8 & 3%		1·746	£193,631
Gross Rents after 2 years		128,625	
Less Management, say	5,500		
Ground Rent	600	6,100	
Net Income		122,525	
Y.P. 54 years at 8 & 3%	11·412		
P.V. £1 in 2 years at 8%	0·857	9·78	£1,198,295
			£1,391,926
		Say	£1,400,000

Note:—The above calculation should be adjusted for income tax on the sinking fund element. For discussion of methods of adjustment see Chapter 14.

11. Urban Regeneration

In March 1988 the Government announced its consolidated programme for the regeneration of inner-city areas in a policy document entitled "Action for Cities". The document contains little in the way of new policies or proposals to take new powers; it merely confirms the Government's intention to attempt to act in a concerted manner in order, finally, to make some real impact on a problem which has plagued successive Governments for the past 30 or more years.

No attempt will be made here to set out the many policies and powers involved (although success in this endeavour could have a very real impact on local, regional and national land values) but merely to note the main ones which affect landed property and, in particular, commercial and industrial property.

In the Local Government, Planning and Land Act 1980,

the Government took powers to designate urban development areas and enterprise zones.

A number of urban development areas, which are areas of run-down, derelict land, were designated and in respect of seven of those areas urban development corporations were set up to secure the regeneration of the areas concerned. The first two, the London Docklands Development Corporation and the Merseyside Development Corporation have been running since 1981. Four others, Trafford Park, the Black Country, Teesside and Tyne and Wear, were announced in 1987, and a further one covering the Lower Don Valley, Sheffield, in 1988. The development corporations are ad hoc bodies whose objectives include bringing land and buildings into effective use, encouraging the development of industry and commerce and ensuring that housing and social facilities are available to encourage people to live and work in the area. The corporations are intended to have a limited life and have powers to acquire land by agreement or compulsorily and receive land transferred by the Secretary of State from public bodies. They are also the local planning authorities for their areas.

Enterprise zones are small areas of land identified "to see how far industrial and commercial activity can be encouraged by the removal of certain tax burdens, and by releasing or speeding up the application of certain statutory or administrative controls". Schemes for the creation of an enterprise zone could be drawn up on the invitation of the Secretary of State by a district or London borough council, a new town corporation or an urban development corporation. The benefits to industrial and commercial firms in such zones, limited usually to a period of 10 years, include exemption from general rates, 100% allowances for corporation and income tax purposes for capital expenditure on industrial and commercial development. Enterprise zones were set up in a number of areas but the Government announced in 1987 that no further zones were to be created.

Other provisions to be noted in this context are:—

Urban Development Grant—purpose is "to promote the economic and physical regeneration of run-down urban areas by encouraging private investment, which would not otherwise take place in such areas, which strengthens the local economy and brings land and buildings back into use". Assistance takes the form of a grant and/or loan and the types of project appropriate include building shops, offices, workshops and warehouses; converting factories, warehouses, offices and other buildings to houses, flats, workshops, offices or shops; providing leisure and tourist facilities, hotel building and refurbishment.

Urban Regeneration Grant—purpose is "to promote the economic and physical regeneration of older urban areas affected by industrial change, by enabling the private sector to redevelop large sites and refurbish large groups of buildings, and by encouraging private investment in such areas. It differs from UDG mainly because it is specifically directed at large-scale schemes." Assistance takes the form of an outright grant, a loan or a repayable grant.

Derelict Land Grant—purpose is "to reclaim land which is derelict through being so damaged by industrial or other uses that it cannot be used without being treated". Assistance takes the form of a grant paid as a percentage of the net loss to the owner or carrying out reclamation work.

City Grant—this grant introduced in 1988 replaces the three types of grant available to private developers referred to above.

Urban Programme—purpose is "to help tackle the economic, environmental and social problems of the inner cities. It provides support for a wide range of projects submitted by local authorities as part of the Inner Area Programme for their district. In particular it provides funding to enable local authorities to make assistance available for private sector projects which contribute to the economic development of inner city areas". Assistance takes the form of loans or grants for such purposes as converting, extending, improving or modifying industrial buildings and converting other buildings into industrial or commercial buildings; towards the rent payable under a new lease of a building intended for industrial or commercial use up to the equivalent of two years' rent; premises and managed workshops for new firms.

Land Registers—purpose is "to bring to the attention of prospective developers details of unused or under-used land owned by public authorities and to assist developers or other members of the public to obtain the release of particular plots of public land of which they are aware". The registers are compiled and maintained by the Department of the Environment.

The effects of enterprise zones on local property markets has been studied and a mid-term assessment was published in a series of articles by Paul Syms and Rodney Erickson in the Estates Gazette in 1986 (279 EG 1162 & 1306 and 280 EG 56).

CHAPTER 21

Valuations for Mortgage, Fire Insurance and Company Assets

1. VALUATIONS FOR MORTGAGE

(a) *Nature of a Mortgage.* A mortgage of freehold or leasehold property is a transaction whereby one party—the mortgagor—grants an interest in his property to another party—the mortgagee—as security for a loan.

The transaction is effected by means of a mortgage deed in which the mortgagor usually agrees to pay interest on the loan at a given rate per cent, and may also enter into express covenants as to the repair and insurance of the property. In some cases the mortgage deed provides for periodical repayments of capital as well as interest (as in the case of a Building Society mortgage).

The mortgagor retains the right to recover his property freed from the charge created by the mortgage deed on repayment of the amount due to the mortgagee. This is known as his "equity of redemption".

Since 1925 a legal mortgage of freeholds can only be made either (i) by the grant of a lease to the mortgagee for a long term of years usually 3,000, with a provision for cesser on redemption, or (ii) by a charge expressed to be by way of legal mortgage.[1]

A legal mortgage of leaseholds can only be made either (i) by a sub-lease to the mortgagee of the whole term, less the last day or days, with a provision for cesser on redemption, or (ii) by a charge by way of legal mortgage.[2]

What is known as an "equitable mortgage" may be effected without a mortgage deed either (i) by a written agreement acknowledging the loan and promising to execute a legal

---

[1] Law of Property Act 1925, Sections 85 and 87.
[2] Ibid., Section 86. A charge by way of legal mortgage places the mortgagee in the same position as though he had been granted a lease or sublease.

mortgage if required, or (ii) by a verbal agreement accompanied by deposit of the title deeds of the property. This type of mortgage does not transfer any interest in the property to the mortgagee.

As a general rule, a mortgage is a sound form of investment offering reasonable security and a fair rate of interest, and although the mortgage deed probably stipulates for repayment at the end of six months it is usual for the loan to continue for a very much longer period.

So long as the mortgagor pays the interest regularly and observes the covenants of the mortgage deed, the mortgagee will usually be content to leave him in possession and control of the property. But if the interest is falling into arrears or the mortgagor is unable to meet a demand for repayment of the loan, the mortgagee must take steps to protect his security.

(*b*) *The Mortgagee's Security.* The mortgagee's security for the money he has lent depends primarily upon the property and upon the sum it might be expected to realise if brought to sale at any time. His security for payment of interest on the loan at the agreed rate depends upon the net income the property is capable of producing.

The usual advance by way of mortgage is two-thirds the estimated fair market value of the property, thus leaving the mortgagee a one-third margin of safety. Trustees may not in any case advance more than two-thirds of a valuation of the property made by a skilled valuer. Other investors, such as building societies, often make larger advances, particularly if some form of collateral security is offered or where provision is made for repayment of capital by instalments over a certain period. On the other hand, when there is a risk of future depreciation in value, an advance of three-fifths, or even one-half may be more satisfactory than the usual two-thirds. In all cases the mortgagee, or his adviser, should consider not only the value of the property in relation to the proposed loan, but also whether the net income from the property is sufficient to provide interest at the agreed rate.

If the mortgagor defaults in payment of interest, observance of the covenants of the mortgage deed or repayment of the loan when legally demanded, the mortgagee has the following remedies against the property—

(i) Under certain conditions[3] he may sell the mortgaged property and apply the proceeds to repayment of the loan and any arrears of interest together with the expenses of sale. Any surplus must be paid to the mortgagor.

(ii) He may apply to the Court for a foreclosure order which will have the effect of extinguishing the mortgagor's equity of redemption.

(iii) He may at any time take personal possession of the income from the property, and after paying all necessary outgoings may apply the balance to paying interest on the mortgage debt, including any arrears. This surplus, if any, must be paid to the mortgagor or applied to reducing the mortgage debt.

(iv) Under the same conditions as in (i) he may appoint a receiver to collect the income from the property and apply it to the purposes indicated in (iii), including payment of the receiver's commission.

It is evident that these remedies will only be fully effective where, in cases (i) and (ii), the market value of the property exceeds the amount due to the mortgagee, or where, in cases (iii) and (iv), the net income from the property, after paying all outgoings and annual charges having priority to the mortgage, is sufficient to discharge the annual interest on the loan with a margin to cover possible arrears of interest.

Although the property itself is the mortgagee's principal security, it is usual for the mortgage deed to include a personal covenant by the mortgagor to repay the loan. This may be reinforced by the personal guarantee of some third party. So that, in addition to the remedies mentioned above, there is that of action on the personal covenant.

The character and position of the borrower and his guarantor (if any) are therefore matters of considerable importance to the mortgagee, both as an additional security for the

---

[3] Law of Property Act 1925, Section 101.

repayment of the loan and also as a guarantee for the regular payment of interest as it accrues due.

The exercise of the mortgagee's remedies may be restricted where the property is one to which the Rent Acts apply.

(c) *The Valuation.* In making a valuation for mortgage purposes the ordinary principles of valuation apply, but the valuer must have regard to the mortgagee's position in relation to the property and to the remedies available to him in the event of default by the mortgagor.

He will bear in mind that it may be necessary to realise the security in the future and that unless the sale price then is sufficient to cover the mortgage debt, arrears of interest and costs, the mortgagee will suffer loss.

While market value will be the basis of the valuation the valuer must consider not only the present market value, but particularly whether that value is likely to be maintained in the future and would be readily realisable on the forced sale of the property.

He will consider very carefully any factors such as probable action by the local authority under the Housing Acts, and other statutes, which may unfavourably affect the value of the property in the future. He should fully consider any possible effects of the development plan for the area. Valuations should be on the basis of existing use value unless planning permission has been granted for development. Even then he should disregard any development value: if an owner wishes to raise capital to carry out development then he will enter into a funding agreement which is different from a straightforward mortgage. He may also have to ask himself whether the existing market is unduly influenced by national or local conditions of a temporary nature which may have caused something like an artificial "boom" in prices. Any likely capital expenditure on the property, such as accrued dilapidations or the estimated cost of future development or reconstruction, must be allowed for as a deduction.

The net income from the property must be estimated with the utmost care, not only as a sound basis for the valuation, but to make sure that it will adequately cover the interest on the proposed loan.

Any future element of value which is reasonably certain

in its nature, such as reversion to full rental value on the expiration of an existing lease at a low rent, may properly be taken into account; but anything which is purely speculative in its nature should be disregarded. The valuer must be cautious when capitalising "full" rents and must consider whether they will be maintained or are likely to fall; this is particularly important where the property is not of a first-class type. The valuer must beware of including in his valuation elements of potential value which may never eventuate.

In the case of business premises, goodwill should be excluded from the valuation.

The valuer should also exclude anything which can easily be sold or removed by the mortgagor, such as timber, unless there are adequate safeguards against such a happening.

Information is sometimes tendered as to the price paid for the property by the mortgagor. This is apt to be misleading. An excessive price may have been paid for a special reason, or market values may since have changed.

The cost of erection of buildings is usually best disregarded for mortgage purposes. Large sums may have been lavished on the gratification of individual tastes, or considerable changes in building costs may have occurred since the property was erected.

(*d*) *Advice on Policy.* In addition to his valuation of the property, the valuer may be required to advise as to the nature of the security afforded and as to the sum which may reasonably be advanced.

In the case of trustees, for example, the loan must be made on the advice of an able, practical surveyor or valuer expressed in a report.

Certain types of property are not desirable securities for mortgage purposes. A vacant site, for instance, may be of considerable value and cost nothing for maintenance: but its value is necessarily of a speculative nature and there is no immediate income forthcoming. If, therefore, the mortgage interest falls into arrear, the taking of possession of the land by the mortgagee will not prevent the accumulation of further arrears of interest pending the time when a purchaser can be found.

In these and similar cases the valuer will no doubt feel

it his duty to accompany his valuation by a clear indication of the risks inherent in the nature of the security, and may advise that, if any advance is made at all, it should certainly be less than the normal two-thirds.

Leaseholds being in the nature of a wasting security, require careful treatment, particularly where the term is comparatively short. In some cases provision is made in the mortgage deed for repayment of a portion of the principal from time to time, or for periodical revaluations to check the security. In any case care should be taken to see that the property is kept in reasonable repair by the mortgagor while in his possession, so as to avoid any risk of forfeiture.

Buildings which are the subject of a mortgage advance should be insured in the names of both mortgagor and mortgagee. A covenant to this effect is usually included in the mortgage deed, and the mortgagor should be required to hand the policy to the mortgagee and to produce to him from time to time the last receipt for premium. The valuer is often asked to name the sum for which the buildings should be insured. Valuations for insurance are considered in the next part of this Chapter.

Very considerable sums of money are lent on mortgage by building societies, mainly to owner-occupiers of small house and shop property. The practice of such societies is to lend money upon the basis of repayment by instalments, usually monthly, which include both interest and principal, fixed according to the term for which the loan is granted, which varies between 10 and 30 years. If the instalments are duly paid the money cannot usually be called in during the term, nor can the instalments be increased, although the rate of interest may be increased except in those cases where the advance was made at a guaranteed rate of interest. The fact that the principal begins to be reduced so soon as the first instalment is paid, and that repayment continues with each instalment, makes it practicable for the two-thirds limit of advance to be exceeded. In the case of small properties 70 per cent or 80 per cent would be a normal rate for a building society advance, while as much as 90 or 100 per cent may be advanced if the society is given collateral security such as the deposit of a sum of money or stock, together with a guarantee by a third party or by an insurance company. Where the proposed mortgagor is a protected tenant who is purchasing the house he occupies, advances are frequently made to cover, not only the whole of the purchase price, but the legal fees as well.

In acting for a building society the valuer is usually only concerned with submitting a valuation and report, the amount of the advance being a question of policy for the society to decide.

Advances are frequently made by insurance companies, the advance being repaid at the end of the term on the maturing of a life assurance policy for the amount of the loan. This gives the borrower the additional advantage that in the event of his death, the property is freed from the mortgage debt. A greater percentage advance can often be obtained by this method which may be more expensive than the usual building society mortgage.

(*e*) *Second or Subsequent Mortgages.* It is possible for there to be more than one mortgage on a property, the second or subsequent mortgages being mortgages of the mortgagor's equity of redemption. Provided they are all registered, the second and subsequent mortgagees will each have a claim on the property in their regular order after the first mortgagee's claim has been satisfied.

It is evident that there will be little security for such an advance unless care is taken to ensure that the total amount advanced, including the first mortgage, does not exceed what may reasonably be lent on the security of the property—normally, two-thirds its fair market value.

On the approach to mortgage valuations of residential property, the valuer is referred to Guidance Notes for Valuers published jointly by the Incorporated Society of Valuers and Auctioneers and the Royal Institution of Chartered Surveyors and on definitions of value to the latter's Guidance Notes on the Valuation of Assets (2nd Edition).

Over the past few years a substantial number of cases have come before the Courts which have been concerned in one way or another with valuations for mortgage purposes. A considerable body of case law is building up on the valuer's

duty in performing mortgage valuations not only to the mortgagee by whom he will have been instructed but also to the
mortgagor and other parties. The cases of *Yianni v. Edwin
Evans & Sons* (1981) 259 EG 969, *Smith v. Eric S. Bush*
[1987] 282 EG 326 and *Harris v. Wyre Forest D.C.* [1987]
05 EG 57 are significant in this context. Other cases have
been concerned with the actual performance of the mortgage
valuation including *Singer & Friedlander v. John D. Wood
& Co.* (1977) 243 EG 212 and *Corisand Investments Ltd.
v. Druce & Co.* (1978) 248 EG 315.

In his judgement in the *Corisand* case Gibson J. stated,
inter alia, that "in order to discharge the duty of care of
an ordinarily competent valuer in valuing property such as
this hotel [for second mortgage purposes] the valuer must
have regard to [certain] matters of principle and of fact".
The principles subsequently examined by the learned judge
follow closely the notes set out above but in commenting
on the valuer's duty in a "boom" market he says "I accept
the view . . . that a mortgage valuation must look for a certain
period into the future. The valuer cannot be expected to
peer very far ahead or to anticipate trends or future changes
of which no indication has been or could then be given to
an ordinarily competent valuer. The valuer, however, can
reasonably be required to be aware of the fact that the market
is "high" or unusually buoyant, when such are the circumstances, and to guard against over-confidence in such market
conditions. He can reasonably be required to consider what
the position of the property may well be in circumstances
of forced sale within six to 12 months of his valuation".

2. FIRE INSURANCE VALUATIONS

(*a*) *Generally*. This is an area which increases in importance
as the risk of loss or damage increases and the cost of fire
insurance premiums increases as a proportion of outgoings.

The basis of the fire insurance valuation is the cost of reinstating the asset damaged or destroyed to its former condition. Full re-instatement cost is determined on the basis

of building costs prevailing at the time of re-instatement[4] and to this must be added the other incidental costs such as architect's fees, site clearance, loss of income to a landlord during the rebuilding period, cost of alternative accommodation during rebuilding in the case of a house, reductions in takings in a shop. So far as the estimation of re-instatement cost is concerned, apart from the general sources of building cost information referred to in Chapter 13, for traditionally built houses the annual "Guide to House Rebuilding Costs for Insurance Valuation" prepared on behalf of the Association of British Insurers by the Building Cost Information Service of the RICS is an authoritative source; many house insurance policies incorporate automatic updating of the sum insured on the basis of the ABI/BCIS House Rebuilding Cost Index.

Although the basic proposition in relation to fire insurance valuations is comparatively simply put it is an area fraught with difficulties.

(*b*) *Effect of Under Insurance.* It is essential that a building should be insured for the full current cost of re-building to whatever standard may be required at the time of re-building. In many cases a building will not be completely destroyed by fire but if the insurance policy contains an average clause the insurers may pay only such proportion of the cost of repairs as the full cost of re-instatement bears to the insured value. Thus if a building costing £40,000 to re-instate is insured for only £20,000 and there is damage by fire costing £5,000 to repair, the insurer may agree to bear only £2,500 of the cost. In cases, such as churches, where the full cost of re-instatement results in an impossibly high premium and in any event the building once destroyed may not be re-instated it may be possible to arrange a fire-loss policy to cover major repairs up to a particular percentage of the full cost of re-instatement.

(*c*) *Public Authority Requirements.* It may not be realistic to assume that a building completely destroyed can be re-instated in its present form, quite apart from any new for

---

[4] In *Glennifer Finance Corporation Ltd. v. Bamar Wood and Products Ltd. and Another* (1978) 37 P & CR 208 this point and the method of estimation were considered.

old aspect. If, for example, a building does not meet current building regulations the cost of providing a new building may be in excess of the cost of re-instatement. In the extreme case it may be that planning permission to rebuild would not be given and such a refusal of permission does not attract compensation. In the former case a sufficient addition should be made to the re-instatement cost to cover additional requirements but the latter case would probably be dealt with by a separate policy to cover the loss of site value.

(*d*) *Cost and Value.* The absence of a definite relationship between cost and value was noted in Part 1. It may be that a building which would cost £50,000 to re-instate is worth on the market only £10,000. In these circumstances for the reasons given in (b) above, insurance cover cannot be confined to value although it may be possible to insure against the average clause being applied.

(*e*) *Incidental Costs other than Building Costs.* Mention was made in (a) of some of the incidental costs, such as architects fees and loss of income which may arise. In most cases it is necessary to identify such costs separately from building costs and some may have to be the subject of separate insurance policies.

(*f*) *Value Added Tax on Building Repairs.* Complete re-building of a building destroyed by fire is treated as new work and zero rated for VAT purposes. This is likely to change in 1989 when re-building of non-residential property will be subject to VAT, although recovery of VAT is possible in certain circumstances. Repair work on a partially damaged building on the other hand is subject to VAT at the going rate. It is probably prudent to add VAT to the building costs and fees.

For a more detailed consideration of fire insurance valuations, the reader is referred to Chapter 21 of "Valuation: Principles into Practice" (3rd Edition 1988) Ed. W. H. Rees.

3. VALUATIONS OF COMPANY ASSETS

Valuers have been required to provide valuations for company purposes for many years. These purposes vary between values to be incorporated in the Balance Sheet or other accounts; values of a company's property assets to be incorporated in a prospectus when the company is going public; values of a company's property assets when it is the subject of a takeover bid; and values of property bonds and the like.

The demand for such valuations has grown over recent years. Until 1974 there were few guidelines for valuers as to how to approach such valuations.

In 1974 the Royal Institution of Chartered Surveyors set up an Asscts Valuation Standards Committee to examine the matter in depth and in 1976 the first Guidance Notes were produced. These are regularly extended and amended and the reader is referred to them for a detailed survey of the approach to the valuation of company assets.[5]

Until 1976, the approach tended to be either open market value or going concern value. The going concern method of valuation was rejected by the Assets Valuation Standards Committee but readers who would like to consider such an approach should see Modern Methods of Valuation (Sixth Edition).

The Basis of Valuation is set out in Guidance Note GN1. The underlying principle is that the value should be the open market value. This is defined in Guidance Note GN22 as being:—

(i) The **Open Market Value** is intended to mean the best price at which an interest in a property might reasonably be expected to be sold by Private Treaty at the date of valuation assuming:

(a) a willing seller;
(b) a reasonable period within which to negotiate the sale, taking into account the nature of the property and the state of the market;
(c) values will remain static throughout the period;
(d) the property will be freely exposed to the market;
(e) no account is to be taken of an additional bid by a special purchaser.

The valuation may arrive at either the "existing use

[5] Op. cit. p. 358.

value"—meaning the value assuming the use of the property for the same purpose as before the time of valuation—or the "alternative use value"—meaning the value allowing for the prospects of an alternative use.

In certain instances, the valuation may be of premises rarely if ever sold separately from the business operating in them, for example oil refineries or chemical complexes. For this reason the only realistic approach to the valuation is to adopt the contractor's test whereby the present day estimated cost of acquiring the site is taken with the written down cost of replacing the premises; such an approach is termed the "depreciated replacement cost".

Where the valuation is to be incorporated in the company's accounts the alternative use basis will not be employed since the accounts postulate the continuance of the business. The alternative use basis will be relevant in assessing the overall performance of the company or in a valuation of the assets in contemplation of a takeover or merger.

For a more detailed consideration of asset valuation the reader is referred again to "Valuation: Principles into Practice", Chapter 16, cited in Section 2 of this Chapter.

CHAPTER 22
Valuations for Rating

1. INTRODUCTION

THE EARLY sections of this Chapter are concerned with the practice and procedures extant for the current Valuation List (as at the time of writing in 1988) but including some forward references to the important changes now proposed by impending legislation. The final section of this Chapter comprises a summary and review of the forthcoming proposals for the next revaluation in 1990 as far as is known at the time of writing.

2. GENERALLY

Local rates are a tax levied as a general rule upon the occupiers of property in respect of the annual value of their occupation in order to defray the expenses of local government.

To ascertain the rate liability of a particular occupier, two things must be known. These are, firstly, the rating assessment of the occupied property expressed in terms of rateable value and, secondly, the amount of rate in the pound in force in the rating area in which the property is situated. Until now, the rate has been fixed periodically, usually annually, by the rating authority and is determined by the authority's own financial needs and those of any precepting authorities. However, from 1990 onwards there is to be a national non-domestic rate or uniform business rate (UBR) applicable to all non-domestic hereditaments, fixed by central government and indexed to allow for inflation; domestic hereditaments will no longer, after that date, be rated as such. The making of assessments for rating purposes has, since 1950, been the responsibility of the Inland Revenue as provided by the Local Government Act 1948 and it is with these assessments that this Chapter is primarily concerned. It is not proposed to deal here with the history and development of the rating system, with the law of rateable occupation, or with the minutiae of procedural details.

3. PRINCIPLES OF PROCEDURE

The main statute governing assessment and valuation procedure is the General Rate Act 1967, which is subject to important amendments for the next revaluation. It consolidated a number of previous Acts but did not introduce any new principles of valuation or rating practice.

In London, the Common Council of the City of London (with two additional authorities in the Inner and Middle Temples) and the various London Borough Councils are the rating authorities for their respective areas. Outside London, the rating authorities are the district councils. Before 1950 the rating authorities were responsible both for making rating assessments in the form of draft Valuation Lists, which were subsequently approved by Assessment Committees, and for the collection of rates. Since the Inland Revenue became responsible for the making of assessments, the responsibilities of rating authorities have been confined to rates collection.

The rating assessments of all rateable properties, known as "hereditaments", within a rating area are entered in the Valuation List for that area. The intended procedure is for new valuation lists to come into force every five years. The current list came into force on 1 April 1973, but the next does not become operative until 1 April 1990, as provided by the New Valuation Lists Order 1987. By virtue of the New Valuation Lists (Time and Class of Hereditaments) Order 1987, the revaluation is restricted to non-domestic properties and 1 April 1988 is the date specified by that Order by reference to which rateable values are to be ascertained for the purposes of the next revaluation.

Briefly, the procedure for the preparation of a new valuation list is as follows. The Valuation Officer of the Inland Revenue sends out return forms, for completion by owners and occupiers, asking for details of such matters as the rent paid, length and date of grant of lease and repairing covenants. Hereditaments are then inspected and valuations prepared. The new list is drawn up and transmitted to the rating authority by the end of December, at whose offices it is available for inspection, before coming into force on the following 1 April.

In respect of the 1973 Valuation List, the Valuation Officer, the rating authority in certain specified circumstances and any person aggrieved on certain specified grounds (as referred to in Section 69 of the General Rate Act 1967) may then, or at any time subsequently, make a proposal for the alteration of a current valuation list. The Valuation Officer's proposals are served on the occupier and the rating authority and there is a right of objection. All other proposals must be served on the Valuation Officer, who will usually object. If the assessment cannot then be agreed between the Valuation Officer and proposer/objector, appeals lie in the first instance to the Local Valuation Court and thence to the Lands Tribunal. On questions of fact the decision of the Lands Tribunal is final but on matters of law appeal lies to the Court of Appeal and thence to the House of Lords.

There are important changes envisaged in the appeals procedure for the 1990 revaluation in that time-limits are proposed on aggrieved persons' proposals, restricting the present rights to owners and occupiers of subject properties, and withdrawing appeal rights from rating authorities. These proposed procedural changes are referred to in more detail in the final section of this Chapter.

4. Exemptions and Reliefs

Until 1963 only a very few persons were required to pay rates on the basis of a full net annual value. The occupiers of agricultural land and buildings were (and still are) entirely exempt. Many occupiers were relieved by way of a deduction from net annual value to arrive at rateable value. The occupiers of dwelling-houses were relieved because their assessments were related to 1939, instead of 1956, rental values. Charities and similar bodies were relieved on the actual amount of rates payable and may still receive relief although the method of giving it has changed.

The main object of the Rating and Valuation Act 1961, the provisions of which were incorporated in the General Rate Act 1967, was to introduce some order and reason into reliefs and exemptions. Without going into details of such reliefs and exemptions, which are not appropriate for inclusion in this book, it is worthwhile recording that exemption from liability or relief from the rates burden may be total or partial. In cases of total exemption, the hereditament itself or the actual occupier may be excluded, or the rating authority may not require payment of rates normally recoverable. In cases of partial exemption or relief, valuation or procedural rules may be varied to produce a lower assessment, or the rating authority may grant rate rebates, or the actual rate in the pound may be lowered for a particular type of property, or a special deduction may be given as between net annual and rateable value in special cases.

5. Statutory Basis of Assessment

The assessment of the rateable value of a hereditament has to be made in accordance with the statutory provisions in Section 19 of the General Rate Act 1967. This Section uses the terms "Gross Value", "Net Annual Value", and "Rateable Value".

The ascertainment of Gross Value is the first step in the assessment of all properties consisting "... of one or more houses or other non-industrial buildings, with or without any garden, yard, court, fore-court, outhouse or other appurtenance belonging thereto, but without other land ...". Appurtenance includes all land occupied with a house or educational establishment. Gross Value is thus relevant to houses, shops, offices, warehouses, hotels and public houses in the current 1973 Valuation List but after April 1990 all rateable hereditaments will be valued direct to Rateable Value (which will have the same statutory definition as Net Annual Value currently adopted in Section 19(3) for determining an assessment direct—see subsequent reference). Domestic properties will no longer be included in the Valuation List or form part of the rating system.

"Gross Value" is defined in Section 19(6) as "the rent at which the hereditament might reasonably be expected to let from year to year if the tenant undertook to pay all usual tenant's rates and taxes and the landlord undertook to bear the cost of the repairs and insurance and the other expenses, if any, necessary to maintain the hereditament in a state to command that rent".

In the case of the types of property mentioned above assessed to Gross Value, in order to find Net Annual Value it is necessary to deduct from the Gross Value a specific sum in respect of "repairs, insurance and other expenses". The Net Annual Value is, unless otherwise provided, equal to the Rateable Value. The sum to be deducted varies according to the amount of the Gross Value. These deductions, known as statutory deductions, are laid down by the Valuation (Statutory Deductions) Order 1973, and are as follows:

(1) *Gross Value*	(2) *Deductions from Gross Value* (to arrive at Net Annual Value and, unless otherwise provided, Rateable Value)
Not exceeding £65	45 per cent of the gross value.
Exceeding £65 but not exceeding £128	£29 plus 30 per cent of the amount by which the gross value exceeds £65.
Exceeding £128 but not exceeding £330	£48 plus $16\frac{2}{3}$ per cent of the amount by which the gross value exceeds £128 subject to a maximum of £80.
Exceeding £330 but not exceeding £430	£80 plus 20 per cent of the amount by which the gross value exceeds £330.
Exceeding £430	£100 plus $16\frac{2}{3}$ per cent of the amount by which the gross value exceeds £430.

In the case of other properties a Gross Value is not required but "Net Annual Value" must be estimated directly. The statutory definition of Net Annual Value in Section 19(3) is "the rent at which it is estimated the hereditament might reasonably be expected to let from year to year if the tenant undertook to pay all usual tenant's rates and taxes and to bear the cost of the repairs and insurance and the other expenses, if any, necessary to maintain the hereditament

in a state to command that rent". Although assessment directly to net annual value applies primarily to industrial
properties it also applies to cemeteries, racecourses, sports
grounds, caravan sites and other similar hereditaments where
the land (as distinct from the buildings) is the predominant
factor.

These problems of differentiation will, of course, be simplified after 1990 when rating valuers will only be concerned
with Rateable Value, which is a concept much closer to current rental evidence as referred to later in this Chapter.

Having determined the Net Annual Value, either by
deduction from Gross Value or directly, the rule is that Net
Annual Value equals Rateable Value. Although it does not
affect the assessment of houses and flats, Section 53 of the
General Rate Act 1967 contains provisions for granting rate
reductions or remissions to residential occupiers on grounds
of poverty.

There are also provisions under Section 48 of the 1967
Act for a reduced rate-poundage to be levied in respect of
dwelling-houses and for half of such reduction to be levied
in respect of "mixed hereditaments". A mixed hereditament
is one in respect of which the apportioned rateable value
of the private dwelling is greater than the apportioned value
of the part used for other purposes.

6. PRINCIPLES OF ASSESSMENT

There are certain general principles to be observed in preparing valuations for rating purposes, the most important
of which are:

(i) The hereditament being valued must be assumed to
be vacant and to let. The statutory definitions assume a
tenancy and it is, therefore, necessary to assume that the
hereditament is available so that the bid of the hypothetical
tenant on the statutory terms can be ascertained.

(ii) The hereditament must be valued "*rebus sic stantibus*"
which means in its actual existing physical state, "as it stands
and as used and occupied when the assessment is made"
Lord Parmoor—*Great Western & Metropolitan Ry. v. Ham-*

mersmith [1916], A.C. 23. This rule does not, however, prevent the assumption of minor changes of a non-structural nature; for example, the modernisation of a cottage or the erection of a garage together with access would not be possibilities which could be considered in estimating the rent. Furthermore, the mode or category of occupation by the hypothetical tenant must be conceived as the same mode or category as that of the actual occupier. Thus possible changes of use may be largely irrelevant, particularly if they arc unlikely to be permitted. A local authority scheme which would involve disturbance at a sufficiently early date might affect the bid of a hypothetical tenant from year to year.

(iii) Prior to *Garton v. Hunter* [1969], R.A. 448, if a property was let at what was plainly a rack rent, then that was the only permissible evidence. However, this case decided that "the actual rent is no criterion unless it indeed happens to be the rent the imaginary tenant might reasonably be expected to pay" and as a result other evidence of value may now be examined, and this includes rents passing on comparable properties.

(iv) Assessments on comparable properties may be considered in the absence of better evidence. In the case of dwelling-houses the General Rate Act 1970 permits the rents of other dwelling-houses of the same or a different description as relevant evidence, together with a consideration of the relationship between these rents and Gross Values. The intention seems to be to correct the present imbalance between the assessment of purpose-built flats, which appear more fully and properly assessed, and houses, which appear to be under-assessed due to lack of rental evidence.

(v) A question of importance is the extent of the rateable hereditament and whether separate assessments should be made in respect of different parts. The rateable unit will normally be taken as the whole of the land and buildings in the occupation of an occupier within a single curtilage. However, the Court of Appeal in *Gilbert v. Hickinbottom & Sons Ltd.* [1956], 49 R. & I.T. 231, ruled that a bakery and a building used for repairs essential for its efficient operation could constitute a single hereditament although separated by a highway as they were functionally essential to each other.

It is not necessary for parts to be *structurally* severed to be capable of separate assessment if the parts are *physically* capable of separate occupation. From the valuation viewpoint, separate assessments usually, but not necessarily, result in a higher total assessment but this would be partly offset by higher statutory deductions where Gross Value is relevant. If parts are separately assessed and one part ceases to be in rateable occupation then there might be no liability for rates on that part.

7. METHODS OF ASSESSMENT

There are different methods of assessment but it is vital to bear in mind that, whichever method may be used, the end product must be the rent on the basis of the statutory definition of either Gross Value or Net Annual Value. The definitions of these two values are similar but Gross Value places the liability for repairs, insurance and other expenses necessary to maintain the hereditament on the landlord, whereas Net Annual Value places it on the tenant. Some comment, therefore, on the interpretation of these definitions of value is appropriate before considering actual methods of assessment.

The "rent" is not necessarily the rent actually paid, but the rent which a hypothetical tenant might reasonably be expected to pay. Hypothetical tenants would include all possible occupiers including the actual occupier.

A tenant from "year to year" can occupy the hereditament indefinitely, having a tenancy which will probably continue but which can be determined by notice. There is therefore a reasonable prospect of the tenancy continuing and no implied lack of security of tenure which would adversely affect the expected rent (*Humber Ltd. v. Jones (V.O.) & Rugby R.D.C.* [1960], 53 R. & I.T. 293).

"Usual tenants' rates and taxes" include general rates, water rates and occupiers drainage rate but not Schedule A Income Tax, and owner's drainage rate which are landlord's taxes.

The statutory deduction, previously referred to, from Gross Value to Net Annual Value is deemed to be the equivalent of the average annual cost of repairs, insurance and other expenses necessary to maintain the hereditament. When Rateable Value has to be found directly, which will be the common practice from 1990 onwards, these expenses are deemed to be the responsibility of the tenant.

The question of lack of repair has been before the Courts on a number of occasions in recent years, particularly in relation to dwelling-houses. The general principle to be derived from the various decisions is that in assessing Gross Value the rental bid by the hypothetical tenant will be unaffected by lack of repair if the defects are capable of being remedied and might reasonably be expected to be remedied having regard to the age and character of the property. Thus, the landlord's repairing liability would involve putting the premises in a reasonable state of repair initially and thereafter keeping them in that condition and the hypothetical tenant would make his rental bid on this assumption. If, however, the state of the hereditament is such that a landlord would not consider putting it in repair but would accept a lower rent, then the lower rent would form the basis of the assessment having regard to the actual and badly maintained condition.

Thus, generally, the state of repair of the hereditament is not relevant to arrive at Gross Value. However, in the case where Net Annual Value is obtained directly and the hypothetical tenant would be liable to repair, the state of repair would affect his rental bid.

The principal methods of assessment used are:

(a) by reference to rents paid, which is usually known as the rental method;
(b) the contractor's test;
(c) the profits basis; and
(d) by formula.

The choice of method to be used is not necessarily a free one. For some types of hereditament a statutory formula is laid down or a Minister is empowered to make an order laying down the method of determining the assessment. Examples are statutory water undertakings, schools in public occupation, certain properties occupied by British Coal, British Gas, the Electricity Boards and the Post Office, and also statutory Docks and Harbour undertakings.

In cases where there is no such restriction the first three methods are appropriate but the general rule is that if the rental method can be used, it should be used in preference to the contractor's test or the profits test although all these are means to the same end, namely, to arrive at a rental value.

Their application to particular types of property is dealt with in section 10 of this Chapter but a brief description of the first three methods is given here.

(*a*) *Valuation by reference to rents paid.* In many cases the rent paid for the property being valued may be the best guide to a rating assessment. However, Gross Value or Net Annual Value can only correspond with rents actually paid provided that (i) the rent represents the fair annual value of the premises at the relevant date and (ii) the terms on which the property is let are the same as those assumed in the statutory definition. The rent paid for any particular property will almost certainly not be the true rental value in cases where property has been let for some time and values in the district have since changed.

Again, properties are often let at a low rent in consideration of the lessee paying a premium on entry, or surrendering the unexpired term of an existing lease, or undertaking improvements or alterations to the premises. In the case of premiums or such equivalent sums, the rent must be adjusted for assessment purposes by adding to it the annual equivalent of the consideration given by the tenant for the lease. This would not, however, apply if the premium was paid in respect of furniture or goodwill. A rent of business premises may also be low if a tenant's voluntary improvement under an earlier lease has been ignored under Section 34 of the Landlord and Tenant Act 1954, as amended by the Law of Property Act 1969. If the tenant has carried out non-contractual improvements, the rental value of these improvements must also be added to the rent paid.

The rent paid may not be equal to the rental value because there is a relationship between the lessor and the lessee.

A typical example is where the property is occupied by a limited liability company on lease from the freeholder who is a director of that company. Rents reserved in respect of lettings between associated companies are often not equal to the proper rental value. Sale and leaseback rents may also differ from rental value.

Adjustments may be necessary in cases where the terms of the tenancy differ from those of the statutory definition of Gross Value. A typical example is that of a shop let on a lease, under which the lessee is responsible for all the repairs. In such a case the rent will certainly be lower than it would have been had the landlord been responsible for the repairs. An addition, in respect of the repairs, must therefore be made to the rent to obtain the Gross Value. As a rule of thumb it has been common practice to add 5% to the reserved rent where the tenant has the responsibility for internal repairs only and 10% where his responsibility extends to both internal and external repairs, as in the example of the shop referred to above.

The relationship between rents in accordance with the statutory definitions and lease rents has been a subject of contention. It has been held by the Courts in a number of cases that rents on leases for up to 21 years did not differ materially from rents from year to year. However, these cases were not recent and it appears most likely that a rent fixed for 21 years without rent review clauses would be held to differ from a rent from year to year, because the rent reserved over the earlier years of the lease would be high to balance a later expected profit rent (*Humber Ltd. v. Jones (V.O.) & Rugby R.D.C.* [1960], 53 R. & I.T. 293). This point is of some importance when comparing and analysing rents paid under leases which appear to be above other market evidence on account of the security of lengthy terms without review, particularly in a rising rental market.

In *Dawkins v. Ash Brothers & Heaton Ltd.* [1969], R.A. 205, the House of Lords by a 3–2 majority decision held that the prospect of the demolition of part of a hereditament within a year was a factor which a hypothetical tenant would consider in making his rental bid. This resulted in a lower assessment but involved complex argument as to the point at which actual facts displaced the hypothetical circumstances to be considered in rating law.

Where the rent actually paid is above or below the rental value, or where a property is owner-occupied, a valuation must be made by comparing the property being valued with other similar properties let at true rental values.

Sometimes a proper rent can be fixed by direct comparison with other similar properties. In other cases it may be necessary to compare their relative size or accommodation and to use some convenient unit of comparison, such as the rent per square metre/square foot.

With certain special types of property a unit of accommodation rather than of measurement may be used, such as a figure per room, or per seat for theatres and cinemas, or per table for billiard saloons, or per car parking space for parking garages.

When using the rents paid for other similar properties as a basis of assessment regard must be had to the terms on which those properties are let, and to making any necessary adjustments to those rents so that they conform with the applicable statutory definition.

Mention may also be made of the principle of "equation of rents". This is a theory based on the assumption that a tenant would pay only a fixed sum by way of rent and rates. If the rates burden increases substantially, as it did on industrial property as a result of the 1963 revaluation and the abolition of derating, then the rent should fall. This, however, may be very difficult to prove and in a case concerning the assessment of a large factory for the 1963 list, the Tribunal decided that there was no evidence of industrial rents falling after the 1963 revaluation. However, this issue of equation could well be of some interest in the 1990 revaluation, which is to be based on rental evidence as at 1 April 1988. A possible point of argument and negotiation is likely to be whether or not these 1988 rental levels were agreed in the full recognition of the potentially significant changes in future rate burdens as a result of the forthcoming revaluation.

(*b*) *The Contractor's Test*. This method is used in cases where rental evidence, either direct or indirect, is not available or is inconclusive; such evidence may take the form of comparisons from other assessments or from accounting evidence as to the occupier's likely expectation of profit. The theory behind the contractor's test is that the owners, as hypothetical tenants, would in arriving at their bid have regard to the yearly cost to them of acquiring the ownership of the hereditament by taking a rate of interest on capital cost or capital value. Examples of properties for which the contractor's basis is appropriate are public libraries, town halls, sewage disposal works, fire stations, colleges, municipal baths, schools, crematoria, specialiscd industrial properties and most rateable plant and machinery. The method has also been used in the case of a motor racing track where no licence is required and there is no quasi-monopoly. If a quasi-monopoly exists, as, for example, with a licensed hotel, then the profits basis based on available accounts would be appropriate.

The contractor's method was described in outline in Chapter 2 and is applied by taking a percentage of the effective capital value of the land and buildings to arrive at the annual value.

There are two possible methods of determining the effective capital value of buildings for this purpose:

(i) by reference to the known or estimated cost, inclusive of fees, of reconstructing the existing building, known as the replacement cost approach. In the case of a new building the effective capital value might well be the actual cost of construction unless there was some form of surplusage, such as excess capacity or other disability, which would justify a reduction in that cost. With an older property, however, the cost of reconstruction would have to be written down to take account of disabilities of the existing building, reflecting its age and obsolescence. Excessive embellishment and ornamentation would normally have to be ignored as it is not something for which the hypothetical tenant would pay more rent.

(ii) by reference to the cost, including fees, of constructing a simple modern building capable of performing the functions of the existing building, being a more refined approach known as the "simple substitute building" solution to the same problem of valuing obsolete or older properties. The cost, for example, of a school based on the present day price per student place as certified by the Department of Education and Science would have to be written down to take account of the extent to which the existing building falls short of the standards of the new substitute building.

In either case the effective capital value which is required is the cost of a modern building less the necessary deductions in respect of disabilities so that the final figure obtained represents as nearly as practicable the value of the old building with all its disadvantages. To this figure must be added the effective capital value of the land, the value being assessed having regard to the existing buildings "*rebus sic stantibus*" and ignoring any prospective development value.

The final stage in the valuation is the conversion of effective capital value into a rental value by the application of an appropriate percentage which theoretically could be argued to be the market borrowing rate for funds. However, the crucial outcome is that the figure so arrived at should correspond to the annual market value of the capital invested in the land and buildings, and there is some judicial guidance on this point.

In *Coppin (V.O.) v. East Midlands Airport Joint Committee* [1970], R.A. 503, concerning the assessment of the East Midlands Airport, Castle Donington, the Lands Tribunal in their decision referred to the fact that both valuers agreed that 5 per cent was the generally accepted rate to be applied to the effective capital value to arrive at Net Annual Value in the normal type of case. It was also mentioned that 3¾ per cent was the rate taken by valuation officers in the decapitalisation of the effective capital value of non-commercial undertakings of local authorities such as sewage disposal works. In *Shrewsbury School (Governors) v. Hudd* [1966], R.A. 439, concerning the rating of a public school, 3½ per cent of the cost of a substitute building, fees and site less 70 per cent for age and obsolescence formed the basis of the Lands Tribunal's decision in arriving at Gross Value, while in a cemetery and crematorium case, *Gudgion v. Croydon L.B.C.* [1970], R.A. 341, the Lands Tribunal adopted 3¾ per cent on replacement cost less surplusage and disabilities to arrive at Net Annual Value.

Various Lands Tribunal decisions have confirmed the following range of percentages:—

Public Schools and Universities	—$3\frac{1}{2}$% to Gross Value
Local Authority Properties (reflecting the Authority's statutory duty)	—$4\frac{1}{2}$% to Gross Value
Special Industrial Properties	—5% to Net Annual Value
Commercial Sports Facilities	—6% to Gross Value

The East Midlands Airport decision is summarised below:

Total Capital Cost of Airport		£1,239,000
Less Excess costs		
(a) excess runway thickness and width		
(b) cost of separately assessed hereditaments		248,070
		990,930
Less for "tone of the valuation list"— $12\frac{1}{2}$%. The reduction was made to convert 1964/65 costs to those appropriate to 1962/63	123,866	
		867,064
Less for disabilities at the terminal building		67,064
Effective Capital Value at $3\frac{3}{4}$%		£800,000 £30,000 N.A.V.

("normal" rate of 5% adjusted to $3\frac{3}{4}$% to reflect the difficulties likely to be met by the hypothetical tenant during the build-up period because the airport was a new venture and did not become operational until April 1965)

It should not be overlooked that the hypothetical tenant's ability to pay the resultant figure of rent arrived at by a contractor's method valuation is a material factor, which could possibly result in an adjustment downwards of the end product.

(c) *The Profits Basis.* This method is also used where rental evidence is absent or inconclusive. The theory is that the hypothetical tenant would relate his rental bid to the profits he would be likely to make from the business he would conduct on the hereditament. It must be emphasised that the profits themselves are not rateable but that they are used as a basis for estimating the rent that a tenant would pay for the premises vacant and to let. Examples of properties to which the profits basis may be applied are racecourses, licensed premises, caravan sites and leisure centres including pleasure piers and the rule is that the method is particularly applicable where there is some degree of monopoly, either statutory, as in the case of public utility undertakings, or factual, as in the foregoing examples.

The method involves the use of the accounts of the actual occupier but if the actual occupier's management skill is below or above the normal level of competence assumed for the hypothetical tenant then consequential adjustment to those accounts will be necessary. From the gross receipts purchases are deducted, after they have been adjusted for variation of stock in hand at the beginning and end of the year, thus leaving the gross profit. Working expenses are then deducted. The residue, known as the divisible balance, is divided between the tenant, for his remuneration and interest on his capital invested in the business as a first charge, the rates and the landlord by way of rent. The tenant's share must be sufficient to induce him to take the tenancy, irrespective of the balance for rent and rates.

The final balance is rent, either on a Gross Value or Net Annual Value basis, plus rates. The rates should not be deducted as an outgoing in making the initial valuation even though the tenant is liable for their payment, because the amount of the rent and the rates are related to one another.

A profits valuation for the assessment of a licensed hotel to a Gross Value is set out in outline below. The method is similar when Rateable Value is required directly, as will be the case for the 1990 revaluation, but with the necessary additions to the working expenses to reflect the tenant's extra liabilities in respect of repairs and insurance of the hereditament.

Licensed Hotel—Assessment to Gross Value for the 1973 Valuation List

		£	
		Receipts	
	less	Purchases	(adjusted
		————	for stock
		Gross Profit	position)

less Working expenses, from the trading figures, which would be appropriate to a tenant from year to year occupying under the terms of Gross Value. The working expenses deducted may be adjusted, if necessary, to reflect those which the hypothetical tenant would allow and need not necessarily be those actually incurred.

————————
Divisible Balance*

less Tenant's share consisting of:
  (i) interest on his capital invested in furniture, equipment, stock and working capital at, say, 7½%
  (ii) remuneration for running the business including risk etc. or capital (an assessed figure—or, say, 10% on tenant's capital or alternatively, say, 20% of the Divisible Balance)

(Tenant's share, rent on a Gross Value basis and rates)

————————
G.V. and rates

(*this Divisible Balance is subject to repairs and insurance
as the valuation is to Gross Value, but in the future such
items will be deducted prior to arriving at the Divisible
Balance so that Rateable Value may be then ascertained
directly)

N.B.
1. The tenant's share is sometimes arrived at by taking
a higher rate, say, 17½%, on his capital invested in the business to comprise both elements of his share.
2. An alternative method of assessing the tenant's share,
which is sometimes used, is to take a percentage of the gross
receipts.
3. The divisible balance is sometimes referred to as the
amount available after interest on tenant's capital at, say,
7½%, has been deducted.

A shortened version of the profits test is frequently used
to value licensed premises, petrol stations, cinemas and
theatres.

8. DATE OF VALUATION AND TONE OF THE LIST

Uniformity of assessment is of paramount importance if
an equitable distribution of the rate burden is to be ensured.
It is for this reason that periodical revaluations take place
over the whole country. These should be made quinquenially
but have usually been made at less frequent intervals.

Sections 19A and 19B were added to the General Rate
1967 by the Local Government, Planning and Land Act 1980,
giving the Secretary of State powers to specify types of hereditament which are to form the subject of future revaluations and to specify dates for such revaluations. There are
also powers to set an antecedent date, prior to the revaluation
date, for the purposes of revaluation. Thus all non-residential
properties form the basis of the Valuation List on 1 April
1990, based on values appertaining on 1 April 1988, but
taking into account physical and other factors existing in
1990.

Prior to the Local Government Act 1966, however, proposals to amend, or add to, the valuation list necessitated in law that the valuation should be based on values prevailing at the date of the proposal. After the list had been in force for some time this would often have resulted in assessments being unfairly high because they would not have been in accordance with the "tone of the list", which means they would not have been consistent with assessments already entered in the list. In such cases the Inland Revenue policy was, in fact, to follow the "tone of the list" but such a course of action could not have been upheld successfully if it was in issue before the Local Valuation Court or the Lands Tribunal.

The position has been remedied by Section 20 of the General Rate Act 1967, re-enacting a provision in the 1966 Act. Section 20 applies the "tone of the list" to all hereditaments except public utility undertakings valued on a profits basis, and there are special provisions as to mines, quarries and public houses.

The valuation "shall not exceed" the value of the hereditament as if it had been subsisting throughout the year before that in which the valuation list came into force, in which case it would have been valued at the general revaluation date on which the valuation is based. If there has been a fall in values then the valuation would be made as at the date of the proposal. Regard is to be had to the state of the hereditament, locality, transport services and other local facilities and matters affecting local amenities at the date of the proposal. This necessitates a valuation of the hereditament in its current use and state in the context of the existing locality but based on rent levels of the current list.

The valuation of public houses must be based on the volume of trade carried on at the proposal date. Mineral valuations must be based upon the quantity of minerals extracted at the same date. In both cases the valuation will have regard to values adopted for the current valuation list.

The current situation for the 1973 Valuation List is that the "tone of the list" sets the ceiling value for the life of the list. However this may not be the case for the 1990 Revaluation and proposals for alteration of values below the tone of the list could well be excluded under proposed new legislation.

9. RATING OF UNOCCUPIED PROPERTIES

Due to the absence of a beneficial occupier unoccupied properties are not normally rateable under general rating law.

The General Rate Act 1967, Section 17 and Schedule 1, as amended by Section 15 of the Local Government Act 1974, gives rating authorities a discretionary power to pass a resolution to levy rates on unoccupied properties. Such a resolution can apply to all such hereditaments or only to particular classes of unoccupied properties within its area, and in so doing defines the percentage of rates payable. There is a limitation of the rates liability of 100% in respect of domestic properties and 50% in other cases. This "empty rate" is payable by the owner in respect of the "relevant period of vacancy" which is after six months in the case of newly erected dwelling-houses and three months in the case of all other hereditaments. These procedures are governed by the Unoccupied Property Rate (Variation of Current Ceiling) Order 1980 but there is a further important variation in the Rating (Exemption of Unoccupied Industrial and Storage Hereditaments) Regulations 1985 which grant total exemption at the present time to industrial and certain defined storage premises.

Additionally, Section 16 of the 1974 Act, again amending the 1967 Act, introduced the empty property surcharge or penal rating. Subject to what is now a long list of exemptions, an owner is required to pay a surcharge additional to the rates payable if for a continuous period exceeding six months a commercial building is not used for the purpose for which it was constructed or has been adapted. The surcharge is levied by doubling the normal rates for the first twelve months of non-use, trebling for the second twelve months, quadrupling for the third and so on. However these penal provisions have been temporarily suspended as from 1 April 1981 by the operation of the Rating Surcharge (Suspension) Order 1980.

10. ASSESSMENT OF VARIOUS TYPES OF PROPERTY

(a) Agricultural properties

Agricultural land and buildings are wholly exempt from rating under Section 26(1) of the General Rate Act 1967. "Agricultural land" is defined in Section 26(3) as "any land used as arable meadow or pasture ground only, land used for plantation or a wood or for the growth of saleable underwood, land exceeding 0·10 hectare used for the purpose of poultry farming, cottage gardens exceeding 0·10 hectare, market gardens, nursery grounds, orchards or allotments, including allotment gardens within the meaning of the Allotments Act 1922, but does not include land occupied together with a house as a park, gardens (other than as aforesaid), pleasure grounds, or land kept or preserved mainly or exclusively for purposes of sport or recreation, or land used as a racecourse".

It will be noticed that the definition includes land used for a plantation or a wood or for the growth of saleable underwood but if such land is kept or preserved mainly or exclusively for the purposes of sport or recreation or otherwise excluded (for example, if it is "occupied together with a house or a park") from the definition of "agricultural land", the exemption will not apply and the hereditament will be assessed in accordance with the special valuation treatment provided in Section 27 (i.e. normally to its value as if let and occupied in its natural and unimproved state, and where such land is used for the growth of saleable underwood then the rateable value will be the value as if let for that purpose).

"Agricultural buildings" as defined in Section 26(4) referred to "buildings (other than dwellings) occupied together with agricultural land or being or forming part of a market garden, and in either case used solely in connection with agricultural operations thereon".

This definition gave rise to some litigation in recent years in connection with buildings used for modern intensive farming practices, particularly broiler houses. In a 1970 House of Lords decision (*Eastwood v. Herrod (V.O.)* [1970] RA 63), Lord Reid expressed the view that the test should be whether the buildings are subsidiary and ancillary to agricultural operations. The particular broiler houses, producing 150,000 birds per week, were in no sense ancillary and they were held to be rateable. Section 2(1) of the Rating Act 1971, however, extended the exemptions by amending the definitions of "agricultural buildings" and "agricultural land" in the General Rate Act so as to include buildings used solely for the keeping and breeding of livestock or for that use together with some agricultural use provided that they are surrounded by or adjoin an area of not less than two hectares of agricultural land.

Section 3 of the 1971 Act extended the exemption to buildings occupied and used for the keeping of bees and a further extension to include buildings used for fish farming was introduced by the Local Government, Planning and Land Act 1980 (see Section 26A of the 1967 Act).

Dwellings are specifically excluded from the definition of agricultural buildings in Section 26(4), but special provision is made for a house occupied in connection with agricultural land and used by a person primarily engaged in carrying on or directing agricultural operations on the land, or employed in agricultural operations on the land and entitled to occupy the house only while so employed. In such a case, Section 26(2) provides that the Gross Value must be estimated on the assumption that the house could not be used otherwise than as an agricultural dwelling-house.

There is little or no evidence of the letting of houses within this statutory definition. Assessments are, therefore, arbitrary, often being arrived at by making a deduction (10 per cent is used in some cases) from the estimated rental value of similar houses not occupied in connection with agriculture in order to allow for the statutory restriction.

(b) Dwelling-houses

For the purpose of the 1956 lists the Gross Value of dwelling-houses had to be related to the 1939 rents. For the 1963 and 1973 lists they were valued in accordance with the statutory definition of Gross Value on the basis of the current rents. It is proposed that all domestic hereditaments should be excluded from the 1990 Valuation Lists and that domestic rates should be replaced by a community charge.

Dissatisfaction with a rental basis of valuation arises from the lack of evidence of rents particularly in areas where the vast majority of houses are owner-occupied. This lack of evidence led, for example, to a disparity between the assessments of houses and purpose-built flats for which the necessary rental evidence existed. The case of *R. v. Paddington (V.O.) ex parte Peachey Property Corporation Ltd.* [1965], R.A. 165, is of interest in this connection because it deals with an attempt to have the 1963 Paddington Valuation List set aside on the grounds of such inconsistencies.

The position is further aggravated by the fact that rents under the Rent Acts are not conclusive evidence of value for rating purposes (*Poplar A.C. v. Roberts* [1922], 2 A.C. 93).

With a view to securing uniformity of assessment, valuers usually adopt the method of analysing the rents of houses in a particular area or locality and reducing them to a "datum" figure for Gross Value of so much per square unit of floor space.

This type of analysis of a number of rents might indicate a datum figure for a particular road of so many pounds per square metre. In assessing the individual houses in the road it may be necessary to vary this figure to reflect differences in age or size or particular advantages or disadvantages. The use of a common datum figure, however, helps to secure some measure of uniformity.

The method of analysis and application varies in practice. Some valuers prefer to utilise outside measurements of the building for quick and easy comparison to arrive at a "reduced covered area" (R.C.A.), while other valuers adopt as a basis the "effective floor area" (E.F.A.), being the floor area of habitable rooms including kitchens.

The danger of these methods is that, if applied too rigorously and without proper discretion, they may result in an old-fashioned, badly-planned house being assessed at a higher figure than a modern, conveniently planned house which, although possessing less floor space, is much more attractive to prospective tenants and would therefore command a higher rent.

In any case, the value of the house must be considered in conjunction with the garden, garages, outbuildings and grounds with which it is enjoyed, but generally no specific account is taken of gardens unless exceptionally large or small for the type of property concerned. However, additions are made for garages, outbuildings, etc. at an appropriate value per unit of area in order to arrive at the total Gross Value shown in the Valuation List.

The methods used for the assessment of cottages and tenements let on weekly tenancies at inclusive rents do not differ in principle from those applied to dwelling-houses generally, except that the amount of the rates and water rate which are paid by the landlord must be deducted from the rent in order to obtain the Gross Value.

As regards structural alterations made after 1 April 1974, Section 21 of the Local Government Act 1974 prevents any increase in domestic assessments to reflect addition value where their cumulative value is equal to or less than 10% of the existing Gross Value or £30, whichever is the less. Furthermore, installation of central heating is to be ignored but Section 21 items may be taken into account in the valuation process before any reductions are given in domestic assessments.

(c) Blocks of Offices and Flats

Consideration of the rents actually paid, checked by comparison with rents paid for other similar premises, usually provide a basis of valuation.

With many properties of this type, the landlord is responsible for some or all of the repairs including repairs to the common parts, such as halls and stairways, and for the provision of services, such as central heating and hot water, lifts, lighting and cleaning the common parts and for porters and lift attendants. Tenants will pay either rents inclusive of services or separate service charges in addition to the rent.

A normal method of valuation is to find the gross rents

from the block, adjust them to bring them to terms of gross value and then deduct the cost of providing the services. The difference is the aggregate gross value of the block and this should be apportioned between the various flats or office suites. The deduction in respect of services would include normal items such as wages and insurance of employees, the running costs of lift service, central heating and domestic hot water, lighting and cleaning the common parts, upkeep of gardens and a sum for supervision of the services. After 1990, flats will be excluded from the Valuation List and offices will be valued direct to Rateable Value, necessitating an appropriate adjustment to the above valuation procedure.

Section 23 of the General Rate Act 1967 now applies in all cases where rents are inclusive of services, including the repair, maintenance or insurance of premises not forming part of that hereditament, or where separate service charges are made for such services in addition to the rents. In this latter case, the rent must be treated as increased by the amount of any service charge. The amount deducted from the rent for the cost of services must not include the cost of repairs, maintenance and insurance of the common parts including rateable plant and machinery, or in respect of profit on the services. For this reason it will be understood that repairs to boilers and the cost of a sinking fund to replace the boilers have been held to be costs which may not be deducted because the boilers formed part of the common part of the hereditament. Costs of repairs of a rateable passenger lift have similarly been held not to be deductible. Management and supervision costs on services are deductible but rent collection costs are not.

(d) Shops

The assessment of shops is governed mainly by consideration of the rents actually paid. In principle, if a property is let at a market rent, then that rent, adjusted if necessary to conform to the definition of Gross Value, should form the basis of the assessment.

If a shop is let on a full repairing and insuring lease, an

addition to the rent of 10 per cent is usually made to convert it into a rent on terms of Gross Value. If the tenant is responsible only for internal repairs, the rent is usually increased by 5 per cent. Such a general practice may be considered too arbitrary and should not be adopted if other figures can be justified and, in fact, the Lands Tribunal have adopted the actual cost of repairs as an increase factor in specified cases. However, these problems will disappear after 1990 when shops are to be valued more realistically direct to Rateable Value. An addition to the rent must also be made for any tenant's expenditure such as the installation of a shop front, particularly in the case of a new shop where the tenant leases and pays rent for only a "shell" and covenants to complete and fit out the shop. It might be thought that the allowance for such expenditure should be obtained by decapitalising at dual rates with allowance for income tax on the sinking fund. The position is by no means clear, however, as in *Caltex Trading and Transport Co. v. Cane (V.O.)* [1962], RA 93 the Lands Tribunal considered that only simple interest on expenditure was correct while in 1967 they agreed with the use of dual rates but excluded allowing for the effect of income tax on sinking fund as a factor which the tenant would not consider (*F. W. Woolworth & Co. Ltd. v. Peck (V.O.)* [1967], R.A. 365). In a later case (*F. W. Woolworth & Co. Ltd. v. Moore (V.O.)* [1978], R.A. 186), this principle was upheld and finishing costs to the hereditament were decapitalised over a 35 year period using a 6% and 3% dual rate table (excluding income tax). The use of simple interest only gives the lowest addition to the rent paid while the use of dual rates with allowance for tax gives the highest. The final figure obtained, in any event, should be the rent which the hypothetical tenant would pay for the completed shop on the basis of the statutory definition. Any necessary adjustment for repairs undertaken by the tenant must be applied to the rent after it has been increased by allowing for tenant's expenditure.

Shops only a short distance apart can vary considerably in rental value because of vital differences in their positions. Any factor influencing pedestrian flow past the shop has its effect on value, such as proximity to "multiples", adequate and easy car parking or public transport, the position of shopping "breaks", bus stops and traffic lights and widths of pavements and streets.

In practice, certain recognised methods of valuation are used with the object of promoting uniformity and facilitating comparison between different properties.

A method in general use for valuing the ground floor of a shop, which is usually a very much more valuable part than the rest of the premises, is the "zoning" method. The front of the shop is the most valuable part as being the most suitable selling space and the value per unit of area decreases as the distance away from the front of the shop increases until a point is reached beyond which any further reduction would not be sensible. The zoning method allows for this progressive decrease in value from the front to the rear.

The first step in the analysis of a rent paid for premises including a ground floor shop is to deduct the rent attributable to all ancillary accommodation, leaving that paid for the ground floor selling space only. This rent is then broken down on the assumption that the front part of the shop, back to a certain depth, is worth the maximum figure, say £x per unit of area, the next portion £x/2 per unit of area, and the remaining portion £x/4. This process, known as "halving back", is used most extensively and can be varied, but usually the number of zones will not exceed three.

The depth of each zone varies according to circumstances and valuers have different opinions as to the most suitable depths to be used. The choice of the depths of zones should, however, be logical and governed by the depths of the shops under review, as it is pointless to halve back after 7 metres if the minimum depth of any shop under consideration is 10 metres. In the past, for example, some valuers have taken a depth of 15 feet for the first zone and 25 feet for the second while others have divided the shop into zones each 20 feet deep.

The first zone (termed Zone A) is measured backwards from the front of the shop, which is usually the glass window. This zone may therefore consist entirely of shop front, arcades and show cases and is clearly the most valuable. The benefits of a return frontage on a corner shop can be reflected by a percentage addition to the value of the shop. As far as sales space on upper or basement floors is concerned this may be valued as a fraction of Zone A value in comparative terms. Other ancillary space is usually taken at a unit value applied to the area concerned.

The Lands Tribunal have indicated that in their opinion the number and depths of the zones to be adopted is not so important provided that the zoning method is applied correctly and consistently according to the actual depths of the shops whose rents are being devalued and that the same method is applied subsequently when valuing (*Marks & Spencer v. Collier (V.O.)* [1966], R.A. 107).

When a large shop is being valued on the basis of rental information derived from smaller shops, a "quantity allowance" is sometimes made in the form of a percentage deduction from the resulting valuation of the large shop. This procedure may be justified on the grounds that there is a limited demand for large shops and that therefore a landlord may have to accept a rather lower rent per unit of area than he would for a small shop. This may be valid when a large shop is in what is basically a small shop position but it is probably invalid when it is in part of a shopping area where large chain stores have established themselves. For this reason, the Lands Tribunal rejected quantity allowances on two shops in Brighton in 1958, in assessments for the 1956 list (*British Home Stores Ltd. v. Brighton C.B.C. and Burton; Fine Fare Ltd. v. Burton and Brighton C.B.C.* [1958], 51 R. & I.T. 665). Later, in a 1963 list reference, concerning a new store built for Marks & Spencer in Peterborough and their old store, which they had sold to Boots, the Lands Tribunal refused quantity allowances on the ground that the limited demand and limited supply of large shops was in balance (*Marks & Spencer Ltd. v. Collier (V.O.)* [1966], R.A. 107). Furthermore, in *Trevail v. C. & A. Modes Ltd.* and *Trevail v. Marks & Spencer Ltd.* [1967], R.A. 124, the Lands Tribunal expressed doubts as to whether the zoning method was not being stretched beyond its capabilities in the valuation of these large walk-round stores. The problems of valuing large stores for rating purposes was comprehensively considered in the Lands Tribunal's decision on the John

Lewis's store in Oxford Street (*John Lewis & Co. Ltd. v. Goodwin (V.O.) and Westminster City Council* [1979], 252 EG 499). An alternative approach is to value such stores on an overall pricing method, but this can only be supported where there is appropriate and reliable rental evidence which has been tested in the market.

Apart from a possible quantity allowance, a disability allowance may be an appropriate deduction in the case of shops with disadvantages such as obsolete lay-out, inconvenient steps, changes in floor level, excessive or inadequate height, lack of rear access, inadequacy of toilets or large and obstructive structural columns, if their values have been based on those of shops without such disabilities.

In order to be able to check an assessment of a particular shop to see if it is fair by comparison with the assessments of other neighbouring shops it is essential to be at least reasonably conversant with the shopping locality.

The following example illustrates the method of analysing the rent of premises comprising a ground floor shop and two upper floors occupied together with the shop for residential purposes. The analysis for the current valuation list is made to ascertain the rental value per unit of area of the front zone of the shop so that it can be compared with the rents of other shops. It is not in this case considered likely that there would be any doubt about the correctness of the figure used for valuing the upper floors.

Example 22–1

Shop premises comprising a ground floor "shell" and two upper floors situated in a good position in a large town were let during the year immediately preceding the coming into force of the valuation list at £5,000 per annum on a full repairing and insuring lease for 15 years with a review in the 5th and 10th years. The tenant spent £4,500 on a shop front and other finishings. Analyse this rent for the purpose of rating assessments. The shop has a frontage of 6 metres and a depth of 20 metres. The net floor areas of the residential first and second floors are 50 square metres each.

Analysis (for the current Valuation List)

Rent reserved	£5,000

Add

Annual equivalent of cost of shop front
and finishings provided by the tenant—

$$\frac{£4,500}{\text{Y.P. 15 yrs at 6\% and 3\%}}$$

$$= \frac{£4,500}{8 \cdot 7899}$$ 512

                                                                     ─────
                                                                     5,512

Add

10% for tenant's full repairing liability	551

Full rental value on terms of Gross Value	£6,063

Deduct

Rental value of upper floors on terms of
Gross Value

100 sq. metres at £7 per sq. metre	700

Leaving for shop rental value on terms of

Gross Value	£5,363

N.B. If this shop were being analysed in terms of Net Annual Value (or Rateable Value in the 1990 List), the figures would be £5,000 (Rent reserved) plus £512 (Annual Equivalent of shop front, etc.) less say £630 (Upper floors), equalling a total of £4,882 for shop rental value in terms of Net Annual Value.

Measurement shows that the effective net area of the shop is as follows:

First 7 metres (often referred to as Zone 'A') 42 sq. metres; Second 7 metres (often referred to as Zone 'B') 40 sq. metres;
Third 6 metres (often referred to as Zone 'C') 32 sq. metres.

Let £x per square metre represent the rental value of the first zone and adopting "halving back":

then $42x + \dfrac{40x}{2} + \dfrac{32x}{4} = £5,363$

$70x = £5,363$

$x = £77$ approximately Zone A rental value per sq. metre on terms of Gross Value.

N.B. On an analysis in terms of Net Annual Value, Zone A would approximate to £70 per sq. metre. However, it is relevant to stress that a rental value basis (as at 1988) would be very many times greater than the figures used in the above example due to the inflation of shop rents over the previous sixteen years.

The above analysed figures can then be compared with other Zone A rents based on the letting of similar shops in the vicinity to assist in obtaining a rent which represents a fair and consistent basis for the assessment of the shops under consideration.

A more convenient approach is that of reducing areas to "equivalent Zone A" areas. Using the above facts, the total area of $42 + 40 + 32$ sq. metres (114 sq. metres) is expressed as:

$$\text{Zone A} \quad 42$$

$$\text{Zone B} \quad 20\left\{\frac{40}{2}\right\}$$

$$\text{Zone C} \quad 8\left\{\frac{32}{4}\right\}$$

Equivalent Zone A area = 70 sq. metres

analysis then becomes $\dfrac{£5,363}{70}$

$= £77$ approximately as above for Gross Value analysis

(or £70 for Net Annual Value)

It must be emphasised that the zoning method, although used very commonly in practice, is merely a means to an end in order to find the true rental value. The fixing of zone depths and the allocation of values to the zones are arbitrary processes and strict adherence to an arbitrary pattern may result in absurd answers in particular cases.

On the other hand, the method is based on a sound practical principle, namely, that the front portion of a shop, including windows, is the part which attracts the most customers and is therefore the most valuable part as selling space. Consequently a shop with moderate but adequate depth is likely to have a higher overall rental per unit of floor space than one with the same frontage but a much greater depth. Similarly, a shop with a frontage of 7 metres and a depth of 15 metres may be worth £6,000 per annum but an adjoining shop with the same frontage of 7 metres and otherwise identical but with double the depth, i.e., 30 metres, will be found to be worth considerably less than £12,000 per annum.

In the above example metric measurements were used throughout. In practice it will be found that in the 1973 List properties were generally valued adopting metric measurements but shop zone depths were measured in feet. This arose because the Inland Revenue converted their records to metric units but lacked the time and resources to re-measure shops adopting metric depth zones. This mixed measurement code may well be used again for the 1990 revaluation if the Valuation Office have not re-measured and/or re-calculated their zone areas.

(e) Factories and Warehouses

Factories are industrial buildings being "factories, mills and other premises of a similar character used wholly or mainly for industrial purposes" as defined in Section 19(6) of the General Rate Act 1967. They are assessed directly to Net Annual Value which is a rent on a full repairing basis.

Warehouses, which are non-industrial buildings used for storage of materials and merchandise, require a Gross Value for the 1972 Valuation List but will be valued directly to Rateable Value for the 1990 Revaluation.

Both factories and warehouses are usually assessed by reference to effective floor space, the value per square metre being fixed by comparison with other similar properties in the neighbourhood. In some cases a flat rate per unit of floor space may be used throughout the building but in other cases it may be more appropriate to vary the rate applied to each floor.

Properties of this type differ considerably in such matters as construction, accommodation, planning and situation. Any special advantages or disadvantages attaching to the property under consideration must be very carefully examined when applying rents of other properties. Particular factors affecting rental values are the proximity of motorways or rail facilities, availability of labour, internal layout, nature of access to upper floors, loading and unloading facilities, natural lighting, heating, ventilation, adequacy of toilets, nature of ancillary offices, canteen facilities, availability of public transport and car parking for staff.

There may be no general demand for certain industrial properties of highly specialised types in some areas and therefore no evidence of rental values which could be used as a basis for comparison, particularly since most are owner-occupied. With such cases as, for example, oil refineries, chemical plants, cement works and steelworks, it will probably be necessary to resort to the contractor's test by taking an appropriate percentage of the effective capital value of the land and buildings as a method of obtaining the Net Annual Value.

Plant and machinery is only to be taken into account in the rating assessment if it is deemed to be a part of the hereditament. Section 21 and Schedule 3 to the General Rate Act 1967, the Plant and Machinery (Rating) Order 1960, and the Plant and Machinery (Rating) (Amendment) Order 1974 specify that five classes of plant and machinery are deemed to be a part of the hereditament and therefore rateable. They are:

Class 1. Machinery and plant used mainly or exclusively for:
    (*a*) the generation, storage, primary transformation or main transmission of power, or
    (*b*) the heating, cooling, ventilating, lighting,

draining or supplying of water to the hereditament or protecting it from fire.

However, machinery used for manufacturing or trade processes is not included even if used for the purposes specified in (b) above.

Class 2. Lifts and elevators mainly or usually used for passengers.

Class 3. Railways and tramway lines and tracks.

Class 4. Plant or machinery, or any part thereof, in the nature of a building or structure including gas holders, blast furnaces, coke ovens, tar distilling plants, cupolas or water towers with tanks.

Class 5. Pipelines, excluding drains, sewers, gas and electricity pipes and pipes forming part of the equipment of and within a factory or petrol storage depot or premises comprised in a mine, quarry or mineral field.

The effect of these provisions is that the rent to be ascertained is that which a tenant would pay for the land and buildings, including rateable plant and machinery, in accordance with the statutory definition.

There may be no difficulty in assessing the rental value, on a unit of floor space basis, of premises including certain rateable plant and machinery such as sprinkler and heating systems. Other rateable plant and machinery may have to be valued separately from the land and buildings on the contractor's test by adopting as its rental value a percentage of its effective capital value. The percentage of the effective capital value to be taken to obtain the rental value will normally be related to the economic life of the plant and machinery. The shorter the life, the higher the percentage that will be justified. On the other hand, under the definition of Net Annual Value, the tenant is assumed to bear the cost of all repairs and maintenance to the plant and machinery.

Three further points should be noted. They are:

(1) Rateable plant and machinery is not restricted to that found on industrial hereditaments except for Class 5 (pipelines); for example, a passenger lift in a department store is rateable.

(2) The statutory provisions regarding plant and machinery do not apply to a valuation made on a profits basis.

(3) The Valuation Officer, if asked to do so by the occupier, must provide written particulars of what plant and machinery he has included in his valuation, as deemed to be part of the hereditament.

(f) Special Properties

Schools

Section 30 of the General Rate Act 1967 requires the assessment of County and Voluntary Schools to be made on a formula basis related to a quasi-contractor's test. The necessary details regarding the "average cost of providing a place for one pupil" are provided by the Department of Education and Science. It is from this figure that the Gross Value of the school can be assessed by means of a modified contractor's test valuation which will need to be reconsidered in terms of Rateable Value for the 1990 Revaluation. At each revaluation the formula is also brought up to date as regards building prices and educational standards. Section 30 also states that regulations may provide that land forming part of, or occupied with, such schools shall be treated as a separate hereditament.

The rating of other privately funded schools is not governed by a formula basis and it will probably be necessary to resort to a contractor's test. Thus, in a 1963 list reference, *Shrewsbury School (Governors) v. Hudd* [1966], R.A. 439, concerning the assessment of a large public school, the Lands Tribunal preferred the contractor's test to a valuation based upon a value per pupil place, although the latter figure can be useful as a comparison between schools. In later cases, *Westminster City Council v. The American School in London and Goodwin (V.O.)* [1980], R.A. 275, and *Imperial College of Science & Technology v. Ebdon (V.O.) & Westminster City Council* [1984], R.A. 244, the major issue was the appropriate rate of interest to be applied to arrive at Gross Value for schools and colleges ($3\frac{1}{2}$%). For the 1990 Revaluation new considerations are required to arrive at assessments in terms of Rateable Value.

Cinemas and Theatres

A method of valuation which has been approved by the Lands Tribunal is a quasi-profits or takings method. It involves finding the gross receipts from the sale of seats plus the takings from bingo, screen advertising, and the sale of ice-cream, cigarettes and sweets. A percentage of this total figure is then taken to obtain the Gross Value. In *Thorn EMI Cinemas Ltd. v. Harrison (V.O.)* [1986], R.A. 125, a percentage of 8·5% was applied to gross receipts (adjusted to 1973 levels) which produced a Gross Value of £7,650 (equivalent to £7·86 per cinema seat). An alternative method of making the assessment is to relate it to a price per seat but very wide variations can be found in analysing assessments by this method.

Licensed Premises

The method of valuation for rating purposes is a shortened profits basis using the direct approach method which assumes the brewer is the hypothetical tenant who will sublet to a tied tenant. Where no brewery is involved, the brewer's over-bid is excluded from the direct approach method. This method is dealt with in detail in Chapter 32.

Hereditaments occupied by Gas Suppliers, Electricity Boards and Statutory Water Undertakings, Railway and Canal Premises

Premises occupied by Gas Suppliers and Electricity Boards are excluded from rating by Sections 33 and 34 of the General Rate Act 1967, respectively, but there are certain exceptions in Sections 33(2) and 34(2), such as showrooms and offices not situated on operational land. These properties must be assessed in the normal way. Both industries make payments in lieu of rates to rating authorities.

Section 31 and Schedule 4 to the Act deal with premises

occupied for the purposes of Statutory Water Undertakings. These are rateable in accordance with a statutory formula.

Hereditaments occupied for the purposes of the British Railways Board, London Regional Transport or the British Waterways Board and subsidiaries, are dealt with in Section 32 and the Schedule 5 to the Act. Except for some important exceptions mentioned in Section 32(2), such as dwelling-houses, hotels, places of public refreshment or premises so let out as to be capable of separate assessment, they are exempt from rating but the owners make payments, in lieu of rates, to the rating authorities, and there are formulae for the calculation and apportionment of these payments.

Caravan Sites

A site used for the parking of caravans is normally assessed as a caravan site only. If however, the caravans remain for a long enough period to constitute the necessary degree of permanence, they may themselves become rateable with the land.

In the absence of good rental evidence caravan sites are normally assessed by a profits test, but a Lands Tribunal decision on a 1963 list reference, *Garton v. Hunter (V.O.)* [1969], R.A. 448, which is summarised below, established that various methods of valuation were admissible but that it was up to the Court to decide the most appropriate.

Gross receipts from letouts	£31,050
Less Working expenses	11,050
Gross Profit	£20,000
Less Tenant's share—the Tribunal preferred to assess a figure, £10,000 in this case, rather than a percentage of the gross receipts or of the divisible balance. It is, incidentally, 50% of the Gross Profit or a little over 32% of the gross receipts	10,000

Rent and Rates	10,000
Less Rates 10s. in the £1 on £6,667	3,333
	6,667
Add Agreed rateable values of facility buildings	1,350
Net Annual Value	£8,017

To help overcome the problems associated with "leisure caravans" the Valuation Officer may, under the Rating (Caravan Sites) Act 1976, "treat all or any of the pitches as forming a single hereditament together with so much, if any, of the site as is in the occupation of the site operator". If certain specified conditions are met the site operator will become the rateable occupier and a single hereditament will be assessed directly to Net Annual Value, including any rateable caravans.

Garages and Service Stations

These are normally valued on a direct profits basis. The rental value depends primarily on throughput, being the quantity of petrol sold. A rental value for a certain throughput (per thousand gallons for the 1973 list) is taken to represent the tenant's bid on the terms of Gross Value. The figure varies on a sliding scale which increases with throughput as the tenant's overheads would be proportionately less as the trade increases. The Gross Value thus arrived at allows for the petrol sales area only. Additions to this rent would need to be made for such other buildings and land as storerooms, showrooms, lubrication bays, workshops, and lock-up garages and other facilities.

For the 1963 valuation lists, the Lands Tribunal in *Petrofina (Great Britain) v. Dalby* [1967], R.A. 143, took a tenant's bid of £3·50 per 1,000 gallons based upon a throughput in that case of 135,000 gallons per annum. For the 1973 Valuation Lists figures ranged upwards to £7·00 per 1,000 gallons for Gross Value, depending upon the level of throughput. For the 1990 Revaluation increasing values plus the need to assess Rateable Value will obviously provide new bases of assessment.

Minerals

The rating of minerals is dealt with in Chapter 33.

11. SUMMARY OF PROPOSED CHANGES IN RATING LEGISLATION

Following the issue of a consultation paper in July 1987 and the Local Government Finance Bill in December 1987, the Government is proposing the following changes in rating legislation and practice.

Domestic Rating

Domestic rates are to be replaced by community charges for the financial years from 1 April 1990.

Non-Domestic Rating

A revaluation of non-domestic hereditaments will take effect from 1 April 1990 and a national non-domestic rate or uniform business rate (UBR) will be introduced to replace local authority rate poundages.

The main proposals arising from the revaluation of non-domestic property can be summarised as follows:—

(i) For the 1990 revaluation all hereditaments will be assessed to Rateable Value, and values will be related to rental evidence as at 1 April 1988. However, the "tone of the list" will no longer operate as a ceiling value as the existing right to reduce assessments below 1988 levels, if values fall during the period following 1990, is to be removed.

(ii) A statutory time-table will be introduced for future rating revaluations to take place every five years.

(iii) The Government may wish to restrict the effects of the UBR by introducing it gradually from 1990 and by setting an upper limit on the annual percentage increases and decreases in rate bills up to 1995. The duty of local authorities to consult with representatives of business in their areas will continue despite the introduction of UBR.

(iv) Following the introduction of the new Valuation List,

rights of appeal will be restricted to occupiers and owners of the subject property over a six month period and normally the only exceptions to the time rule would be upon grounds of material changes in circumstances or an error of fact in the List. However, there is to be an additional right to make a proposal within six months of any change of occupation, provided that the right of appeal has not previously been exercised in the currency of the List. Apart from the above, there will, therefore, be no right of appeal after October 1990. Furthermore, it appears that local authorities will no longer have the right to make proposals or objections as third parties, but this point is under consideration by the Minister.

(v) The present Local Valuation Court is to be re-named "The Valuation and Community Charge Tribunal" and this Tribunal will have new powers of increasing an assessment where it considers this justifiable.

(vi) The right of a ratepayer to withhold 50% of an increase in rate liability where an appeal is made after the revaluation is to be replaced by a payment of interest on any rates refunded.

(vii) The Secretary of State is to be given new powers to prescribe additional categories of empty properties to be rated.

(viii) The Government will be reviewing the various statutory formulae to bring them up to date in 1990 and it proposes to replace all the existing statutory provisions relating to formula rating with a simple enabling power.

(ix) The Government is taking the power to prescribe the decapitalisation rate used in the method of valuation known as the Contractor's Test in order to secure harmonisation of rateable values for a particular class of hereditament, but it is hoped to achieve harmonisation not by legislation but rather by consultation with industry, the profession and those others responsible for the revaluation.

(x) There will be special rules to avoid over-valuation of properties in terminating Enterprise Zones, permitting the Valuation Officer to offset any clement in rents which reflects the benefit of the non-payment of rates.

CHAPTER 23

Capital Gains Tax, Inheritance Tax and Income Tax

1. CAPITAL GAINS TAX ON LAND AND BUILDINGS

TAXATION OF CAPITAL GAINS— CAPITAL ASSETS AND STOCK IN TRADE

BEFORE 1962 a capital gain was generally free from taxation. In the Finance Act 1962 provisions were introduced to treat gains made in a short period, normally 1 year but 3 years for land, as income to be taxed accordingly. The Finance Act 1965 introduced a comprehensive system for the taxation of long term capital gains, the 1962 Act provisions being abolished finally in 1971. Thus since 1965 there has existed a scheme for the taxation of capital gains, by which is meant gains realised when a capital asset is disposed of and the proceeds exceed the costs incurred in acquiring the asset. The provisions of the 1965 Act with subsequent amendments were consolidated in the Capital Gains Tax Act 1979.

These provisions apply to assets of a capital nature. In the case of property these would be the land and buildings owned by a person or company which they occupy or let as an investment. It is important to note that in some instances such property will not be regarded as capital but as stock in trade which is not subject to the provisions applicable to capital gains.

The determination of whether or not property is held as stock in trade is not always clear. Broadly stock in trade refers to those instances where a property was purchased with the purpose of making a profit. A clear example is land purchased by a company engaged in house building. The company buys land on which to build houses and the land is as much a raw material as the bricks and timber which go into the houses themselves. Such land is clearly not a capital asset since the company will sell the houses with the land as soon as possible and so move on to the next site. Thus the cost of buying the land is one of the general costs of the business whilst the sale proceeds from the disposal of the houses constitute its income. Any gain in respect of the land is therefore a part of the company's profits to be treated as income.

On the other hand, if the company owns an office building wherein its staff are housed, such a building is a capital asset since the offices were not purchased with a view to selling on for a profit. If the company does choose to sell its offices at any time, any gain realised would be subject to capital gains tax legislation. This legislation is examined below.

CAPITAL GAINS TAX UNDER THE CAPITAL GAINS TAX ACT 1979

(a) Occasions of Charge

Capital gains tax is payable on all chargeable gains accruing after 6 April 1965, on the disposal of all forms of assets including freehold and leasehold property, options and incorporeal hereditaments.

An asset may be disposed of by sale, exchange or gift. Disposal also includes part disposals and circumstances where a capital sum is derived from an asset. Death is not a disposal.

A part-disposal arises not only when part of a property is sold but also when a lease is granted at a premium. By accepting a premium the landlord is selling a part of his interest and the lessee is purchasing a profit rent. Premiums may be liable to both income tax under the Income and Corporation Taxes Act 1988, which deals with taxation of premiums and also to capital gains tax under the 1979 Act. The Act contains provisions for avoiding double taxation on any part of the premium.

A capital sum is derived from an asset when the owner obtains a capital sum from it. Thus it would include payments received to release another owner from a restrictive covenant or to release him from the burden of ancient lights and would also include compensation received for injurious affection on compulsory purchase.

It also includes capital sums received under a fire insurance policy although if the money is wholly or substantially applied to restore the asset no liability will arise.

The transfer of an asset out of fixed assets into trading stock is deemed to be a disposal. This would arise, for example, if an owner occupier of commercial premises decided to move elsewhere and to carry out a redevelopment with a view to selling the completed new property.

Where a disposal is preceded by a contract to make the disposal, the disposal is taken to occur when the contract becomes binding. This typically occurs on the sale of property where the parties enter into a contract with completion at a later date. If the contract is conditional, for example subject to grant of planning permission, it becomes binding on the date when the planning permission is granted which will be the date of disposal.

(b) Computation of Gains

The general rule applicable to the disposal of non-wasting assets, which includes freeholds, and leases with more than 50 years unexpired, is that in arriving at the net chargeable gain certain items of allowable expenditure are deductible from the consideration received on disposal. These items are:—

(1) Expenditure wholly and exclusively incurred in disposing of the asset. This includes legal and agents' fees, advertising costs and any capital gains tax valuation fees.

(2) The price paid for the asset together with incidental costs wholly and exclusively incurred for the acquisition such as legal and agents' fees and stamp duty.

(3) Additional expenditure to enhance the value of the asset and reflected in the asset at the disposal date, including expenditure on establishing, preserving or defending title. A typical example would be improvements to the property carried out by the taxpayer such as extensions.

Any item allowed for revenue taxation cannot be allowed and thus only items of a capital nature are deductible. Special rules apply where expenditure has been met out of public funds.

Certain of the above-mentioned items will need to be apportioned in the case of a part-disposal and further modifications will be required to meet special circumstances, as described later.

Example 23–1

A purchased a freehold interest in a shop in 1982 for £200,000. In 1987 A sold his interest for £400,000.

Proceeds of Disposal		£400,000
Less Agents' fees on sale, say	£4,000	
Advertising for sale, say	800	
Legal fees on sale, say	2,000	6,800
Net Proceeds of Disposal		393,200
Less Acquisition Price	200,000	
Add Agents' fees on purchase,		
say	2,000	
Legal Fees on Purchase, say	1,000	
Stamp Duty	2,000	5,000	205,000
Gain		£188,200

(c) Disposals after 5 April 1988

The Finance Act 1988 introduced a significant reform of the capital gains tax rules in respect of disposals on or after 6 April 1988. The general provisions are noted elsewhere but one change requires specific attention. This concerns cases where the asset, the subject of the disposal, was acquired before 1 April 1982. In such cases the taxpayer may elect (irrevocably) for capital gains and losses on all assets held at 31 March 1982 to be calculated by reference to values at that date. This relieves those who make the election of the need to maintain records going back beyond that date.

The gain is determined by deducting from the net proceeds of disposal the market value of the asset as at 31 March 1982 in lieu of the actual price paid at the actual time of acquisition. The effect of this is to charge to CGT only the gain arising after 31 March 1982. Where no election is made, special provisions apply where adopting the 1982 value would produce an anomaly such as turning an actual gain into a notional loss.

(d) Indexation

Provisions were introduced in 1982 to make some allowance for the effects of inflation on the amount of gains realised. This is achieved (from 1985) by deducting from the actual gain arising after 31 March 1982 the gain which would have arisen if the growth in value had merely been in line with inflation. If the inflation gain is less than the actual gain then only the balance of the gain attracts CGT. Where the inflation gain exceeds the actual gain then this excess is treated as a capital loss.

The indexation allowance is calculated by applying the percentage increase in the Retail Price Index (RPI) between 31 March 1982 and the date of disposal to the market value on 31 March 1982, or, if acquired after 31 March 1982, the percentage increase between the date of acquisition and disposal to the acquisition price.

RPI figures are calculated and published each month by the Government in relation to the RPI Index. The Index was re-based in January 1987 to 100. However, the earlier figures of RPI have been re-calculated against the 1987 base so that, for example, the RPI figure for March 1982 is 79·44 on the 1987 Index (313·4 in the previous Index).

Thus if an asset was sold in January 1987 and which was acquired before 31 March 1982, the indexation allowance would be:

$$\frac{RPI\,(Jan\,'87) - RPI\,(Mar\,'82)}{RPI\,(Mar\,'82)}$$

$$= \frac{100 \cdot 00 - 79 \cdot 44}{79 \cdot 44}$$

= 25·88% of Market Value on 31 Mar '88 (i.e. general inflation between March 1982 and January 1987 was 25·88%).

Example 23–2

As for *Example 23–1*, A purchased a freehold interest in a shop in January 1982 for £200,000 and sold the interest in January 1987 for £400,000.

Proceeds of Disposal		£400,000
Less Incidental Costs (as before)		6,800
Net Proceeds of Disposal		393,200
Less Acquisition Costs (as before)		205,000
	Gain	£188,200
Less Indexation Allowance:—		
Market Value 31 March 1982,		
say	220,000	
RPI increase	0·2588	56,936
Gain Chargeable to CGT		£131,264

(e) Rates of Tax

In the years before 1987 the rate of tax was 30 per cent for all taxpayers. In the Finance Act 1987 the rate of tax for companies changed to the same rate of tax which applied to their general profits (corporation tax rate). In 1988 this approach was extended to individuals, the rate of tax being the taxpayer's marginal income tax rate.

Hence if an individual realises a chargeable gain and his income tax rate is the basic rate, then that rate will be applied to the gain. If his income tax rate is the higher rate then that rate will be applied. In cases where the gain, if added to other income would take the taxpayer into the higher rate, the rate of tax will be the basic rate on the amount equal to the difference between other income and the higher rate threshold, with the higher rate on the balance.

The first part of a gain is exempt for individuals, with half that amount for trustees. This varies from year to year. In the year 1988/89 the exempt amount is £5,000.

(f) Exemptions and Reliefs
1. Exempted Bodies
Certain bodies are exempt from liability including charities, local authorities, friendly societies and scientific research associations and superannuation funds.

2. Owner-occupied houses
Exemption from capital gains tax is given to an owner in respect of a gain accruing from the disposal of a dwelling-house (including a flat) which has been his only or main residence, together with garden and grounds up to one acre or such larger area as may be appropriate to the particular house. The exemption does not apply, however, if the intention of the transaction was to realise a capital gain.

The degree of exemption is proportionate to the period of owner-occupation during ownership. Full exemption is given if the owner has lived in the house throughout the whole of his period of ownership. To cover the circumstances where a house is vacant after the owner has moved and is looking for a purchaser, the exemption includes the last two years of ownership. Certain other periods of absence have also to be disregarded under the Act, such as where the taxpayer has to live elsewhere temporarily as a condition of his employment.

Thus, if a property is sold and was not owner-occupied for the whole period of ownership, the degree of exemption depends upon the ratio between the period of owner-occupation (including in any event the last two years of ownership) and the total period of ownership.

If, therefore, X buys a house on 1 April 1986, and lives in it for two years until 1 April 1988, when he lets it, subsequently selling the house on 1 April 1992, the proportion of any capital gain which is exempt from capital gains tax is:

$$\frac{2+2}{6} = \frac{2}{3}$$

Where premises are used partly as a dwelling and partly for other purposes, the exemption applies only to the residential part and it will be necessary to apportion any capital gain on the whole property between the two portions. This apportionment should be made on a value basis. Thus if a house is half let and half owner-occupied, the gain on disposal is not necessarily apportioned on a 50:50 basis. It is likely that more value is attributable to the owner-occupied part and that the growth in value is greater for that part. The apportionment should reflect these circumstances.

The exemption also applies to one other house which is occupied rent free by a dependent relative if the house was bought before 6 April 1988, and also where trustees dispose of a house which has been occupied by the beneficiary under the trust.[1].

3. Replacement of business assets

Where trade assets, including fixed plant and machinery and goodwill are sold and the whole of the proceeds devoted to the replacement of the assets with other trade assets, the trader may claim to defer any capital gains tax which ordinarily may have been payable on the sale. He may choose, instead of paying the tax which arises, to have the actual purchase price of the replacement written down by the amount of any capital gain on the sale of the original assets. This process may be repeated on subsequent similar transactions so that tax on the accumulated capital gain will not be paid until the assets are sold and not replaced. To qualify for this relief, the acquisition of the new assets must be within a period commencing one year before and ending 3 years after the sale of the old assets. The Act also deals with circumstances where not all the proceeds of sale are re-invested.

---

[1] For further details see CGT 4, issued by The Board of Inland Revenue and available from Tax Offices free of charge.

Example 23–3

X purchases a freehold shop in 1967 for £15,000, the expenses of acquisition being £500 and commences trading as a grocer. In 1979, he sells this shop for £40,000, his expenses of sale being £900. He immediately purchases a new shop for £45,000, incurring expenses of £1,000 and continues in business in the same trade.

X may claim relief from the payment of tax in 1979 on the sale for £40,000 but the cost of acquisition of the new shop will be dealt with as follows:

Proceeds of Disposal		£40,000
Less Expenses		900
Net Proceeds of Disposal		39,100
Less 1967 Cost	£15,000	
Expenses of Purchase	500	15,500
Chargeable Gain		23,600
Cost of Replacement Asset		45,000
Less Gain on Sale of Old Asset		23,600
Notional Cost of Replacement Asset		£21,400

If the replacement shop was sold in 1983 for £50,000, the expenses of sale being £1,200, the owner then ceasing to continue in business, liability to capital gains tax would then arise as follows (ignoring indexation relief):

Proceeds of Disposal		£50,000
Less Expenses		1,200
Net Proceeds of Disposal		48,800
Less Notional Acquisition Price	£21,400	
Expenses of Acquisition	1,000	22,400
Chargeable Gain		£26,400

Thus the actual net gain in respect of the new asset of £50,000 − (£45,000 + £1,200) = £2,800 is boosted by the previous gain of £23,600 carried (or 'rolled') over to give a terminal gain of £2,800 + £23,600 = £26,400. These provisions are termed "rollover relief" for reasons which are obvious − the gain is rolled over into the new asset.

X may, however, be eligible for relief from this charge if he retired on the disposal (see 4 below).

4. Retirement relief

On retirement at age 60 or later, an owner may be exempted from capital gains tax on gains of up to £125,000 which accrue to him from the disposal by way of sale or gift of a family business or of shares or securities in a family trading company. On gains above £125,000, only half of the next £500,000 of gains is brought into tax. He must have been in the business for ten years or more. A similar relief is given to persons who are forced to retire before the age of 60 due to ill-health.

5. Holdover relief

A gift is a disposal for capital gains tax purposes. Relief is available to the parties whereby they may elect to have any liability deferred until the time of subsequent disposal by the donee.

(g) Losses

A capital loss might arise as a result of a disposal, say where the asset is sold for less than the price paid for it. Such a loss is allowable if a gain on the same transaction would have been chargeable. The loss would normally be set off against gains accruing in the same year of assessment but if in a particular year losses exceed gains, the net loss can be carried forward and set off against gains accruing in the following or subsequent years.

(h) Part disposals

The rule for calculating any gain or loss on a part disposal is that only that proportion of the allowable expenditure which the value of the part disposed of bears at the date of disposal to the value of the whole asset can be set against the consideration received for the part. Thus it is necessary to value the whole asset and this necessitates a valuation of the retained part, since for these purposes the value of the whole asset is treated as being the aggregate of the values of the part disposed of and the part retained. The proportion disposed of is then:

$$\frac{A}{A+B} =$$

$$\frac{\text{Consideration on part disposal (A)}}{\text{Consideration on part disposal (A)} + \text{value of retained part (B)}}$$

Thus if X buys an asset in 1977 for £100,000, including costs, and later sells part of it for £60,000, no disposal costs being involved, the first step is to value the part retained, say £90,000. The proportion of the asset disposed of is:

$$\frac{£60,000}{£60,000 + £90,000} \text{ or 40 per cent}$$

i.e. he is realising 40 per cent of the value of the asset.

Allowable expenditure of costs of acquisition and enhancement expenditure is therefore taken to be 40 per cent, thus 40 per cent of £100,000 = £40,000 and the chargeable gain is £60,000 less £40,000 = £20,000. Where enhancement expenditure relates solely to the part sold it is fully allowable: where it relates solely to the part retained then none is allowable on the part disposal.

An alternative basis of calculating the cost of a part disposal of an estate for capital gains purposes avoids having to value the unsold part of the estate. Under this alternative basis the part disposed of will be treated as a separate asset and any fair and reasonable method of apportioning part of the total cost to it will be accepted e.g., a reasonable valuation of that part at the acquisition date. Where the market value at 6 April 1965 or 31 March 1982, is to be taken as cost of acquisition a reasonable valuation of the part at that date will be accepted.[2]

The cost of the part disposed of will be deducted from the total cost of the estate (or from the balance) to determine the cost of the part retained. This avoids the total of the separate parts ever exceeding the whole. Thus in the above example, the total costs were £100,000. Of this, £40,000 was treated as the cost of the part disposed: the remaining £60,000 is carried forward as the cost of the retained interest.

The taxpayer can always require the general rule to be applied except in cases already settled on the alternative basis but if he does so it will normally be necessary to adhere to the choice for subsequent part disposals.

Where a small part of a holding is disposed of for £20,000 or less, such consideration being not more than 20% of the value of the whole holding, the taxpayer can elect to pay no capital gain on such a part disposal. This is effected by deducting the consideration from the acquisition costs. Thus, in the above example, if the value of the whole is taken to be £150,000 at the time of disposal, a disposal of part at £20,000 would be less than 20% of the whole. No tax would arise, but the acqusition cost of the retained land would be £100,000 − £20,000 = £80,000.

(i) The market value rule on certain disposals

In a normal case the actual sale price will be treated as the consideration received on disposal. On certain occasions, however, the Act provides for a deemed sale at market value at the date of disposal. This rule on market value operates in the case of gifts. It also applies in the case of other dipositions not by bargain at arms length, such as transfers between closely related or associated persons. The rule applies to both transferor and transferee so that if X gives a property to his son worth £10,000, he will be deemed to have sold for that sum and will be assessed for capital gains tax accordingly.

---

[2] This alternative basis is an extra-statutory concession introduced by the Inland Revenue.

The son can then adopt £10,000 as his cost of acquisition on a subsequent disposition. Market value is the price which the asset might reasonably be expected to fetch on a sale in the open market.

(j) *Assets owned on 6 April, 1965*

Capital gains tax is designed to tax any increase in value accruing since 6 April, 1965. Where assets disposed of were acquired before this base date, it is necessary to ascertain the amount of any gain or loss which is attributable to the period since 6 April, 1965.

The normal rule is one of time apportionment. Any gain is deemed to have accrued at a uniform rate from the date of acquisition to the date of disposal. Where the date of acquisition was before 6 April, 1945, it will be deemed to have been acquired at that date.

Thus if an asset was purchaed on 6 April, 1957, for £3,000 and twenty four years later, on 6 April, 1981, is sold for £93,000, the total gain is £90,000 but the chargeable gain would be that proportion of the whole gain accruing in the sixteen years from 6 April, 1965, that is 16 years since 6 April 1965 out of 24 years since 6 April 1955, being 2/3 of £90,000 = £60,000. The Act provides a formula to be applied to the overall gain $T/P + T$ where T = period from April 1965 to time of disposal and P = period from time of purchase to 6 April 1965. Where an asset was purchased before 6 April 1945 it is treated as having been purchased at that date (but at the price actually paid) so that the maximum value of $P = 20$.

The owner may elect for an alternative basis of computation, in which case he would be treated as having sold and re-purchased the asset on 6 April 1965, at market value. The chargeable gain is then the excess of the disposal price over that figure. He would elect for the basis if it would produce a lesser gain or a greater loss. The election must be made within two years of the date of disposal and cannot be revoked.

Valuers are frequently called upon to make valuations as at 6 April, 1965. This has obvious problems: in many cases imagination is required by the valuer to put himself back

to this date. Regard must be had to the circumstances then
obtaining. Thus a cottage may be sold in say 1981 with vacant
possession but in April 1965 it may have been worth only
a fraction of the vacant possession value particularly if it
was then occupied by a protected tenant. Where appropriate
the tenant's possible bid in April 1965 may be taken into
account. Similarly land may be sold in 1981 with planning
consent but in April 1965 no permission would have been
granted. In this case the possibility of obtaining consent on
appeal or in the future may take effect to give "hope value".

If the disposal price of land includes development value
so that the price obtained exceeds current use value, broadly
value ignoring development value, the time apportionment
basis is not applicable and the gain must be calculated by
reference to the market value of the land on 6 April 1965.
Special provisions in the Act deal with unfair results from
the operation of this rule. Thus, for example, the chargeable
gain must not exceed the actual gain made during the whole
period of ownership.

In practice taxpayers rarely elect for adopting market value
as at 1965 because the general rate of growth since 1965
greatly exceeds that before 1965. The time apportionment
approach thus gives a favourable result to the taxpayer.
Further, for disposals after 5 April 1988, the right to elect
to adopt market value as at 31 March 1982 as the acquisition
price will almost always give a yet more favourable result
so that time apportionment or valuations as at 1965 are likely
to become abandoned as methods of computation.

(k) Sale of Leasehold Interests

A long lease, that is a lease with more than 50 years unexpired, is not treated as a wasting asset and the whole of
the original acquisition cost and other expenditure can be
set against the consideration received on the sale of the lease.

A lease with 50 years or less to run, however, is treated
for capital gains tax purposes as a wasting asset and on the
sale of such an interest the whole of the acquisition cost
and other expenditure cannot be deducted. Instead, it is
deemed to waste away at a rate which is shown in a table
of percentages in paragraph 1 of Schedule 3 of the 1979 Act.

Only the residue of the expenditure which remains at the date of disposition can be set against the consideration received.

The table of percentages is derived from the Years Purchase 6 per cent Single Rate table, although as they are concerned with depreciation of a leasehold interest, a dual rate table would have been a more logical basis. The Y.P. for 50 years is taken to be 100. Thus against 40 years the figure is 95·457 and against 25 years, 81·100. This implies that the value of the lease with 40 years to run should be 95·457 per cent of its value when it had 50 years to run, and 81·100 per cent with 25 years to run. Similarly the value of the lease with 25 years to run should be 81·100/95·457 per cent of the value when it had 40 years to run. If, therefore, a lease having 40 years unexpired was purchased for £5,000 and sold for £8,000 when it had only 25 years to run, the whole of the expenditure of £5,000 would not be allowable, but only that part of it that has not notionally wasted away. In this case the lease should have wasted away to:

$$\frac{81 \cdot 100}{95 \cdot 457} \times £5,000 = £4,248$$

Thus the gain in the case is not £8,000 − £5,000 = £3,000 but £8,000 − £4,248 = £3,752.

The Act provides a formula for writing down acquisition costs whereby there is deducted P1 − P3/P1 from the costs where P1 = figure from the Table in Schedule 3 relating to years to run at time of purchase and P3 = figure from Table relating to years to run at time of sale.

It is suggested that a more convenient approach is to multiply the acquisition cost by P3/P1.

If a lease which has more than fifty years to run is purchased, the appropriate percentage at acquisition will be 100 and it will commence to be a wasting asset when it has less than fifty years unexpired.

Where an election is made to adopt market value at 6 April 1965 or 31 March 1982, it should be remembered that this is a (deemed) acquisition cost which is also subject to writing down by applying P3/P1.

(*l*) *Premiums for Leases Granted out of Freeholds or Long Leases*

The receipt of a premium on the grant of a lease is treated as a part disposal of the larger interest out of which the lease is granted. Against the premium may be set the appropriate part of the price paid for the larger interest and any other allowable expenditure as determined by the formula applicable to part disposals.[3]

Where a lease for a period of fifty years or less is granted at a premium a part, at least, of the premium will be liable for income taxation under Schedule A.[4] To avoid double taxation the part of a premium for a lease which is thus chargeable to income tax is excluded from liability to capital gains tax. This necessitates a modification to the normal formula applicable to ascertain allowable expenditure.

Example 23–4

X purchased a freehold shop for £50,000 (inclusive of costs) in 1977. In 1988, he grants a 25-year lease at £6,000 per annum net, taking a premium of £75,000.

Step 1. Calculate the amount taxable under Schedule A.
The amount taxable is the whole premium less 2 per cent of the premium for each complete year of the term except the first year. Hence:

Whole premium	£75,000
Less 2 (25 − 1)% of £75,000	36,000
Part subject to Sch. A	£39,000

£39,000 is excluded from any capital gains tax liability, leaving £36,000 as the amount of premium on which to base capital gains tax.

Step 2. Allowable expenditure is then to be considered in accordance with the part disposal formula[5] but there

---

[3] See section (h) of this Chapter.
[4] See Part 3 of this Chapter.
[5] See section (h) of this Chapter.

is to be excluded from the consideration in the numerator of the fraction (but not in the denominator) that part of the premium taxable under Schedule A.

The application of the formula involves a valuation of the interest retained, which includes the capitalised value of the rent reserved under the lease:

Rent reserved	£6,000	
Y.P. 25 years at 6%	12·78	76,680
Reversion to estimated full rental value (net)	£12,000	
Y.P. perp, deferred 25 years at 6%	3·88	46,560 £123,240
Value of Retained Interest	say	£123,000

Using the modified part disposal formula, the chargeable gain is

$$£36,000 - \left\{ £50,000 \times \frac{£36,000}{£75,000 + £123,000} \right\}$$

$$= £36,000 - £9,090$$
$$= \text{Chargeable gain } £26,910 \text{ (subject to indexation)}.$$

(*m*) *Premiums for Sub-leases Granted out of Short Leases*

As the larger interest is a wasting asset, the normal part disposal formula does not apply. Only that part of the expenditure on the larger interest that will waste away over the period of the sub-lease in accordance with the table of percentages[6] can be set against the premium received.

Thus if a person acquired a 40 years lease for £5,000 and when the lease had 30 years to run, he granted a sublease for 7 years at the head lease rent, taking a premium of £6,000, the following percentages from the table are required:

40 years 95·457 (percentage when interest acquired);
30 years 87·330 (percentage on grant of sub-lease);
23 years 78·055 (percentage on expiration of sub-lease).

---

[6] See section (k) of this Chapter.

The percentage for the 7 years of sub-lease is therefore 9·275 and the expenditure which is allowable against the premium of £6,000 is

$$£5,000 \times \frac{9 \cdot 275}{95 \cdot 457} = £486$$

The capital gain is therefore £6,000 − £486 = £5,514.

(*N.B.*–The allowable expenditure has to be written down if the sub-lease rent is higher than the head lease rent.)

In this case $2(7-1)\% = 12$ per cent of the premium is not taxable leaving £5,280 liable to income tax under Schedule A. The method of avoiding double taxation is different in this case. The amount of the premium chargeable to income tax is deducted from the capital gain of £5,514 and only the balance of £5,514 − £5,280 = £234, is subject to capital gains tax.

2. Inheritance Tax

(a) General

The Finance Act 1975 repealed the long established provisions for taxing the value of a deceased's estate at death by the imposition of estate duty. The Act replaced estate duty with a new tax, Capital Transfer Tax. The provisions relating to this tax were incorporated in the Capital Transfer Tax Act 1984. The Finance Act 1986 abolished capital transfer tax and replaced it with Inheritance Tax. Since many of the features of inheritance tax are the same as capital transfer tax, the 1984 Act was renamed the Inheritance Tax Act 1984.

(b) Taxable Transfers

Inheritance Tax (IHT) applies when there is a transfer of value. This will arise where a person makes a gift in his lifetime or his estate passes in its entirety on his death. A gift may be an absolute gift, whereby an asset is passed to another without any charge, or where an asset is sold to another at an "under value" by which is meant the sale price is deliberately low so as to confer an element of gift in the price—there is an intention to confer a gratuitous benefit.

(c) Basis of Assessment

Since IHT relates to the transfer of value, the value on which the tax is assessed is not the value of the asset itself but the diminution in the value of the donor's estate caused by the transfer. This will commonly be the same figure as the value but not necessarily so. For example, suppose that a person owns a home which is vacant and which he lets to his son at a nominal rent of £100 p.a. for 20 years. The grant of the lease at a low rent—under value—is a gift to his son. The value of the house before the gift, with vacant possession, is say £30,000, but after the gift when subject to the lease is say £8,000. The value of the lease is say £12,000. Although the subject of the gift, the lease, is worth £12,000, he has actually made a transfer of value of £30,000 (pregift) − £8,000 (post-gift) = £22,000 which will be subject to IHT.

Sums which may be set against the transfer of value are any incidental costs incurred in making the transfer and any capital gains tax payable on the gift. Note that it is the capital gains tax itself and not the whole gain so that there is an element of double taxation.

Since it is the transfer of value which is to be taxed it is important to establish who is paying the tax as IHT may be paid by the donor or donee in the case of a lifetime gift. If the donee pays, then the IHT is assessed on the value transferred. If for example, the value transferred were £12,000 and the tax rate was 40 per cent, the donee would pay 40 per cent of £12,000 = £4,800. On the other hand if the donor pays, the transfer value is not only the asset but also the IHT payable out of the estate. Hence it is necessary to gross up the value transferred before determining the tax so that the grossed up value less IHT equals the value transferred. Following the above example, where the value transferred is £12,000, this is grossed up by

$$\frac{100}{100 - 40} \times 12,000 = £20,000$$

Thus IHT at 40 per cent of £20,000 = £8,000, leaving £12,000 as the value transferred.

(d) Rates of Tax

The rates of tax depend on whether the transfer is made on death, or during life with special rules if made within seven years before death. In the case of lifetime gifts the rates of tax are half the death rates. Prior to 1988 there were several rates of tax on bands of value, the rates and bands changing yearly. The Finance Act 1988 introduced a greatly simplified system whereby the first £110,000 of value are exempt from IHT, a rate of 40% being the rate on all value in excess of this sum.

(e) Exemptions and Reliefs

i. General. There are several exemptions and reliefs of a general nature such as exemptions for transfers between husband and wife, certain gifts to charities, lifetime gifts up to £2,000 per annum, and wedding gifts up to £5,000.

ii. Potentially Exempt Transfers. Where a gift is made by an individual to another individual or into certain trusts, no IHT liability will arise if the donor lives for seven years after making the gift. In such cases the gift is an exempt transfer. However, if the donor dies within 7 years IHT becomes payable although there is tapering relief whereby a proportion only of the tax is charged. The tapering relief is:—

Years between Gift and Death	% age of full IHT payable
0—3	100
3—4	80
4—5	60
5—6	40
6—7	20

IHT is charged at the rate of tax applicable at the time of

death but on the value at the time of making the gift. Thus if an asset was given to another individual in June 1984 with a value of £100,000 and the donor dies in September 1988 when the asset has a value of £150,000, the IHT liability will be 60% of 40% of £100,000.

iii. Business Assets. Where a person owns a business as the sole proprietor, or otherwise has a controlling interest (husband and wife being treated as one), on the transfer of any business assets the transfer value is reduced by 50 per cent; or 30 per cent where the transferor has a minority shareholding, or the interest is in property used by a controlled company or a partnership.

iv. Agricultural Property. Where a person occupies property for agricultural purposes and is engaged in agriculture—the "working farmer"—he is entitled to relief on any transfer of that property of 50 per cent of the agricultural value of the property. In the case of tenanted agricultural land the relief is 30 per cent of the agricultural value.

Agricultural value is the value assuming it will always be used for agricultural purposes, so any value attributable to non-agricultural use is ignored, particularly development value or hope value. Hence assume 10 acres of agricultural land were given by a farmer to his son which had a possibility of residential development. The residential value is £1,000,000 but the value as farmland is £20,000. The residential value would be taken into account in arriving at the transfer value but the relief would be 50 per cent of £20,000. Similarly when farm cottages are the subject of the transfer, the agricultural value is determined by assuming that they could only be occupied by farm workers, and so ignoring any enhanced value if they were to be sold as say "weekend cottages".

v. Woodlands. Where on death the deceased's estate includes woodlands, an election may be made to exclude the value of the timber from the value of the estate. Thus no IHT will be payable on the value of the timber at that time. If there is a subsequent disposal or transfer of the timber in the new owner's lifetime then IHT becomes payable at the deceased's marginal rate of IHT on the disposal proceeds. If the new owner retains the timber to his death, then no

IHT will be payable on the original owner's estate at death in respect of the timber.

In determining the value of the deceased's estate where this relief is claimed, the value of the land on which the woodlands grow is included at what is often termed "prairie value". Since it is land covered with trees the value will be relatively low.

Where a person owns and runs woodlands as a commercial enterprise the business relief referred to above may be claimed.

(f) Valuation

The general principle for determining the value of a person's estate the subject of a transfer is to assume a sale at market value being the price which might reasonably be expected to be fetched if sold in the open market at the time of the transfer. No reduction is to be made because such a sale would have "flooded the market". Further it is to be assumed that the assets would be sold to achieve the best price, which means that if a higher overall price would be achieved by selling parts rather than as a single lot, then it is to be assumed that the sale would follow that approach.[7]

3. INCOME TAX ON PROPERTY—SCHEDULE A

Income tax is charged under Schedule A of the Income and Corporation Taxes Act 1988, on income from rents and certain other receipts from property after deductions have been made for allowable expenses.

A former charge to tax under Schedule A had been abolished in 1963. It related to the payment of income tax on annual value arising from the ownership of landed property. Liability to income tax now only arises from the receipt of income from property, so that the value of beneficial occupation to owner-occupiers or to occupying lessees enjoying a profit rent is not now subject to tax, as it was at one time.

Liability under Schedule A extends to rent under leases of land and certain other receipts such as rentcharges. Pre-

7 *Duke of Buccleuch* v. *I.R. Comrs.* (1967) I A.C. 506.

miums receivable on the grant of a lease for a term not exceeding fifty years are also subject to taxation under Schedule A. The amount of the premium taxable is the whole premium less 2 per cent for each complete year of the lease, except for the first year.[8]

Deductions from the gross rents receivable may be made in respect of allowable expenses incurred including cost of maintenance, repairs, insurance, management, services, rates and any rent payable to a superior landlord. Items of a capital nature, such as expenditure on improvements, additions or alterations, cannot be deducted except for writing down allowances of the cost of certain specific categories. These include expenditure on such items as the provision or improvement of agricultural or industrial buildings and the provision of certain plant and machinery. These allowances generally take the form of annual allowances such as 4% of the cost of industrial or agricultural buildings, and 25% of plant and machinery on a reducing cost basis. A deduction may also be made if a premium has been paid to a superior landlord in consideration for the grant of a lease for a term not exceeding fifty years.

Rents receivable from furnished lettings are similarly chargeable to income tax on the gross rents less allowable expenses. The whole of the rent will be charged under Case VI of Schedule D but the landlord may elect for the profit arising from the property itself to be assessed under Schedule A, the profit from the furniture continuing to be assessed under Case VI. A writing-down allowance may be claimed in respect of furniture and any other items provided. As an alternative to this, the taxpayer may choose to deduct the expenses of renewing these items.

---

[8] See Part 1(l) of this Chapter for Capital Gains Tax provisions concerning premiums.

CHAPTER 24

Compensation Under the Town and Country Planning Acts—I. Compensation Governed by the "Unexpended Balance"

THE MODERN law on this subject is in its essentials a direct survival from the immediate post-war period when the Town and Country Planning Act 1947 was passed. Despite many changes, therefore, the law today can only be properly understood in its historical context, which must be described briefly by way of introduction.

1. LOSS OF DEVELOPMENT VALUE: THE 1947 ACT

Under the system of planning control instituted by the Town and Country Planning Act 1932, any owner whose property was depreciated in value by the coming into operation of a town planning scheme or by the doing of work under it was—subject to a number of important exceptions—entitled to compensation, which might include loss suffered by restrictions on development imposed during the interim period. Compensation was also payable in respect of a number of other matters connected with the coming into operation or enforcing of schemes.

On the other hand, the responsible authority were entitled to recover 75 per cent of any increase in value due to an operative town planning scheme. But, owing to the very small number of schemes actually in operation and to the difficulty of determining what increases in value were directly attributable to a scheme, this provision for the recovery of "betterment" was, in practice, a dead letter.

The Town and Country Planning Act 1947 dealt with this "compensation-betterment problem", as it is often called, on entirely different lines. An outline of the Act is given in Chapter 15, but certain of its financial provisions require re-examination at this stage. The guiding principle of the

515

Act was that, as from 1 July, 1948, all "development values" in land should be under the control of, although not actually vested in, the State, and that, as a consequence, transactions in land should in future take place on a basis of "existing use value" only.

The Act sought to achieve this by means of provisions to the following effect:—

(i) Whenever planning permission was refused, or granted subject to conditions then—unless the proposed development came within Part 2 of the Third Schedule of the 1947 Act—no compensation was payable for any consequent loss of development value to the owner.

(ii) Whenever permission to develop was granted, then—with certain exceptions, including development within the scope of the Third Schedule or covered by the Development Charge Exemptions Regulations 1948—a "development charge" was levied equal to 100 per cent of any increase in value due to that permission.

This charge was based on the amount by which:—

(a) the value of the land with permission to carry out the proposed works or change of use ("consent value") exceeded

(b) the value of the land without that permission ("refusal value").

Both (a) and (b) were valuations of the fee simple in possession of the land, irrespective of the interest held by the particular developer. If permission was given for a limited period only, the charge was adjusted accordingly.

(iii) Whenever land was acquired compulsorily or by agreement, under statutory powers, the basis of compensation was (with a few exceptions) the "existing use value" of the owner's interest—i.e., its market value assuming that planning permission would only be given for those forms of development listed in the Third Schedule to the 1947 Act.

Like development value accruing subsequently, development value *existing at 1 July, 1948*, would be lost to the owner in consequence of these provisions; but in respect of it an owner was entitled to submit a once-for-all claim under Part VI of the Act based on the difference between (a) the value of his interest in the land if restricted to existing use value only ("Restricted Value"), and (b) the value his interest would have had if the Act had not been passed ("Unrestricted Value"). Both valuations were based on prices current immediately before 7 January, 1947. Such claims were to have been met out of the "£300 million Fund" established under the Act and already referred to in Chapter 15.

The above financial provisions of the 1947 Act were substantially amended by the Town and Country Planning Acts of 1953 and 1954.

The Act of 1953 abandoned the attempt to collect increases in value due to the grant of planning permission by abolishing the levying of Development Charge as from 18 November, 1952.

The Act also suspended the distribution of the "£300 million Fund" established under the 1947 Act—which was due to take place in July, 1953—leaving it to the Town and Country Planning Act 1954, to introduce new provisions on the subject of compensation for loss of development value.

The guiding principles underlying these provisions of the Town and Country Planning Act 1954, were:—

(i) that there should not be any general requirement for compensating an owner for loss of development value of land in consequence of adverse planning decisions since 1 July, 1948;

(ii) but that compensation should be payable (a) in certain circumstances specified in the 1954 Act, subject to a maximum figure attributable to development value existing at 1 July, 1948, which was the subject of an established "Part VI Claim" under the 1947 Act, and (b) in certain other circumstances specified in the 1954 Act without being subject to that maximum figure.

Until 1 January, 1955, the right to secure any payment dependent upon a Part VI claim was known under the Act as a "claim holding" and was a purely personal right.

On and after 1 January, 1955, the value of any "claim holding" (or holdings) still existing in respect of any property was converted into a figure of "original unexpended balance of established development value" which thereafter has been treated as attached to the land itself and is not the personal property of any one owner.

There were three distinct classes of case in which payments were provided for under the Town and Country Planning Act 1954, subject to a maximum amount attributable to development value existing at 1 July, 1948 and covered by a "Part VI claim":—

(1) Cases where, before 1 January, 1955, transactions in land were based on the 1947 Act principle that development values were vested in the State, subject to owners' claims on the £300 million Fund.

Payments in these cases were made under Parts I and V of the Act and were limited by the value of the "claim holding".

They are now so much a matter of history that it is not proposed to make any further reference to them. Should the reader require further details they can be found on pages 289–291 of the Fifth Edition of this book.

(2) Cases where, on or after 1 January, 1955, planning permission should be refused or granted subject to conditions. Payments in these cases are now made under Part VII of the Town and Country Planning Act 1971, and are still limited by the amount of the "unexpended balance" attached to the land. They are considered in detail below.

(3) Cases where, on or after 1 January, 1955, land should be acquired or injuriously affected under the exercise of statutory powers.

Up to October, 1958, payments in class (3) were made under Part III of the 1954 Act and were also limited by the amount of the "unexpended balance". They are now a matter of history. As from 30 October, 1958—under the provisions of the Town and Country Planning Act 1959, later incorporated in the Land Compensation Act 1961—compensation in these cases has been based on the value of the land in the open market and no payment has been made in respect of any "unexpended balance" (see Chapter 27).

Cases in which compensation was to be payable without

being limited by reference to a "Part VI claim" are examined in the next Chapter.

To sum up, the effect of the Act of 1947 was broadly to deprive landowners of the substance of development value—the excess of "unrestricted" over "restricted" value—and leave them "existing" or "current" use value; the effect of the subsequent legislation was broadly to restore "unrestricted" value in cases where planning permissions were granted but not—except to the limited extent that compensation was made available—in cases where they were refused (or granted only subject to burdensome conditions).

2. Claims under Part VI of the 1947 Act

(*a*) *Basis of the Claim*. Unlike the case of valuation for determining development charge, the valuer was concerned here with a particular interest in land—e.g. that of a freeholder, lessee or sub-lessee.

The claimant might choose the unit of land to which his claim related—e.g. his claim might relate to the whole of a particular piece of land in which he had an interest, or part only.

The basis of claim was the amount by which the "restricted value" of the claimant's interest in the land on 1 July, 1948, was less than its "unrestricted value". The difference between those two figures was the "development value" for loss of which *in 1948* the owner was claiming.

Restricted Value meant the market value of the interest in land on the assumption that planning permission would be granted for development of any class specified in the Third Schedule to the Act, but would not be granted for any other development.

Unrestricted Value meant the market value of the owner's interest in the land on the assumption the Act had not been passed and that development therefore continued to be permissible in accordance with pre-existing law.

The general tendency of the provisions of the Act regarding (i) planning control, (ii) development charges, and (iii) compensation for compulsory purchase, was to reduce the market price of land broadly to its existing use value. But in

calculating "unrestricted value" the valuer had to assume
that these provisions did not exist and that the land could
be valued with the benefit of all potential development, subject only to such statutory or other restrictions as existed
prior to the coming into operation of the Act. The latter
would, in general, include any restrictions imposed under
the Town and Country Planning Acts 1932 and 1943, or under
the Restriction of Ribbon Development Act 1935.

The two principal rules governing the calculation of both
"restricted" and "unrestricted" values were as follows:—

(i) Subject to the statutory assumptions referred to above,
     the value of the claimant's interest was the price it
     might be expected to realise if sold in the open market
     by a willing seller—value to one particular purchaser[1]
     and value due to illegal or unhealthy user to be
     ignored.
(ii) Except in certain special cases, the interest was to be
     valued as it existed on 1 July, 1948, subject to all inci-
     dents, restrictive covenants, easements, public or
     other rights affecting it at that date. But the valuation
     was to be made by reference to prices current immedia-
     tely before 7 January, 1947.

(*b*) *Exclusion of Small Claims.* No claim for loss of development value could be entertained unless the development
value, averaged over the land, exceeded £20 per acre and
also exceeded one-tenth of the restricted value.

(*c*) *Making and Determination of Claims.* Claims for loss
of development value under Part VI of the 1947 Act had
to be made to the Central Land Board by 30 June, 1949.

After a claim had been made, the Central Land Board
(acting in practice through the Land Valuation Department
of the Inland Revenue) considered the claim and eventually
served a notice on the claimant stating what they considered
to be the "development value" and the amounts of the
"unrestricted" and "restricted" values.

---

[1] In December 1950, however, the Chancellor of the Exchequer authorised the
Central Land Board to take this factor into account in assessing claims in respect
of land suitable for the extension of existing buildings. This was legalised by the
1954 Act (section 1 and First Schedule, para. 10).

The claimant might object, stating the grounds of his objection and specifying the amounts which in his opinion should be substituted. The Board then considered the objection and finally determined the "development value" (and the "unrestricted" and "restricted" values).

If the claimant disputed the amount of the claim as finally determined by the Board, he might appeal to the Lands Tribunal.

A Part VI claim agreed with the Central Land Board or determined by the Lands Tribunal, in default of agreement, was known under the 1954 Act as an "established claim".

(*d*) *Person Entitled to Claim.* The right to a Part VI claim vested in the person who was the owner of the particular interest on 1 July, 1948. But that right could be transferred by operation of law (e.g. on death) or by assignment, which had to be notified to the Central Land Board.

(*e*) *Exemptions.* No claim could be made for loss of development value in the case of land certified by the Minister of Town and Country Planning as "ripe for development" under Section 80 of the 1947 Act, because such a certificate would also exempt the land from liability to the development charge—i.e. the imminence of its development made it expedient to treat such land as if it had been developed already. Nor—subject to certain conditions specified in Sections 82–85—could any such claim be made in respect of lands of local authorities, statutory undertakings or charitable trusts, there being a corresponding exemption from development charge in these cases also.

(*f*) *Example.* The following example illustrates the lines on which a Part VI claim might be made. The facts stated are those assumed to exist at 1 July, 1948, related to 1947 prices.

Example 24–1

A rectangular area of land of 2 acres has a frontage of 400 ft, depth 220 ft. At the rear is a field of 5 acres. The whole was used for agricultural purposes on 1 July, 1948. In 1947, it is estimated that the value of the front land was £10 per foot frontage and that it would be four years before it could be developed due to licensing restrictions. The value of the 5 acres for building purposes was £500 per acre. As agricultural land the holding was worth £50 per acre.

The valuation for loss of development value would be:—

Unrestricted Value:—

Agricultural value, say	£14 p.a.	
Y.P. 4 years at 4%	3·63	£51

360 ft (allow 40 ft for access road to land at rear) at £10 per ft	£3,600	
5 acres at £500 per acre	£2,500	
	£6,100	
P.V. £1 in 4 years at 5%	0·81	£4,941
		£4,992

Restricted Value:

7 acres at £50 per acre	£350
Development Value, say	£4,640

Note.—In this case the same period of deferment is taken for the back land as for the front land, the difference in value being due to the development costs.

(g) *Special Payments in Respect of War-damaged Land.*

These were authorised by a scheme prepared by the Treasury under Section 59 of the 1947 Act and known as the Planning Payments (War Damage) Scheme, 1949.

They are now a matter of history and it is not proposed to make any further reference to them. Details can be found, if required, on pages 286 and 287 of the Fifth Edition of this book.

3. "ESTABLISHED CLAIMS" AND "CLAIM HOLDINGS" (PARTS I AND IV OF 1954 ACT)

Under the 1954 Act the term "established claim" meant a claim for loss of development value which was agreed with the Central Land Board, or determined by the Lands Tribunal under Part VI of the 1947 Act; while the "benefit of an established claim" meant the prospective right to a payment in respect of that claim.

In some cases, however, the "benefit of an established claim" might have become split up between two or more persons since the time when the claim was originally agreed or determined. The 1954 Act therefore used the following expressions in relation to rights existing in respect of an established claim during the period 1 July, 1948, to 31 December, 1954:—

"Claim holding" = "benefit of an established claim".

"Area of claim holding" = the land which forms the subject of the claim holding.

"Value of the claim holding" = the whole or part of the original claim of which the "claim holder" has the benefit.

Example 24–2

X was the owner-occupier of the area of freehold land ABCD shown below. In 1948 X submitted a "Part VI claim" which was agreed at £1,200

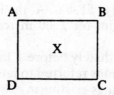

Provided no rights under the claim were assigned, until 1 January 1955, X was the "holder" of a "claim holding" the area of which was ABCD and the value of which—subject to the possible deductions referred to later—was £1,200.

Supposing, however, that in March, 1951, X sold his freehold interest in part of the land EBCF to Y, together with such part of the established claim as was reasonably apportionable to it (say £500). Then the position under the 1954

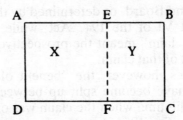

Act from that date up to 1 January, 1955, would have been as follows:—

> X would be the "holder" of a "claim holding" whose "area" was AEFD and whose value was £1,200—£500 = £700.
>
> Y would be the "holder" of a "claim holding" whose area was EBCF and whose value was £500.

Example 24–2

"Greenacre" was a large house standing in about 3 acres of land, 2 acres of which could profitably be developed by the erection of six smaller houses.

In 1948 B, who held the property on a long-term lease, submitted a "Part VI claim" in respect of his leasehold interest which was agreed at £1,400. A, the freeholder, succeeded in establishing a claim for £300 in respect of the freehold reversion.

In this case, immediately before 1 January, 1955—subject to any of the deductions referred to later—there would have been two claim holdings existing in respect of Greenacre:—

  (i) A's "claim holding"—value £300
  (ii) B's "claim holding"—value £1,400

each of which would at that stage have been the personal property of the particular "claim holder".

There were a number of cases under the 1954 Act in which the value of a claim holding might be reduced or extinguished altogether. These are now so much a matter of history that it is not thought necessary to refer to them in detail.

4. UNEXPENDED BALANCE OF ESTABLISHED DEVELOPMENT VALUE

(Sections 17 and 18 of the 1954 Act, now re-enacted in Sections 135–145 of the Town and Country Planning Act 1971.)

Broadly speaking, what is known under these Acts as the "original unexpended balance of established development value" in relation to any particular piece of land consists of eight-sevenths of the value of any claim holding, or holdings, subsisting in that land immediately after 1 January, 1955. The additional one-seventh corresponds roughly to interest at $3\frac{1}{2}$ per cent for the period 1948–55, less tax at the standard rate; this is capital and not interest: *Re Hasluck, Sully v. Duffin* [1957] 1 WLR 1135; [1957] 3 All E.R. 371.

Example 24–4

ABCD is the area of a single claim holding subsisting at 1 January. 1955, whose value was £1,400.

The "original unexpended balance of established development value" attaching to the land as from 1 January, 1955, would be:—

$$1,400 \times \text{eight-sevenths} = £1,600$$

Example 24–5

Taking the same area of land as in *Example 24–4* assume that X the freeholder had a claim holding of £800 and Y the lessee had a claim holding of £1,300, both in respect of the whole area ABCD.

Then the "original unexpended balance of established

development value" attaching to ABCD as from 1 January, 1955, would be:—

$$(£800 + £1,300)\ £2,100 \times \text{eight-sevenths} = \underline{£2,400}$$

It must again be emphasised at this point that, whereas the "claim holding" was a species of intangible personal property ("chose in action") belonging to the "claim holder", the original unexpended balance of established development value is not the subject of separate ownership. It is, in effect, a notional fund attached to the land. Until it is exhausted, it enables any persons now or hereafter entitled to an interest in the land, irrespective of whether or not they themselves made a Part VI claim in 1948–9, to obtain compensation from the Secretary of State, under the provisions of the 1971 Act, in respect of future planning restrictions.

It will be clear from this that, since the "unexpended balance" is there to be used up until exhausted, it is a wasting asset, whereas losses in development value which it exists to compensate may succeed one another indefinitely. One obvious result of this is that the compensation payable to any one owner out of this notional common fund affects all other owners with interests in the same land. It also follows that whenever an occasion for compensation under the Act arises in the future it will be necessary to determine the amount of the "unexpended balance" existing at that particular date.

This may be the "original" unexpended balance—e.g., the £1,600 or £2,400 in *Examples 24–4* and *5*—or it may be that figure less any compensation paid on previous occasions, since 1 January, 1955, to one or more persons interested in the land.

Because the "unexpended balance" exists to compensate owners for being deprived of development value, it must be taken as being used up not only if compensation is paid but also if an owner obtains the same asset in alternative form, namely as actual land value, which of course happens if and when a planning permission is eventually granted and market demand is such that development value accrues as a result. A further deduction may therefore have to be made from the "unexpended balance" for the value—at the date when the unexpended balance has to be calculated—of any "new development" for which planning permission has been given.

"New development" is defined in Section 22(5) of the Act of 1971 as being any development outside the limited group of categories in what is now Schedule 8 to the Act of 1971 (formerly the Third Schedule to the Acts of 1947 and 1962), being development involving no substantial departure from the existing use of the land in question. For instance, if in (say) 1980, "new" development was carried out on Blackacre and later, in (say) January, 1988, permission for further development was refused, it would be necessary, in finding the unexpended balance available for compensation at the later date, to deduct the value of this previous new development. This value will be assessed as at January, 1988—not at 1980 when the development was initiated.

Under Section 141 and Schedule 16 of the 1971 Act, the value of the new development has to be calculated on the assumption that:—

(a) the development has not been carried out and the land has remained in the state in which it was immediately before the development was initiated[2] (except that if the development involved clearing the site, the state of the land before development means the site after it had been cleared but before development had begun) and

(b) the development could lawfully be carried out (apart from the 1947, 1962 and 1971 Acts) at the time when the value of the development is being calculated.

The "value of the development"—i.e., the sum to be deducted from the unexpended balance—will be the amount by which in these circumstances:—

---

[2] New development shall be taken to be initiated:—

(a) if the development consists of the carrying out of operations, at the time when these operations are begun;

(b) if the development consists of a change in use, at the time when the new use is instituted;

(c) if the development consists both of the carrying out of operations and of a change of use, at the earlier of the times aforesaid. (1971 Act, Section 290(5)).

(a) the value of the land with unconditional permission
    for the new development (or subject to any conditions
    which were in fact imposed) granted immediately
    before the valuation date, would have exceeded
(b) its value if permission had been refused immediately
    before that date, and it could be assumed that per-
    mission for that and any other "new development"
    would be refused on a subsequent application.

It would appear from the wording of the Act that the two
valuations are to be based, not on the interest in the land
of the particular developer, but that of an assumed freeholder
in possession.

If the development was initiated subject to a condition
expressed by reference to a specified period (e.g., a consent
for a limited term) then in the calculation of the value of
the development, the conditions to be assumed attaching
to the planning permission are deemed to include a like
requirement for the same duration (beginning at the valuation date) as the period originally specified.

The value of the development has to be found by reference
to prices current at the date of the valuation which—as has
already been noted—may be several years after the time
when the development was initiated.

If the development, the value of which has to be calculated,
was not completed at the time when the value has to be
ascertained, the calculation is to be made by construing references to permission for the development as references to
permission for so much of the development as has been completed at the date of the calculation.

As in other cases under the Act "value" is to be estimated
on the basis of the price which the land might be expected
to realise if sold in the open market by a willing seller. Value
attributable to illegal or unhealthy user is to be disregarded;
but for the purpose of Schedule 16, value to one particular
purchaser or value attributable solely to the statutory powers
of a particular authority may be taken into account.[3]

If "new development" is carried out partly on land having
an unexpended balance and partly on other land, it will be

---

[3] See section 163 of the 1971 Act

necessary for purposes of deduction, to estimate what proportion of the value of the development can properly be
attributed to the land with the unexpended balance.

Example 24–6

A is the freeholder of 4 acres of land about a mile from the
centre of a town of 50,000 inhabitants. The land was used
for grazing until December, 1982, when planning permission
was granted for its use as a caravan site for a term of 10 years.

A claim under Section 58 of the Town and Country Planning Act 1947 was submitted and agreed: Unrestricted Value
£2,000: Restricted Value £250.

On obtaining planning permission, A let the land to B
on a 10 year lease at a rent of £3,000 per annum with provision
for upward only review after 5 years, lessee paying all outgoings. On review in 1987 the rent was increased to £4,000
per annum.

In 1989 planning permission for residential development
was refused and it is required to find the amount of the unexpended balance at that time.

Original unexpended balance of established development
value:—

Claim under Section 58 Town and Country Planning Act 1947		£1,750
Add one-seventh		250
Original unexpended balance		£2,000
Less value of new development in 1989:—		
Value of land in 1989 with 10 year permission for use as caravan site;		
Rental value, say	£4,500 p.a.	
Y.P. 10 years at 10%	6·145	
		£27,653
Reversion to value as grazing land in 1999, say	£15,000	
P.V. £1 in 10 years at 10%	0·386	5,790
		£33,443

Less value of land in 1989 had
the above permission been
refused   £15,000   £18,443

*Amount of Unexpended Balance of Established
Development Value in 1989*   NIL

It has already been noted that when compensation
becomes payable on some future occasion under the Act—
e.g., an adverse planning decision—the effect will be to
reduce or extinguish the unexpended balance on the land.
If the particular act or decision affects only part of the land,
the unexpended balance on the whole will have been apportioned, and compensation will only be payable out of such
part of the balance as is properly attributable to the land
affected.[4]

Apart from occasions arising under the Act, it may be
desirable to know whether or not land, which is perhaps
the subject of some private transaction, has an unexpended
balance attaching to it, since this may have a bearing on
market value. Information on this point was formerly obtainable from the Central Land Board in the form of a certificate
under Section 48 of the 1954 Act.

The Central Land Board was dissolved as from 1 April,
1959, and the information is now obtainable from the Department of the Environment.[5] The certificate is only bound
to show the original balance attaching to the land, together
with a statement of what was taken to be the state of the
land on 1 July, 1948. But the Secretary of State may, at
his discretion, include additional information as to acts or
events which may result in a deduction from this figure. Failing such information, the applicant must ascertain such facts
or events for himself and work out the appropriate deductions
to arrive at the current figure of unexpended balance.

If "new development" has been carried out, it will in any
case be impossible to arrive at a precise figure of unexpended

[4] See section 144(2) of the 1971 Act.
[5] See now section 145 of the 1971 Act.

balance by means of such a certificate because the appropriate deduction in respect of such development can only be calculated at the date of an occasion under the Act; until then—owing to the possibility of changing values—only the roughest of estimates can be made.

5. PLANNING DECISIONS REFUSING PERMISSION FOR "NEW" DEVELOPMENT

(*a*) *Generally*. The general effect of Part VII of the 1971 Act is that where planning permission is refused, or is granted subject to restrictive conditions, for "new development" on any land having an unexpended balance of development value then—subject to the important exceptions referred to later in this Chapter—compensation for any depreciation in value due to the decision will be payable by the Secretary of State up to the limit of the unexpended balance attached to the land affected.

If no part of the land affected has an "unexpended balance" there is no right to compensation. The owner's only possible remedy is the service of a purchase notice under Section 180 of the 1971 Act, but this cannot succeed unless the adverse planning decision renders the land incapable of reasonably beneficial use.

Where—as sometimes happens in practice—proposals for certain works, such as the construction of a service road by the would-be developer, are included in a planning application because the applicant has reason to think that without them he is unlikely to get planning permission for his proposed development, then, if permission is given and the Secretary of State certifies that he is satisfied that the work in question was only included in the application for the above reason, the applicant may get compensation as though the doing of that work had been one of the conditions of the grant of permission.[6]

It may conveniently be noted at this point that the right to compensation under Part VII of the 1971 Act is not

---

[6] Section 150 of the 1971 Act.

confined (as it is under Part VIII of the Act, which will be discussed in the next Chapter) to cases where the planning decision is given on a direct reference to the Secretary of State, or on appeal to him. It arises as soon as an adverse decision is given by the local planning authority—although, as will be noted later in this Chapter, the local planning authority's decision may subsequently be amended by the Secretary of State, with consequent reduction in the amount of compensation ultimately payable.

(*b*) *The Right to Compensation* (*Section* 146). To entitle a person to compensation under Part VII of the Act:—

> (i) he must own an interest in land to which the adverse planning decision relates, or in land which includes that land;
> (ii) the whole or part of the land affected by the decision must have an unexpended balance attached to it;
> (iii) the owner's interest in the land affected must be depreciated in value by the adverse decision.

But even if these conditions are satisfied, the right to compensation may be excluded under Sections 147 and 148 of the Act either on account of (i) the type of restriction or the reason for its imposition, or (ii) the fact that planning permission is available for certain other forms of development.

(*c*) *Exclusion of Compensation.* Under Section 147 no compensation is payable under Part VII of the Act in respect of the following types of adverse planning decisions:—

> (i) Refusal of permission for any development which consists of or includes the making of any material change in the use of buildings or other land[7]—for example,

---

[7] Under Section 290 of the 1971 Act, "use" in relation to land does not include the use of land by the carrying out of building or other operations thereon. For example, the erection of a dwelling-house on land formerly used as agricultural land, with planning permission to use it as a dwelling-house when erected, is development comprising both a building operation and a change of use.

refusal of permission to carry out alterations for the purpose of converting a dwelling-house into offices.

(ii) Any decision in regard to the display of advertisements.

(iii) Imposition of conditions in respect of the following matters:—

(a) the number or disposition of buildings on the land;

(b) the dimensions, design, structure or external appearance of any building or the materials to be used in its construction;

(c) the manner in which any land is to be laid out for the purposes of the development, including the provision of parking, loading and fuelling facilities on the land;

(d) the use of any buildings or other land;

(e) the location or design of any " means of access to a highway",[8] or materials to be used in construction;

(f) the winning and working of minerals;

(iv) Refusal of permission on the grounds that the development is "premature" having regard to (a) the order of priority (if any) for development indicated in the development plan for the area, (b) any existing deficiency in the provision of water supplies or sewerage services and the period within which any such deficiency may reasonably be expected to be made good.

But if seven years have elapsed since the last application, the development cannot again be held to be "premature" on the same grounds.

(v) Refusal of permission on the grounds that the land is unsuitable for the proposed development because of its liability to flooding or subsidence.

Note:—If permission to develop land is granted subject to a condition prohibiting development of a specified part

---

[8] This phrase does not include a service road.

of the land, this must be treated as a decision refusing permission as respects that part. (Section 147(6).)

So that if permission were given to erect houses on a particular estate provided no building was done on two acres of the land which were liable to flooding, this would amount to a refusal of permission in respect of the two acres but, under (v) above, would not entitle the owner to compensation.

Under Section 148, compensation for refusal of planning permission is also excluded if, immediately before the Secretary of State gives notice of his findings in respect of the claim, there is a grant of, or undertaking by him to grant, planning permission for some alternative form of "development of a residential, commercial or industrial character, being development which consists wholly or mainly of the construction of houses, flats, shops or office premises, or industrial buildings (including warehouses) or any combination thereof". For example, no compensation would be payable for refusal by the local planning authority of planning permission to erect a garage on a particular piece of land, if the Secretary of State were to grant, or undertake to grant, planning permission for the erection of shops on the site, either unconditionally or subject to such conditions as are referred to in (iii) (a)–(c) above.

(*d*) *Procedure in Making Claims (Sections* 38, 154 *and* 155). A claim for compensation under Part VII of the Act must be made within six months of the date of the planning decision which gives rise to it, or within such extended time as the Secretary of State may allow in any particular case.

The procedure is governed by the Town and Country Planning (Compensation and Certificates) Regulations 1974.

The claim is made to the local planning authority who must forward it to the Secretary of State together with the information required by the Regulations.

The Secretary of State may notify the claimant that, in his opinion, no compensation is payable. But, except where a claim is withdrawn, he must give notice of the claim to every other person who appears to have an interest in the land to which the planning decision relates.

Except where claims are withdrawn, the Secretary of State

may review any planning decision giving rise to a claim and may substitute a decision "more favourable"[9] to the claimant, or may give permission for some other form of development. But before making such a direction he must give the local planning authority and the claimant or claimants an opportunity of being heard.

It follows that, although a party may have what may be called a prima facie right to compensation when the local planning authority gives the adverse planning decision, the actual compensation (if any) to which he may be entitled will be determined having regard to any direction given by the Secretary on his review of that decision.

(*e*) *Amount of Compensation (Sections* 152 *and* 153). For the purpose of these sections land which has an unexpended balance of development value, is referred to as "qualified land".

Broadly speaking, the amount of compensation payable will be either

  (i) the depreciation in the value of the claimant's interest, so far as it subsists in "qualified land",

or

  (ii) the amount of the unexpended balance—whichever is the less.

Since the amount of the unexpended balance is derived from values in 1947/8, it is almost always found in practice, due to the increase in values during the last three decades, that compensation is (ii) above.

Example 24–7

A parcel of 20 acres of land lies on the edge of a suburb of a town. The land forms part of a farm and has an

---

[9] More favourable" means:—
  (a) in relation to a refusal of permission—a decision granting permission either unconditionally or subject to conditions, and either as respects the whole or part of the land; and
  (b) in relation to a grant of permission subject to conditions—a decision granting the permission applied for unconditionally or subject to less stringent conditions.

unexpended balance of established development value of £16,000. The most profitable development for the land today would be by the erection of dwelling-houses at a density of 10 houses per acre but the land lies within the "green belt".

The owner has applied to the local planning authority for permission to develop the land by erecting 200 houses, but permission has been refused. The value today with the benefit of the planning permission applied for would be £250,000 per acre and the value now, after the refusal, is £2,000 per acre. It is required to assess the compensation payable under Part VII of the Town and Country Planning Act 1971.

Compensation

The amount of compensation payable is the lesser of:—

(i) The depreciation in the value of the freeholder's interest:—

(a)	Value had permission been granted—	
	20 acres at £250,000 per acre	£5,000,000
less (b)	Value taking account of the refusal—	
	20 acres at £2,000 per acre	£40,000
		£4,960,000

or (ii) The unexpended balance of established development value:—	£16,000
Compensation	£16,000

If there is more than one claimant with an interest in the "qualified land" and the aggregate of the claims does not exceed the "unexpended balance" on the land, then each party will receive as compensation the depreciation in the value of his interest. But if the aggregate of the claims exceeds the "unexpended balance", then the latter—which is the limit of compensation payable—must be divided between the claimants in proportion to the depreciation in the value of their respective interests.

Example 24–8

A's interest in the land affected by an adverse planning decision is depreciated to the extent of £700. The depreciation in the value of B's interest is £300. The "unexpended balance" on the land is £800. The compensation payable to the parties under Part VII of the Act will be:—

$$\text{A} \quad £800 \times \frac{700}{1,000} = £560$$

$$\text{B} \quad £800 \times \frac{300}{1,000} = £240$$

Note:—Special rules[10] prescribed by Section 152 have to be applied where:—

(i) part of the land affected by a planning decision is not "qualified land"—i.e., land which has an unexpended balance;

and/or

(ii) one or more interests in the land affected relate to part only of that land.

The depreciation in the value of the claimant's interest will be taken to be the amount by which:—

(i) the value of the claimant's interest at the time of the "relevant decision", and taking into account the effect of that decision, is less than

(ii) the value it would have had if the decision had been to the contrary effect—i.e., if it had been granted instead of refused, or if it had been granted subject only to the type of conditions already referred to, which do not attract compensation.

"Value" is to be determined in accordance with Rules 2 to 4 of Section 5 of the Land Compensation Act 1961.

In making the calculation, regard must be had to any grant of, or undertaking to grant, planning permission made after

---

[10]For a detailed explanation of these rules see Lawrance and White's "A Guide to the Town and Country Planning Act 1954" (Estates Gazette) at pp. 67–68.

the decision giving rise to the claim and in force immediately
before the Secretary of State gives notice of his findings on
the claim. It must also be assumed that (apart from such
grant or undertaking to grant permission) planning permission after the date of the "relevant decision" would only
be given for Schedule 8 development.[11]

(*f*) *Apportionment and Registration* (*Section* 158). If the
compensation exceeds £20 and it appears practicable to the
Secretary of State to do so, he must apportion the amount
of the compensation between different parts of the land to
which the claim relates according to the way in which he
thinks those parts are differently affected by the decision.

Details of any compensation exceeding £20 (together with
any apportionment) are registered with the local authority
in the register of local land charges and are known as "compensation notices".

(*g*) *Determination of Claims* (*Section* 39). Under the Town
and Country Planning (Compensation and Certificates)
Regulations 1974, notice of the Secretary of State's findings
as to the compensation payable to any claimant must be given
(i) to the claimant himself and (ii) to all other claimants
in respect of the same planning decision. Each of the parties
concerned will therefore know the amount of the compensation proposed to be awarded to any other party interested
in the land affected.

Details of any apportionment will appear in the Secretary
of State's findings and must be given not only to the claimants
but also to any other person whose interest in the land may
be materially affected.

There is a right to appeal to the Lands Tribunal against
the Secretary of State's findings or against any apportionment
of the compensation over the land affected.

(*h*) *Effect of Payment of Compensation on Unexpended
Balance* (Section 140(1)). The amount of any compensation
payable under Part VII will be deducted from the amount
of the unexpended balance when next it becomes necessary
to determine the amount (if any) of the balance still attaching
to the land.

---

[11] Schedule 8 as modified by Schedule 18—see next Chapter.

6. Repayment of Compensation on Subsequent Development

When a "compensation notice" is registered in respect of land, no "new development" of the types specified below may be carried out on that land until an appropriate sum in respect of that compensation has been repaid to the Secretary of State or secured to his satisfaction (Sections 159–160). The repayment may take the form of a lump sum, or a series of instalments of capital and interest, or a series of other annual or periodic payments at the discretion of the Secretary of State.

"New development" is (it must be remembered) development other than that covered by Schedule 8 of the 1971 Act, and the types of "new development" which may involve repayment of compensation are:—

  (i) development of a residential, commercial or industrial character;

 (ii) the winning and working of minerals; or

(iii) development whose probable value is such that in the opinion of the Secretary of State the provision as to repayment ought to apply.

But where, in the opinion of the Secretary of State development is likely to be discouraged by the obligation to repay compensation, he has discretion to remit the whole or part of any sum which would otherwise be recoverable.

Also, where compensation was paid on account of planning permission being given subject to conditions, no question of repayment will arise when development is carried out in accordance with those conditions.

If the area on which "new development" is to be carried out—known as "the development area"—is the same as, or includes, the whole of the land comprised in the "compensation notice", the whole of the sum specified in the notice will be recoverable. If "the development area" comprises or includes part only of the land comprised in the "compensation notice", the amount recoverable will be an appropriate part of the sum specified in the notice.

What is "an appropriate part" in the latter case will depend on whether or not the Secretary of State's decision on compensation included an apportionment. If there is no apportionment, the compensation is assumed to be distributed rateably over the whole area—e.g., if a quarter of the area is to be developed, a quarter of the compensation will be repayable. If there is an apportionment, then the amount repayable will depend on the sums allocated by the apportionment to the part or parts of the area to be developed.

Once compensation has been repaid under these provisions, no further sum will be repayable in respect of further development at a later date, with the possible exception of those cases where the Secretary of State has previously remitted part of the sum repayable.

Where compensation has been repaid and it subsequently becomes necessary to determine the unexpended balance (if any) attached to the land, no deduction will be made in respect of so much of the original payment of compensation as was attributable to that land, since this has, in effect, been cancelled out.

The effect of the above provisions on value is that a prospective purchaser of land for development purposes will inquire as to the existence of any "compensation notice" and that the price he will be prepared to pay will, theoretically, be influenced by the liability for repayment which he is likely to incur under it. However, the sum involved is likely to be insignificant when measured against present day values.

The recovery by the Secretary of State of any compensation money due to be repaid depends on the registration of the "compensation notice" as a local land charge, as stated above. This is because the land may have changed hands in the meantime, and the new owner is entitled to be made aware of the liability. If he or his solicitor makes the customary search of the local land charges register, in due form, and the registry fails to disclose the "compensation notice", the new owner is not liable to repay the money. If asked he should refuse to do so; the Secretary of State will then have his remedy in damages by bringing an action in tort for negligence against the local authority responsible for the registry (*Ministry of Housing and Local Government v. Sharp* (1970)). On no account should the owner repay the money to the Secretary of State on demand and himself sue the local authority, because his loss will then be his own fault (*Stock v. Wanstead and Woodford Borough Council* (1962)).

CHAPTER 25

Compensation Under the Town and Country Planning Acts—II Compensation Payable as of Right

1. GENERAL PRINCIPLES

UNLIKE the compensation for planning restrictions discussed in the previous Chapter, the compensation discussed in this Chapter is not dependent on the existence of any "unexpended balance" relating to the land. Where the conditions precedent to the payment of planning compensation in these cases are met—that is to say where the particular kinds of compensatable loss are established—compensation may be claimed "as of right". It is perhaps not too much to say that the kinds of adverse planning decision referred to in the pervious chapter occur frequently in practice and the kinds referred to in this chapter do not.

Compensation which depends on the existence of an "unexpended balance" is dealt with in Part VII of the Town and Country Planning Act 1971; but compensation claimable "as of right" is dealt with in Part VIII, except for compensation in respect of (i) pedestrian precinct orders under Section 212 (in Part X of the Act which deals with highways) and (ii) ancient monuments under the Ancient Monuments and Archaeological Areas Act 1979 Part I (Sections 7–9). And whereas the compensation dependent on an "unexpended balance" is payable by the Secretary of State, who is responsible for those balances, any compensation claimable "as of right" is (except in the case of ancient monuments) payable instead by local planning authorities.

The varieties of compensation "as of right" can be grouped as follows. First, there is compensation payable on a refusal (or restrictive grant) of planning permission, in those cases where the development prevented is not "new development" as discussed in the previous chapter but is contained within

544 Modern Methods of Valuation

the relatively narrow limits of Schedule 8 to the 1971 Act
(as modified). Second, there is the compensation payable
on revocation (or modification) of permission already
granted for *any* kind of development; and since this will,
in fact, usually comprise "new development" there are special rules whereby the Secretary of State may voluntarily
contribute any element relating to the "unexpended balance"
to the overall amount claimable as of right from the local
planning authority (there are also provisions for the *repayment* of compensation when "new development" is subsequently undertaken). Third, there is compensation payable
when a discontinuance order is served putting an end to authorised uses of (or works on) land. Fourth, there is a group
of miscellaneous cases of compensatable planning restrictions
concerning trees, special buildings, long-established advertisements, stop notices, pedestrian precincts and ancient
monuments.

2. DECISIONS RESTRICTING SCHEDULE 8 DEVELOPMENT
(Secs. 169, 178 and 179—Town and Country Planning Act 1971)

Section 169 of the 1971 Act provides that where, on appeal
from a local planning authority's decision, or, on reference
of the application to him, the Secretary of State refuses permission for any type of development specified in Part II of
Schedule 8 to the 1971 Act, or grants it subject to restrictions,
any owner of the land whose interest is depreciated in value
in consequence may claim compensation from the local planning authority, provided he does so within six months.

Schedule 8 is to be construed subject to modifications contained in Section 278 and Schedule 18 (derived from the Town
and Country Planning Act 1963) and in Subsection 6A
inserted into Section 169 by the Town and Country Planning
(Compensation) Act 1985.

The basis of compensation will be in effect the difference
between:

  (i) the value of the interest if permission had been uncon-
      ditionally granted, and

(ii) its value subject to the refusal of planning permission or its grant subject to conditions, as the case may be.

The valuation will be made in accordance with rules contained in Section 5 of the Land Compensation Act 1961, ignoring any mortgage to which the interest may be subject.

In making the valuation it is to be assumed that any similar application in the future would be treated in the same way; but regard must be had to any alternative development for which the Secretary of State may have undertaken to grant permission. An example of this type of case is given later in this Chapter.

Where the Secretary of State grants planning permission subject to conditions, he may, in effect, direct that no compensation shall be payable in respect of any such conditions regulating the design, external appearance, size or height of buildings if, having regard to local circumstances, he considers it reasonable to do so.

No compensation is payable where the refusal or the restrictions relate to the two types of development specified in Part I of Schedule 8—i.e., rebuilding, or the use as two or more dwelling-houses of a building previously used as a single dwelling-house—although the value of such development will be included in the compensation payable if the property should be compulsorily purchased.

The general purpose of Schedule 8 is to indicate a range of categories of prospective development which do not involve any substantial departure from, or can be regarded as marginal to, the existing or previous use of particular land. The prospective development value which they add to the strict existing use value of land is regarded as if (in general terms) it is value to which the landowner is entitled whereas the development value attributable to the prospect of development outside the categories of Schedule 8 is value to which he is regarded as not being absolutely entitled (though he may often secure it in fact).

This distinction was made in the Act of 1947. The value of prospective development within Schedule 8 (it was then the Third Schedule) is broadly conceded to owners on the footing that (i) they can normally expect to obtain planning permission for such development but (ii) if, untypically, they are denied such permission they will be fully compensated therefor. The compensation may in some cases be obtained directly as planning compensation applied for after an adverse planning decision, and may in any case be obtained indirectly, by inclusion within compensation for compulsory purchase.

The Act of 1947 drew a distinction within the Third Schedule. The first two categories of development within the Schedule were placed within Part I, and the remaining six were placed within Part II. Development value within Part II, if denied to an owner, was to be (and is) compensatable in the form of either planning compensation or compulsory purchase compensation, according to circumstances. But development value within Part I, if so denied, was not to be compensatable in the form of planning compensation; therefore an owner denied such value by an adverse planning decision could (and can) only realise it in the form of compulsory purchase compensation. If no authority intends to purchase the land compulsorily the owner can serve a purchase notice on the local authority; but this will only succeed if the land has been rendered "incapable of reasonably beneficial use".

These principles are still the law. The categories of development within what is now Schedule 8 to the 1971 Act have never had any official description; but in practice they are often (paradoxically) called "existing use development". Development going beyond them has since 1954 been termed "new development".

In the cases in which restrictions on Schedule 8 development give rise to planning compensation, i.e. development within Part II of the Schedule, the relevant section of the 1971 Act is 169 (discussed above).

Schedule 8 is set out as follows exactly as stated in the 1971 Act; but it is modified by Sections 169(6A) and 278 and Schedule 18 of that Act in terms which will be set out subsequently.

SCHEDULE 8

Development not Constituting New Development

PART I

Development not ranking for compensation under section 169.

1. The carrying out of any of the following works, that is to say—

 (a) the rebuilding, as often as occasion may require, of any building which was in existence on the appointed day, or of any building which was in existence before that day but was destroyed or demolished after the seventh day of January, nineteen hundred and thirty-seven, including the making good of war damage sustained by any such building;

 (b) the rebuilding, as often as occasion may require, of any building erected after the appointed day which was in existence at a material date;

 (c) the carrying out of works for the maintenance, improvement or other alteration of any building, being works which affect only the interior of the building or which do not materially affect the external appearance of the building and (in either case) are works for making good war damage,

so long as (in the case of works falling within any of the preceding sub-paragraphs) the cubic content of the original building is not exceeded—

 (i) in the case of a dwelling-house, by more than one-tenth or seventeen hundred and fifty cubic feet, whichever is the greater, and

 (ii) in any other case, by more than one-tenth.

2. The use as two or more separate dwelling-houses of any building which at a material date was used as a single dwelling-house.

PART II

Development ranking for compensation under section 169.

3. The enlargement, improvement or other alteration, as often as occasion may require, of any such building as is mentioned in sub-paragraph (a) or sub-paragraph (b) of paragraph 1 of this Schedule, or any building substituted for such a building by the carrying out of any such operations as are mentioned in that paragraph, so long as the cubic content of the original building is not increased or exceeded—

 (a) in the case of a dwelling-house, by more than one-tenth or seventeen hundred and fifty cubic feet, whichever is the greater, and

 (b) in any other case, by more than one-tenth.

4. The carrying out, on land which was used for the purposes of agriculture or forestry at a material date, of any building or other operations required for purposes of that use, other than operations for the erection, enlargement, improvement or alteration of dwelling-houses or of buildings used for the purposes of market gardens, nursery grounds or timber yards or for other purposes not connected with general farming operations or with the cultivation or felling of trees.

5. The winning and working, on land held or occupied with land used for the purposes of agriculture, of any minerals reasonably required for the purposes of that use, including the fertilisation of the land so used and the maintenance, improvement or alteration of buildings or works thereon which are occupied or used for those purposes.

6. In the case of a building or other land which, at a material date, was used for a purpose falling within any general class specified in the Town and Country Planning (Use Classes for Third Schedule Purposes) Order, 1948, or which, having

been unoccupied on and at all times since the appointed day, was last used (otherwise than before the seventh day of January nineteen hundred and thirty-seven) for any such purpose, the use of that building or land for any other purpose falling within the same general class.

7. In the case of any building or other land which, at a material date, was in occupation of a person by whom it was used as to part only for a particular purpose, the use for that purpose of any additional part of the building or land not exceeding one-tenth of the cubic content of the part of the building used for that purpose on the appointed day, or on the day thereafter when the building began to be so used, or, as the case may be, one-tenth of the area of the land so used on that day.

8. The deposit of waste material or refuse in connection with the working of minerals, on any land comprised in a site which at a material date was being used for that purpose, so far as may be reasonably required in connection with the working of those materials.

PART III

Supplementary provisions.

9. Any reference in this Schedule to the cubic content of a building shall be construed as ascertained by external measurement.

10. Where, after the appointed day, any buildings or works have been erected or constructed, or any use of land has been instituted, and any condition imposed under Part III of this Act, limiting the period for which those buildings or works may be retained, or that use may be continued, has effect in relation thereto, this Schedule shall not operate except as respects the period specified in that condition.

11. For the purposes of paragraph 3 of this Schedule—

  (a) the erection, on land within the curtilage of any such buildings as is mentioned in that paragraph, of an additional building to be used in connection with the original building shall be treated as the enlargement of the original building; and

  (b) where any two or more buildings comprised in the same curtilage are used as one unit for the purposes of any institution or undertaking, the reference in that paragraph to the cubic content of the original building shall be construed as a reference to the aggregate cubic content of those buildings.

12. In this Schedule "at a material date" means at either of the following dates, that is to say:

  (a) the appointed day, and

  (b) the date by reference to which this Schedule falls to be applied in the particular case in question;

Provided that sub-paragraph (b) of this paragraph shall not apply in relation to any buildings, works or use of land in respect of which, whether before or after the date mentioned in that sub-paragraph, an enforcement notice served before that date has become or becomes effective.

13. (1) In relation to a building erected after the appointed day, being a building resulting from the carrying out of any such works as are described in paragraph 1 of this Schedule, any reference in this Schedule to the original building is a reference to the building in relation to which those works were carried out and not to the building resulting from the carrying out of those works.

(2) This paragraph has effect subject to Section 278(4) of this Act [which states that it does not affect the meaning of "new development"].

It is important to note that, although Schedule 8 re-enacts in detail the Third Schedule to the Act of 1947, this is nevertheless subject to an important modification as to time. The original Third Schedule classes were applicable by reference to the "appointed day", namely 1 July, 1948, and not later. But by the Town and Country Planning Act 1954 they were made of continuing application; and this remains the law under Schedule 8 to the 1971 Act. The wording "at a material date" (i.e., when the Schedule is being currently applied) achieves this effect. It was the problems to which this change gave rise (for example, extending the "ten per cent tolerances" indiscriminately to buildings put up later than 1 July, 1948) that prompted the passing of the Town and Country Planning Act 1963, in which the complex provisions now contained in Section 278 and Schedule 18 of the 1971 Act (described below) first made their appearance.

The modifications to which Schedule 8 is subjected are as follows. Section 169(6A) states:—

"For the purposes of subsection (1) of this section paragraph 3 of Schedule 8 to this Act shall be construed as not extending to the enlargement of a building which was in existence on the appointed day if—

(a) the building contains two or more separate dwellings divided horizontally from each other or from some other part of the building; and

(b) the enlargement would result in either an increase in the number of such dwellings contained in the building or an increase of more than one-tenth in the cubic content of any such dwelling contained in the building." [inserted by Section 1(2) of the Town and Country Planning (Compensation) Act 1985].

Section 278(2) states:—

"In the application of the said Schedule 8 . . .

(a) paragraph 3 of that Schedule shall be construed as not extending to works involving any increase in the cubic content of a building erected after the appointed day (including any building resulting from the carrying out of such works as are described in paragraph 1 of that Schedule); and

(b) paragraph 7 of that Schedule shall not apply to any such building".

This means that the "ten per cent tolerances" (in terms of cubic content) which are applied to development by way of (a) alteration to a building, and (b) extension of use within a building, no longer benefit any building erected later than 1 July, 1948. Thus the prospect of altering a building and increasing its cubic content by up to ten per cent, or of extending an existing use of part of a building by up to ten per cent of the cubic content of that part, continues to be development within Schedule 8 provided that the building was built on or before 1 July, 1948; but it will not be such development if the building was built later; and compensation rights will fall to be determined accordingly. But even if the building was built on or before 1 July, 1948 the prospective development will nevertheless still not be within Schedule 8 if the requirement as to gross floor space in Schedule 18 (about to be discussed) is not complied with. Tolerances applicable to blocks of flats built before 1 July 1948 are subjected to the further restriction that no additions can be envisaged to the number of flats in such a block, and that the 10 per cent cube limit applies not only to the block as a whole but also to each separate flat in it.

Section 278(1) of the 1971 Act restricts the scope of Schedule 8 still further, as follows:

"In any case where the value or depreciation in value of an interest in land falls to be determined on the assumption that planning permission would be granted for development of any class specified in Schedule 8 to this Act, it shall be further assumed, as regards development of any class specified in paragraph 1 or 3 of that Schedule, that such permission would be granted subject to the condition set out in Schedule 18 to this Act."

The condition set out in Schedule 18 provides as follows:

Schedule 18

Condition Treated as Applicable to Rebuilding and Alterations

1. Where the building to be rebuilt or altered is the original building, the amount of gross floor space in the building as rebuilt or altered which may be used for any purpose shall not exceed 10 per cent of the amount of gross floor space which was last used for that purpose in the original building.
2. Where the building to be rebuilt or altered is not the original building the amount of gross floor space in the building as rebuilt or altered which may be used for any purpose shall not exceed the amount of gross floor space which was last used for that purpose in the building before the rebuilding or alteration.
3. In determining under this Schedule the purpose for which floor space was last used in any building, no account shall be taken of any use in respect of which an effective enforcement notice has been or could be served or, in the case of a use which has been discontinued, could have been served immediately before the discontinuance.
4. For the purposes of this Schedule gross floor space shall be ascertained by external measurement; and where different parts of buildings are used for difference purposes, floor space common to those purposes shall be apportioned rateably.
5. In relation to a building erected after the appointed day, being a building resulting from the carrying out of any such works as are described in paragraph 1 of Schedule

8 to this Act, any reference in this Schedule to the original building is a reference to the building in relation to which those works were carried out and not to the building resulting from the carrying out of those works.

The meaning of the term "original building" is not altogether clear in this Schedule; but the implication appears to be that any building dating back to 1 July 1948 is to be regarded as "original", whereas any building built later than 1 July, 1948 is "original" only if it is substantially a building on a virgin site and not one resulting from works for rebuilding a previous building on the same site. This being so, it follows that, in consequence of Schedule 18, the prospect of rebuilding or altering a building in such a way as to increase its floor space for any use by up to ten per cent can be development within Schedule 8 provided that the building is or was "original", i.e., not erected later than 1 July 1948 as a rebuilding of a previous building on the same site. It will not be within Schedule 8 if the building was in fact erected in those circumstances; and compensation rights will fall to be determined accordingly. But even if the building is or was "original" the prospective development will nevertheless still be outside Schedule 8 if the limits on increasing the cubic content (discussed above) are not complied with.

It is to be noted that paragraphs 3 and 7 of Schedule 8 (except insofar as the latter refers solely to land) can only apply to a building currently in existence. But paragraph 1 (rebuilding) can apply not only to a building currently in existence but also to a building which has ceased to exist, provided that its destruction or demolition occurred later than 7 January, 1937.

3. REVOCATION OR MODIFICATION OF PLANNING PERMISSION

(Sections 45, 164, 168, 178 and 179—Town and Country Planning Act 1971)

Under Section 45 of the 1971 Act a local planning authority may, by means of an order confirmed by the Secretary of State, revoke or modify a planning permission already given provided they do so:

(a) before building or other operations authorised by the permission have been completed, in which case work already done will not be affected by the order,
or
(b) before any change of use authorised by the permission has taken place.

Notice of the proposed Order must be given to the owner and occupier of the land affected and to any other person who, in the opinion of the local planning authority will be affected by the Order. Any such person is entitled to object to the Order and to be heard by a person appointed by the Secretary of State.

In the event of the Order being confirmed, Section 164 of the 1971 Act provides for the payment by the local planning authority of compensation under the following heads:

(i) expenditure on work which is rendered abortive by the revocation or modification—including the cost of preparing plans in connection with such work or other similar matters preparatory thereto.

But no compensation will be paid in respect of work done before the grant of the relevant planning permission—e.g., in anticipation of such permission being granted.

(ii) Any other loss or damage directly attributable to the revocation or modification.

No compensation of this kind was payable under the 1947 Act for depreciation in the value of land unless either (a) a development charge had been paid, or (b) the land was exempt from the charge under Part VIII of that Act.

But where the order for revocation or modification is made on or after 1 January, 1955, compensation for depreciation in the value of the claimant's interest in the land may be payable, under Section 164 of the 1971 Act, whether or not the original planning decision related to "new development" and irrespective of whether or not the land has an unexpended balance of development value.

In accordance with the provisions of Section 178 of the 1971 Act, compensation for depreciation in the value of an interest in land will be calculated on a market value basis as prescribed by Section 5 of the Land Compensation Act 1961, ignoring any mortgage to which the interest may be subject. The measure of compensation will be the amount by which the value of the claimant's interest with the benefit of the planning permission exceeded the value of that interest with the planning permission revoked or modified.

In calculating such depreciation it is to be assumed that planning permission would be granted for development within Schedule 8 of the Town and Country Planning Act 1971.

It follows from this that there will be a difficulty in the rare but conceivable type of case in which it is a planning permission for development within Schedule 8 itself which is revoked or modified. Since the assessment of compensation goes on the assumption that this is precisely what has *not* happened, the only available course is to re-apply for such permission, and then claim compensation under Section 169 (described earlier in this Chapter) on refusal. The difficulty here is that if the development for which permission is in this manner revoked and refused lies within Part I of Schedule 8 (e.g. converting a house into flats), as distinct from Part II, no planning compensation is payable, and consequently (in the absence of compulsory purchase, by purchase notice or otherwise) there can be no redress.

Section 165 of the 1971 Act applies the above provisions as to compensation where planning permission given by a Development Order is withdrawn—whether by revoking or amending the Order or by making a direction under it[1]— and, on an express planning application being then made, permission is refused or is granted subject to conditions other than those imposed by the Development Order. In cases where the Development Order is itself revoked or modified, the express planning application must be made within a year thereafter.[2]

Disputes as to the compensation payable under Sections

[1] For example a "direction" made by the Secretary of State or the local planning authority under Article 4 of the General Development Order 1977.

[2] Section 165(1A), inserted by the Town and Country Planning (Compensation) Act 1985, Section 1(1).

164 and 165—including any sum for depreciation in the value
of the land—are referable to the Lands Tribunal (Section
179(1)). Special provisions are laid down for compensation
in cases of revocation or modification of planning permission
for mineral development (see Sections 164A, 178A–C).

Revocation or modification of planning permission may
entitle the owner to serve a purchase notice under Part IX
of the Act.[3]

As in the case of claims under Part VII of the Act, provision
is made[4] for the apportionment of compensation for
depreciation in value exceeding £20 between different parts
of the land, where practicable, and for the registration of
the "compensation notice" as a land charge.

Also—as under Part VII of the Act—compensation so
registered will be repayable in whole or in part if permission
is subsequently given for "new development" on the whole
or part of the land affected by the revocation order, except
where the registered compensation was paid in respect of
a local planning authority's order modifying planning permission previously given and the subsequent development
is in accordance with that permission as modified.[5]

Where the circumstances are such that, had the original
planning decision been to the same effect as the order for
revocation or modification (i.e. an adverse decision), compensation would have been payable by the Secretary of State
under Part VII of the Act, the Secretary of State may pay
to the local planning authority a sum equal to such compensation as, in his opinion, would have been payable. Provided
that the amount of such contribution shall not exceed:

(a) the amount of compensation for depreciation paid by
    the local planning authority; or
(b) the amount of the unexpended balance at the date
    when the order for revocation or modification is
    made.[6]

Any sum so paid may be deducted from any unexpended

[3] Section 188. See Chapter 27.
[4] Section 166.
[5] Section 168—for meaning of "new development", see Chapter 25.
[6] Section 167.

balance attached to the land. But interested parties must be notified of the Secretary of State's intention to make such a payment and may object that no compensation would, in fact, have been payable under Part VII or that the amount of the compensation would have been less than the proposed contribution. There is a right of appeal on this point to the Lands Tribunal.[7]

4. INTERFERENCE WITH AUTHORISED USER OR WORKS: DISCONTINUANCE ORDERS

(Sections 51, 170 and 178—Town and Country Planning Act 1971)

By means of an order confirmed by the Secretary of State, a local planning authority may at any time require the discontinuance or modification of an authorised use of land (as in *Blow v Norfolk County Council* (1966), in which the authorised use of land as a caravan site was required to be discontinued) or the alteration or removal of authorised buildings or works.[8]

Any person who suffers loss in consequence of a discontinuance order, either through depreciation in the value of his land, or by disturbance, or by expense incurred in complying with the order, is entitled to compensation provided his claim is made within six months. An example of this type of case is given later in this Chapter. As an alternative to claiming compensation for depreciation in the value of his land, the owner of the interest may be able to serve a purchase notice (see Chapter 26). Special provisions apply to certain discontinuance orders relating to mineral development (see Sections 170 A–B, 178 A–C).

---

[7] Town and Country Planning (Compensation and Certificates) Regulations, 1974.

[8] Where, on the other hand, uses or works are "unauthorised", i.e., have been begun or carried out without the grant of planning permission or contrary to conditions attached to such permission, the local planning authority may proceed by means of an "enforcement notice" under Section 87 of the T. & C.P. Act 1971, so that no compensation is payable. On this, see Chapter 15.

5. Other Cases Under The 1971 Act

Compensation on account of planning requirements may also be payable in connection with the following matters under the 1971 Act:

  (i) Refusals, or restrictive grants of consents; or directions for replanting trees without financial assistance from the Forestry Commission under tree preservation orders (Sections 60 and 174–5).

 (ii) Protection of buildings of special interest by refusals, or restrictive grants, of "listed" building consents, or by building preservation notices, where such buildings are not "listed" (Part IV and Sections 171–3).

(iii) Cost of removal of advertisements in certain special and limited circumstances (Sections 63 and 176).

 (iv) Stop notices (Sections 90 and 177, as amended).

  (v) Pedestrian precinct orders (Section 212).

Compensation is payable in these cases, as in those mentioned earlier in this Chapter, by the local planning authority to whom application has to be made within six months of the official decision giving rise to the claim (twelve months for decisions made under tree preservation orders). Compensation is not, however payable for refusals of consent to demolish "listed buildings".

Refusals, or restrictive grants, of consent to alter "listed buildings", and the making of pedestrian precinct orders (insofar as they cause properties to lose vehicular access to highways), entitle owners to compensation for depreciation in value of the properties affected. (i) Tree preservation restrictions; (ii) pedestrian precinct orders; and (iii) stop notices and building preservation notices which fail (in effect) for lack of justification; all entitle persons affected by them to compensation for resultant "loss or damage", except where the refusal, or restrictive grant, of a consent under a tree preservation order is accompanied by a certificate (not quashed on appeal) that specific trees are to be preserved "in the interests of good forestry" or by reason of their "outstanding or special amenity value". In *Bell v, Canterbury City Council* (1988) 22 EG 86, the Court of Appeal held that "loss or damage" in relation to the refusal of consent to remove protected trees included not only the value of the timber but also the reduction in the existing use value of the land on which the trees stood. Compensation in respect of advertisements is payable only "in respect of any expenses reasonably incurred" in carrying out works (i) to remove advertisements, or (ii) to discontinue use of any site for advertising, dating back (in either case) to 1 August 1948.

6. Ancient Monuments

Part I of the Ancient Monuments and Archaeological Areas Act 1979 empowers the Secretary of State to make a "schedule of monuments" (rather on the lines of the list of buildings of special architectural or historic interest made under Section 54 of the 1971 Act) in order to protect ancient monuments. Consents are then required for carrying out works affecting ancient monuments and the Secretary of State must pay compensation to anyone who "incurs expenditure or otherwise sustains any loss or damage" in consequence of a refusal, or conditional or short-term grant, of consent by him (Sections 7–9).

7. Examples

Example 25–1

Claim for refusal to permit Schedule 8 (Part II) development (Section 2 of this Chapter).

A freehold factory is situated on the outskirts of a large town in an area predominantly residential. The buildings comprise a two-storey office block and a single-storey factory. The total internal floor space is 12,500 sq. ft. The total cubic content is 200,000 cu. ft. The premises were erected in 1935. At the side of the factory there is a plot of land between the factory and adjacent houses in the same road, with a frontage of 50 ft and a depth of 100 ft. Owing to the expansion of the business carried on, the premises have become very congested and the occupier has had plans prepared for the erection of a single-storey loading bay for packing, loading and unloading of goods. The building is to be erected on the vacant plot and will have a total floor space of 1,200 sq. ft and a cubic content of 18,000 cu. ft.

An application for planning consent has been refused by the planning authority on the grounds that the factory is a non-conforming use within a residential area and that no further expansion should be permitted.

On appeal to the Secretary of State, the refusal is confirmed. You are asked to advise on the claim that should be submitted under Section 169 of the Town and Country Planning Act 1971.

Calculation of Compensation:

The proposed extension is within the limits prescribed by Part II of Schedule 8 as modified by Section 278 and Schedule 18 of the 1971 Act, i.e. the addition to the cube and, presumably, the gross floor space is less than 10 per cent. Thus a Section 169 claim is justified.

As a result of an inspection it is considered that the new loading facilities will enhance the value of the property to an extent that if the development were carried out, the property might reasonably be valued at £20 per sq. ft whereas in the absence of these facilities the value would be £18 per sq. ft.

Value with extension:

	sq. ft		
Present area	12,500		
Extension	1,200		
Total area	13,700 at £20 per sq. ft		£274,000
Deduct cost of extension, say		£25,000	
Add for fees and contingencies and profits, say 25%		6,250	
			31,250
Value with permission			£242,750
Value at present without permission to develop	12,500 at £18 per sq. ft		225,000
Claim			£17,750

Example 25–2

Claim for discontinuance of an existing use—(Section 4 of this Chapter).

A factory has been established in its present building for many years. The building was constructed 50 years ago and the accommodation is on two floors, each of 3,000 sq. ft. There are no offices other than "works offices" and the site is fully covered.

The area is a residential one and is allocated for this use in the local plan. The local authority, following complaints about lorry traffic, smells and noise by local residents have ordered that it shall cease to be used for its present purpose.

It is required to assess the compensation payable under Section 170 of the Town and Country Planning Act 1971, in respect of the discontinuance of the authorised use. No other premises are available in this area.

The planning authority has indicated that consent would be given for the erection of a single dwelling-house on the site.

Calculation of Compensation

Value of premises as a factory		
Ground floor—3,000 sq. ft at £1·50 per sq. ft		£4,500 p.a.
First floor—3,000 sq. ft at £1·00 per sq. ft		£3,000 p.a.
Estimated net rental value		£7,500 p.a.
Y.P. in perpetuity		7
		£52,500
Value of site with planning consent to erect a single dwelling-house, say	£12,500	
Less: Cost of demolition of existing buildings, say	3,000	£9,500
Depreciation in value of freehold interest		£43,000

In addition, the freeholder would be entitled to claim for incidental losses due to "disturbance", such as are discussed in Chapter 29.

CHAPTER 26

Compensation Under the Town and Country Planning Acts—III. Purchase and Blight Notices

1. COMPULSORY PURCHASE INSTIGATED BY LAND OWNERS

AN ALTERNATIVE type of remedy provided for landowners who suffer from adverse planning decisions or proposals is afforded by the provisions of Part IX of the Town and Country Planning Act 1971 (as supplemented by later legislation). This involves procedures under which local authorities and other public bodies are, in certain circumstances, compelled to buy land affected by such decisions or proposals.

Planning compensation as described in the two previous Chapters is, of course, claimable only on the basis that the claimant retains the land in question and is reimbursed for depreciation or other loss relating to such land. But where a purchase or blight notice takes effect the land is transferred and not retained; in other words there is a compulsory purchase, and the compensation payable is, in fact, compulsory purchase compensation. This, of course, does not in principle prevent the claimant from receiving lost development value in terms of money, just as he does in planning compensation cases, but he will only do so to the extent that the principles of compulsory purchase compensation allow. There is in addition a special type of case in which compensation is payable even though a purchase notice is prevented from taking effect.

2. PURCHASE NOTICES

(Sections 180–191—Town and Country Planning Act 1971)

If, in any case, planning permission is refused, either by the local planning authority or by the Secretary of State,

561

or is granted subject to conditions, then if the owner[1] of
the land claims that it is incapable of reasonably beneficial
use:

  (i) in its existing state;
 (ii) if developed in accordance with conditions imposed
      (if any);
(iii) if developed in any other way for which permission
      has been, or is deemed to be, granted under the Act,
      or for which the Secretary of State or the local plan-
      ning authority have undertaken to grant permission;

he may, within twelve months[2] of the planning decision
in question, serve a "purchase notice" on the local authority
for the district, requiring them to purchase his interest in
the land.

The Council on whom a purchase notice is served shall,
within three months of such service, themselves serve a counter-notice on the owner to the effect either:

  (a) that they are willing to comply with the purchase
      notice; or
  (b) that another specified local authority, or statutory
      undertakers, have agreed to comply with it in their
      place; or
  (c) that, for reasons specified in the notice, neither the
      council nor any other local authority or statutory
      undertakers are willing to comply with the purchase
      notice, and that a copy of the purchase notice has been
      sent to the Secretary of State on a date specified in
      the counter-notice together with a statement of the
      reasons for their refusal to purchase.

In cases (a) and (b) above, the Council on whom the purchase notice was served, or the specified local authority or
statutory undertakers, as the case may be, will be deemed

---

[1] "Owner" means the person entitled to receive the rack rent of the land, or
who would be entitled to receive it if the land were so let—Section 290(1). (See
Corporation of London v. Cusack-Smith (1955)).
[2] Town and Country Planning General Regulations 1976, reg. 14.

to be authorised to acquire the owners' interest in the land and to have served a notice to treat on the date of the service of the counter-notice.

In case (c), where the purchase notice is forwarded to the Secretary of State, the following courses of action are open to him:

(i) to confirm the notice, if satisfied that the land is in fact incapable of reasonably beneficial use in the circumstances specified in Section 180;[3]

(ii) to confirm the notice but to substitute another local authority or statutory undertaker;

(iii) not to confirm the notice but to grant permission for the required development or to revoke or amend any conditions imposed;

(iv) not to confirm the notice but to direct that permission shall be given for some other form of development;

(v) to refuse to confirm the notice, or to take any action, if satisfied that the land has not in fact been rendered incapable of reasonably beneficial use.

"Reasonably beneficial use" is to be judged in relation to the present use of the land.

In considering whether or not the use of any land is "reasonably beneficial" the Secretary of State must not take account of the possibility of any development outside those types specified in Schedule 8 to the 1971 Act.[4]

"Incapable of reasonably beneficial use" signifies that the land in question must be virtually useless and not merely less useful, because practically any planning restriction will

---

[3] But even in this case the Secretary of State is not obliged to confirm under certain special circumstances relating to land, forming part of a larger area, which has a restricted amenity use by virtue of a previous planning permission—Town and Country Planning Act 1971 Section 184. Thus, if planning permission is given to build houses on a field, subject to a condition that for amenity reasons trees are to be planted along the road frontage, the developers cannot after building and selling the houses claim that the road frontage land which they retain is "incapable of reasonably beneficial use" so as to justify serving a purchase notice (for the previous law, see *Adams & Wade v. Minister of Housing and Local Government* (1965)).

[4] As modified by Section 278 and Schedule 18 (see Chapter 25).

result in land being less useful (*R. v. Minister of Housing and Local Government, ex parte Chichester R.D.C.* (1960)).

Before taking any of the steps enumerated above—including refusal to confirm—the Secretary of State must give notice of his proposed action to the person who served the purchase notice, the local authority on whom it was served, the local planning authority and any other local authority or statutory undertaker, who may have been substituted for the authority on whom the notice was served. He must also give such person or bodies an opportunity of the hearing if they so desire. If after such hearing it appears to the Secretary of State to be expedient to take some action under the Section other than that specified in his notice he may do so without any further hearing.

If the Secretary of State confirms the purchase notice, or fails to take any action within six months, the local authority on whom it was served will be deemed to be authorised to acquire the land compulsorily and to have served a notice to treat on such date as the Secretary of State may direct, or at the end of the period of six months as the case may be. The notice to treat is deemed to be authorised as if the acquiring authority required the land "for planning purposes" under Part VI of the 1971 Act.

Any party aggrieved by the decision of the Secretary of State on the purchase notice may, within six weeks, make an application to the High Court to quash the decision on the grounds that either (i) the decision is not within the powers of the Town and Country Planning Act 1971, or (ii) the interests of the applicant have been substantially prejudiced by a failure to comply with any relevant requirements.

If the Secretary of State's decision is quashed, the purchase notice is treated as cancelled; but the owner may serve a further purchase notice within six months.

Where a purchase notice takes effect—i.e., the authority are deemed to have served a notice to treat—the compensation payable to the owner will be assessed, as in any case of compulsory acquisition, under the provisions of the Land Compensation Act 1961. (See Chapter 27.)

Where the Secretary of State does not confirm the purchase notice but directs instead that permission shall be given for some alternative development, then if the value of the land for such alternative development is less than its "existing use value"[5] the owner is entitled to compensation equal to the difference between the two values (Section 187). But this is subject to any direction by the Secretary of State excluding compensation in respect of any conditions as to design, external apperance, size or height of buildings, or number of buildings to the acre.

Example 26–1

Example of compensation following refusal of Secretary of State to confirm a purchase notice.

A site having a frontage of 30 ft. and a depth of 75 ft. stands on the inside of a sharp bend in a main road carrying heavy traffic. A shop with upper part on three floors was erected on the land in 1910 and was entirely destroyed by fire last year. The freeholder immediately applied for planning permission to build a replacement shop and upper part on the site but permission was refused on the grounds that the re-erection of the premises would obstruct the view of traffic approaching the corner.

The freeholder served a purchase notice on the local authority. They referred it to the Secretary of State who refused to confirm it. He indicated in his decision that he would permit a single-storey lock-up shop to be erected on the corner to be set back so that the effective site depth would be only 45 ft.

If the original premises were to be reinstated on the site, they would have a net rack rental value of £20,000 per annum producing a site value of £75,000.

The lock-up shop for which permission would be granted would be worth only £10,000 per annum producing a site value of £40,000.

---

[5] i.e., in these cases, the value assuming planning permission would only be given for the forms of development specified in the Third Schedule to the 1947 Act, as originaly anacted, but subject to the modifications prescribed by Section 278 and Schedule 18 of the Town and Country Planning Act 1971, for the corresponding paragraphs (1, 3 and 7) of Schedule 8 of the 1971 Act.

Assess the compensation payable under Section 187.

Compensation:
"Existing use" value i.e. value of site with
permission to rebuild the former shop and
upper part worth £20,000 per annum:
    Site Value   £75,000
Value of site for erection of lock-up shop
    worth £10,000 per annum:
    Site Value   £40,000

                       Compensation   £35,000

Purchase notices may also be served when land has been rendered "incapable of reasonably beneficial use" in consequence of a revocation or modification or discontinuance order, or a refusal (or restrictive grant) or revocation or modification of a "listed building" consent (Sections 188–190 of the 1971 Act). In theory they may be made available under advertisement regulations or tree preservation orders (Section 191), but this depends on provision being made in the Regulations issued.

Purchase notices are also met within housing legislation. Under Section 287 of the Housing Act 1985, the owner of an "obstructive building", being one which, although it is not (if a house) unfit for habitation, the local authority wish to have demolished because its nearness to other buildings makes it injurious to health (i.e., it is a sound building in a slum area), may offer to sell to the authority (i.e. require them to buy) his interest in it. The order to demolish it must give a period of two months for the building to be vacated, and the offer may be made within that time. There is no need to prove that the property is "incapable of reasonably beneficial use". The same is true of Section 227 of the Housing Act 1985. This states that a person having control of a substandard dwelling in respect of which the local authority have served an "improvement notice" may, within six months thereafter, require the authority to buy his interest in the dwelling.

3. BLIGHT NOTICES

(Sections 192–208—Town and Country Planning Act 1971)[6]

Planning proposals which will eventually involve the compulsory acquisition of land may very well depreciate the value of a property or even make it virtually unsaleable.

It is true that such depreciation will be ignored—under Section 9 of the Land Compensation Act 1961—in assessing the compensation when the property is actually acquired. But this will not help the owner in the meantime if he wants to sell his property in the open market.

For instance, the owner-occupier of a house affected by such proposals may, for personal reasons, be obliged to move elsewhere and may suffer considerable hardship if he has to sell at a very much reduced price.

In partial mitigation of such cases a strictly limited class of owner-occupier is given power to compel the acquisition of interests in land provided that the claimant in each case can prove that he has made reasonable efforts to sell his interest, but has been unable to do so except at a price substantially lower than he might reasonably have expected to obtain but for the threat of compulsory acquisition inherent in the proposals.

(i) The "Specified Descriptions".

The first requirement which the claimant must meet is to show that the land in question comes within one of the "specified descriptions". These comprise (in effect) a list of the kinds of situation in which official proposals have reached a stage that points to the acquisition of the claimant's land by some public authority, referred to as the "appropriate authority".[7] As set out in Section 192(1) of the 1971 Act and amplified by Sections 68–76 of the Land Compensation Act 1973, they are as follows, namely that the claimant's land is:

(a) indicated in a "structure plan" either as land which may be required for the functions of a government department, local authority, statutory under-

---

[6] As amended by Sections 68–81 of the Land Compensation Act 1973.
[7] Town and Country Planning Act 1971, Section 205(1).

taking or the National Coal Board, or a public telecommunications operator; or

(b) allocated for the purpose of such functions by a "local plan" or defined in such a plan as the site of proposed development for any such functions; or

(bb) indicated in a unitary development plan as land required for any such functions;[8] or

(bc) allocated in a unitary development plan as a site for proposed development for any such functions; or

(c) indicated in a development plan as required for a new, improved or altered highway; or

(d) on or adjacent to the line of a highway proposed to be constructed, improved or altered as shown in an order or scheme under Part II of the Highways Acts 1959 or 1980 relating to trunk roads, special road or classified roads, with availability of compulsory purchase powers; or

(e) shown on plans approved by a local highway authority as land comprised in the site of a highway to be constructed, improved or altered; or

(f) a site in respect of which the Secretary of State has given detailed notification of his intention to provide a trunk road or special road; or

(g) subject to a compulsory purchase order empowering any authority to acquire rights over the land as distinct from acquiring the land itself, but notice to treat has not been served; or

(h) subject to a local authority's published intent to acquire it for a general improvement area under Part VIII of the Housing Act 1985; or

(i) authorised by a special enactment to be compulsorily acquired; or

(j) a site in respect of which a compulsory purchase order is in force but notice to treat has not yet been served.

Categories (a), (b), (d), (g) and (j) were extended by the Land Compensation Act 1973,[9] to benefit claimants at an earlier stage, namely when the proposals are published in draft before being formally approved. That Act[10] also introduced additional categories of "specified description", as follows, namely that the claimant's land is:

(k) included in a plan approved by resolution of a local planning authority as shown to be needed for the functions of a public body or included in the plan to safeguard it for development for any such function; or

(l) included in an order (approved or published in draft) designating the site of a New Town; or

(m) included in (or surrounded by or adjoining) a slum clearance area, if the local authority intend to acquire it (which they are now allowed to deny on receiving the blight notice); or

(n) included in a plan approved by resolution of a local authority which proposes to acquire it under Section 22 of the 1973 Act (for mitigating adverse effects of highways) or indicated by the Secretary of State (in writing to the local planning authority) as proposed to be acquired by him under that Section for a trunk or special road; or

---

[8] Paragraphs (bb) and (bc) were added by the Local Government Act 1985.

[9] Sections 68, 69, 70, 74, 75.

[10] Sections 71, 72, 73, 74, 76.

(o) included within the minimum width prescribed for a new street and comprising all or part of a dwelling (or its curtilage) built when that width was prescribed (in this case the authority are not allowed to deny an intention to acquire on receiving the blight notice).

It should be noted that Section 79 of the Land Compensation Act 1973, recognises that an "agricultural unit" may be only partially "blighted"—i.e. that only part of it falls within the "specified descriptions". The part "blighted" is the "affected area" and the remainder is the "unaffected area". In a case of this sort the owner-occupier can serve a blight notice which extends to the "unaffected area" as well as the "affected area" if he can show that the "unaffected area" as such is not capable of being reasonably farmed even with any other available land which the claimant can add to it.

(ii) Interests "Qualifying for Protection".

The second requirement which the claimant must meet, under Section 192(3)–(5) of the 1971 Act, is to show that he has an interest in the land "qualifying for protection". He must in any case be an owner-occuper, or else the mortgagee[11] (with a power of sale currently exerciseable) or the personal representative[12] of an owner-occupier, being:

(a) a "resident owner-occupier" of the whole or part of a dwelling-house (without any limit of rateable value); or

(b) the "owner-occupier" of the whole or part of any other hereditament the annual value of which does not exceed a certain prescribed limit (at present £2,250);[13] or

(c) the "owner-occupier" of the whole or part of an agricultural unit—e.g., a farm.

The term "owner-occupier" is defined in some detail in Section 203 of the 1971 Act. The claimant must have an

[11] Town & Country Planning Act 1971, Section 201. The mortgagee cannot serve a blight notice if his mortgagor has already served one which is still under consideration (and the converse is also true).

[12] Land Compensation Act 1973, Section 78.

[13] Town & Country Planning (Limit of Annual Value) Order, 1973 (S.I. 1974, No. 425).

"owner's interest" in the land—i.e., the freehold or a lease
with at least three years to run—and must have been in physical occupation of the property for at least six months up
to the date of service of the blight notice, or up to a date
not more than twelve months before such service provided
that (in such a case) the property (unless it is a farm) was
unoccupied in the intervening period. If an owner-occupier's
mortgagee is entitled to serve a blight notice, the relevant
period is extended by six months for his particular benefit.

(iii) Blight Notice Procedure.

The notice to purchase the owner-occupier's interest must,
under Section 193 of the 1971 Act, relate to the whole of
his interest in the land, be in the prescribed form,[14] and
be served on the "appropriate authority" (that is, the authority who, it appears from the proposals, will be acquiring
the land).

Within two months of the receipt of the claimant's notice,
the "appropriate authority" may serve a counter-notice of
objection, in the prescribed form,[14] on any of the following
grounds:

  (a) that no part of the hereditament or agricultural unit
     is land of any of the "specified descriptions";
  (b) that they do not, unless compelled, propose to acquire
     any part of the hereditament, or of the "affected area"
     of the agricultural unit, affected by the proposals;
  (c) that they propose to acquire a part of the hereditament
     or "affected area" but do not, unless compelled, pro-
     pose to acquire any other part;
  (d) that, in the case of land within paragraphs (a) or (bb)
     or (c) of the list of "specified descriptions" in Section
     192(1) of the 1971 Act, but not paragraphs (d), (e)
     or (f), they do not, unless compelled, propose to
     acquire any part of the hereditament or "affected
     area" within fifteen years[15] from the date of the coun-
     ter-notice;

[14]Town & Country Planning General Regulations, 1976 (S.I. 1976, No. 1419).
[15]They can specify a longer period.

(e) that the claimant is not currently entitled to an interest in any part of the hereditament or agricultural unit;
(f) that the claimant's interest is not one "qualifying for protection" under the Act—e.g., he is not an "owner-occupier";
(g) that he has not made "reasonable endeavours" to sell; or that the price at which he could sell is not "substantially lower" than that which might reasonably have expected to get but for the planning proposals.[16]

Within two months of the counter notice, the claimant may, under section 195 of the 1971 Act, require the authority's objection to be referred to the Lands Tribunal who may uphold the objection or declare that the claimant's original notice is a valid one. If, in case (c), the authority's objection is upheld, or is accepted by the claimant, they will, of course, have to purchase the part referred to in the counter-notice as land they intend to acquire.

If the authority object on grounds (a), (e), (f) or (g) above, the claimant must satisify the Lands Tribunal that the objection is "not well-founded"—in other words the burden of proof lies on the claimant to show that the land is within the "specified descriptions",[17] that his interest is one "qualifying for protection", and that he has made reasonable but unsuccessful attempts to sell at a fair market price.

But if they object on grounds (b), (c) or (d) it is for the authority to satisfy the Lands Tribunal that the objection is "well-founded"—in other words the burden of proof lies on *them* to show that they have no intention to acquire the land (or part of the land) in question, within 15 years or at all. In *Duke of Wellington Social Club and Institute Ltd. v. Blyth Borough Council* (1964), the Lands Tribunal held that an objection that the authority do not intend to acquire can be held to be "not well-founded" if there would be hardship on the claimant as a result; but in *Mancini v. Coventry*

---

[16] Section 194 of the 1971 Act, as amended.
[17] In *Bolton Corporation v. Owen* (1962), the Court of Appeal held that statements in a development plan which "zone" the claimant's land for residential use are not sufficient to bring it within the "specified descriptions" as being required for the "functions of a local authority", even if the likelihood is that it will be redeveloped for council housing and not private housing.

572 _Modern Methods of Valuation_

City Council (1982) the Court of Appeal doubted whether hardship could be relevant to an authority's intention not to acquire.

Section 80 of the Land Compensation Act 1973, empowers the authority serving a counter-notice in response to a blight notice relating to a farm which includes an "unaffected area" (i.e., part of the farm is not land within any of the "specified descriptions", as described above) to challenge the assertion that the "unaffected area" is incapable of being reasonably farmed on its own (or with any other available land added to it). Indeed, the authority must challenge that assertion if they claim an intention to take part only of the "affected area" (i.e., of the "blighted" part of the farm). If in either circumstance the Lands Tribunal uphold the counter-notice they must make clear to which (if any) land the blight notice will apply, and specify a date for the deemed notice to treat.

Where no counter-notice is served, or where the claimant's notice is upheld by the Lands Tribunal, the appropriate authority will be deemed under Section 196 of the 1971 Act to be authorised to acquire the claimant's interest in the hereditament, or (in the case of an agricultural unit) in that part of the unit to which the proposals which gave rise to the claim relate. But if the authority succeed in an objection that they should only take part of a claimant's property, Section 202 of the 1971 Act preserves the right to compel them to take all or none in accordance with Section 8 of the Compulsory Purchase Act 1965, on proof that otherwise the property, if it is a "house, building or manufactory" will suffer "material detriment", or that if it is "a park or garden belonging to a house" the "amenity or convenience" of the house will be seriously affected.[18]

In general, notice to treat will be deemed to have been served at the expiration of two months from the service of the claimant's notice or—where an objection has been made—on a date fixed by the Lands Tribunal.

The general basis of compensation, where an authority are obliged to purchase an owner-occupier's interest under the 1971 Act, will now be that generally prescribed by the

[18]See Chapter 16.

Land Compensation Act 1961, subject to the special rules applicable to such properties as unfit houses ("site value" compensation under Part XVIII of the Housing Act 1985). Thus, in principle, the market value figure that the claimant has tried in vain to secure by his own efforts in a private sale becomes payable to him by the "appropriate authority".

Except where the authority have already entered and taken possession under their deemed notice to treat, a party who has served a blight notice may withdraw it at any time before compensation has been determined, or within six weeks of its determination. In this case any notice to treat deemed to have been served will be deemed to have been withdrawn.

CHAPTER 27

Compulsory Purchase Compensation—I.
Compensation for Land Taken

1. INTRODUCTORY

THE BASIS of compensation for land compulsorily acquired has from time to time been affected by the provisions of the following statutes:

(a) *The Lands Clauses Consolidation Act 1845.* This Act was concerned with procedure rather than with the assessment of compensation, which, like early statutes, it assumed to be a strictly technical matter for valuers. But certain general principles were established as the result of judicial decisions based on its provisions. It should be realised, however, that the characteristic procedure, envisaged under the Act was arbitration; and arbitration in its essential common law form is a question of contract; so that the characteristic proceeding for enforcing proper compliance with arbitrations is a common law civil action for enforcement of arbitration contracts known as an "action on the award". The judicial decisions just referred to could be actions of this kind; alternatively cases could reach the courts by reason of an arbitrator stating a "special case" on one or more points of law. In recent years, however, the distinction between public law and private law has come to be more clearly drawn, and compulsory purchase cases are undoubtedly within the public law field. They mostly arise as appeals by way of "case stated" from the Lands Tribunal (see below) to the Court of Appeal; alternatively there are judicial review cases, or statutory challenges (e.g. to compulsory purchase orders), in procedural or jurisdictional disputes where the fundamental question is whether or not the relevant authority has acted *ultra vires*.

Since 1 January, 1966, in the majority of compulsory purchase cases, the provisions of the Lands Clauses Consolidation Act 1845, are replaced by corresponding provisions in the Compulsory Purchase Act 1965. But since there is little change in the wording, these new provisions do not appear to affect the general principles established by the courts in their interpretation of the 1845 Act.

(b) *The Acquisition of Land (Assessment of Compensation) Act 1919.* Section 2 of this Act prescribed six rules governing the compensation payable for interests in land acquired compulsorily by any Government department, local or public authority or statutory undertaking. The general basis prescribed was the price the land might be expected to realise if sold in the open market by a willing seller—known in practice as "open market value".

The Act also replaced the various earlier procedures (arbitrations, and verdicts of juries) by a standardised arbitration process conducted by a panel of official arbitrators, who were in turn superseded (with effect from 1 January, 1950) by the Lands Tribunal. Arbitrators could (and can) "state a case" for decision by the Queen's Bench Divisional Court of the High Court; and this method of taking legal points for further adjudication was an alternative to "actions on the award" as a source of early case law. From 1950 appeal from the Lands Tribunal has been by way of "case stated" (on points of law only) direct to the Court of Appeal.

(c) *The Town and Country Planning Act 1944.* During the period 17 November, 1944 to 6 August, 1947, "open market value" for compensation purposes was to be estimated by reference to prices ruling at 31 March, 1939.

(d) *The Town and Country Planning Acts 1947–54.* These Acts applied to compensation payable under notices to treat served after 6 August, 1947, and before 30 October, 1958.

The general basis of compensation was "existing use value"—i.e. open market value assessed on the assumption that planning permission would only be given for such limited forms of development as were specified in the Third Schedule to the 1947 Act.

(e) *The Town and Country Planning Act 1959.* This replaced the Town and Country Planning Acts 1947–54, in the case of notices to treat served on or after 30 October, 1958.

It restored "open market value", as defined by the 1919 Act, as the basis of compensation subject to certain additional rules, and subject also to certain prescribed assumptions as to the forms of development for which planning permission might reasonably be expected to be obtained.

(*f*) *The Land Compensation Act 1961.* As from 1 August, 1961, this Act incorporates and re-enacts the Acquisition of Land (Assessment of Compensation) Act 1919, and the basic compensation provisions of the Town and Country Planning Act 1959. The Act applies to all cases where land is authorised to be acquired compulsorily, including acquisitions made by agreement but under compulsory powers (which in compensation terms count as compulsory acquisitions).

(*g*) *The Land Compensation Act 1973.* This Act contains a variety of matters and deals only incidentally with purchase price compensation. Special compensation rules attributable to it and to other recent Acts will be referred to as appropriate.

It will be clear from the above summary that the code of law now governing the basis of compensation for all interests in land compulsorily acquired consists of

(i) Those general principles established by judicial decisions based on the provisions of the Lands Clauses Consolidation Act 1845.

(ii) The principles embodied in the provisions of the Land Compensation Act 1961, and subsequent amendments.

It makes no difference *in principle* if what is acquired is only part of an owner's interest and not the whole (e.g., part of the garden of a dwelling-house, taken for road widening; or part of a farm, taken for a motorway), or even if it is a new and lesser right not hitherto in existence (e.g., an easement or wayleave, or even a new leasehold) though the House of Lords, in *Sovmots Ltd.* v. *Secretary of State for the Environment*,[1] has held that clear statutory authority must always be shown to justify acquisitions in the form of "new rights". Such authority now exists for local authorities

---

[1] [1977] 2 All E.R. 385.

(*not* other public bodies) in general terms, under the Local
Government (Miscellaneous Provisions) Act 1976.

2. GENERAL PRINCIPLES OF COMPENSATION

The general principles, established by judicial decisions
under the Lands Clauses Consolidation Act 1845, and which
apply to all cases of compulsory purchase and acquisition
by agreement under compulsory powers, unless expressly or
impliedly excluded by Statute, may be briefly summarised
as follows:

(i) Service of the acquiring body's notice to treat fixes the
property to be taken and the nature and extent of the owner's
interest in it. This is because the notice is a semi-contractual
document and a step towards the eventual conveyance to
the acquiring body of a particular owner's leasehold or freehold (as the case may be). Indeed, the courts have said that
notice to treat plus compensation (when settled) in fact constitutes a specifically enforceable legal contract.[2] Any freehold or leasehold in respect of which notice to treat is *not*
served therefore remains unacquired. The effect of Section
20 of the Compulsory Purchase Act 1965, is that holders
of yearly tenancies and lesser interests are not entitled to
receive notices to treat, the assumption being that the acquiring authority acquire the reversion to such an interest and
the interest is then terminated at common law (e.g., by notice
to quit) though compensation will have to be paid if it is
terminated sooner.

Equitable as well as legal freeholds and leaseholds are subject to acquisition (e.g., options and agreements for leases[3])
and compensation will have to be assessed accordingly.

It should be remembered that where general vesting declarations are used, in place of notices to treat and conveyances of the normal kind, a notice to treat is deemed
to have been served, so that what has been said applies in
those cases equally.

[2] As stated by Upjohn, J., in *Grice v. Dudley Corporation* [1957] 1 All E.R.
673.
[3] On this, see *Oppenheimer v. Minister of Transport* [1941] 3 All E.R. 485,
and *Blamires v. Bradford Corporation* [1964] 2 All E.R. 603.

(ii) The old leading case *Penny v. Penny* (1868) was assumed to have established a rule that the value of the property acquired must be assessed as at the date of notice to treat. But in *Corporation of Birmingham v. West Midlands Baptist (Trust) Association*[4] the House of Lords held that this supposed "rule" was without foundation, and expressed the view that the appropriate date for assessing the value of the land is either:

(a) the date when compensation is agreed or assessed; or

(b) the date when possession is taken (if this is the earlier); or

(c) the date when "equivalent reinstatement" can reasonably be started, if that mode of compensation is to be applied (as it was in the *West Midlands Baptist* case itself).

(iii) If the owner can prove that he has suffered loss between the date of service of notice to treat and the date at which compensation is assessed—for instance, through uncertainty of tenure created by the notice to treat—he may include this loss in his claim.[5]

(iv) Compensation must be based on the value of the land in the hands of the owner, not its value to the acquiring body.[6] It is the former value which is "market value" because it is the vendor, not the purchaser, who is at liberty (in a sale by agreement) to market the land or not as he chooses. Any increase in value solely attributable to the scheme involving the acquisition is not a market factor and must be disregarded.[7]

(v) Covenants, easements, etc., already in existence and affecting the land, whether by way of benefit or of burden,

---

[4] [1969] 3 All E.R. 172. (1969) R.V.R. 484.

[5] *Cranwell v. The Mayor and Corporation of London* (1870), L.R.5 Ex. 284.

[6] *Cedar Rapids Manufacturing Co. v. Lacoste* [1914], A.C. 569; *In Re Lucas and Chesterfield Gas and Water Board* [1909], 1 K.B. 16.

[7] *Pointe Gourde etc. Transport Co. Ltd. v. Sub-Intendent of Crown Lands* [1947], A. C. 565. In this case however the disallowed item of claim was not in fact attributable to land value at all, only to estimated savings to the Crown of transport costs, etc.

must be considered in assessing compensation.[8] For
instance, the property may enjoy the benefit of a covenant
restricting building or other works on adjoining land, or it
may itself be subject to the burden of such a covenant and
be less valuable in consequence.

Similarly, it may be a "dominant tenement" with the benefit of an easement of way, support, light, etc., over adjoining
property; or on the other hand it may be a "servient tenement" subject to such a right which benefits adjoining property. Also the possibility of the removal or modification of
restrictive covenants under Section 84 of the Law of Property
Act 1925, as amended, is a factor which might properly be
taken into account.

(vi) Where a lessee has a contractual or statutory right
to the renewal of his lease that right will form part of the
value of his leasehold interest; but the mere possibility of
a lease being renewed is not a legal right existing at the date
of notice to treat and cannot be the subject of compensation.[9]

(vii) An owner is entitled to compensation not only for
the value of the land taken but also for all other loss he
may suffer in consequence of its acquisition.[10] For example,
the occupier of a private house compulsorily acquired will
be put to the expense of moving to other premises and will
suffer loss in connection with his fixtures. An occupier of
trade premises will suffer similar losses and in addition may
be able to claim for loss on sale of his stock or for injury
to the goodwill of his business. It will be convenient to discuss
the "disturbance" compensation payable under these heads
in Chapter 29. But it is important at this point to recognise
them as part of the compensation to be paid to the owner
for the compulsory taking of his interest in the land.

(viii) Where part only of an owner's land is taken, Section
63 of the Lands Clauses Consolidation Act 1845, and the
corresponding provision in Section 7 of the Compulsory Pur-

---

[8] *Corrie v. MacDermott* [1914], A.C. 1056.
[9] See *Re Rowton Houses' Leases, Square Grip Reinforcement Co. (London) Ltd.
v. Rowton Houses* [1966] 3 All E.R. 996.
[10] *Horn v. Sunderland Corporation* [1941], 2 K.B. 26; *Venables v. The Department
of Agriculture for Scotland* (1932), S.C. 573.

chase Act 1965, make it quite clear that the owner is entitled not only to the value of land taken, but also to compensation for severance or injurious affection of other land previously held with the land taken which he retained after the acquisition.

(ix) There are Acts, for example the Local Government (Miscellaneous Provisions) Act 1976, which expressly give specified bodies the power to acquire "new rights" (e.g., easements, leases, etc., not currently in existence) and the appropriate payment for those (in principle) will presumably be the prevailing market figure for the grant of such a right.

The underlying principle throughout is that a normal compulsory purchase is in truth a compulsory assignment of an existing freehold or leasehold right in land; and consequently the fundamental question which a valuer should ask himself is—what capital sum would a purchaser of this freehold or leasehold expect to pay to acquire it in the open market? In this Chapter we concentrate upon the question of compensation for land actually taken, with that principle in mind. Before considering the matter in further detail it is important to reconsider and distinguish a general principle referred to under (iv) above arising from *Pointe Gourde etc. Transport Co. Ltd. v. Sub Intendent of Crown Lands* commonly referred to as the "Pointe Gourde Principle".

The "Pointe Gourde Principle"

In *Pointe Gourde Quarrying and Transport Co. v. Sub-Intendent of Crown Lands* (1947), land in Trinidad containing a quarry was acquired for a naval base. The owners claimed, in addition to land value and disturbance, a sum apparently representing savings to the government by reason of having stone from the quarry conveniently on hand to build the base installations instead of needing to transport it there from afar. This item was rejected, being (in the words of the Privy Council) "an increase in value which is entirely due to the scheme underlying the acquisition". The reported facts of the case would show the reader the difficulty of understanding how the disputed item could have been justified and how the amount could have been assessed.

The true justification of the decision is that all compensatable items had already been accounted for in the sums agreed by the parties and that the particular benefit accruing to the government over building materials was of no concern to the claimant owners whatever. For the Privy Council to speak of the disallowed figure as "an increase in value" was most unfortunate, because it was in fact an increase in claim, which is a totally different thing. The error has given rise to a "Pointe Gourde principle", that tends to distract the attention of lawyers and valuers, to say nothing of courts and tribunals, from the "willing seller" rule, which is the true rule of market value. Where it produces results at variance with those of the "willing seller" rule, the "Pointe Gourde rule" is dubious; and where the results are the same it is redundant.

The leading cases in compulsory purchase which illustrate the problem show that the "Pointe Gourde rule" works irrationally and unpredictably. In *Wilson v. Liverpool City Council* (1971) it deprived the claimant of some of the development value which on the facts clearly accrued to his land. Conversely in *Jelson Ltd. v. Blaby District Council* (1978) it gave the claimant development value which, on the facts, his land did not possess (this happened because it was said that the "rule" requires valuers to "disregard a decrease", as well as an increase, if it is "entirely due to the scheme underlying the acquisition"). In *Trocette Property Co. Ltd. v. Greater London Council* (1974) it gave the claimant's leasehold interest in a cinema substantial "marriage value" in respect of redevelopment prospects which did not in fact exist because no such redevelopment was permitted (whether it could be assumed to be permitted, under Sections 14–16 of the Land Compensation Act 1961, might profitably have been considered instead). Yet in *Birmingham District Council v. Morris and Jacombs* (1976) the "rule" was not applied when valuing a piece of access land which could in fact have been used for additional housing development had this use not been prohibited. The contrast between this and the Jelson decision is remarkable. Moreover the three last-mentioned cases all arose on acquisitions under purchase notices, where there can be no relevant 'scheme" at all because the authority are acquiring against their will and therefore without any kind of functional purpose in view.

The "Pointe Gourde rule" has no true foundation either in law or in valuations, that is to say it is justified neither by precedent nor by usage.

3. MARKET VALUE

Six Basic Rules of Valuation

Section 5 of the Land Compensation Act 1961 (re-enacting with some slight amendments Section 2 of the 1919 Act), prescribes six rules for assessing compensation in respect of land. Five of these rules relate to the valuation of land and interests in land; the sixth preserves the owner's right to compensation for disturbance and other loss not relating to land value which is suffered in consequence of the land being taken from him.

Rule 1. No allowance shall be made on account of the acquisition being compulsory.

In assessing compensation under the Act of 1845 it had become generally recognised custom to add 10 per cent to the estimated value of the land on account of the acquisition being compulsory. This addition was no doubt intended originally to cover the cost of reinvesting capital and other incidental expenses to which the owner might be put and in that sense may be regarded as part of the value of the land to him. There was nothing in the Act of 1845 which expressly authorised such an allowance. It is now expressly excluded. (Percentage additions made in order to attempt to quantify *development* value are another matter. The modern law concerning the inclusion of development value in compensation is considered later in this Chapter).

Rule 2. The value of land shall, subject as hereinafter provided, be taken to be the amount which the land if sold in the open market by a willing seller might be expected to realise.

The purpose of this rule is to indicate the true basis of compensation as being open market value, which is what the courts meant in earlier cases by stressing "value to the owner". It takes for granted that there will be a "willing buyer"—i.e., that there exists a demand for the land—presumably because of the compulsory nature of the acquisition. Yet whether in the open market there would be a willing buyer at a price acceptable to a willing seller is a question which may well cause problems in certain cases. (Some of these problems may be solved by applying Rule 5—below.)

Where interests in land are purely of an investment nature there is probably no difference in any valuer's mind between value to owner and value in the open market. In other cases the rule should put it beyond doubt that there must be excluded from the valuation any element which would have no effect on the price obtainable for the property under normal conditions of sale and purchase—i.e., anything that distorts a proper calculation of "market value".

The meaning of the words "amount which the land if sold in the open market by a willing seller might be expected to realise" was fully examined by the Court of Appeal in the case of *Inland Revenue Commissioners v. Clay and Buchanan*,[11] as follows:—

(i) "In the open market" implies that the land is offered under conditions enabling every person desirous of purchasing to come in and make an offer, proper steps being taken to advertise the property and let all likely purchasers know that it is in the market for sale.

(ii) "A willing seller" does not mean a person who will sell without reserve for any price he can obtain. It means a person who is selling as a free agent, as distinct from one who is forced to sell under compulsory powers.

(iii) "Might be expected to realise" refers to the expectations of properly qualified persons who are informed of all the particulars ascertainable about the property

[11][1914], 3 K.B. 466—In that case the judgment of the court was directed to almost identical words used in the Finance (1909–1910) Act 1910, in regard to taxation. See also *Re Hayes's Will Trusts*, [1971] 2 All E.R. 341, where Ungoed-Thomas, J:, speaks of "... a range of price, in some circumstances wide, which competent valuers would recognise as the price which 'property would fetch if sold in the open market'" (The judge was dealing with estate duty valuation.)

and its capabilities, the demand for it and likely buyers.

In assessing compensation, then, it must be assumed that the owner is offering the property for sale of his own free will, but is taking all reasonable measures to ensure a sale under the most favourable conditions. The compensation payable will be *that price which a properly qualified person, acquainted with all the essential facts relevant to the property and to the existing state of the market, would expect it to realise under such circumstances.*

An estimate of market value on this basis will take into account all the potentialities of the land, including not only its present use but also any more profitable use to which, subject to the requisite planning permission, it might be put in the future—i.e., prospective development value as well as existing use value.

For example, if land at present used as agricultural land is reasonably likely (having regard to demand) to become available for building in the future, the prospective building value may properly be taken into account under Rule 2 provided that it is deferred for an appropriate number of years. Again, if buildings on a well-situated site have become obsolete or old-fashioned, so that the rental value of the property could be greatly increased by capital expenditure on improvements and alterations (again, having regard to demand), compensation may properly be based on the estimated improved rental value, provided that the cost of the necessary works is deducted from the valuation.

It should be emphasised, however, that in the case of land capable of further development, the price which it might be expected to realise under present-day conditions of strict planning control depends very largely on the kind of development for which planning permission has already been obtained, or is reasonably likely to be given having due regard to the provisions of the development plan for the area. But it is essential to bear in mind the words used by Lord Denning, M.R., in *Viscount Camrose v. Basingstoke Corporation*:[12]

[12][1966] 3 All E.R. 161.

"Even though (land may) have planning permission, it does not follow that there would be a demand for it. It is not planning permission by itself which increases value. It is planning permission coupled with demand."

Thus existing use value rests on demand, whereas development value rests on demand plus planning permission; in principle, both go to make up "market value" of land.

In practice, a prospective purchaser in the open market would probably obtain permission for his proposed development before deciding the price he was prepared to pay. This factor is normally absent in compulsory purchase cases, and the Land Compensation Act 1961, therefore, provides that, besides taking into account any existing planning consents, certain assumptions shall be made as to the kinds of development for which planning permission might reasonably have been expected to be granted but for the compulsory acquisition. These assumptions are considered in detail later in this Chapter.

In general compensation will be based on the value—as at the date of assessment or of entry on the land—of the interests existing at the date of the notice to treat. But in all cases to which the Acquisition of Land Act 1981, applies[13] the Lands Tribunal "shall not take into account any interest in land or any enhancement of the value of any interest in land, by reason of any building erected, work done or improvement or alteration made", if the Tribunal "is satisfied that the creation of the interest, the erection of the building, the doing of work, the making of the improvement or the alteration, as the case may be, was not reasonably necessary and was undertaken with a view to obtaining compensation or increased compensation".[14] This does not prevent recognition of a merger or surrender as between landlord and

---

[13] Section 4 (re-enacting a similar provision in earlier legislation).

[14] The provision applies not only to the land being acquired but also to "any other land with which the claimant is, or was at the time of the erection, doing or making of the building, works, improvement or alteration, directly or indirectly concerned . . .". This section is equally applicable in slum clearance cases (Housing Act 1985 Section 598).

tenant, provided that compensation claimed as a result is based on a reasonable market figure.[15]

In the case of leasehold interests there seems no doubt that their value should be determined by reference to the length of the unexpired lease at the date when the valuation is made.

Rule 3. The special suitability or adaptability of the land for any purpose shall not be taken into account if that purpose is a purpose to which it could be applied only in pursuance of statutory powers, or for which there is no market apart from the special needs of a particular purchaser or the requirements of any authority possessing compulsory purchase powers.

Under the Lands Clauses Acts, if land could be shown to be specially suited or adapted to a particular purpose so that anyone requiring it for that purpose might be expected to pay a higher price on that account, this "special adaptability" might be regarded as giving the land a special value in a certain limited market and thereby increasing its value in the hands of the owner.

Thus in *Manchester Corporation v. Countess Ossalinski*[16] the fact that land was specially suitable and adaptable for the construction of a reservoir for a town's supply was held to enhance its value to the owner; and, in later cases under the Lands Clauses Acts, it was held that such "special adaptability" might properly be considered even where the land could only be used for the purpose for which it was best suited by bodies armed with statutory powers. This is because there exists no rule that a "market" situation requires a minimum of (say) two prospective purchasers; the fact that in a particular case there is a sole purchaser, who happens to be armed with statutory powers, does not affect the principle as such.

Rule 3 restricts the consideration of "special suitability

[15] *Banham v. London Borough of Hackney* (1970), 22 P. & C.R. 922. But if a residential tenant is rehoused by a local authority, under Section 39 of the Land Compensation Act 1973, after the date of his landlord's notice to treat, the landlord's interest is to be valued without regard to the tenant's giving up possession (Section 50(2) of the 1973 Act). Conversely a tenant whose leasehold is expropriated must not be given less compensation by reason of his being rehoused by, or by arrangement with, the acquiring authority (Section 50(1)).

[16] Tried in Q. B. D. of the High Court on 3 and 4 April, 1883, but not reported. However, extracts from the judgment are contained in the report of the decision in *Re Lucas and Chesterfield Gas and Water Board* [1909] 1 K.B. 16.

or adaptability" of the land, provided however that this relates to its use for a "purpose" and not merely to the position of any party to the transfer. In relation to any "purpose", either the fact that there is a sole purchaser or the existence of statutory powers, if that purpose would not otherwise apply, suffices to bring the rule into operation. For instance, the circumstances existing in *Manchester Corporation v. Countess Ossalinski* could not now affect the compensation payable for land, if there were no likelihood of its being used for the purpose of a reservoir except under statutory powers. Again, the exceptional price which one particular purchaser might be willing to pay for premises, because of their special convenience for his purpose, will not now affect the assessment of their market value in accordance with Rule 2.[17]

It is clear that "purpose" in Rule 3 means some prospective physical use of the land itself and does not extend to a purpose connected with the use of the products of the land—e.g., minerals—nor to a factor such as the special attraction of a landlord's reversion to a "sitting tenant" (i.e., to the latter the purchase of the reversion means an enlargement of his interest; to anyone else it means merely the acquisition of an investment).[18] If, therefore, "special suitability" of the land for "any purpose" is not established, then the mere fact that there is only one prospective purchaser does not bring Rule 3 into play.

Rule 4. Where the value of the land is increased by reason of the use thereof or of any premises thereon in a manner which could be restrained by any Court, or is contrary to law, or is detrimental to the health of the inmates of the premises or to the public health, the amount of that increase shall not be taken into account.

The general purpose of this rule seems clear and requires no further comment. Little attention is given to it in practice.

Rule 5. Where land is, and but for the compulsory acquisition would continue to be, devoted to a purpose of such a nature that there is no general demand

---

[17] In *Inland Revenue v. Clay and Buchanan* [1914] 3. K.B. 466, it was held that the special price *already offered and paid* for a house by the adjoining owner who wanted the premises for the extension of his nursing home was properly taken into account in assessing market value for the purposes of the Finance (1909–10) Act 1910.

[18] See *Pointe Gourde, etc., Transport Co. Ltd. v. Sub-Intendent of Crown Lands*, [1947] A.C. 565; and *Lambe v. Secretary of State for War*, [1955] 2 Q.B. 612.

or market for land for that purpose, the compensation may, if the Lands Tribunal is satisfied that reinstatement in some other place is bona fide intended, be assessed on the basis of the reasonable cost of equivalent reinstatement.

There are certain types of property which do not normally come upon the market and whose value cannot readily be assessed by ordinary methods of valuation, such as that of estimating the income or annual value and capitalising it. Such properties include churches, alms-houses, schools, hospitals, public buildings and certain classes of business premises where the business can only be carried on under special conditions.[19]

Rule 5 gives statutory authority to assessing compensation on the basis of the cost of providing the owner, so far as reasonably possible, with an equally suitable site and equally suitable buildings elsewhere—as an alternative to assessment on the basis of market value—provided that:

   (i) the land is devoted to a purpose for which there is no general demand or market for land;

  (ii) compensation is limited to the "reasonable cost" of equivalent reinstatement; and

 (iii) the Lands Tribunal is satisfied that reinstatement in some other place is bona fide intended.

"Equivalent reinstatement" would seem to imply putting the claimant in the same position, or in an equally advantageous position, as that which he occupied when his land was acquired.

In certain cases the only practical method of reinstatement may be the provision of a new site and new buildings. But where, for instance, claimants are using an old building which has been adapted to their purposes, the term "equivalent reinstatement" might cover the cost of acquiring another similar property, if that is possible, together with the expenses of any necessary adaptations.

In a leading decision of the House of Lords[20] the point

---

[19] See *Festiniog Rail Co. v. Central Electricity Generating Board*, (1962) 12 P. & C.R. 248.

[20] *West Midlands Baptist (Trust) Association (Incorporated) v. Birmingham City Corporation*, [1969] 3 All E.R. 172; (1969) R.V.R. 484. For the phrase "devoted to a purpose" see *Zoar Independent Church Trustees v. Rochester Corporation*, [1974] 3 All E.R.5.

at issue was whether the cost of reinstatement should be assessed as at the date of notice to treat (14 August, 1947)—agreed at £50,025—or as at the earliest date when the work might reasonably have been begun (30 April, 1961)—agreed at £89,575. It was unanimously decided by the House of Lords (confirming the decision of the Court of Appeal and reversing a decision of the Lands Tribunal) that the later figure was the proper basis for compensation.

Bearing in mind that, subject to the "special suitability" concept in Rule 3, there is no reason in strict principle why one prospective purchaser should not constitute a "market", it will be apparent that the application of Rule 5 depends not on there being "no market" but on there being "no *general* market".[21] What therefore matters is that the Lands Tribunal should be satisfied that the facts of the case require Rule 5 to be applied.

Equally important is the question of development value. The wording of Rule 5 takes account only of the existing use of the land in question. If the existing use of land in circumstances envisaged by Rule 5 points to a (restricted) market value figure of (say) £1,000 and the reasonable cost of equivalent reinstatement is assessed at £20,000, it is obviously reasonable for the owner to claim the latter figure. If, however, that land has genuine development value assessed at £30,000 it is reasonable to claim this figure instead; but if there is development value assessed only at £15,000 there seems no reason in principle why "equivalent reinstatement" should not be claimed in preference to it.

Rule 6. The provisions of Rule 2 shall not affect the assessment of compensation for disturbance or any other matter not directly based on the value of the land.

[21] This distinction was endorsed by the House of Lords in *Harrison and Hetherington v. Cumbria County Council*, (1985) 50 P. & C.R. 396, in which the claimants were held to be entitled to equivalent reinstatement compensation for the site of the old cattle market in the centre of Carlisle; the demand for land for cattle markets normally extends only to one such site at a time in any given town, and therefore that demand, though genuine, cannot be described as "general". In *Lambe v. Secretary of State for War*, [1955] 2 Q.B., 612, the court accepted that "market value" to a sitting tenant may well be different from (and higher than) "market value" to an investment purchaser when a reversion is sold; so presumably the demand (if any) from a sitting tenant for the reversion to his tenancy is not "general", though of course the question of equivalent reinstatement is not likely to arise for the reversioner.

This rule merely preserves an owner's right (established under the Lands Clauses Acts) to be compensated not only for the value of his land but for any other loss he suffers through the land being taken from him, chiefly "disturbance". This is discussed in Chapter 29.

4. ADDITIONAL RULES OF ASSESSMENT

Sections 6 to 9 of the Land Compensation Act 1961 prescribe three additional rules to be applied in assessing market value for compensation purposes.

(a) *Ignore notional increases or decreases in value due solely to development under the acquiring body's scheme.*

Section 6 and Schedule 1 of the 1961 Act give statutory authority to a principle that certain increases and decreases in value must be ignored. These are increases and decreases which are not attributable to market factors but are purely hypothetical. It is made clear, by the use of the words "other land", that what is in question is a modification of the value assessed for the claimant which is made because of what has happened, or is thought likely to happen, *on neighbouring land also being acquired.*

In principle, there is, of course, no objection to modifying an assessment of value for reasons of this kind. Section 6 and Schedule 1 therefore exclude such modifications only in the following circumstances:

(i) the "other land" is being acquired in order to be developed for the same purposes as the claimant's land because it is included in the same compulsory purchase order or in the same area of comprehensive development or town development or of a New Town; *and*

(ii) an increase or decrease in value of the claimant's land is being envisaged on the hypothesis that it is not being acquired for those purposes—contrary to the reality of the situation, since its value is being assessed precisely because it is in fact being so acquired; *and*

(iii) such an increase or decrease in value cannot be justified independently in the way that it would be justified if the development would be "likely to be carried out" in other circumstances (that is to say, if there had been a market demand for such development and a likelihood of its being permitted).

In other words, what is being ruled out is an unreal modification of value, dependent on the blatant contradiction that the land is assumed *not* to be acquired, when assessing the price for its acquisition.

In assessing compensation in any of the cases referred to in Table A below, no account is to be taken of any increase or decrease in the value of the interest to be acquired due to the development of the kind noted against that particular case.

"Development"—which includes the clearing of land—refers both to development which may already have taken place and also to proposed development—being in either case development which would not have been likely to be carried out except for the compulsory acquisition (or, in cases other than Case 1, if the areas mentioned had not been designated).

In Case 1 of Table A the rule would apply to the effects on value of the development, or the prospects of development of other land acquired under the same compulsory purchase order or Special Act. In the remaining cases, which deal with large-scale undertakings, the rule extends to actual or prospective development of other land within the defined area of the scheme.

TABLE A

Type of case	Ignore increase or decrease in value due to the following, if they are unlikely to occur but for the compulsory acquisition or designation (as the case may be):—
Case 1 All cases where the purpose of the acquisition involves development of any of the land to be acquired.	Development for the purposes of the acquisition, of any land authorised to be acquired, other than the land to be valued.

Case 2	Where any of the land to be taken is in an area designated in the current development plan as an area of comprehensive development.	Development of any other land in that area in accordance with the plan.
Cases 3 and 3A	Where on the service of notice to treat any of the land to be taken is in an area designated as the site of a New Town under the New Towns Act 1965,[22] or an extension of a New Town, designated in an order taking effect after 13 December, 1966.[23]	Development of any other land in that area in the course of the development of the area as a New Town or extension as the case may be.
Case 4	Where any part of the land to be taken forms part of an area designated in the current development plan as an area of town development.	Development of any other land in that area in the course of town development within the meaning of the Town Development Act 1952.
Case 4A	Where any part of the land to be taken forms part of an area designated as an urban development area.[24]	Development of any other land in that area in the course of development or redevelopment of the area as an urban development area.

In *Davy v. Leeds Corporation*[25] the claimant's land was acquired (at "site value", because it comprised houses unfit for habitation) as part of a clearance area. He claimed that the prospect of clearance and redevelopment of the adjoining land in the area would increase the value of his own land if it were not being acquired, and that Section 6 did not rule out this notional increase because it was not justifiable to say that the clearance "would not have been likely to be carried out except for the compulsory acquisition". This contention depended on the possibility that the clearance might have been brought about in circumstances other than

[22] See Part II of the First Schedule for special provisions applying where notice to treat is served on or after the date on which the new town development corporation ceases to act. The current general Act is the New Towns Act 1981.

[23] New Towns Act 1966.

[24] By an order made under the Local Government, Planning and Land Act 1980, Section 134.

[25] [1965] 1 All E.R. 753.

compulsory purchase by the local housing authority. The
House of Lords rejected this argument, on the ground that
the facts made it inconceivable that the clearance would have
come in any other way. Section 6, therefore, applied, and
the argument for an increase in value failed.

(b) *Set off increases in value of adjacent or contiguous land
in the same ownership.*

Where land is acquired compulsorily it may well be that
other adjoining land belonging to the same owner is increased
in value by the carrying out of the acquiring body's undertaking on land taken. Neither the Lands Clauses Acts nor the
Acquisition of Land (Assessment of Compensation) Act
1919, made any provision whereby the acquiring authority
might benefit from this increase in value. But a number of
special Acts, including the principal ones under which land
is taken for road works, expressly provide that, in assessing
compensation for land taken, any increase in the value of
adjoining and contiguous lands of the same owner due to
the acquiring body's scheme shall be deducted from the compensation payable.

The Land Compensation Act 1961, now applies this principle of "set-off" to all cases of compulsory acquisition, as
follows.

The effect of Section 7 is that where, at the date of notice
to treat, the owner has an interest in land contiguous or
adjacent to the land acquired, any increase in the value of
that interest in the land retained due to development
under the acquiring body's scheme, is to be deducted from
the compensation payable for the interest in the land
acquired.

As under Section 6, "development" refers to either actual
or prospective development under the acquiring body's
scheme which would not be likely to be carried out but for
the compulsory acquisition. In this case, however, the prospect of development on the land acquired must be considered as well as development on other land taken under
the same compulsory order, or special Act, or included in
the same area of development.

The following table, based on the First Schedule to the
1961 Act, may help to make the position clear:—

TABLE B

	Type of case	Set off increase in value of contiguous or adjacent land of same owner due to the following, if unlikely to occur but for the compulsory acquisition or designation (as the case may be):—
Case 1	All cases where the purpose of the acquisition involves development of any of the land to be acquired.	Development for the purposes of the acquisition, of any land authorised to be acquired including the land to be valued.
Case 2	Where any of the land to be taken is in an area designated in the current development plan as an area of comprehensive development.	Development of the land taken, or any other land in the area designated, in accordance with the plan.
Cases 3 and 3A	Where on the service of notice to treat, any of the land to be taken is in an area designated as the site of a New Town or extension of a New Town.	Development of the land taken, or any other land in the area designated.
Case 4	Where any part of the land to be taken forms part of an area designated in the current development plan as an area of town development.	"Town development" on the land taken, or any other part of the area designated.
Case 4A	Where any part of the land to be taken forms part of an area designated as an urban development area.	Development or redevelopment on the land taken, or any other land in the urban development area.

The above provisions as to "set-off" do not apply to acquisitions under certain existing Acts—specified in Section 8(7)—which already provide for "set-off", nor to acquisition under any local enactment which contains a similar provision. In these cases the question of "set-off" will be governed by the express provisions of the particular Act. But any provision in a local enactment which restricts "set-off" to any increase in "the existing use value" of contiguous or adjacent land will cease to have effect.

Under the above provisions as to "set-off", the compensation payable to an owner may be reduced by the increase in the value of his interest in adjacent land. But there are also cases where the compensation for land taken will be increased on account of the injurious affection to other land held with it due to the acquiring body's scheme. In either case, if such adjacent land is subsequently acquired, the operation of Section 6, which requires increase or decreases in value due to the scheme to be ignored, might result in an owner either being paid a certain amount of compensation twice over or deprived of it on two occasions.

Section 8 therefore provides as follows:—

(i) If, either on a compulsory purchase or a sale by agreement, the purchase price is reduced by setting off (under Section 7 or any corresponding enactment) the increase in the value of adjacent or contiguous land due to the acquiring body's scheme, then if the same interest in such adjacent land is subsequently acquired that increase in value (which has served to reduce the compensation previously paid) will be taken into account in assessing compensation and not ignored as it otherwise would have been under Section 6.

(ii) Similarly, if a diminution in the value of other land of the same owner due to the acquiring body's scheme has been added to the compensation payable for land taken, then if the same interest in that other land is subsequently acquired that depreciation in value (for which compensation has already been paid) will be taken into account in assessing compensation and not ignored as it otherwise would have been under Section 6.

If in either of the above cases part only of the adjoining land is subsequently acquired a proportionate part of the set-off or injurious affection will be taken into account.

Section 8 also ensures that where several adjacent pieces of land of the same owner are acquired at different dates—although perhaps under the same compulsory purchase order—an increase in value due to development under the acquiring body's scheme which has already been set off against compensation on one occasion shall not be set off again on the subsequent acquisition of a further part of the lands in question.

The underlying principle in Sections 6–8 can perhaps be best put by saying that Sections 7 and 8 require genuine market increases and decreases in value be taken properly into account, whereas Section 6 requires that increases and decreases which are not genuine market calculations be disregarded. It should, however, be noted that "set-off" under Section 7 is, of its very nature, somewhat capricious in its incidence because the increase in value to which it relates can only be taken into account if the owner is losing other land by compulsory purchase, and not beyond the amount of the compensation payable in respect of that other land.

(c) *Ignore loss of value due to prospect of acquisition.*

Section 51(3) of the Town and Country Planning Act 1947, provided that in assessing compensation no account should be taken of any depreciation in the value of the claimant's interest due to the fact that the land had been designated for compulsory purchase in the development plan. Section 9 of the Land Compensation Act 1961, extends this principle to depreciation in value due to any proposals involving the acquisition of the claimant's interest, whether the proposals are indicated in the development plan—by allocation or other particulars in the plan—or in some other way. For instance, no account should be taken of depreciation in the value of the land due to its inclusion in a compulsory purchase order which has been publicised under the Acquisition of Land Act 1981, or any comparable provisions.

5. DEVELOPMENT VALUE

Assumptions as to Planning Permission

Section 14 to 16 of the Land Compensation Act 1961, prescribe certain assumptions as to the grant of planning permission which are to be made in assessing the market value of the owner's interest in the land to be acquired.

These assumptions are to be made without prejudice to any planning permission already in existence at the date of the notice to treat—whether, for instance, given by the local planning authority or under a General Development Order. It may be that the land in question enjoys additional value by way of development value because of an actual planning permission to an extent that makes the "planning assumptions" superfluous; but if so this is coincidental, and its occurrence is uncommon. The valuer must make such one or more of the prescribed assumptions as are applicable to the whole or part of the land to be acquired, and compensation will be related to whichever of these assumptions is most favourable from the point of view of value in the open market.

But the fact that, under the Act, land may be assumed to have the benefit of planning permission—e.g., for residential purposes—does not necessarily imply a demand for that land for those purposes. It is important always to remember the words of Lord Denning, M.R., referred to earlier in this Chapter, about the elements necessary for development value: "It is not the planning permission by itself which increases value: it is planning permission coupled with demand."[26] In some cases normal demand—apart from the acquiring authority's scheme—might be so far distant as to warrant only a "hope" value for development.

Again, the fact that these assumptions are to be made does not imply that planning permission for other forms of development would necessarily be refused. So the possibility that prospective purchasers might be prepared to pay a higher price for land in the hope of being able to obtain permission for a certain form of development may be a factor in assessing market value, even although the permission in question is not covered by the assumptions to be made under the Act. But in deciding whether permission might reasonably have been expected to be granted—and might therefore influence the price a prospective purchaser might be expected to pay— regard is to be had to any contrary opinion expressed in any certificate of "appropriate alternative development" which may have been issued under Section 17 of the Act[27] (as amended).

In applying these provisions of the Act one must also have regard to the possible incidence of other planning legislation.

If, for instance, compensation in respect of the unexpended balance of established development value has already been paid under the Town and Country Planning Act 1971 (or corresponding earlier legislation) in respect of an adverse planning decision, or the revocation of permission previously granted, then the fact that such compensation will be repayable if permission for "new development"—such as might be covered by one of the statutory assumptions—is given

---

[26] *Viscount Camrose and Another v. Basingstoke Corporation* [1966] 3 All E.R. 161.
[27] Such certificates are considered below.

in the future will certainly affect the price which a prospective
purchaser might be expected to pay for the land.

Again, although any "unexpended balance of development
value" does not form part of the compensation payable for
land acquired, its existence may have an indirect effect on
market value through the compensation provisions of the
Town and Country Planning Acts, in regard to adverse planning decisions. Thus cases may arise where no development
of land to be acquired, other than of an "existing use" type
(within Schedule 8, as amended by Sections 169(6A) and
278, and Schedule 18, of the Town and Country Planning
Act 1971), can be assumed under the terms of the 1961 Act,
and yet if planning permission for "new development" were
in fact refused, or granted subject to conditions, the owner
might be entitled to compensation under Part VII of the
Town and Country Planning Act 1971, not exceeding the
amount of the unexpended balance attached to the land.
Here, if the possibility of such compensation might fairly
be assumed to affect the price which a prospective purchaser
might be prepared to pay for the land, there seems no reason
why this factor should not be taken into account in assessing
market value under Rule 2 of Section 5 of the 1961 Act.
(Such an imaginary purchaser would obviously pay very special attention to the limitations on the right to compensation
imposed by Sections 147 and 148 of the 1971 Act). But the
most compelling reason for including any "unexpended
balance" in the compensation for compulsory purchase is
that Section 142 of the 1971 Act provides that any such purchase results in the extinction of any "unexpended balance"
attributable to the interest acquired. Although neither the
1961 Act nor the 1971 Act expressly deals with this point,
it must follow that Section 142 of the 1971 Act justifies the
inclusion in compulsory compensation of development value
to the extent of the amount of an outstanding "unexpended
balance", irrespective of the assumptions as to "planning
permission" in the 1961 Act.[28]

The assumptions to be made under Sections 14–16 of the

---

[28] On these matters see the foregoing Chapters on Planning Compensation
(Chapters 24–26).

Land Compensation Act 1961, may be described broadly as (1) general assumptions and (2) assumptions related to current development plans.

(1) *General Assumptions as to Planning Permission*

(i) Where the acquiring authority's proposals involve development of the whole or a part of the land to be acquired, it shall be assumed that planning permission would be given for such development in accordance with the authority's proposals. (Section 15(1) and (2).)

But where a planning permission for the proposed development is already in force at the date of the notice to treat, its terms will take the place of any assumed permission, unless it is personal only and does not enure for the benefit of all persons interested in the land.

As a general rule then, the possibility of carrying out the type of development for which the land is acquired may be reflected in the compensation payable. For instance, if the local authority require land for housing, it will be assumed that planning permission is available for the kind of housing development which the local authority propose to carry out.

But where the proposed development is for a purpose to which the land could only be applied in pursuance of statutory powers, the assumption of planning permission will not necessarily affect the compensation, since this element of value may well be excluded by Rule 3 of Section 5 of the Act.

(ii) It shall be assumed that planning permission would be granted for any form of development specified in Schedule 8 (as amended) of the Town and Country Planning Act 1971 (Section 15(3) and (4)).

But this rule is subject to the following exceptions to avoid compensation being paid twice over:

(a) Where at any time before service of notice to treat planning permission was refused, or was granted subject to certain conditions, in respect of some form of development in Part II of Schedule 8 and compensation has become payable under Section 169 of the 1971 Act, planning permission shall not be assumed for that particular development, or shall only be assumed subject to the conditions already imposed, as the case may be.

(b) Where before the date of notice to treat an order was made under Section 51 of the 1971 Act, for the removal of any building or the discontinuance of any use, and compensation became payable under Section 170 of that Act, it shall be assumed that planning permission would be granted for the rebuilding of that building or the resumption of that use, as the case may be.[29]

(iii) It shall be assumed that planning permission would be granted for development of any class specified in a "certificate of appropriate alternative development" which may have been issued under Part III of the Act. (Section 15(5).)

But this assumption is governed by the terms of the certificate which may indicate that planning permission would not be granted until some date in the future and/or subject to certain conditions.

The cases in which such certificates may be issued and the procedure in connection with them are considered later in this Chapter.

(2) *Assumptions as to Planning Permission related to current Development Plans*

Where at the date of notice to treat land to be acquired is comprised in a current development plan—whether the original plan or some amended form of it—certain assumptions as to planning permission are to be made according to how the land, or any part of it, is dealt with in the plan.

In some cases land may be "defined" in the plan as the site for some specific development—e.g., a new road, a public building, a public park. In other cases land may be "allocated" (or zoned) for some more general purpose—e.g., for

---

[29] The actual wording of Section 15(3) and (4) of the 1961 Act speaks of provisions in the Town and Country Planning Act 1947; but Schedule 24. para. 2 of the Town and Country Planning Act 1971, requires the modern equivalents to be read in place of the original provisions in cases of this kind, where the original enactment has been repealed, and replaced by corresponding provisions in the 1971 Act. It is important to remember that Schedule 8 to the 1971 Act is modified by Sections 169(6A) and 278, and Schedule 18, to that Act (as described earlier in Chapter 25).

agricultural, residential or industrial user. Or again, the land may be defined in the plan as an "area of comprehensive development" or "action area"—i.e., one which, in the opinion of the local planning authority, should be developed or redeveloped as a whole.[30]

In all the cases (i) to (iv) set out below the assumptions made as to planning permission must be subject to:—

(a) any conditions which might reasonably have been expected to be imposed on the grant of the planning permission in question; and

(b) any indication in the development plan—whether on any map or in the written statement—that such permission would only be granted at some future time, thus suggesting that the benefit of the assumed permission should be deferred for an appropriate period.

Cases (i)—(iii) which follow refer to land which is not in an area of comprehensive development.[31]

Case (i): Land defined in the development plan as the site for development of a specific description. (Section 16(1).)

In this case it is to be assumed that planning permission would be given for the particular development.

In many cases where the land is defined as the site of development for which there is no demand except by bodies armed with statutory powers, this assumption will have little or no effect on the market value of the land. In such cases the owner may be advised to apply for a certificate of "appropriate alternative development" under Part III of the Act (see below).

Case (ii): Land allocated in the development plan for some primary use (Section 16(2)).

---

[30]The Town and Country Planning Act 1971, Section 11(4), defines an "action area" as any part of a local planning authority's area "which they have selected for the commencement during a prescribed period of comprehensive treatment, by development, redevelopment or improvement of the whole or part of the area selected, or partly by one and partly by another method".

[31]"Area of comprehensive development" is to be construed as an "action area" for which a local plan is in force under Part II of the Town and Country Planning Act 1971, according to Section 291 and Schedule 23 of that Act. See preceding footnote.

In this case it is to be assumed that planning permission would be given for any development which:—

(a) is within the specified primary use; and
(b) is of a kind for which planning permission might reasonably have been expected to be granted but for the compulsory acquisition.

For example, land may be zoned primarily for "residential purposes", a term which may include a number of different forms of development—e.g. houses or blocks of flats, with varying densities per ha. Here planning permission must be assumed for the type of residential development for which it might reasonably have been expected to be granted had the land not been acquired compulsorily.

In some cases there may be a reasonable possibility that permission would have been given for the development of the whole or part of the land for some purpose ancillary to the purpose for which the area is primarily zoned—e.g., a terrace of shops in an area zoned for residential use. In such a case it would seem that, although definite planning permission can only be assumed for the specified primary use, it would be permissible to consider any possible effect which the reasonable expectation of planning permission for the ancillary use might have had on the open market value.

Case (iii): Land allocated in the development plan primarily for two or more specified uses (Section 16(3)).

In this case it is to be assumed that planning permission would be given for any development which:—

(a) is within the range of uses specified in the development plan;
(b) is of a kind for which planning permission might reasonably have been expected to be granted but for the compulsory acquisition.

Case (iv): Land defined in the development plan as an area of comprehensive development. (Section 16(4) and (5).)

As stated above, an area of comprehensive development is one which, in the opinion of the local planning authority, should be developed or redeveloped as a whole.[32] The development plan, in addition to defining the area in question, will also indicate the various uses to which it is proposed the different parts of the area should be put on redevelopment.

In this case, in assessing compensation for the land to be acquired, regard is to be had to the range of uses proposed for the area, but the proposed distribution of those areas under the development plan must be ignored, together with any development which at the date of notice to treat has already taken place in the area in accordance with the plan.

The open market value of the land in question must then be assessed on the assumption that planning permission would be granted for any form of development—within the range of uses proposed for the area—for which permission might reasonably have been expected to be granted if the area had not been defined as an area of comprehensive development.

6. CERTIFICATES OF APPROPRIATE ALTERNATIVE DEVELOPMENT

Where an interest in land is proposed to be acquired by an authority possessing compulsory powers and that land, or part of it, does not consist or form part of an area:—

(a) defined in the current development plan as an area of comprehensive development (or "action area"); or
(b) shown in the current development plan as allocated primarily for residential, commercial or industrial uses, or a combination of any of those uses with other uses.

[32] See footnotes 30 and 31 above. An "area of comprehensive development" is much the same as an "action area', although its definition (which dates back to the Act of 1947) is less elaborate. Both kinds of area have been intended usually, though not invariably, for achieving town-centre redevelopment (or "urban renewal") by redistribution of sites to private developers or public authorities, for redevelopment in accordance with the requirements of the local planning authority as specified in the plan for the area.

Section 17 of the Land Compensation Act 1961, as amended by Section 47 of the Community Land Act 1975, enacts that either the owner of any interest to be acquired, or the acquiring authority, may apply to the local planning authority for a certificate stating for what development (if any) permission would have been granted if the land had not been subject to compulsory purchase. When the certificate is issued, planning permission for such development as is indicated in the certificate will be assumed in assessing the market value of any interest in the land for compensation purposes, in accordance with Section 15(5) of the 1961 Act (referred to earlier in this Chapter).

This provision is intended to cover cases where not sufficient guidance is given by the development plan as to the kind of development for which planning permission would have been given, or where the plan favours development of the land in question of a kind which is not likely to give rise to an appreciable amount of development value.

Typical cases where such a certificate might be applied for are:—

   (i) land defined in the development plan as the site for some purely public development—e.g., a sewage disposal works or a public open space;
  (ii) "white area" land not allocated in the plan for any form of development—e.g. land in the green belt;
 (iii) land in an area not covered by a current development plan.

The right to apply for a certificate arises where land is "proposed to be acquired", i.e.:

  (a) where any required notice in connection with the acquisition is duly published or served; or
  (b) where notice to treat is "deemed to have been served"; or
  (c) where an offer in writing is made on behalf of an acquiring authority to negotiate for the purchase of the owner's interest in the land.

Provisions as to the issue of certificates and appeals therefrom are contained both in the Act and in the Land Compensation Development Order, 1974.[33] The following is a summary of the procedure.

The application for a certificate, accompanied by a plan or a map, may be made at any time before the date of any reference to the Lands Tribunal to determine the compensation in respect of the applicant's interest in the land. But it cannot be made after that date except with the written consent of the other party or by leave of the Tribunal.

The applicant must specify one or more classes of development which in his view would be appropriate for the land in question if it were not being acquired compulsorily. He must also state the date on which a copy of the application has been or will be served on the other party. Not earlier than twenty-one days from this latter date, but within two months from the receipt of the application, the local planning authority must issue a certificate to the applicant stating either:—

    (a) that in their opinion planning permission for development of one or more specified classes (which may or may not be classes specified in the application) would have been granted if the land were not proposed to be acquired, or

    (b) that in their opinion planning permission would not have been granted for any development other than the development (if any) which the acquiring authority propose to carry out.[34]

Where, in the opinion of the local planning authority, the permission referred to in (a) above would only have been granted subject to conditions or at some future time, or both subject to conditions and at some future time, the certificate must say so.

The local planning authority are not necessarily bound by the provisions of their development plan in determining what

[33]S.I. 1974, No. 539 (made under Section 20 of the 1961 Act).
[34]This type of certificate tends to be called a "nil certificate".

sort of development might reasonably have been permitted on the land in question.

If a certificate is issued for development other than that specified in the application, or contrary to written representations made by the owner of the interest or the acquiring authority, the local planning authority must give their reasons and also state the right of appeal to the Secretary of State.

When a certificate is issued to either owner or acquiring authority a copy must be served on the other interested party. A copy must also be sent to the local authority in whose area the land is situated.

Section 18 of the 1961 Act provides that either the owner or the acquiring authority may appeal against a certificate to the Secretary of State for the Environment who, after giving the parties and the local planning authority an opportunity to be heard, may either confirm the certificate, or vary it, or cancel it and issue a different certificate in its place.

Appeal may also be made to the Secretary of State if the local planning authority fail to issue a certificate within two months of an application to them to do so, although this time may be extended by agreement of the parties. In this case the appeal will proceed as though the local planning authority had issued a certificate to the effect that planning permission could not normally have been expected to be granted for any development other than that which the acquiring authority propose to carry out.

Appeals to the Secretary of State must be made within one month of the date of issue of the certificate, or the expiry of the time limit of two months (or extended time), as the case may be.

Section 19 of the Act contains special rules for applying the procedure in respect of certificates of appropriate alternative development to cases where an owner is absent from the Kingdom or cannot be found. Section 21 gives the right to challenge the legal validity of a decision given by the Secretary of State on appeal (within six weeks) by means of an application to the High Court, which may quash the decision if it is found to be ultra vires the 1961 Act or to involve some procedural error substantially prejudicing the applicant.

7. Special Compensation Rules in Particular Cases

(a) *Houses Unfit for Human Habitation*

Under the Housing Act 1985, Section 585, where houses unfit for human habitation are compulsorily acquired, compensation is in principle (and subject to various exceptions) assessed on a "cleared site value" basis.

The provisions of that Act are considered in detail later, in Chapter 30. What is relevant here is that in certain other special cases also of compulsory acquisition an unfitness order can be made declaring a house to be (a) unfit for human habitation and (b) incapable of being rendered fit at reasonable expense, in consequence of which the Land Compensation Act 1961 (Section 10 and Second Schedule) provides that compensation will be assessed at "site value", and not at full market value (of site plus house) if that is assessed at a higher figure.

These are cases of compulsory acquisition under:—

(a) section 6 of the Town Development Act 1952; or

(b) Part VI of the Town and Country Planning Act 1971;[35] or

(c) the provisions of Part IX of the Town and Country Planning Act 1971,[36] which relate to purchase and blight notices; or

(d) the Development of Rural Wales Act 1976, by an acquiring authority under the new towns code within the meaning of that Act; or

(e) section 104 of the Local Government, Planning and Land Act 1980, by the Land Authority for Wales; or

(f) section 141 of that Act, by an order vesting land in an urban development corporation; or

(g) section 142 of that Act, by such a corporation directly; or

(h) Orders under Section 1 of the New Towns Act 1981, designating land as the site of a new town; or

---

[35] This authorises acquisitions for "planning purposes" (see Chapter 16 above: compulsory purchase in planning).

[36] Discussed above (see Chapter 26).

(i) the New Towns Act 1981, or any enactment as applied by the provisions of that Act, being acquisition by a development corporation or a local highway authority or the Secretary of State; or

(j) Part VIII of the Housing Act 1985, concerned with general improvement areas.

The procedure in all the above cases is for the local authority to submit the unfitness order to the Secretary of State for the Environment, at the same time serving a notice on every owner and mortgagee of the land, or part of it, stating the effect of the order and the time within which objections to it must be made. The Secretary of State must consider any objections and must hold an enquiry if any objector or the local authority so desires. Successful objectors may qualify for an award of costs (Appendix to D.O.E. Circular 2/87).

Provided the order declaring the house to be unfit is confirmed by the Secretary of State the basis of compensation will be the open market value of the cleared site ignoring the value of any buildings on it.

In certain circumstances, specified in the Housing Act 1985, the owner may also be entitled to a supplementary payment as an "owner-occupier" or in respect of a "well-maintained" house. These payments are considered in detail in Chapter 30.

It is quite possible, however, that the open market value of the site, cleared of buildings and available for development, may exceed the value of the unfit house as it stands, for the latter figure would have to take into account such items as existing cost of maintenance, difficulty of securing possession from existing tenants, and the cost of demolishing dilapidated buildings.

Section 589(1) of the Housing Act 1985 therefore provides, in effect, that the *maximum* compensation payable for an "unfit" house shall be the market value of the property as it stands, estimated in accordance with the general provisions of the Land Compensation Act 1961. In other words, although "cleared site value" is prima facie assumed to be lower than the value of the site-plus-house, the reverse is sometimes the case: if so the compensation must not exceed the value of site-plus-house (i.e. whichever sum is lower is the one that is paid, where the property comprises an unfit house). None of these provisions precludes payment of development value, if the rules in the Land Compensation Act 1961 permit this; indeed it is in development value cases that the value of site-plus-house is likely to be lower than "cleared site value". Section 589(2) of the Housing Act 1985, however, also provides that in the case of an owner-occupier of a private dwelling the *minimum* compensation for his interest—including any "well-maintained" or "owner-occupier" supplement, but leaving aside compensation for disturbance, injurious affection or severance—shall be the gross value of the house for rating as shown in the current valuation list. Where part only of the house is owner-occupied the gross value must be suitably apportioned by the district valuer.

(b) *Statutory Undertakers' Land*

Under the Town and Country Planning Acts 1947–54, the compensation for certain special types of property was assessed on the assumption that planning permission would be granted for development whereby the use of the land could be made to correspond with that prevailing on contiguous and adjacent land.

The properties in question included those held by local authorities for general statutory purposes, operational land of statutory undertakers and land held and used for charitable purposes.

This "prevailing use basis", as it was called, was abolished by the Town and Country Planning Act 1959, and now, under Section 11 of the Land Compensation Act 1961, compensation in these cases will, in general, be assessed on the same basis as for any other type of property.

But where land is acquired from statutory undertakers who themselves have acquired the land for the purpose of their undertaking, compensation will be assessed in accordance with certain special rules contained in Section 238 of the Town and Country Planning Act 1971.

It may be conveniently noted here that nothing in the 1961 Act shall apply to any purchase of the whole or part of a statutory undertaking under any enactment which prescribes the terms on which such a purchase is to be effected (Section 36).

(c) *Outstanding Right to Compensation for Refusal, etc., of Planning Permission*

It has already been noted in relation to development value that where a right to compensation exists in consequence of some planning decision or order already made—e.g., a refusal of permission, or its grant subject to conditions, or the revocation or modification of a permission already given—the fact that this compensation, or part of it, may be repayable under Section 159 of the 1971 Act if permission for "new development" is given in the future will naturally affect the assessment of market value if the land is compulsorily acquired.

The liability to repay actually only arises under Section 159 provided that "a compensation notice" has been registered as a land charge. But the effect of Section 12 of the 1961 Act is that the factor of liability for repayment of compensation can be taken into account in the assessment of "market value" whether a "compensation notice" was registered before the notice to treat or on or after that date, and whether or not a claim for compensation in respect of the adverse planning decision has yet been made.

It follows, therefore, that if no claim for compensation in respect of the adverse decision has in fact been made, the owner should proceed with it in spite of the fact that his land is being acquired.

8. Summary of General Basis of Compensation

It may be useful at this point to summarise briefly and in very general terms the basis of compensation for land taken prescribed by the 1961 Act.

Essentially it is the best price which the owner's interest might be expected to realise if voluntarily offered for sale in the open market. But in many cases it may be necessary to make two or more estimates of the value of the property, each based on different assumptions permitted by the Act in order to determine what that "best price" is and (in particular) whether in addition to the existing use of the land the assessment should also take account of the prospect of development (having regard to "planning permission coupled with demand", in the words of Lord Denning, M.R., quoted earlier in this Chapter).

The possible bases for these estimates of value may be formulated from the valuation standpoint as follows:—

(i) The value of the property as it stands, but having regard to the possibility of any future development within the limits of Schedule 8 of the 1971 Act (as amended), and taking into account also the terms of any planning permission already existing at the date of notice to treat, but not yet fully implemented by development.

In the case of a very large number of properties, both in built-up and in rural areas, this will represent the highest price obtainable in the open market.

(ii) The value of the land, as in (i), but with the assumption that planning permission would be given for the development which the acquiring body propose to carry out.

This may or may not give a higher value than (i) according to whether permission to carry out this kind of development would be of value (a) to purchasers generally or (b) only to bodies armed with statutory powers or one particular purchaser—in which case the element of value might be excluded under Section 5 Rule 3 of the Land Compensation Act 1961 if the development is for a purpose which can only be carried out by that body or purchaser.

(iii) The value of the land subject to such of the prescribed assumptions as to planning permission—based on the provisions of the current development plan—as are applicable to the particular case.

This does not necessarily rule out of consideration the possibility that one or more purchasers might be prepared to pay a higher price in the hope that permission might be obtainable for some other form of development.

(iv) The value of the land subject to the assumption that planning permission would be given for one or more classes of development specified in a "certificate of appropriate alternative development"—in cases where the development plan gives little or no guide to the kind of development which might be permitted.

In all the above cases the valuation will exclude any increase or decrease in the value of the land attributable to actual or prospective development under the acquiring body's scheme, either on the land taken or on other land, also any decrease in value due to the threat of acquisition.

Where the owner has an interest in other land held with that taken, additional compensation for severance and injurious affection may be payable under the provisions of the Lands Clauses Consolidation Act 1845, or, in the great majority of cases, the corresponding provisions of the Compulsory Purchase Act 1965.

Where the owner has an interest in land adjacent or contiguous to that taken, any increase in the value of such land due to actual or prospective development under the acquiring body's scheme, either on the land taken or on other land, is to be deducted from the compensation.

If a dwelling-house is certified as unfit for habitation, compensation will, subject to various qualifications, be based on the value of the bare site. This matter is dealt with in Chapter 30.

Where development properties are acquired under the compensation provisions of the Land Compensation Act 1961, the problem is mainly one of the choice of basis most favourable to the claimant. The following examples illustrate the choices available:—

Example 27–1

Open land under grass acquired for housing and allocated as such in development plan, programmed 1–5 years.

Housing value £250,000 per acre.
Agricultural value £2,000 per acre.
Compensation—£250,000 per acre.

Note: The value for purpose acquired and for allocation in development plan are the same.

Example 27–2

Suppose the same land is acquired for allotments.

Housing value £250,000 per acre.
Agricultural value £2,000 per acre.
Allotment value £3,000 per acre.
Compensation—£250,000 per acre.

Note: The value for allocation in the development plan gives the highest figure.

Example 27–3

As for *Example 27–1* but programming 6–20 years. Acquired for school purposes.
Compensation—£250,000 per acre deferred for length of time market would allow. For example, this could be three years if the programme is likely to be accelerated. It could alternatively be 15 years if (say) no drainage is available until then.

Note: Here again the value is that for the allocation in the development plan since the value for school purposes is unlikely to be as great.

Example 27–4

Open land under grass acquired for housing. Land is shown in a "white area" on the development plan.

Values as in previous examples.
Compensation—Housing value, say, £250,000 per acre.
   (Value for purpose acquired).

Example 27–5

Open land under grass allocated in development plan for school purposes and acquired for use as such. The land is

in the middle of a residential area in the development plan.
Values as in previous examples.

Compensation. In this case the claimant should apply to
the planning authority for a certificate of appropriate alternative development, asking for a certificate to be granted for
residential development.

If granted—Compensation £250,000 per acre.
(Value for certified purpose).
If refused—"School value" or existing use value.
Compensation, say, agricultural value £2,000
per acre.

Example 27–6

Land as before, but local planning authority's certificate
states that planning permission could not reasonably have
been expected except for school purposes. The land has an
unexpended balance of established development value of
£720 and "School Value" is taken in this case to be less
than agricultural value (£2,000 per acre).

Compensation. £2,000 per acre plus £720 (discounted for
time and trouble of collection) since this is a case where
the owner could have claimed compensation up to £720 under
the Town and Country Planning Act, if the planning permission for residential development had been refused, as
seems probable.

Example 27–7

Land in a "white area" is to be acquired as a recreation
ground. There is some possibility that the development plan
might be changed to a residential allocation on review. The
agricultural value is £2,000 per acre. Recreation ground value
£5,000 per acre. A speculator would give £20,000 per acre
in the hope that the allocation will be changed.

Compensation—£20,000 per acre.

In practice in the absence of direct evidence of recent comparable sales in the same area it is difficult to prove "hope
value".

Example 27–8

3 acres of land in a green belt is to be acquired for housing. Compensation equal to the original unexpended balance of established development value of £2,000 was paid for planning refusal in 1956.

Compensation. Housing value, say £150,000, less £2,000 which would be repayable if planning permission for housing were now to be granted, i.e., £148,000.

Example 27–9

A freehold building used until recently as a private house is to be acquired compulsorily: it is in an area of comprehensive development. It is now vacant. The development plan shows that the area is to be redeveloped for industrial and shopping purposes. If converted into a shop, the premises would be worth £12,500 per annum—the cost of conversion would be £50,000.

The site area is 350 sq. yds. Industrial land is worth £100 per sq. yd.

(i) Value with permission to convert into a shop:

Net rental value	£12,500 p.a.
Y.P.	12
	£150,000
Less: Costs, etc., say	65,000 (to include fees, profit, etc.)
Compensation, say	£85,000

OR

(ii) Value as industrial land

350 sq. yds. at £100 per sq. yd.	£35,000

OR

(iii) Value as a house, say   £50,000

In this case basis (i) would be chosen by the claimant. Here the claimant is entitled, in any case, to the existing use value of £50,000. He could only claim £85,000 as compensation if he could show that planning permission for conversion to a shop might reasonably have been expected to be granted if the area had not been defined as an area of comprehensive development.

CHAPTER 28

Compulsory Purchase Compensation—II.
Compensation for Injurious Affection

1. GENERAL PRINCIPLES

THE PRINCIPLES governing the right to compensation for injurious affection were considered in Chapter 16 where a distinction was drawn between:—

(i) claims for injurious affection to (i.e., depreciation of) land owned by the claimant in consequence of the acquisition, under statutory powers, of adjacent land some or all of which was formerly "held with" it; and

(ii) claims for injurious affection to land owned by the claimant in consequence of the exercise of statutory powers on adjacent land none of which was formerly "held with" it.

The right to compensation in both cases derives either from the Lands Clauses (Consolidation) Act 1845, or—in the majority of cases nowadays—from the corresponding provisions of the Compulsory Purchase Act 1965. The relevant Sections are 63 and 68 of the 1845 Act (for (i) and (ii) respectively) and 7 and 10 of the 1965 Act (similarly).

The following diagram may help to make this fundamental distinction clear:—

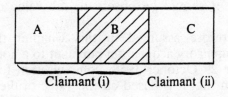

Claimant (i)   Claimant (ii)

Land "B" is being acquired under statutory powers. Claimant (i), from whom it is being acquired, is entitled to claim compensation not only for its market value on acquisition but also for any injurious affection under Section 7 of the 1965 Act to his other land "A" which, until the acquisition, has been "held with" it. Claimant (ii) is only entitled to claim compensation for any injurious affection to his land "C" under Section 10 of the 1965 Act because none of land "B" has been "held with" it. Land "B" is being "severed" from land "A", but not from land "C".

Lands such as "A" and "B" are "held with" each other even if the claimant's rights in them are not the same (as in *Oppenheimer v. Ministry of Transport* (1941) where the claimant's property right in the land taken was merely an option) and even if not actually contiguous, provided they are such that "the possession and control of each" gives "an enhanced value to the whole" (*Cowper Essex v. Acton Local Board* (1889)); and this is a valuation question of obvious practical importance.

The view is often expressed that compensation under this head is not governed by the provisions of the Land Compensation Act 1961. While this is undoubtedly true in regard to many items in the nature of disturbance which may arise where part only of the land is taken, it is submitted that, insofar as the claim for compensation is based on depreciation in the "value" of the land, it comes within the scope of Rule (2) of Section 5 of the Land Compensation Act 1961. Section 5 expressly applies in general terms to "Compensation in respect of any compulsory acquisition"; and the exception from its scope which is contained in Rule (6) is expressly confined to "disturbance or any other matter not directly based on the value of land"— not merely, it should be observed, the value of the land acquired.

It is therefore assumed in this Chapter that, in all cases of compulsory acquisition pursuant to a notice to treat served after 29 October 1958, compensation for injurious affection—in that it is based on the value of the land—will represent the depreciation in the value of that land in the open market.

It would appear, however, that the assumptions as to planning permission to be made under Section 14–16 of the 1961

Act, in the case of lands taken, do not apply to assessments of market value in the case of lands injuriously affected.[1]

2. COMPENSATION WHERE PART ONLY OF THE LAND IS TAKEN

This is "severance". Cases of this type frequently occur, particularly in connection with the construction of new roads or the widening of existing roads or town-centre redevelopment. An example occurred in *Ravenseft Properties Ltd. v. London Borough of Hillingdon* (1968): though in that case the acquiring authority were eventually compelled to buy the whole of the property in dispute instead of severing it as they had intended by acquiring part of the garden.

It is necessary to consider the principal losses likely to be suffered in connection with the land formerly "held with" the land taken and the bases on which claims for compensation should be prepared.

Compensation where part of a property is taken falls under three main heads: (a) land taken; (b) severance and other injurious affection to land held therewith; (c) other incidental losses resulting from the compulsory taking. Other matters which may have to be considered are (d) accommodation works, and (e) apportionment of rents.

(*a*) *Land Taken*. The area of land to be taken will usually be indicated on the plan accompanying the notice to treat. In the case of a road this will necessarily include the land required not only for the road itself but also for the slopes of any cuttings or embankments.

The compensation for the land taken will be assessed, in accordance with the principles prescribed by the Land Compensation Act 1961 (as amended). In the case of agricultural land its "value" will probably be estimated by reference to prices paid for small areas of land of the same type in the district; but this is, of course, a point of valuation rather

---

[1] Sections 14–16 apply to the "relevant interest" and "relevant land". Section 39(2) defines these, "in relation to a compulsory acquisition in pursuance of a notice to treat", as (respectively) "the interest acquired in pursuance of that notice" and "the land in which the relevant interest subsists", and no mention is made of any land retained by the claimant.

than of law, and in law it is justifiable in principle just as valuation by reference to comparable properties is justifiable generally.

In addition to the value of the land itself the owner is entitled to compensation for the loss of any buildings or fixtures or timber on the land, whether or not these items are included in the overall purchase price or are subject to a separate valuation. Obviously the same item of value must not be compensated for twice over. The tenant or owner-occupier of agricultural land may also have a claim for "tenant-right", which will be discussed in more detail under the heading of "other incidental losses". The relevant principles have been discussed above, in Chapter 27.

(*b*) *Severance and other Injurious Affection*. It is important to remember that "severance" compensation is one variety of "injurious affection" compensation. That is to say an owner suffers compensatable loss (referred to in Section 7 of the 1965 Act as "damage") because his "other land" which he retains is depreciated whether by severance or some other factor. The loss by "severance" is loss whereby the market values of the land taken and the land retained amount to less than the total market value of the land before it was severed. A classic case is *Holt v. Gas Light & Coke Co.* (1872) in which a small portion of certain land used as a rifle-range was compulsorily purchased. The part taken was peripheral only, but so situated that the safety area behind the targets was no longer sufficient and the land retained could not in future be used as a range.

A typical modern example is where part of a farm is separated from the rest of the farm, including the farmhouse and farm buildings, by the construction of a road across the property, or where the area of a farm is significantly reduced in size by the taking of part even though the part remaining is not split up.

Such severance is likely to result in increased working costs. For example, if a portion of arable land is cut off by severance of intervening land there will probably be an increase in the cost of all the normal operations of ploughing, sowing, reaping, carting, etc., as well as additional supervision necessitated by the separation of the land from the rest of the farm. If the severed portion is pasture land, extra labour and supervision may be required in driving cattle to pasture as well as possible risk of injury to cattle, as for instance in crossing a busy new road. These additional expenses are likely to involve some reduction in rental value of the land which, capitalised, will represent the injury due to severance.

The main kinds of severance can perhaps be best understood diagrammatically:—

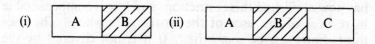

Land "B" is acquired from the owner and severed from lands "A" and "C" which the owner retains. The essential "severance" is that of land "B" from the other land; the severance of land "A" from land "C" is a secondary matter (though none the less important). More complicated forms of severance may, of course, cause further fragmentation of an owner's land; but the basic principles of compensation are not affected by this.

The extent of loss from severance will naturally vary greatly according to the nature of the undertaking and other circumstances, for example, whether or not a new road or railway is situated on a level with the land remaining or is put on an embankment or viaduct or in a cutting or tunnel, and whether or not "accommodation works" such as a private bridge or "underpass" are carried out to enable the owner to cross the road or railway. It must not be forgotten that land ownership extends physically downwards and upwards from the land surface, so that viaducts and tunnels involve "severance" of land in principle just as surface works do; though it may be that the financial loss caused to an owner by having a tunnel made below his land surface will in some circumstances be nil (see *Pepys v. London Transport Executive* (1974)).

In whichever sense it is "severed", the property as a whole may suffer depreciation in value by reason of the fact that it can no longer be occupied and enjoyed as one compact holding.

The valuer must be careful to include in the claim for compensation any injury likely to be caused to the rest of the property by the authorised user of the works. At one time this only applied to such user insofar as it occurred on the land acquired from the claimant—i.e., land held by him with the injuriously affected land until the severance—as was held by the Court of Appeal in *Edwards v. Ministry of Transport* (1964). But Section 44 of the Land Compensation Act 1973, has now abolished this restriction, and loss is compensatable in respect of the user of the works as a whole. The user must, however, be *authorised*. If it is not covered by the statutory authorisation conferred on the acquiring authority they will be liable instead to damages in a civil action.

Here "injurious affection" arises "otherwise" than by severance, and is akin to depreciation actionable at common law in the tort of nuisance. For example, the use, as a major road, of a strip of land across a residential estate may seriously depreciate the value of the mansion by reason of noise, fumes and loss of privacy. Such factors (other than loss of privacy) are actionable nuisances if they occur to any significant degree. All of them (including loss of privacy and any other non-actionable loss) can and should be taken into account in claiming injurious affection compensation in cases where land retained is depreciated (leaving aside the actual fact of severance) in consequence of the carrying out of the acquiring body's project.

Here the leading authority is the decision of the House of Lords in *Buccleuch (Duke of) v. Metropolitan Board of Works* (1872), when part of the garden of the claimant's house (in fact its entire riverside frontage) was compulsorily acquired for the construction of the Victoria Embankment at Westminster. The full depreciation of the claimant's property was held to be payable, on the basis of severance and injurious affection in combination, insofar as the insignificant purchase price or market value of the strip of garden actually taken was insufficient of itself to make up the total loss in land value which the claimant had suffered (i.e. on a "before and after" valuation).

In the case of agricultural land, the possibility of crops being damaged by fumes or dust from a new road, or the yield of milk from pasture land being reduced by disturbance of cattle due to heavy traffic on the road, may result in loss of rental value.

Every head of damage which can reasonably be anticipated should be included in the claim, since no further claim can be made later for damage which might have been foreseen at the time when the land was taken.

The claim for depreciation in value of the land retained will be based on its market value which will take into account the benefit of any actual planning permission already given. It may be permissible, in some cases, to consider the effect on value of the possibility that planning permission might have been given, having regard to the terms of the development plan and other circumstances. But no assumptions of planning permission can be made, as in the case of land taken, because the relevant provisions of the Land Compensation Act 1961, do not refer to land retained; thus nothing other than genuine "hope value" existing independently of the actual grant of planning permission could possibly be justified in any relevant valuation.

The Land Compensation Act 1973, Section 8(4A), requires that there be entered in the local land charges register details of: (a) the works for which the land taken is required, and (b) that part of the land which is not taken. This is to avoid duplication of compensation in the event of a possible claim under Part I of the Land Compensation Act 1973 (discussed below).

(*c*) *Other Incidental Injury.* In addition to the value of the land taken and injurious affection to other land held therewith, the owner is entitled to compensation for all other loss and expense which he may incur in consequence of the compulsory acquisition. The generic term for these items of compensation is "disturbance", which is the subject of the next Chapter. But some may in practice be closely connected with claims for severance and injurious affection compensation and can for the sake of convenience be touched on here. Such losses will vary with the circumstances of each case, so that it would be misleading to attempt to suggest

an exhaustive list of possible items. A consideration of some
of the principal heads of damage likely to arise in connection
with the taking of a strip of land through an agricultural
estate will indicate the general nature of items which may
be included with this part of the claim. They may be briefly
summarised as follows:

(i) *Disturbance and Tenant-Right on the Land Taken.*
Either an owner-occupier or a tenant is entitled to compensation for any loss suffered through having to quit a portion
of farm land at short notice. Such loss may arise from the
forced sale of stock which can no longer be supported on
the reduced acreage of the farm, or from the forced sale
of agricultural implements. He may also claim for other similar consequential losses, for example, temporary grazing and
storage. Improvements to the land made at a tenant's expense
may have to be taken into account. Both the owner-occupiers
and tenants may claim for "tenant right".[2]

(ii) *Damage During Construction.* It is almost unavoidable
that during construction a certain amount of damage should
be caused to crops, etc., on land immediately adjoining the
works. It is also likely that certain parts of the farm, particularly those portions which are to be severed, will be more
difficult to work during this period, so that a claim for
increased labour costs or total loss of rental value may be
justified. If the works are being carried out close to the mansion or farmhouse, the disturbance to the occupier may be
considerable and in extreme cases it may be necessary for
him to obtain temporary accommodation elsewhere.

(iii) *Reinstatement Works.* Owing to the construction of
the undertaking on the land taken, the owner or occupier
may be forced to carry out various works to the remaining
land. For example, small awkward-shaped pieces of land may
be left on either side of the works which it will be necessary
to throw into adjoining fields by rearranging fences, grub-
bing-up hedges, filling in ditches, etc.

---

[2] Additional compensation for reorganisation of the tenant's affairs, up to four
times the annual rent of the part taken, may also be payable under the Agriculture
(Miscellaneous Provisions) Act 1968, Section 12, (as amended by the Agricultural
Holdings Act 1986, Schedule 14). The significance of this is best considered in
connection with "disturbance" compensation (see the next Chapter).

(*d*) *Accommodation Works*. In the case of railway undertakings the acquiring body was obliged under Section 68 of the Railways Clauses Act 1845, to provide certain "accommodation works" for the benefit of owners of land adjoining the undertaking. These included bridges and other means of communication between severed portions of land, the adequate fencing of the works, means of drainage through or by the side of the railway and provision of watering places for cattle. These works tended to reduce the effect of severance and other injury likely to be caused by the construction of the railway and were, of course, taken into account in assessing compensation.

In the case of other undertakings there is no such obligation on the acquiring body to provide accommodation works, or on the owner to accept in lieu of compensation. But in practice it is frequently agreed between the parties as a matter of joint convenience that the acquiring body will carry out certain "accommodation works" or "works of reinstatement", and that compensation shall be assessed on the basis of these works being provided. For instance, where a new road is constructed across agricultural or accommodation land, the acquiring body will not only fence along the boundaries of the road, but will also provide new gates where convenient. If part of the front garden of a house is taken under a street widening scheme, the acquiring body will probably agree to provide a new boundary wall and gates, to plant a quickset hedge to screen the house, to make good the connection to the house drains and similar works.

All these are items for which compensation would otherwise have to be included in the claim. It is usually convenient for both parties that the acquiring body should do them while the works are still in progress. Details of the works agreed upon will therefore be included in any settlement of compensation by agreement, or in case of dispute may be handed to the Lands Tribunal and considered by them in awarding compensation.

It is also important in road cases to come to an understanding as to the maintenance of slopes, banks and retaining walls, and as to the owner's right of access to the road. The acquiring body will usually undertake responsibility for slopes, banks and retaining walls. Normally any retaining wall built to support a highway, or wall built to prevent soil from higher land falling on the highway will be part of the highway. The owner will usually stipulate for access to the new road across any intervening slopes or banks and the right to lay sewers, and also for public services such as gas and water mains, electric cables, etc., to be permitted in the soil of the road.

(*e*) *Apportionment of Rent* (Compulsory Purchase Act 1965, Section 19). Where part of land subject to a lease is taken it may be necessary to apportion the rent between the part taken and that which is left. Naturally the lessee should not be required to continue to pay the same rent, particularly if the portion taken is considerable; but it is often difficult for the lessor and lessee to agree on the amount of the deduction to be made. The lessee can only demand a fair apportionment of the rent paid, not of the annual value of the property. Also, he cannot include in the reduction of rent any figure representing reduced value to the rest of the property. That loss should be met by compensation from the acquiring body to the lessor or lessee as appropriate.

In view of these difficulties it is a common practice, particularly where small portions of urban properties are taken for road widening purposes, to agree on a nominal apportionment of, say, one pound a year on the land taken. Under this arrangement the lessee will continue to pay the rent reserved under his lease for the balance of his term, but on the other hand will receive full compensation for the loss of rental value from the acquiring body; while the freeholder will be compensated for the injury to his reversion.

Where a freehold property is subject to a building lease at a ground rent and sub-lease at the full annual value or rack rent, apportionment might be agreed on a nominal basis of 1p per annum on the part taken as regards the rent under the ground lease and £1 per annum for the part taken as regards the rent under the sub-lease.

Any dispute as to apportionment of rent under a lease may be referred to the Lands Tribunal. But in that case the apportionment must be a true apportionment as distinct from a nominal one. The costs of apportionment are not covered by the words "costs of all conveyances" in Section 23 of the Compulsory Purchase Act 1965 and so are not automatically borne by the acquiring body (*Ex parte Buck* (1863)).

(f) Example 28–1

A Highway Authority is about to acquire a strip of land through a farm of 80 ha for the construction of a road 30 m wide, running roughly north and south and likely to carry a considerable volume of traffic. Where the road first enters the farm at the north, it will run for approximately 100 m on an embankment of a maximum height of 3 m. For the remainder of its course it will be on the level. The total area of land acquired, including the slopes of the embankment will be 3 ha.

The farm consists of 64 ha of pasture, 15 ha of arable, and the rest roads and buildings. It is occupied by the owner. Similar land in the neighbourhood but without buildings has sold recently for £6,000/ha.

The new road will sever 24 ha of the best land from the homestead and interfere with the water supply and land drainage of three fields.

The Highway Authority will fence along the whole length of the road, and at two points will provide underpasses giving access from the fields on one side of the road to those on the other. They will provide adequate land drainage along the sides of the road and to the slopes of the embankment and will make good any interference with the water supply.

Notice to treat was served on 25 March last. Estimate the compensation payable to the owner-occupier.

Valuation

Land Taken—
  3 ha at £6,000/ha   £18,000

Injury Due to Severance
  24 ha will be severed from the farmhouse and
  buildings and extra labour and risk will be
  involved in driving cattle to and from those
  fields.

Loss of value, say £600/ha on 24 ha	14,400
Disturbance on land taken, including possible loss on sale of stock, say	2,000
Tenant-right on land taken, say	1,000
Interference during construction of works:—	
(i) Depreciation of rental value on 24 ha for say, 6 months at £80/ha	
(ii) Total loss of rental value on 8 ha immediately adjoining the works, say	640
Cost of re-arranging fences between fields and ploughing up small area of pasture	2,000
Re-arrangement of land drainage to three fields	1,500
Compensation	£39,140

Plus surveyor's fees and legal costs.

Note:—The works of fencing, draining, etc., which the Highway Authority have undertaken to provide come under the heading of "accommodation works" or "works of reinstatement".

3. Compensation where No Part of the Land is Taken

The four rules which govern the right to compensation for injurious affection in this type of case in consequence of the decision of the House of Lords in *Metropolitan Board of Works v. McCarthy* (1874), have already been mentioned in Chapter 16. It should be remembered that these cases are treated very differently from those arising where some land has been taken from the claimant, as discussed above. Whereas in the latter cases compensation is paid in full for any injurious affection that is shown to occur, in these cases such proof is quite insufficient if the four *McCarthy* rules cannot be satisfied in full.

The four rules can be briefly recapitulated as follows:—

  (i) the works causing the injurious affection must be authorised by statute;

(ii) the harm must be of a kind which would be actionable in the civil courts but for that authorisation;

(iii) the loss to be compensated must be confined to land value (e.g., not business loss or other "disturbance");

(iv) the cause of the harm must be the *execution* of the works and not their *use* (e.g., the building of a new road or railway, not the effects of the traffic on it when opened).

Typical examples of successful claims are where authorised development by the acquiring body deprives an adjoining owner of the benefit of some easement attached to his land— such as a private right of light, as in *Eagle v. Charing Cross Rail Co.* (1867), or a private right of way—or is in breach of some restrictive covenant to the benefit of which the adjoining owner is entitled, as in *Re Simeon and the Isle of Wight Rural District Council* (1937).

Since the greatest stumbling-block to claimants has in most cases in practice been caused by rule (iv)—though rule (iii) also in practice frustrates claims from time to time, as shown in *Argyle Motors* (*Birkenhead*) *Ltd. v. Birkenhead Corporation* (1974)—Parliament enacted Part I of the Land Compensation Act 1973 to give owners (on and after 23 June, 1973) a right to compensation for depreciation to their land caused by the use (as distinct from the execution) of public works. The use must have begun on or after 17 October 1969, and must give rise to depreciation by reason of certain prescribed "physical factors", namely "noise, vibration, smell, fumes, smoke and artificial lighting and the discharge on to the land in respect of which the claim is made of any solid or liquid substance". The "responsible authority" which has promoted or carried out the works is liable, including the Crown (but no claim may be made in respect of "any aerodrome in the occupation of a government department"). The claimant must hold an "owner's interest" in the depreciated land, namely the freehold or a leasehold with three or more years to run. If it is a dwelling it must be his residence if his interest entitles him to occupy it; landlords of dwellings may also claim. If it is a farm he must occupy the whole even though his interest need only be in part. If it is any other kind of property his interest and occupation must relate to all or a "substantial part" of it and the rateable value must not exceed £2,250 (in respect of the valuations in force since April 1973). Claims for £50 or less are ignored.

The period for submitting a claim begins one year after the date when the use of the works began (the "relevant date"), subject to certain exceptions, and the normal six-year limitation period under the Limitation Act 1980 then starts to run. Prospective development value outside the Eighth Schedule to the Town and Country Planning Act 1971 (as amended), is not compensatable. Corresponding benefit to other land of the claimant will be "set off" against the compensation (if any). There must be no duplication of any compensation otherwise payable (e.g., under Section 7 of the 1965 Act, or as damages in tort for nuisance). Availability of grants for soundproofing must be taken into account.

The use giving rise to compensation must be taken to include reasonably foreseeable future intensification. Beyond this, subsequent alterations to works, or changes of use apart from mere intensification and apart from aerodromes or highways, will give an additional right to compensation. "Physical factors" caused by aircraft as such give no right to compensation except in respect of new or altered runways, "taxiways" or "aprons".

Once the legal right to compensation is established, it is then a question of determining the depreciation in the market value of the land due to the injury complained of. A claim made under Part I of the Land Compensation Act 1973, in *Hickmott v. Dorset County Council* (1975) failed because the claimant could show nothing beyond an increased fear of danger to property from passing traffic in consequence of road widening.[3] It is clear from *Pepys v. London Transport Executive* (1974) that in order to establish depreciation in market value it is not sufficient to show merely that a sale at a higher figure fell through by reason of the authority's works while a sale at a lower figure went ahead subsequently.

---

[3] See also *Streak and Streak v. Royal County of Berkshire* (1976): failure to attribute depreciation to proximity of new motorway. But the claimant in *Davies v. Mid-Glamorgan County Council* (1979), succeeded in a claim based on depreciation attributed to successive extensions to an airfield near his land.

The usual method is to make two valuations of the property—(i) as it previously stood, and (ii) after the interference with the legal right in question.

This "Before and After" method, as it is often called, can be used both in this type of case and also in cases where part of land has been taken. It is considered in detail in the next Section of this Chapter.

4. "Before and After" Method of Valuation

Besides the case where no part of the owner's land is taken, this method is also used in many cases of the taking of part of a property where, in practice, it is often very difficult to separate the value of the land taken from the injurious affection likely to be caused to the rest of the land by the construction and use of the undertaking.

As applied to this latter type of case it will involve two valuations—(i) of the property in its present condition unaffected by statutory powers, and (ii) of the property as it will be after the part has been taken and the undertaking is constructed and in use. The amount by which valuation (i) exceeds valuation (ii) will represent the compensation payable both for the loss of the land taken and also for injurious affection to the remainder. In addition, the owner might be entitled to claim for injury during the carrying out of the works, and it would be necessary to come to an understanding as to the works of reinstatement which the acquiring body are prepared to provide.

An example is the taking of a strip of land forming part of the garden or grounds of a house. Here it is usually very difficult to assign a value to the strip of land taken without at the same time considering all the consequences of the taking. For instance, suppose that the strip forms part of a garden of a fair sized house and is to be used in the construction of a new road, the following are some of the questions which will naturally suggest themselves in assessing the fair compensation to the owner:—

(i) Will the land remaining be reasonably sufficient for a house of this size and type? (ii) Will the proposed road be on the level, on an embankment, or in a cutting? (iii) Will it be visible from the house, and if so from what parts of it? (iv) What volume of traffic may be expected? (v) How close will the house be to the road and to what extent is it likely to suffer from loss of privacy, noise, fumes and other inconvenience?

It is obvious that the most realistic approach to the problem is that of comparing the value of the house as it now stands with its estimated value after a portion of the garden has been taken and the new road is in full use (as in the *Duke of Buccleuch's* case, above).

In theory, at any rate, there are two statutory obstacles to the use of this method—(i) the fact that the statutory assumptions as to planning permission apply to land taken, but not to land injuriously affected; (ii) the fact that Section 4(2) of the Land Compensation Act 1961, requires that the owner's statement of claim shall distinguish the amount claimed under separate heads and show how the amount claimed under each head is calculated.

Even so, it is probable that the valuer's first approach to a problem of this kind will be along the lines of a "before and after" method and that, having in this way arrived at what he considers a reliable figure, he will then proceed to apportion it if necessary as between compensation for land taken and compensation for severance and injurious affection to the remaining land.

The Lands Tribunal accepted the method in *Budgen v. Secretary of State for Wales* [1985] 2 EGLR 203 and in *Landlink Two Ltd. v. Sevenoaks D.C.* [1985] 1 EGLR 196 but in *A. D. P. & E. Farmers v. Dept. of Transport* [1988] 18 EG 80 preferred separate valuations of land taken and land retained.

Example 28–2

The factory illustrated below consists of a brick and slated building on two floors, in a reasonable state of repair, and is held on ground lease having 41 years still to run, the ground rent being £15 p.a. The leaseholder-occupier is a manufac-

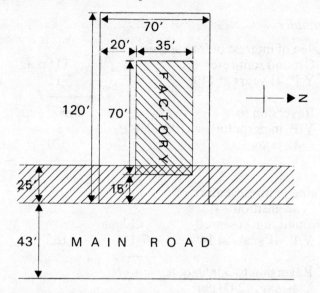

turer and the estimated rack rental is £13,500 p.a. (£3 per sq. ft.). The total floor space is 4,500 sq. ft. and the apportionment of the ground rent on the land to be taken has been agreed at £3 p.a.

A Highway Authority are acquiring a strip of land 25 ft wide on the west side of the main road for road-widening purposes and notice to treat was served on all interested parties in December last.

The forecourt is used for loading and unloading goods, the entrance doors being at present in front. It may be assumed that the Highway Authority will not permit lorries to stand on the new road for these purposes, and that the claim put forward by the owners of the two interests concerned, that the whole of the premises should be acquired, will not be upheld.

It is required to assess the compensation payable and to list the probable "accommodation works" to be agreed.

Valuation

> *Note:*—The statutory assumptions do not appear to affect the case, and the "Before and After" method of approach is therefore adopted.

Freeholder

Value of interest before acquisition:—

Ground rent reserved	£15 p.a.	
Y.P. 41 years at 14%	7·11	£106
Reversion to	£13,500 p.a.	
Y.P. in perpetuity at 10% deferred 41 years	·20	2,700
		£2,806

Value of interest after acquisition:—

Ground rent reserved	£12 p.a.		
Y.P. 41 years at 14%	7·11	£85	
Reversion to 3,900 sq. ft. at, say, £2·00 per sq. ft.	7,800 p.a.		
Y.P. in perpetuity at 11% deferred 41 years	·13	£1,014	£1,099
Compensation for land taken and injurious affection			£1,707

Note:—The Years' Purchase and rental value per square foot used in the "after acquisition" valuation are lower than those used in the "before acquisition" valuation as the property will then be less desirable, e.g., no forecourt loading and side entrance.

If it is required to divide this between the land taken and injurious affection the amount of the former could be obtained as follows:—

Loss in ground rent	£3 p.a.	
Y.P. 41 years at 14%	7·11	£21

Loss in rental value in reversion 600 sq. ft. at
£3 per sq. ft.   1,800 p.a.
Y.P. in perpetuity at 10%
deferred 41 years   ·20   360
                                                                   ————
Land taken, say   £381
Injurious affection   1,326
                                                                   ————
Compensation as above   £1,707
                                                                   ————

Leaseholder

Value of interest before acquisition:—
Rental value   £13,500 p.a.
Ground rent   15
                                                ————
Profit rent   £13,485
Y.P. 41 years at 12 and 3% (Tax
at 30%)   7·24   £97,631
                                                ————
Value of interest after acquisition:—
Net rental value   £7,800 p.a.
Ground rent   12
                                                ————
Profit rent   £7,788
Y.P. 41 years at 13 and 3% (Tax
at 30%)   6·75   £52,569
                                                ————
Compensation for injurious affection and
land taken   £45,062
Cost of internal re-arrangement of factory due
to entrance doors being at side and rear,
say   20,000
Temporary loss of net profits while production
impaired, say   15,000
                                                           ————
Total   £80,062
                                                           ————

Note:—If required, the sum of £45,062 mentioned could be
apportioned between "land taken" and "injurious
affection" in a similar manner to that done above
in respect of the freehold interest.

The accommodation works would probably include:—

Demolition of existing front wall, erection of new wall
and making good.
Making side entrances and rear yard fit for traffic, e.g.,
tarmac surface, etc.
Any re-arrangement of drainage necessary.
Forming opening in side or rear wall and provision of
entrance doors.
New front gates and boundary walls.

5. ADJUSTMENT OF UNEXPENDED BALANCE

Where, in connection with a compulsory acquisition, or
corresponding sale by agreement, compensation is paid for
severance or injurious affection, in respect either of land
held with land taken or land not so held, the Town and
Country Planning Act 1971 (Section 143(1) and (2)), provides
that any unexpended balance which may attach to the land
will in future be deemed to be reduced by a sum equal to
the amount by which:—

(i) the compensation payable exceeds
(ii) the compensation which would have been payable had
the value of the land been calculated on an "existing
use" basis.[4]

In other words, the unexpended balance is reduced by
so much of the compensation as represents injury to the
development value of the land. The question of the unexpended balance of established development value has been
discussed already in Chapter 24.

---

[4] That is on the assumption that permission would only be granted for development within Schedule 8 (as amended) and not for "new development".

Example 28–3

A sports ground with a total area of 8 acres is let by the freeholder to a club on annual tenancy at a rent of £8,000 per annum. The whole of the land is zoned residential at a density of 10 houses to the acre in the Development Plan and it was anticipated that development would commence in two years' time when the land would be worth £500,000 per acre. An original unexpended balance of £2,400 is attached to the land.

The freeholder has just been served with a notice to treat in respect of 3 acres of the land which is required for a car park and for the erection of public conveniences.

The acquisition will not delay development of the land not being acquired but it is considered that its value for residential development will be only £400,000 per acre and that as a sports ground it will let for £3,000 per annum.

Assess the compensation payable to the freeholder for the land taken and injurious affection to the remainder.

Valuation

The most profitable assumption will be the value for the purpose for which the land is zoned and the claim will be made on this basis.

Value of interest before acquisition:—			
Rental value as			
sports ground	£8,000 p.a.		
Y.P. 2 years at 10%	1·74		£13,920
Reversion to			
building value—			
8ac. at £500,000			
per acre	£4,000,000		
P.V. £1 in 2 years at			
13%		·78	£3,120,000 £3,133,920

Value of interest after acquisition:—		b/f £3,133,920
Rental value as sports ground	£3,000 p.a.	
Y.P. 2 years at 10%	1·74	£5,220
Reversion to building value—5 ac at £400,000 per acre	£2,000,000	
P.V. £1 in 2 years at 13%	·78	£1,560,000 £1,565,220
Compensation for land taken and injurious affection		£1,568,700

1. Compensation for land taken

Rental value as sports ground—3 ac at £1,000 per acre	£3,000 p.a.	
Y.P. 2 years at 10%	1·74	£5,220
Reversion to building value—3 ac at £500,000 per acre	£1,500,000	
P.V. £1 in 2 years at 13%	·78	£1,170,000 £1,175,220

2. Compensation for injurious affection   £393,480

Effect of acquisition on unexpended balance:—

Assume that unexpended balance is spread rateably over the whole area.

The original unexpended balance on the land taken, £900, will be extinguished.

The original unexpended balance on the land not taken, £1,500, will be reduced on the next occasion when it becomes necessary to know whether or not a balance is attached to the land (e.g., if planning permission is refused in 2 years' time for the erection of houses and a claim is made for compensation), by the amount by which the compensation for injurious affection exceeds the depreciation in the existing use value.

Compensation for injurious affection			£393,480
Existing use value before acquisition:—			
Rental value—5 ac at			
£1,000 per ac	£5,000 p.a.		
Y.P. perp. at 10%	10	£50,000	
Existing use value after acquisition:—			
Rental value—5 ac at			
£600 per ac	£3,000 p.a.		
Y.P. perp. at 10%	10	£30,000	£20,000
Excess			£373,480

The unexpended balance will, not surprisingly, be extinguished.

Note:—In calculating the compensation payable, allowance would have to be made for any compensation payable by the landlord to the sports club as tenants under Part II of the Landlord and Tenant Act 1954.

CHAPTER 29

Compulsory Purchase Compensation—III. Compensation for Disturbance

1. DISTURBANCE COMPENSATION AND DISTURBANCE PAYMENTS

DISTURBANCE COMPENSATION is an element of compulsory purchase compensation, that is to say it is a sum added to the purchase price of land compulsorily acquired. It is not payable in respect of land retained by a claimant—a point reaffirmed in *Argyle Motors* (*Birkenhead*) *Ltd. v. Birkenhead Corporation*, (1974)—and is therefore a totally separate head of compensation from severance and injurious affection. It has been evolved as a principle of case law, without express authorisation in any statute (apart from Rule 6 of Section 5 of the Land Compensation Act 1961, which provides that the rules governing the assessment of land value "shall not affect the assessment of compensation for disturbance...."). It is therefore in a sense "parasitic", because there must first be an acquisition price and, if there is, disturbance compensation can then be included in it. In *I.R.C. v. Glasgow & South Western Rly. Co.* (1887) 12 App. Cas. 315, Lord Halsbury L.C. referred to acceptable claims for such well-known disturbance items as "damages for loss of business" and "compensation for the goodwill" but added: "in strictness the thing which is to be ascertained is the price to be paid for the land...."

Disturbance *payments*, on the other hand, are authorised by statute (Sections 37–8 of the Land Compensation Act 1973) in certain cases in which disturbance compensation is not payable because, although a compulsory acquisition has in fact taken place (or some comparable occurrence—see below), the claimant himself has not had any interest compulsorily acquired from him but instead has merely been dispossessed. These are situations in which a tenant holding under

643

a short term leasehold has not had that term renewed by
the acquiring authority which has taken his landlord's place
on acquiring the latter's reversion. The dispossession must
have occurred on or after 17 October, 1972, in consequence
(i) of the acquisition of the reversion under compulsory
powers, or (ii) of an order or undertaking under the Housing
Acts, or (iii) of redevelopment by an authority holding the
land for a purpose for which the reversion was acquired under
compulsory powers. Licensees cannot claim these payments
as of right, though authorities have a discretion to pay them.
Agricultural land is excluded. But an occupier from whom
a dwelling is compulsorily purchased *at site value without
owner—occupier's supplement* can claim a disturbance payment, since site value precludes disturbance compensation.

Section 38(1) of the 1973 Act provides as follows:

"The amount of a disturbance payment shall be equal to:—
(a) the reasonable expenses of the person entitled to the payment in removing
    from the land from which he is displaced; and
(b) if he was carrying on a trade or business on that land, the loss he will sustain
    by reason of the disturbance of that trade or business consequent upon his
    having to quit the land".

If a business tenant would also be entitled to compensation
for loss of security of tenure under Section 37 of the Landlord
and Tenant Act 1954, he is entitled to choose whichever
amount is the higher, the payment under that Section or
the disturbance payment, but not both (1973 Act, Section
37(4)). It should be observed that this provision is worded
in pretty broad terms; though whether the Lands Tribunal
(which settles disputes as to amounts, in the first instance)
and the courts will interpret it broadly remains to be seen.
Regard, however, must be had to the probable length of
time for which the land from which the claimant has been
dispossessed would have been available for his use, and also
to the availability of other land, when "estimating the loss"
(Section 38(2)).

It is important to remember that disturbance payments
(under the 1973 Act) are claimable by a tenant who has been
dispossessed but not expropriated; whereas disturbance compensation is claimable by any tenant or freeholder who has
been *both* dispossessed *and* expropriated because it is

included in (and treated as part of) his expropriation compensation. It follows from this that it is rare for a landlord to justify a claim for disturbance compensation, since he is not being dispossessed even though he may be expropriated. In *Lee v. Minister of Transport*, (1966) 1 Q.B. 111, Davies L.J. said: "Disturbance must, in my judgment, refer to the fact of having to vacate the premises." Thus, if premises are let by a freeholder to a periodic tenant, the former may be expropriated but not dispossessed while the latter (if served with a notice to quit and not notice to treat or notice of entry) will be dispossessed but not expropriated. The tenant would now qualify for a disturbance payment: but neither would be entitled to claim disturbance compensation.

An exception may, however, be recognised when both landlord and tenant are corporate bodies sufficiently closely connected with one another to be treated virtually as the same person, for example if they are related companies with the same directors and their separate identity is a mere matter of form. In *D. H. N. Food Distributors Ltd. v. London Borough of Tower Hamlets* (1975) 30 P. & C.R. 251, the Court of Appeal held this to be the case for two companies with the same directors, of which one company owned the freehold of the acquired premises and the other occupied them as licensee; and the directors were awarded disturbance compensation. But in *Woolfson v. Strathclyde Regional Council*, (1978) 38 P. & C.R. 521, the House of Lords insisted that normally where there are two companies they must expect to be treated separately, since they are in law two separate "persons". Their Lordships distinguished the *D.H.N.* case narrowly upon its own special facts. In *Woolfson* there were two companies, as in *D.H.N.*, one owning the acquired premises and the other occupying them under a licence; ownership and membership of the two companies was not identical, even though there was a very considerable overlap as regards both shareholders and directors.

If a periodic tenant or any tenant whose term does not exceed a year is in fact turned out (by notice of entry) before his tenancy is terminable at common law, then Section 20 of the Compulsory Purchase Act 1965, requires the acquiring authority to compensate him accordingly, since he is being expropriated. The market value of his interest may well be small, or nominal, but the right to compensation in principle carries with it the right to include disturbance items, which may well constitute the bulk of the claim in such a case.

2. DISTURBANCE COMPENSATION: ITEMS WHICH MAY BE CLAIMED

(a) *Residential Premises*

Where a dwelling-house is compulsorily acquired, the occupier, if he be a freeholder, or a lessee enjoying an appreciable profit rent, will be entitled to compensation based on the market value of his interest in the property, estimated in accordance with the statutory provisions already described. If he be a lessee or tenant holding under a contractual tenancy and paying approximately the full rack rental of the premises, the value of his interest in the land will be negligible, but he will be entitled to some measure of compensation for being forced to quit before the expiration of his term—similarly, when the interest is no greater than that of a yearly tenant and the tenant is required to give up possession before the expiration of his interest. No definite basis can be prescribed for these types of cases; but where the lease still has a number of years to run, a figure of one year's rent is often allowed for what may conveniently be called "extinction of lease". But if the acquiring body have compulsorily purchased the reversion they will become the tenant's new landlord, and they may well be content to await the termination of his tenancy contractually by effluxion of time or notice to quit, in which case there will be no purchase price in which disturbance can be included.

In addition to the value of his interest in the land, or a suitable allowance for the termination of that interest, and in theory part of it, the occupier will then also be entitled to disturbance compensation in respect of (i) disposal of fixtures, (ii) cost of removal, and (iii) other incidental expenses caused by having to leave the premises.

Fixtures. The occupier may remove any fixtures to which he is entitled, or he may insist on the acquiring body taking them as part of the premises. If he moves them he is entitled to compensation for any depreciation they are likely to suffer in the process of removal and fixing elsewhere—in practice an allowance of 50–75 per cent of their value is often adopted as a convenient basis for this item. If the fixtures are taken with the premises, the owner is entitled to their fair value as fixtures to an incoming tenant.

Cost of Removal. This item will include not only the actual cost of moving the owner's furniture to other premises but also any other expense incidental thereto, such as temporary storage of furniture, cost of adapting various items of furnishing, such as blinds and curtains to the new premises, change of address on stationery, etc.

Incidental Expenses. In addition to cost of removal, there may be other incidental expenses incurred by an owner-occupier in consequence of being dispossessed of his premises.

In *Harvey v. Crawley Development Corporation,*[1] Romer, L.J. summarised the principle governing the inclusion of such items in the claim as follows: "The authorities . . . establish that any loss sustained by a dispossessed owner (at all events one who occupies his house) which flows from a compulsory acquisition may properly be regarded as the subject of compensation for disturbance provided, first, it is not too remote and secondly, that it is the natural and reasonable consequence of the dispossession of the owner." In the case in question the claimant, who was required to sell and give up possession of her house, was entitled to recover legal costs, surveyor's fees and travelling expenses incurred in finding another house to live in, together with similar expenses incurred to no purpose in connection with the proposed purchase of a house on which she received an unfavourable report from her surveyor. Such fees are a genuine loss; whereas a purchase price paid for new premises, large or small, represents not a loss but "value for money".

Legal and other professional fees incurred after notice to treat in connection with the preparation of the owner's claim are also recoverable under Rule 6 of Section 5 of the Land Compensation Act 1961. This practice was sanctioned by

[1] [1957] 1 Q.B. 485.

the Court of Appeal in *London County Council v. Tobin*, [1959] 1 All E.R. 649. But the same Court, in *Lee v. Minister of Transport* [1966] 1 Q.B. 111, held that these items, though within Rule 6, are not "disturbance" but are covered by the words "any other matters not directly based on the value of the land". Thus solicitors' and surveyors' fees incurred in obtaining new premises count as "disturbance" items; but solicitors' and surveyors' fees incurred in preparing the compulsory purchase claim itself count as "any other matter". As an exception to the general position the legal fees incurred in conveying the interest to the authority are reimbursed under Section 23 of the Compulsory Purchase Act 1965.

(b) Business and Professional Premises

Like the householder, the occupier of business premises will be entitled on compulsory purchase to compensation for (i) the value of his interest in the land or for "extinction of lease", (ii) loss of or injury to fixtures, and (iii) cost of removal. In addition, a trader or business man may have a claim for loss on stock and trade disturbance.

Compensation for Interest in Land. As in the case of house property, if a lessee is enjoying a substantial profit rent he will be entitled to compensation for loss of his leasehold interest based on the ordinary principles of compulsory purchase valuation as explained above, in Chapter 27.

It is submitted that a claim of this kind is not affected by the provisions of the Landlord and Tenant Act 1954. For although under that Act the tenancy will automatically continue after the termination date, the landlord, by serving the necessary notice under the Act, can ensure that the new tenancy shall be at a rent at which (having regard to the other terms of the tenancy) the holding might reasonably be expected to be let in the open market. In any case the Land Compensation Act 1973, Section 47, requires that both the business tenancy and the reversion to it be valued on the basis that the tenancy enjoys statutory protection.

Where the rent already paid under the lease is approximately the full rack rental value of the premises, the additional security of tenure given by the Landlord and Tenant

Act 1954, would appear to strengthen the tenant's claim for compensation for "extinction of lease", although it must be remembered that this factor may well be reflected in the claim for "injury to goodwill" or "trade disturbance".

At all events, there is no justification for any item of loss being paid twice over, no matter what head of claim it may appear under. As stated above, whenever business premises are compulsorily purchased (as distinct from being terminated at common law) the purchase price, of the tenancy and of the reversion alike, is determined on the footing that the tenancy enjoys security of tenure under the Act of 1954. The authority's right to obtain possession is ignored for this purpose; though if the landlord has in fact an independent ground to terminate the tenant's security of tenure, that must be taken into account. (This is enacted in the Land Compensation Act 1973, Section 47).

In the case of a tenant from year to year, or for any lesser interest, whose right to compensation depends on Section 20 of the Compulsory Purchase Act 1965 replacing Section 121 of the Lands Clauses Consolidation Act 1845, Section 39 of the Landlord and Tenant Act 1954, as amended by Section 47 of the Land Compensation Act 1973, expressly provides that the total compensation paid to him is not to be less than that which, in certain circumstances, he might have received under Section 37 of the 1954 Act if a new tenancy had been refused—i.e., an amount equal to three times the rateable value, or to six times the rateable value where the tenant or his predecessors in business have been in occupation of the holding for the past 14 years.

Fixtures. The occupier will probably insist on these being taken with the premises, since the possibility of transferring and adapting them to other premises usually is somewhat problematical. He nevertheless has this choice open to him on the authority of *Gibson v. Hammersmith and City Rail Co.* (1863). In *Tamplin's Brewery Ltd. v. County Borough of Brighton* (1970) the acquiring authority made new premises available to the claimants, and the outstanding question of compensation related to equipment. The claimants bought new equipment and relinquished the old. They then claimed the cost of the new equipment as an item of compensation, reduced only by an amount representing a saving in operating costs. The Lands Tribunal accepted this in principle, though with a reduction in the total sum. Yet it would seem that the claimants, in obtaining new equipment, got "value for money" in so doing; and this may cast doubt on the principle of the award in this case.

Cost of Removal. This will often be substantial, including in the case of industrial premises such items as the cost of moving machinery and its reinstallation in new premises.

Incidental Expenses. These will include notification of change of address to customers, new sign writing, stationery, etc. As in the case of private houses, there is authority for the inclusion of legal and surveyors' fees incurred in connection with the acquisition of new premises and also legal and other professional fees incurred in connection with the preparation of the claim.[2]

Loss on Stock. This may consist either of depreciation in the process of removal to other premises, or loss on forced sale in those cases where no other premises are available, or where the trade likely to be done in new premises will be of a somewhat different class, or where the stock will not bear removal.

Loss on depreciation may be expressed as a percentage of the value in the trader's books, but may be covered by the cost of taking out an insurance policy before the move. Loss on forced sale is likely to be high—possibly 33–50 per cent on retail prices.

Trade Disturbance. "Trade disturbance" is the term applied to the loss likely to result from a trader or business man being dispossessed of his premises. The capital value of the business, as distinct from that of the premises, is its "goodwill", and depends on the profits made in the course of trading. "Goodwill" is capital, and profits are income; but since the one is derived from the other it is important always to remember that the same loss is not compensatable twice over.

It will be convenient to discuss the nature of this loss in

[2] See *London County Council v. Tobin* [1959] 1 W.L.R. 354; also *Rowley v. Southampton Corporation* (1959) 10 P & C.R., 172.

relation to retail trades and then to see to what extent the same considerations apply to the wholesale trader, the manufacturer or the professional man.

The "goodwill" of a business has been defined as the probability of the business being carried on at a certain level of profit. In effect it is the business itself as a capital asset, distinct from (a) the premises, (b) the stock-in-trade and other chattels, (c) the profits and income from the business. Where a trader has been in business in certain premises for a number of years he will have acquired a circle of regular customers on whose patronage he can rely; he will also be able to count on a fairly steady volume of casual custom. As a result, by striking an average over three or four normal years he can make a fairly accurate estimate of his annual profits. It is the probability of those profits being maintained, or even increased, in the future which constitutes the "goodwill" of the business.

Although goodwill is a capital item assessable on the prospect of continuing profits in future years, the profits to be earned in the course of current trading are another matter. They are the subject of compensation in their own right (*Watson v. Secretary of State for Air*, [1954] 2 All E.R. 582) if the compulsory acquisition prevents their being earned in fact because it cuts short the commercial activity which would, if continued, have produced them.

In *Bailey v. Derby Corporation* [1965] 1 All E.R. 443, the Master of the Rolls, Lord Denning, in regard to the claimant's demand for compensation in respect of the goodwill of his business, said: "All that is acquired is the land. The compensation is given for the value of the land, not for the value of the business." But the reason why the claim for goodwill failed in this case was that the claimant could have disposed of it on the open market had he tried. His excuse for not trying, namely age and ill-health, was not in fact valid, because age and ill-health need not prevent such a transaction being put in hand. It is to be noted that the claimant succeeded in obtaining £1,200 for loss of profits.

The sequel to this case was the enactment of Section 46 of the Land Compensation Act 1973. This allows claimants aged 60 or over (irrespective of health) to require compensation to include extinguishment of goodwill if they have not independently disposed of that asset. They must give an undertaking not to dispose of it nor to carry on the business themselves within a reasonable area and period to be specified, on pain of having to repay the amount in question. The premises must not have a rateable value in excess of £2,250. Special rules apply where a claim is made by a partnership or company.

The various factors which go to make goodwill can usually be divided into two classes—(i) those which, being of a personal nature, do not depend on the situation of the premises, e.g., the name and reputation of the firm or the personality of the proprietor; (ii) those which are dependent on situation, e.g., the advantage derived from being on the main shopping street of a town or in a street or district which is the recognised centre for businesses of a particular type.

When business premises are taken under compulsory powers the tradesman's goodwill is not necessarily destroyed but it may be seriously damaged. How seriously depends upon whether the goodwill is mainly personal in character or largely dependent upon the situation of the premises. The test of whether goodwill can legitimately be said to have been partially or totally extinguished, thus justifying a claim for compensation, is to consider whether or not it could reasonably be sold on the open market and whether its marketability, if any, has been reduced because of the circumstances of the compulsory purchase.

The usual method of assessing this class of loss is by multiplying the average annual net profits by a figure of Years' Purchase which varies according to the extent of the injury likely to be suffered. In most cases the figure of net profits is based on the past three years' trading as shown by the trader's books. The accounts are often supplied to the valuer by the claimant's accountant.

Usually, however, the figures given will not have taken into account interest on the capital employed in the business, and as the trader could earn interest upon his capital by investing it elsewhere, the annual profit due to the business is really not the figure taken from the books, but that figure less interest on capital. The tenant's capital would comprise the value of the fixtures and fittings, stock, etc., and the necessary sum to be kept in hand for working expenses. The latter item would obviously be larger in the case of a credit business than in a cash business. The valuer needs, therefore, to examine the figure supplied to him as the average net profits and to make a deduction for interest on capital if that has not already been done.

He must also ascertain what rent has been charged in the books. Usually the actual rent paid is charged in the accounts, and if the valuer estimates that the property is worth more than the rent paid, he must deduct the estimated profit rent. While in the case of a freehold, if no rent has been charged, the estimated annual rental used for arriving at the value of the property must be deducted.

The wages of assistants employed in a firm will naturally be deducted in finding the net profits. But it was held by the Lands Tribunal in *Perezic v. Bristol Corporation*[3] that there was no evidence that it was customary to deduct a sum in respect of the remuneration of the working proprietor of a one-man business.

In a later case—*A. V. Speyer v. City of Westminster*,[4] the Tribunal expressed the view that whether such a deduction was appropriate or not must depend on the effect of the disturbance on the earning capacity of the claimant.

In *Appleby & Ireland Ltd. v. Hampshire County Council*[5] a considerable number of adjustments to the net profits shown in the accounts were made including adjustments in respect of directors' reasonable remuneration (as against actual salaries paid), bad debts, and exceptional expenditure on research.

Such of these deductions as are applicable having been made, and true net profits having been found, the next step is to fix the multiplier which should be applied to this figure in order fairly to compensate the trader for injury to his goodwill.

Where the taking of the premises will mean total extinction of trade the full value of the goodwill may be allowed as

[3] (1955) 5 P. & C.R. 237.
[4] (1958) 9 P. & C.R. 478.
[5] (1978) 247 EG 1183.

compensation. In the case of retail businesses, this normally ranges between 2 to 5 Years' Purchase of the net profits. The figure used will be influenced, amongst other things, by whether the profits appear to be increasing or decreasing.

Where the trade will not be totally lost but may be seriously injured by removal to other premises, a fair compensation may be about half what would be paid for total extinction. But a much lower figure will be given where the trade is likely to be carried on almost as profitably as before.

A cash tobacconist adjoining the entrance of a busy railway station may lose the whole trade if the premises upon which the trade is carried on are taken from him. In such a case, up to the full value of the business may be appropriate compensation—possibly 3 Years' Purchase of the net profits.

A milkman, on the contrary, knowing all his customers by reason of delivery of milk daily at the houses, may face removal with little risk of loss of that portion of his trade, and a baker or family butcher may be much in the same category, although any of these may suffer some loss of casual custom, and also in respect of some items sold over the counter. In such cases a half-a-year's profits would often be proper compensation.

It is obvious that since the variety of trades is so great and the circumstances of each case may vary so widely, every claim of this sort must be judged on its merits. But the following are amongst the most important considerations likely to affect the figure of compensation:—

(i) The nature of the trade and the extent to which it depends upon the position of the premises. For instance, a grocer or confectioner or draper whose business is done entirely over the counter will suffer considerable loss if he has to move to premises in an inferior trade position. Probably 1½–2 Years' Purchase of his net profits would not be excessive compensation. On the other hand, a credit tailor would be far less likely to be injured by removal since his customers might be expected to follow him.

Where the trade is partly cash and partly credit, the valuer may think it proper to separate the profits attributable to the two parts and to apply a higher figure of Years' Purchase to the former than to the latter.

(ii) The prospects of alternative accommodation. For instance, in many cases a shopkeeper turned out of his present premises will find it impossible to obtain a shop elsewhere in the town and a claim for total loss of goodwill may be justified. Or, again, the fact that the only alternative accommodation available is on a secondary shopping street may considerably affect the figure.

(iii) The terms on which the premises are held. The compensation payable to a trader holding on a lease with a number of years to run will probably be substantially the same as that of a claimant in similar circumstances who owns the freehold of his premises—particularly in view of the additional security of tenure enjoyed under the Landlord and Tenant Act 1954. But a shopkeeper who holds on a yearly tenancy only can scarcely expect as high a level of compensation.

The question of compensation payable to wholesale traders and manufacturers involves similar considerations to those already discussed. It will usually be found, however, that the probable injury to trade is much less than in the case of retail business, since profits are not so dependent upon position. Provided other suitable premises are available, the claim is usually one for so many months' temporary loss of profits during the time it will take to establish the business elsewhere, rather than any permanent injury to goodwill (e.g. see *Appleby & Ireland v. Hampshire County Council*).[6]

In this type of case the sum claimed for temporary loss of income has been regarded as not subject to income tax because compulsory purchase compensation, regardless of its particular components is supposed to be "one sum" in the nature of a "price to be paid for the land" (*Inland Revenue Commissioners v. Glasgow and South Western Rail Co.* (1887), 12 App. Cas, 315—a decision of the House of Lords). It was therefore held in *West Suffolk County Council v.*

[6] [1978] 247 EG 1183.

Rought Ltd.,[7] that the Lands Tribunal, in assessing the compensation payable for temporary loss of profits, should have deducted their estimate of the additional taxation which the claimant company would have had to bear if it had actually earned the amount which the interruption to its business prevented it from earning, because if earned in fact that amount would have been liable to tax as income. On this basis acquiring authorities for some time paid compensation to companies net of tax. However, changes in the tax status of compensation payments flowed from provisions in the Finance Acts 1965 and 1969 and the Income and Corporation Taxes Act 1970, and the current position based on the decision of the Court of Appeal in *Stoke-on-Trent City Council v. Wood Mitchell & Co. Ltd.* (1978) 248 EG 870, is that temporary loss of profits, loss on stock and such revenue items as removal expenses and interest, are paid gross by the acquiring authority and then taxed as receipts in the hands of the claimant company.

In the case of professional men, such as solicitors or surveyors, the goodwill of the business is mainly personal and is not very likely to be injured by removal. But the special circumstances of the case must be considered, particularly the question of alternative accommodation. For instance, a firm of solicitors in a big city usually requires premises in the recognised legal quarter and in close touch with the courts, although this consideration might be of less importance to an old-established firm than to a comparatively new one.

In some cases of trade disturbance a basis somewhat similar to that of reinstatement is used in making the claim.

Thus, a claimant forced to vacate his factory, shop, etc., may show that he is obliged to move to other premises, which are the only ones available, and will base his claim for trade disturbance on the cost of adapting the new premises plus the reduced value of his goodwill in those premises.

The latter figure may be due to reduction in profits on account of increased running costs (other than rent) in the

---

[7] [1957] A.C. 403—a decision of the House of Lords following the House's decision in *British Transport Commission v. Gourley* [1956] A.C. 185, which applied this principle to payments of damages in tort.

new premises. For instance, heating and lighting may cost more, transport costs may be higher, it may be necessary to employ more labour owing to the more difficult layout of a production line.

Or, again, the new position may not be so convenient for some customers as was the old. Or it may involve some change in the nature of the business which tends to make the profits rather less secure. For instance, in *L.C.C. v. Tobin*[8] the Court of Appeal approved a figure for trade disturbance although it appeared that the profits in the new premises were likely to be higher than in the old. The compensation was based on the difference between the value of the profits in the old premises multiplied by 3 Y.P. and those in the new premises multiplied by $1\frac{1}{2}$ Y.P., the lower figure being justified by changes in the general circumstances of the business in the new premises.

To justify a claim based on reinstatement of the business in other premises a claimant must show that he has acted reasonably and taken only such premises as a prudent person would take in order to safeguard his interests and mitigate his loss. In *Appleby & Ireland v. Hampshire County Council*[9] the Lands Tribunal held that the claimants should have moved to premises in the town where they were when acquired and compensation was assessed on the notional move rather than costs and losses incurred in the actual move to another town.

If there are no premises to which he can remove, except at a cost much out of proportion to what he is giving up, he may be justified in taking those premises; but he may in certain circumstances, particularly in the case of a trader, be compelled to allow a set-off from the cost of so reinstating himself in respect of the improved position he enjoys.

An acquiring body may sometimes offer alternative accommodation with a view to meeting a claim for trade disturbance.

Thus, if a retail trader claims that his business will suffer complete loss by the taking of the premises in which it is

[8] [1959] 1 W.L.R. 354
[9] [1978] 28 EG 326.

carried on, it is open to the acquiring authority to indicate premises which can be acquired for the reinstatement of the trade, or even to offer to build premises on land belonging to themselves, available for the purpose, and to transfer the premises to the claimant, in reduction of his claim. Arrangements of this kind are usually a matter of agreement between the parties. A claimant cannot be forced to accept alternative accommodation, although he may find it difficult to substantiate a heavy claim for trade disturbance in cases where it is offered.

In *Lindon Print Ltd v. West Midlands C.C.*[10] the Lands Tribunal accepted that the onus of proof is on the acquiring authority to show that the claimant has not mitigated his loss.

3. DISTURBANCE AND DEVELOPMENT VALUE

In *Horn v. Sunderland Corporation*,[11] Lord Greene, M.R., said that Rule 6 "does not confer a right to claim compensation for disturbance. It merely leaves unaffected the right which the owner would, before the Act of 1919, have had in a proper case to claim that the compensation to be paid for the land should be increased on the ground that he has been disturbed".

In the same case this right was described as "the right to receive a money payment not less than the loss imposed on him in the public interest, but on the other hand no greater".

It is true that, in practice, the value of the land itself will be assessed in accordance with Rule 2 and another figure for disturbance may be arrived at under Rule 6. But these two figures are, in fact, merely the elements which go to build up the single total figure of price or compensation to which the owner is fairly entitled in all the circumstances of the case and which should represent the loss he suffers in consequence of the land being taken from him.

It follows that an owner cannot claim a figure for distur-

---

[10] [1987] 2 EGLR 200.
[11] [1941] 2 K.B. 26; 1 All E.R. 480.

bance which is inconsistent with the basis adopted for the assessment of the value of the land under Rule 2.

For instance, in *Mizzen Bros. v. Mitcham U.D.C.* (1929)[12] it was held that claimants were not entitled to combine in the same claim a valuation of the land on the basis of an immediate sale for building purposes and a claim for disturbance and consequential damage upon the footing of interference with a continuing market garden business since they could not realise the building value of the land in the open market unless they were themselves prepared to abandon their market garden business. The existing use value of the land as a market garden was about £12,000, and the disturbance items totalled £4,640. These items when aggregated still fell short of the development value of the land for building, which was £17,280, but they could not justify any additional claim on top of that sum by way of disturbance, even though they were in fact being disturbed.

On the other hand, where a valuation on the basis of the present use of the land, plus compensation for disturbance, may exceed a valuation of the land based on a new and more profitable user, the owner has been held entitled to claim the former figure, though not both.

The facts in *Horn v. Sunderland Corporation* were that land having prospective building value and containing deposits of sand, limestone and gravel was compulsorily acquired for housing purposes. The owner occupied the land as farm land, chiefly for the rearing of pedigree horses.

The owner claimed the market value of the land as a building estate ripe for immediate development and also a substantial sum in respect of the disturbance of his farming business.

The official arbitrator awarded a sum of £22,700 in respect of the value of the land as building land, but disallowed any compensation in respect of disturbance of the claimant's business on the grounds that the sum assessed could not be realised in the open market unless vacant possession were given to the purchaser for the purpose of building development.

It was held by a majority of the Court of Appeal that

---

[12]Estates Gazette Digest, 1929, p. 258; reprinted "Estates Gazette", 25 January, 1941, p. 102.

the arbitrator's award was right in law provided that the sum of £22,700 equalled or exceeded—(i) the value of the land as farm land, plus (ii) whatever value should be attributable to the minerals if the land were treated as farm land, plus (iii) the loss by disturbance of the farming business.

If, however, the aggregate of items (i), (ii) and (iii) exceeded the figure of £22,700 the claimant was entitled to be paid the excess as part of the compensation for the loss of his land.

Claims for disturbance must relate to losses which are the direct result of the compulsory taking of the land and which are not remote or purely speculative in character. Loss of profits in connection with a business carried on on the premises and which will be directly injured by the dispossession of the owner is a permissible subject of claim. But where a speculator claimed, in addition to the market value of building land, the profits which he hoped to make from the erection of houses on the land, the latter item was disallowed.[13] It was quite distinct from the development value of the land, which was a legitimate item of claim on the basis just described. The point at issue was succinctly put by Lord Moulton in a decision of the Privy Council (*Pastoral Finance Association Ltd. v. The Minister (New South Wales)*, [1914] A.C. 1083), when he said that "no man would pay for the land, in addition to its market value, the capitalised value of the savings and additional profits which he would hope to make by the use of it". Again, where an owner of business premises compulsorily acquired was also the principal shareholder in the company which occupied the premises on a short-term tenancy, a claim in respect of the depreciation in the value of her shares which might result if the acquiring body gave the company notice to quit was held to be too remote for compensation.[14]

In *Palatine Graphic Arts Co Ltd v. Liverpool C.C.*[15], the Court of Appeal decided that a regional development grant

---

[13] *Collins v. Feltham U.D.C.* [1937] 4 All E.R. 189; and see *McEwing & Sons Ltd. v. Renfrew County Council* (1960) 11 P & C.R. 306.
[14] *Roberts v. Coventry Corporation* [1947] 1 All E.R. 308.
[15] [1986] 1 EGLR 19.

paid to claimants should not be deducted from their compulsory purchase compensation.

4. HOME LOSS AND FARM LOSS PAYMENTS

The Land Compensation Act 1973, makes additional provision for compensation broadly within the scope of disturbance, namely "home loss" and "farm loss" payments. These do not depend on the distinction between dispossession with expropriation and dispossession without expropriation, and therefore cut across the dividing line which separates disturbance compensation from disturbance payments.

Home loss payments may be claimed under Sections 29–33 of the 1973 Act by a freeholder, leaseholder, statutory tenant or employee, in respect of a dwelling substantially occupied by him (in that capacity) as his main residence for the last five years, from which he has been displaced against his will on or after 17 October, 1972 in circumstances similar to those giving rise to a disturbance payment as described earlier in this Chapter. (Caravan-dwellers also can claim a home loss payment on proof of five years' residence within a caravan site). The claim must be made within six months of the displacement. If the claimant has been resident for five years but not in a capacity described above (i.e., he has been a mere licensee for part of the time), the period can be made up by adding the period of occupancy of his predecessors. The payment consists of a set figure, which is three times the rateable value of the dwelling, subject to a maximum of £1,500 and a minimum of £150. A home loss payment has been upheld in respect of displacement from a "pre-fab" which was due for removal and replacement by a more substantial dwelling: *R v. Corby District Council ex p. McLean*, [1975] 2 All E.R. 568.

Farm loss payments may be claimed under Sections 34–6 of the 1973 Act, but only by freeholders or leaseholders with three years unexpired whose interest is compulsorily purchased with the result that they are (on or after 17 October, 1972) displaced from their farms ("agricultural units") against their will. Yearly tenant farmers are thus debarred from obtaining these payments. A claimant must begin to farm another "agricultural unit" in Great Britain not more than three years after being displaced, and at some time between the date when the acquiring authority were authorised to acquire his original farm and the date when he begins to farm the new one he must acquire a freehold, or a lease with at least three years to run, in the latter. The amount of the payment is calculated as the average annual profit from the original farm during the three years immediately before the displacement, or during such shorter period as the claimant has been in occupation, deducting (i) an amount representing a reasonable rent (regardless of the actual rent) if the claimant is a tenant responsible for outgoings and (ii) any items already included in a claim for disturbance compensation. If the new farm is not so valuable as the old, the payment must be scaled down accordingly. This is done by reference to the existing use value of each unit (ignoring development value, that is to say) in accordance with market prices at the date when the new unit is begun to be farmed, as regards that property, and at the date of displacement, as regards the original property. The main dwelling on each property, if there is one, must also be excluded from the calculation; but the "willing seller" rule and attendant rules in Section 5 of the Land Compensation Act 1961 are to be applied. It should also be noted that if the purchase price of the original property includes development value the amount of the development value will be deducted from the farm loss payment. Claims must be made within one year after the farming of the new unit begins, and disputes over the amount claimed are to be settled by the Lands Tribunal. Interest is payable, at whatever rate is currently prescribed for compulsory purchase compensation, from the date of the claim, as also are sums for reasonable legal and valuation costs.

One most important complication in regard to farm loss payments is that no such payment can be claimed by a farmer already entitled to a payment for "re-organisation of affairs" under Section 12 of the Agriculture (Miscellaneous Provisions) Act 1968 (as amended by Schedule 14 of the Agricultural Holdings Act 1986). This is so regardless of whether the payment under the 1968 Act is the full amount, namely four times the yearly rent, or a mere fraction of that figure no matter how small. Section 12 of the 1968 Act provides that, in the event of a compulsory purchase, the full amount is payable in principle, but that where a term of two years or more is expropriated there is a "ceiling" on the compensation which is fixed at the amount of compensation which would be paid to a yearly tenant subject to compulsory purchase of the property. This means that a farmer with a short-to-medium length agricultural tenancy which is compulsorily purchased might be entitled to a compulsory purchase payment (including disturbance, which will normally be a major item in it) such that the "ceiling" is approached but not actually reached, which in turn means that a small fraction of the Section 12 payment under the 1968 Act is still to be added in order to reach that "ceiling". In turn, this means, under the 1973 Act, that if a Section 12 payment (however small) is due, no "farm loss payment" can be claimed. But the ceiling does not apply to the compulsory purchase compensation as such, which may reach or exceed it. If so a "farm loss payment" is claimable under the rules mentioned above. The interrelation of these various compensation provisions is clearly a difficult and complicated matter and must be considered with great care in each particular case.[16]

[16]For a further consideration of compulsory purchase compensation, including disturbance, the reader is referred to Chapter 9 of "Valuation: Principles into Practice" (3rd Edition) Ed. W. H. Rees (Estates Gazette).

CHAPTER 30
Compensation Under the Housing Acts[1]

INTRODUCTORY

THE "Principal Act" is now the Housing Act 1985, which consolidated a great number of earlier Housing Acts, the most notable of these being the Housing Acts 1957, 1961, 1964, 1969, 1974 and 1980, and also the Housing (Financial Provisions) Act 1958, the Housing Finance Act 1972, the Housing Rents and Subsidies Act 1975, the Housing (Homeless Persons) Act 1977, the Housing and Building Control Act 1984 and the Housing Defects Act 1984.

In addition there are the following statutes passed at the same time as the Housing Act 1985, namely the Housing Associations Act 1985, which is concerned with the functions and finance of housing associations, housing trusts and the Housing Corporation, the Landlord and Tenant Act 1985, which is concerned with the implied covenants for upkeep of various tenanted dwellings (and also rent-books and service charges), and the Housing (Consequential Provisions) Act 1985, which is procedural.

Valuations for compensation purposes may be required in connection with the following matters dealt with in the "principal Act":—

(A) Clearance Areas.
(B) Insanitary Houses.
(C) Obstructive Buildings.
(D) Provision of new Housing Accommodation.

As regards (A) an alternative method of procedure is available under the Town and Country Planning Act 1971; while

---

[1] This Chapter is confined to the question of compensation. Various books have been published on other aspects of Housing Law; but the most comprehensive information is to be sought in the annotated texts of (i) the Encyclopedia of Housing and (ii) Current Law Statutes (1985 Vol. 4).

as for (D) housing accommodation is also frequently provided under the New Towns Act 1981, and the Town Development Act 1952.

Thus, although slum property may be dealt with in a "clearance area" under the Housing Acts, alternatively it might
be designated in the county planning authority's structure
plan—or any subsequent amendment of it—as an "action
area", and its detailed redevelopment along with non-residential property indicated in the district planning authority's
"action area plan" made thereunder. It could then be
acquired by the local authority under a compulsory purchase
order, confirmed by the Secretary of State, for purposes of
general redevelopment.

The fact that alternative powers are available does not
prevent a local authority from proceeding under the Housing
Acts. The authority will be a district council acting in the
capacity of "housing authority". These procedures, which
are still widely used, present a number of special features
which directly or indirectly affect the valuation of houses
in general and are therefore dealt with in some detail in
this Chapter.

(A) CLEARANCE AREAS[2]

If in any area in a local authority's district the following
conditions exist:—

(a) The houses are unfit for habitation or are dangerous
or injurious to health because of their bad arrangement
or the narrowness or bad arrangement of the streets;
and

(b) the other buildings are dangerous or injurious to health
for the like reason; and

(c) the best solution is the demolition of all buildings in
the area;

the local authority may define the area by means of a map,
in such a way as to exclude from the area any building which
is not unfit for human habitation or dangerous or injurious

[2] Housing Act 1985, Parts IX and XVII.

to health, and may pass a resolution declaring it to be a "clearance area". A copy of the resolution must be sent to the Secretary of State for the Environment.

It should be noted that, in determining for any purpose of the Housing Act 1985, whether a house is unfit for human habitation, regard shall be had to its condition in respect of the following matters, namely:—(a) repair; (b) stability; (c) freedom from damp; (d) internal arrangement; (e) natural lighting; (f) ventilation; (g) water supply; (h) drainage and sanitary conveniences; and (i) facilities for preparation and cooking of food and for the disposal of waste water; and the house will be deemed to be unfit if, and only if, it is so far defective in one or more of these matters that it is not reasonably suitable for occupation in that condition.[3]

In practice the clearance area is defined on the "Area Map" by colouring it red. The area having been declared a "clearance area", the local authority may proceed to secure the clearance of it by acquiring the land and demolishing the buildings, either by agreement or by compulsory purchase.

It should be noted that local authorities are given power to postpone the demolition of houses acquired by them if, in their opinion, such houses, though "unfit", can be rendered capable of providing accommodation of a standard which is adequate for the time being.[4] But this does not necessarily exempt them from liability under the Public Health Act 1936 if such houses are in a state "prejudicial to health" or "a nuisance"—*Salford City Council v. McNally* [1975] 2 All E.R. 860.

There used to be an alternative procedure to acquisition, namely that of "clearance orders" whereby the local authority could require the owners of unfit houses in a clearance area to demolish them so that the land should be available for redevelopment. But this was abolished by the Housing Act 1974. Sections 303–306 of the 1985 Act, however, set out a procedure whereby buildings of special architectural or historic interest in clearance areas can be specially dealt with. If after inclusion in a compulsory purchase order such

---

[3] Housing Act 1985, section 604.
[4] Housing Act 1985, sections 300–302.

a building is "listed" under the Town and Country Planning Act 1971, Section 54, the authority can, within three months, apply to the Secretary of State to nullify the "listing" by allowing them to demolish it. If he refuses, the building must remain, and will be excluded from the clearance area, unless already owned by the authority, in which case it is "appropriated" to housing or planning purposes and the compensation paid must, where necessary, be supplemented to bring it up to full market value. If excluded it must be subjected to a repair notice or closing order, as appropriate, if it had been included in the first place merely by reason of unfitness for habitation.

Another procedure, under section 299 of the Housing Act 1985, is the "rehabilitation order". A house in a clearance area acquired by the local authority before 2 December, 1974, or included in a compulsory purchase order made in draft before that date and confirmed before 2 March, 1975, if unfit for habitation but capable of improvement to the "full standard" for which "intermediate grants" are payable under Part XV of the 1985 Act (see above, Chapter 19), may be subject to a "rehabilitation order" made by the authority and confirmed by the Secretary of State. The house must then be improved to the "full standard". If the authority own the house it will be "appropriated" to housing or planning purposes and the compensation paid must if necessary be supplemented to bring it up to full market value. If they do not own the house, it will be excluded from the clearance area.

COMPULSORY PURCHASE ORDERS

(a) Procedure[5]

The local authority may decide to acquire part or the whole of any land in a clearance area. They may also acquire any land surrounded by the area which is needed to secure a cleared area of convenient shape and size, and any adjoining land which is required for the satisfactory development or use of the cleared area.

---

[5] Housing Act 1985, Section 290 and Schedule 22. The Acquisition of Land Act 1981, does not apply to compulsory purchases for slum clearance.

If the local authority cannot acquire the land they want by agreement, they must submit a draft compulsory purchase order to the Secretary of State for the Environment for confirmation. The order must be advertised and opportunity given for the making of objections. If any objections are raised, the Secretary of State must hold a local inquiry, or give the objector an opportunity of being heard privately, before confirming, unless he is satisfied that the objections relate exclusively to matters which can be dealt with by the Lands Tribunal by whom the compensation is assessed.

The procedure is regulated by Schedule 22 of the Housing Act 1985.

The compulsory purchase order and the map accompanying it must distinguish between:—

(i) Unfit properties included in the clearance area—in practice coloured red or pink on the plans of the scheme;

(ii) properties included in the clearance area only because of bad arrangement—usually coloured pink hatched yellow;

(iii) properties not in the clearance area, but included in the scheme of acquisition for the purpose of making clearance and redevelopment efficient—usually coloured grey

If a person objects to a compulsory purchase order on the grounds that his property is not unfit for habitation, he is entitled to a written notice specifying the defects complained of at least 14 days before the local inquiry or private hearing is held.

The question of the category in which his property is placed on the map accompanying the compulsory purchase order is of considerble importance to the owner, since it will affect the amount of compensation to which he is entitled. He should carefully inspect the map as soon as the making of the order is advertised, since the only opportunity he will have of protesting against the inclusion of his property as unfit property will be at the local inquiry or private hearing held by the Secretary of State for the Environment. The point cannot be raised once the scheme is confirmed.

The compulsory purchase order, when confirmed by the Secretary of State, will incorporate Parts II and III of Schedule 2 to the Acquisition of Land Act 1981 (formerly sections 77–85 of the Railway Clauses Consolidation Act 1845) relating to mines and minerals under the land. The Compulsory Purchase Act 1965, will govern the procedure for acquisition after the order comes into effect. Section 8 of that Act provides that part only of a "house, building or manufactory" or a park or garden belonging to a house, may be taken if, in the opinion of the Lands Tribunal, it can be taken without "material detriment" to the remainder.

There is a general direction that any building erected or improvement or alteration made, or any interest in land created, after the date on which notice of the order having been made is published, is to be ignored in assessing compensation if, in the opinion of the Lands Tribunal, it was not reasonably necessary and was carried out with a view to obtaining or increasing compensation.[6]

Compensation will be assessed under the provisions of the Land Compensation Act 1961, but its basis will be affected according to whether the property acquired consists of (i) houses in the clearance area unfit for habitation, or (ii) other property in or outside the clearance area.

(b) Compensation for unfit houses in the clearance area[7]

In the case of houses in the clearance area unfit for human habitation the basis of compensation prescribed by section 585 of the 1985 Act, is the value of the site cleared of buildings and available for development in accordance with building regulations. The value of the site is to be estimated as at the date when the valuation is made.

Under the Land Compensation Act 1961, the basis of compensation is the price which the cleared site might be expected to realise if sold in the open market by a willing seller, having regard to the assumptions as to planning permission to be made under the Act.

In the case of land with market demand and zoned for

---

[6] Housing Act 1985, section 598.
[7] Housing Act 1985, sections 585–592.

some valuable purpose, which would give rise to development value, this basis might give a higher figure than the value of the unfit property as it stands. The 1985 Act, therefore, provides that the compensation payable under this part of the Act, shall in no case exceed the compensation which would have been payable if it had not been assessed on a site value basis.[8]

In practice, the cleared site value of a property is usually based on a figure of so much per unit of site area varying with the situation of the clearance area and the position of the particular site within the clearance area. Development value is unlikely to be obtainable unless several properties are amalgamated into a block in one ownership.

Where there are several interests in the property acquired, each party's interest must be valued as an interest in the cleared site only. For example, if a house is held for a term of years at a ground rent and is let at weekly rents to a number of tenants, the freeholder's interest will be treated, for compensation purposes, as an unsecured ground rent receivable for so many years, followed by a reversion to the cleared site value. Similarly, in estimating the lessee's compensation, the weekly rents must be ignored, since the site is assumed to be cleared of buildings, and the lessee's profit rent (if any) will be deemed to consist of the difference between the ground rent payable to the freeholder and the rental value of the cleared site. If the rental value of the site is the same as, or less than, the ground rent payable, the lessee will receive a purely nominal figure of compensation for the taking of his legal interest in the property although he may be in receipt of quite a substantial income from weekly rents.

Well-Maintained Payments

The local authority, if satisfied that a dwelling-house, although properly included in a compulsory purchase order as unfit for habitation, has in spite of its sanitary defects

---

[8] Housing Act 1985, section 589.

been well maintained,[9] may make an additional payment in respect of the building, depending on whether the house is wholly or partially well-maintained.[10]

The sum payable in respect of a wholly well-maintained house is an amount equal to fourteen times the rateable value or such other multiplier as the Secretary of State may by order prescribe.[11] Half of this amount is payable for a partially well-maintained house, where either the interior or exterior, but not both, has been well-maintained, for example where the tenant has done his best to maintain the interior but the landlord has neglected the exterior, or vice versa.

The amount of a wholly or partially well-maintained payment must not exceed the amount (if any) by which the full value of the house exceeds the site value. The full value of the house means the amount of compensation which would have been payable if the house had been purchased compulsorily but not as being unfit.

In general terms, the payment is made to the person to whose efforts the good maintenance of the house is attributable.

Owner-Occupier Supplements

Section 587 and Schedule 24 of the Housing Act 1985, make provision for the payment of supplemental compensation to owner-occupiers of certain premises if their interests are acquired at site value, or they are required to vacate their house under a demolition, closing or clearance order. Owner-occupiers are entitled to this supplementary payment in cases where clearance action has been formally initiated by the local authority provided the house was owner-occupied either on 13 December 1955 or (if later) throughout

[9] Housing Act 1985, section 586 and Schedule 23. A landlord, tenant, occupier or mortgagee may make representations to the Secretary of State if dissatisfied by the local authority's decision not to make a payment to him. See *Hoggard v. Worsborough Urban District Council* [1962] 2 Q.B. 93.

[10] "Well-maintained" is not defined, and has to be interpreted as a question of fact and degree in each case.

[11] Housing (Payments for Well-Maintained Houses) Order, 1982 (S.I. No. 1112). The multiplier originally was four.

a period of 2 years ending with the date on which the local authority took action as set out in paragraph 1 of the Schedule.

This requirement of the two-year period was included to stop collusive sales between landlord and tenant in anticipation of clearance action to increase the amount of compensation. However, paragraph 2(2) of Schedule 24 provides for payment in those cases where an owner-occupier bought within the two-year period but was genuinely unaware of the likelihood of clearance action.

The additional compensation payable under these provisions is equal to the full compulsory purchase value of the interest less the compensation paid on a site value basis. In other words, the total compensation payable is equal to the full compulsory purchase value including disturbance.

Provision is made for the payment of supplements of similar amount to owners of houses used for business purposes.

Disturbance Compensation and Disturbance Payments

It was formerly the law that any occupier of premises who was displaced but not expropriated in the course of compulsory purchase might be paid such sum for cost of removal as the local authority in their discretion thought fit.[12] Had the occupier been not only displaced but expropriated in consequence of the compulsory purchase—i.e., forced to sell his freehold or leasehold interest (if any) in the land to the authority—he would have been entitled as of right to include items of this sort in his compensation, as "disturbance". But it is often possible for authorities to turn out occupiers under short-term tenancies at common law without expropriating them, by taking their landlord's place and then serving on them a notice to quit; there is then no compulsory purchase compensation for the "disturbance" to be included in.

These principles are of general application in compulsory

---

[12]Housing Act 1957, section 63 (now repealed by the Land Compensation Act 1973). For further discussion, see Chapter 29.

purchase and by no means confined to acquisitions under the Housing Act.

It is true that in many cases displaced tenants of business premises could (and can) obtain compensation as of right from the acquiring body as their landlord under Part II of the Landlord and Tenant Act 1954. But it was decided that short-term occupiers ought to be allowed compensation as of right by virtue of the compulsory purchase. As a result, sections 37–8 of the Land Compensation Act 1973 now provide that compensation is payable as of right for losses incurred in consequence of removal, by the acquiring authority to the displaced occupiers of residential and business premises; and business occupiers can also obtain compensation for business loss. Claimants have to have been "in lawful possession", which excludes licensees (though discretionary payments may be made to these). Displacement must arise from compulsory purchase, from the making of a demolition or closing order, from acceptance of an undertaking to do repair works to a dwelling, or from redevelopment by the public authority concerned. It should also be noted that even an expropriated owner can get a "disturbance payment" if he is being deprived of an unfit house and is not having his "site value" compensation made up to full market value: this is because his house is disregarded (as being unfit) for compensation purposes and therefore he will get no "disturbance compensation" in respect of it.

Furthermore, under sections 29–33 of the Land Compensation Act 1973, anyone displaced from a dwelling that has been his main residence for five years, whether or not he is also expropriated, is entitled to a "home loss payment" of three times the rateable value (but not less than £150 nor more than £1,500).

Minimum Compensation Payable

When a person owns and occupies a private dwelling-house at the date of the compulsory purchase order, and continues to own the interest at the date of the notice to treat, or until his death, if sooner, the compensation payable to him on a cleared site value basis (including the amount of any well maintained allowance or any supplementary compensation under Schedules 23 or 24 of the 1985 Act) shall not be less than the gross value of the premises as shown in the current valuation list.[13]

(c) Compensation for property other than unfit houses[14]

In the case of (i) property not in the clearance area itself, and (ii) property included in the area only because of its bad arrangement in relation to other buildings, or on account of the narrowness or bad arrangement of the streets, compensation will be on the normal basis as prescribed by the Land Compensation Act 1961.

(d) Rights-of-way, etc.[15]

When land is acquired under this part of the Act all private rights-of-way and all rights of laying down, erecting, continuing, or maintaining any apparatus on, under, or over the land, and all other rights or easements in relation to the land are extinguished, and any such apparatus shall vest in the local authority.

Any person who suffers loss by the extinguishment of vesting of any such right or apparatus is entitled to compensation assessed in accordance with the Land Compensation Act 1961.

(B) INDIVIDUAL UNFIT HOUSES[16]

If, in the opinion of the local authority, an individual house is unfit for human habitation, but is capable of being rendered fit at a reasonable expense, a notice may be served on the person having control of the house specifying the work to

---

[13] Housing Act 1985, section 589(2).
[14] Housing Act 1985, section 578. See Chapters 27–29, above.
[15] Housing Act 1985, section 295. Special rules apply to statutory undertakers (sections 296–8).
[16] Housing Act 1985, sections 192, 300.

be done and requiring him to execute it within a reasonable time.[17]

If, on appeal against the notice to repair, the County Court finds that the house cannot be made fit for human habitation at a reasonable cost, the local authority may purchase the house by agreement, or may be authorised to do so compulsorily by means of a compulsory purchase order confirmed by the Secretary of State for the Environment.

Compensation will be assessed in accordance with the Land Compensation Act 1961; but section 585 of the Housing Act 1985 provides that the basis of assessment will be the value as a cleared site available for development in accordance with building regulations, and the compensation may include well-maintained payments and owner-occupier supplements, as described earlier in this Chapter in relation to unfit houses in clearance areas.

Subject to a right of appeal to the county court, a local authority may require the demolition of any house which is unfit for human habitation and which, in their opinion, is not capable at a reasonable expense of being rendered so fit. The owner may offer to render the house fit for habitation or undertake not to use it for habitation until it has been rendered fit. But if no such offer or undertaking is made or accepted, or if an offer is not carried out, the local authority must serve a demolition order or may purchase the house in lieu of making any such order. This power of purchase may be exercised when, in the opinion of the local authority, the house (in spite of its unfit state) is or can be rendered capable of providing accommodation of a standard which is adequate for the time being. Subject to the service of notices and a right of appeal to the county court, the local authority may then purchase the house by agreement or may be authorised by the Secretary of State to acquire it compulsorily. Compensation will be on the same basis as in the case—referred to above—of a house unfit for habitation and incapable of being made so at reasonable expense.

If only part of a house is unfit, or if an unfit house supports

---

[17]Housing Act 1985, section 189. Section 190 enables an authority to serve such a notice if the house is in "substantial disrepair", even if it cannot be shown to be "unfit" for habitation. The meaning of "unfit" is discussed earlier in this Chapter.

an adjoining building, or if it is of special architectural or historic interest, or if a non-residential use can be found for it, then demolition is inappropriate and a closing order should be substituted for the demolition order.

(C) OBSTRUCTIVE BUILDINGS[18]

An obstructive building is one which by reason only of its contact with, or proximity to, other buildings is dangerous or injurious to health. A local authority may order the demolition of the whole or part of an obstructive building after first notifying the owner of their intention and giving him the opportunity to be heard.

The owner or owners may offer to sell his or their interests to the local authority provided the acquisition of the interest or interests in question will enable the local authority to carry out the demolition. The purchase-price will be assessed as if it were compensation for compulsory purchase subject to the rules prescribed by section 585 of the Housing Act 1985, which have already been considered above for properties in clearance areas other than unfit houses.

If no offer to sell is made, the owner or owners must demolish the building within a given period, failing which the local authority will demolish it and sell the old materials.

Where the building is demolished, either by the owner or by the local authority, the local authority must compensate the owner or owners for any loss arising from the demolition. The general principles of compensation referred to above will then apply, subject to the fact that the owner is being compensated not for the compulsory purchase of the property but only for the loss of the building.

(D) PROVISION OF NEW HOUSING ACCOMMODATION[19]

(a) Procedure
Local housing authorities are empowered under Section 17 of the Housing Act 1985 to acquire by agreement any land, including any houses or other buildings thereon, as

[18] Housing Act 1985, sections 283–8.
[19] Housing Act 1985, Part II.

a site for the erection of houses. They may also acquire houses, or other buildings which are, or may be made, suitable as houses, and have power to alter and adapt such houses and buildings as necessary. Land may also be acquired for various ancillary purposes.

Failing purchase by agreement the land can be acquired compulsorily by means of a compulsory purchase order made and submitted by the local housing authority to the Secretary of State for the Environment and confirmed by him in accordance with the provisions of the Aquisition of Land Act 1981.

The definition of "house" in the Housing Act 1985, section 56, includes any part of a building which is occupied or intended to be occupied as a separate dwelling. In *Sovmots Ltd. v. Secretary of State for the Environment* (1976) part of the "Centre Point" complex of buildings in London had been built for (private) residential use in the form of maisonettes although the use of the remainder of the property was commercial. The local authority made a compulsory purchase order for the acquisition of the maisonettes, under Part V of the Housing Act 1957 (now Part II of the 1985 Act). The House of Lords, when the order was challenged, quashed it, stating that although the statutory powers authorised part of a building to be acquired they did not go further and authorise the compulsory creation of new easements, such as rights of access, services and support, necessary for the separate use of such part in the particular circumstances. (The same is true of other newly granted rights, including new leaseholds). In this case the maisonettes were not at ground level but situated above commercial premises, hence the need for such easements after the ownership had been severed. The compulsory creation of leases, easements, etc., however, is authorised in particular circumstances by various statutes, notably the Local Government (Miscellaneous Provisions) Act 1976 which now allows this wherever a local authority possesses compulsory purchase powers.

(b) Basis of Compensation

Compensation will be assessed on the normal compulsory purchase basis as prescribed by the Land Compensation Act 1961, as is the case for acquisition of property in clearance areas other than unfit houses, discussed earlier in this Chapter.

In assessing compensation the Lands Tribunal may disregard any increase in value due to interests in land created or work done on land if satisfied that the creation of the interest or the doing of the work, as the case may be, was not reasonably necessary and was undertaken with a view to obtaining or increasing compensation (Acquisition of Land Act 1981, section 4).

Example 31–1

A block of 22 unfit terraced houses was included in a Clearance Area and a Compulsory Purchase Order under the Housing Act 1985, has recently been confirmed in respect of the whole block. The houses front on two parallel streets and each house stands on a site with a frontage of 12 ft. and a depth of 50 ft.

Twenty of the houses in a block occupying a site 120 ft. by 100 ft. are held on ground lease with 22 years unexpired at a rent of £30 per annum. The houses are occupied by weekly tenants on rents exclusive of general rates and water and drainage charges and are producing the maximum permitted gross income of £10,000 per annum.

The remaining two houses are owner-occupied by the free-holders; one purchased five years ago and has been in occupation since; the other purchased from the former landlord less than two years before clearance action was initiated but before purchase he made enquiries of the local authority to ascertain if clearance action might be taken and was informed that such action was unlikely.

Each house is assessed for rating purposes at R.V. £128.

All of the houses are in an area zoned for shopping purposes in the development plan.

The Secretary of State has directed that a well-maintained payment should be made in respect of the owner-occupied house purchased five years ago and that partially well-maintained payments should be made in respect of six of the leasehold houses, four relating to external condition and two relating to internal condition.

Notices to treat have just been served in respect of all interests. Assess the compensation payable.

Valuations—

Twenty Leasehold Houses

(i) Freeholder's Compensation. Value for purpose for which land zoned assuming a cleared site available for redevelopment in accordance with building regulations.

Next 22 years—ground rent	£30 p.a.	
Y.P. 22 years at 14%	6·74	£202
Reversion—to value as shop		
site, say	£50,000	
P.V. £1 in 22 years at 12%	·083	£4,150
		£4,352
	say	£4,350

But the compensation payable must not exceed what would have been paid if the interest was not being acquired at site value. Thus, the compensation would be restricted to—

Ceiling Value—			
Next 22 years—approx. as before			£202
Reversion—to gross rentals		£10,000 p.a.	
Less Repairs, say	2,500		
Insurance	600		
Management	1,150	£4,250	
Net income		£5,750 p.a.	
Y.P. Perp. at 14% deferred 22 years			
		·4	£2,300
			£2,502
		say	£2,500

(ii) Lessee's Compensation—

Ground rental value as shop site	£4,000 p.a.	
Less Ground rent payable	30	
Profit rent	£3,970 p.a.	
Y.P. 22 years at 10 and 3%		
(tax at 35%)	6·65	£26,401
Add Partially well-maintained		
payments, say 4 × 7 R.V. £128		£3,584
		£29,985
		say £30,000

Ceiling Value—

Net income from houses	£5,750 p.a.	
Less Ground rent	30	
Profit rent	£5,720 p.a.	
Y.P. 22 years at 16 and 3%		
(tax at 35%)	4·75	£27,170
		say £27,200

The lessee's compensation would, therefore, be restricted to £27,200.

(iii) Tenants' Compensation. The tenants have no valuable interest in the land but are entitled to be re-housed by the local authority and to receive disturbance and, if they have occupied for the requisite 5 year period, home loss payments.

With regard to the two partially well-maintained payments relating to internal condition, it is evident that cleared site value is well in excess of the value of the standing house, therefore no partially well-maintained payments would be made.

Owner-Occupied House Purchased Five Years Ago

The cleared site afforded here, 12 ft. by 50 ft. is too small for shop or residential purposes. This could mean that the value would be restricted to a "conventional" compensation value for small individual sites but it could be argued that "hope" value would attach because of the possibility, even in the absence of compulsory acquisition, that at some time in the future this site could be included in a larger redevelopment scheme. This hope must, however, be disregarded unless it springs from the possibility that redevelopment will at some time be undertaken by some agency other than the local authority and not solely from the action which the local authority is at present taking or any alternative action which the local authority might have taken—see *Davy v. Leeds Corporation*, (1964) 16 P. & C.R. 24, referred to in Chapter 27.

Site value, say		£200
Add		
Supplemental compensation— difference between full compulsory purchase value and site value		
Full value as house, say	£5,000	
Disturbance, say	1,500	
Compulsory purchase value	£6,500	
Less Site value	200	£6,300
		£6,500
Home loss payment 3 × R.V. £128		384
Total		£6,884

The well-maintained payment will not be made as the owner-occupier is already entitled to receive full compensation for his loss.

Owner-Occupied House Purchased Less Than Two Years Before Action Initiated

Although the owner-occupier has not been in occupation for the qualifying period of 2 years, it appears that this is only because the local authority advanced its slum clearance

programme. In these circumstances the compensation paid
would include the owner-occupier's supplement. Thus the
computation would be on similar lines to the previous one
but it is reasonable to assume that this house is in worse
condition than the other.

Site value, say		£200
Add		
Supplemental compensation—		
Full value as house, say	£4,500	
Disturbance, say	1,500	
Compulsory purchase value	£6,000	
less Site value	200	5,800
Total		£6,000

The owner-occupiers are entitled to be re-housed in the
same way as tenants and no deduction should be made from
their compensation for any "value" which might be said to
attach to a local authority tenancy.

CHAPTER 31

Electricity Wayleaves, Sewer Easements, Pipe-Lines and Gas Installations[1]

1. ELECTRICITY WAYLEAVES

STATUTORY PROVISIONS

IN THE past there have been numerous electricity authorities and undertakings throughout the country concerned with the supply of electricity for light and power in particular areas; in the future it is intended that the industry should be privatised. What follows is the state of play at the time of writing.

Under the Electricity Acts 1947–1958, the authorities now concerned in England and Wales are the Electricity Council, the Central Electricity Generating Board and 12 Area Electricity Boards. The Electricity Council is primarily a co-ordinating and advisory body and the functions of generation, transformation and transmission are performed by the other authorities.

It is proposed to summarise briefly the current statutory powers vested in electricity authorities for the use of land for electricity purposes before considering the practical question of compensation likely to arise where these powers are exercised.

Under section 22 of the Electricity (Supply) Act 1919, any authorised undertakers may place any electricity line:—

    (a) below ground, across any land, and
    (b) above ground, across any land other than land covered by buildings or used as a garden or pleasure ground.

---

[1] The reader is referred also to Chapter 20 "Valuation: Principles into Practice" (3rd Edition 1988) Ed. W. H. Rees; also to the various booklets published by the Country Landowners' Association, which have the advantage of regular updating, in particular A.15/87 "Electricity Wayleaves"; A16/87 "Telecommunications Wayleaves"; A.17/87 "Commercial Pipelines"; A.14/87 "Private Underground Pipelines and Cables".

Notice must first be served on the owner and occupier, who may give their consent on such terms as to compensation, etc., as may be agreed. But if they fail, within 21 days, to give consent, or will only do so on terms unacceptable to the undertakings, an application must be made to the Secretary of State for permission to lay the line.

The Secretary of State, after giving both parties an opportunity to be heard, may give consent either unconditionally or subject to such terms, conditions and stipulations as he thinks just. But any question of disputed compensation will be settled under the Land Compensation Act 1961.[2]

Where an owner enters into an agreement with an electricity authority for a wayleave through or over his land, it is usual to reserve the right to terminate it at any time by twelve months' notice. But under section 11 of the Electricity (Supply) Act 1922, the authority may insist on retaining the line in position subject to the same procedure as though the line were being newly laid under section 22 of the 1919 Act. At any time while the line is so retained in position the authority may apply to the Secretary of State for a revision of the original terms and conditions, in which case also the matter will be treated as though the line were being newly laid. In either case the Secretary of State will have no power to deal with any question of pecuniary compensation connected with the retention of the wayleave.

Under section 9 of the Electricity Act 1947, the Secretary of State may authorise any Electricity Board to purchase compulsorily any land which they require for any purpose connected with the discharge of their functions. The expression "land" is expressly stated to include easements and other rights over land, and the Secretary of State may authorise any Electricity Board to purchase compulsorily a right to place an electric line across land, whether above or below ground, and to repair and maintain the line, without purchasing any other interest in the land.

The procedure in connection with the grant of these compulsory powers is governed by the Acquisition of Land Act

---

[2] *West Midlands Joint Electricity Authority and Minister of Transport v. Pitt and Others* (1932) 2 K.B. 1.

1981. Compensation, if in dispute, will be assessed in accordance with the Land Compensation Act 1961.

Under section 34 of the Electricity (Supply) Act 1926, an electricity authority may serve a notice requiring the lopping or cutting of any trees or hedges which obstruct or interfere with any electric line, subject to payment of the expense incurred in complying with the order. Or, if the order is not complied with within 21 days, the authority may do the work itself. Any owner or occupier is entitled to object to the terms of such an order within 21 days, in which case the matter is referred to the Secretary of State, who may make such order as he thinks fit and also determine what compensation (if any) and expenses are to be paid.

CLAIMS FOR COMPENSATION

(a) *Generally*. There are two main types of case which may arise under the Electricity Acts:—

(i) Where land is acquired compulsorily for the erection of generating stations, distributing stations, and other purposes;

(ii) where "wayleaves" are acquired, i.e., rights to carry electric lines under land, or over land by means of poles or pylons.

Case (i) does not differ in principle from any other case of compulsory acquisition where the compensation is governed by the Land Compensation Act 1961.

The acquisition of "wayleaves" under case (ii) may include the following:—

(a) The carrying of overhead conductors[3] across land by means of supports erected on the land;

(b) the carrying of overhead conductors across land without any supports being erected on the land itself— sometimes referred to as "oversails";

(c) the carrying of conductors underground.

---

[3] The term "conductor" is used to indicate the wire or cable which conveys the current.

In (a) damage is likely to be caused when the line is erected, and thereafter certain parts of the land will be permanently occupied by the supports. The nature of these supports will vary according to the voltage to be transmitted. For the larger voltage lines, lattice-work steel towers are used with a base measurement 15 ft. × 15 ft. and upwards. The smaller voltage lines may be supported by smaller steel towers, by concrete towers or by double or single wood poles.

In (b) there is no actual occupation of the land itself and, in the case of purely agricultural land, the presence of the oversail may have little, if any, effect on value, although the minimum height at which the conductor crossses the land is always a matter for consideration.

In (c) the damage during construction will be greater than in (a), but, on the other hand, the land will probably be little affected once the conductor is laid. Subject to fair compensation being paid for any injury done during the laying of the line or any subsequent inspection or repair of it, annual rentals at a nominal figure per yard or metre run have commonly been agreed in this type of case. Conductors are not laid underground when it can be avoided, owing to the high cost of this method as compared with overhead lines.

Questions of compensation for overhead electricity wayleaves involve consideration of the following points: (i) the compensation to be paid for the wayleave itself, and (ii) the compensation to be paid for other loss suffered. It may also be necessary to distinguish between loss suffered by the owner and loss suffered by the occupier.

The first point for the owner to decide is whether he will grant a wayleave at an annual rent, or whether he will require a lump sum in full and final settlement. If the compensation is referred under the Land Compensation Act 1961, it would seem that the Lands Tribunal is bound to award a lump sum of compensation.

In most cases, however, owners will probably be willing to enter into agreements on reasonable terms to accept an annual rent for the wayleave, provided a right is reserved to terminate the agreement at any time by, say, twelve months' notice or less. It is true that the right to determine will be subject to the authority's power, under section 11 of the 1922 Act, to insist on the line being retained, but in that case the whole question of compensation is re-opened and any changes in the circumstances of the land can be taken into account.

The terms of such agreements will provide for (i) a yearly rent or wayleave in respect of the use of the land and interference with agricultural operations caused by the presence of poles or towers, and (ii) compensation for any damage done in erecting the line and for any subsequent injury.

(*b*) *Compensation for Wayleave.* Agreement is reached annually by the Central Electricity Generating Board and the 12 Area Electricity Boards in England and Wales with the CLA and NFU about rates of wayleave payment to be made to owners and occupiers for grid and distribution lines over agricultural land. The terms of these agreements, which cover rent and compensation for interference with agricultural operations, are published in the professional press, and in CLA Publication A.15/87 referred to in footnote 1.

The compensation payments are intended to meet the costs of keeping the site of a pole or tower clean and of avoiding it in course of cultivations, the loss of profit on the area rendered unproductive and any diminution of crop immediately outside that area.

(*c*) *Other Compensation.* In addition to any such annual sum as is suggested above, compensation may be payable for a number of other losses suffered by owner or occupier.

These may include loss of crops or tenant right on the land on which the towers are erected, together with any injury to crops and interference with agricultural operations on adjoining land while the work is being done. The above is based on the assumption that agreement has been or will be reached on these items and that fair compensation will be paid for any damage which may subsequently be caused by the Board's servants or by accident due to the presence of the cable.

A line passing through woodlands generally requires the cutting of a ride 13 metres or 40 feet wide; compensation will be payable for the trees felled and for possible injury to the rest of the wood and to sporting rights.

In the great majority of cases electricity conductors are

carried over open country—i.e., arable or grassland, or moorland.

If it were proposed to carry a line over ripe building land, the owner's best course would be to make representation to the Secretary of State offering an alternative route.

If the original proposal were persisted in, then the effect on the value of the estate of the erection of pylons on certain plots and the presence of high-voltage cables over other plots would have to be considered. In such a case a claim for depreciation in the value of the land affected could be made. The amount could be arrived at—by the "before and after" method—by valuing the estate before the line was placed over the land and deducting from this amount the value of the estate after the line had been erected.

In a case before the Lands Tribunal[4] a claim was successfully established for depreciation in the value of a manor house following the erection of pylons and the laying of overhead wires. The award included a sum for the value of the land taken and for legal and surveyors' fees prior to the reference.

2. SEWERS AND WATER MAINS

STATUTORY PROVISIONS

Under the Public Health Act 1936, as amended by the Water Act 1973, a water authority may construct a sewer "in, on or over any land not forming part of a street after giving reasonable notice to every owner and occupier of the land". Similar powers may be exercised in respect of water mains.[5]

It is clear from the wording of the Act that the sewer or main may be carried below ground, or on the surface, or partly in one way and partly in another.

When the sewer is constructed it will vest in the water authority.[6]

---

[4] *Radnor Trust, Ltd. v. Central Electricity Generating Board* (1960) 1 R. & V.R. 9.

[5] Public Health Act 1936, sections 15 and 119.

[6] Ibid., section 20(1)(b).

The power to construct the sewer includes the provision of means of access or ventilation in the shape of manholes, ventilating shafts, etc.; and since the water authority is under obligation to maintain the sewer[7] there is an implied right of entry from time to time for purposes of inspection and repair.

An owner is, in general, entitled to claim "full compensation" for any damage he suffers through the exercise of an authority's powers under the Act.[8] But where compensation is claimed in respect of the construction of a sewer or the laying of a water main the tribunal which assesses compensation is directed to determine also by what amount, if any, the value to the claimant of any land belonging to him has been enhanced by the construction of the sewer or main, and the authority is entitled to set off that amount against the amount of compensation awarded.[9]

Section 278(2) of the Act provides that compensation for damage caused by the exercise of a water authority's powers shall be determined by arbitration—or by justices if the claim does not exceed £50 and either party so requires. But the case of *Thurrock, Grays and Tilbury Joint Sewerage Board v. Thames Land Company Ltd.*[10] appears to be authority for saying that, by virtue of the vesting in the water authority of that part of the land which comprises the pipeline, questions of disputed compensation for the laying of sewers or water mains should be determined under the Land Compensation Act 1961, by the Lands Tribunal. From time to time, authorities have questioned their liability to pay any compensation at all to a landowner for laying a pipe across his land. Landowners and their advisers now have the benefit of a number of Lands Tribunal decisions[11] which illustrate the

---

[7] Ibid., section 23.

[8] Public Health Act 1936, section 278.

[9] *Ibid.*, section 278(4) and see *Rush & Tomkins Ltd. v. West Kent Sewerage Board* (1963) 14 P. & C.R. 469.

[10] (1925) 23 L.G.R. 648.

[11] *Quartons (Gardens) Ltd. v. Scarborough RDC* (1955) 5 P. & C.R. 190: *Frost v. Taunton Corporation* (1957) 9 P. & C.R. 123: *Lucey's Personal Representatives & Wood v. Harrogate Corporation* (1963) 14 P. & C.R. 376.

See also The Chartered Surveyor, March 1963, pages 503–8, "Water Mains, Sewers and other pipelines: compensation payable to the landowner."

amount of compensation payable in such cases. These cases support the view that owners are entitled to payment not only for permanent damage to the value of the surface land but also for the presence in the land of the pipe itself, implying as it does rights of entry for inspection and other purposes in the future.

A decision of the Lands Tribunal[12] on a preliminary point of law established that compensation can be claimed for damage sustained by reason of the construction of a public sewer in a street either under section 278 of the 1936 Act or section 22 of the Water Act 1973.

CLAIMS FOR COMPENSATION

(*a*) *Temporary Damage.* A certain amount of damage will almost certainly be caused by the actual laying of the sewer or main. In the case of agricultural land this may include such items as injury to fences, gates and land drainage, cost of making good the surface, loss of tenant right, and temporary interference with agricultural operations while the works are in progress. In the case of residential property damage might include the cost of reinstating flower beds, paths, lawn, etc., and temporary loss of amenity or rental value to the house. Except in so far as they may be made good by the authority, the owner is entitled to compensation for all such items of "temporary" damage.

(*b*) *Permanent Depreciation in Value.* Compensation may also be claimed for any depreciation in the value of the property due to the presence of the sewer or main in the land.

Even if the sewer is entirely underground, the owner is entitled to some compensation for the vesting of the subsoil in the authority and for any inconvenience likely to be caused by the exercise of their rights of access for maintenance and inspection purposes. There may also be manholes, lampholes and ventilating shafts whose presence may cause some loss of a value to the land. If the sewer is laid wholly or in part above ground the effect is likely to be more serious; not only will the strip of land occupied be quite unuseable, but

[12] *George Whitehouse Ltd.* (*Trading as Clarke Bros.* (*Services*)) *v. Anglian Water Authority* (1978) 247 EG 223.

the use of amenities of the property as a whole may be substantially interfered with.

For many years it was common practice to claim compensation for what was described as the "pipe easement"—a misleading term to apply to a water authority's interest in the pipe line, since an easement can only exist as appurtenant to the ownership of a "dominant tenement".

Compensation for the so-called "easement" was based either on the value of the strip of land occupied by the sewer or main or was taken at a figure of so much per yard run. Reference to the cases listed at footnote 11 above, indicates that a figure of so much per yard run seems to be preferred.

In the case of land ripe for building, the fact that no building may be erected over the sewer without the water authority's permission[13] may be a matter for serious consideration. When the pipe is laid above ground the loss of value will be much greater and may include injury to the rest of the property by severance or injurious affection. Water authorities will often undertake to move a pipe or to pay extra compensation if land is given consent after pipes have been laid.

A possible example in the case of a country estate might be depreciation in the value of the house due to a line of ventilating shafts across the park or a length of sewer carried above ground on an unsightly embankment.

On the other hand the provisions of the Public Health Act regarding "set-off" must be borne in mind in cases where the owner will have a right of connection to the pipe line.

(c) *Manholes, Ventilating Shafts, etc.* Compensation for these is usually taken at lump sum figures, according to the type of land in which they occur and the position in which they are placed.

For instance two or three manholes at intervals along the line of a hedge on agricultural land may be of little or no consequence, whereas a manhole or ventilating shaft close to a residential property may cause appreciable injury.

Again, a manhole in the middle of an arable field can be a potential danger to farm implements, and weeds tend

---

[13] Public Health Act 1936, section 25.

to grow round them which will have to be removed from time to time.

Lampholes are usually taken at about half the figure for manholes or ventilating shafts.

Here, again, the present tendency is to regard conventional figures with suspicion and the valuer must be prepared to make out a good case for damage actually sustained.

3. PIPE-LINES

Under the provisions of the Pipe-Lines Act 1962, compulsory purchase orders can be made for the acquisition of land and "compulsory rights orders" for the acquisition of rights over land required for the construction of private pipe-lines.

Where land is acquired under these provisions the Land Compensation Act 1961 applies, subject to minor modifications set out in the Third Schedule.

Where rights are acquired by a compulsory rights order the Act provides[14] that compensation can be claimed:—

(a) for any depreciation in the value of an interest in land which comprises or is held with the land to which the order applies: and

(b) for any other loss suffered by reason of damage to, or disturbance in the enjoyment of, any land or chattels. This includes damage to land drainage, access roads and drives. Compensation is now generally paid to the owner or occupier in respect of his time and expenses dealing with contractors, statutory undertakers, etc., including secretarial expenses and telephone calls.

4. GAS INSTALLATIONS

Under the Gas Act, 1986, British Gas plc is charged with the duty of developing and maintaining a gas supply and given powers to discharge these functions including powers to acquire compulsorily any land including easements or other rights. Compensation is payable in accordance with

[14] Section 14.

the provisions of the Land Compensation Act 1961, and is assessed in accordance with the normal rules. British Gas is also authorised under the Gas Act, to obtain a "storage authorisation order" for the storage of gas underground and compensation is payable in accordance with the rules laid down in the Act.

CHAPTER 32
Licensed Premises

1. GENERALLY

THE TERM "licensed premises" is a very wide one and includes all those properties which are licensed for the sale of intoxicating liquors, such as hotels, public-houses, refreshment rooms, restaurants and "off-licences".

A valuation of this type involves not only a careful inspection of land and buildings but an enquiry into the nature and extent of the licensed trade carried on at the premises, and an estimate of the future prospects of that trade.

In practice this class of work is largely confined to specialists and only a broad outline of the principles involved will be attempted here.

2. TYPES OF LICENCE

The retail sale of beer, wines and spirits can, with some exceptions, only be carried on under the authority of a licence granted by the Licensing Justices.

There are two principal types of licence—(i) the "on-licence", which permits the sale of intoxicating liquors for consumption on or off the premises; (ii) the "off-licence", which permits their sale for consumption off the premises only.

A full on-licence covers the sale of beers, wines and spirits; but a more restrictive on-licence may be granted to premises such as Wine Bars, limiting sales perhaps to wine only.

Conditional forms of on-licences granted to hotels and restaurants are described as "a residential licence", a "restaurant licence" or "a residential and restaurant licence".

Following the Licensing Act 1988, an on-licence will be granted for three years, whereas previously it was granted for one year only. Licensing Justices can however revoke a licence during its currency on grounds which would have previously led to a licence renewal being refused.

It is much more difficult to obtain a new on-licence, than to renew an existing one, and it may be subject to such conditions as the Licensing Justices think fit to impose in the public interest.

An off-licence may cover the sale of beers, wines and spirits for consumption off the premises, or it may be limited to the sale of beer, cider and wine only. In recent years off-licences have become much more readily obtainable than was formerly the case, and are now held by most supermarkets and grocers.

3. "Free" and "Tied" Houses

A "free" public-house is one in which the licensee is free to purchase his liquor from anyone he pleases. A "tied" public-house is one in which the licensee is bound to purchase his beers, and often wines and spirits from a particular firm of brewers.

A "tied" house is created by a brewer obtaining a freehold or leasehold interest in licensed premises and putting in a tenant to run the business on the condition that he shall purchase his liquors from his landlord. Sometimes the tied tenant holds a lease of the premises from the brewer. More frequently he holds a yearly tenancy.

The prices paid by tied tenants for certain types of alcoholic liquors may be higher than those paid by free tenants. In the past this was normally the case, the difference consisting of the extra discount a brewer or supplier may allow to free trade customers, who are those able to purchase liquors where they please. The tied tenant's trade is secured to the brewer by contract, whereas free trade must be obtained in competition with other brewers. Because of these discounts the tied rent may be less than the rent the premises would produce if let to a free tenant, on otherwise similar terms.

Although this two-tiered price structure with "tied" cost prices higher than "free" trade prices, is still operated by some brewers, the trend in recent years has been towards a single price structure for both tied and free trade, with a consequent increase in tied rents to a level which may be similar to that paid by the free tenant.

Recent EEC legislation has restricted the extent of the tie which can be imposed by a brewer with the consequences that some brewers have totally "freed" their tenants for wines and spirits, permitting them to buy from any source they wish. However this is normally compensated for by an increase in rent, off-setting the loss in wholesale profits.

The value of a tied house to a brewer consists, therefore, partly in the tied rent and partly in the profits he may expect to make on the purchases from him secured by the tied tenancy.

Instead of letting to a tied tenant some houses are under the management of the brewer, thus securing the retail profits in addition to profits on supplies, or wholesale profits.

In recent years some brewers have sold off a number of their more isolated or lower barrelage houses. Such houses, which provide a home as well as a business to owner occupiers, are generally much in demand and the prices paid for them may reflect residential values as much as commercial potential. When a house with a good trade comes on the market it may fetch a high figure by reason of the competition amongst brewers to secure an additional outlet for their supplies.

4. Trade Profits

A valuation of licensed premises for whatever purpose will almost certainly involve some enquiry into the trade done and the actual or estimated profits.

(*a*) *Brewer's profits*—In the case of a tied house it may be necessary to consider the profits which the brewer makes from the supply of liquor under the "tie".

These vary, for there is no uniformity of practice regarding the terms on which tied houses are let. In some houses the tied rent may be low and the prices charged for liquor unusually high. In others the reverse may be the case, though the tendency continues to be towards a (lower) free trade price structure, with consequent higher rents.

The value of the beer trade also depends largely on the class of beers sold. Brewers earn a better profit upon higher priced beers, and consequently the value of such barrelage is more.

The figures of profits taken in the examples are to illustrate method and should not be regarded as representing actual profits in any particular case.

(*b*) *Tenant's profits*—In some cases, for instance, in estimating the rental a tenant would be willing to pay, it may be necessary to inquire into the profits made by the licensee.

His gross profits will, of course, consist of the difference between purchases and sales. This may be found by reference to the accounts or may be estimated by taking a percentage on the purchase prices of beers, wines, spirits, etc.

The latter method requires a considerable amount of practical experience, but is often useful as a check on actual takings as shown by the books.

In either case it is desirable to consider the figures for a number of years in order to strike a fair average and to allow for any tendency towards appreciation or depreciation in the trade.

Gross profit having been found, a deduction for reasonable overhead and working expenses must be made to arrive at a figure of net profit.

Overhead and working expenses will include such items as rates and water rate, wages and keep of staff, insurances, accountancy, tenant's share of repairs, lighting, heating and other incidentals, and interest on tenant's capital. The last item is usually calculated at about 10 per cent on the value of stock, fixtures and fittings and working cash capital.

Repairing liability varies from one brewer to another, but generally the Brewery will be responsible for structural and external repairs, and often many, if not all, of the internal repairs also. This is an important factor in the valuation of public houses because repair costs are high with this type of property.

5. Principles of Valuation

A valuation of licensed premises may be required for various purposes—for sale or purchase, for mortgage, for probate, for grant or renewal of a lease, for rating, or for compulsory purchase.

Valuations for rating will be considered in a later Section of this Chapter.

It is proposed to deal here with estimates of capital value in the open market such as would be required for purposes of sale, mortgage, probate and compulsory purchase, and to illustrate the principles involved by reference to the case of the public-house with a full on-licence.

A valuation of a freehold or leasehold interest in a "free" house may be made by capitalising the retail net profits by an appropriate figure of years' purchase, and maybe by having regard also to the value of the residential accommodation.

The result would reflect the value of the property in the open market to a free licensee. This method might be applied also where the type of property is such that a large proportion of the business is in non-alcoholics such as catering, letting and gaming machine income.

Where however, by reason of the volume of sales in beers, wines and spirits the property is likely to prove attractive to a brewer a different method would be appropriate.

In such a case the value would be arrived at by capitalising the estimated brewer's profits on liquors and adding the capitalised estimated or actual tied rent (or capitalised net retail profits assuming the house would be under management).

An example of this type of valuation is as follows:—

Example 32–1

Estimated Brewer's profit from the sale of beers, wines and spirits*	£12,700	
Years' purchase	10	£127,000
Estimated net tied rental	£10,000	
Years' purchase	12	£120,000
Market Value		£247,000

* for calculation of Brewer's profit see final section of *Example 33–2* below.

The appropriate figure of years' purchase will vary according to the age and type of house, level of trade, location and the circumstances generally.

A further method would be to arrive at the capital value direct by reference to the weekly or yearly barrelage (one barrel equals thirty-six gallons), or "converted barrelage" which would also reflect the wine and spirit trade.

For simplicity, if one considers the beer barrel as the unit of comparison, the figure taken per barrel is based upon an analysis of sales of comparable properties. For example, a public house with a trade of 6 barrels of draught and bottled beer per week might be valued at £15,000 per weekly barrel, giving a capital value of £90,000. As the price per barrel might vary between say £6,000 and £50,000 the successful application of this method would clearly depend to a great extent on the skill and experience of the valuer.

When dealing with a licensee's interest, he will often be found in practice to be holding on a short tenancy from a firm of brewers to whom he is tied for the supply of his liquors. In this case he may have no valuable interest in the property and in the event of his death, or a change of tenancy, all that would fall to be valued would be the loose effects and stock and such of the fixtures and fittings as may belong to him.

If the licensee holds the residue of a lease, an estimate of the rent which a tenant might reasonably be expected to pay for the premises may show that he is sitting at a profit rent. In this case, the capitalised profit rent, plus the value of his goodwill, based on so many years' purchase of his net profits according to the length of the term, plus the value of the stock, fixtures and fittings, will represent the total value of his interest in the premises. Sometimes brewers make a loan to tenants which is repayable during the term of the lease. Any such sum still outstanding will, of course, be deducted from the above figure.

No definite rules can be laid down as to percentages in the valuation of licensed premises, as the security of income is largely dependent upon the nature and prospects of the trade and wide variations are found in practice.

The valuer will naturally consider the character and situation of the house and its age and condition. He will have regard to the trading facilities—e.g., the number of bars, their type and accommodation, facilities for catering, the nature of the living accommodation and rooms for guests, the general layout of the house, cellarage, etc. He will also consider the nature of the surrounding district, the density of the population, possible movements of population due to housing schemes and other causes, the extent of the competition from other licensed premises and similar factors.

An important element in the valuation will be the class of purchaser to which the property is most likely to appeal. It has already been pointed out that a "high trading" free house will often command a high price owing to the competition of two or more brewers anxious to secure the trade of the house by a profitable tie. Equally the low barrelage house, particularly those in pleasant locations, may have particular appeal to the prospective free occupier with limited capital, anxious to acquire a home and business of his own.

Freehold ground rents on licensed premises, unless very well covered, usually fetch a lower figure of years' purchase than those secured on other premises owing to the risk of the licence being lost and the security thereby diminished. Owners of ground rents may insure against this risk.

The following example of the compulsory purchase of tied licensed premises illustrates the method of valuing the landlord's and the licensee's interests respectively. The additional items for removal, fixtures, etc., are similar to those met with in disturbance claims in other compulsory purchase cases.

Example 32–2

A licensed property is to be acquired compulsorily by a local authority. You are acting for the freeholder, a brewer, and also for the lessee. Determine the compensation payable to all interested parties. The house was originally leased at £5,000 p.a. rent, but the property has since increased in value. The lease has 10 years to run. The lessee is tied for beers, wines and spirits and for the past few years the trade has varied very little.

Purchases last year amounted to £80,000 and takings to £140,000. The trade expenses, including the rent, were £37,500. The stock was recently valued at £6,000 and fixtures and fittings at £12,000. There is no brewer's loan on the property. The lessee pays for all repairs.

Details of purchases are as follows:—

Draught Beer	350 barrels
Bottled Beer	1,200 doz. pints
	(50 barrels)
Wine	100 gallons
Spirits	250 gallons

Valuation:—

Lessee's Interest.—This consists of two factors:—(i) his profit rent, (ii) his interest in the trade.

(i) His profit rent arises largely from inflation since the lease was granted. In order to ascertain the profit rent it is proposed to estimate, by reference to the trade, the rent which a tied tenant would be prepared to pay at the present day, assuming he held on the same conditions as to repairs, etc., as the lessee.

Estimate of present tied rental value—

Gross profit			£60,000
Deduct trade expenses	£37,500		
Less rent paid	£5,000		£32,500
			————
			£27,500
Allow for "tenant's share":			
Stock	£6,000		
Fixtures and Fittings	£12,000		
Cash capital, say	£7,000		
	————		
Interest on tenant's capital at 10% on	£25,000	£2,500	
Tenant's remuneration		£15,000	£17,500
		————	————
Fair tied rent on lease			£10,000 p.a.
			————

Lessee's Compensation
  (i) *Interest in lease*:

Fair tied rent on lease	£10,000	
Rent reserved	£5,000	
Profit rent	£5,000 p.a.	
Y.P. 10 years at 9% and 3%— allowing for Income Tax	4·66	£23,300

  (ii) *Trade*:

Gross Profit		£60,000
Less:		
Expenses	£37,500	
Profit rent	£5,000	
Interest on capital	£2,500	£45,000
Net		£15,000
Y.P. 10 years at 15% and 3%— allowing for Income Tax	3·64	£54,600
Depreciation of value of fixtures and fittings, say 80% of £12,000		£9,600
Loss on sale of stock, say 10% on £6,000		£600
Cost of removal		£600
Compensation to lessee, say		£88,700

In addition, a lessee/tenant occupier may also qualify for a home-loss payment under the Land Compensation Act 1973, based on the Rateable Value attributed to the living accommodation. A tied tenant on an annual tenancy may also qualify for compensation under Sec. 37 of the Act, if he is not offered a similar house by the brewery.

Brewer's Interest.—This also will consist of two factors:— (i) the tied rent, (ii) the profits from the tie. Since a brewer will already have all the production facilities and organisation, it will cost him little extra to produce another ten or twenty barrelsofbeeraweekconsequentlymakinghigherthanaverage profits on these. He will probably therefore, when making his valuation for a single property adopt these resultant higher "marginal profits" in the calculations, rather than his "overall" profits per barrel, which would be substantially lower.

(i) In valuing the tied rent we must consider (a) the rent of £5,000 reserved under the lease for the next 10 years, and (b) the rent receivable thereafter.

Brewer's Compensation			
Tied Rent for 10 years	£5,000 p.a.		
Y.P. 10 years at 8%	6·7		
			£33,500
Reversion to full net			
rental value	£10,000 p.a.		
(N.B.—this figure			
depends largely on			
the maintainable			
level of trade and is			
not so well secured as			
the £5,000)			
Y.P. perp. at 8½%	11·76		
Y.P. 10 years at 8½%	6·56	5·2	£52,000
Trade: The brewer's marginal			
profit may be accepted at the			
following figures:—			
Draught Beer—350 barrels at			
£30·00	£10,500		
Bottled Beer—50 barrels at			
£30·00	£1,500		
Wines and Spirits—350			
gallons at £2·00	£700		
	£12,700*		
Y.P. perp. at 9%	11·1		£141,000
Compensation, say			£226,500

* calculation referred to in *Example 32–1* above.

In addition the brewer may receive a share of the income from the Gaming Machines, which should be capitalised. In practice it would be normal to have regard to market evidence also, since calculations such as above cannot readily reflect movements in the market from time to time.

6. VALUATIONS FOR RATING

In valuing licensed properties for rating purposes, as in the case of all other properties, it is required to ascertain the rent which a tenant might reasonably be expected to pay from year to year on the terms of a yearly tenancy.

Obviously this will depend upon the profit which can be made by entering into a tenancy by competitive parties including licensees, brewers and others, and the likely degree of competition is an important factor.

There was a fundamental change in the valuation of licensed premises for rating purposes following the decision of the House of Lords in *Robinson Bros. (Brewers) Ltd. v. Houghton and Chester-le-Street Assessment Committee (1938), A.C. 321.*

Prior to the case the judgment of the High Court in *Bradford-on-Avon Union v. White* (1898), 2 Q.B. 630, had been followed for many years. The effect of the judgment was that, in assessing the rent a hypothetical tenant might be expected to pay for licensed premises, the possible competition of brewers could not wholly be excluded from consideration, but the rents they might be prepared to give, owing to special considerations relating to their trade profits, should be excluded, except so far as the possibility of such special rents being obtained might raise the market generally.

It was found difficult to interpret the *Bradford* judgment in a practical way and as a general rule the competition of brewers does not appear to have been taken into account in rating assessments, at any rate quantitatively. A quite common method of valuation was to estimate (a) the volume of trade the house was capable of doing, and (b) the gross profit obtainable assuming the house was "free"; working expenses were then deducted, leaving a balance to be divided between (i) tenant's remuneration and interest on capital,

(ii) the fixed charges, viz., rates, water rate and licence duty, and (iii) the landlord's rent. In short, the object of the method was to find what profit a hypothetical free tenant, intending to occupy as licensee, could make, in order to estimate the rent he would be likely to bid.

The *Robinson* judgment established the principle that the hypothetical tenant may reasonably be expected to pay the rent which, in the letting market for such premises, would be offered as a result of the competition existing in that market. It is for the valuing authority to gauge both the extent of the competition in the market and the rent likely to be offered and accepted in that market.

Evidence of the rents which brewers would be prepared to pay for the tenancy of the house, whether they proposed to sub-let it to a tied tenant or to occupy it themselves by a manager, is both competent and relevant in estimating the rent which the hypothetical tenant might be expected to pay. There is no justification for including brewers among the competitors, but excluding from consideration the rent they would offer.

Logically, therefore, it appears necessary in any particular case to consider the profits which brewers might expect to receive by securing the tenancy of the house. Usually the brewer would sub-let to a tied tenant and his profit would consist of (i) the tied rent, and (ii) the profit on the alcoholic goods supplied to the tenant under the "tie". It is out of the profits that he would make his bid.

The proportion of his estimated income which a brewer might be prepared to pay away in the form of rent depends on the volume of the trade, the degree of local competition and other factors.

With the 1973 Valuation List still in force, those values relevant to 1973 are used. Wholesale profit figures for Beers, Wines and Spirits are based on those adopted for the 1973 Valuation List, and the Tied Rent will have been assessed on a "units" basis related to Draught Beer barrels, Bottled Beer barrels, and Wines and Spirits gallons, having regard to the type of house and trade. So, although any actual tied rent being paid will include the value of any catering or letting, the tied rent in a rating valuation, assessed on a "price

per unit" basis, relates essentially to the wet trade and
tenants' accommodation. Having assessed the Gross Value
of the wet trade by taking the "Brewers Bid" on the Brewers
Income from wholesale profit and tied rent, one then has
to make certain additions to reflect the rental value (to the
brewer tenant) of other income earned on the premises such
as from catering or letting, and to take account of the effect
on the rental value of the property of having one or more
Gaming Machines on the premises.

The following illustrates the method of valuation, known
as the Direct Method, which has been approved by the Lands
Tribunal.

Example 32–3

A fully licensed property occupied by a tied tenant. The
actual tied rent was £600 per annum. The average three years
trade was 230 Barrels Draught Beer, 100 Barrels Bottled
Beer, 240 Gallons Wines and Spirits.

Estimated future maintainable trade—

Draught Beer—230 barrels at £5·00 profit per barrel	£1,150
Bottled Beer—100 barrels at £6·50 profit per barrel	£650
Wines and Spirits—240 gallons at 90p profit per gallon	£216
Estimated Brewer's wholesale profit	£2,016
Estimated fair Tied Rent, say	£550
Total Brewer's Income	£2,566
Brewer/Tenant Share 60%	£1,540
Brewers Rental Bid (Gross Value) 40%	£1,026
Catering—£2,300 p.a. at 5%	£115
Gaming Machines—One	£60
	£1,201

Rating Assessment—Gross Value say £1,200.

1. GENERALLY

IN THIS book it is only possible to give a brief outline on aspects of this specialised subject. There are, however, a number of surface minerals, for example, sand and gravel, brick earth, chalk and limestone, which can come within the province of general practice.

Valuations of minerals may be required for the purpose of assessing capital or rental values, compulsory purchase, rating, taxation, probate, planning refusals and restrictions. In addition valuations may be required in connection with the purchase or sale of a business including the land, buildings, plant and machinery.

The first essential is for the valuer to obtain sound background knowledge of the industry in question and the problems it encounters in the excavation and processing of the mineral and its marketing. Two areas of mineral bearing land may appear comparable but there can be many factors which affect their respective ease of working and future rate of extraction which, in turn, will have a marked effect on their value.

The valuation of surface mineral bearing land involves the valuation of an asset which is destroyed as excavations proceed and ultimately the land loses its mineral value. In most cases there will be some residual value after the mineral has been worked and possibly an interim surface value for agricultural purposes on part while the excavation proceeds. One area of land might have a total value reflecting a sequence of uses with varying periods of deferment—this could start with an immediate agricultural value to be enjoyed for a few years, then a period of mineral extraction during which the landowner might enjoy the receipt of royalties, then a period of restoration during which tipping royalties might be received leading to the ultimate reclamation of the land for agriculture or possibly some recreational use.

The Town and Country Planning (Minerals) Act 1981, established a new regime for the planning control of mineral workings and associated development. This regime is now fully in place (see Section 9).

Planning control has a vital bearing on the valuation of mineral bearing land and it is necessary for the valuer to explore the planning position on any land with which he is concerned. Many Planning Authorities have produced Minerals Local Plans within the framework of their Structure Plans and it is necessary for the valuer to look carefully at these to assess the degree of hope value and deferment he applies to a proven deposit that has no planning permission.

Due to the effect on the environment that can be caused by mineral extraction and a reluctance to release high grade agricultural land difficulty is often experienced in obtaining planning permission. Many planning consents result from a successful Appeal against a refusal of permission and when granted can be subject to stringent conditions which regulate the method of working and restoring the land and can impose after care obligations. These factors can have a material effect on the value of mineral bearing land and need careful consideration by the valuer. In summary the existence of a proven deposit of economically valuable mineral land does not mean it has any great value in the open market. It is the prospect of a planning permission or the grant of it together with an established demand for the mineral that will bestow any mineral value on mineral bearing land.

2. Factors Affecting Value

The value of minerals ultimately depends on the prospects of a mineral operator's profit from their exploitation.

Factors to consider when valuing mineral bearing land are:—

(1) The quantity of the mineral.
(2) Its quality and suitability for the market it will serve.

(3) The ease or difficulty of winning and working which will include a consideration of such matters as contamination, geological faults, water table, overburden, etc.

(4) A consideration of the planning conditions which have been or may be imposed particularly in relation to reinstatement.

(5) The level of output that the market to be served would justify.

(6) The estimated profitability bearing in mind likely development and operating costs.

(7) The residual value of the land having regard to the requirements of the planning permission.

3. Capital Method of Valuation

The best evidence of capital value is usually to be found in directly comparable properties but with minerals it can be difficult to find such evidence. It is clearly relevant to establish whether the sale of a comparable property had the benefit of planning permission for mineral extraction. There will be instances where without a valid permission an enhanced price is realised reflecting "hope value" in anticipation that the necessary permission will be obtained in due course. This reinforces the need to investigate the extent of consented reserves in the area to enable an estimate of deferment to be made.

Where the market for the particular mineral is not restricted there may be sufficient evidence of current transactions to justify the valuer basing his valuation on the area of the land.

The particular circumstances of a prima facie comparable transaction should be investigated and there are many reasons why the evidence could be misleading. For example, an unduly high price may have been paid by a mineral operator whose existing reserves are near exhaustion. Also the operator may have efficient processing plant which has been written down and rather than face heavy capital expenditure in establishing a new plant and buildings on an alternative site, he may have paid a high price to maintain production at his existing works. Conversely there will be cases where agricultural land is bought by mineral operators from owners unaware of the mineral value. Sale prices achieved in such circumstances afford little assistance for the purposes of comparison.

Apparently comparable land may have widely differing contents per hectare and the valuer must investigate the mineral content of the land and its quality. Where appropriate the mineral should be proved by means of borings or trial holes possibly put down in conjunction with an electrical resistivity or seismic survey.

Provings should indicate the depth of topsoil and overburden, the depth of the mineral, and any major faults in the mineral. The question of proving the land is a specialist matter and an inadequate number of random boreholes could give a misleading result as to "quantity" which will affect the valuation. It is also important to know the "quality" of the mineral for the proposed end product. Where the geological formation is uncertain it is desirable for comprehensive tests to be taken. By way of example, where the deposit is of sand and gravel it is vital to know if the material when washed and graded will provide good concreting aggregates or whether it is only suitable for sale as a low grade granular fill.

Although land may contain high quality mineral in sufficient quantity it may have little or no value if the potential market is distant or is already adequately served from existing sources with ample reserves.

On the other hand, where the supply of a particular mineral is limited, for example, in the case of sand and gravel in certain districts, there may be an urgent requirement from the aggregates industry for further reserves to be made available. Planning control thus tends to aggravate shortages and enhance values and this reinforces the need for the valuer to have thorough knowledge of the planning position and the existence of other sources of the mineral in question within the catchment area of the property he is valuing.

4. ROYALTY METHOD OF VALUATION

Where there is no evidence of capital transactions an alternative approach is to capitalise the notional annual royalty income the land should yield during the estimated life of the minerals. A royalty is the amount paid under a mineral lease or agreement for each unit of mineral output and in most modern leases the tonne is the usual unit of measurement although the royalty might be expressed in cubic metres.

This method of valuation is dependent upon a number of assumptions and the final answer should be converted to a value per hectare as a check.

The valuer must estimate the probable rate of output from the undertaking and from this determine the likely life of the deposit having regard to the workable reserves. This involves appraisal of the market potential and investigating the level of output and reserves of other operators in the area who are already serving the market.

When the reserves are required to extend existing workings guidance may be obtained from the present level of output although the prospect of increased output over the normal demand for a specific project should be taken into account as this would enhance value. For example, major road construction work might call for large quantities of aggregates in a particular area for a limited period. Particular care is needed in determining the royalty to be applied and the valuer should search for any evidence of current royalties being paid for comparable minerals. The royalty chosen should reflect such variables as the situation, the quality of the mineral and the likely working costs. By way of example, if the overburden is exceptionally thick or there are onerous or expensive restoration requirements attached to the planning consent an operator would, *prima facie*, offer a lower royalty compared with a deposit where such problems were not present. Also the distance of the pit or quarry from the market is a major factor in the case of bulky and relatively low value aggregates due to the cost of transport.

5. CAPITALISATION OF ROYALTIES

In the past the traditional method of capitalising the estimated annual royalty has been to use dual rate valuation tables with allowance for tax on the sinking fund instalment.

The reason is that minerals are a wasting asset and consequently their valuation involves similar considerations to those applied when valuing a leasehold interest. A number of valuers have for some time contended that single rate tables are more appropriate.

Except in the case of academic valuations, the practice of using dual rate tables has declined primarily due to the fact that mineral operators do not necessarily apply this approach when acquiring their land. When therefore it is necessary to capitalise a royalty for valuation purposes, particular care is needed in the selection of the interest rates used and the result should be considered in relation to any evidence the valuer can find of sales of comparable land.

The following example illustrates the royalty method of valuation:—

Example 33–1

    6 hectares of sand & gravel
    Estimated total mineral reserves 750,000 tonnes.
    Estimated rate of working 50,000 tonnes per annum.
    Estimated life of quarry 15 years.
    Estimated royalty value 75p per tonne.

Annual royalty value 50,000 tonnes at 75p	£37,500
Y.P. 15 years at 15 and 3%	
(Tax at 35%), say	4·3
	£161,250

This is equivalent to about £27,000 per hectare.

The valuation of a freehold interest subject to a mineral lease would proceed in a similar manner to the capital royalty valuation described above. The following general points should be noted in relation to mineral leases, licences and agreements.

In addition to the royalty reserved under a mineral lease, it is usual for the lessee to pay a certain or minimum annual rent whether any working takes place or not. This ensures that the lessor will receive a certain regular income irrespective of output and guards against the risk that the lessee may leave the minerals unworked. In such cases the royalty usually merges with the minimum rent. For example, if the royalty is 50p per tonne geared to a rent of £25,000 per annum, the minimum rent ceases to apply once the output exceeds 50,000 tonnes per annum. There is no hard and fast rule and a minimum rent might be established at, say 50% of the estimated annual royalty income.

Many leases incorporate a short-working clause whereby, if the output falls below the level prescribed by the minimum rent, the deficiency can be set off in subsequent years against royalty payments in excess of the minimum rent. In the example, if the output was 40,000 tonnes in the first year then the lessee would pay the minimum rent of £25,000 but would be entitled to carry forward £5,000 short workings. If in the second year the output inceased to 70,000 tonnes his payment would be £35,000—£5,000 equalling £30,000, which could be expressed as £25,000 minimum rent plus £5,000 royalties.

A surface rent may also be payable to compensate for the loss of agricultural land or the occupation of surface land during the period of excavation. This is normally based on the agricultural rental value.

6. Residual Value

In addition to the value of the mineral it is necessary to consider if value should be added to reflect any deferred potential development value after the mineral has been extracted. In many cases the land will revert to agricultural use with no further development prospects and any such value will be deferred to reflect the timescale before the land is restored to agriculture. In such cases the residual value will probably be insignificant and make little difference to the open market value. However in some cases the "void" created by the excavation may have interim value as a landfill site particularly if situated close to a built up area where there is an ever increasing demand for tipping facilities. Here it will be necessary to make a suitable addition to reflect this potential and the value will depend on the type of filling permitted. A void consented for household refuse is more valuable than one restricted to excavated materials. It should be borne in mind that in addition to planning consent for tipping, it is also necessary to obtain a licence under the Control of Pollution Act 1974.

There is a general presumption that valuable minerals should not be sterilised and there are cases where planning permission may be granted for extraction prior to some other permanent development. In such cases where permission for prior extraction is granted a substantial addition may need to be made to reflect the residual value which may not be long deferred. The valuer must consider the time that would elapse before the land would be suitable and available for its ultimate development.

In some cases the extraction of the minerals will result in the formation of lakes where the natural water table is high. With suitable landscaping such lakes can be attractive amenity features and may be used for a variety of recreational purposes. Angling, sailing and water ski-ing are now popular and the residual value for such uses is a matter for consideration by the valuer.

7. VALUATIONS FOR RATING IN ENGLAND AND WALES

Mineral properties are rateable and the current statutory provisions flow from two principal sources. The Poor Relief Act 1601 made coal mines expressly rateable and as only coal was mentioned, other minerals were not rateable. This anomalous situation was changed by the Rating Act 1874, which extended rateability to mines of every kind. Section 7 prescribed the method of assessing tin, lead and copper mines.

The current statutory provisions flow from Section 16 of the General Rate Act 1967, Section 19 and Schedule 3 of the Local Government Act 1974 and the Mines and Quarries (Valuation) Order 1983.

It is outside the scope of this book to comment on the formula basis for coal mines and open-cast workings vested in British Coal.

The valuer will normally be dealing with pits or quarries producing sand, gravel, clay, chalk, limestone, etc.

The rateability of these is covered by Section 16(d) of the General Rate Act 1967, which refers to "mines of every other description other than a mine of which the royalty or dues are for the time being wholly reserved in kind".

Mineral properties are assessed direct to Net Annual Value and the method follows the recommendations of the former Central Valuation Committee and their Resolution No. 63 dated 22 March 1929 on Mineral Producing Hereditaments is still worthy of study.

A royalty based on evidence is adopted for rating purposes having regard to the considerations and general principles of value referred to earlier. This royalty is applied to the actual or estimated annual output. To this is added the Net Annual Value of any rateable plant and buildings.

The purpose is to ascertain the rent at which the property might reasonably be expected to let from year to year having regard to the rating hypothesis and the definition of Net Annual Value under Section 19(3) of the General Rate Act 1967. Evidence of actual open market royalties passing may be relevant in ascertaining the hypothetical rating royalty providing the evidence is up to date. A tender royalty may however be suspect as the successful tenderer may have over-bid and if negotiations had been carried out in the market place a lower royalty might have been agreed.

The factors affecting royalty values should be considered to enable comparisons to be made between pits and quarries in the same locality and any royalty evidence obtained from leases or licences should be carefully analysed.

The Inland Revenue Valuation Office send out statutory forms of return requiring information on the preceding year's output. Assessments are dealt with by the Mineral Valuer, who revises them annually on up to date output and reflects any alterations to the rateable plant and buildings.

Once the hypothetical rating royalty has been agreed at the time of a revaluation this is applied for the period of the Valuation List, subject to variations for changes in working conditions, which may give rise to arguments for adjustment. The rating royalty for any new hereditament must conform to the statutory tone of the list procedure under Section 20 of the General Rate Act 1967.

In some small undertakings there is no rateable plant. However where there is a processing plant the effective capital value of the rateable elements has to be ascertained in accordance with the current Plant and Machinery (Rating) Order. A percentage is then applied to arrive at the Net Annual Value on the contractor's basis with an addition for the value of any buildings plus a rental value for the plant site. It is usual for a static figure to be agreed for the rateable plant and buildings which is a constant addition on the annual revision of assessment subject to any alterations and additions. However if a plant is substantially under-utilised consideration should be given to writing down the value for rating purposes to ensure that surplus capacity is not reflected. It is also worth considering if there is a case for an adjustment where plant is absolete or where the lay-out is poor.

Under the Mines and Quarries (Valuation) Order 1983 the method of determining the Rateable Value of any hereditament which consists of or includes a mine or quarry is prescribed. Such assessments are made on the assumption that only one half of the royalty is to be treated as rent with a 50% reduction from Net Annual Value to Rateable Value. This adjustment applies to that part of the assessment attributable to the winning and working, grading, washing, grinding and crushing of minerals. The rateable plant and buildings do not qualify for this adjustment but the value of the site they occupy does.

Example 33–2

A gravel pit has a washing and grading plant producing concrete aggregates and the effective capital value of the rateable plant is £60,000. Last years' output was 100,000 tonnes and a fair hypothetical rating royalty is 50p per tonne.

1. Output—100,000 tonnes at 50p	£50,000
2. Rateable plant & buildings—	
effective capital value £60,000 at 5%	3,000
3. Plant site rent	1,000
Net Annual Value	£54,000

Items 1 and 3 qualify for 50%
reduction under Mines & Quarries
(Valuation) Order 1983.
Rateable Value   £28,500

8. COMPULSORY PURCHASE

The general provisions relating to compulsory purchase
and the assessment of compensation are found in the Land
Compensation Acts 1961 and 1973 and the Compulsory Purchase Act 1965. Any minerals in land will normally be
acquired and their value will depend on the valuation principles discussed earlier, in particular the prospect or existence
of planning permission.

However minerals are excluded from a compulsory purchase if the Order applies the Mining Code. This is covered
in Schedule 2 of the Acquisition of Land Act 1981 which
re-enacts Sections 77 to 85 of the Railway Clauses Consolidation Act 1845. Briefly this code enables the acquiring authority to buy land without the underlying minerals and if the
owner subsequently gives notice of his intention to work them
the acquiring authority have the option to pay compensation
and thus sterilise the minerals.

Broadly speaking, the basis of compensation under the
Land Compensation Act 1961 is current open market value
taking into account the various planning assumptions described in Chapter 27. Mineral working may be permitted
in areas where no other form of development could be considered, for example in the Green Belt or in an Area of
High Landscape Value. In such circumstances the certificate
procedure in Part 3 of the 1961 Act may be useful. The existence of a planning permission for mineral working does not
necessarily preclude a claim in respect of some other form
of surface use providing it can be shown that such potential
is reflected in the open market value. The valuer should
consider claiming for any loss of filling value or any other
potential deferred values to which reference has been made
earlier.

9. COMPENSATION UNDER TOWN AND COUNTRY PLANNING LEGISLATION

Minerals are subject to special provisions and regulations under the Town & Country and Country Planning Act 1971 and the Town and Country Planning (Minerals) Act 1981 which in certain circumstances adapt and modify the general rules relating to compensation for revocation and modification of planning permissions and other planning restrictions.

(A) *Revocation or Modification of Planning Permission*

The position with minerals is similar to other forms of property in that full compensation is payable except in those cases where a reduction is required under the terms of the Town and Country Planning (Compensation for Restrictions on Mineral Working) Regulations 1985, referred to below. Not only can compensation be claimed in respect of the full market value of the land but, in addition, compensation is payable for abortive expenditure and other loss or damage. It should, however, be noted that Regulation 5 of the Town and Country Planning (Minerals) Regulations 1971, enables the Lands Tribunal to sever a claim in respect of buildings, plant or machinery from the remainder of the claim. The claimant must show that the buildings, plant and machinery cannot be used except at the loss claimed. As an example, if a revocation considered by itself would virtually render the buildings, plant and machinery valueless and subsequently the claimant is able to acquire further mineral land which can be processed in the existing plant, then this fact will be taken into account in assessing the loss or damage resulting from the revocation. This provision could well reduce the claim in respect of the buildings, plant and machinery.

(B) *Planning Restrictions*

The Town and Country Planning Act 1971 contains powers which enable permissions to be revoked or modified but such powers have rarely been exercised in connection with mineral workings due to the claims for substantial compensation that would flow in many cases. One of the main objectives of the Town and Country Planning (Minerals) Act 1981 was to reduce the amount of compensation payable should mineral planning authorities wish to modify existing mineral permissions to bring them into line with current planning standards. Special mineral compensation provisions are now laid down.

The 1981 Act imposes a duty on mineral planning authorities to undertake periodic reviews of mineral sites in their areas with a view to varying the terms of planning permissions so that extraction, restoration and after-care can be regulated. Apart from this general duty of periodic review of mineral planning permissions, mineral planning authorities are given specific powers to make Modification, Revocation, Discontinuance, Suspension and Prohibition Orders in relation to mineral working sites.

Where certain "mineral compensation requirements" are met the Town and Country Planning (Compensation for Restrictions on Mineral Workings) Regulations 1985 make provision for a reduction in the full compensation that would otherwise be payable following the making of such Orders.

Modification, Revocation and Discontinuance Orders
(Sections 45 and 51 of the 1971 Act and the 1985 Regulations)
In the case of Orders under these headings the full compensation is to be reduced by the greater of—
(a) The sum of £2,500, or (b) 10% of the sum (known as the "threshold") calculated by multiplying Annual Value of the right to work minerals by a specified multiplier which increases in accordance with the estimated life (subject to a maximum deduction of £10,000). A number of detailed pre-conditions have to be met for the "mineral compensation requirements" to be satisfied. In particular the order cannot impose restrictions on the size of the area to be worked, the rate or period of working or the quantity to be extracted.

Prohibition and Suspension Orders (Sections 51A and 51B of the 1971 Act and the 1985 Regulations)
In the case of these Orders which prohibit the resumption of operations and require steps to be taken to protect the

environment where mineral working has been suspended, the full compensation is reduced by £5,000 provided the minerals planning authority carried out specific prior consultations about the making of the Prohibition or Suspension Order.

(C) Compensation for Planning Refusals

Claims for compensation arising as a result of planning refusals or conditions attached to planning permissions are governed by Part VII of the Town & Country Planning Act 1971.

No claim can arise unless the land concerned has an unexpended balance of established development value. The general principles underlying such claims as described in Chapter 24 apply to minerals, the basis of compensation being the difference between the value of the land with and without the planning permission subject to the ceiling of the unexpended balance of established development value attaching to the land. A suitable reduction must be made from the unexpended balance to allow for the value of new development which is valued on the basis of Schedule 16 to the 1971 Act having regard to the current values at the date of the planning decision.

No compensation is payable in respect of conditions attached to a planning permission for mineral working unless the condition in effect prohibits the working of a specified part of the land (Section 147(6) of the 1971 Act). For example, conditions may be imposed restricting the working of minerals within a specified distance from neighbouring development or from a highway boundary or limiting the depth of excavation.

The provisions of Section 148 of the 1971 Act apply so that in the event of alternative permission being available for residential, commercial or industrial purposes no compensation is payable.

Regulation 9 of the Town & Country Planning (Minerals) Regulations 1971, provides for the creation of separate claim holdings where since 1 July 1948, the freehold in the minerals has been severed from the freehold interest in the remainder of the land. The claim holding or the unexpended balance of established development value is apportioned between the minerals and the remainder of the land whereupon the minerals and the remainder of the land are treated as separate claim areas.

10. TAXATION

Prior to the Finance Act 1965 which introduced capital gains tax, capital receipts had been free of tax. However income receipts from mineral bearing land were taxed as income.

Finance Act 1965

This Act introduced taxation of capital gains made on the disposal of assets, including land, whether by outright sale or the grant of a lease. The general principles and computation of gains is described in Chapter 23. Nevertheless the historical distinction in connection with minerals remained important since the rate of capital gains tax on a capital receipt was considerably lower than the maximum rate of income tax levied in respect of a royalty under a lease. This situation led to an increasing reluctance on the part of mineral owners to grant mineral leases.

Finance Act 1970

This Act attempted to overcome the problem by recognising that royalties paid under a mineral lease are, because minerals are a wasting asset, partly in the nature of rent and partly in the nature of a capital payment. Accordingly rent and royalties received after 6 April 1970, irrespective of whether the mineral lease was granted before that date, were divided, one-half being regarded as income liable to tax at income tax rates (or in the case of a company to corporation tax) and one-half being deemed to be capital and treated as a capital gain.

However, the usual capital gains procedure is not adopted and the half of the annual royalty payment which is not subject to income tax is treated as a gain without any off-setting allowance for expenses. Nevertheless in certain circumstances a balancing relief is available to owners on termination of the lease.

Finance Act 1988

For individuals from 6 April 1988, capital gains are taxed at the individual's marginal rate of income tax removing any advantage or penalty that accrued under the previous rules.

11. CAPITAL ALLOWANCES UNDER FINANCE ACT 1986

Revised taxation allowances were introduced for expenditure incurred in a "trade of mineral extraction" after 31 March 1986 to bring the minerals industry more into line with industry generally. For expenditure prior to that date allowance was given in accordance with the provisions of Section 60 of the Capital Allowances Act 1968.

Total allowances under the Finance Act 1986 are limited to the "qualifying expenditure" incurred in connection with a trade of mineral extraction and allowances are given in a chargeable or base period calculated on:—

Acquisition of a mineral asset	10%
Other qualifying expenditure	25%

Allowances for subsequent periods are calculated by applying the same percentages to the balance of expenditure after adjustment for disposal receipts and allowances and charges given or made for earlier periods.

"Qualifying expenditure" includes expenditure on:—

(a) mineral exploration and access;
(b) acquisition of a mineral asset;
(c) construction of works in connection with the working of a source.

Where expenditure includes the acquisition of an interest in land an amount equal to the "undeveloped market value" must be excluded. Undeveloped market value is the open market value of the land at the time of the acquisition ignoring the mineral deposits and assuming development of the land is, and remains, lawful.

When an asset on which qualifying expenditure has been

incurred ceases permanently to be used in a trade of mineral extraction the disposal value must be brought into account. This will give rise to a balancing charge or allowance.

A balancing charge arises if the disposal receipts for that and earlier periods and net allowances made for earlier periods exceeds the expenditure. The balancing allowance arises when sale receipts are less than unexpired expenditure.

Where an asset is acquired from another person and that person or an earlier owner incurred qualifying expenditure, allowances will be calculated on the amount incurred by the most recent previous owner net of any allowances made to that person.

TABLE OF STATUTES

STATUTORY INSTRUMENTS

TABLE OF CASES

737

Index